THE FABER DICTIONARY OF EUPHEMISMS

THE
FABER DICTIONARY OF
EUPHEMISMS

R. W. Holder

faber and faber

LONDON · BOSTON

First published in Great Britain in 1987 as
A Dictionary of American and British Euphemisms
by Bath University Press
This revised edition published in 1989
by Faber and Faber Limited
3 Queen Square London WC1N 3AU

Photoset by Parker Typesetting Service Leicester
Printed in Great Britain by Richard Clay Ltd Bungay Suffolk
All rights reserved

British Library Cataloguing in Publication Data is available

ISBN 0-571-15125-6 (Pbk)
ISBN 0-571-14253-2 (USA only)

Contents

An Explanation

This book is developed from another which was completed in 1985 and entitled *A Dictionary of American and British Euphemisms*, although some thought the sub-title 'The language of evasion, hypocrisy, prudery and deceit' more appropriate. In deciding what constituted a euphemism, I relied on Fowler's definition: 'Euphemism means (the use of a) mild or vague or periphrastic expression as a substitute for blunt precision or disagreeable truth.'

A second, and perhaps simpler, test is that the euphemistic word or phrase must once have meant, or prima facie today still means, something else. In most cases I give the reader credit for knowing what the proper, or non-euphemistic, meaning was or is. Where there may be doubt, I explain the proper meaning too. Thus in the entry 'equal pay' you will see 'Properly, paying everyone who does precisely the same job the same money'. The definition 'inequitable remuneration' will be familiar to those who have taken part in any kind of formal wage bargaining or worked in a unionized shop, and the entry goes on to explain why this is.

Words which I have come across only in other dictionaries have been left out. The temptation to which lexicographers are particularly subject is plagiarism and I was delivered from this because there was nothing to copy. Nobody had selected euphemisms, defined them, suggested their etymology and, where appropriate, illustrated their use. The original work was far advanced when Hugh Rawson's *Dictionary of Euphemisms* came out. I found it great fun but his approach was different to mine.

Euphemisms are often concerned with taboos, and the taboos of one generation are not always those of the next. We are less obsessed than the Victorians with brothels and prostitution, less prudish about courtship, childbirth and legs, less terrified of bankruptcy. In turn we are reluctant to admit that our society includes dull schoolchildren, cripples or poor folks in receipt of charity: or that peoples who were once oppressed can themselves act oppressively. I have tried to take a photograph of the language, using a long exposure to capture euphemisms enshrined in literature which is still widely read, those in common use today and a few others which have caught my fancy.

The choice has of necessity been subjective.

Many taboos surround sexual or distasteful matters. Sometimes, as with 'lavatory', we have no non-euphemistic word in the language and elsewhere the only definition which is not itself euphemisitic is crude, offensive to many and tedious if repeated too often. I therefore use the euphemistic 'copulate' rather than 'fuck' and the inelegant 'sexual mistress' in place of any alternative circumlocution. Other problem words, such as 'lover', are dealt with in the text. In the end I was persuaded to deal with sexual matters, repetitive and tedious as they become, as fully as with other entries. To preserve my earlier analogy, the photograph you see is of yourselves and your ancestors. This is the language they used and we use.

There is no satisfactory answer to the problems of geography. Each country develops its own euphemisms, and so does each region, each trade and even each family. There is some conformity in Great Britain and the Republic of Ireland because London and Dublin respectively dominate government, the arts, television, business and so on. It is not so in North America where distance and a federal system of government have combined to create many focal cities. Fortunately literature is common from San Diego to Aberdeen but a New Englander would be inadequate for this task in Chicago, let alone an Englishman. This work in effect confines itself to the English of the Northern Hemisphere, the area in which I have travelled frequently. Some Indian usages have crept in (although I was at first defeated by a Delhi headline a few weeks ago which read 'Eve harrassment riots' – female students were protesting about the attentions of males, it was suggested). The fertile Australian soil I have left untilled.

I try not to define one euphemism by another. Where in the text an entire entry is bracketed, I have included a non-euphemism because I thought it of interest. A bracketed comment within an entry indicates that I am conscious of being overly intrusive.

The way in which certain subjects are treated euphemistically, so revealing current social attitudes and mores, has been historically of great interest. The language used by Mayhew and Dickens tells us unconsciously almost as much about mid-Victorian England as their reporting and story-telling. So too for other periods and the evidence is of special value because it is contemporary information which is passed down to us unaware. Certain examples, such as the status of the unmarried nineteenth-century woman, are referred to in the text.

The entries are classified in an Index. The Bibliography is confined to books quoted from or mentioned in the text among which Joseph Wright's *English Dialect Dictionary* stands supreme. Many of the entries have been expanded from my earlier work and others added, reflecting the development of the language during three years, and my own further reading. I have changed one etymological explanation but none of the definitions. I am grateful to Robert McCrum, from whose *Story of English* I picked up my etymological error, for allowing this volume to appear in an unedited, perhaps idiosyncratic, form.

I must again record my thanks to Sam Allen, of Old Haddam, who helped me with the American entries, to Dr Michael Allen of Bath University for support in many ways and to Professor John Bayley who, with his wife, Iris Murdoch, and Michael Allen, saw a draft of the original book at an early stage and encouraged me to complete and publish it.

West Monkton
January, 1989.

Abbreviations

Geographical

Am.	America or American
BI	British Isles
Br.	Britain or British
Eng.	England or English
Ire.	Ireland
Sc.	Scotland or Scottish

General

abbr.	abbreviation
c.	century or approximately
CB	Citizen's Band
cf.	compare
fig.	figurative(ly)
ob.	obsolete
q.v.	refer across to
rh.	rhyming
SE	Standard English
sl.	slang
tr.	translation
usu.	usual(ly)
WW	World War
?	perhaps
....	indicates that part of a passage has been omitted from a quotation
...	follows the quoted text

Reference

see under Bibliography

Bibliography

Dictionaries and other reference books included in the bibliography are marked*. Some of these books are referred to in the text by an abbreviation, and these abbreviations are listed first.

The quotations were included in the text to show how each word or phrase was used, and when. As with all libraries, mine is subject to continual depredations and in a handful of cases I have been unable to verify the title of a work from which I have quoted. The date given refers to the first publication or to the edition which I have used. Where an author has deliberately used archaic language, I mention that in the text.

BDPF   The Dictionary of Phrase and
            Fable
            Brewer (1978)
CBSLD   The 'Official' CB Slanguage
            Language Dictionary
            Dill (1976)
CED   Collins English Dictionary
            (1979)
DAS   Dictionary of American Slang
            Wentworth and Flexner (1975)
DDE   The Dictionary of Diseased
            English
            Hudson (1977)
DHS   A Dictionary of Historical
            Slang
            Partridge and Simpson (1972)

DNB   The Dictionary of National
            Biography (1978)
Dr Johnson A Dictionary of the English
            Language (1755)
DRS   A Dictionary of Rhyming
            Slang
            Franklin (1961)
DSUE   A Dictionary of Slang and
            Unconventional English
            Partridge (1970)
EDD   The English Dialect
            Dictionary (1898/1905)
FDMT   The Fontana Dictionary of
            Modern Thought
            Bullock and Stallybrass (1977)
Grose   Dictionary of the Vulgar
            Tongue (1811 edn.)
MBD   Mrs Byrnes's Dictionary of
            Unusual Obscure and
            Preposterous Words
            Byrnes (1974)
ODEE   The Oxford Dictionary of
            English Etymology
            Onions (1978)
ODEP   The Oxford Dictionary of
            English Proverbs
            Smith and Wilson (1970)
OED   The Oxford English
            Dictionary (1979)
SOD   The Shorter Oxford English
            Dictionary (1968)
WNCD   Webster's New Collegiate
            Dictionary (1977)

Agnus (1900)   Jan Oxber
Agrikler (1872)   Rhymes in the West of
    England Dialect
Ainslie (1892)   A Pilgrimage to the Land of
    Burns
Alexander (1875/1882 edn.) Sketches of Life
    among my Ain Folk
Allbeury (1985)   Palomino Blonde
    (1976)   The Only Good German
    (1976)   Moscow Quadrille
    (1978)   The Lantern Network
    (1979)   Consequence of Fear
    (1980)   The Twentieth Day of January
    (1980)   The Reaper
    (1981)   The Other Side of Silence
    (1981)   The Secret Whispers
    (1982)   All our Tomorrows

Allen (1975)   Plain Tales from the Raj
    (1979)   Tales from the Dark Continent
Amis (1978)   Jake's Thing
    (1980)   Russian Hide-and Seek
    (1986)   The Old Devils
Anderson D. (1826)   Poems Chiefly in the
    Scottish Dialect
Anderson R. (1805/1808 edn.)   Ballads in
    the Cumberland Dialect
Anderson W. (1851/1867 edn.)   Rhymes,
    Reveries and Reminiscences
Andrews (1899)   Bygone Church Life in
    Scotland
Antrobus (1901)   Wildersmoor
Archer (1979)   Kane and Abel
Armstrong A. (1890)   Ingleside Musings
    and Tales

Armstrong L. (1955)   Satchmo
Aubrey (1696)   Collected Works
Axon (1870)   The Black Knight of Ashton

Bacon (1627)   Essays
Bagley (1982)   Windfall
Bagnall (1852)   Songs of the Tyne
Ballantine (1869)   The Miller of Deanhaugh
Banim (1823)   O'Hara
Barlow (1892)   Bogland Studies
Baron (1948)   From the City From the
   Plough
Barr (1861)   Poems and Songs
Bartram (1897)   The People of Clopton
   (1898)   The White-headed Boy
Beattie (1801)   Fruits of Time Parings
Beatty (1897)   The Secretar
Behr (1978)   Anyone here been raped &
   speaks English
*Bernard and Lauwerys (1963)   A Hand-
   book of British Educational Terms
Besant and Rice (1872)   Mortiboy
Binchy (1985)   Echoes
Binns (1889)   Yorkshire Dialect Words
Blanch (1954)   The Wilder Shores of Love
Block (1979)   Mayday
Blythe (1969)   Akenfield
Bogarde (1972)   A Postillion Struck by
   Lightning
   (1978)   Snakes and Ladders
   (1981)   Voices in the Garden
   (1983)   An Orderly Man
Boldrewood (1890)   A Colonial Reformer
Boswell A. (1803)   Songs
   (1871)   Poetical Works
Boswell J. (?1762/3)   London Journal
Boyd (1981)   A Good Man in Africa
   (1982)   An Ice-Cream War
Boyle (1979)   The Climate of Treason
Bradbury (1959)   Eating People is Wrong
   (1985)   Stepping Westward
   (1975)   The History Man
   (1976)   Who Do You Think You Are
Brand (1789)   The History and Antiquities
   of Newcastle-upon-Tyne
*Brewer (1978)   The Dictionary of Phrase
   and Fable
Brierley (1865)   Irkdale
   (1880)   Treadlepin
   (1886)   The Cotters of Mossburn
*Brown (1958)   Words in our Time
*Browning (1962)   Everyman's Dictionary
   of Literary Biography
Bryce (1888)   The American Constitution
Buchan (1898)   John Burnet of Barns
Buckman (1870)   John Darke's Sojourn in
   the Cotswolds
*Bullock and Stallybrass (1977)   The
   Fontana Dictionary of Modern Thought

Bunyan (1680/4)   The Pilgrim's Progress
Burgess (1959)   Beds in the East
Burmester (1902)   John Lott's Alice
Burnley (1880)   Poems and Sketches
Burns (1786/96)   Poems, Songs and Letters
Burton (1621)   The Anatomy of Melancholy
Butler (1903)   The Way of All Flesh
*Byrnes (1974)   Mrs Byrnes's Dictionary of
   Unusual Obscure and Preposterous Words
Byron   Works
Bywater (1839)   The Sheffield Dialect
   (1853)   The Shevvild Chap's Annual

Caine (1885)   The Shadow of a Crime
Carleton (1836)   Fordorougha the Miser
Carrick (1835)   The Laird of Logan
Chambers (1870)   Popular Rhymes of
   Scotland
Chamier (1837)   quoted in ODEP
Chandler (1934)   Finger Man
   (1939)   Trouble is my Business
   (1940)   Farewell my Lovely
   (1943)   The High Window
   (1944)   The Lady in the Lake
   (1950)   The Big Sleep
   (1951)   The Little Sister
   (1953)   The Long Good-bye
   (1958)   Playback
Christie (1939)   Evil under the Sun
   (1940)   Ten Little Niggers
Clare (1827)   The Shepherd's Calendar
Clark (1839)   John Noakes and Mary Styles
Cleland (1749)   Memoirs of a Woman of
   Pleasure (Fanny Hill)
Cobbett (1823)   Rural Rides
Coghill (1890)   Poems, Songs and Sonnets
*Collins English Dictionary (1979)
Collins (1981)   Chances
Colvil (1796)   The Whig's Supplication
Colville (1985)   The Fringes of Power
Condon (1966)   Any God Will Do
Congreve (1695)   Love for Love
Cookson (1967)   Slinky Jane
   (1969)   Our Kate
Corley (1961)   Democratic Despot
Crisp (1982)   The Brink
Crocker (1862)   Fairy Legends & Traditions
   of South Ireland
Crocket (1894)   The Raiders
   (1896)   The Grey Man
Cromwell O. (1643)   Letter
Cross (1844)   The Disruption
Cussler (1984)   Deep Six

Davidson (1978)   The Chelsea Murders
Defoe (1721)   Moll Flanders
Deighton (1972)   Close-up
   (1978)   SS-GB
   (1981)   XPD

(1982) Goodbye Mickey Mouse
(1985) London Match
Dickens C. (1840) The Old Curiosity Shop
  (1853) Bleak House
  (1861) Great Expectations
Dickens M. (?1940) Mariana
Dickinson (1866) Scallow Beck Boggle
Dickson (1978) The Official Rules
*Dictionary of National Biography (1975)
Diehl (1978) Sharky's Machine
*Dills (1976) The 'Official' CB Slanguage
  Language Dictionary
Dixon (1846) Ancient Poems, Ballads and
  Songs of the Peasantry of England
Doherty (1884) Nathan Barlow
Douglas (1901) The House with the Green
  Shutters
Doyle (1855) Polly's Gaon
Dryden (1668/98) Poetical Works

Egerton (1884) Sussex Folks and Sussex
  Ways
Eliot (1871/2) Middlemarch
Ellis (1750) The Modern Husbandman (?)
Emerson (1890) Wild Life on a Tidal Water
Erdman (1974) The Silver Bears
  (1981) The Last Days of America
  (1986) The Panic of '89
*Evans (1962) Comfortable Words

*Farmer and Henley (1890/1904) Slang and
  its Analogues
Farran (1948) Winged Dagger
Fergusson (1773) Poems on Various Subjects
Fielding (1729) The Author's Farce
  (1742) The History of the Adventures of
  Joseph Andrews
Fletcher (?1618) Valentinian
Follett (1978) The Eye of the Needle
  (1979) Triple
Forbes B. (1983) The Rewrite Man
  (1986) The Endless Game
Forbes C. (1983) The Leader and the
  Damned
  (1985) Cover Story
  (1987) The Janus Man
Ford (1891) Thistledown
Forsyth (1984) The Fourth Protocol
*Foster (1968) The Changing English
  Language
*Fowler (1957) Modern English Usage
Fowles (1977) The Magus (revised)
  (1985) A Maggot
Fox (1982) White Mischief
Francis D. (1962) Dead Cert
  (1978) Trial Run
  (1982) Twice Shy
  (1982) Banker
  (1985) Break In

Francis M. (1901) Pastorals of Dorset
*Frank (1955) Heavens to Betsy and Other
  Curious Sayings
Franklin (?1758) The Way to Wealth
Fraser (1969) Flashman
  (1970) Royal Flash
  (1971) Flash for Freedom
  (1973) Flashman at the Charge
  (1975) Flashman in the Great Game
  (1977) Flashman's Lady
  (1982) Flashman and the Redskins
  (1985) Flashman and the Dragon

Galloway (1810) Poems
Galt (1821) The Ayrshire Legatees
  (1823) The Entail
  (1826) The Last of the Lairds
Gannel-Milne (1933) Wind in the Wires
*Garmonsway and Simpson (1969) The
  Penguin English Dictionary
Gascoigne (1576) quoted in ODEP
Gaskell (1863) Sylvia's Lovers
Genet (1969) Funeral Rites (in tr.)
Gissing (1890) A Village Hampden
Goebbels (1945) Diaries – The Last Days
  (in tr.)
Gordon A. (1894) Northward Ho!
Gordon F. (1885) Pyotshaw
Gordon J. F. S. (1880) The Book of the
  Chronicles of Keith
Gosling and Warner (1960) The Shame of
  a City
Graham (1883) The Collected Writings
Grant (1884) Lays and Legends of the
  North
Graves (1940) Sergeant Lamb of the Ninth
  (1941) Proceed Sergeant Lamb
Gray (1811) Poems
Grayson (1975) The Last Alderman
Green (1979) Rachman
Greene G. (1932) Stamboul Train
  (1934) It's a Battlefield
  (1967) May We Borrow Your Husband
  (1978) The Human Factor
Greene G. A. (1599) Works
*Grose (1811) Dictionary of the Vulgar
  Tongue
Guinness (1985) Blessings in Disguise

Hailey (1973) Wheels
  (1975) The Money-Changers
  (1979) Overlord
  (1984) Strong Medicine
Hall (1969) The Ninth Directive
  (1979) The Scorpion Signal
Hallam (1866) Wadsley Jack
Hamilton (1897) The Outlaws of the
  Marches
  (1898) The Mawkin of the Flow

Hardy (1874) Far From the Madding Crowd
(1888) Wessex Tales
*Harland and Wilkinson (1867) Folk Lore
Harris (1925) My Life and Loves
Hartley (1870) Heart Broken
Harvey (1628) Anatomica de Motu Cordis etc.
Hayden (1902) From a Thatched Cottage
Heath (1650)
Hector (1876) Selections from the Judicial Records of Renfrewshire
Hemingway (1941) For Whom the Bell Tolls
Henderson G. (1856) The Popular Rhymes, Sayings and Proverbs of the County of Berwick
Henderson W. (1879) Notes on the Folk Lore of the Northern Counties etc.
Herd (1776) Ancient and Modern Scottish Songs
Herr (1977) Dispatches
Herriot (1981) The Lord God Made Them All
Hetrick (1826) Poems and Songs
Heywood (1546) Works
Hibbert (1822) A Description of the Shetland Islands
Higgins (1976) Storm Warning
Hogg (1822) Perils of Man
(1866) Tales and Sketches
*Holt (1961) Phrase and Word Origins
Hood (c. 1830) Poems
Horrocks (1960) A Full Life
Horsley (1887) Jottings from Jail
Housman (1896) Poems
*Howard (1977) New Words for Old
* (1978) Weasel Words
*Howat (1979) Who Did What
*Hudson (1977) The Dictionary of Diseased English
* (1978) The Jargon of the Professions
Hughes (1856) Tom Brown's Schooldays
Hunt H. (1854) Letter
Hunt R. (1865 and 1896 edn.) Popular Romances of the West of England
Hutchinson (c. 1650) Letter
Hynd (1949)

Iacocca (1984) Iacocca
Ingelo (1830) Reminiscences
Inglis (1895) Oor Ain Folk
Innes (1982) The Black Tide
Irvine (1986) Runaway

James (Surgeon) (1816) Journal
James (1972) An Unsuitable Job for a Woman
(1975) The Black Tower
(1980) Innocent Blood
(1986) A Taste for Death
Jane (1897) The Lordship, the Passen and We
*Jennings (1965) Personalities of Language
Jefferies (1880) Hodge
*Johnson Dr S. (1755) A Dictionary of the English Language
Johnstone (1891) Kilmallie
Jolliffe and Mayle (1984) Man's Best Friend
Jones and Marriott (1970) Anatomy of a Merger
Jones R. V. (1978) Most Secret War
Jonson (Ben) (1598/1633) Works
Joyce (1922) Ulysses

*Kay and Stevens (1974) Beyond the Dictionary in English
Keith (1896) The Indian Uncle
Kelly (1721) A Complete Collection of Scottish Proverbs
Keneally (1979) Confederates
(1982) Schindler's Ark
(1985) A Family Madness
Kennedy (1867) The Banks of the Boro
Kersh (1936) Night and the City
Kinloch (1827) The Ballad Book
Kirkton (1817) The Secret and True History of the Church of Scotland etc.
Kyle (1975) The Semenov Impulse
(1983) The King's Commander

Lacey (1986) Ford
Lauderdale (1796) A Collection of Poems
Lavine (1930) The Third Degree
Lawless (1892) Grania
le Carré (1962) A Murder of Quality
(1980) Smiley's People
(1986) A Perfect Spy
Lewis (1795) The Monk
Liddle (1821) Poems on Different Occasions
*Lingemann (1969) Drugs from A to Z
Linton (1866/7) Lizzie Lorton of Greyrigg
Lodge (1962) Ginger You're Barmy
(1975) Changing Places
Londres (1924) The Road to Buenos Ayres (in tr.)
Longstreet (1956) The Real Jazz Old and New
Lowson (1890) John Guidfollow
Ludlum (1979) The Materese Circle
(1984) The Aquitaine Progression
Lumsden (1892) Sheep-head and Trotters
Lyall (1965) Midnight Plus One
(1969) Venus with Pistol
(1972) Blame the Dead
(1975) Judas Country

(1980)   The Secret Servant
(1982)   The Conduct of Major Maxim
(1985)   The Crocus List
Lyly (1579)   Euphues, the Anatomy of Wit
Lynn and Jay (1981)   Yes Minister
(1986)   Yes Prime Minister

McBain (1981)   Heat
McCarthy (1963)   The Group
(1967)   Vietnam
MacDonagh (1898)   Irish Life and
Character
McKenzie of Coul, see Prebble (1963)
MacLaren (1895)   Beside the Bonnie Brier
Bush
MacManus (1898)   The Bend of the Road
*McNair (1973)   A Guide to Hip Language
and Culture
MacTaggart (1824/1876 edn.) Encyclopaedia
Maidment (1844)   Spottiswoode Miscellany
(1868)   A Book of Scotch Pasquils 1568–
1715
Mailer (1965)   An American Dream
*Major (1970)   Black Slang. A Dictionary of
Afro-American Slang
Manchester (1968)   The Arms of Krupp
Mann (1902)   The Fields of Dulditch
Manning (1960)   The Great Fortune
(1962)   The Spoilt City
(1965)   Friends and Heroes
(1977)   The Danger Tree
(1978)   The Battle Lost and Won
Marshall (1811/7/8)   Review and Abstract of
the County Reports to the Board of
Agriculture etc.
Marvell (c. 1670)   Poems
Mason A. E. W. (1927)   No Other Tiger
Mason W. (1815)   A Statistical Account or
Parochial Survey of Ireland
Masters (1976)   The Himalayan Concerto
Mather (1862)   Songs
Matthew (1978)   The Diary of a Somebody
(1983)   How to Survive Middle Age
Mayhew (1851)   London Labour and the
London Poor
(1861)   Mayhew's London
(1862)   London Underworld
*Mencken (1940/8)   The American Language
Mitford J. (1963)   The American Way of
Death
Mitford N. (1945)   The Pursuit of Love
(1949)   Love in a Cold Climate
(1956)   Noblesse Oblige
(1960)   Don't Tell Alfred
Moir (1828)   The Life of Mansie Wauch
Monsarrat (1978)   The Master Mariner
Morison (1790)   Poems
Mortimer (1895)   Tales from the Western
Moors

Moss (1985)   Moscow Rules
Moss W. S. (1950)   Ill Met by Moonlight
Moynahan (1983)   Airport International
Mucklebackit (1885)   Rhymes
Muggeridge (1972)   Chronicles of Wasted
Time
Muir (1816)   The Clydesdale Minstrelsy
Murdoch A. (1873)   Lilts on the Doric Lyre
(1895)   Scotch Readings
Murdoch I. (1977)   Henry and Cato
(1978)   The Sea, The Sea
(1980)   Nuns and Soldiers
(1983)   The Philosopher's Pupil
(1985)   The Good Apprentice
Murray D. (1886)   Rainbow Gold
1890   John Vale's Guardian
Murray E. (1977)   Caught in the Web of
Words

Nares (1822)   A Glossary or Collection of
Words etc.
*Neaman and Silver (1983)   Kind Words: A
Thesaurus of Euphemisms
*New Larousse Encyclopedia of Mythology
(1968)
Nicholson W. (1814)   Poetical Works
Nicholson and Burn (1777)   The History
and Antiquities of the Counties of
Westmoreland and Cumberland

O'Reilly (1880)   Sussex Stories
Ogg (1873)   Willi Waly; and other Poems
Olivier (1982)   Confessions of an Actor
Ollivant (1898)   Owd Bob, the Grey Dog of
Kenmuir
*Onions (1975)   The Oxford Dictionary of
English Etymology
*Original Selection of New Words (1986)
*Oxford English Dictionary (1979)

Parker (1944)   The Portable Dorothy Parker
*Partridge (1947)   Shakespeare's Bawdy
*   (1959)   Origins
*   (1969)   A Dictionary of Slang and
Unconventional English
*   (1972)   A Dictionary of Clichés
*   (and Simpson)   A Dictionary of
Historical Slang
*   (1973)   Usage and Abusage
*   (1977)   A Dictionary of Catch Phrases
Pass the Port (1976)   An Anthology
Payn (1878)   By Proxy
Peacock E. (1870)   Ralf Skirlaugh, the
Lincolnshire Farmer
Peacock F. (1890)   A Soldier and a Maid
Pease (1894)   The Mark o' the Deil
Pegge (1803)   Anecdotes of the English
Language
*Pei (1969)   Words in Sheep's Clothing

* (1978) Weasel Words
Pennecuik (1715) Description of Tweeddale and Poems
Pepys (1662) Diaries
Peshall (1773) Ancient and Present State of the City of Oxford
Picken (1813) Miscellaneous Poems and Songs
Pindar (Wolcot) (1816) Works
Pinnock (1895) Tom Brown's Black Country Annual
Playboy's Book of Limericks (1972)
Pope (1735) Poetical Works
Pope-Hennessy (1967) The Sins of the Fathers
Praed (1890) Romance Station
Prebble (1963) The Highland Clearances
Price (1970) The Labyrinth Makers
  (1971) The Alamut Ambush
  (1972) Captain Butler's Wolf
  (1974) Other Paths to Glory
  (1975) Our Man in Camelot
  (1978) The '44 Vintage
  (1979) War Games
  (1982) The Old Vengeful
  (1985) Here Be Monsters
Proudlock (1896) The Borderland Muse
*Pythian (1979) A Concise Dictionary of Current English

Quiller-Couch (1888) The Astonishing History of Troy Town
  (1890) I Saw Three Ships
  (1891) Naughts and Crosses
  (1893) The Delectable Duchy

Rabelais (1532) Pantagruel (in tr.)
  (1534) Gargantua (in tr.)
*Radford and Smith (1973) To Coin a Phrase
Ramsay A. (1737) Collection of Scots Proverbs
  (1800 edn.) Poems
Ramsay E. (1858/61) Reminiscences of Scottish Life and Character
*Rawson (1981) A Dictionary of Euphemisms and Other Doubletalk
Ray (1678) A Collection of English Proverbs
Read (1986) The Free Frenchman
Rees (1980) Graffiti
Richards (1933) Old Soldiers Never Die
  (1936) Old Soldier Sahib
Ritchie (1883) The Churches of St Baldred
Robbins (1981) Goodbye Janette
Roberts (1951) The Estate of Man
Rock (1867) Jim an' Nell
Rodger (1838) Poems and Songs
Rogers (*see* Treddlehoyle)

*Roget's Thesaurus (1966)
*Ross (1956) Noblesse Oblige
* (1973) Words in Sheep's Clothing
Russell (c. 1900) A Strange Voyage

Salinger (1951) The Catcher in the Rye
Sale (1930) The Specialist
Sanders (1970) The Anderson Tapes
  (1973) The First Deadly Sin
  (1977) The Second Deadly Sin
  (1977) The Tangent Objective
  (1978) The Marlow Chronicles
  (1979) The Sixth Commandment
  (1980) The Tenth Commandment
  (1980) Caper
  (1981) The Third Deadly Sin
  (1982) The Case of Lucy Bending
  (1983) The Seduction of Peter S.
  (1984) The Passion of Molly T.
  (1985) The Fourth Deadly Sin
  (1986) The Eighth Commandment
Saxon (1878) Galloway Gossip Sixty Years Ago
Scott A. (1805) Poems
Scott P. (1968) The Day of the Scorpion
  (1971) The Towers of Silence
  (1973) The Jewel in the Crown
  (1975) A Division of the Spoils
  (1977) Staying On
Scott W. (1803) Minstrelsy of the Scottish Border
  (1814) Waverley
  (1815) Guy Mannering
  (1816) The Antiquary
  (1817) Rob Roy
  (1818) The Heart of Midlothian
  (1819) The Bride of Lammermoor
  (1822) The Fortunes of Nigel
  (1824) Redgauntlet
Service (1887) The Life and Recollections of Dr Duguid of Kilwinning
  (1890) Thir Notandums
Seymour (1980) The Contract
  (1982) Archangel
  (1984) In Honour Bound
Shakespeare Plays as noted and sonnets
Shankland (1980)
Sharpe (1973) Indecent Exposure
  (1974) Porterhouse Blue
  (1975) Blott on the Landscape
  (1976) Wilt
  (1977) The Great Pursuit
  (1978) The Throwback
  (1979) The Wilt Alternative
  (1982) Vintage Stuff
*Sheppard (1970) A Dictionary of Railway Slang
*Shipley (1945) A Dictionary of Word Origins

Shirer (1984)　The Nightmare Years 1930–
　1940
Sidney (1586)　Works
Simon (1979)　Jupiter's Travels
*Slang Dictionary (The) Etymological,
　Historical, and Analytical (1874)
Slick (1836)　Clockmaker
*Smith　A Smaller Latin–English Dictionary
Smith M. C. (1981)　Gorky Park
Smith W. (1979)　Wild Justice
*Smith and Wilson (1970)　The Oxford
　Dictionary of English Poverbs
Smollett (1748)　Roderick Random
　(1751)　Peregrine Pickle
　(1771)　Humphrey Clinker
Solzhenitsyn (1974)　The Gulag
　Archipelago (2) in tr.
Somerville and Ross (1897)　Some
　Experiences of an Irish RM
　(1908)　Further Experiences of an Irish
　RM
Spence (1898)　From the Braes of the Carse
Steinbeck (1961)　The Winter of our
　Discontent
Stewart (1892)　Shetland Fireside Tales
Stoker (1895)　Waller's Mou
*Story of English (The) (1986)　McCrum,
　Cran and MacNeil
Strachey (1918)　Eminent Victorians
Strain (1900)　Elmslie's Drag-net
Styron (1976)　Sophie's Choice
Sutcliffe (1900)　Shameless Wayne
　(1901)　Mistress Barbara Cunliffe
*Sutherland (1975)　The Oxford Book of
　Literary Anecdotes
Swift (1723/38)　Works

Tarras (1804)　Poems
Taylor (1890)　Miss Miles
Tennyson (1859)　The Idylls of the King
　(1889)　Owd Roä
Tester (1865)　Poems
Thackeray (1837/55)　Works
Theroux (1971)　Jungle Lovers
　(1973)　Saint Jack
　(1974)　The Black House
　(1975)　The Great Railway Bazaar
　(1976)　The Family Arsenal
　(1977)　The Consul's File
　(1978)　Picture Palace
　(1979)　The Old Patagonian Express
　(1980)　World's End and Other Stories
　(1981)　The Mosquito Coast
　(1982)　The London Embassy
　(1983)　The Kingdom by the Sea
Thom (1878)　The Courtship and Wedding
　of Jock o' the Knowe
Thomas H. (1961)　The Spanish Civil War
Thomas L. (1977)　Bare Nell

　(1978)　Ormerod's Landing
　(1979)　That Old Gang of Mine
　(1981)　The Magic Army
　(1986)　The Adventures of Goodnight
　and Loving
Thomas M. (1980)　Green Monday
　(1982)　Someone Else's Money
　(1985)　Hard Money
　(1987)　The Ropespinner Conspiracy
Torriano (1642)　quoted in ODEP
Townsend (1982)　The Secret Diary of
　Adrian Mole Aged 13¾
Treddlehoyle (Rogers) (1846/1892/1893)
　Bairnsla Annals (reprinted in Leeds
　Mercury Supplement etc.)
Trevanian (1972)　The Eiger Sanction
　(1973)　The Loo Sanction
Trevor-Roper (1971)　Introduction to
　Goebbels' Diaries
Trollope (1885)　The Land-Leaguers
Turner (1968)
Tweeddale (1896)　Moff

Ustinov (1966)　The Frontiers of the Sea
　(1971)　Krumnagel

Vachell (1934)　The Disappearance of
　Martha Penny
Van Lustbaden (1983)　Black Heart
Vedder (1832)　Orcadian Sketches
Verney (1870)　Lettice Lisle

Wallace (1693)　A Description of the Isles of
　Orkney
Wambaugh (1975)　The Choirboys
　(1981)　The Glitter Dome
　(1983)　The Delta Star
Ward M. (1895)　The Story of Bessie
　Costrell
Ward T. (1708)　Some Queries to the
　Protestants etc.
Wardrop (1881)　Johnnie Mathison's
　Courtship and Marriage
Waugh A. (from *Private Eye* diaries as dated)
Waugh E. (1930)　Labels
　(1932)　Remote People
　(1933)　Scoop
　(1955)　Officers and Gentlemen
　(1956)　Noblesse Oblige
*Wentworth and Flexner (1975)　Dictionary
　of American Slang
*Webster's New Collegiate Dictionary (1977)
Webster J. (1623)　The Duchess of Malfi
West (1979)　Proteus
Westall (1885)　The Old Factory
Weverka (1973)　The Sting
Whitehead A. (1896)　Legends of Penrith
Whitehead S. (1876)　Daft Davie
Willock (1889)　Rosetty Ends

Wilson (1836)   Tales
Wilson (1915)   Ruggles of Red Gap
Wilson T. (1843)   The Pitman's Pay
Wilson (1603)   The Bachelor's Banquet
Wodrow (1721)   The History of the
  Sufferings of the Church of Scotland etc.
*Wood (1962)   Current English Usage
*Wood and Hill (1979)   Dictionary of
  English Colloquial Idioms

Wouk (1951)   The Caine Mutiny
*Wright (1898/1905)   The English Dialect
  Dictionary

Young (1721)   The Revenge

Zack (Keats) (1901)   Tales of Dustable Weir

A

A amphetamine used illegally
'A' is also used by addicts for LSD. The punning 'A bomb' is a combination of illicit narcotics, from the effect on the user. A 'B bomb' is a benzedrine inhaler used illegally.

à trois three people living together in a sexual relationship
Abbr. of 'ménage à trois'. Often of a married couple and the outside sexual partner of one of them: 'I've been living *à trois* with a married couple. Do I shock you?' (Murdoch, 1977).

Aaron's rod a penis
Properly, an ornamental rod with a serpent entwined round it, from the plant Verbascum Thapsus, which has tall erect spikes of yellow flowers. Aaron used his rod for producing miracles in Egypt and when planted in the ground, it produced almonds.

abandoned working as a whore
Properly, forsaken and epitomizing the formal 19c. attitude to prostitution: 'The foolish idea . . . . that once abandoned she must always be profligate' (Mayhew, 1862, of a whore). The punning 'abandoned habits' were the flashy clothes whores wore when riding in London's Hyde Park.

abbess a female bawd
An old use, partly humorous and partly based on the supposition that nunneries were not solely occupied by chaste females: '. . . who should come in but the venerable mother Abbess herself' (Cleland, 1749, of a bawd).

abdomen a man's genitalia
Properly, the lower cavity of the trunk. A convenient evasion for sports commentators when a player has been incapacitated by a blow in his testicles. Also as 'lower abdomen'. An 'abdominal protector' in genteel language is a shield for the genitalia.

ablutions a lavatory
Properly, the religious rite of washing, whence washing the body on any occasion and the place in which you washed: 'We were told to choose a bed site . . . shown where the Ablutions were' (Bogarde, 1978, of being drafted into the army – here and elsewhere note the capital letter for a word used euphemistically). An army usage.

abnormal homosexual
Heterosexuality is the norm: '. . . lived an institutional life with other men in uniform without ever seriously arousing the suspicion that he was what is called abnormal' (P. Scott, 1975). Of either sex. 'Abnormality' is homosexuality: 'The fact that he revealed a hatred of "abnormality" was only to be expected. "What a filthy Lesbian trick," he said' (McCarthy, 1963).

aboard (1) drunk
The imagery is from loading a ship. In dialect use, 'something aboard': 'He's sum'uts aboard today; he could nobud just sit e' his gig' (EDD). ? ob.

aboard (2) copulating with
Male usage, from getting above the female: 'I was aboard Lily Langtry long before he was' (Fraser, 1970 – the 'he' was King Edward VII).

abode of love a brothel
Where 'love' imports copulation: 'These abodes of love seen from the other side are strangely transfigured. All is order, cleanliness and respectability' (Londres, 1928, in tr.).

above ground respectable or legitimate
Usu. of a changed pattern of behaviour after a period of shameful or illegal conduct: 'She starred in dozens of blue movies before coming above ground' (Deighton, 1972). 'Above', like 'no', is a prefix in many euphemistic expressions; thus an 'above critical' nuclear reactor is very unsafe. The converse 'underground' has implications of illegality or impropriety in many phrases.

abuse yourself to masturbate
Properly, to misuse your body in any respect, as by eating too quickly. Of males rather than females and *see* **self-abuse**. 'Mutual abuse' is masturbation by each other of any combination of males and females. To 'abuse a bed' was to copulate extra-maritally: 'See the hell of having a false woman. My bed shall be abused' (Shakespeare, *Merry Wives of Windsor*).

Abyssinian medal an undone and visible trouser fly-button
Various 'medal' phrases found favour after successive military campaigns until the zip replaced buttons. The Abyssinian Campaign lasted from 1893 to 1896, to be followed by a similar adventure in Egypt with its medals, real and euphemistic, and so on until the emergence of the general **medal showing** (q.v.).

AC/DC indulging in both homosexual and heterosexual practices

The imagery is from the ability to use inter-changeably alternating and direct electric current: 'Young attractive housewife, AC/DC would like to meet married AC/DC people to join well-endowed husband for threesomes or moresomes' (*Daily Telegraph*, May 1980 – *see* **threesomes** for the rest of the story).

academic dismissal expulsion from college
Not just the end of classes for the day: 'No student ever gets expelled any more, though he may suffer "academic dismissal"' (Jennings, 1965).

academy a brothel
Properly, a school, from the garden where Plato taught: '. . . the show of a shop was shut, the academy open'd; the mask of mock-modesty was completely taken off' (Cleland, 1749). In the same sense whores were styled 'academicians'. ob.

Acapulco gold marijuana
The plant is grown near the Mexican city with 'gold' punning on the colour, the quality and the cost: 'Charters produced very strong, very good Acapulco Gold. He had two joints already rolled' (Collins, 1981). This is an example of many similar geographical evasions used by addicts.

accident (1) involuntary urination or defecation
Properly, anything which happens, whence in common use anything undesirable: 'I've never punished him, the way our mothers and nurses did, when he has an "accident"' (McCarthy, 1963 – here and elsewhere note the use of inverted commas for a word or phrase used euphemistically). Mainly used of young children.

accident (2) an unwanted pregnancy
To treat impregnation as though it were an unforeseen happening may seem unduly innocent or optimistic: 'I have the means to prevent any . . . . accident. I promise I'll be very careful' (Styron, 1976). The child born under these circumstances may also be called an 'accident'.

accident (3) a collision which damages a vehicle or causes injury
We all want to attribute the blame for a mishap to forces beyond normal expectation, in so far as we cannot blame someone else: 'Threequarters of the road accidents are not accidents at all . . . . Most of the deaths and injuries are due to "carelessness, speeding, improper overtaking, not obeying traffic

signs or effects of drink or drugs"' (*Daily Telegraph*, May 1981, omitting poor vehicle maintenance, aggression, inexperience and trying to reverse while looking the other way).

accommodate yourself to urinate
Not seeking lodging as well: '. . . our guide stopped on the path and accommodated himself in a way that made me think that his reverence for the spot was far from fanatical' (E. Waugh, 1932, on being guided to a holy place).

accommodation collar *see* **collar** (2)

accommodation house a brothel
'Accommodation' means supplying needs, of which man has many other than for extra-marital copulation: '. . . take him along to one of the accommodation houses in Haymarket, and get him paired off with a whore' (Fraser, 1973, writing in 19c. style). In the same sense to 'accommodate' was to copulate with extra-maritally: '. . . nothin' but the best gentlemen to accommodate' (Fraser, 1982 – a bawd was speaking of her classy clientele). ob.

accouchement the period of childbirth
What was a euphemism in French becomes doubly so in SE use. cf. **lie in**.

account for to kill legally
Of animals by hunters and humans by soldiers. It might imply a reckoning of the numbers slain but you can 'account for' a single victim. Sir Walter Scott used 'go on the account' for engaging in piracy.

ace to kill
From the ability to take a trick at cards, although 'trump' might seem more appropriate: 'The gaunt man, his hands enclosed in blood-covered surgeon's plastic gloves, looked up at him. "Somebody's aced the lady."' (Diehl, 1978). Am.

ace of spades the vagina
Punning on the highest card in the pack and the appearance of pubic hair in a brunette. Am.

acid lysergic acid diethylamide
Better known as 'LSD' and only to chemists as $C_{20}H_{25}N_3O$. To 'drop acid' is to illegally ingest LSD: '. . . he was dropping acid and bombed out of his gourd' (Sanders, 1977). An 'acid-freak' is someone addicted to LSD. 'Acid Fascism' was the violence induced by Manson, the Californian cult leader, and others under its influence.

acorn academy an institution for lunatics
Where you might expect to find a **nut** (q.v.):
'"Your Honor, were these the acts of a sane
man?" – and Dan would be hidden away in
an acorn academy for a period of years'
(Sanders, 1973). Am.

acorns testicles
A less common Am. variant of **nuts** (q.v.):
'. . . shrieked as the spray hit him in the
acorns' (Wambaugh, 1975).

acquire to steal
Properly, to obtain possession of legally.
Mainly army use, of which DSUE in Volume
I says 'Not a euphemism, for it is used
jocularly' and then 'Army euphemistic coll:
1939 – 45' in Volume II. cf. **gain** and **win**
(1).

act (the) copulation
An abbr. of any of the phrases which follow
but rarely also used alone as 'My prepuce
contracted so that the act would have been
difficult' (Harris, 1925). 'Act of shame'
indicates extra-marital copulation: 'She with
Cassio hath the act of shame A thousand
times committed' (Shakespeare, *Othello*).
Specifically as 'act of generation': 'The
embrace of the sexes in the act of generation'
(EDD); 'act of intercourse': 'An act of intercourse took place, in the course of which
both partners achieved climax' (Amis, 1978);
'act of love': 'It was the time after the act of
love' (West, 1979); and 'the sexual act': 'The
sexual act is fully covered, but not in these
pages' (Longstreet, 1956). However 'a sexual act' implies something short of copulation.

act like a husband to copulate with a
female extra-maritally
But not of a transaction with a whore: 'Jessie
confessed that her sister accused her of letting me "act like a husband. She must have
seen a stain on my chemise"' (Harris, 1925).

Actaeon to cuckold
In the legend, Actaeon was no more than a
casual observer of Artemis' nakedness, and
she had no husband to take offence. Never-
theless she turned him into a stag and set his
own pack on him: 'Divulge Page himself for
a secure and wilful Actaeon' (Shakespeare,
Merry Wives of Windsor). Now literary use
only.

action (1) the proceeds of vice or illegality
Usu. of illegal gambling, narcotics or prostitution: '. . . one waits, while Federal authorities, mayors, and the Mafia decide . . . . how

much of the action they want' (Allbeury,
1976). A 'piece' or 'slice' of the action may
also be an unmerited share in a dubious
enterprise started by someone else: 'He has
claimed a piece of the action in the video
production of operas at Covent Garden'
(*Private Eye*, May 1981).

action (2) the brutal harassment of supposed opponents
The 'Aktion' of the Nazis: 'Schindler did
not dare believe that this red child had survived the Aktion process' (Keneally, 1982, of
such a round-up).

action (3) the availability of females for
extra-marital copulation
The vice itself, rather than its proceeds as in
action (1) (above): 'Then he stared around
to check the action' (Sanders, 1982 – a man
had gone to a bar to pick up such a woman).

active not crippled by illness or age
Of those Am. geriatrics who have retained
mobility: 'Active Adult Golf Community'
(advertisement at Gainesville, Florida,
November 1987 for houses close to a golf
course).

active (air) defence *see* defence

activist a person who uses illegality for
political purposes
The former meaning, a supporter of the
philosophical concept of activism, has
entirely given way to this use which seeks to
imply that those pursuing similar aims legally
are passive and ineffective.

actress a whore
Until a liberating decree of Charles II,
female roles on stage were played by males.
Therefore until the late 19c. acting was not
considered a respectable profession for a
woman: 'The actress and the singer were
considered nothing much more than prostitutes with a sideline' (Longstreet, 1956, of
New Orleans prior to 1917). The connection
between the stage and the couch persists:
'Miss Keeler, 20, a freelance model, was
visiting Miss Marilyn Rice-Davies, an
actress' (*Daily Telegraph*, December 1962).

acute environmental reaction
cowardice
Am. Vietnam jargon for the nervous illness
induced by the shocks of war: 'Most Americans would rather be told that their son is
undergoing acute environmental reaction
than to hear that he is suffering from shell
shock' (Herr, 1977).

Adam a public lavatory for males
A tasteless, but happily uncommon, variant in hotels, etc. for men (q.v.) with 'Eve' as its counterpart. In the 19c. 'Adam's arsenal' was the male genitalia: 'It wasn't just that she was unusually partial to Adam's arsenal' (Fraser, 1971, writing in 19c. style – the lady liked copulating). Of the same time and tendency, 'Eve's custom-house' was the vagina, where Adam was supposed to have made his first entry (Grose).

adapt to dye
Of woman's hair: 'She "mutates" or "adapts" or "colour-corrects" her hair' (Jennings, 1965).

adjourn to urinate
From the formal suspension of a meeting. Usu. in the form 'May I adjourn' – I want to urinate; or 'I suggest we have a short adjournment' – this gives everyone a chance to urinate. cf. **stretch your legs**.

adjust to increase
Commercial jargon when prices go up. When they go down, the reduction needs no glossing over. An 'adjustment' is such an increase: 'Price adjustment adds £5m to Carsington bill' (*Waterbulletin*, August 1983). But cf. **currency adjustment**.

adjustment (1) *see* **adjust**

adjustment (2) a bribe
The cost of re-arranging affairs in a manner which you find acceptable as by having a criminal charge withdrawn: 'They caught him molesting a child in a public school in Queens. The desk sergeant had enough sense not to book him. The final adjustment cost about eighteen thousand dollars' (Condon, 1966). Am.

adjustment (3) the cure of the mad or the punishment of the prisoner
You are correcting the deviation from your norm: 'Lucy is a very disturbed child, and a long way from adjustment' (Sanders, 1982). An 'adjustment centre' in an Am. prison is a cell for solitary confinement.

adjustment (4) a military defeat
The front, defensive position or line is adjusted under the compulsion of the enemy.

adjustment (5) a theft
Military use, when you 'adjust' the rights of ownership: 'No sirree, captain, there will be no theft. There will be adjustments' (Keneally, 1979 – the conscripts then had their clothing taken from them).

adjustment (6) the subjective alteration of published accounts
Usu. to record an improvement on what actually transpired but sometimes, in a private company, to conceal profit and thereby reduce tax: 'The purpose of the "adjustments" was to put the bank in the best possible light when the year-end figures ultimately appeared in the annual report' (Erdman, 1986). With most trading corporations the only verity is cash which, short of detectable fraud, can seldom be misstated; this does not prevent inventories being commonly manipulated. Banks, whose inventory is cash, are allowed to play the game by special rules.

admirer a man with whom a woman regularly copulates extra-maritally
Jane Austen uses 'admire' and 'admirer' in the sense of having no more than proper heterosexual desire for, but by mid 19c. the euphemistic use had developed: '. . . met her admirer at a house in Bolton Row that she was in the habit of frequenting' (Mayhew, 1862, of a married woman's extra-marital copulation). ? ob.

Adriatic tummy diarrhoea
Caught by foreign tourists in Italy and Yugoslavia: 'In the end a bout of Adriatic tummy had persuaded them to cut their losses and fly home a week early' (Sharpe, 1982).

adult (1) pornographic
Things so described are certainly unsuitable for children. An 'adult movie' is a pornographic film; an 'adult novelty' is a mechanism supposed to enhance sexual pleasure; an 'adult book store' is a shop which sells explicit pornography: '. . . nothing but taverns, junkyards, and adult book stores' (Sanders, 1980). It is difficult to believe that these are the normal tastes of the fully grown human.

adult (2) excluding children
Parts of the State of Florida abound with 'adult' trailer parks implying not that these facilities have achieved maturity but that geriatrics who live there will not be pestered by children. *See*, too, **active** (above).

adventure (1) a war
Properly, a chance happening and usu. of a conflict in which the aggressor sees only easy gains: 'Stalin will (not) allow himself to be dragged into the Pacific adventure' (Goebbels, 1945, in tr.).

adventure (2) an act of extra-marital copulation

Again from the proper sense, a chance or exciting event: 'I cannot have an adventure with Martin. He would boast of me' (Theroux, 1980). 'Adventure' is also used of a series of such acts.

adventuress a female who regularly copulates extra-maritally
Although not a whore, she has many **adventures** (2) (above): '... she was also an adventurer, in the precise sense of the word – one who has adventures, as opposed to an adventuress .... one who has lovers' (Blanch, 1954).

(adverse weather conditions describes any meteorological phenomenon which disrupts Br. public transport: '... drifts half an inch deep, known to British Rail as Adverse Weather Conditions' (*Private Eye*, December 1981). Dysphemism more than euphemism.)

adviser the representative of an imperial power in a client state
Often put there in an attempt by an unpopular government to stay in power: 'The Spanish Communist leaders moved out in the wake of their Russian "advisers"' (Boyle, 1979).

aesthete a male homosexual
Properly, he who affects a higher appreciation of beauty than others: '... aesthetes – you know – those awful effeminate creatures – pansies' (N. Mitford, 1949). Whence 'aestheticism', male homosexuality: 'He had been at the House, but remarked with a shade of regret that he had not found any aestheticism in his day' (E. Waugh, 1930, of a homosexual).

aesthetic procedure cosmetic surgery
Not the sexual practices of a homosexual but an operation to enhance beauty: 'They were concerned that my teeth never showed, even when I smiled, but they said the cure was simple. They had what they called an aesthetic procedure' (Iacocca, 1984).

affair a relationship which involves extramarital copulation
Properly, any business or proceeding. Originally of the wife so involved but now of either sex: '... having a vigorous and even dangerous wife, and an affair problem' (Bradbury, 1975). In the same sense further disguised as the French *affaire*: 'He comes only to see the singer Floriana. He's her latest *affaire*' (Manning, 1960 – here and elsewhere observe how the euphemism is printed in italics). Some homosexual use, as 'His affairs with men had been few' (P. Scott,

1971) which must not be confused with the 'man of affairs'. For Fanny Hill an 'affair' was a penis: '... draws out his affair, so shrunk and diminish'd' (Cleland, 1749).

affinity a sexual mistress
Properly a natural liking for anything, whence a relationship, as by marriage: 'Q: Why is a Model T like an affinity? (*Affinity* was the vogue euphemism for 'mistress' in the 1920s) A: Because you hate to be seen on the streets with one' (Lacey, 1986). Am. ob.

affirmative action giving unfair preference to Black people
Not just treating Black and White even-handedly: 'And of course, there's Affirmative Action. Apparently there aren't too many black or Hispanic Masterwomen .... How many spics and jigaboos you got working here, anyway?' (M. Thomas, 1982, highlighting the prejudice which the policy seeks to overcome). Mainly Am. but: '... would pursue stepped up "affirmative action" policies, i.e. favouring blacks for jobs' (*Daily Telegraph*, April 1983, of London).

afflicted crippled
Properly, suffering from a disease but used of those who are not. Now largely supplanted by 'handicapped'. In ob. Br. use it also meant drunk and 'afflictions' were mourning clothes.

African black marijuana
From the colour and perhaps the source. Mainly Am.

after lusting for
Of either sex, homosexually or heterosexually, from the pursuit: 'She's after you, or was. Probably moved on to somebody else by now' (Amis, 1978).

after part the buttocks
A rare form of **behind** (q.v.).

after shave a perfume used by males
The ostensible justification was the alleviation of smarting following a shave with a blunt razor: 'His sweet-whisky fragrance of after-shave lotion stung my eyes' (Theroux, 1982). I suppose the macho brand names relieve the doubts of those who affect these cosmetics.

afterlife death
Used especially by Quakers, Spiritualists and other bodies who have confidence that death is not the necessary end: '"It is the smell of afterlife." "It smells more like that of afterdeath," said Jessica' (Sharpe, 1978).

afternoon man a debauchee
He is supposed not to get up in the morning:
'They are a company of giddy-heads, afternoon men' (Burton, c. 1633). Probably ob.
despite its use by Anthony Powell in his
1931 novel title.

afterthought a child born within wedlock
following an unplanned conception
Of the processes associated with the event,
thought is usu. the least prominent: 'Being
the youngest in the family – what is commonly called an "afterthought" – she was
also a little spoilt' (Read, 1986).

agent a taboo subject or job
In espionage, a spy, more of your own side
than of the opposition and specifically as
'secret agent'; in buggery, the donor – the
recipient is the 'patient'; in warfare, bombs
etc. with a 'chemical warfare agent' as a
noxious poison. We also use 'agent' of our
jobs to enhance our prestige. Thus the Br.
'estate agent' is in law the agent of neither
the buyer nor the seller and there is an
infinite variety of Am. 'agents', often no
more than junior employees.

aid (1) military repression
Abbr. of 'aid to the civil power' and a common usage in the Br. empire where individual Britons commanded quite small native
police forces with responsibility over large
and often hostile populations: 'Such a
request for aid was, in a sense, really only a
call to stand by' (P. Scott, 1973, of India –
when the military became actively involved
in riot control, you issued live rounds only to
a sniper, who fired at the ringleaders).

aid (2) a gift from a rich country to a poor
one
Usu. of food and munitions and seldom with
as much altruism as the donor would have
you believe. 'Tied aid' means that the
recipient has to spend the money buying
goods from the donor.

air (the) peremptory dismissal from
employment or courtship
Both the giver and the receiver use the term:
'If Victoria wants to give Jamie the air, it's no
business of ours' (Deighton, 1982, of a
broken engagement). Perhaps from the ejection from a building in which you were
working. Mainly Am.

air support attacking the enemy from
aircraft
Military jargon for the dropping of bombs
etc. to help your own troops. The usage is so
common that we seldom think of the logical

meaning of the phrase, including the
phenomenon whereby a laminar flow of air
maintains an aircraft in flight.

Ajax *see* jakes

alcohol an intoxicant
The SE use is an abbr. of 'alcohol of wine',
from the meaning a condensed spirit, which
in turn was derived from 'the fine metallic
powder used in the East to stain the eyelids,
etc.' (SOD).

alcove the vagina
Viewed sexually by a male. Properly, a recess
in a room. Not common.

Alderman Lushington *see* lush

alienate to pilfer
I suspect this comes from the meaning to
make less close or affectionate rather than
from the legal jargon, to transfer ownership:
'You can "alienate" as much pineboard as
that?' (Keneally, 1982, of stealing from a pile
of lumber). ?ob.

all-nighter a contract with a whore to stay
with her all night
Prostitutes' jargon of obvious derivation:
'The price of a short-time with massage
stayed the same, and an all-nighter cost only
an extra three-fifty' (Theroux, 1972). In ob.
Br. use an 'all-night man' dug up recent
corpses to sell for medical dissection. Wide
belief in the resurrection of the dead led to
an understandable reluctance to donate your
body for medical purposes in case you might
be faced in due course with a piecemeal
return to earth.

all right prepared to copulate extra-
maritally
Of a female, often described by males as a
'bit of all right' despite her manifest moral
turpitude. In modern use, it is likely to refer
only to sexual attractiveness.

all-rounder a person of both homosexual
and heterosexual tastes
The imagery is from sport, where it denotes
ability in various aspects of a game, or in
many games: 'She was a bit of an all-
rounder. Both sexes, general fun and games'
(Davidson, 1978).

all the way copulation with full penetration
Usu. teenage use, to distinguish from the
intermediate stages of caressing: '"Have you
had sex together?" He blushed. "Well, ah,
not exactly. I mean, we've done . . . things.
But not, you know all the way"' (Sanders,
1981, of a man's relationship with a school-

girl). In rare adult use, the phrase may mean copulation without contraception: 'I *want* you, Nimrod. *All the way*. Now' (Hailey, 1979, of a wife to her impotent husband's friend).

all up with about to die
From the sl. 'all up', ended: 'It's all up with him, poor lad . . . . His bowels is mortified' Fraser, 1971).

alley apple a horse turd dropped on the highway
A perhaps ob. Am. version of **horse apples** (q.v.).

alley cat a whore
Both tend to frequent narrow lanes: 'These alley cats pluck at your sleeve as you pick your way along the steep cobbled footpath' (Theroux, 1975). To 'alley-cat' means to copulate promiscuously with many partners: '. . . couldn't stand the thought of the guy alley-catting around' (Sanders, 1977).

alleyed dead
WW I army usage. Probably from 'tossing in the alley', to acknowledge defeat in the game of marbles, but WW I soldiers did wonderful things with French verbs, including 'aller', to go.

along the passage to the lavatory
The place where a guest may be asked if he wishes to go, but it could as well apply to the kitchen or the fuel store in most houses.

alter to castrate
Of domestic animals in 19c. prudery: '. . . *to castrate* became *to change, to arrange, or to alter*' (Mencken, 1940).

alternative opposed to existing social arrangement or convention
The use infers that the methods proposed can lead to a better life without corresponding hardship; as by solar energy replacing normal methods of electrical production, homeotherapy replacing drugs etc.: 'Eva Wilt's . . . . Alternative Medicine alternated with Alternative Gardening and Alternative Nutrition and even various Alternative Religions' (Sharpe, 1979). Politically it may imply the acceptance of violence to achieve change: 'I'm into . . . Marxist esthetics. I'm interested in alternative education' (Bradbury, 1976). Militarily it means opposed to nuclear weapons and countering your enemy's arsenal of hydrogen bombs with gunpowder: '. . . an "alternative defence workshop" led by Mrs Joan Ruddock, CND Chairman' (*Daily Telegraph*, November

1983). 'Alternative sexuality' is homosexuality: 'Homosexuality, with the inevitable personal disorientations it generates, was shrugged off as "alternative sexuality"' (*Daily Telegraph*, November 1979).

amateur a female who copulates promiscuously without payment
Properly, a person who loves doing something, whence a performer who does it without payment: '. . . stark except for her riding boots. That took me aback, for it ain't usual among amateurs' (Fraser, 1971). In the 19c. it meant a whore who had other employment: '. . . working before losing their virtue, at some trade or other . . . . called the "amateurs" to contra-distinguish them from the professionals' (Mayhew, 1862).

amatory rites copulation
The formalities of **love** (q.v.) within or outside marriage: '. . . my two friends soon transferred both their sleeping arrangements and their deafening amatory rites to the bed in Nathan's quarters' (Styron, 1976).

ambidexterous having both homosexual and heterosexual tastes
Of men or women, from the facility to use either hand with equal skill.

ambivalent having both homosexual and heterosexual tastes
Properly, entertaining two opposite emotions at the same time: 'Sexually I'd say some of the company was on the ambivalent side' (P. Scott, 1975).

ambrosia an intoxicant
Properly, the food, and less often the drink, of the gods: 'Bring your own ambrosia or take pot luck' (Sharpe, 1976). 'Nectar' would be more accurate except that it implies sweetness.

ambulance chaser a disreputable lawyer
He likes, fig. at least, to follow an ambulance to hospital in the hope of being briefed in a contingency suit which he may persuade the victim to bring: 'Madder was a shyster in the Quorn Building. An ambulance chaser, a small time fixer, an alibi builder-upper' (Chandler, 1939). Am.

amenity the purchase of priority or privacy during illness
An evasion of the Br. National Health Service where the principle of free medical treatment on demand for all in practice involves delays in treatment, summary summonses for consultation and little privacy; but the imperfections must not be directly

mentioned. Thus 'amenity' beds and wards for 'private', or paying patients.

America first isolationism
Very common before Pearl Harbor: 'Sloan did not care if Hitler gobbled up the whole of Europe – he was for America First' (McCarthy, 1963). Whence 'America Firster': 'FDR has said, "all aid short of war". And the America Firsters would raise an almighty hue and cry' (Archer, 1979). Not yet ob.

ammunition (1) lavatory paper
Of the same tendency as the ob. jocular 'bum fodder', which now hides its origins in the abbr. 'bumf', masked still further as 'bumph', meaning no more than an excess of paperwork: 'Astounding how the bumph accumulated during even a short absence .... Minutes! More like bloody hours' (Grayson, 1975).

ammunition (2) a towel worn during menstruation
Possibly adverting to the red danger sign on explosives, or on its expendability. In ob. Br. naval use an 'ammunition wife' was a whore, lively in performance but expendable.

amorous favours etc. copulation
Of either sex and see **amatory rites** and **favours**: 'It had become embarrassingly and sickeningly plain that the fickle Kim was bestowing amorous favours simultaneously on Melinda' (Boyle, 1979, of Philby and Maclean's wife). For 'amorous sport', see **sport**. An 'amorous tie' is a commitment to another which involves extra-marital copulation: 'I have few friends and no "amorous ties", I am alone and free' (Murdoch, 1978).

amount of investment in the service funeral expenses
The jargon of funeral arrangers who seek to extract as much as they can out of the bereaved by linking expenditure with grief: 'Am important error to guard against .... is referring to "cost of casket". The phrase "amount of investment in the service" is a wiser usage' (J. Mitford, 1963). Am.

amour an extra-marital sexual partner
Properly, love or affection. An 'amour' may also less often be a single act of extra-marital copulation: 'Those women who live in apartments, and maintain themself by the product of their vagrant amours' (Mayhew, 1862). Rarely in this sense in the singular: '... the jolly athletic amour so obviously and exquisitely enjoyed' (Styron, 1976, of noisy copulation).

ample fat
Only of women. Properly, wide and commodious: '... a generous figure. "Ample", she used to call it, or, in a kinder manner, "my Edwardian body"' (Bogarde, 1978).

amply endowed see **well endowed** etc.

anarchistic groups those opposed to Communism
Communist jargon. If you are a Marxist, those who advocate an alternative to authoritarian rule which is implicit in the system, must be advocating no rule at all: 'The word strike has continuously featured alongside the customary poisonous euphemisms ("anti-Socialist elements", "anarchistic groups") in the columns and even the headlines of the party Press' (*Sunday Telegraph*, August 1980, of Poland).

angel a male homosexual playing the masculine role
He tries to secure devotion with gifts which indicates derivation from the 'angel' who backs plays.

angel dust heroin
Usu. synthetic. 'Angel' from the short-lived heavenly sensation: 'And that shooting .... wasn't just some kid on angel dust' (Deighton, 1981). In ob. use 'angel foam' was champagne.

angle with a silver hook to bribe
This meaning, which I have heard spoken but not read, replaces the 19c. use, to pretend to have caught a fish which you have bought. cf. **catch fish with a silver hook**.

Anglo-Saxon crude or vulgar
Of language from the supposition that most obscenities in English have that ancestry.

anoint a palm see **palm** (1)

Anschluss a military conquest
Properly in German, a meeting, as of roads at a fork. The word was used by the Nazis of their 1938 annexation of Austria and so became a euphemism in both German and English.

answer the call (1) to die
Usu. of those killed in war, called to arms and then to life eternal.

answer the call (2) to urinate
The 'call' is a **call of nature** (q.v.) with perhaps jocular reference to dying: '... was answering an urgent call behind bushes when they stopped close by' (Cookson, 1967).

anti- avoiding a statement of your allegiance
If a cause you wish to promote may have few adherents, you declare yourself as being against something which well-meaning and gullible people are also likely to abhor. Thus an 'anti-Fascist' is a Communist. A very old trick; in the 5c. Athenasius set himself up as an anti-Aryan, and millions today repeat his doctrinal niceties each Sunday.

anti-freeze a spirituous intoxicant
It warms in cold weather. Rarely, too, of heroin, but with less justification.

anti-personnel designed to kill
It could merely mean opposed to people: '"Anti-personnel weapon" is a sophisticated euphemism for "killer weapon"' (Pei, 1969). Weapons, too, can be sophisticated, which means they are complicated, cause more destruction and kill more people.

anticipating pregnant
An Am. version of **expectant** (q.v.).

antics in bed copulation
The posture adopted may well be described as grotesque: 'There were even married women in my time who did not connect their husbands' antics in bed with the conception of children' (Fraser, 1969, writing of the 19c.).

antisocialist elements *see* **anarchistic groups**

any extra-marital copulation
Of either sex and of a single or repeated encounters. An inquisitive and lewd person may ask another known to be courting whether he or she gave, had, got, etc. 'any'.

apartheid *see* **separate development**

ape mad
Usu. of a temporary condition, from the supposed simian behaviour: 'Victor had something Jake will never have. It drove him ape' (Sanders, 1977). Mainly Am.

appeasement the avoidance of war at the expense of another
To 'appease' is properly to pacify, whence to seek to pacify by conceding demands. Specifically used of the Br. and French attitude to Hitler prior to WW II and the abandonment of the Czecho-Slovaks.

appendage a penis
Properly, something attached or hung on, but men don't so speak of their big toes: '. . . her mean little hand ready to perform its spiritless operation on my equally jaded appendage' (Styron, 1976, of masturbation).

appetite a desire to copulate
Properly, desire of any kind and usu. only to eat food. It acquires greater sexual significance in the plural: '. . . consigned to an early grave by his wife's various appetites' (Sharpe, 1974). Also of homosexual activities.

apple polish to bribe
A shiny skin is said to indicate good fruit, but the imagery remains obscure: 'Why try to apple-polish the dinge downstairs?' (Chandler, 1939 – he could mean merely to flatter). Am.

appliance medical equipment worn on the body
Properly, any thing which is applied for a specific purpose. An abbr. of 'surgical appliance', which is a euphemism in its own right, because a scalpel might as well be so described. Usu. of a truss but also of wooden legs, hearing aids or anything else you don't want to be too precise about.

appropriate to steal
Originally it meant to take for your own use, without taint of impropriety: 'All old *mali* had actually ever done, though, was appropriate his fair share of what he had hoed and sweated to grow' (P. Scott, 1977 – the mali had been dismissed for theft). The now redundant 19c. 'misappropriate' was introduced to cover the illegal conversion of property.

appropriate technology torture
A choice of technology gives you the answers you want. Used by the Home Affairs Minister in Mugabe's Zimbabwe: 'In the House of Assembly, Harare's Commons, he called it "appropriate technology", a euphemism for electric shock treatment that drew appreciative nods from his colleagues' (*Daily Telegraph*, September 1983, of Ushekowokunza and the torture of White Air Force officers).

approved school a penal institute for children
The 'approval' was by the Br. Home Office as being suitable for young criminals. You would be wrong to assume that educational establishments not so described lack the blessing of society.

apron-string-hold the occupation by a man of his wife's property
The use satirizes Br. land tenures, freehold, leasehold and copyhold: 'A man being possessed of a house and large orchard by apron-string-hold, felled almost all his fruit trees, because he expected the death of his sick wife' (Ellis, 1750). I include this ob. entry because it indicated what people

thought of a man who lived off his wife's estate, whose property in those days vested automatically in her husband, for her lifetime or beneficially.

Arctic explorer a person who illegally ingests cocaine
From his use of **snow** (1) (q.v.). Am.

Arkansas toothpick a dagger
I'm not sure whether this Am. usage mocks the uncouthness of the inhabitants or applauds the robustness of frontier life. This is a sample entry; as perusal of the ODEP shows, many common objects preceded by a geographical description indicate a weapon thought to be common in or particular to the region.

arm a policeman
An Am. use, probably from the cliché, the long arm of the law. In New York, perversely, the 'arm' is an organization of criminals. The perhaps ob. Br. 'arm-bend' is not to assault or bribe the constabulary but to drink intoxicants: 'He was busy arm-bending in the public house when the tattoo sounded' (EDD).

armour a contraceptive sheath
As Boswell reports: 'I took out my armour, but she begged that I might not put it on, as the sport was much pleasanter without it.' ob.

army form blank lavatory paper
Some military use and also by former soldiers, to let you know that they, too, have served. It is said to be the only paper found in the Br. army without a form number on it.

around the horn *see* **run round the Horn**

arouse to cause sexual excitement in another
Properly, to waken from sleep. It is used of either sex, heterosexually and homosexually: '... he aroused her in a way that her husband had never done' (Allbeury, 1976, and not by a new alarm clock). Whence 'arousal', such excitement and specifically an erection of the penis: '... the muted talk of women made him excited and he had to roll onto his stomach to conceal his arousal' (Boyd, 1982).

arrange *see* **alter**

arrangement a pot for urine
The action of arranging, until after WW II, was to place it under the bed for use in the night, partly because there were fewer lava-tories in private houses and hotels and partly because wandering down corridors by males was discouraged. In ob. use to 'make arrangements' was to copulate extra-maritally: 'Give a gal a drop of beer, and make her half tipsy, and then they makes their arrangements. I've often heard the boys boasting of having ruined girls' (Mayhew, 1851). In Am. funeral jargon, an 'arrange-ments conference' is the taking of an order for burial services: '"The arrangements conference" (in which the sale of the funeral to the survivors is made) . . .' (J. Mitford, 1963).

arse a person viewed sexually
Properly the buttocks but because they were the subject of taboos, the old name for don-key was called in aid, until 'ass' acquired its own connotations. Thus in ob. Br. use, polite ladies were reduced to calling a jack-ass a 'Johnny Bum', 'Jack' and 'ass' being vulgar while 'bum' was still respectable. (And if you think that odd, *see* 'rooster-swain' under **game chicken**.) The com-moner use is by the male of the female, as a 'bit' or 'piece' of 'ass' or 'arse': 'Am I to believe you would risk something like this for a piece of ass?' (Diehl, 1978). Less often by a female of a male: 'The stewardesses all agreed he was a piece of ass' (Follett, 1978 – they desired him sexually). Male homosexual use too, and of male and female prostitutes, who may be called 'arse pedlars'. An 'arse man' may be a homosexual or a man who copulates promiscuously: '. . . sexy as he smiled at the girl who was one of Engineer-ing's assistants. He was the house ass-man' (M. Thomas, 1982).

article any object the subject of a taboo
Thus it may be a pot for urine, as an abbr. of 'article of furniture' which is also euphemis-tic: 'Article (meaning "chamber-pot") is non-U' (Ross, 1956); or anything which has been stolen; or, in white slave jargon, a potential whore: 'Some "articles" are from seventeen to twenty kilos, i.e. women from seventeen to twenty years old' (Londres, 1928, in tr.); etc.

artillery a hypodermic needle used for illicit narcotic injection
From landing its charge and the explosive effect: '. . . a piece of community artillery passed from junkie to junkie' (Wambaugh, 1975). Am.

aryan without Jewish ancestry
Nazi jargon in their anti-Jewish dogma, although a pure German's ancestors' blood

was permitted to have been so mingled prior to 1750. In proper use an 'aryan' is one of the 'descendants of those who spoke the Aryan language' (SOD), which would include Slavs, Persians and Celts as well as Teutons.

as Allah made him naked
The way he was born: 'Recognizably not wearing anything . . . as Allah made him' (Davidson, 1978). In the same sense others ascribe the manufacture to God.

asbestos drawers relating to female promiscuity
They are wearing **hot pants** (q.v.): 'Needs asbestos drawers, I hear. Another little number from the sticks with a rich husband and hot pants' (M. Thomas, 1982).

ashes hauled *see* **haul your ashes**

asleep dead
A tombstone favourite, often amplified to 'asleep in Jesus', etc. And *see* 'fell asleep' under **fall** (3).

ass *see* **arse**

assault to attack sexually
Properly, to use any force against another without consent. Of boys homosexually and women heterosexually: 'If I'd been assaulted by men of my own race I would have been an object of pity' (P. Scott, 1973, of a woman raped by a gang of Indians). Explicitly as 'indecent assault'.

assembly centre a prison
Am. WW II name for the place of confinement of those Americans of Japanese descent. They spent most of the war where they were assembled. cf. **relocation camp**.

assignation a meeting for extra-marital copulation
Properly, the allotment of something, whence a tryst, which remains the SE meaning: 'I have never really seriously thought of marriage . . . . What suits me best is the drama of separation, of looking forward to assignations and rendezvous' (Murdoch, 1978).

assist the police *see* **help the police (with their inquiries)**

assistance a regular payment to the poor from public funds
Properly, help of any kind, even across a busy street. Often as public or national 'assistance'. To be 'on assistance' carries the inference of unemployment and poverty. This usage has had an unusually long life in the sequence of expressions which try to cloak the charitable and perhaps degrading nature of state payments to the indigent.

association (1) the regular copulation with other than a spouse
Properly, the action of combining together for any purpose; but a housewife who forms an 'association' with the milkman is doing more than confirming her requirement for dairy produce.

association (2) a cartel
Commonly formed by traders selling a similar range of products. The impressive titles and expressions of public benevolence may mask the objects of spying on each other, keeping up prices and restricting competition. Because many of their discussions are illegal under the laws of some countries in which they operate, Zurich zoo has become a favoured venue for delicate meetings.

astride copulating with
Equine imagery and normally of the male: '"Harry – you are *sure* you have not been astride Mrs Lade?" . . . . "Eh? Good God, girl, what d'you mean?" "Have you mounted her?"' (Fraser, 1977).

asylum an institution for the mad
Properly, a place where pillage was sacrilegious, which is why there was so much fuss about Henry II's murder of Becket who, as Chancellor, had supported his conquests. Then it became any safe place or benevolent institution. Now abbr. of SE 'lunatic asylum'.

at a rope's end death by being hanged
With your head in the noose: 'I'll have thee at a rope's end yet' (Fowles, 1985, writing in archaic style of a threat).

at half mast with a trouser zip undone
From a flag incorrectly hoisted. Normally used as a hint from one male to another in mixed company.

at liberty involuntarily unemployed
Actors' jargon and it is certainly correct that they are free to take another role: '"Laurence Olivier" (very careful checking every time for correct spelling) "at liberty"' (Olivier, 1982, of an advertisement when he was out of work). *See*, also, **between shows**.

at-need after death
Funeral jargon for doing business when you have a corpse to dispose of: 'In 1960 preneeds of graves and crypts outnumbered "at-need" sales by four to one' (J. Mitford, 1963). Am.

at rest etc. dead
A tombstone favourite which might seem to discount the prospects of an after-life. On the other hand a regimen of eternal harp-playing and hymn-singing might be restful, if tedious. Also as 'at peace'.

athlete a male profligate
Copulation is thought to provide the male with good exercise: 'Erroll was the greatest "athlete" in Kenya . . . . and was undoubtedly the love of Diana's life' (Fox, 1982).

athletic supporter a brief tight under-pant
Not a football fan: 'The speaker stumbled sleepily past him towards the Silex, dressed in nothing but an athletic supporter' (Wouk, 1951).

athwart your hawse copulating with you
A 'hawse' is a rigid cable and, in this naval usage, the female is astride it: 'I was near crazy, with that naked alabaster beauty squirming athwart my hawse, as the sailors say' (Fraser 1973).

attaché a spy
It is a convention that certain members of an embassy are charged with the function of espionage and given a nominal role with diplomatic status so that they can be quietly repatriated if their conduct becomes too offensive to the host nation: 'At the embassy Jerry Cole, whose ostensible post was Assistant Military Attaché, was waiting for him' (Allbeury, 1981, of a spy).

attend to copulate with
Properly, to see to the needs of, which in this usage and the judgment of the male, is a need to copulate with him: 'I'm goin to 'tend to this li'l beauty right here an' now' (Fraser, 1971, of a man about to copulate with a woman).

attendance centre a place to which young criminals report for disciplinary training
They have to go as part of their sentence, but it might equally apply to a discotheque or a skating rink. BI.

attentions extra-marital copulation
There is a distinction between 'paying attention', which indicates heterosexual courtship, and 'pressing attentions', copulation with the male doing the pressing: '. . . dancing partners of wealthy widows and lonesome wives, ready to pay for attentions accorded them' (Lavine, 1930).

au naturel naked
Am. rather than Br. borrowing from the French to describe a condition still more subject to taboos in parts of the New World than in the Old. In New England they still don't like you changing swimming trunks on a beach under the cover of a towel.

auld is the Sc. form of 'old' and appears in many names for the devil – see **old a' ill thing, etc.** The 'auld kirk' is whisky, from the name given to the established church of Sc.: 'Whisky for me – a dram o' guid Auld Kirk' (Coghill, 1890). I have not traced the etymology beyond recalling that after a Sc. sermon in a Sc. church without much heating in a Sc. winter, you need some kind of restorative.

aunt (1) an elderly whore
The modern Am. use recalls Shakespeare: 'Summer songs for me and my aunts. While we lie tumbling in the hay' (*The Winter's Tale*).

aunt (2) a lavatory
To whom mostly women pay a mythical visit and in Victorian days, your Aunt Jones, or Mrs. Jones. cf. **uncle**. If the punning 'Aunt Flo' is visiting you, you are menstruating.

aunt (3) an elderly male homosexual
Those so described are normally a generation older than those whose company they seek: 'Some mincing auntie in a cell with flowered curtains' (Ustinov, 1971).

auto-da-fé killing by burning
Properly the 'act of faith' of the 'inquisition', itself no more in its own eyes than an inquiry. In Spanish 'auto de fe' and no more palatable, but the souls of heretics had to be destroyed as well as their bodies, and there was no other way.

auto-erotic habits masturbation
Of either sex. It might have meant merely thinking sexy thoughts or seeing a pornographic film.

avail yourself of to copulate with extra-maritally
Usu. of a male: 'Any man who availed himself of the "tree rats" or "grass bidis" was properly dealt with' (Allen, 1975). An 'available' female can be expected to consent to extra-marital copulation, with or without payment: 'Aileen was the only girl who had ever turned him down. The rest were always available – however nice – however respectable' (Collins, 1981).

away (1) dead
The use is ob. but the concept survives in

'gone': 'Rachel mournynge for hir children and wolde not be comforted, because they were awaye' (Coverdale, *Jeremiah* xxxi 15; the Authorised Version says 'because they were not').

away (2) in prison
The use was more common when the stigma of imprisonment was greater. In ob. Br. usage 'away the trip' meant pregnant, from the vacation far from home which young unmarried females took under those circumstances. There were also many regional euphemisms, some alluding to landmarks or towns which a pregnant girl might pass or go to for a discreet childbirth. Thus from Cheshire comes 'She has given Lawton Gate a clap': 'Spoken of one got with child and going to London to conceal it. Lawton is on the way to London from several parts of Cheshire' (Ray, 1678, quoted in ODEP).

awful experiment the prohibition of sale and consumption of intoxicants in the USA
'Awful' for those denied intoxicants or forced into illegality to obtain them; much more awful for the impetus to organized crime which bedevils parts of the country still: 'A generation or so has come between us and the Awful Experiment' (Longstreet, 1956).

awkward pregnant
Of women, from the clumsiness which is a consequence of the extra weight and size. Of quadrupeds it denotes being on their backs and unable to get to their feet without help.

ax(e) (the) peremptory dismissal from courtship or employment
The instrument severs quickly and, it is hoped, cleanly: 'They were brought to Berlin and axed' (Shirer, 1984, of two German Socialist leaders handed over by Pétain in 1940 and executed by the Nazis). In ob. use 'the axe' was death by execution, usu. but not necessarily by beheading.

Aztec twostep etc. diarrhoea
An affliction of visitors to Mexico – you have to keep dancing to a lavatory. Also as 'Aztec hop' and cf. **Montezuma's revenge**.

B

B anything taboo beginning with the letter B.
The common candidates are benzedrine,
bitch, bloody and bugger – a 'B-pill' is benzedrine used illegally; a 'silly B', if a woman,
is being insulted as a silly bitch; a 'B fool' is a
bloody fool; and you may be told to 'B off'
which is not 'be off' but 'bugger off'. The
military spoken alphabet 'baker' is sometimes used in the same way, as in **baker
flying** (q.v.). For 'B bomb', *see* A; for 'B girl',
see **bar**; for 'BO', *see* **body odour**; for 'B
Special', *see* **special** (3).

baby marijuana
Perhaps because it is the common introduction to illegal narcotics with more damaging
qualities. Am.

baby-snatcher etc. a person with a much
younger sexual partner
The imagery is of a child taken from the
cradle, as in **cradle-snatcher** (q.v.). Some
homosexual use but mainly heterosexual for
anything outside the normal male/female
age pattern. Thus the woman may be very
little older but the man has to transgress the
rule of half his age plus seven years: 'He had
been living with an older woman . . . . baby-
snatching, as everybody called it' (Murdoch,
1978). The punning 'baby-farmer', used in
the same sense, is rare.

bacchanalian drunken
Properly, anything to do with Bacchus, or
Dionysus, who was the god of wine: 'Burgess fell from grace again at the Foreign
Office as a result of another bacchanalian
holiday trip' (Boyle, 1979). A 'devotee', 'son'
or 'priest' of Bacchus is a drunkard and
'bacchanals' – Bag o'Nails in Eng. pub signs
– a carouse.

bachelor's wife a whore
Only of transitory relationships with any
man. A 'bachelor girl' is a single woman who
may place a career before marriage.

back indicates copulation by a female, from
the position commonly adopted
Thus the Br. WW II slogan 'Back to the
Land', which was introduced to spur agri-
cultural production, became, as 'Backs to the
Land', the supposed motto of the 'Women's
Land Army', the young women who
replaced absent farmworkers on the tractor
and in the shippen – and too often the
farmer's wife in the bed. 'On your back'
means copulating: 'One way to travel. On my
back' (L. Thomas, 1977, of a whore).

back door *see* **front door (the)**

back-door man a woman's extra-marital
sexual partner
In Am. he fig. leaves by this exit when the
husband arrives at the front door. In ob.
Eng. use, the 'back-door trot' was diarrhoea,
punning on the location of the lavatory and
the anus: 'Are teh poorly? – Ay, ah've been
on t'back-door trot this mony a day' (EDD).

back-gate parole the natural death of a
prisoner
Am. prison use – I suppose the corpse is
taken out that way. Major in *Black Slang*
gives 'back-gate parlor', which looks like a
misprint.

back passage etc. the anus
Medical jargon which has common vulgar
use. Until this meaning became explicit, it
also described a corridor to the rear of a
house. The 'back garden' or 'back way' for
the anus are less common.

back teeth afloat wanting to urinate
You have raised your bodily liquid level to
your mouth: 'I've got to go to the john first.
My back teeth are floating' (Sanders, 1973).

backfire to fart
The extra-cylindrical combustion of a motor
coupled with the location of the exhaust pipe
provides this male vulgarism.

backhander a bribe
Properly, a blow with the back of the hand.
The recipient of a bribe fig. rotates his palm
to accept payment. In ob. Br. use a 'backhander' was also a glass of wine taken out of
turn, when the bottle had in error circulated
in the wrong direction.

backside the buttocks
This SE use ignores the other parts of the
body, from the back of the skull to the heels,
which would equally qualify, if they were the
subject of taboos: 'But then it was just my
. . . . backside was at risk' (Price, 1978 –
spoken by a cultured woman). 'Backseat' is
rarer and more explicit. In ob. Br. use a
'backside' was a lavatory, from its location
behind the house.

backward (1) very dull
In educational jargon, it indicates an IQ of
between 70 and 84. Lay people use it of
idiots. It might have meant merely doing
poorly in a class of normal children.

backward (2) poor and uncivilized
Of sovereign states and perhaps the first of the series of post-colonial euphemisms which mask the differing abilities of people when it came to governing themselves again: '... countries which have progressively and with increasing euphemism been termed backward, underdeveloped, less-developed and developing' (FDMT). *See*, too, **south** and **third world**.

backward (3) through the anus
I give this entry as a lone example in these pages of Pepys' vulgar frankness: '... and so to Mrs Martin and there did what je voudrais avec her, both devante and backward, which is also muy bon plazer'. ob.

bad working as a whore
A judgment on morals rather than job proficiency: '... lost her place for staying out one night with the man who seduced her; he afterwards deserted her and then she became bad' (Mayhew, 1862). 'Bad girls' are whores: '"Bad girls here," said the tonga driver when he dropped me in a seedy district of the old city; but I saw none, and nothing resembling a Lahore house' (Theroux, 1975).

bad lad etc. the devil
Mainly Sc. usage and perhaps ob. Also as the 'bad man': 'The gite has a drop o' the bad man's bluid on it' (Johnstone, 1891 – a 'gite' is a dress) and as the 'black lad': 'The auld black lad may hae my saul, if I ken but o' ae Macnab' (Ford, 1891).

bad mouth to denigrate a competitor to third parties
Commercial jargon and owing nothing to gingivitis: 'This legendary trio were busy bad-mouthing the Segal/Fitzwalter management' (*Private Eye*, May 1981).

bad news menstruation
For those wishing to copulate: '"Shall we go to bed, Maggie?".... "Yes I'd like that.... But I'm afraid I have some rather bad news for you"' (Trevanian, 1973). But it can be good news for those fearing an unwanted pregnancy.

bad power a fart
My assumption that the use comes from the slow and smelly combustion of a faulty charge in a firearm is reinforced by hearing people say it has been 'burnt' or 'let off'. Mainly used by men.

bad week menstruation
From its normal duration. A woman normally uses the phrase of herself – 'my bad week'.

badge bandit a policeman on highway patrol
From the arbitrary extraction of on-the-spot fines for traffic violation. Am.

badger a whore
Formerly a licensed huckster who had to wear a badge, from which the SE meaning, to importune excessively. The use survives in the 'badger game' where the victim is led by a whore into a sexually compromising position and then blackmailed: 'Any man who accompanies a night-club or dance-hall hostess to her apartment .... runs a risk of being robbed or subjected to the well-known badger game' (Lavine, 1930).

bag (1) to steal
From concealing and taking away the loot in a bag. Still particularly a schoolroom favourite, as in Tom Brown's schooldays: 'The idea of being had up to the Doctor for bagging fowls, quite unmans him' (Hughes, 1856). The Am. 'bag job' is burglary by a government agency. Private documents are removed without judicial approval for later examination, to secure evidence of treason or to discredit a political opponent.

bag (2) dismissal from employment or courtship
A rare and perhaps ob. form of **sack** (q.v.).

bag (3) to kill by hunting
Of birds and usu. small mammals, which are put in the hunter's bag; but you may fig. 'bag' a rhinoceros, despite its bulk and threatened extinction. A 'bag' of partridges etc. indicates how many were killed on a particular occasion. SE.

bag (4) a supply of illicit narcotics
Originally it indicated a certain quantity of heroin, although that quantity seems to have differed from place to place. Now of any narcotic wrapped in paper.

bag (5) *see* **in the bag**

bag (6) *see* **baggage**

bag job *see* **bag (1)**

baggage a whore
Formerly in SE a worthless person, male or female. Shakespeare uses the euphemism in one of his more complex sexual puns: 'No barricado for a belly; know't; It will let in and out the enemy with bag and baggage' (*The Winter's Tale* – 'bag and baggage' is the impedimenta of any 16c. army, with whores

among the other female camp-followers). The white-slave jargon use came from the pimps taking the girls with them to S. America etc. as so much merchandise: 'The "baggage" consisted of two "underweights" who had travelled as stowaways' (Londres, 1928, in tr. – an 'underweight' would be a girl barely past puberty). A 'bag', an unprepossessing whore, may be an abbr. of 'baggage', or come from, the phrase 'bag and baggage', or from the current sl. meaning, an ill-favoured woman of any age. In ob. Br. use a 'bag-shanty' was a brothel.

bagged drunk
An Am. use, perhaps from **bag** (3) (above), as you often feel like death afterwards: 'Al Mackey giggled. He was more than half bagged' (Wambaugh, 1981). The ob. Br. meaning pregnant probably puns on the girl having being caught by a hunter, and on the resulting swelling: 'Well, Venus shortly bagged, and ere long was Cupid bred' (Nares, c. 1820).

bagnio a brothel
The common bathing imagery: '. . . he had seen her some two or three months since entering a bagnio behind St James' (Fowles, 1985, of an 18c. whore going into a brothel). ob.

bags trousers
An abbr. of 'leg-bags', which came from the 19c. taboo on trousers: 'The shapeless flannels which he called his "bags"' (Manning, 1965). Now dated sl. 'bags of' anything denotes an excess and not a form of packaging. The phrase can be used euphemistically as: 'She knew "bags of stamina" was a euphemism for "not much finishing speed"' (Francis, 1985, of a racehorse).

baker see B

baker flying menstruating
In the US Navy a red quartermaster (or baker) flag is flown to indicate danger when a boat is loading fuel or ammunition, warning other craft to stand well clear. Am.

balance of mind disturbed a purely temporary insanity
Br. legal jargon of suicides where people want to bury the corpse in consecrated ground or merely to reject the probability that someone had been driven to suicide: 'The verdict at the inquest was that he took his life while the balance of his mind was disturbed. I know little of my son's mind but I reject that comfortable euphemism' (James, 1972).

bale out (1) to urinate
A Br. naval usage, from the removal of surplus water from small boats.

bale out (2) to jump by parachute from a damaged aircraft
Again from the action of throwing water over the side of a small boat: 'I once baled out of a Provost' (Price, 1970 – a Provost is a jet trainer). In flying circles you do not talk of aircraft failure. In WW II you might also have said that you had been 'on the silk', from the material from which some parachutes were made. Whence the fig. 'hit the silk', to seek to escape, to unload, to cash in etc.: 'In markets like these, if that happens, everyone'll try to hit the silk at once and no one'll get out the door' (M. Thomas, 1987).

baling searching the beaches for marijuana
When they think they are about to be caught, smugglers of illegal narcotics to Florida jettison bales which can be recovered from the sea or beaches: 'If I had that ol' cat right now, I could go baling' (Sanders, 1982 – a 'cat' is a catamaran).

ball to copulate with
Probably punning on the sl. meaning, an orgy and on the testicles although it is used of copulation by either sex: 'Sure I balled Victor. I wish he had bathed more often, but sometimes that can be fun, too' (Sanders, 1977). The ob. Br. 'ball money' was extortion at a wedding, being not a kind of copulation-fee but money ostensibly taken from guests by onlookers to pay for a football for the parish. In practice the recipients pocketed what they obtained.

balloon room a place where marijuana is commonly smoked
An addict usage, perhaps punning on the practice of storing the narcotic in rubber balloons and the feeling of levitation sometimes induced. Am.

balls the testicles
Men use the word more than women. There are also two common fig. usages; as a derisive riposte, when some suppose it is an abbr. of 'balderdash'; and to denote courage, the testicles being a feature of manliness: 'I hate to admit it, but I got to admire him for that. The balls!' (Sanders, 1980). However I begin to doubt my etymology when I find the phrase used of a female: 'Maybe Mama even hustles him right here: she's got the balls for it' (Sanders, 1977).

balmy drunk
From the mild or fragrant sensation which

may come over you at one stage. The sl.
meaning, insane, is usu. spelt 'barmy'.

bamboozled drunk
Properly, hoaxed and perhaps adverting to
the old excuse you can be deceived in liquor.
Am.

banana copulation
Perhaps from the sl. meaning, a penis.
Oddly then a man 'has a banana with' a
woman – never the reverse. If he has his
banana 'peeled', he ejaculates.

bananas mad
The etymology has escaped me, although I
suspect it comes in corrupted form from
another language. It is often used of mild
hysteria: '. . . there's a poor cop called Captain Salvatore going bananas' (L. Thomas,
1979).

bandit a political opponent
Pejorative Communist jargon for internal
critics and dissidents. If you question the
value of Communism you are criminal, if not
mad. Dysphemism rather than euphemism.

bandwagon a cause or chance for profit
which attracts opportunists
Properly, a vehicle carrying musicians in a
circus parade: 'I'm on the bandwagon with
him' (N. Mitford, 1960, of someone who
had joined a scheme in which easy profits
were made). Whence a 'band-wagoner':
'. . . sufficiently politically confused to rank
either as band-wagoner or a half-baked pain
in the neck' (P. Scott, 1973, of Mahatma
Ghandi in 1942 – it is useful to have had one
writer who ignores the myths).

bang (1) to copulate with
Properly, to beat and using the common
violent imagery for the male role: 'It'd be
amusing to bang her under all those ducal
Gainsboroughs' (M. Thomas, 1980). And of
a single act of copulation by a male: 'Did you
ever give the maid a bang?' (Mailer, 1965).
The ob. 'bang-tail', abbr. to 'banger', was a
whore: '. . . that little brown banger . . . . she
was a lissome little wriggler' (Fraser, 1975
writing in 19c. style). A 'gang-bang', also in
the Am. forms of 'gang-shay' or 'gang-shag',
is successsive copulation with a woman by a
number of males in each others' company.
'Bang and biff' is syphilis, from rh. sl. on
'syph', and perhaps punning on the copulation and the unhappy outcome.

bang (2) an illicit narcotic
Usu. taken by injection and so having an
immediate result, cf. **shot** (3) and **artillery**.

banish your bed to refuse to copulate
with
Usu. a female sanction but also a kingly
gesture: 'I banish her my bed and company'
(Shakespeare, 2 *Henry VI*). ob.

bank to fail in business
It was the bench on which Italian moneylenders conducted their business, which was
turned over – 'rupted' – if they failed to meet
their commitments. In the late 19c. banks
were still failing regularly and the phrase was
still in use: 'Dunnot ye know at Turner's is
banked' (Taylor, 1890). A 'banker' was a
bankrupt, which sounds odd to us today as it
is the bankers who do most of the bankrup-
ting. ob.

bar a place for the sale and consumption of
intoxicants
A plank was used both as a counter and a
barrier, giving the world perhaps its most
multi-national word; even the French Academy doesn't claim it comes from the sea-
perch via fish restaurants. Many derivatives
and compounds, like 'bar-fly', a drunkard,
'bar steward', a bastard and the Am. 'bar
girl', a whore: 'Paul was getting anxious to fix
me up with a bar girl' (Simon, 1979). 'Bar
girls' formerly looked for trade in bars but
now may be any casual or inferior prostitute,
and 'B girl' puns on 'bar' and 'B' for second
quality: 'He's got a finger in the B-girl rackets' (Theroux, 1973).

bareback copulating without a contraceptive sheath
The common equine imagery, but this time
without a saddle: 'I always ride bareback
myself' (Wambaugh, 1981, of copulation).
Men or women can be 'bareback riders':
'. . . no females except the local bareback
riders' (Fraser, 1971 – by inference they had
venereal disease).

barker a handgun
Neither a fairground tout nor a dog, but
from the noise: 'You knew you'd have to
carry a barker on this job?' (Sanders, 1970).
Am. sl.

barley cap a person who habitually drinks
whisky
From the grain used in the manufacture.
'Barley fever' is drunkenness: 'This was the
first time he ever had fallen a victim to the
barley-fever' (Moir, 1828). 'Barrel fever' was
also drunkenness but could also be illness
caused by dipsomania. 'John Barleycorn',
sometimes knighted, was whisky: 'Inspiring
John Barleycorn. What dangers thou canst

make me scorn' (Burns). I suspect all these uses are ob.

barrack-room lawyer an opinionated but well-informed know-all.

Usu. an old soldier who has refused promotion and combines experience in the ways of the army with knowledge of military regulations and bloody-mindedness: '"Who says that, now?" cries this barrack-room lawyer' (Fraser, 1982, of such a person). In Am. a 'barracks lawyer' and in the navy a 'sea lawyer' or 'ship's lawyer' play the same part.

barred window boys private operators of institutions for the mentally ill.

Lunacy and other conditions or addictions affecting the mind are embarrassing to the rest of the family who may want the sufferer hidden away without publicity: 'The barred window boys . . . small private sanatoriums or what have you that treat alcoholics and dopers and mild cases of mania' (Chandler, 1953). Am.

barrel-house a brothel

Originally a cheap Am. saloon, where the intoxicants were served from barrels: 'The cribs, saloons, sinister dancing-schools, the barrel-houses . . .' (Longstreet, 1956).

basement a lavatory

From its frequent location there in shopping malls, public rooms, etc. There is no connection with the sl. anatomical meaning, the stomach. Usu. in the query, 'Where's the basement?' Am.

baser needs copulation by a male

From the dated assumption that regular copulation improves a man's health but is at the same time reprehensible: 'What you need is a sensible wife to take care of your baser needs' (Sharpe, 1982). Having cooked meals is even more basic.

bash to work as a whore

The sl. 'bash' means to walk, as in the army 'square bashing': 'Lettin' a woman bash on the bloody streets' (Kersh, 1936). 'On the bash' is so working: 'Anybody would think that I was asking you to go on the bash' (ibid.).

bash the bishop to masturbate

Of a male, from the likeness of the penis to the chessman. Also as 'flog the bishop' but cf. **shake hands with the bishop**, which means to urinate.

basket (1) a bastard

The two words sound alike and this is only used fig. and often jocularly. Do not say it to an ill-educated person, for it is likely to be a deadly insult still. In ob. Br. use the punning 'basket-making' was extra-marital copulation by a male.

basket (2) the male genitalia seen through tight trousers

Homosexual jargon: 'The movement arched his entire body and made his basket bulge under the cloth of his trousers' (Genet, in 1969 tr.). Very rarely too in heterosexual use, the vagina.

basket case a poor person unable to maintain himself

Groceries given to the poor were delivered in wicker hampers: 'You cock teasers have turned millions . . . . into a generation of sexual basket cases' (Styron, 1976). A community or country may also be so described: 'Poland, which is economically a basket case' (*Daily Telegraph*, February 1982).

Basra belly diarrhoea

Another of the many alliterative phrases, this time for those passing through the Persian Gulf.

basted drunk

The common culinary imagery which in this Am. instance likens the subject to a joint of meat being roasted and periodically covered with molten fat.

bat (1) a whore

No doubt from flitting around at night. The ob. 19c. Eng. use has re-emerged in 20c. Am. A 'bat-house' is a brothel.

bat (2) a drunken carouse

Possibly from an innings at cricket or baseball, except that a 'bat' was an habitual drunkard. 'Over the bat' means drunk.

bath-house a chamber for mass killing

The Nazis stripped their victims and herded them into gas-chambers on the pretence that they were going for decontamination: 'Of four thousand in the next four trainloads, two and a half thousand went at once to the "bath-houses"' (Keneally, 1982, of Auschwitz).

bathroom a lavatory

In the long line of euphemisms which associate washing with urination and defecation; in this instance from the former location of lavatories in bathrooms: '. . . asked where the bathroom was. The restroom was filthy' (Diehl, 1978 – and what was the lavatory like?). The standard Am. use which leads to untold confusion in Europe.

bats (in the belfry) madness
The wild ideas circle in your head like the mammals living in the church tower at twilight: 'Dear man, you've got bats in the belfry' (Mason, 1927). Abbr. to 'bats' or 'batty', the words are also used of varying degrees of eccentricity.

battered drunk
Am. culinary imagery again, but also punning on the feeling that you have been roughly handled.

batting and bowling having both homosexual and heterosexual tastes
As this is a Br. usage, the imagery has to come from the game of cricket, in which most players tend to specialize in one or the other. cf. **all-rounder**.

battle fatigue cowardice
Properly, acute neurosis induced by periods of fighting and much more even in that sense than the tiredness resulting from constant combat: '. . . wondering suddenly how much guilty truth and how much honest battle fatigue there had been' (Price, 1978, of an officer who had admitted being a coward). The WW II equivalent of WW I 'shell shock'.

battle of the bulge a desire to slim
The 'bulge' is the evidence of obesity around the waist or hips. This female use puns on the German Ardennes offensive of December 1944, but the modern campaigns seldom last so long or achieve comparable losses.

bawd the keeper of a brothel
It means no more than dirt: 'Like sanctified and pious bawds, The better to beguile' (Shakespeare, *Hamlet*). 'Bawdy' has many of the moral meanings of **dirty** (q.v.), of which 'bawdy house', a brothel, survives: 'I would not wreck it, turn it into a bawdy house, or receive any members of the press here' (Bogarde, 1978, of conditions on his lease).

bay window a fat person's stomach
Normally used kindly of a male, from the architectural feature which often protrudes from the lower floor only.

be excused to urinate or defecate
Properly, politely to obtain release from the company of others. Perhaps the first thing we all learnt when we started school.

be nice to to copulate with extra-maritally
Usu. of a female, from the supposed wish to accommodate or please. Rarely of a male, as 'wouldn't you like to be nice to Dasha?'

(Amis, 1980 – she meant, would you like to fuck me).

be with to copulate with extra-maritally
Of either sex: 'The girl talked. We know you've been with her' (Mailer, 1965 – the police had evidence of recent copulation). It is a reflection on the human condition that mere proximity imports such a conclusion.

beach to dismiss from employment
Usu. of a sailor, from the former practice of leaving one you needed no more on a foreign shore, to find another ship or his own way home. 'On the beach' is out of work as a sailor: 'You hear that, you Port Mahon bumboatman, you? You ought to be on the beach!' (Fraser, 1971).

bear (1) to be pregnant or to give birth
The SE use makes us forget that anyone who lifts an infant thereby bears a child and is of child-bearing age: 'Asses are made to bear, and so are you' (Shakespeare, *Taming of the Shrew*, using both meanings). Conversely when a mother 'bears' a child, she no longer bears it; it is born but no longer borne.

bear (2) a policeman
The common Am. use probably comes from the threat and the violence, characteristics which the quadruped and the officer of the law are thought to have in common. There are many derivatives, some of which come from CB radio. 'Bear bait' is a speeding car without CB and therefore likely to be pulled in; a 'bear cage' is a police station; a 'bear in the air' is a police helicopter, especially if it is on traffic duty; 'bear food' is any speeding vehicle; 'bear bite' is a ticket for speeding; a 'bear trap' is police radar, illogical in that it is the 'bears' who do the trapping; the 'bears are crawling' means that the police are switching from one direction of the highway to another, to counter warnings of their presence on CB; a 'state bear' is a state trooper; the punning 'bearded buddy' is any policeman, probably from the cartoon character, Yogi Bear; a 'lady bear' is a policewoman; etc.

beard (1) the female pubic hair
In ob. Br. use a male who parted it in the act of copulation was a 'beard splitter'. A 'bearded clam' is the vagina viewed sexually by a male: 'I've ate close to three hundred bearded clams in my time' (Wambaugh, 1975).

beard (2) a male who falsely adopts the role of a woman's extra-marital sexual partner
The purpose is to protect another man

performing that role and the derivation from
the false beard worn as a disguise: 'He's the
"beard". That's what they call the other man
who pretends to be the lover' (Sanders,
1981).

beast with two backs copulation
From the facing posture of the parties. The
'beast' may be 'made': 'Your daughter and
the Moor are now making the beast with two
backs' (Shakespeare, *Othello*); or 'played':
'She had the goods on me; in an idle
moment I played the beast with two backs
with her' (McCarthy, 1963). Also as the
'two-backed beast': 'I . . . . know what it had
been like with Deborah and him, what a hot
burning two-backed beast' (Mailer, 1965);
or as the 'two-backed game': 'She had a
hearty appetite for the two-backed game'
(Fraser, 1977). I have traced one use of
homosexuality: 'This was an embrace, and
as the girls on stage made the beast with two
backs, the man in the film hopped into the
missionary position' (Theroux, 1975).

beastliness male masturbation
Hardly fair, as most animals don't masturbate: '. . . the detrimental effects on
sportsmen of masturbation, referred to in
the sermon as beastliness' (Sharpe, 1982). In
the 19c. it meant copulation, of the male,
when it was thought proper for women so to
regard the occupation: 'While you were at
your beastliness . . .' (Fraser, 1971, writing
of something which happened during copulation, in 19c. style).

beat on *see* **raise a beat** etc.

beat the gong to smoke opium
From an Am. association of Oriental ideas.
However, a 'beat pad' is a place where marijuana is smoked communally, usu. characterized by the impurity of the product.

beat the gun to copulate with a proposed
spouse before marriage
The 'gun' is the starter's pistol. Used specifically of conception before marriage even if
only evident afterwards, cf. **cheat the
starter**.

beat the mattress to copulate
Punning on the domestic chore of beating a
flock mattress to make it more even and the
movements of the copulating pair: '. . . we
beat the mattress regularly as far as Council
Grove' (Fraser, 1982).

beat your meat etc. to masturbate
yourself
Of a male and *see* **meat**: '"To see that you

don't beat your meat", said the constable
coarsely' (Sharpe, 1976, explaining why a
prisoner was oept underobservation). Less
often as 'beat your dummy' – a 'dummy' is a
penis. Also as 'beat off': 'Twenty minutes,
he'll beat off and save the money' (Diehl,
1978 – a male was waiting impatiently for a
whore).

beau a woman's male sexual partner
Not necessarily beautiful, but paying court to
her and, if married, implying that she is
copulating with him: '"You don't do it
famously," . . . . "I haven't heard a word of
complaint from any new beau"' (Mailer,
1965).

beauty care the attempted concealment of
signs of ageing
Cosmetic and similar routines for women
are thus described. The object is to persuade
the subject that she is thus preserving her
looks rather than donning a deceptive mask.
Such routines may take place in a 'beauty'
salon or parlour and involve the concealment
or imposition of a 'beauty spot', a facial
blemish.

beaver the vagina
From the sl. meaning, a beard, and thus the
pubic hair: 'He gobbles one beaver and gets
promoted' (Wambaugh, 1975, of cunnilingus). A 'beaver-shot' is a photograph
which shows the exposed vagina. cf. **three-
legged beaver**.

Bechuana tummy diarrhoea
An African variant of the enteric indisposition common to places with impure water
and poor sanitation. It is also used of the
stomach pains which may follow
drunkenness.

bed (1) childbirth
The bed is the symbol of birth, marriage and
copulation. In certain societies and times the
marriage ceremony is not complete until the
witnesses have seen the bride and groom
tucked up together, or 'bedded'. To be
'brought to bed' is SE for being delivered of
a child: 'At the height of the gale a soldier's
wife was brought to bed' (Graves, 1940, of
childbirth).

bed (2) to copulate with
The normal location: 'Woo her, wed her and
bed her' (Shakespeare, *Taming of the Shrew*)
and in modern use: '. . . what made the English "Doctor X" bed as many young girls'
(Lyall, 1980). 'In bed' means copulation:
'Afghan women were always hungry for men
. . . . and very active in bed' (Fraser, 1969).

'Bed down' usu. implies extra-marital copulation, with the male taking the active part: 'Did you really think of bedding me down right there in the middle of that cocktail party?' (Diehl, 1978). In ob. use, a 'bed-faggot' was a whore and a 'bed-house' an establishment to which you might take a female for extra-marital copulation, paying corkage, as it were. 'Bed-hopping' is promiscuous copulation: 'Given more privacy, some bed-hopping might have developed' (Hailey, 1979). 'Bed and breakfast' is a single act of extra-marital overnight copulation, punning on what a guest-house offers: 'No mention of any bed-and-breakfast work, setting up ex-military members of parliament for possible blackmail' (Lyall, 1980). 'Beddable' means nubile: 'I'm wary of strong, clever women, however beddable they may be' (Fraser, 1973). 'Bedwork', copulation, puns on the proper meaning, a job so easy you could do it in bed. 'Bedworthy' describes a woman who it is thought might benefit from having a child born to her. A 'bedfellow'. is a person with whom you copulate extra-maritally: 'I've had better bedfellows, mistresses more given to the art of love' (Harris, 1925). A woman with 'bedroom eyes' invites extra-marital copulation: 'A redheaded number with bedroom eyes' (Chandler, 1939). To be 'privy to a bed' was not to be a commode but to copulate with a woman extra-maritally: 'Now, before you knew Dick was privy to her bed, had you marked any understanding between them?' (Fowles, 1985). etc. etc.

Bedfordshire bed
An ancient pun on the Eng. county: '... sleepy knaves, we pulled them out of Bedforshire' (Thomas of Woodstock, 16c.). Used for children who want to stay up, perhaps from fear of the dark; and for adults who should have got up earlier.

bedewed sweating
Of a female, who is not supposed to sweat in public or, in some circles, at all. The liquid excreted is likened to the pure morning dew: '... a lady might get "bedewed", but she didn't sweat' (Jennings, 1965).

bedpan see pan

bedwetting urinating in bed
Usu. of children involuntarily. This SE use makes us forget that there are many other ways of making a bed damp.

bee a quantity of illicit narcotics
An inexact unit of measurement, probably based on the size of the insect rather than its ability to sting. Am.

beef copulation
Just as Africans may refer to any meat as 'beef', so in euphemism the two words are largely interchangeable: '... feeding him beef like a shogun in a geisha house' (Wambaugh, 1975). 'Beef' may also mean a penis, any woman viewed sexually by a male or a whore. 'Beefcake', copying **cheesecake** (q.v.), is the photograph of a naked man for female erotic gratification.

been having urinated
Polite usage and effectively the past tense of the verb 'to go': 'Hari's realization that I hadn't "been" rather cast a blight on his evening' (P. Scott, 1973 – an Indian youth was entertaining a White girl). Rarely too of defecation. 'Been into' is almost explicit of male copulation: 'He had never been into a girl either' (Bradbury, 1975). An unmarried female said to have 'been there' has copulated.

beg a child of to copulate with
Male usage, perhaps from a wish to generate an heir: 'I think he means to beg a child of her' (Shakespeare, 3 *Henry VI*). ob.

beggar a mild oath
A corruption of **bugger** (q.v.).

behind the buttocks
It could be any part of you, from your head to your heels: '... reference to a female buttocks as her "behind"' (Jennings, 1965 – but it is used equally of males). Rarely as the anus: 'It was a serious insult, because that was the hand they used to wipe their behinds' (Simon, 1979). There is also some male homosexual use: 'This bee-hind is for sale, boy' (Mailer, 1965).

bell money the money extracted from a bridegroom at a wedding
Not a corruption of 'ball money' – see **ball** – but from payment demanded by the ringers: 'At a wedding, the boys and girls of the neighbourhood assemble in front of the house, calling out "Bell money, bell money, shabby waddin, canna spare a bawbee." Money is then given to them' (N & Q 1855, quoted in EDD – such rudeness hardly deserved rewarding). I include this ob. Sc. entry to remind us that weddings have often been the occasion for extortion and wilful delay, even before the photographer made his appearance.

belle mère a mother-in-law
A French euphemism doubly euphemistic in English. In the same vein as calling The Furies 'the Kindly Ones', the devil 'the Goodman', etc.

belly plea a claim that the defendant is pregnant
A pregnant woman could not be hanged and therefore so advised the judge if she were convicted on a capital charge: 'My mother pleaded her belly, and being found quick with child . . .' (Defoe, 1721). To 'wear the belly high' is merely to be pregnant.

belly to belly copulating
Am. use from a position adopted by the participants. In ob. Eng. use a 'belly-piece' was a whore, punning on the meaning, an apron.

belly up bankrupt
Usu. of Am. companies, with piscine imagery: '. . . no government on earth in the mid-1980s let a company like MDC go belly up' (Erdman, 1981).

bellyful of lead *see* lead

below stairs employed as a domestic servant
The construction of town houses afforded day accommodation for the servants in cellars or semi-basements and sleeping space in the attics, communicating through the 'back-stairs' of gossip fame. Servants might also be described in general terms as 'downstairs'.

below the salt socially inferior
The salt was put in the middle of the table, with the more important people on one side of it, the less on the other. Of several saline classifications, this only has passed into general fig. use, but note: '. . . it's a big dinner and you'll be well above the salt' (N. Mitford, 1960).

belt (1) to take any violent or wrong action
Of many taboos, such as copulating extra-maritally, smoking marijuana or becoming very drunk. To 'belt your batter' is to masturbate yourself, perhaps a vulgar culinary pun on the sl. 'batter', a penis. A 'belter' is a cheap whore, but not with any special penchant for bondage. To 'belt' is to drive a vehicle at an excessive speed, but beware of doing so on an Am. 'belt-way', or ring road.

belt (2) a drink of spirituous intoxicant
Usu. drunk fast and to excess: 'Dundee and Spencer had a couple of belts on the drive into Manhattan' (Sanders, 1984). cf. **belt** (1).

bench to cause to withdraw from active participation
From being relegated to the substitutes' bench while others do the playing: '. . . if I say you're benched, you're benched' (Deighton, 1982 of a commander grounding a flier). A 'bench-warmer' in Am. is a less competent athlete.

bend to drink intoxicants to excess
Probably an abbr. of the euphemistic 'bend the elbow', from the locomotion of the drinking vessel: 'Bend well to the Madeira at dinner' (Ramsay, 1859). In modern use an 'elbow-bender' is a drunkard and 'elbow bending' drinking intoxicants: 'Alrazi was a major leaguer at elbow-bending' (M. Thomas, 1980). 'Bent' means drunk, 'on the bend' is being engaged in an alcoholic debauch and a 'bender' a drunken carouse. The 19c. New England 'benders' were the human legs in that age of prudery.

bend sinister an imputation of bastardy
It runs from the upper right to the lower left corner of a coat of arms. To suggest that someone, whether or not entitled to a coat of arms, has a 'bend sinister' is to infer that he is actually or fig. a bastard.

bend the rules to act illegally
The inference is that the law has not really been broken: '. . . if he sometimes "bent the rules" . . . . he believed that the end justified the means' (P. Scott, 1973). 'Bent' means stolen or dishonest: 'Having sold a stolen or *bent* car to a complainant' (Lavine, 1930). And the awful punning cliché, a 'bent copper' for a dishonest policeman.

bends (the) menstruation
Properly decompression sickness and its painful symptoms: 'She was having her damned period, she said, a real bastard, cramps, the bends, you name it' (le Carré, 1986).

benefit state aid paid to the poor
Properly, an advantage, whence the specific advantage of being a member of a fund from which you could draw if you were ill. If the illness lasted too long, or you failed to keep up your contributions, you went 'out of benefit'. The modern use is of regular or ad hoc payments: 'Jobless CSE candidates "should be given £13 benefit"' (*Daily Telegraph*, December 1980 – the Certificate of Secondary Education was designed for English and Welsh children unable to sit the harder General Certificate of Education examinations).

benevolence an arbitrary tax
It means generosity. Eng. monarchs extracted it from their rich subjects under the guise of loans which were never repaid, until the 1689 Bill of Rights brought this method of royal fund-raising to an end. The Br. WW II 'post-war credit' was a similar device except that it was repaid decades later in a depreciated currency.

Bennett buggy a motor car drawn by a horse
It was named after the Canadian Prime Minister during the Great Depression: '. . . took the engine out, welded shafts on, hitched up a horse, and drove with reins through the windshield' (*National Geographical Magazine*, 1979, of the 'Bennett buggy'). I include this entry because, as well as giving rise to many ob. euphemisms, the Depression led to a poverty beyond the understanding of those whose memories do not antedate WW II.

benny (1) a benzedrine pill used illegally
The abbr. puns on the male name. In ob. Br. army usage, it meant involuntary adult urination, a phenomenon not unknown to those of us who have occupied the lower bunk in a barrackroom. I cannot even make a guess at the etymology: 'What with the cold, and having the wind up so badly, the man must have been producing bennies at half-hour intervals throughout the night' (Richards, 1936).

benny (2) slow-witted
From a character so-named in the long-running but now ended television series *Crossroads*. Used to describe someone who has acted stupidly, especially as a 'right benny'. To 'throw a benny' is to have a tantrum. BI.

bent (1) *see* **bend the rules**

bent (2) *see* **bend**

bent (3) homosexual
Usu. of a male – he deviates from 'straight', or heterosexual, inclinations: '. . . he's bent as a tin spoon' (Bogarde, 1981, of a male homosexual).

berry an indication of displeasure
Probably an abbr. of **raspberry** (1) (q.v.). Holt refers to the dialect 'rasp', to belch, wrongly, I think. 'Berries', the testicles, is rare.

besom a whore
Properly, a broom, whence the aged menial who wielded it, with connotations of the pre-ferred method of transportation of witches. In the 19c.: 'A girl described as "a besom" without a qualifying adj. would imply unchastity' (EDD) and a 'besomer' was a promiscuous person of either sex. If in N. Eng. you decided to 'hang out the besom', you lived riotously during your wife's absence from home; probably because inn signs were poles with tufts on them, which looked like besoms, and punning on the meaning, a whore. But a woman 'hanging out the broomstick' was scheming to get herself a husband, again from the sign advertising that the place was open for business. All these uses are ob.

bespattered a mild oath
For those who wanted to imply but avoid the once taboo 'bloody'. ? ob.

bestiality the copulation of a human with an animal
Literally, appertaining to beasts, but cf. **beastliness**. Legal jargon for such a relationship with a mammal quadruped by either sex and also of a man with a bird. The case of *r. vs Brown* established the unlikely principle of Eng. law that you can be convicted of attempting an offence which it is impossible to commit. As 'bestiality' embraced only such a relationship with cattle and Brown's amorous attentions were directed towards a duck, he was convicted of attempted bestiality. Cattle, in Eng. law, includes geese because they graze and I was present in court in Wells, Somerset when a male was convicted of bestiality with a gander. It was generally thought he deserved a medal for bravery rather than six months. 'Bestiality' is also used rarely of obscenities.

bestride to copulate with
Of a male, with the common equine imagery: 'The tools of the fools who bestrode her' (*Playboy's Book of Limericks*).

bestseller a book of which the first impression is not remaindered
Publishers' puff. An 'international bestseller' is one in which the spellings 'honor', 'traveler', etc. are used to avoid re-setting the Am. edition. An 'instant bestseller' indicates an expensive pre-release advertising campaign.

betray to copulate with a third party while married
From the sense of proving false. There are two nuances – the male may 'betray' the female by copulating with her extra-maritally, despite her acquiescence in the

transaction: '. . . servant girls ceased to be seduced and began to be betrayed' (Mencken, 1940); and either spouse may 'betray' the other by so acting.

better country etc. life after death
The belief or hope of those who profess certain religions: '. . . strive to take it with faith and patience, looking to a "better country"' (Sir James Murray in a 1915 letter. His stern faith was admirable but led to a fundamental flaw in the OED, the omission of taboo words and phrases.) Also as 'better place', or 'better' or 'next' world, etc.

between shows involuntarily unemployed
Theatrical jargon, and not used of those rehearsing for a new part: '"I worked on lots a pictures a his over the years." "Did he know you were between shows?"' (Wambaugh, 1981, of an out-of-work dancer).

between the sheets copulating
From the bed linen but not only of copulation in bed: 'We still suited very well between the sheets' (Fraser, 1970, of a wife). Shakespeare used 'twixt the sheets': 'Twixt my sheets, Has done my office' (*Othello*).

between the thighs copulation with a female
Used only of extra-marital copulation: 'A man can learn more between the thighs of a good woman than he ever needs to know' (Sharpe, 1974 – academically and anatomically incorrect, for all its vivid imagery).

beverage an intoxicant
Properly a non-alcoholic drink, such as tea. Now standard Am. use for any alcoholic drink served – 'Would you like a beverage, sir?' – in a bar or 'beverage room' by a barkeep or 'beverage host'.

beyond salvage condemned to death
Espionage jargon for a defector who cannot be safely brought back to his former allegiance: 'The case against me is beyond salvage . . . . I'll be executed at the first opportune moment' (Ludlum, 1979).

bibi a whore
In Hindi, it means a lady, whence the 19c. Br. Indian use, a White wife married to a White man: 'The *bibi*, or white wife, was a great rarity; but the *bubu*, or native wife, was an accepted institution' (Blanch, 1954). Later a 'bibi' in Br. Indian army use became any Indian whore: 'Sahib, you want nice Bibi, me drive you to bungalow of nice half-caste, plenty clean, plenty cheap' (Richards, 1936). You may also find it spelt 'bidi' and as

'grass' bibi or bidi. The army or colonial service carried the use into Africa: '. . . African mistress, also known as "native comfort", "*bibi*" (Anglo-Indian) or "*bint*" – young woman (Arabic)' (Allen, 1979).

biddy a woman with whom you might copulate extra-maritally
In Ire. it meant a chicken and in Am., as an abbr. of 'Bridget', a maid-servant when many such were Irish: '. . . for a pound of sausages you could find a biddy who would actually chuck her old man out of bed and send him to sit downstairs till you'd finished' (Seymour, 1980, of Germany immediately after WW II).

big pregnant
Abbr. of 'big with child', but used also before the swelling is visible: 'They said shoo'r big, but doctor said 'twor nought at all but cowld' (Doyle, 1855). More explicitly, a 'big belly' means pregnancy, without any suggestion of overeating: '. . . the consequence of which was a big belly, and the loss of place' (Cleland, 1749 – a pregnant servant might expect summary dismissal).

big-boned fat
Of adults and children, suggesting that their frame needs that excess covering: '. . . in his beefy adolescence his mother had tactfully described him as "big-boned", though "burly" was how he now liked to see himself' (Boyd, 1981).

big brother a totalitarian tyranny
Fig. use from the character in Orwell's *1984*. Technical progress in communication systems and computers has kept pace with the passing years since he wrote, and it now all seems possible. In Am. CB sl., 'big brother' is a policeman.

big C cancer
A mainly Am. use for the most feared of all groups of disease. The 'big D' is death.

big girl a large and sexually unattractive young woman
Males use the term in a derogatory sense, because they need some physical dominance over a female, who therefore should not be larger or stronger than her master. A mother so describing her exceptionally large adolescent daughter does so kindly, to imply that she has merely grown quickly and all will be well in due course. Unfairly a 'big man' is assumed to have the virtues of generosity and virility.

big house etc. a prison
Am. usage, from the size of the building: 'She has other worries besides trying to keep her ex-lover out of the Big House' (Lavine, 1930). Also as 'big pasture' or, for male convicts, 'big school', the 'little school' being a prison for women or children. In ob. Br. use, a 'big house' was an institution for the destitute, or the common name for the residence of the squire.

big jobs defecation
Nursery usage in several forms: '. . . done our bigs and wiped our bottoms' (Amis, 1978). 'Little jobs' or 'littles' is urination.

big prize (the) copulation
A male wins it extra-maritally after lesser awards during courtship: '. . . allowing moist liberties but with steel-trap relentlessness withholding the big prize' (Styron, 1976).

bijou inconveniently small
Br. estate agents' jargon which seeks to persuade you that a tiny apartment is a jewel.

bikini wax the removal of women's pubic hair
To prevent hair escaping from the scanty lower garment: 'Her fag hairdresser gives a great bikini wax' (Sanders, 1982). It is the skin which is waxed, not the bikini.

bill a policeman
Perhaps from the weapon once carried by constables: '"Eyes front", said Murf. "It's Bill." A policeman in a helmet and gleaming rain-cape was coming towards them' (Theroux, 1976). Also as 'old bill'.

Billingsgate foul language
It was used by women sellers of fish rather than by male porters in the London market closed in 1982. According to Dryden 'Parnassus spoke the cant of Billingsgate' and in modern use: '. . . his ears had surely overflowed with such billingsgate' (Styron, 1976).

bin an institution for the mad
Properly, a container, and abbr. of 'loony bin': 'We shall be found stark staring mad with horror and live sixty more years in an expensive bin' (N. Mitford, 1949). Now less used because of our heightened understanding or taboos about lunacy.

bind to cause constipation
Properly, to tie fast whence, in medical jargon, to curb diarrhoea: 'Then the water will be madly binding' (N. Mitford, 1945, of a hypochondriac). 'Bound' means constipated.

binge a drunken carouse
The verb means to soak and in 19c. use referred to drinking too much beer: 'A man goes to the ale-house to binge himself' (EDD).

bint a whore
The Br. army picked up the Arabic word for girl and carried it across the world: 'The women put it down to the rations we got, and the men down to the bint, as they called it' (Bogarde, 1978).

biographic leverage blackmail
Espionage jargon: 'Jonathan smiled at the cryptic jargon . . . . "biographic leverage" meant blackmail' (Trevanian, 1972).

bird (1) a whore
When Holman Hunt wrote in 1854 of his 'bird in a gilded cage', the Br. meanings covered the spectrum from girl through sweetheart and sexual mistress to whore. An Am. 'bird-cage' is still a brothel but a 'bird' today is any young girl viewed sexually.

bird (2) imprisonment
From the cage. To do 'bird' is to be incarcerated. A 'birdcage' is a prison cell.

bird (3) the vagina
A male use, and the 'bird's nest' is a female's pubic hair: 'This bitch wears these short shorts . . . . when I'm down on my knees . . . . I kneel there and look right at her bird' (Wambaugh, 1975).

bird dog (1) a small gambler who follows the betting pattern of heavy gamblers
From the animal that retrieves the quarry brought down by its master. But he is not that stupid; those who habitually bet large sums are likely on occasion to be party to criminal interference with the runners. Am.

bird dog (2) an apparently respectable person aiding but publicly concealing his collusion with a criminal
Again from picking up the game and bringing it back to the hunter, for a reward: 'Your bird dog, the State Senator?' (Chandler, 1939, of such a relationship).

bird in the air a police helicopter watching traffic
A 'bird' is an aircraft and this may be a corruption of the CB 'bear in the air' (q.v. under **bear** (2)). A 'bird circuit' is not their flying pattern but the saloons frequented by Am. male homosexuals in a vicinity where you can visit several.

bird lime bird shit
The colour is the same as lime, and it goes powdery when dry. SE.

bird's nest *see* bird (4)

birth control the prevention of conception during copulation
The phrase accurately describes the stratagems of midwives to prevent the arrival of babies at weekends or other times inconvenient to themselves. A more accurate term would be 'conception prevention'.

birthday suit etc. nakedness
What you were born in: 'I went in the morning to a private place, along with the housemaid, and we bathed in our birthday soot' (Smollett, 1771 – I am sure he meant they had one each). Also as 'birthday' attire, gear or the ob. finery: '. . . the figure I made . . . . outshone all other *birthday* finery' (Cleland, 1749, of a naked woman).

bisexual having both homosexual and heterosexual tastes
In biology, etc. it means having both sexes in the same plant or animal. Often abbr. to 'bi'.

bit a woman viewed sexually by a male
Almost interchangeable with **piece** (1) (q.v.): '"Opale," said Cicero. "Whose bit is that?"' (Londres, 1928, in tr. of a whore). Often as a 'bit' of all right, arse, ass, crumpet, fluff, goods, hot stuff, jam, meat, muslin, skirt, stuff, you-know-what, etc., most of which are elaborated under those headings so that one illustration will suffice: 'One of them . . . . was his own bit of goods. She was a married woman whose husband was away working' (Richards, 1936). A 'bit' can also be extra-marital copulation by either sex: '. . . taking a little bit now and then from her husband's valet' (Condon, 1966). A 'bit on the side' is regular copulation with other than your regular sexual partner, adverting to the 'side', or additional, plate served with a formal meal: 'She had been used, had been just the fun you can't get when you're married, a bit on the side' (Bradbury, 1976).

bit on a bet
Racing jargon, abbr. of a 'bit of money bet on', and seeking to show that the wager was a modest one. I don't think there is any pun on the 'bit' the horse has in its mouth.

bitch a male homosexual
Am. homosexual jargon, of someone thought to be spiteful or vindictive as the woman so described. In ob. use a 'bitch' was a whore and to 'bitch' was to be a regular user of brothels.

bite a swindler
'A cheat; a trick; a fraud; in low and vulgar language' says Dr Johnson, and of 'biter', 'A tricker; a deceiver'. 'Is this wench an idiot, or a bite?' (Fielding, 1742) uses an ob. word but we still say 'the biter bit'. The Am. 'bite' meant to borrow before its present criminal connotations, such as 'put the bite on', to extort by threats: '. . . put the bite on you and you paid him a little now and then to avoid scandal' (Chandler, 1951). All uses have dental origins.

bite the dust *see* lick the dust

black and whites the police
Perhaps from the uniform or from the common car colouring: '. . . didn't even notice the cops gliding up in the black-and-white' (Wambaugh, 1981). Am.

black beauty an illegal narcotic pill
Usu. biphetamine and punning on the horse in the story: 'Librium and Valium in fives and tens; Quaaludes; Dexamyls and Benzedrines; Nembutols and Amyl Nitrate; black beauties' (M. Thomas, 1982).

black economy the sum of goods and services provided without tax or other official cognizance
The international phenomenon of rich nations where all wish to avoid paying taxes and some wish to continue to draw unemployment pay despite working. In the USA it is 'underground production', '*schwarzarbeit*' in Germany, '*sotto governo*' in Italy, etc. 'All public-spirited citizens will want to help the Inland Revenue in its battle against this "black economy" of untaxed income and benefits' (A. Waugh, *Private Eye*, March 1981 – the satirist meant that the tax collector would get no help from the public).

black-eyed Susan a whore
Probably the song came first. Of whores working sea ports: '. . . the sailors' wives and black-eyed Susans would . . . . haunt the quays in sailing days' (Fowles, 1977). ? ob.

black gentleman etc. the devil
The Prince of Darkness, he was also thought to enter a house by the chimney in the days of coal fires and soot. Also as the 'black' lad, man, prince, Sam, spy, etc.: 'The Black Man would gi'e her power . . . . to kep the butter frae gatherin' in the kirn' (Service, 1890). But 'black George' was a poacher in SE and in Sc. 'black fishing' was poaching fish

by night: 'Blackfishers, poachers and smugglers are a sort of gentry that will not be much checked' (W. Scott, 1824). Most of these uses are ob. as we don't have to refer allusively to the devil these days.

black hole   a prison
Most Br. towns had one, so called because it was insanitary, unlit and below ground: 'Naething but law and vengeance, black-hole and fining' (Cross, 1844). Also abbr. to 'hole': 'They'l other foin us, or else send us to't oil' (Bywater, 1839). I include this ob. Br. entry because generations of schoolchildren think the only 'black hole' was the 1756 Calcutta version in which the native ruler had the effrontery to incarcerate some foreigners of whose activities he disapproved.

black ivory *see* **blackbird**

black market   the illegal dealing in rationed goods
Here, as elsewhere, black indicates illegality: 'A black market is beginning to appear, in sharp contrast to the orderly arrangements . . . . in the food markets' (Goebbels, 1945, in tr.). 'In the black' meant trading in such commodities, punning on 'black market' and the profitability, as bank statements used to show credit statements in black ink. Debit accounts were shown in red and despite modern monochrome print-outs, we still talk about being 'in the black' – in credit– or 'in the red' – overdrawn.

black money etc.   cash gained illegally
It can be the excess profits from a gambling establishment which are concealed to avoid tax; the proceeds of any vice; a bribe received by a politician; etc. In each case there is a need to pass the funds through a lawful enterprise before spending it: 'Hasn't the wily oriental got black money tucked away?' (Davidson, 1978). Also as 'black' pounds, dollars, etc. '. . . to do with black dollars . . . . after returns from the orient' (ibid.). But 'black marks' are not wrongly acquired German banknotes.

black operator   a secret agent or spy
This CIA jargon does not mean he isn't a White man. In ob. Eng. use 'black work' was the burial of corpses: '. . . employed in black work, or who, in other words, worked for an undertaker' (Egerton, 1884). Similarly the punning 'black art' was the business of arranging funerals, a 'black job' was a funeral and 'blacks' were mourning clothes.

black order (the)   Himmler's military Nazi organization
The Schutzstaffel, better known as the SS, consisted of men 'racially pure since 1750'. Also known as 'blackshirts' from their dress, as were other non-German Fascists who aped them and their uniform.

black pox   syphilis caught from a black woman
see **pox** – White males so infected thought that the disease took a more virulent form: 'John Lawrence, who got black pox, as he called syphilis, caught from a Negress . . .' (Harris, 1925).

black stuff etc.   opium
Also as 'black' pills or smoke: 'Imagine a clergyman peddling the black smoke' (Fraser, 1985, writing in archaic style of an opium smuggler). The 'white stuff' is cocaine and cf. **black beauty**.

black velvet   a dark-skinned whore
Originally used by Br. soldiers in India but the pun is now general: 'In sophisticated circles Black Velvet is a mix of champagne and Guinness. But in the outback the phrase has a different meaning derived from an obscure Ugandan dialect' (*Private Eye*, January 1982 – *see* **Uganda** for the equally obscure in-joke).

blackbird   a negro slave
The jargon of Whites engaged in the slave trade or owning such slaves. Trading in slaves was 'blackbirding': 'I had recently forsaken African blackbirding in favour of river dealing' (Fraser, 1971). The trade was also the 'blackbird trade': 'Things were making life more difficult in the blackbird trade' (ibid.) or 'blackbird pie': 'The old swine had his fingers in the blackbird pie' (ibid., of a Br. businessman). A 'blackbirder' was either a transporter of or dealer in slaves: 'When the stinking ships of the blackbirders crossed the bars below the delta' (Longstreet, 1956). The slaves in the mass were known as 'black cattle': '. . . wi' a full load of black cattle' (Fraser, 1971, of a ship full of slaves); or as 'black hide': 'There won't be a black hide aboard to show against us' (ibid. – when slavery became illegal you might avoid conviction by pushing weighted slaves overboard to drown, before being boarded by the enforcement vessel); or as 'black sheep': 'You're tender of black sheep' (ibid.); or as 'black pigs': 'I was shipping black pigs when you were hanging at your mother's teat' (ibid.); or, because of their value, as 'black ivory': '. . . a cargo of black ivory going over

the Middle Passage' (ibid.). Moral condemnation may be expected, of all the White people involved through several generations, directly and indirectly, and of the Black chiefs and agents who provided the cargoes. I confine my comment to quoting von Longau in Longfellow's translation: 'Though the mills of God grind slowly, yet they grind exceeding small'; and to referring you to Pope-Hennessy's 1967 *Sins of the Fathers*, a title aptly taken from Exodus XX 5 except that the ultimate price will be payable long after the third and fourth generation.

(**blackmail** is SE for extorting money by threats, usu. on more than one occasion. It comes from the tribute paid by the Lowland Scots to the Highlanders: 'And what is black-mail? A sort of protection money that Low-country gentlemen . . . . pay to some Highland chief that he may neither do them harm nor suffer it be done to them by others' (W. Scott, 1814. Dr Wright, in EDD, with the innocence and assurance of the late Victorians, calls the use obsolete.)

blackshirt *see* **black order**

blank (1) a mild oath
A blank space may be left in print for the taboo swearword, which means that the euphemism is never written. The adjectival 'blanking' is both spoken and written.

blank (2) to kill
From the void into which the victim is sent: '. . . none of whom seemed particularly distressed by the sudden blanking of Victor Maitland' (Sanders, 1977). Am.

blanked drunk
As a WW I usage, and knowing what Br. soldiers did to the French language, it probably came from drinking too much 'vin blanc' rather than from rendering yourself senseless.

blanket drill self masturbation
In some tropical stations an afternoon siesta on your charpoy was compulsory, the period being called 'blanket drill', although the last thing you needed was a blanket. In the heat and boredom there was ample opportunity for masturbation and the phrase was also used of copulation.

blast (1) to kill
By shooting, and so it probably refers to the explosion: 'We just got a message for the guy. We don't blast him. Not today' (Chandler, 1939). Am.

blast (2) a mild oath
The etymology is uncertain. It could come from the meanings a 'puff of air', or 'lightning'. Partridge in DSUE says of 'blasted', 'a euphemism for bloody' and of 'bleating', 'Among the lower classes a euphemism for bloody', but he didn't explain what led him to these conclusions.

blast (3) to take narcotics illegally
Perhaps from the feeling of levitation induced: 'I'm higher than a giraffe's toupee. I started blasting when I was 13' (Longstreet, 1956). An Am. 'blast party' is where illegal narcotics are ingested communally. Rarely too a 'blast' may be an intoxicant: '. . . get me another blast, will you? Easy on the ice' (Sanders, 1982).

blazes hell
The fires burned you, without consuming your body or rendering you insensible to pain: 'You can count on J.B. to blazes and beyond' (Fraser, 1977). 'Old blazes' was the devil, who found the environment not uncongenial. Heretics had to be burned on earth without access to the eternal fires because that was the only way of destroying their soul and ensuring they would have no body for subsequent resurrection. It was very logical, if you believed in a medieval hell.

bleach to dye
Of hair, and normally on women. Dyeing hair means you are vain or trying to conceal your age but natural bleaching in the sun would not be anything to be ashamed of.

bleed to extort on a regular basis
Am. underworld sl., of obvious derivation. The ob. Br. 'bleed the monkey' was to steal rum, taking a little at a time through a straw from the mess tub, or 'monkey'.

(**bleeding** is today a mild oath, used for 'bloody', but each is about as harmless or offensive as the other.)

blighty a serious wound
It comes from the Hindi 'bilayati', foreign, which effectively meant Great Britain for the soldiers and subjects of the Br. Indian empire. WW I usage of a wound serious enough for you to be sent home and so released, for a time at least, from the horror of the Western Front: 'What we used to call "a nice blighty one"; sent me back to England' (Price, 1974).

blind a drunken carouse
It should be because it makes you 'blind

drunk' but the use seems to predate both the cliché and its Sc. form 'blind-fou'. Now often called a 'blinder'.

blind pig an unlicensed place for the consumption of intoxicants
Hidden from the police, perhaps? Other unsocial activities like the sale of illegal narcotics and prostitution might be found, the customers being usu. Blacks: 'Howison had raided it as long ago as February, 1966, and had discovered that it was, in fact, the front for a blind pig' (Lacey, 1986). Am.

blip off to kill
'Blips' indicate that an oscilloscope or other monitoring equipment is working. They vanish if the instrument malfunctions, or is switched off. Am.

blitzed drunk
The consequent feeling of devastation is not much like a WW II air raid by the Germans on Eng., a 'blitz' from the lightning war. Oddly this is an Am. rather than a Br. use.

block to copulate with
Of a male, with obvious imagery: 'There was a young lady of Thun, Who was blocked by the man in the moon' (*Playboy's Book of Limericks*). The punning 'block her passage' is more explicit.

blockbuster a real estate dealer who induces Whites to sell their homes through threat of Blacks moving into the area
The use puns on the WW II bomb and the breaking up of 'blocks' of property occupied solely by Whites, for which higher prices might be obtained on redevelopment. Am.

blocked under narcotic influence
I suppose from the sense hemmed or shut in.

bloke cocaine taken illegally
An Am. addict use which could be rh. sl. for 'coke', cocaine – or merely rhyming with it.

blood disease etc. syphilis
The condition was doubly taboo as incurable and contracted in a shameful manner. This Am. use just survives but 'blood poison' for syphilis is ob.: '*Syphilis* became transformed into *blood-poison, specific blood poison* and *secret disease*' (Mencken, 1940, writing on 19c. Am. evasions).

blood money extortion
Properly, a reward for bringing about another's death, or compensation paid to surviving relatives in respect of a killing: '. . . collecting "blood money", that is, shaking down prostitutes, poor peddlars, &c.' (Lavine, 1930). Am.

bloody menstruating
Female usage, from the visual symptom and in other expressions like 'the bloody flag is up'. (The expletive 'bloody' may refer to menstruation, or come from the ob. popular oaths like 'God's blood', or by a corruption of 'by Our Lady'. A 'Bloody Mary' is an intoxicant consisting of vodka and tomato juice – for my taste with ice, tabasco, salt, pepper, a slice of lemon and Worcestershire Sauce – after the Br. queen who caused many protestants to be killed. A 'Virgin Mary' or 'Bloody Shame' is the tomato juice without alcohol for the person who does not or dare not take an intoxicant: '"Just tomato juice for me," the sergeant said stolidly. "A Virgin Mary," the waiter nodded wisely. "Also known as a Bloody Shame"' (Sanders, 1977 – the sergeant had been an alcoholic).

blooming a mild oath
I suppose it is for 'bloody', as most etymologists say so.

blot out to kill
From the extinction of life: 'You can even blot me out suddenly so that I don't know about it' (Fraser, 1977).

blow (1) to copulate
This use is perhaps ob., although you may still hear that a male may 'blow through', 'blow the loose corns' or 'blow the groundsels', which last is done on the floor. 'Blow off' is to ejaculate semen, during copulation or otherwise, with imagery from the whale: 'Blew off all over the booth' (*Playboy's Book of Limericks*). In ob. use a 'blow', or the Am. 'blowen', was a whore. These meanings have today been almost entirely submerged by the sense, orally to excite the penis or vagina, homosexually or heterosexually: 'He was cruising down the interstate and his daughter's husband is blowing him' (Diehl, 1978). A 'blow job' is usu. fellatio by a whore: '"You want for me to give you a blow job?" She got off the bed and came towards him' (Sharpe, 1976). But for thieves a 'blow job' may still be the use of explosives to gain access to a building or safe.

blow (2) to fart
And as 'blow off ' – both uses are common. 'Blow a raspberry' is to make a similar noise with the lips: 'The bank man blew the Mar-

seilles equivalent of a raspberry and went home' (L. Thomas, 1977).

blow (3) to boast
This perhaps ob. use comes from puffing yourself up like a frog: 'Bonapart, loud vaunting smart, It was a fearfu' blaw that' (A. Scott, 1805). In modern imagery you may 'blow your own horn' or 'trumpet'; or 'blow smoke', like a distant ship advertising its presence: 'You think I'm blowing smoke?' (Sanders, 1984 of someone accused of exaggeration).

blow (4) a mild oath
Brewer says 'A play on the word Dash me, which is a euphemism for a more offensive oath' (BDPF) – how I wish those Victorians were more explicit. I suspect it is of the same tendency as **blast** (2) (q.v.).

blow (5) to betray to authority
Espionage jargon, from 'blowing', or allowing to escape, secret information: 'Did you tell the man to blow me?' (Hall, 1979, of a betrayed spy). In the underworld of crime, to 'blow the whistle' is to inform to authority, from a referee's action in stopping a game: 'He was a number one hitman for the Cosa Nostra and he blew the whistle on them' (Diehl, 1978). The Br. 'blow the gaff' has the same meaning.

blow (6) an ingestion of illicit narcotics
Through the mouth, and I suppose you blow some of it out again. You may also 'blow' a stick, Charlie, horse, snow, etc. To 'blow a fix' is to fail to penetrate a vein when attempting to inject yourself.

blow away to kill
Usu. by gunfire at short range, although the corpse is left for disposal: 'He got blown away. I went to his funeral' (Sanders, 1977). Am.

blow one give me a draught beer
The summary Am. request is to the barkeep who then scoops, or rarely, blows off the froth which has resulted from pouring bottom-fermented beer under pressure direct into a glass. 'Blown', drunk, is not from drinking the beer – indeed 'blown out' would be more appropriate – but from the exhaustion of a horse.

blow the whistle to inform against
The action which brings the game to an end: ' – and we hate to ruin Kealy's career . . . . So we'd feel bad about blowing the whistle on him' (Sanders, 1984).

blow your cool etc. to do an irrational or unexpected act
An imprecise Am. phrase which can confuse foreigners. If you 'blow' your cool, cork, lump, noggin, roof, stack, top etc. you may commit suicide, be angry, talk indiscreetly, drink intoxicants to excess, ingest illegal narcotics or indulge in any other off-beat behaviour.

blue (1) a policeman
Mainly Am. use, from the normal colour of the uniform: 'Okay, it was on the sixth floor when the first blues got to the Kipper townhouse' (Sanders, 1980, of the elevator). A policeman is also a 'bluebottle', 'bluebird', 'blue-belly', 'blue man', 'blue jeans' or 'blue and white' and the 'men in blue' are the police. In BI a 'man in blue' or a 'bluecoat' is a policeman and the 'blue lamp', a police station, from the standard exterior sign. Internationally the 'blue police' are those in uniform and operating to known rules as different from more sinister varieties: '. . . speak to the SS man, to the Ukrainian auxiliary, to the Blue Police and to OD details' (Keneally, 1982, of Nazi-occupied Poland; German control rested in the army and these four organizations, the OD being Jews in authority over other Jews).

blue (2) erotic
Probably from the French 'bibliothèque bleu', a collection of seamy works of literature, rather than from the colour of the brimstone fires which await the evil: 'She starred in dozens of blue movies before coming above ground' (Deighton, 1972).

blue (3) drunk
The dialect 'blue' was a jug of ale but this Am. use probably comes from post-alcoholic depression. Also as the punning 'blue-eyed'.

blue balls a sufferer from gonorrhoea
I suppose from one of the male symptoms. Am.

blue box an electronic device to avoid paying for toll telephone calls
A 'black box' by another name. It persuades a pay phone not to demand money, as if it were being tested or the charge transferred to another subscriber. Am.

blue cheer etc. an illegal narcotic
From the colour of the pill, or from its supposed ability to drive away the 'blues' – depression. Also as 'blue' devil, flags, heaven, jay (sodium amytal), velvet etc. In ob. N. Br. dialect 'blue stone' was inferior whisky, punning on the word for vitriol.

'Blue ruin' was any cheap intoxicant – usu. gin – from the colour and the consequences: 'My ole man and me want some blue ruin to keep our spirits up' (Mayhew, 1862). The ob. 'blue-devil factory' was not an illegal distillery but a mad-house, from one of the common delusions of lunatics: 'I saw him off for the last time to the blue-devil factory in the country where he died bawling with delirium tremens' (Fraser, 1975, writing in 19c. style).

blue hair an old woman
From the dye, or 'blue rinse', applied to the hair: 'This joint is where you find busloads a blue-hairs when they get off the freaking cruise ships' (Wambaugh, 1981).

blue room a lavatory on an aircraft
Crew jargon, perhaps from the subdued lighting: '. . . a passenger deliberately burnt himself to death in the right aft "blue room" or toilet' (Moynahan, 1983).

blue veiner an erection of the penis
From the prominence of the veins when erect: 'Even now he got a blue veiner every time he held a bar of soap' (Wambaugh, 1975).

board to copulate with
Of the male, usu. extra-maritally, from naval imagery: 'I am sure he is in the fleet: I would he had boarded me' (Shakespeare, *Merry Wives of Windsor*). Or, less subtly: 'I tried to board her at Kiva, but the caravanserai was too crowded' (Fraser, 1975 – he lusted after a woman in the party). The 19c. Br. 'board lodger' was a whore who obtained her finery from a pimp, thus staying under his control; or a whore working on her own but paying commission to the bawd of the brothel to which she brought men: 'Board lodgers are those who give a portion of what they receive to the mistress of the brothel in return for their board and lodging' (Mayhew, 1862). For 'board a train', *see* **pull a train**.

boat people the refugees from Vietnamese Communism
Not those normally living or working on boats but the victims of Hanoi's tyranny and its **new economic zones** (q.v.). In ob. Eng. use to 'boat' was to send convicts to penal settlements abroad, whence to imprison anywhere.

bobby a policeman
The name comes from Sir Robert Peel, who reorganized the London police with his New Metropolitan Police Act of 1828. It is often forgotten that as Secretary for Ireland

he had done the same service there somewhat earlier. Still commonly used of Br. police.

bobtail a dishonourable discharge from the army
US Army jargon – the bit about 'honorable and faithful service' was clippped off the bottom of the printed certificate of discharge. In ob. Eng. use a 'bobtail' was either a eunuch, from 'bob', to cut off; or a whore, from 'bob', to move up and down and 'tail', what she might be moving.

bodily functions urination and defecation
The equally important breathing, sweating, digesting, etc. do not count: 'You slept there, bathed, performed your bodily functions' (Sanders, 1973).

bodily wastes urine and faeces
Discharged in the **bodily functions** (above): '. . . the fan is full of bodily wastes' (M. Thomas, 1987 in fig. use).

body a corpse
Contraction of 'dead body': 'At Worster must his bodie be interr'd' (Shakespeare, *King John*). If you 'count bodies' it can be of the living or the dead but a 'body count' is only of the living.

body odour stale sweat etc.
The advertising invention of Lifebuoy Soap, which claimed to correct the condition. Now normally abbr. to 'BO': 'SA and BO, perfect rubbish and bosh – one was a beauty or a *jolie laide* and that was that' (N. Mitford, 1949 – 'SA' was sex appeal).

body rub masturbation by a whore
One of the services offered, usu. to males, in a 'massage parlour' by a 'body worker'. But 'body wax' is not what you get in your ears, or to help with removing hairs on the body, but a turd.

body shaper etc. a corset
An invention of advertisers to persuade fat women that they are neither fat nor buying a corset. Also as 'body' briefer, hugger, outline, etc. Mainly Am.

boff (1) to copulate with
Of a male and as it probably comes from sl. 'boff', to hit, with the common violent imagery: 'He boffs her or he doesn't boff her. She leaves' (Sanders, 1977, of a man who might have copulated with a woman). On the other hand, it could be a corruption of 'buff', to rub and that is surely the etymology of the other sexual meaning, to masturbate, of a male.

boff (2) to fart
Common Br. school usage. The etymology
is obscure.

bog a lavatory
Abbr. of 'bog-house', probably from the
marshy ground which used to surround it
before the advent of the cesspit or the septic
tank: '. . . been in the bog a little while . . . .
What do you suppose he's doing there?'
(Theroux, 1973). In male speech, to 'bog' is
to defecate.

bogy a policeman
Probably from the meaning, a devil,
although a 'bogy' was really an apparition
with special powers of inducing nursery
terrors, making you lose your way in the
dark, causing you to be chased by phantoms,
etc.: 'Well, the bloody bogies are cleaning
the streets up. There won't be a girl about'
(Kersh, 1936, of clearing whores from the
London streets prior to a coronation).
Horses reared, or 'boggled', when they saw a
bogy in the path, as our minds do in the
modern cliché.

boiled drunk
The common Am. culinary imagery: 'A
crowd that can get boiled without having to
lie up with Dr Verringer' (Chandler, 1953).

boiler house an unscrupulous seller of
shares
From the intense heat applied and the international successor to the bucket shop (q.v.
under **bucket** (2)). Also as 'boiler' room or
shop: 'The Dutch authorities are finally
acting to close down the "boiler-shop"
share-pushing operations based in Amster-
dam' (*Daily Telegraph*, August 1986).

boilerplate disclamatory provisions in a
public document to protect professional
advisers from liability
As used on old battleships, with an inference
of elaborate and excessive protection: '. . . so
that the attorneys for the underwriters could
satisfy themselves on matters of title and
other boilerplate' (M. Thomas, 1982).

bolt to leave your husband for another man
The imagery is from an unmanageable
horse: 'He mightn't want to send you off, but
he'll be jolly pleased now you've bolted'
(Murdoch, 1978). A 'bolter' is a woman who
so acts.

bolt the moon etc. *see* **moonlight flit**

bomb (1) an atomic bomb
The taboo is against nuclear weapons rather
than high explosives: 'The French say they
will soon have a Bomb' (N. Mitford, 1960).

bomb (2) *see* **bomber**

Bombay milk-cart a vehicle used to
empty the contents of lavatories
Like the Eng. milk-cart, it had two wheels
and carried its load in a churn: 'Waste from
the latrines was collected by the sweepers
and removed in a conveyance drawn by a
pair of oxen and known as the "Bombay
milk-cart"' (Allen, 1975, writing of India).

Bombay oyster a laxative
This compound of milk and castor oil was
given to young Br. sailors. As with an oyster,
you just swallowed it down.

bomber a marijuana cigarette
I suppose from its effect on the smoker. Also
as a 'bomb' or a 'bombita', a little bomb in
Spanish and sometimes cocaine. 'Bombed
out' is under narcotic influence or drunk:
'. . . he was dropping acid and bombed out of
his gourd most of the time on pills and
booze' (Sanders, 1977).

bona-roba a whore
From the fine clothes she wore to atttract
custom: 'She was then a bona-roba'
(Shakespeare, 2 *Henry IV*, of Jane Nightwork). ob.

bondage the satisfaction of sexual desire by
physical constraint or abasement
Properly, a condition of slavery, or of being
tied up. Prostitutes' and sexual deviants'
jargon.

**bonds of life being gradually
dissolved** dying slowly
A saunter through old churches and churchyards can reveal many similar evasions. I
especially recommend an hour or so in Bath
Abbey, whence this example, and which also
provides a potted geography of the British
Empire: 'The Bonds of Life being gradually
dissolved She winged her Flight from this
World in expectation of a better, the 15th
January 1810'. A 'long illness' in a modern
obituary indicates death from cancer.

bone (1) to steal
'Bone' may mean a finger, which has overtones of thieving as in **finger-blight** (q.v.);
or there could be an allusion to the ossivor-
ous habits of canines: 'From her grave in
Mary-bone They've come and boned your
Mary' (Hood, c. 1830 – he certainly worked
on his puns, of which this is by no means the
feeblest). Grose gives 'boned' as 'taken up by
a constable'. The modern Am. 'boning' is

enrichment through sharp practice, perhaps from improving the edible weight of meat by removing the bone before sale.

bone (2) an erect penis
From the rigidity. 'Bone-ache', syphilis, probably comes from the general bodily malaise, or it may be a pun.

bone (3) associated with human death
What is eventually left after burial, along with the teeth, if any. Many ob. uses like 'bone-house', a coffin; 'bone hugging', carrying a corpse to the grave; 'bone-orchard' or 'bone-yard', a burial ground; etc. You may still meet rare jocular use, as '. . . we usually plant one or two in the bone-orchard before we start for home' (N. Mitford, 1960, of a party of elderly tourists in Spain). 'Make old bones' is to live long but used normally in the negative as a prediction of a short life. The modern Am. 'make bones' is to kill, with special significance in the Mafia where a candidate must 'make his bones' – kill someone – before qualifying for full membership.

bonk to copulate
The usu. violent imagery, from sl. 'bonk', to hit rather than punning on the other sl. meaning, the **head** (4) (q.v.). The *Mail on Sunday* of 9 August 1987 devoted an article to the etymology which was speculative rather than enlightening. 'Bonkers' has long meant slightly mad or, in ob. Br. naval sl., intoxicated.

booby a madman
Properly, a fool. A 'booby hutch' is an institution for the insane: 'Check the booby hutches . . . . for escapees' (Sanders, 1981).

book a sentence in prison
In Am. 'a book' is a sentence for a year, 'the book', a sentence for life. cf. **throw the book at**, which may explain the derivation. In ob. use 'books' or the 'devil's books' were playing cards and to 'plant the books' was to cheat by stacking the pack.

book club *see* **club** (2)

bookmaker a person who accepts bets for a living
'Book' is a 19c. abbr. of 'betting book' and this punning SE use developed soon after, to be followed by other euphemisms for this profitable but once disreputable profession.

boom-boom (1) defecation
Am. nursery usage, the image coming perhaps from the firing of ordnance.

boom-boom (2) copulation
Again from the firing of a gun? That would imply male activity, but it is used of either sex: ' "No more boom-boom for that mamma-san," the Marine said, that same tired remark you heard every time the dead turned out to be women' (Herr, 1977). As you might expect 'boom-boom-boom' is repeated copulation: 'You get that madam into bed, boom-boom-boom – why, she's glad to lodge you for a week' (Fraser, 1971). A 'boom-passenger' was not a passive partner on such an occasion, but a Br. convict who was chained to the boom on deck during his sea voyage to a penal colony.

boondock to court sexually
Supposedly from the Tagalog 'bundok', a mountain, the isolated place where the car might be parked, thus to Am. via the Philippines. 'Boondagger', a female homosexual taking the male role, may be a punning corruption of 'boondocker'.

boost (1) to steal
Properly, to give a lift to: 'You were in Fulton Superior Court apologizin' for boosting car radios' (Diehl, 1978). A 'booster' is such a thief, perhaps concealing the proceeds in a 'booster bag' or 'booster bloomers'.

boost (2) to make or accept a fraudulent bid at auction
Am. auctioneers' jargon, again from giving something a lift.

boot (1) **(the)** summary dismissal from employment
From the kick to speed the departing servant, which today would land you in court if not in hospital: 'You know they can't sack teachers. You've got to do something really drastic before they give you the boot' (Sharpe, 1976).

boot (2) to inject mingled blood and narcotics into a vein
Presumably because it gives an extra kick. The blood is your own.

bootleg smuggled
Usu. of spirituous intoxicants, from the flat bottles concealed against the leg used when carrying illegal supplies to the Am. Indians. The term came into its own during the era of Prohibition: '. . . had got his hands on some bootleg liquor and was giving a party' (Theroux, 1978). Today it is mainly used of stolen intoxicants.

(booze intoxicants is almost certainly a corruption of a German root meaning 'drink', although Coptic, Gaelic, Latin and Russian scholars offer other explanations. The 19c. Philadelphian distiller, Mr E. G. Booze, has his proponents too, but they must have been unaware of Burns' 1798 lines: 'There let him bowse and deep carouse.')

boracic indigent
From rh. sl. 'boracic lint', skint. Usu. of a temporary embarrassment when the sufferer will describe himself as 'brassic'. BI.

border incident *see* incident

born in a now rare way of indicating that someone is subject to an imperfection associated with the supposed natal place. Thus 'born in a mill' denotes deafness; 'born in a barn', the failure to close a door; etc. However if you were 'born in the vestry', you are a bastard, because your parents were not married in church.

borrow to steal
An army usage if the article has substantial value: 'In the Army it is always considered more excusable to "win" or "borrow" things belonging to men from other companies' (Richards, 1936 – you must not steal from your mates). Also of social or trivial consumption, like a match, 'borrowed' to light a cigarette, but never repaid. In ob. use 'borrowed time' was life after 70, the biblical three-score years and ten.

both hands a prison sentence for ten years
Am. underworld sl., from the number of fingers.

both oars in the water mentally normal
Always in the negative, from the uneven progress of a boat propelled with one lateral oar: 'They're not exactly demented, but neither Isaac Kane nor Sylvia Mac has both oars in the water' (Sanders, 1985). Am.

bother an unwelcome male approach for copulation
Within marriage and from the sense to trouble rather than to fight: '... grandma whispering hoarsely, "Leave me alone, will you?" .... I only knew he was "bothering her"' (Cookson, 1969, of a child sharing her grandparents' bedroom).

bottle (1) **(the)** an addiction to intoxicants
Bottles and intemperance have long gone together, especially if the preference is for wine and spirits: 'The bottle was enjoyed by both as a launching pad for the missile of social grace' (Ustinov, 1971). To 'take to the bottle' is to be an alcoholic: 'Mitzi had taken to the bottle, since reality was too bleak for her' (Ustinov, 1966). The regimen of the baby invites many puns like 'on the bottle', drinking intoxicants to excess. 'Bottled' means drunk: 'We none of us were ever quiet when we was bottled' (Cookson, 1967).

bottle (2) urination
From the shaped glass container used by the recumbent male in hospital or sickbed: 'You don't want the bottle, or anything like that? You're ready to see your visitor?' (Price, 1979, of a male hospital patient).

bottle (3) male prostitution
Rh. sl. for 'bottle and glass', arse, but I have yet to see this Am. use outside a dictionary.

bottom the buttocks
Not the soles of your feet, which might be more logical: 'God gave them bottoms to be smacked on' (Bradbury, 1976). An Am. 'bottom woman' is illogically a pimp's favourite whore. A 'bottomless' woman is naked, usu. working as a waitress at one remove from **topless** (q.v.).

bought and sold bankrupt
From the disposal of the debtor's possessions: 'For Diccon, thy master, is bought and sold' (Shakespeare, *Richard III*). ob.

bought it killed or severely wounded
A wartime usage, perhaps from notionally acquiring the missile which hits you; or it could just be from 'buying' your ticket back to your homeland: 'They bought it – all except me. I'd gone for a walk .... You know, with a spade' (Manning, 1978 – a soldier's mates had been killed while he was defecating). The Am. 'buy the farm', to be killed in wartime, probably refers to a city dweller's dream of retirement: 'Who knows when M. M. will buy the farm?' (Deighton, 1982, of a fighter pilot).

bounce (1) to copulate
From the motion, especially on a sprung mattress: 'We all bounced about in bed together from time to time and enjoyed it' (Fraser, 1970). A 'bounce', or 'bouncy-bouncy', is an act of copulation: 'One bounce with that female Russian shotput and you'd bust your truss' (Sharpe, 1977).

bounce (2) to be dishonoured by non-payment
Of cheques, because they are returned to the person who drew them, like a rubber ball dropped to the ground and caught again.

bounce (3) peremptorily to dismiss from employment
Again from the rebounding after hitting another surface, such as the sidewalk: 'If the case is cleared, or I get bounced, the two of you go back to your regular duties' (Sanders, 1985). The 'bounce' or 'grand bounce' is such dismissal, and also the ending of courtship, especially by the female. A 'bouncer' evicts the unruly or unwanted from a club etc.

bounce (4) to persuade by violence
Criminal and police jargon, of extortion, forcibly extracting a confession, etc.: 'You push the victim on the floor. When he comes out this time we're going to grab him and bounce him a little. Nothing heavy' (Sanders, 1977). The word is also used of rushing another party into an ill-considered contract: 'Soviet support for the heavy Cuban involvement in Angola . . . . was achieved . . . . through "bouncing" the Russians' (*Sunday Telegraph*, November 1983).

bowel movement defecation
Medical jargon and *see* **move your bowels**: 'Most constipation is "imagined". A daily bowel movement can be a needless fetish' (Hailey, 1979).

bowler hat the premature discharge of an officer from the services.
The former standard business headgear replaced the uniform cap: 'Command in the desert was regarded as an almost certain prelude to a bowler hat' (Horrocks, 1960, of Br. armies in N. Africa). The phrase can also be used of routine retirement and a 'golden bowler' is a substantial payment to a young officer compelled to retire because of an overall reduction in the forces.

box (1) a coffin
Today people tend to this use when reference is made to their own death, as 'When I'm in my box . . .' Formerly to 'box' was to place a corpse in a coffin for burial: 'Ol Joe Sharman died. Donald made the coffin and they'd boxed him' (Emerson, 1892). To 'box the Jesuit and get cockroaches' was not to bury a priest, but to masturbate of a male, involving a choice of unsavoury puns.

box (2) a shield for the male genitalia
Mainly sporting use but now extended to riot protection: 'The cricket boxes issued to constables as items in their "new protective equipment range" are made of nasty plastic with very little room for accommodation' (*Police*, July 1981).

box (3) the vagina
Viewed sexually as a container for the penis: 'Her box is so big she wouldn't even feel your hand unless you wore a wristwatch' (Wambaugh, 1975). Am.

boy an adult male
Of any age, including geriatrics: 'Boy. He must be forty-four' (Collins, 1981). Only White people used the word for a Black servant, which is now considered offensive as well as inaccurate.

boy scouts State police
They enjoy less status than some of their colleagues and often wear clothes like a Baden-Powell scoutmaster. CB sl. Am.

boyfriend a male extra-marital sexual partner
In heterosexual use, he can be any age over puberty: '. . . occasional liaisons which she alluded to by saying . . . . "He's an old boyfriend of mine"' (Theroux, 1976). In homosexual use, usu. of an adult: 'It is not known whether he will take his South African boy friend, ballet dancer, (a masculine name), with him' (*Private Eye*, March 1981). 'Girl friend' – usu. two words – is used in the same way, of a sexual mistress or of a woman's regular homosexual partner: 'What was he so worried about? Maybe he'd got himself a girlfriend' (Kyle, 1978). The phrases are equally used of normal courtship.

boys (1) a lavatory for exclusive male use
A variant of **men** (q.v.) but not reserved for juveniles: 'I went into "Boys" and looked around' (Theroux, 1979, of a lavatory). And as with 'men's room', so with 'boys' room': 'You should know we never lock the boys' room' (Sharpe, 1977, of a lavatory).

boys (2) any men engaged in a nefarious enterprise
In this use, they are never juveniles. 'The boys' may mean members of a criminal gang. The Am. 'boys in the backroom' are those who dictate policy to elected politicians, etc. as different from the 'backroom boys', who innovate on behalf of an employer. Also Am., the 'boys upstairs' control vice without making an appearance in person, from the normal location of managerial offices relative to the workplace of other employees: 'Snyder had appealed to Christiansen for a reduction of his weekly quota. Christiansen . . . . said he'd talk to the boys upstairs' (Weverka, 1973). The Am. 'boys uptown' are the corrupt political bosses anywhere,

from the location in New York City of Tammany Hall, which housed the crooked Democrat politicians who ran the city through those whose elections they contrived. In Rhodesian use, the 'boys in the bush' were the Black terrorists supplied from Zambia and Mozambique: 'There are still going to be some boys in the bush dreaming of marching into Salisbury' (*Sunday Telegraph*, December 1970), etc.

brace to kill
Not, I think, from the putting of arms (bras) around, from which the SE meaning to strengthen comes; perhaps from an Am. sl. meaning, to waylay; but most likely from the rigor mortis. All these suggestions are guesses. 'You and your friend go up to brace him' (Sanders, 1973, of a killing). In criminal use, 'bracelets' are handcuffs.

bracer an intoxicant
Properly, something which stiffens, whence a tonic of any kind. It refers only to a spirituous drink.

Brahms drunk
From the rh. sl., 'Brahms and Liszt', pissed. cf. **Mozart**, which is rarer. BI.

branch water water which is offered from a bottle
It is supposed to come from an unpolluted tributary, or branch, of a stream and therefore not to spoil the taste of your whisky with the taint of chlorine. Only bartenders can say how much 'branch water' does not come out of the common faucet. Am.

brand X a competitor's product
Advertising jargon, to avoid being sued for defamation when you have said how inferior it is to your own. As you will have subjected both to selective and unscientific tests and then paid a woman to purport to examine the test results before endorsing your claim, it is sensible to use evasive language. For a manufacturer, 'brand X' may be your competitor's product, possibly better than your own, about which you need to know more before writing the specification for development work.

brass a whore
Rh. sl. for 'brass nail', tail. We now meet it only in the cliché 'as bold as brass'.

(brassière a garment to contain women's breasts, has no other Eng. meaning. It is properly in French a sleeved garment, becoming euphemistic there before its adoption in English covered the taboo breasts

with a double evasion. With 'bust bodice' we tried to coin our own euphemism and as soon as that became explicit, we reduced it to its initials, 'BB'. After the admirers of Brigitte Bardot had appropriated those punning initials for her, their 'bébé', the confusion and association of ideas caused the usage to lapse. We can note with relief that the Am. 'boobytrap' failed to gain popularity.)

break a lance to copulate
Of a male, punning on 'lance', to copulate, and the rigid 'weapon' which returns to a flaccid state – is 'broken' – after that kind of use. The Am. prostitutes' jargon, 'break luck', means merely to secure the first customer of the day.

break the news to obtain a confession or other information by violence
The Am. criminal is forcibly made aware of the extent of his predicament: '"Breaking the news" .... and numerous other phrases are employed by the police .... as euphemisms to express how they compel reluctant prisoners to refresh their memories' (Lavine, 1930).

break the pale to copulate extra-maritally
The 'pale', as in 'paling', was a piece of wood, then a fence, then a fenced-in curtilage and finally a district under the control of a centre with hostile natives prowling round outside. Properly, to 'break the pale' was to get where you shouldn't be: 'He breaks the pale, And feeds from home' (Shakespeare, *Comedy of Errors*). ob.

break wind to belch or fart
see **wind** (1). It is respectable of belching although Shakespeare indicated farting in his complex vulgar pun: 'A man may break a word with you, sir; and words are but wind; Ay, and break it in your face, so he break it not behind' (*Comedy of Errors*). And in modern use: 'I'll kill the first son of a bitch who even breaks wind' (West, 1979). The Am. 'break the sound barrier', to fart or to belch, refers to a sonic boom.

break your elbow etc. to give birth to a bastard
The fracture was sometimes caused by a fig. bed: 'And so she broke her elboe against the bed' (Heath, 1650, of a woman who had a child while unmarried). But if she 'broke her elbow at the church', she was no worse than a poor housekeeper after marriage. To 'break your knee', a direct translation of a French euphemism, was to copulate extra-

maritally for the first time, of a woman. An unmarried pregnant woman might also be said to 'break her leg above the knee', referring to a ruined horse and to the location of her vagina: 'If her foot slip and down fall she, And break her leg above the knee' (Fletcher, 1618). The putative father, if brought to book, was also said to have 'broken his leg'. All these Br. uses are ob.

break your neck to have an urgent desire to urinate
Normally of a male, with no fear of suicidal tendencies. It originally meant that 'breakneck speed' was needed for any activity.

break your shins against Covent Garden rails *see* Covent Garden

breathe your last to die
Perhaps circumlocution and evasion rather than euphemism, as you cannot expect to live more than two or three minutes after the event: '. . . the quicker that one breathed his last, the better, so I hurried up with my lance . . . . and drove it into his throat' (Fraser, 1969).

breezy drunk
An Am. use, from the bonhomie which may be detected in some at a certain stage of drunkenness.

brethren of the coast the pirates on the N. Am. eastern seaboard.
The traffic and terrain were well suited to piracy which flourished to an extent that local communities were dependent on and supported the pirates. Also as the 'brotherhood of the coast': 'You must wait for twenty years, till you are the most famous captain in the brotherhood of the Coast' (Monsarrat, 1978, writing of the 18c.).

brew to be destroyed by internal fire
Of an armoured vehicle, from the habit of Br. soldiers who brewed tea over an open fire often raised by burning petrol allowed to soak into sand: 'You'll have seen a tank being brewed, Johnny' (Seymour, 1980). Br. WW II tanks were usu. inferior to their German opposition and their crews were burnt to death if hit by anti-tank weapons.

brewer's goitre frontal obesity in a male
The thyroid gland is placed elsewhere but the cause is often persistently drinking too much beer: ' – the crenellated face, the brewer's goitre slung under his belt' (Keneally, 1985 – in fact the belt is often ineffectively slung under the protuberance).

brick a kilogram of marijuana
In Am. it may be packed in the form of a block, the size of a normal building brick.

brick short of a load imbecile
Of the same tendency as **fifty cards in the pack** (q.v.). 'Who is Sir James Goldsmith anyway? . . . . Is he a brick short of a load?' (*Private Eye*, March 1983).

Bridport dagger a hangman's rope
The Dorset town was, and still is, famous for its rope, twine and net-making, the industry developing from the facility with which flax was once grown in the vicinity. To be 'stabbed with a Bridport dagger' meant to be killed by hanging. Perhaps still some literary use.

brig a prison
Abbr. of 'brigantine', a ship often used as a naval prison: 'I'm not saying he'll end up in the brig, but he'll lose all rank' (Higgins, 1976). Civilian as well as military use.

Brighton pier a male homosexual
Rh. sl. for 'queer'. An ob. Br. use – there were two piers for trippers to the Sussex town.

bring off (1) to cause to achieve a sexual orgasm
Of either sex, in copulation or masturbation: 'He remained in her for what seemed like hours . . . . bringing her off again and again' (M. Thomas, 1980).

bring off (2) to cause the abortion of a foetus
It is physically removed from the mother: 'I was left in the club . . . . like any tiresome little skivvy, but unlike her we were able to arrange to have it brought off' (P. Scott, 1975).

bring out the highlights to dye blonde
The jargon of barbers and of manufacturers of dyestuffs for women's hair. The pretence is that human hair, which is dead matter, has lively properties which can be brought into play by the application of a lotion.

bring your heart to its final pause to die
Unless you experience an extra-systole, prior pauses are unlikely: '. . . and bring his heart to its final pause' (Eliot, 1871).

(British justice, the handing down of an unexpected or perverse judgment, is technically meaningless as there is no such thing as British Law, only England and Wales sharing legislation: 'You've been through it all and got off. British justice has forgiven you' (Murdoch, 1985). Those, acquitted though guilty or successful through perjury, like to pretend that right was on their side and will be heard on the courtroom steps expressing their faith in this notional commodity.)

broad a whore
The 15c. meaning, vulgar, survives only when we speak of humour or the accents of country folk. As an abbr. of 'broad woman', it alludes to her moral laxity and not to her girth: 'Give me some pictures where the good guys get the dough and the broads once in a while' (Deighton, 1972). In ob. Br. use 'the broads' were not a collection of such females but playing cards, with a suggestion of cheating: 'Will you have a . . . . touch of the broads with me?' (Mayhew, 1851, of an invitation to play cards). 'Broad' coves, fakers, men, pitchers, etc. were common cheats. The 'Norfolk Broads' are no more than shallow inland lakes resulting from the widespread mediaeval digging of peat for fuel.

brodie to kill yourself by jumping from a high building or bridge
In 1886 Steve Brodie claimed to have jumped into the river from Brooklyn Bridge, and to have survived. ?ob.

Bronx cheer a fart
The Bronx is one of the less fashionable quarters of New York City, where such activity, or mention of it, may not be taboo. Mainly Am. use.

broomstick match *see* **jump (3)**

(**brother** was used to denote a calling thought socially undesirable, if not criminal. Thus a 'brother of the bung' was a brewer, a 'brother of the gusset', a pimp, etc. Today, the accident of birth apart, our 'brothers' are fellow socialists or trade unionists, who wish to proclaim thus ostentatiously their faith in the brotherhood of man, so long as he is like-minded. In ob. Br. use a 'brother starling' was a man with whom you shared a sexual mistress, building, as Grose puts it, in the same nest.)

brought to bed *see* **bed (1)**

brown (1) *see* **brown-hatter**

brown (2) dead
Rh. sl. in London for 'brown bread', but you would hear it as 'brahn'.

brown-hatter a male homosexual who indulges in buggery

From the anal content of the patient: 'Harrison's are a lot of wankers and Slymne's go in for brown-hatting' (Sharpe, 1982). Some fig. abusive use, as 'A lot of brown-hatters and word-merchants' (Sharpe, 1974). Sometimes abbr. to 'brownie'. To 'do a brown' is to bugger a male or a female.

brown paper bag an unmarked police car
Nothing on or about it advertises its identity in this CB Am. use. To 'brown bag' is to take your lunch to work with you and eat it at your desk.

brownie (1) *see* **brown-hatter**

brownie (2) a spirituous intoxicant
Whisky or brandy, from the colour: 'I had to toddle off to the sherbert cupboard and administer a stiff brownie and water' (*Private Eye*, July 1981).

brownie (3) an amphetamine tablet
Again from the colour, in illegal use.

brownie points an attempt to curry favour at the expense of a fellow worker
The younger girls in the organization established by Baden-Powell are called 'Brownies', from the colour of their uniform and the benevolence of the creatures which are supposed to perform good deeds around the house by night. You obtain promotion in your pack, to the exalted position of 'sixer' or beyond, by winning points for good works or achievement. The phrase is much used in industry of snide behaviour by ambitious managers.

browse to steal and consume food within a store
From the selective feeding of animals. In this refinement of supermarket theft, you carry the stolen goods past the check-out in your alimentary canal.

brushfire war a war in which a major power is not directly involved
It involved fig. the undergrowth and not the timber: 'The language of the mad foments (violence) . . . . "Brushfire wars", "limited actions", "clean atom bombs"' (West, 1979).

bucket (1) defecation
A male usage, especially where a smaller tin for urination is inside communal living quarters and defecation on a larger receptable takes place outside. Also some fig. use: 'Get off the bucket, I'm serious' (Theroux, 1978).

bucket (2) a prison
Br. rh. sl. for 'bucket and pail', a jail. In ob.
Eng. use, the 'bucket' was also peremptory
dismissal from employment, probably from
the phrase 'kick the bucket', to die. A
'bucket shop' does not offer pails for sale but
is an office which tries to persuade the public to buy securities of little or no value.

bucket (3) to kill kittens by drowning
A favoured way of disposing of an excess:
'Hadn't someone better bucket them at
once?' (N. Mitford, 1960, of newly-born
kittens).

buckle to to copulate with
Properly, to tackle a task vigorously:
'. . . threatening to feed me to the sharks
unless she buckled to with him' (Fraser,
1977). However, the perhaps ob. Eng.
'Bucklebury' is buggery, of which DSUE says
'Ex the Berkshire locality'; for the good
name of the residents I suggest that it is from
the phonetic similarity.

budget cheap
Advertising jargon. The inference is that the
cost will not exceed the amount which you
have allowed for the purpose.

(buff the bare skin is an abbr. of (flenched)
buffalo, and has been used in this sense
since the late 18c. In the 19c. it came also to
mean to embrace sexually, from the concepts
of nakedness and rubbing: 'I wor fit for
booath cooartin' and buffin'' (Mather,
1862). 'In the buff' still means naked.)

bug (1) to conceal an apparatus for eaves-
dropping
From its size, colour and shape: 'He was
ready to give me permission to bug his
church pew' (Diehl, 1978). A 'bug fix' is
introduced to foil or detect such activity by
your opponent: 'It took us months to crack
the "bug fixes" and find our way inside'
(Deighton, 1981).

bug (2) a mark indicating the use of union
labour in manufacture
Mainly in the Am. printing trade, perhaps
punning on **bug** (1) (above). The mark is not
authorized but condoned by the employer.

bug-house mad
In Am. use it suggests that you have insects
in your head. It is also an institution for the
insane.

bug out a retreat
This Korean war usage came from the Am.
sl. meaning, to quit rapidly.

(bugger a person who participates in anal
penetration by the penis, is a corruption of
Bulgar, via the French. The association
arose from the activities of Bulgarian clerics
exiled to France rather than from the sexual
preference of the majority of males in their
Balkan homeland.)

built-in emphasis padding
Advertising jargon, especially of garments
for females who know they have small
breasts, want to appear to have bigger ones
but do not wish to admit to undue artifice:
'. . . her bra comes with "built-in emphasis"'
(Jennings, 1965).

bull (1) to copulate with
Of a male, from the function for which
uncastrated animals are mainly preserved:
'He would guarantee all his female slaves
had been bulled by his crew' (Fraser, 1971 –
a Black slave pregnant by a White man is
said to have commanded a premium). Rarely
also as 'bullock': '. . . giggling about how
he'd bullocked the headman's wife on his
last leave' (Fraser, 1975). A 'bull' is also a
male who regularly seeks to copulate extra-
maritally: 'He is the village bull. The women
dare not refuse him' (Manning, 1960, of a
priest).

bull (2) egocentric boasting
Abbr. of 'bullshit': 'You're full of bull this
morning' (Steinbeck, 1961) – but not an
abbr. of 'bullshitter', a person who boasts or
acts officiously. In army use 'bull' is no more
than compliance with military standards of
drill or tidiness. The initials 'BS' apply both
to 'bullshit' and 'bullshitter' in all senses:
'He was a great romancer and wrote the
biggest B.S. of them all' (Richards, 1933).
The uses may come from the 19c. term
'bull-scutter' defined by Dr Wright properly
as 'the liquid excrementum of a bull after
gorging new grass' and fig. as 'anything
worthless or nasty' (EDD).

bull (3) a policeman
Perhaps from his size and aggressive mien,
as it is an Am. use. Originally only a detective: 'Only on rare occasions will the cop . . . .
offer any information to the "bull" or
"dick"' (Lavine, 1930). Now applied to any
uniformed protector of property. A 'bullpen'
is either a prison: '. . . ordered them thrown
into the bull pen' (ibid., of men arrested) –
or any common dormitory for males.

bull (4) a female homosexual taking the
male role

I think just an abbr. of 'bull-dyke', meaning the same thing: 'So you gave that old bull a key' (Theroux, 1976, of an elderly female homosexual) and 'I know the model. Bull dyke' (Sanders, 1977).

bullet (the) peremptory dismissal from employment
The imagery comes from **fire** (q.v.) and at second remove from the SE 'discharge'. A 'bullet' also means death by shooting, especially in espionage fiction: '. . . never knowing whether they're getting a medal or a bullet' (le Carré, 1980). Fatalistic soldiers say that the bullet which hits them has their name on it: '. . . he could no more remove the name from his heart than avoid the bullet which had his name on it' (Price, 1978).

bum a whore
Properly in Am. sl. an idle person who hangs round saloons, etc. 'Bum', the buttocks, was once a genteel usage although 'bum-shop', a brothel and 'bum-fighting', copulation were not. 'Bum' is also the male counterpart of **bunny** (1) (q.v.) in various sports. For a dissertation on 'bum fodder', see **ammunition** (1).

bump (1) (the) peremptory dismissal from employment
From the sudden displacement. Less often as 'bump off': 'They got bumped off the staff of the hospital' (Chandler, 1938). In Am. use 'the bump' can either be contriving the dismissal of a senior in a hierarchical system, to obtain that post for yourself, or posting an unwanted senior employee in a union shop from one task to another, each less attractive than the last, until he ends up cleaning the lavatories and hands in his own notice. This process circumvents strict 'first in, first out' labour contracts.

bump (2) (the) pregnancy
Properly, any swelling in the body, usu. caused by a blow. This rather tasteless use is uncommon. A 'bumper' is not the putative father but a stripper in an erotic stage show.

bump (3) to copulate
Probably from the renewed pushing of the bodies against each other: 'One could imagine brother and sister bumping like frogs in broad daylight' (Theroux, 1978, of incest). Rarely as 'bump bones'.

bump (4) a killing
From striking heavily: 'Normal routine in the case of a bump is to stay clear' (Hall, 1969, of a murder). 'Bump off', to kill by violence, is commoner: '"He had to take

risks". "Like bumping chaps off?"' (le Carré, 1980). Sometimes abbr. in Am. to 'bump': 'I don't go round bumping everyone I meet, you know' (Keneally, 1985 – in an Australian novel). An Am. 'bump man' is a professional killer.

bump (5) to cause a pre-booked passenger to travel by a later aircraft
Airline jargon for the practice of ensuring that staff and those in a position to cause trouble about overbooking are not among those left behind: '17 passengers were "bumped" in all: although after the desk closed he heard the girl being told to allow for six to eight extra Sudan Airways personnel on the flight' (*Private Eye*, December 1981).

bump off see **bump** (1) (4)

bun a whore
This leads us to the mariner's fetish about rabbits, which must not be mentioned before a voyage if you wish to avoid ill luck. The taboo dates back to the days when fraudulent chandlers supplied cheap rabbit meat, which doesn't keep when salted, for pork, which does. The scrupulous had, before a trip, to touch the tail of a hare or, if none were to hand, the pubic hair of a woman, including one who might for a fee allow hers to be touched. Thus the 'bun' was an abbr. of 'bunny', itself the diminutive for the rabbit, the hair and the whore. In ob. Br. use a 'buttered bun' was a whore who copulated successively with different men on the same occasion – perhaps punning lewdly on the seminal deposits of previous partners. Grose however says of such a whore: 'She is said to have a buttered bun'.

bun in the oven (a) pregnancy
WW II service use, punning on the rising of cake mixture and the hidden growth of the foetus: 'I rather fancied she had a bun in the oven' (Theroux, 1971, of a pregnant woman).

bun on (a) drunkenness
Perhaps an abbr. for bundle, a quantity of anything. Am.

bun-puncher a person who never drinks intoxicants
Br. army usage, where abstention from intoxicants can be as taboo as drunkenness in civilian life: 'If a teetotaller he was known as a "char-wallah", "bun-puncher" or "wad-shifter"' (Richards, 1933 – he was a tea and cake man).

bunch of fives a punch with a clenched fist
Hardly euphemistic when it refers to the fist alone, but the implication is always that it is to be used aggressively, 'given' or 'handed out' to the victim.

bundle to copulate extra-maritally with the consent of your family
Properly, a package of things brought together. The 'New England custom of "bundling", namely the supposedly chaste lying in bed together of young, affectionate, unmarried persons of opposite sexes for the sake of company and the saving of fuel' (Graves, 1941, writing of the 18c. – the partners nearly always married each other). Similar customs obtained in S. Scotland and elsewhere. The Eng. dialect 'bundle with' can still mean to marry: 'My God! do you expect to bundle with that 'un?' (Cookson, 1967, of a male suitor).

bung (1) a drunkard
Properly, a stopper for a cask: 'Away . . . . you filthy bung' (Shakespeare, *2 Henry IV*). 'Bung' also meant drunk, as you were if someone said you had been to 'Bungay fair', punning on the Suffolk market town. All uses are ob.

bung (2) contraception by the use of a pessary
From the method of vaginal introduction and the function it is expected to perform: 'I used to be Bung but now I'm Pill' (Bradbury, 1975).

bung up and bilge free copulating
The phrase properly describes how a rum cask should be stored aboard ship, whence to the meaning, in good order. The Br. naval use puns on that and on the mechanics of copulation, but without any inference that the woman has opted for any special method of contraception.

bunk flying boasting
Am. air force usage. The exploits which redound to your credit are dreamed or otherwise invented in bed.

bunny(1) a homosexual who takes the female role
It can be a male or female but, if a male, usu. a prostitute. The use may come from **bun** (above) but I doubt it because 'bunny' is a pet name given to someone with timid and feminine characteristics. Beach, jazz, ski, surf etc. 'bunnies' are heterosexual girls who consort with males adept at those pastimes – 'bums' – with whom they copulate promiscuously.

bunny (2) a towel worn during menstruation
From its shape and feel? I have seen no literary use.

buoys a lavatory for exclusive male use
Punning on 'boys', and favoured by Am. restaurants near the sea where females are confronted, perhaps perplexed, by 'gulls' for girls.

burial of an ass no burial at all
The hole had to be too big in rocky terrain: 'He shall be buried with the burial of an ass, drawn, and cast forth beyond the gates of Jerusalem' (Jeremiah). ob.

buried in prison
From your withdrawal from Am. society,

(Burke to murder, comes from the celebrated Irishman who killed people to replenish his stock of corpses which he sold for dissection. He was killed by hanging in Edinburgh in 1829. Do not confuse with 'berk', a stupid person, which comes from the rh. sl. 'Berkshire Hunt' – or 'Berkeley' – a cunt, viewed fig. rather than anatomically.)

burn (1) to infect with venereal disease
From one of the symptoms felt by the male: 'Light wenches will burn. Come not near her' (Shakespeare, *Comedy of Error*). Whence 'burned', so infected: 'No heretics burned, but wenches' suitors' (Shakespeare, *King Lear*). A man who 'burned his poker' was so infected and a 'burner' was the infection. All ob.

burn (2) to kill
Originally by electrocution, from the singeing of contact points on the corpse. Latterly in Am. of any violent death, especially by shooting: 'Do you really think Knorr burned Kipper and Stonehouse' (Sanders, 1980, of two killings).

burn (3) to extort from criminally or to cheat
Probably derived from the phrase 'put the burn on', to compel through fig. application of heat or literally by contra-rotating the skin at the wrist: 'I thought he was the one who burned me' (Theroux, 1976, of a cheat). There are two Am. narcotic uses – to take money for illicit supplies and fail to deliver; and to give information to the authorities about another's addiction.

burn out to withdraw from narcotic addition
Especially of an older addict, with obvious imagery. Mainly Am.

burn with a low (blue) flame to be very drunk
The imagery is from a dying fire, about to go out. Am.

burner an aircraft which uses excessive fuel
Airline jargon applied to old civil jets whose engines are inefficient; nothing you say must imply that the airframe too is old: 'The "burners" go on the shorter hauls where fuel consumption is less critical' (Moynahan, 1983). A fuel-efficient, new aeroplane is a 'spanker', spanking new.

burra peg *see* **chota peg**

burst to have an acute need to urinate
What you fear will happen to an over-extended bladder and usu. in the cliché, 'I'm bursting', with 'for a pee' left unsaid. Mainly male use; females tend to 'bust'.

bury a quaker to defecate
In Irish use a 'quaker' was a turd. Apart from a lack of sympathy for their beliefs among those strongly committed to Rome, the etymology escapes me. A 'quaker's burial ground' was a lavatory.

busby a woman's pubic hair
Properly, the tall fur hat of a soldier: '. . . she had him growling in her busby' (Sanders, 1982, of cunnilingus).

bush (1) the pubic hair
Of male and female. Partridge says 'Low (mid-c. 19 – 20) after being a literary euphemism' (DSUE). Still widely used: 'The small, trimmed bush, soft as down' (Sanders, 1982, of a naked female). The Am. 'bush patrol' means extra-marital copulation, punning on the pubic hair, the seclusion sought and the military exercise so named. In parts of the world where jungles persist, a 'bush marriage' is performed without due ceremony: '. . . most of them were bush marriages performed by some joker wearing a coconut mask and a feathered jock-strap' (Sanders, 1977). In the same areas, a bastard may be said to have been 'made in the bush': 'Yeboa had been "made in the bush", and was lighter in colour than Anokye' (ibid.).

bush (2) marijuana
Another form of the sl. 'grass'. The ob. Br. 'bush house' was a private house which sold beer or cider on fair days, hanging out a bush to denote it was open: 'Starting from the "Bush-house" where he had been supping too freely on the fair-ale' (EDD, 1886).

bushwack to ambush
Properly, to hack a path through woods or to propel a craft upstream by pulling on over-hanging foliage: '. . . had bush-wacked a Russian baggage train and were busy looting it' (Fraser, 1973).

business any taboo or criminal act
Of defecation and, less often, urination – in humans: 'Frensic finished his business in the lavatory' (Sharpe, 1977), or in animals: 'Clem, a pedigree Labrador, evidently feeling at home, did his business' (Sharpe, 1976).Of copulation, usu. extra-marital and often prefixed with 'amorous', 'night's' etc.: '. . . gave her the business for all I was worth on top of her dressing-stool' (Fraser, 1982). Of illicit narcotic aids like eye-droppers, bent spoons, syringes, etc., perhaps alluding also to the theatrical jargon meaning. Of prostitution, where to be 'in the business' is to be a whore: 'Mine was a large lady, already in the business for some time' (Londres, 1928, in tr.) and a 'business woman' is the whores' jargon for a whore. Of killing: '. . . you'd tried to give the Führer the business' (Price, 1978, of someone who had tried to kill Hitler), etc.

business-like and friendly totally unproductive
The phrase is used to describe a meeting of parties with inflexible and opposing views which neither modified during the discussions.

bussing the obligatory transfer of children to distant schools to try to achieve balance between Blacks and Whites in classes
The Am. intention is to provide equal advantages and disadvantages in education regardless of skin pigmentation and the waste of the children's time on additional daily journeys.

bust (1) any conduct the subject of a social taboo
Of financial ruin, a drunkard, a drunken carouse, the violent entry of police into a gathering, a violent robbery, etc.: 'Professor Philip Swallow . . . . was among sixteen people arrested on Saturday . . . . "I've never been busted before," he said' (Lodge, 1975). In Am. the word is particularly used of police action against illegal narcotic use, but the addict 'bust a cap' is to ingest an illicit narcotic, from the breaking of the seal on the phial.

bust (2) *see* **burst**

bust bodice *see* **brassière**

bust your nuts to achieve a sexual orgasm
The Am. phrase is used of both sexes, despite the masculinity and function of the 'nuts', the testicles. In fig. use, merely to try hard.

busy a policeman
Probably an abbr. of 'busybody': '... don't hang around. The bloody street's alive with busies' (Kersh, 1936). Eng. ?ob.

butch a female homosexual playing the male role
Probably from 'Butch', a 'Benjamin', the youngest male child of a family who tends to be spoilt, whence any rough or uncouth male. Also used adjectively. Rarer use of a male homosexual acting in a masculine way: 'He marked them down as very butch guys' (B. Forbes, 1986, of two homosexuals). In Manx dialect a 'butch' was a witch, but without any suggestion of homosexuality.

buttered bun *see* **bun**

butterfly a male homosexual
From the light and pretty appearance of the diurnal insect: '... if it ever comes out that Dunce's top aide is a butterfly, it's not going to do his candidacy any good' (Sanders, 1984).

buttock a whore
I suppose from a part of the body brought into play. A 'buttock ball' was copulation, according to Capt. Grose. A 'buttock and twang' was just a whore but a 'buttock and file' was a whore who would rob you. To 'buttock' was to copulate extra-maritally, whence 'buttock-mail', a fine if you were found out: 'Yer buttock-mail, and yer stool of repentance' (W. Scott, 1814). I think all these Br. uses are ob.

button (1) the vagina viewed sexually
Perhaps from the appearance. It is to be found in both ob. Br. and modern Am. sl. The punning 'button-hole' was to copulate and a 'button-hole factory' was a brothel.

button (2) a professional killer
Presumably you press him for action when you need it: 'Know what a button is, DeLoroza? A shooter' (Diehl, 1978). Also as a 'button man': 'His head was alive and jumping with notions of button men' (M. Thomas, 1980). Am.

button (3) a policeman
From those on his uniform: 'The buttons won't have any time to worry about what's going down on East 55th Street' (Sanders, 1980). Am. sl.

buxom fat
Of women. There was formerly an inference of comeliness, like Dr Spooner's barmaid: 'In the daytime she is fair and buxom' (Old Saw).

buy it etc. *see* **bought it**

buy jawbone *see* **jawbone**

buy love to copulate with a whore
Normally of a man but perhaps some homosexual use: '"I don't buy love," I warned her, "but how much do you generally get?" "From one dollar to five"' (Harris, 1925). Like other song writers, the Beatles were not averse to punning lyrics.

buyer a person addicted to illegal narcotics
Addict jargon – he probably also buys food and clothing from time to time: 'The label is drugs .... Converse was a heavy buyer' (Ludlum, 1984).

buzz on (a) mild drunkenness or narcotic influence
From the ringing in the ears? '... we'd drink, get a little buzz on, and then go into the ocean to swim and sober up' (Theroux, 1973). The WW II 'buzzed', meaning killed, may have come from the noise of the bullet which hit you.

by(e) an indication of bastardy
Properly, ancillary to. 'By(e)' -blow, -chap, -scape, etc. meant a bastard and 'by(e)' -come, -begit, etc., bastardy. Still used despite the fact that bastardy is almost respectable: 'I really was a niece of a one-time Governor and not some by-blow of Lili Chatterjee's family' (P. Scott, 1973). In ob. Br. use 'by-courting' was done on the sly without intention of marriage: 'Bitterly did I regret I had done my by courtings so near home' (Crockett, 1896). A 'by-shot' was an elderly unmarried woman, though not because Cupid's aim was poor: 'If she cannot restrain her loquacity, she is in danger of bearing the reproach of a by-shot' (Tarras, 1804 – reminding us of the old Sc. taboo in respect of unmarried females).

by yourself mad
The etymology is unclear. We would not use the old form: 'But monie a day was by himself, He was so sairly frighted' (Burns, 1785), although we retain the cliché 'by himself with rage'.

C

C anything taboo beginning with the letter C
If disease, it is the dread cancer, which is the 'big C'; if narcotics, heroin as the successor to cocaine.

cabbage (1) to steal
'Cabbages' were odd snippets of cloth which were traditionally the perquisite of tailors in employment, who often made sure good material fell into the same category: 'If I cabbage that ring tonight, I shall be all the richer tomorrow' (N & Q, 1882, quoted in EDD). Still in common Br. use.

cabbage (2) the vagina
Modern male Am. use, but ob. in BI, from a supposed visual resemblence.

cactus juice an intoxicant
Because it is supposed to be able to save the life of a traveller dying of thirst in a waterless desert.

(cadge to beg in modern SE, formerly meant to pilfer: 'A thieving set of magpies – cadgin' 'ere and cadgin' there' (Ward, 1895). Dr Johnson gives 'cadger A huckster; one who brings butter, eggs and poultry, from the country to market' from which an itinerant vendor who had a reputation for thieving as he went.)

cage a prison
Dysphemism perhaps. The derivation is obvious but there was a 19c. reference to the yellow clothes worn by dangerous convicts, coloured like the popular cage-bird, the canary.

Cairo crud *see* **crud**

California blankets newspapers used by the destitute as bedding
Am. Depression use but destitute people still pad their clothes with sheets of newsprint as insulation against the cold. A 'California widow' was an Am. woman anywhere who had been deserted by her husband on the pretext that he was off to find gold. 'California sunshine' is LSD.

call (the) death
Your God needs you elsewhere: 'Hersel' was the first gat the ca'' (Grant, 1884, of a dead woman). We no longer 'call souls' from a flat tombstone on Sunday mornings, when deaths might be announced along with any other gossip: 'Last Sunday fwornuin, after service . . . . the clark caw'd his seale' (Ander-

son, 1805). The rare 'call it a day' is to die from the meaning, to finish work. 'Called', dead, is usu. amplified by the addition of a destination such as 'home' or 'away': 'He had been ca'ed awa atween the contract an' the marriage' (Wilson, 1836, of the death of an engaged man). God is also referred to as a lender requiring satisfaction: 'So he was only sixty-six when God called in the loan' (Lyall, 1985). 'Called to higher service' is perhaps my favourite euphemism, embodying in one phrase an avoidance of direct reference to death, an implication that the dead person was specifically wanted by a deity, the recognition of meritorious work of a religious nature on earth, and the acknowledgement that heaven is the destination.

call-button girl a whore
She usu. operates in airport hotels where there is a constant harvest of transient males: 'Prostitutes, "call-button girls" as they call themselves, roam from airport to airport, operating from the airport hotels' (Moynahan, 1983). cf. **call girl**.

call down to announce publicly that you will not pay your wife's debts
I give this ob. Br. usage to remind us that it was not very long ago that a married woman had no property rights and could only pledge her husband's credit for food and clothing, called by the jargon word 'necessities'. The 'calling down' was done by the Town Crier and exonerated the husband from meeting any debts contracted by his wife in his name from then on. Failing a Town Crier, notice might be inserted in the local newspaper.

call girl a whore
She used to operate from or in a 'call house', a particularly depraved class of brothel, before the advent of the telephone by which she may now be summoned: 'A low-church missionary who was discovered as being the business manager of a ring of syphilitic call-girls' (Ustinov, 1971). Today 'call girls' tend to be elegant, expensive and free from disease so that their services can safely be bought to bribe businessmen and politicians. The rare 'call boy', apart from summoning performers to the stage on cue, is a male prostitute: 'He made an additional two hundred as a call boy for discriminating gay customers' (Wambaugh, 1981).

call it eight bells let us drink intoxicants
Noon, or eight bells of the watch, is the earliest time in Br. naval etiquette when intoxicants can be drunk publicly.

call of nature urination or defecation
The visit is demanded by your bodily mechanism: 'I was probably off the road, behind the bush, answering a call of nature' (Follett, 1978). The imagery appears in several phrases: '"When nature calls, heh, heh, heh," he'd said . . . . and made his way out into the trees' (M. Thomas, 1980).

call off the bets to die
If a horse is withdrawn from a race under certain conditions in Am., the wagers are invalid.

call the tricks *see* **trick**

called etc. *see* **call (the)**

caller (a) menstruation
A female usage which is as common as **visitor** (q.v.) and shares the imagery of a temporary affliction or imposition.

callisthenics in bed copulation
'Callisthenics' is training in graceful movement for girls: '. . . other than callisthenics in bed, and from what rumours I hear, you're getting plenty of that' (Hailey, 1979, of a libertine).

calorie counter a fat person
Advertising jargon, subtly suggesting that blame for obesity does not attach to the sufferer: '. . . don't risk offending them by calling them fat. Their ads are addressed to "weight watchers" and "calorie counters"' (Jennings, 1965).

camera a police radar set
I suppose from the resemblance and from its ability to hold a record of the speed indicated for inspection by the motorist. In Am. CB sl. a 'folding camera' is a speed monitoring device carried in a police patrol car.

camisole a straitjacket
Properly, a woman's bodice, which can look something like a straitjacket. Am. medical jargon.

camp (1) homosexual
The word is used of either sex. I find none of the suggested etymologies satisfactory, and the use may not be euphemistic. DSUE quotes Ware as saying 'probably from the French', but hardly from 'bien campé . . . . well set-up (fellow)' (Harrap). Partridge himself prefers a derivation from a 19c. dialect meaning, uncouth, adding 'see esp. the EDD'. Unlike most of his readers, I have a copy to hand and Dr Wright gives us plenty to choose from: 'an ancient form of the game

of football', 'gyrating in the air', 'gossiping' and even 'a heap of potatoes or turnips earthed up in order to be kept thoughout the winter' – but we will never know which Partridge found illuminating. WNCD wisely says 'origin unknown' and both ODEE and OED (1979 edition) ignore the use. The meaning seems probably to have developed after WW II from theatrical sl. meaning effeminacy: 'The Red Shadow is at large. Did you ever see anything quite as camp?' (P. Scott, 1975 – the dialogue about a male homosexual set in 1946 is anachronistic). To 'camp it up' is to display or accentuate male homosexual symptoms and, in Am., to take part in a male homosexual orgy. However, 'to camp about' may mean no more than to act jokingly: '. . . just words, they weren't meant seriously, I was just camping about' (Bogarde, 1981).

camp (2) *see* **concentration camp**

camp down with to cohabit and copulate with extra-maritally
Permanence is implied in the arrangement but not homosexuality: 'Race left Linda with a weeks-old baby and camped down with his House of Commons harpie/secretary' (*Private Eye*, July 1981).

camp follower a whore
From the days when armies had a trail of tradesmen and providers of services moving about with them: '. . . to prevent their men from contracting certain indelicate social infections from – hem hem – female camp-followers of a certain sort' (Fraser, 1975, writing in 19c. style). ob. in military use.

(campaign a pressure group, has less sinister overtones than **front (1)** (q.v.) despite sharing its military imagery. One 'campaign' – for Real Ale – may bring together like-minded and discriminating people while another – for Nuclear Disarmament – disparate adherents ranging from the saintly to the subversive. A sanguine historian may reflect that if a Papal Bull could not outlaw the cross-bow, humanity is unlikely to abandon an even more unthinkable weapon, however desirable that might be.)

can (1) a lavatory
Originally of the bucket which was emptied from time to time but now used of all degrees of plumbing sophistication: 'Snyder had paced the small office and gone to the can a couple of times' (Weverka, 1973). Mainly Am.

can (2) to dismiss from employment
The dismissed person is fig. put in the

ash-can, or even in the can (1) (above): 'He worked for maybe a month and then he was canned' (Sanders, 1980). There is also an Am. college jargon meaning, dismissal of a student for misconduct or academic failure.

can (3) a prison
From the meaning, a container. Usu. of a short-stay location in a confined cell: 'You wanna sit in the can for twenty years?' (Weverka, 1973, seeking to emphasize the boredom of close confinement). Am.

can (4) *see* canhouse

can on (a) drunkenness
Probably from the Am. use of 'can' as a drinking vessel (WNCD) and the phrase antedates the fashion of selling beer in cans. 'Canned' means drunk with 'half-canned' no less so. A 'can' may also be an ounce of marijuana and 'can on' and 'canned' probably are already used in speech for narcotic stupefaction.

canary an informer to the police
He 'sings' out information about criminals, as in the cliché 'singing like a canary', of a suspect who tells all. A 'canary' or 'canary-bird' was a dangerous convict, because of the yellow clothing he had to wear. In ob. Br. use, a female 'canary' was either a sexual mistress – 'kept' in her fig. 'cage' – or a burglar's assistant: 'Sometimes a woman, called a "canary", carries the tool, and watches outside' (Mayhew, 1862).

candy illegal narcotics
Specifically at one time cocaine, and then marijuana or LSD on a sugar cube, but now any narcotic. 'Nose-candy' is sniffed: 'C'mon t'daddy little girl. C'mon an' get your nose candy' (Collins, 1981). The punning 'candy man' is a dealer in illegal narcotics. Mainly Am.

canhouse a brothel
'Can' is rare sl. for the buttocks, whence in ob. use, a whore: 'The little girls, looking so sweet and demure, knew all the words for canhouses . . . . and seemed ready to illustrate them with anyone' (Longstreet, 1956). Am.

canned *see* can on (a)

canned goods a person who has not copulated
Usually of adult females, untainted – free from disease; and unopened – with maidenhead intact. Rarely of a male. Am.

cannibal a person who practises fellatio or cunnilingus

Usu. of a whore, 'eating' the penis of her Am. customer.

cannon a pickpocket
The imagery is from the pool table – you bump into your victim, make him stumble and rob him in the confusion which follows. In underworld sl. a handgun may also be called a 'cannon'.

canoe to copulate extra-maritally
If a young man took a woman for a trip in such a craft, there was no room for a chaperone which gave them unwonted seclusion when they went ashore: 'Her Old Man . . . . had been hearing about me and Daisy canoeing from the first night we'd got together' (L. Armstrong, 1955, meaning copulation and not aquatic sports). The modern 'canoodle', to fondle sexually, is perhaps a compound of 'canoe' and 'cuddle', although you can't do the latter in the former unless you want to swim: 'Helen had fallen from a balcony while canoodling with a Dutch sea captain' (*Private Eye*, May 1981).

canteen medal an exposed trouser fly-button
A 'canteen', properly a wine cellar, is a place of refreshment for soldiers. This Br. use scorns medals awarded other than for acts of bravery. (Along with most WW II soldiers I shared this prejudice and scorned to collect my 'campaign' medals.)

cap (1) a mechanical contraceptive device worn by the female
An abbr. of 'Dutch cap' which appears under **Dutch** (below). A woman who says she is 'cap' indicates that she habitually copulates, uses contraception and indicates the method chosen.

cap (2) to buy, open or use illicit narcotics
This Am. addict use comes from the seal on the phial which is broken prior to use, or from an abbr. of 'capsule'.

capital involving killing
Properly, to do with the head, but the form of death now has nothing to do with beheading. A 'capital crime' is murder, involving a suspect in a 'capital charge' before the courts and, in some places, 'capital punishment', death.

capital act (the) copulation
The head would seem to play a minor role in the proceedings, nor is the activity confined to a principal city: '. . . crashed through the top of the bed into the fireplace, and com-

pleted the capital act among the warm embers' (Fraser, 1985).

capon a male homosexual
Properly, a castrated cock. In ob. SE it meant a eunuch but the current Am. use may merely infer that his sexual activity does not lead to procreation.

captain is at home (the) I am menstruating
From the Br. officer's red coat. Now perhaps ob.

cardiac incident a malfunction of the heart
'Cardiac' means pertaining to the heart and an 'incident' is a happening. Medical jargon, but every heartbeat might properly be so described. 'Cardiac arrest' is a jargon way of saying a heart stops beating.

cardigan a contraceptive sheath
This Am. use is at two removes from the Crimea where the pugnacious earl gave his title to an article of clothing.

cardinal is at home (the) I am menstruating
From the red biretta. Now perhaps ob.

cards (your) dismissal from employment
Br. revenue stamps were affixed weekly to cards, originally to provide various insurance and pension rights but latterly as a tax on employment paid by employer and employee. Without your 'cards' properly stamped you might not draw state aid when unemployed or for long retain any new employment: 'Get your cards! You take a week's pay and you get out of my place' (Deighton, 1972). The dismissal is not necessarily peremptory and an employee, wishing to leave employment, might 'ask for his cards'.

care the removal of children from parental control
Often they are confined in an institution. Criminal and educational Br. jargon where the children are unruly or criminal, or have parents unfit to look after them. A child subject to such removal is said to be 'in care', which is not to say that children living normally at home with their families are uncared for. cf. **caring**.

career interest inventory possible jobs
Am. educational circumlocution which may be euphemistic for some teachers who have not worked other than in a school and prefer to refer allusively to the world outside the educational system.

careful (1) stingy
From the old concept that thrift is praiseworthy – though not included in the Seven Virtues – while meanness is odious. SE.

careful (2) using a contraceptive during copulation
Originally applied to the prevention of impregnation but today as relevant in the context of disease: 'If you can't be good, be careful. If you can't be careful, remember the date' (Old Saw).

caress yourself to masturbate
Of a female, from the proper meaning, to touch gently: 'She admitted having caressed herself ever since she was ten' (Harris, 1925).

cargo any valuables fortuitously received
A generic term, especially in the S. Pacific, for manufactured articles, food, etc. which strangers may abandon for the natives. A 'cargo cult' is the religion in such places of looking skywards for 20c. manna.

caring the ostentatious display of social conscience
I first defined this entry as 'interfering', but interference is merely a symptom of the condition: 'They will probably become nuns or prison wardresses or join the "caring" professions' (A. Waugh, *Private Eye,* July 1980). In the same sense 'uncaring' means cruel, selfish or insensitive, often in a double negative: 'Ulyatt, who was not a cruel man, or an uncaring one, simply shut his eyes' (Kyle, 1978). Much pejorative use, especially among those sharply aware of hypocrisy or self-advertisement in others.

carnal pertaining to copulation
It should mean no more than to do with flesh. Legal jargon and SE in various phrases. A 'carnal act' is copulation: '. . . the only time I've completed the carnal act with my nose full of water was in Ranava Ilona's bath' (Fraser, 1977). 'Carnal knowledge' is always extra-marital and usu. with a taint of illegality: '"Know you this woman?" "Carnally, she says"' (Shakespeare, *Othello*). 'Carnal necessities' is rare, alluding to the supposed ill-health of men denied copulation: 'I have been afflicted for ninety years by the carnal necessities of women' (Sharpe, 1978 – the venerable speaker was a libertine). 'Carnal relations' is copulation, of either sex: 'Maitland had had carnal relations with several other women during this period' (Condon, 1966). A 'carnal stump' is

an erect penis: 'To see some brawny, juicy rump Well tickled with my carnal stump' (Rabelais, in tr.), etc.

carpet (1) to reprimand
Unlike the workshop or servants' quarters, the master's room had a carpet on which the defaulter had to stand. Whence 'on the carpet', liable for punishment but beware the French 'sur le tapis', which merely means up for consideration.

carpet (2) a wig
Worn by an Am. male and a variant of **rug** (q.v.): '. . . snowy-white hair. If it wasn't a carpet, it had enjoyed the attention of an artful coiffeur' (Sanders, 1979).

carpet-bagger a plunderer
Originally an absconding Am. banker, who so carried the reserves with him, but in wide use of the Northerners who sought pickings in the defeated South after the Civil War. Modern use is of touts for merchant bankers etc. in rich but primitive societies, whose activities may reflect the cultured fee-grubbing of some of their principals in London, New York etc. SE.

carry (1) to be pregnant
Of the same tendency as **bear** (1) (q.v.) and long SE. A pregnant woman may be said to be 'carrying', without specification of the burden: 'She was in the seventh month of pregnancy and carrying big' (Collins, 1981). To 'carry a child' is specific: 'Mrs Thrale is big, and fancies that she carries a boy' (Dr Johnson).

carry (2) to have an illegal narcotic on you
An abbr. of 'carry drugs'. Because of the risk of detection in a body search, an addict rule says 'Never carry when you can stash'.

carry (3) to be in possession of a handgun
An abbr. of 'carry a gun' but, unlike 'carrying' narcotics, this covers both legal and nefarious possession: '"Ahh, I'm carrying", Boone said. "Someone will spot the heat"' (Sanders, 1977, of a policeman). Am.

carry (4) to drink intoxicants without overt drunkenness
With or without intermittent urination: '. . . as gentlemen should, carried their two bottles of an evening' (Strachey, 1918).

carry a card to be a member of the Communist Party
The use developed in the 1920s, when such membership was not flaunted because it might lead to ostracism: 'Maurice Dobb, who was probably the first academic in

Britain to carry a card' (Boyle, 1979). Today a 'card-carrying Communist' describes a member of the party who publicly acknowledges such membership.

carry a (heavy) load to be drunk
This common Am. expression refers to the weight consumed, although not necessarily of beer. *See* also **load** (1).

carry a torch for to desire sexually
But not within marriage. The imagery probably comes from the religious processional light: 'Maggie Young-Hunt came in today. Out of coffee, so she said. I think she's carrying a torch for me' (Steinbeck, 1961 – a male was talking about a woman who was stalking him).

carry off to kill
An epidemic or sudden illness is said to 'carry off' the person who dies. And in the passive: '. . . if one of the characters did happen to be carried off in the course of nature' (N. Mitford, 1949). SE.

carry on with to copulate with regularly and extra-maritally
Of either sex. Perhaps the 19c. use meant no more than to consort with heterosexually: 'I carry on with him now and he likes me very much' (Mayhew, 1862 – a young woman was speaking of her swain). In modern use the relationship is explicit and censurable: '. . . administered a public wigging to Princess Margaret when she was carrying on with that nancy-boy pop singer' (*Private Eye*, April 1981).

carry the banner to be out of work
Perhaps from the activities of the Salvation Army, whose members may so advertise their faith and always try to help the poor or unfortunate. The Am. 'carry the balloon' has the same meaning, and refers to the 'balloon' or bedroll of the itinerant which is carried above the pack.

carry the can to get undeserved punishment while the culprit goes free
If the 'can' were the receptacle for urine, the derivation might be deduced. The fuller version, 'carry the can back', suggests a less malodorous and burdensome journey, possibly back to the cookhouse with an empty communal food container. The phrases are also used of a guilty person who is singled out for punishment among several miscreants. Also as 'take the can (back)': 'Nobody wanted to take the can back' (B. Forbes, 1986, of people trying to avoid blame).

carrying *see* **carry** (1)

case (1) a brothel
From the Italian 'casa' and sometimes so spelt: 'Four casas, four women, often four Frenchwomen, to the square hectare' (Londres, 1928, in tr. of Buenos Aires). Grose reports that a 'case vrow' was 'A prostitute attached to a particular bawdy house'. The form 'caso' survived into the 1930s at least: 'Some people used to call her Caso Maggie. She got her money out of girls' (Kersh, 1936). A 'casita' was a small brothel: '. . . the representative of the law hurries to the *Casita* and the woman pays at once' (Londres, 1928, in tr.). A 'case' was also a lavatory or, in Dr Johnson's definition: 'A building unfurnished'. While all these uses may be ob., a 'casino' remains a room in which the public may gamble.

case (2) anything the subject of a taboo
In medical use, where it may be a breach of confidence to divulge the name of the patient. And in funeral jargon, of a corpse: 'We cremate quite a few cases' (J. Mitford, 1963), etc.

cash flow problem an insolvency
'Cash flow' is properly the difference between the receipts and payments of a business on a continuing basis. It becomes a 'problem' when companies knowingly continue to trade while insolvent, which makes the directors personally liable for the debts then contracted: 'Once *that* word gets round we are to have what is euphemistically called a cash flow problem' (Sharpe, 1977). You may also hear the expression used, perhaps humorously, of temporary indigence.

cash in your checks etc. to die
Equally common in the form 'cash in your chips', both Am. phrases alluding to the gambling counters for which you get money when you leave the game, there being an assumption that you may be going to your final reckoning. In similar fashion, 'checks' or 'chips', may be 'passed in'. But if you announce in company that you are going to 'cash a check', you are leaving to urinate.

cast to give birth prematurely
A SE usage, normally of animals, from the meaning, to cause to fall: 'Just a pair still-born at the hinner een', Puir dwarfed last anes, Wee, deid, cast anes' (Lumsden, 1892, of lambs). Whence perhaps the two punning phrases which meant to give birth to a bastard; 'cast a girth' used equestrian imagery and 'cast a laggin girth' came from the dis-placement of the hoop which held the staves of a tub, causing them to spill outwards: '. . . slipping a foot, casting a leglin-girth or the like' (W. Scott, 1822). In ob. Br. use if you were 'cast for death', you were not playing Julius Caesar but terminally ill, 'casting' being divination by magic: 'He's cassen her planets, and he's sure she'll dee' (Peacock, 1870).

cast your pellet to defecate
From 'cast', to let drop: '. . . the squatting early morning figures of male labourers casting their pellets upon the earth' (P. Scott, 1973, of India).

casting couch (the) extra-marital copulation between a female seeking a favour and a male in a position to grant it
Originally of actresses seeking roles: '. . . married a veteran Hollywood stunt man . . . . saved her from being just another hooker working the casting couches' (Collins, 1981). Less often outside the theatre: 'Young lady, I do not need a casting couch, I can have any woman I want' (*Private Eye*, May 1981, quoting a male journalist).

casual (the) an institution which housed the destitute
An abbr. of the Br. 'casual ward', 'casual' meaning coming at uncertain intervals. Those who used such accommodation were also known as 'casuals'.

cat (1) a whore
Still found in Am. but ob. in BI. 'Cat-house', a brothel, is used generally: '"What are those places?" asked Treece. "Ware-houses," said Jenkins. Treece thought he said whore-houses . . . . They didn't look like his idea of a cathouse' (Bradbury, 1959). A 'cat' may now also be a male prostitute: 'If you want to bugger a male cat, that means you're a queer' (Theroux, 1973) or any male who frequents brothels: 'These cats comin' here for a good time' (Collins, 1981, of a brothel).

cat (2) the vagina
Probably from the resemblence of the female pubic hair to the feline fur and *see* **pussy**: 'The rest of them were putting cigarettes in their cats and puffing on them' (Theroux, 1975). Mainly Am.

catch a rich marriageable adult
The imagery is from fishing and the 'catcher' improves status or security through a marriage. Anyone described as a 'good catch' may well have so far eluded the matrimonial net. In Pidgin 'catch' also means to

copulate with, along with 'infinite different meanings' (Jennings, 1965).

catch a cold (1) to contract gonorrhoea
WW II Br. army use, punning on the sl. meaning, to get yourself into trouble. Perhaps Shakespeare had the same thing in mind when he wrote 'A maid, and stuft! there's goodly catching of cold' (*Timon of Athens*).

catch a cold (2) to have a trouser zip inadvertently undone
An oblique warning from one male to another, received by me on the quay at Destin, Florida in November, 1987.

catch a fox *see* **foxed**

catch a packet to be killed or severely wounded
'Packet' is a diminutive of 'pack', and the use meant being struck by something solid, such as a shell, in WW I. After that war, it meant getting into any kind of serious trouble until WW II when two distinct new meanings developed. Of a locality, it meant being subjected to a heavy attack from the ground or air: 'The same thing's happening to the 2nd Northants, they've caught a packet too' (Price, 1978, of a badly mauled regiment) or, of a WW II serviceman, that he had caught a venereal disease.

catch fish with a silver hook to pretend to have caught fish which you have bought
An expression among anglers, where such behaviour is opprobrious. Unlike **angle with a silver hook** (q.v.) it does not also mean to bribe but cf. **shoot with a silver gun**.

catch the boat up to have contracted venereal disease
Naval usage, from the period in hospital ashore when your ship has sailed elsewhere, so that you have to travel to rejoin it.

cattle (1) negro slaves
They were herded, exploited, bred and sold like animals: 'Could be payin' (a right nice price) for the right kind of cattle' (Fraser, 1971, of early 19c. Southern States).

cattle (2) to copulate
Rh. sl. for 'cattle truck', fuck but now only used fig.: 'I don't give a flying cattle if you give me fifteen thousand pounds a week' (Kersh, 1936). 'Cattle', sometimes also defined as whores, seems to be based in that sense solely on Evelyn's 'Nelly . . . . concubines and cattell of that sort'. The diarist might as easily written 'people of that sort'

and this seems slim evidence on which to assume that 'cattell' are sui generis with Mistress Gwynne and concubines.

(Caucasian of White descent, comes from the 1781 skull classification of Blumenbach. Although both misleading and useful as an evasion, it is not euphemistic.)

caught (1) pregnant
The 'catching' takes place when she copulates and is impregnated. Mainly female usage, of unwanted pregnancies: 'If the girl gets caught and pregnancy results . . .' (Harris, 1925).

caught (2) infected with venereal disease
Medical practitioners tell me that this is the commonest way in which their diseased and embarrassed young patients introduce the subject of their visit.

caught short an urgent desire to urinate or defecate in an inconvenient place
The use is by both sexes, mainly of urination. I suspect it comes from the days when coaches or trains stopped at regular intervals but afforded no lavatory accommodation between one station and the next: 'Well, this virus carried a gun. I nearly got caught short' (Steinbeck, 1961). (I vividly recall an account by my mother of a long childhood journey in a train without a corridor during which her father laid newspaper on the floor so that she could defecate when 'caught short' of Carlisle.)

cavalry whores who solicit from motor vehicles
I have not met this use in Am. or BI but it is common in the English-speaking Far East. The 'infantry' solicit on foot.

CC pills US army laxatives of WW II
And some civilian use thereafter. The 'CC' is not, I think, from cubic centimetre, common carrier, chief clerk, cricket club, closed circuit or carbon copy.

cease fire a continuation of fighting
You meet this when the opponents are operating under different rules, and especially if the politicians on one side wish to pretend that the war is coming to an end: 'It is mined by the Viet Cong – even more furiously since the cease-fire (which is, willy-nilly, a painful euphemism)' (Theroux, 1975).

Cecil a penis
One of the male forenames adopted – *see* **Jock**, **John Thomas** etc.: 'I know all he

wants is to dip Cecil in the hot grease'
(Sanders, 1981, of copulation).

celebrate to drink intoxicants to excess
It is a social convention that intoxicants
should be available on a festive occasion. But
when a drunk person is said to have been
'celebrating', there is no suggestion of prior
festivities.

celebrity a nonentity employed as an entertainer
Properly, deserving fame. Jargon of the
entertainment industry: 'On the fringe of the
famous . . . . constantly invaded by idle chatter and envious gossip which inevitably, it
seems, surrounds what is euphemistically
called today a celebrity' (Bogarde, 1978).

cement to prevent defecation
Of medicine taken after an attack of
diarrhoea, although 'concrete' might seem
more appropriate: 'I'd already got the trots.
They're supposed to cement you up' (P.
Scott, 1975, of pills). And in various compound uses, as 'The water came from a
communal tap down by the road, so it was
cement-sandwich country as far as I was
concerned' (Lyall, 1972 – he wished to avoid
defecating). In Am. addict jargon 'cement' is
a poor quality illegal narcotic.

cement shoes etc. murdered and hidden
Am. underworld use, from the practice of
setting the lower legs in a concrete block to
prevent subsequent floating and discovery of
the corpse: 'There were more bodies down
there at the bottom of the lake with cement
shoes than there was garbage' (Weverka,
1973). 'Cement boots' is rarer.

certain age (a) old
The precise figure is often uncertain: 'They
were a certain age; they had humps and
braces and wooden legs' (Theroux, 1979).

certain condition (a) pregnancy
The phrase is used even though the condition may be one of considerable uncertainty
for the pregnant woman: 'He said that a
young woman who was obviously in "a certain condition", but not having a ring . . .'
(Lodge, 1975).

certain regarder a person who condones
violence to achieve a political aim
A Welsh use at a time when there is anxiety
that the advantages of economic integration
with England and Europe should not swamp
the naturally surviving Welsh culture and
language: 'In Wales called "certain regar-
ders", that is, people who say "I hold no

brief for violence, but I have a certain regard
for those who may think they have been
driven to it"'(*Daily Telegraph*, December
1980).

certified compulsorily confined in an institution for the mad
Under Br. law two medical doctors and a
magistrate had to certify that a lunatic should
be involuntarily incarcerated: 'He's out of
his skull . . . . he's ready for certifying'
(Bogarde, 1981). 'Certifiable' means either
mad but still at liberty: 'I won't put him in an
asylum. He really and truly isn't certifiable'
(McCarthy, 1963) or, loosely, irrational by
the commission of a single stupid act.

chair (the) killed by electrocution
From the furniture to which the victim is
strapped: 'We get a lock on the case, you
could face the chair' (Mailer, 1965). In ob.
use your 'chair-days' were your old age: 'In
thy reverence and thy chair-days, thus To
die in ruffian battle' (Shakespeare, 2 *Henry
VI*).

challenged crippled
Not by a sentry or in a duel: 'Part of a trend
to find new euphemisms for disabilities'
(*Original Selection of New Words*, 1986).

chamber a receptacle for urine
Abbr. of 'chamber-pot', from the room in
which it is kept in a small cupboard or under
the bed. The punning modern Am. 'chamber of commerce' is a lavatory but in ob. use
was a brothel. The ob. 'chamber-lye' was
fomented bottled urine, used in the washing
of clothes, in dressing wheat, etc.: 'We leak
in the chimney; and our chamber-lye breeds
fleas like a loach' (Shakespeare, *1 Henry IV*).

chamber of commerce *see* chamber

chambering copulation
The activity normally takes place in an
upstairs room: 'Harriet heard more than she
wanted of the chambering next door' (Manning, 1978).

champagne trick a rich customer for a
whore
Prostitutes' jargon and not the ability to open
a bottle without spilling any. 'Champagne'
for the expense and *see* trick.

chance conceived out of wedlock
From the unplanned nature of such impregnation. In many SE and dialect forms like
'chance-' bairn, begot, born, child, come,
etc., etc.: '"Chance children", as they are
called . . . . are rare among the young women
of the costermongers' (Mayhew, 1851). A

'chanceling' was a bastard, both literally and as an insult: 'Offspring of a pair a conn-celins' (Bywater, 1853).

change (1) (the) the menopause
Female usage and abbr. of the SE 'change of life'.

change (2) to be an idiot child
Babies born wise and beautiful grew up stupid and mischievous if the jealous fairies did a switch in the cradle: 'My granny never liked her, said she was "changed"' (Service, 1887). Thus a 'changeling' was an idiot. This entry is an example of how those in isolated communities rationalized the results of their incest and other inbreeding. ob.

change (3) *see* **alter**

change (4) to replace by a clean one a soiled napkin on a baby
The baby remains unchanged, albeit usu. cleaner and sweeter smelling: 'The baby now began to scream. "I expect he wants changing," said David' (N. Mitford, 1960).

change your luck to copulate extra-maritally with a Black woman
The use is by a White Am. male, from switching to black in the game of roulette after failure to win on the red.

channel a vein into which narcotics are illegally injected
Usu. in the crook of the elbow and scars there can indicate such practices.

chant falsely to describe a horse for sale
Properly, to sing. I include this ob. Br. use to illustrate that horse dealers had the same reputation and used the same deceits as salesmen of second-hand cars today. Thus a 'chanter' or 'horse-chanter' lied about the beast's age, temper, hooves, soundness, teeth, coat, etc. - or you might say about its mileage, roadworthiness, tyres, compression, petrol consumption, bodywork, etc.

chap a male suitor
Properly, a buyer, and then in colloquial use, any man: 'On the suspicion of an offence, the "gals" are sure to be beaten cruelly and savagely by their "chaps"' (Mayhew, 1851). 'Chapping', courting by a female, is ob. The 'old chap' was the devil: 'Speak truth, then ye needna fear Tae meet the auld chap face to face' (Thomson, 1881).

chapel of ease etc. a mortuary
Properly, a place of worship for the con-venience of parishioners who live a long way from the parish church. Now funeral jargon:

'From "undertaker" tout court to "funeral parlor" to "funeral home" to "chapel" has been the linguistic progression' (J. Mitford, 1963). Also, from the supposition that the body is biding its time against its resurrec-tion, as 'chapel of rest': '"James" had already mercifully been removed to the "Chapel of rest"' (Murdoch, 1978). In ob. Br. use a 'chapel of ease' was a lavatory, punning on the ecclesiastical sense and on 'ease yourself', to urinate.

chapter eleven *see* **go (2)**

character conventional
Real estate jargon. The SE word comes from a Greek instrument for graving (SOD), whence anything distinctive. But a 'charac-ter' bungalow can be expected to offer no more than repetitious banality.

charge (1) an erection of the penis
DAS suggests derivation of this Am. use from 'activation through an electric charge and/or the sensation of electric shock'. Many males would find the concept and imagery less appealing than that of loading a piece of ordnance.

charge (2) an illegal narcotic injection
The same imagery, of revitalizing, appears in that stupidest of clichés, 'a shot in the arm'. 'Charged up' means under illegal narcotic influence. (I am always incensed to read that a gift of money, say, to a troop of Brownies provided 'a shot in the arm' as though the small girls and Brown Owl were about to behave with unnatural vigour under narcotic influence.)

charity girl a female who copulates free of charge and restraint
She was usu. of respectable family and responded in this fashion to the early Am. chauvinism of WW II. A 'charity dame' was her mother, acting in the same sense, or lack of it.

Charlie a substitute word for a taboo subject
It may, according to the context, mean a policeman, a homosexual male, a whore, an idiot (or 'right' Charlie), the genitalia of the male or the female, menstruation (in the phrase 'Charlie's come') and, for a time, a Viet Cong adherent: 'They could sure as shit believe that Charley was shooting them' (Herr, 1977, of Vietnam). Some espionage use, too, of the Central Intelligence Agency, from the phonetic alphabet: 'It's just the sort of kit Charlie would have been supplying' (Lyall, 1985). In the Br. meaning, a ponce, it

is rh. sl. for 'Charlie Ronce', although neither he nor his namesake 'Joe Ronce' have earned a mention in the DNB. If you are told that 'Charley's dead', you are receiving an oblique warning that your trouser zip is undone. The Br. army 'Charlie Uncle', a fool, took two letters of the phonetic alphabet, the 'cu' of 'cunt' used fig. The 19c. 'charlies', a woman's breasts, is ob., along with 'dairies' and 'bubbies' (*The Slang Dictionary*, 1874).

charms the anatomical parts of a female which excite male lust
A 'charm' was properly the singing of a song, whence a magic incantation and so to 'charms', which work such magic: 'I had a full front-view of all her charms' (Cleland, 1749, of a woman stripped for copulation). In ob. use to 'charm' was to cure by magic: 'Soom folk says it's hall bosh about charmin' yer cock . . . . Mah feyther took a feather o' his cock to t'old witch an' she charmed un' (*Good Words*, 1869, quoted in EDD – an avian remedy was supplied, not an aphrodisiac). A 'charmer' was a good intentioned or 'white' witch and 'charming', in good health: 'An' how's Coden Rachel? – She's charmin', thankee' (Quiller-Couch, 1890).

charter of labour the feudal conditions of work in Nazi Germany
Industrial and farm workers were tied to their jobs by a repressive law dated 20 January, 1934, which stifled trade union rights and freedom to choose or change your job. Presented as a law to guarantee workers' rights, this 'Law Regulating National Labour' was one of a series of acts taken by the Nazis as soon as they won power to suppress individual liberty.

charwallah a teetotaller in the army
Properly, the 'wallah', or man, who brought round the 'char', or tea, for the sale to Br. troops serving in India, whose expression it was. And *see* **bun-puncher** for a fuller explanation.

chase to seek to copulate with extra-maritally
Of a male, from following in a predatory way. In Am. you normally 'chase' something specific, like 'hump', 'skirt' or 'tail': '. . . known to tipple a bit and chase hump' (Mailer, 1965, of a drunken womanizer).

chaser an intoxicant different in kind from that just taken
It follows the previous libation down the throat. Usu. of beer after spirits or vice versa, but sometimes too of a further portion of what you have just drunk.

chauffeur a spy
Properly in French the person who stoked the boiler, but a 'chauffeuse' remains a foot-warmer. Communist usage where reciprocal arrangements with the host nation restrict the size of a diplomatic mission below that needed for espionage, subversion, forestalling defection etc.: 'Was the rank of chauffeur a cover? No Major of KGB covert intelligence seemed to give a shit what his title was abroad' (Seymour, 1982, of a Russian spy in London).

cheap John a brothel
Properly, a low or dilapidated saloon and perhaps punning on **john** (1) or (2) (q.v.). I have not seen this Am. expression in print outside a dictionary.

cheap money a policy of allowing money in circulation to increase faster than the creation of wealth
Unhappily it leads to inflation and wasted resources, because legislators seeking Utopia or re-election are unable to repeal the law of supply and demand. A 'cheap money' proponent, the Br. Old Etonian socialist Hugh Dalton, will be remembered for his undated 2½% Consols – 'Daltons' – long after his Budget indiscretion and his booming voice are forgotten.

cheat to copulate with other than your regular sexual partner
Of either party, within or outside marriage, from the deception usu. involved: 'Eight months married and cheating on me with a piece of merchandise like that' (Chandler, 1943).

cheat the starter to conceive a child before marriage
Sporting imagery, from starting a race before the signal to go. As with **beat the gun** (q.v.) the phrase may refer to any detected pre-marital copulation, even without impregnation.

cheaters cosmetic padding
From the attempt to deceive. They are worn by Am. women to improve the appearance of thighs, buttocks, chest etc.

check out to die
The imagery is said to have come from medical examination on demobilization, but leaving a hotel or cashing in when you quit gambling are just as likely: 'If you get found,

you check out. See you in the morgue'
(Chandler, 1953). Mainly Am.

check the seat covers look in that car for
an attractive woman
The advice is sent on Am. CB radio from
one trucker to another.

(cheeks the buttocks, comes directly from
the SE meaning, something arranged
laterally, whether doorposts or flesh and, if
the latter, on the face or on the hams. Grose
indicates which when he writes of the
'cheeks near cunnyborough').

cheesecake an erotic picture of a female
The word puns on the sweet confection and
the smile-inducing 'cheese' demanded by
photographers. Mainly WW II use and cf.
'beefcake' under **beef**.

chef a person who prepares opium for
smoking
Am. addict use, from the heating, whence
too the 'lamp habit', ingesting it. (Note how
the 'chef' or principal cook is the only one,
just as the 'Ober' needs no underlings.)

chère amie a sexual mistress
The French euphemism is carried into English and even rarely translated as 'dear
friend', retaining its meaning: 'Phryne, the
chère amie of a well-known officer in the
Guards' (Mayhew, 1862).

cherry the hymen
From the colour and appearance? '. . . asking
me to look after you was the most risky thing
she could do if you wanted to hang on to that
cherry of yours' (P. Scott, 1968 - a libertine
was talking to a virgin). Whence 'cherry',
being a virgin: 'Were you cherry when you
got married?' (Sanders, 1981). The punning
'cherry-picker' is a libertine who likes young
females for extra-marital copulation.

chew to practise fellatio
From the action of masticating: '"He
wanted you to gobble ze goo?" she asked.
"What?" "Chew on his schlong," Maddie
said impatiently' (Sanders, 1981).

chew a gun to kill yourself
You put the barrel in your mouth and aim
upwards: 'Doing good deeds apparently
keeps people from chewing on guns' (Wambaugh, 1981). Am.

chi chi of mixed White and Indian ancestry
A derogatory use. It means dirty in Hindi.

chic sale a primitive outdoor lavatory
From the Am. humorist Chic Sales whose

The Specialist is devoted to the construction
and location of outside lavatories.

chick a whore
The common avian imagery and rarely also
of a male prostitute in homosexual use. Also
of any young female viewed sexually by a
male: 'What was the name of the chick with
the big behind who sat on my knee in the
car?' (Bradbury, 1959). The Am. 'chickie' is
always a whore: 'Mayhew got himself a little
number down at China Beach, little chickie
workin' the scivvie houses there' (Herr,
1977). A 'chicken ranch' is a brothel.

chicken a youth attractive to homosexuals
cf. **chick** and owing nothing, I think, to the
sl. meaning, cowardly. A 'chickenhawk' is a
homosexual male who seeks out boys for
sexual purposes, punning on the preying
sparrow-hawk: 'I just happen to like boys
. . . . but I don't do chicken-hawks' (M.
Thomas, 1980). **No chicken** (q.v.) does not
mean heterosexual.

child of God a member of the Untouchable class in Hindu society
Dirty work, especially the collection of
human excreta, is their monopoly and any
other Hindu touching one is defiled: 'She
decided he was a Harijan, a child of God, an
untouchable' (P. Scott, 1971).

child of sin a bastard
The 'sin' was extra-marital copulation, at
least so far as the mother was concerned: 'I
have fallen! I am a mother, and my poor dear
boy is the child of sin' (Mayhew, 1862). The
concept and use are now ob.

child of Venus a whore
She has been mothered by the Goddess of
Love. The phrase is also used of a female
who enjoys copulation: '. . . a merry little grig
and born child of Venus' (Harris, 1925 - a
'grig' is a lively, jolly person).

chill to kill
The common cooling imagery: 'A hundred
guys could have chilled this little wart'
(Chandler, 1939, of a corpse).

Chinese copy a production model stolen
from another's design
Usu. exactly copied without acknowledgement, consent, licence, royalty, etc.: '. . .
some big-time outfit'll Chinese-copy his
equipment and take his market away by
underpricing him' (M. Thomas, 1982). The
tradition is kept alive by the Taiwanese.

Chinese three-point landing a crash
on the runway

An elaboration of the WW I 'Chinese landing', which punned on the mythical Oriental, Wun Wing Lo. WW II usage.

Chinese tobacco opium
From the smoking and the association of opium with China. But 'China-white' is heroin of good quality, perhaps from the colour: '. . . offered me a whole piece of unstepped-on China white' (Wambaugh, 1981, of pure heroin).

Chinese wall the pretence by a firm of advisers that it is justified in taking fees at the same time from clients with conflicting interests
F. D. Roosevelt first used the phrase in this context in 1927. Now a device often called in aid to try and stop a client going to a competitor when in dispute with another client. 'Chinese walls' also allow the trading department of a bank etc. to continue speculating at a time when another part of the same organization possesses price-sensitive information. This is all part of **self-regulation** (q.v.).

chippy (1) a low grade whore
Possibly from 'chip', a bit or piece: 'He pays some chippie fifty to gobble his pork' (Diehl, 1978, of fellatio). A 'chippie-joint' is an Am. brothel.

chippy (2) to take illegal narcotics on an irregular basis
Where illicit narcotic ingestion is the norm, non-addiction may be taboo. In such a culture a non-addict may wish to avoid being thought stuffy by not entirely eschewing narcotics, as it were merely chipping at a mass. Lingeman suggests a derivation from '*chippying*, dallying with (a chippy): hence *chippy-user*, one who uses narcotics infrequently' – but that seems unnecessarily complex. In Am. Black sl. a 'chippy' may also ingest regularly strong illicit narcotics, which adds to our knowledge and confusion, if not to elucidation of the etymology.

chips *see* **cash in your checks etc.**

chirp to be an informer to the police
This Am. underworld sl. uses the common 'singing' imagery.

chisel to steal or cheat
The imagery is from removing slivers by a sharp instrument. Thus the thefts may be minor and repetitious and the cheating mean: 'Gotham liked to chisel whatever "float" it could over the weekend' (M. Thomas, 1980, of the banking practice of stealing the interest on customers' money by being dilatory on Fridays). 'On the chisel ' is so behaving: 'He'd be pretty sore if I was on the chisel. Not that I don't like money' (Chandler, 1955). There is a further new Am. use, to avoid compliance with an unpopular law.

choke your chicken to masturbate
Of a male, from the likeness of an erect penis to a chicken's plucked neck: 'I went to Chi Town to clean up, but I ended up choking my chicken' (CBSLD – the speaker sought copulation in Chicago). A 'chicken choker', or masturbator, is said to be 'a friendly term truckers use for each other' (ibid.).

chokey prison
The Hindi 'chauki' is a space surrounded by walls, whence a prison in Br. Indian use and common Br. sl.: 'I've got to cart Voluptia off to chokey. She's been interfering down in the circumcision booths' (Bradbury, 1976).

chop (1) to kill
Originally SE of the killing of an animal before sportsmen had been given an opportunity of hunting it to death, but now used of killing humans: 'Unless he chopped us both (which seemed far-fetched, pirate and Old Etonian though he was)' (Fraser, 1977). To 'get the chop' is to die, especially in wartime. In newspaper jargon a 'chop shot' is a picture of a death: 'You don't get many chop shots these days' (M. Thomas, 1980, of a public execution).

chop (2) (the) sudden dismissal from employment
The imagery is from the act of chopping and is used of individual rather then multiple dismissals. To 'chop' is so to dismiss: 'Joint editor Allan Segal was chopped last month' (*Private Eye*, May 1981). 'For the chop' is to be a candidate for dismissal: 'Tusker had been for the chop the moment Solly Feibergerstein set eyes on him' (P. Scott, 1977).

chopper (1) a machine gun
Underworld jargon from army use, referring to the chopping down of the victim and *see* **chop** (1): 'The man with the chopper' (Chandler, 1950, of someone so armed). A 'chopper' may also be a killer by firearm or, in aviation sl., a helicopter.

chopper (2) a penis
Perhaps from its divisive sexual function in its erect state. (My daughter, whose job included editing etymological puzzles, once erred by passing 'a butcher's chopper' as a

crossword clue for 'cleaver', which calls to mind Dr Wright's definition: 'Broach - a butcher's prick' (EDD). If she had studied Grose she might also have had qualms about 'cleaver' – 'One that will cleave; used of a forward or wanton woman' and to 'cleave' was to copulate: 'How many different men have cleft thee this last six month?' (Fowles, 1985, writing in archaic style).)

chota peg a spirituous intoxicant
'Chota' is small in Hindi, although the measure may not be, and *see* **peg**: 'Better a few too many chota pegs than the possible alternative' (P. Scott, 1968). A 'burra peg' is a large measure of spirits. These Br. Indian uses are now seldom heard in BI.

chubby fat
Properly, like the thick, coarse-fleshed fish, whence agreeably plump, especially of babies. Used in advertisements to avoid disturbing mothers who have to select capacious clothes for an obese child.

chuck (the) peremptory dismissal from employment or as a suitor
The inference is (wrongly) that the parting is effected by force. In ob. English to 'chuck seven' was to die, there being no seven on a dice cube.

chucked drunk
Probably from the feeling of rotation, like an object being turned in the chuck of a lathe and owing nothing to being 'chucked out' of an inn for drunkenness. The Am. 'chuck horrors' are either the acute symptoms which may follow withdrawal from narcotic dependence; or the claustrophobic symptoms of someone confined or afraid of being confined in a prison cell.

church house an institution for destitutes
I give this entry to explain the many 'Church House Inns' in Devon, which you will find near the church and parsonage: 'Wi' croping church-house grules long fed' (Rock, 1867 – the grules were miserly).

church triumphant the dead
A Christian use, especially of those considered to have faithfully served the 'church militant here on earth', while others of us supposedly languish among the vanquished.

churning unnecessarily dealing in a client's securities to inflate commission
Mainly Am. stock dealing jargon and practice. The imagery is from constantly turning the milk to obtain butter or cream, the prin-cipal being milked and the agent getting the cream.

circus an obscene stage performance
Am. jargon of those who promote pornographic shows. The round or oval Roman amphitheatre gave its name to the performances held there and thence to the modern clown and elephant routines.

cissy a male homosexual
Properly, an effeminate man, probably from the abbr. female name: 'You know how cissies hate pregnant ladies' (N. Mitford, 1949 – in fact, I did not know).

civil reception *see* **house**

civil rights the assertion that illegal action is justified for a good cause
Properly no more than the assertion and enjoyment of what you are entitled to as a citizen. However a 'Civil Rights' person may select what is right even if that involves holding that the law is wrong, and once you accept that, various propositions follow. The Am. and N. Ire. 'civil rights movements' are examined in FDMT where, inter alia, the manipulation of well-meaning dupes by extremists is noted.

claim to steal
This Eng. use seeks to put a gloss of legality on the taking, usu. of items of low value. To 'claim responsibility for' arson, murder, etc. is terrorist jargon for admitting to the perpetration of the crime specified. To claim is also used journalistically as a device for imputing a lie: '"He claims he saw . . ." was synonymous with "He is lying when he says he saw . . ."' (D. Francis, 1985, of a scurrilous newspaper).

claimant a poor person supported in part or whole by the state
From the 'claiming' of money from public agencies: 'Reductions for Students, OAPs and Claimants' (Theatre Wales poster, October 1981 – it would not have availed a self-sufficient person to have 'claimed' indulgence). There is also a Br. 'Claimants Union', which exists to help the poor obtain their full entitlement from society, other than by earning a wage.

(clap, gonorrhoea, is venerable sl. Dr Johnson gives merely 'A venereal infection' and Pope was clearly under a medical misapprehension when he wrote 'Time, that at last matures a clap to pox'. In ob. London use you had caught gonorrhoea if you 'came home by Clapham', an outer suburb in those

days. I think DAS is incorrect even for Am.
use in saying 'esp. syphilis'.)

claret blood
Boxing jargon, from the colour, and usu. of
bleeding from the nose, or 'claret-jug'.

class warfare etc. the tension between
various citizens in a non-Communist state
Marxist jargon, dogma and justification. The
manual workers are supposed to be in permanent conflict with the rest, because they
were seen to be oppressed in 19c. factories.
Today if no such conflict exists, it should be
fomented or invented. The Communists use
many compounds of the same tendency,
which it would be tedious to analyse, including 'class-' conflict, education, law, literature
etc.

classic pretentious and costly
Properly, a book used in class, whence one
written in Latin or Ancient Greek, and then
any work which remains in vogue over a long
period. Its advertising jargon use may owe
something to 'classy', or 'superior', which
did not at one time prevent the Br. 'Classic'
cinema chain specializing in pornographic
films.

classic proportions obesity
Of women, because Rubens and other
'classic' painters seemed to favour plump
women.

clean free from unpleasant or illegal taint
see **dirty**, of which in many uses this is the
opposite. Thus if you are 'clean-living', you
refrain from extra-marital copulation: 'VD is
dangerous. Clean living is the real safeguard'
(L. Thomas, 1977) and 'clean' indicates the
absence of venereal disease: 'I was a lucky
devil to drop on such a lovely clean skirt'
(Richards, 1936 – the female was disease-
free). A 'clean' atom bomb has less fall-out
than a 'dirty' one: 'The language of the mad
. . . . "Clean atom bombs"'(West, 1979). A
'clean' locality' may be free of the enemy:
'. . . this village is clean and this village is all
Charley' (Theroux, 1975, of Vietnam). You
are 'clean' if you are not illegally carrying
narcotics or a handgun: '"What's the point if
he's clean?" "If he's carrying something?"'
(Kyle, 1978 – a person was suspected of
having a pistol). A miscreant may escape –
'get clean away' – or avoid arrest: 'Drunk as
he'd been the night before, he thought he'd
made it home clean' (M. Thomas, 1980). To
have 'clean hands' is not to be involved in
bribery.

clean up (1) to bring the proceeds of vice
into open circulation
A variant of **launder** (q.v.) using the same
imagery: 'The money from this stuff needed
cleaning up' (Davidson, 1978). Or the
money may be sent 'to the cleaners' for the
same purpose: 'Black money tucked away
ready to go to the cleaners' (ibid.).

clean up (2) to copulate extra-maritally
Of a male, from the sl. meaning, to have a
successful foray: 'I went to Chi Town to
clean up' (CBSLD). Am.

cleaners (the) the actuality of being robbed or cheated
A losing gambler or a dupe by any trickery
within or outside the law may be said to have
been, been sent, been taken or gone 'to the
cleaners', punning on the removal of extran-
eous matter from clothing in the dry-
cleaning process.

cleanse (1) to free from enemy occupation
Vietnam variation of **clean** (above), achieved
by bombing or otherwise dominating formerly hostile villages etc.: '. . . paramilitary
elements trained and drilled in a special
school and sent to "cleanse" (US word)
"pacified" hamlets ' (McCarthy, 1967).

cleanse (2) to remove the placenta from
domestic cattle
Veterinary jargon: 'I was "cleansing" a cow
(removing the afterbirth)' (Herriot, 1981).

cleansing lotion a liquid other than soapy
water
An expensive concoction used by some
women for washing their faces: 'Simple
Cleansing Lotion contains no perfume or
colouring addition. 130ml. By SIMPLE
SOAP LTD' (label on a bottle in my wife's
toiletry). Not just for simple females then,
but those perhaps beguiled by clever packaging. Br. 'cleansing personnel' may be garbage collectors.

clear-out (a) defecation
Medical jargon and male vulgarism. Of defecation whether or not associated with the
taking of a purge.

clear up to desist from regular use of illegal
narcotics
Properly, to tidy up or to redress any ill. Am.
addict use.

cleavage the visible division between a
clothed woman's breasts
Properly, the action of splitting apart. With
the relaxation of taboos concerning the
breasts, now SE.

cleft the vagina
As viewed sexually by a male, from the
proper meaning, a crack or fissure in a rock:
'Oh! let me view the small, dear, tender cleft'
(Cleland, 1749, of a vagina).

click to steal
Properly, to snatch or seize hold of, the EDD
giving many dialect uses associated with robbery. When Wright and Murray disagree,
then comes the tug-of-war, but this time I
suspect the OED is the loser because click is
more than a corruption of the Sc. 'cleek':
'. . .wanting to cleik the cunzie (that is to
hook the siller)' (W. Scott, 1814). In ob. use
an Englishman might have bought stolen
goods at 'Clickem Fair' or have been robbed
at 'Clickem Inn'; and a 'clicker' was a body-
snatcher or a pestering touting shopkeeper.

clicket copulation
Properly, a latch or something which shuts
with a click (OED, which adds: '. . . supposed
by some to be a she-fox'; however Dr Wright
says 'Of the fox or hare: to be *maris
appetans*'). SE of copulation by foxes, rarely
by deer and hares, fig. only by humans.

(client, a customer, is pompous rather than
euphemistic. Originally a person under
another's patronage, a 'client' became someone who consulted and paid a lawyer, who
did him a favour by allowing himself to be
hired. It went on to mean any buyer, even of
the services of a whore.)

climax a sexual orgasm
Properly, the culmination of anything. Hudson attributes the first euphemistic use in
this sense to Marie Stopes. 'A climax was
never reached by either of them, but that did
not spoil their pleasure' (P. Scott, 1968, of
copulation).

climb to copulate with
Of a male, from the action of 'mounting' the
female: 'You mean you are looking to climb
some gorgeous chorus girl' (Condon, 1966).
'Climb in with' refers to no higher an ascent
than the female's bed: 'I'd just as soon go to
bed with a giant clam as climb in with Eva
Wilt' (Sharpe, 1979). 'Climb into bed' is
specific: '. . . sufficient affection and desire
for her still to want to climb into bed if I got
half a chance' (Fowles, 1977).

climb the ladder on your back to secure promotion through readiness to copulate
extra-maritally
Of a female who hopes to turn advances to
advancement and advantage. In ob. use 'to
climb the ladder' was to be hanged, either

from the ascent to the scaffold or because
the 'ladder' itself was the scaffold: 'When he
was upon the ladder he prayed that God
would inflict some visible judgement on his
Uncle' (Wallace, 1693).

climb the wooden hill *see* **wooden hill**

clink a prison
Originally the jail in Southwark but then
used generally, helped no doubt by the
onomatopoeic attractions of keys in locks
and heavy doors shutting: '. . . the more
troublesome firebrands . . . . were popped
neatly into clink' (P. Scott, 1971). The ob.
Sc. 'clink off' was to die, from a meaning, to
depart: 'In God's gude providence she just
clinkit off hersell' (Ramsay, 1859).

clip (1) to swindle or rob
From the shearing of sheep. Now usu. of the
picking of pockets. A 'clip-artist' is a
swindler and a 'clip-joint' a night club etc.
where customers are overcharged and otherwise cheated.

clip (2) to hit with a bullet
Properly, to cut or shear, whence to mark as
by removing cardboard from a ticket. In Am.
the person 'clipped' is usu. killed but in the
BI only slightly wounded, without being
incapacitated. The rare 'clip the wick', to
kill, comes from snuffing out a candle by
cutting it below where it is burning: 'Maitland found out. So they clipped his wick'
(Sanders, 1977, of killing, not circumcising).

cloakroom a lavatory
Coats are commonly stored in or near lavatories: 'To a small boy looking urgently for
the cloakroom . . .' (Jaeger in *Pass the Port*,
1976). Very common Br. usage but the abbr.
'cloaks' refers normally to the storage of
outer garments.

clobbered drunk
From 'clobber', to beat up, with the common
imagery of disarray and general malaise
which is met at some stage of drunkenness.
Am.

cloot the devil
Properly, one of the divisions of a cloven·
hoof, a physical characteristic shared by
Satan and cattle: 'I hate ye as I hate auld
Cloot' (Barr, 1861). And as 'clootie': 'Auld
Hornie, Satan, Nick, or Clootie' (Burns,
1785). I think this Sc. usage is ob. and
doubtfully euphemistic, but I give it, as with
good man (q.v.) to illustrate the superstition
of our quite recent forebears, who set aside
and left untilled 'clootie's croft' in the hope

that the devil, having his own piece of land, would leave the rest of the farm alone: 'The moss is soft on Clootie's craft' (Henderson, 1856 – I suppose all the thanks the farmer got was a seeding harvest of weeds).

close *see* **near** (1)

close friend *see* **friend**

close its doors to fail
Of a bank, which in fact closes its doors with some care every evening and usu. opens them not at all over the weekend, when it would be convenient for customers: '. . . if the run persisted, cash reserves would be exhausted and FMA obliged to close its doors' (Hailey, 1975).

close stool a portable lavatory
Originally for use in the **closet** (1) (q.v.) but now in any sick-room: 'Your lion, that holds his pole-axe sitting on a close-stool, will be given to Ajax' (Shakespeare, *Love's Labour's Lost* – *see* **jakes** for the punning 'Ajax').

close the bedroom door to refuse to copulate with a spouse
The female usu. does the closing: 'From the moment he had been a gubernatorial candidate she had closed the bedroom door' (Allbeury, 1980). I have heard the phrase used fig. where spouses have continued to share a bedroom but have ceased at the instance of one to copulate with each other.

close your eyes to die
Or explicitly, 'close your eyes for the last time'. If you 'close' another's eyes, he is already dead and you are arranging the corpse.

closet (1) a lavatory
Properly, a small or private room. It is normally used with the descriptive prefixes 'earth' or 'water', whence the initials 'EC' and 'WC'.

closet (2) concealing in public your homosexuality
Again from the small or private room where you act according to your true inclinations. Usu. of a male, as a 'closet' queen or queer, and rarely of a female: 'I often wondered if she was a closet lez' (Sanders, 1977). In rare and convoluted use, a 'closet homosexual' may be a male who affects homosexuality so as to avert the suspicions of a cuckolded husband: 'Dexter Dempster, New York's leading closet homosexual' (M. Thomas, 1980, of a man who so behaved).

clout to steal
Probably from the meaning to hit, whence by transference from the Am. 'hit', to rob. Normally of minor thefts from shops or cars. In ob. Br. use a 'clout' was a cloth worn to absorb urine or menstrual discharge: 'Their bottles o' pap, an' their mucky bins, an' the clats an' the clouts' (Tennyson, 1885). The saw 'ne'er cast a clout till May be out', refers to clothing and the tree blossom, but millions have sweated unnecessarily through torrid springs: '. . . do keep them on up to the middle of May at least' (Kersh, 1936, of winter woollies).

clown a country policeman
Am. CB sl. for a sheriff or deputy in a small community, with limited training or experience.

club (1) *see* **in the club**

club (2) a firm promoting the sale of a specific product
There is usu. an attempt by the promoter to involve customers – 'members' – in a continuing obligation to buy, as with a 'Book Club', but no true association of like-minded people.

club (3) a business which contrives to evade regulations
Usu. selling intoxicants without a licence, with customers being enrolled as 'members', whence the Br. 'club licence', permission to sell intoxicants to a restricted clintele. Also of cinemas showing pornographic films where full public display would be illegal, etc.

clunk a corpse
Properly, the sound of a blow, or a dull person, neither of which elucidates the origin of this Am. use: 'He'll be a clunk before he hits the floor' (Sanders, 1973, of a killing).

cluster the male genitalia
They are certainly proximate, and even more so in tight trousers: '"The cluster," he replied, "is prominent these days"' (Matthew, 1983 – a shop assistant was trying to sell tightly-cut trousers).

co-belligerent a former enemy helping the winner in continuing war
By 1943 **collaborator** (q.v.) had become pejorative and 'the word "co-belligerent" was invented to proclaim her new status' (Jennings, 1965, of Italy). The wise Italians had shown little belligerence before the

about-face, and had no reason to show any more after it.

co-operate (1) voluntarily to assist an invader of your country
Properly, to work with: '. . . people in his area have begun to "co-operate" with the Americans - the word "collaborate" is avoided' (McCarthy, 1967).

co-operate (2) to assist another through fear or duress
Usu. of criminals supplying information to the police. The term is usu. in the mouth of the party applying the pressure; thus the Russian name for the economic control of its European subject states is the 'Economic Co-operation Council', or Comecon.

co-ordination ensuring submission to totalitarian rule
Nazi jargon and concept, largely implemented through an 'Enabling Act', which conferred absolute power on Hitler. (This is one of the many lessons the Nazis taught the Communists – have ready and put into effect a law which gives the leader absolute and irreversible power as soon as you seize control.)

co-pilot a person who watches another who has illegally taken LSD.
The hallucinogen can convince the taker that he can fly. Even if he remains earthbound, he may injure or kill himself under the narcotic influence.

co-respondent a male accused in court of having copulated with another's wife
Legal jargon for the man who has to 'respond' jointly with the wife to a husband's petition for divorce on the grounds of adultery: 'Merrick was, in his romantic way, a sort of professional co-respondent' (Bradbury, 1959). If you wear 'co-respondent's shoes' or, less often, other articles of clothing so described, you are dressing in a style affected by men thought to be philanderers. An Am. 'correspondent' can be a woman: '. . . doubled as a paid correspondent in divorce cases – "the Woman Taken in Adultery"' (McCarthy, 1963). Under Eng. divorce law, the woman whom the wife names as having copulated with her husband is the 'party cited', so that she may defend her good name, if she has one, but without any liability for the payment of damages or costs to the wife.

coast to be under the influence of illegal narcotics
Freewheeling, usu. on heroin. Am.

cobbler a forger
Criminal or espionage use, for someone who prepares bogus credit cards, passports, etc. To 'cobble' is to mend any article in an untidy or rough way, although we expect a neat job from the person who mends our shoes.

cobblers the testicles
Rh. sl. from 'cobblers' awls', balls. DRS says surprisingly 'Accepted as a euphemism and not recognized as reduced rhyming slang' – with which I cannot agree. Mainly fig. use, in the sense that 'balls' means nonsense – 'a lot of old cobblers'. The ob. N. Eng. 'cobs', the testicles, probably came from the meaning, small stones and was not an abbr. of 'cobblers' or a variant of the Am. 'nuts'.

cock to copulate with
The treatment of this word by Dr Wright in EDD differentiates him from other lexicographers (Vol. I pp. 680 to 684). Suffice it to say here that the meaning, a penis, is venerable: 'Pistol's cock is up' (Shakespeare, *2 Henry IV* – another of his vulgar puns) and that to 'cock' was to use your penis in copulation. In modern speech we 'cock a leg' across, athwart or over a female, which is not punning on the 'penis' meaning: '. . . to prevent him cocking his lustful leg over my loving Elspeth' (Fraser, 1975) and '. . . all the more difficult for me to cock a leg athwart Miss Fanny' (Fraser, 1971). A 'cocksman' is a philanderer, from the penis and not the leg movement: 'He didn't think of himself as a cocksman but every now and then . . . . something would get loose in his system' (M. Thomas, 1982). In Black Am. use, a 'cock' is also the vagina, as is 'cockpit' generally, punning on the scene of avian contest and the repository for the penis: '. . . the rose-lipt overture presenting the cockpit so fair' (Cleland, 1949) and the WW II vulgarism 'She was only a pilot's daughter but she kept her cockpit clean'. The ob. Br. 'cock-chafer' was a treadmill, punning on Melolontha Vulgaris: 'He "expiated", as it is called, this offence by three months' exercise on the "cockchafer" (treadmill)' (Mayhew, 1851). I think Partridge is wrong when he says of 'by cock, they are to blame' (Shakespeare, *Hamlet*) that '*Cock* is a euphemism of God'. Because everyone knows that it is vulgar to refer openly to a penis and 'cock' is the commonest word for it, prudery has led to many evasions which I examine under **game chicken**.

cock-eyed drunk
Properly, askew, which is what your clothing might be, or your gait. The ob. 'cocked', drunk, may have come from a pistol prepared for firing with, as normal in drunkenness, the half equalling the whole: 'Half cock'd and canty, hyem we gat' (Wilson, 1843 – 'canty' means cheerful).

cock the leg to urinate
Normally of a dog, but not of a bitch: 'The poodle . . . . shivered and cocked its leg nervously against the front door' (Bogarde, 1978). Sometimes used humorously by and of male humans.

cock the little finger to be a drunkard
From the manner in which some hold a cup: 'Some say she cocks her wee finger. . . . In short that she's gien to the drink' (Barr, 1861). The phrase is also used of addiction to alcohol short of dipsomania.

cocked *see* cock-eyed

cocktail (1) an alcoholic mixed drink
I like to think the derivation is from the Aztec xoc-tl, after the maiden Hochitl who introduced the king to a concoction devised by her father, thereby winning his heart and immortality. Etymology based on a feather used for stirring, or the French 'coquetel', a mixed intoxicant, is much less interesting, whatever the probabilities. A late contender came to my notice when I read the wholly admirable *The Story of English* (1986) which tentatively suggests derivation from the Krio 'koktel', a scorpion. Commoner in Am. than BI where it tends to mean a mixture based on a spirit and no more: 'They had started having cocktails every night' (McCarthy, 1963 – which would have included beer or straight spirits). And you find 'cocktail' bars, hours, lounges, etc. everywhere. In ob. uses a 'cocktail' was a flaming tankard of ale in Yorks; a six-oared boat used by smugglers in Kent; and in BI a whore, involving an obvious pun: 'Such a coxcomb as that, such a cocktail' (Thackeray). A 'cockatrice' was also a whore, as well as being the fabulous serpent which killed by its glare.

cocktail (2) a cigarette of tobacco and other illicit narcotics
From the mixed components. In Am. sl. it is also a tobacco cigarette used to enable you to smoke in its entirety the butt of a marijuana cigarette.

coffee grinder a whore
From the rotary motion of the pelvis rather than the pigmentation of the skin. The term

also means a belly dancer or stripper, and the three callings are not mutually exclusive. Am. The 19c. Br. 'coffee shop' seems also to have been 'a watercloset, or house of office' (*The Slang Dictionary*, 1874).

coffin varnish inferior whisky
This Am. phrase puns on the look, the taste and the container in which you may precipitately find yourself if you drink much of it.

cohabit to copulate with extra-maritally on a regular basis
Properly, merely to live with in the same abode, as do parents and children: 'My staff are all highly trained in the Swedish technique and strictly forbidden to cohabit with the customers' (B. Forbes, 1986, of a bawd). In fact 'cohabitors' normally share a residence as well as a bed.

coil (the) a mechanical contraceptive device used by a woman
From its shape: 'Zoya thumbed a dish of birth control pills, Polish pills. She refused to use the coil' (M.C. Smith, 1981). A person who describes herself as 'coil' indicates that she copulates regularly, seeks to avoid conception and uses this device.

coke cocaine used illegally
Probably no more than an abbr. with no pun on the beverage: 'Out of the apartment houses came cokies and coke peddlers, people who look like nothing in particular' (Chandler, 1943). 'Coked' is under narcotic influence: '. . .''coked'' or ''bopped up'' gunmen' (Lavine, 1930). A 'coke-hound' is a cocaine or heroin addict: 'He's a coke-hound and he talks in his sleep' (Chandler, 1939) etc.

cold (1) dead
Usu. but not exclusively of hot-blooded creatures, and sometimes of unconsciousness – 'knocked out cold' – rather than death despite the retention of body heat. A source of many phrases alluding to death in morbid 19c. humour, some of which have survived or been reinvented, like 'cold meat', a corpse: 'If you bother with us, I will make meat of you – see! – cold meat' (Harris, 1925). A 'cold-meat' party is a funeral; a 'cold-box', a coffin; a 'cold-cart', a hearse; a 'cold cook', an arranger of funerals; 'cold storage', the grave; etc.

cold (2) not easily susceptible to sexual excitement
The opposite of **hot (1)** (q.v.) but also of someone who fails to be sexually aroused on

a specific occasion: 'I have often been asked why on my African travels I was so cold in regard to the native women' (Harris, 1925 – what strange inquisitors he must have had). As in Shakespeare's 'cold chastity', more of women than of men.

cold feet cowardice or fear
There is a physical justification for this SE use – we have all shivered with fear: 'I think I must have the merest touch of claustrophobia – or cold feet as they would call it in the mess' (Price, 1978, of a tank commander who admitted fear).

cold turkey etc. the effect of sudden deprivation of illegal narcotics
From the resemblance of the sufferer to a bird when it has been plucked. Less often of withdrawal from alcoholism: 'You can't suddenly sign the pledge, go cold turkey' (B. Forbes, 1986). In Am. use other birds may replace the 'turkey' in this phrase.

cold-water man a person who drinks no intoxicants
A perhaps ob. Sc. use in a society where abstinence is taboo: '"Dae ye drink?" "He's a cauld-water man"' (Gordon, 1894).

collaborator a traitor
He works disloyally for the conqueror and not loyally with another like-minded person: 'The English so often have these unknown French friends.... Collaborators one and all' (N. Mitford, 1960 – the wide acceptance by the French in 1940 to 1943 of their subservience to the German conqueror and their freeing by the Anglo-Saxons remain factors in their national attitudes and policies today). 'Collaborationist' is specific: 'I told him I was not a collaborationist, that I was a doctor' (Fowles, 1977, of a Greek in WW II). To 'collaborate' is so to act: 'They express their readiness to collaborate' (Goebbels, 1945, in tr. of foreign workers under German control). Similarly 'Mitarbeiter' is police jargon in Russian-occupied Germany for a person who regularly spies and reports on his fellow workers.

collapsible container a contraceptive sheath
Am. police jargon which transfers the collapsing to the contraceptive: 'In any police report when you refer to a collapsible container, it's a rubber' (Wambaugh, 1981).

collar (1) to steal
Of any small object, probably from putting a collar on a dog to secure it.

collar (2) an arrest
From the act of grabbing a suspect by his collar and perhaps so leading him away: 'But the evidence is of such a nature that it doesn't justify a collar – an arrest' (Sanders, 1973). An Am. 'accommodation collar' is an arrest made to fill a quota and so show a superior that you are working well. By transference, a 'collar' may also be an Am. policeman.

collect to accept a bribe
Usu. of taking bribes on a regular basis: 'Woe to the cop who collects anything.... and doesn't "see the sergeant"' (Lavine, 1930). This Am. use is of the same tendency as the ob. Br. 'collector', a highway thief, who asked you to stand and deliver.

colleen an erect penis
Rh. sl. on the colleen Bawn, the heroine of 'Lily of Killarney', and horn. I suspect this Br. use is now ob.

colonial old
Am. real estate jargon of buildings which were not always there before the 1780s. 'Ante-bellum', referring in the same sense to the 19c. civil war, is more likely to be authentic.

colony a distant territory ruled by expatriates
Properly, a place to which people emigrate in order to live but most Br., French and Italian 'colonies' were populated by their indigenous population under the military, economic and political control of London, Paris or Rome. Today the Br. 'Crown Colony' of Hong Kong has over 98 per cent of Chinese residents and under 2 per cent of others, including British.

colour-tinted etc. dyed
Of hair, where it is more than circumlocution because the process is more drastic than the variation of a shade: 'For dry, damaged, bleached or colour tinted hair' (instruction on bottle, 1980). Also as 'colour-corrected': 'She "mutates" or "adapts" or "colour-corrects" her hair' (Jennings, 1965).

coloured not of exclusively White ancestry
No human skin pigmentation is colourless and those with pale skins go to considerable expense and discomfort to darken them by exposure to ultra-violet rays, under sun lamps or distant skies: 'There are already white tables so why not have a table for the coloured fellers?' (Theroux, 1973, but not of foresters). This popular evasion replaced for

a while 'Black', except in S. Africa where it relates to those of mixed ancestry.

colt (1) to impregnate a woman
From the service of a mare, perhaps punning on the meaning, to cheat: 'She hath been colted by him' (Shakespeare, *Cymbeline*). ob.

colt (2) a fine extracted from a recruit by old employees
The money was then spent on communal intoxicants in a process known as 'shoeing the colt'. I give this ob. W. Eng. example of a widespread practice in the days when apprenticeships were hard to secure but ensured a good livelihood once completed.

Columbian gold high quality marijuana
From the colour and the profits. It is grown near Baranquilla in Columbia, where the millionaire traders are called 'marijuaneros': 'Pot-smokers the world over recognize the taste of its product, known as Columbian Gold' (Theroux, 1979).

come to achieve a sexual orgasm
Of both sexes and a similar euphemism in French and German. Much use both spoken and written: '"I don't know why I let you come this evening," says Flora. "You haven't let me come," says Howard' (Bradbury, 1975). The alternative 'come off' is more of male than of female orgasms. 'Come' is also the fluid secreted by the male and the female respectively during copulation: '"It's Bernard Shaw's semen." . . . . "You mean it's come?" "Yes"' (Bradbury, 1976). There are three ob. phrases meaning to copulate which are probably not punning on the achievement of an orgasm – 'come about', a female use of a male copulating with her, stems from the meaning, to visit for a purpose; 'come over' puns on the attitude assumed by the male and his authority over his mistress: 'To have no man come over me' (Shakespeare, *Much Ado*); and 'come together' was a SE use, indicating physical proximity rather than simultaneous orgasms: 'When as his mother Mary was espoused to Joseph, before they came together, she was found with child by the Holy Ghost' (Matthew, 1 18). The ob. 'come aloft' was to have an erection of the penis: 'I cannot come aloft to an old woman' (Dryden, 1668).

come across (1) to do something unwillingly under coercion
Properly, to accede to a suggestion. In Am. use, of extortion or bribery: '. . . ask why he had to pay when the other bird didn't come across' (Lavine, 1930).

come across (2) to copulate extramaritally
Again from the meaning, to accede to a suggestion. Of a female usu. on a single occasion.

come across (3) to defect
Espionage jargon, from the actual or fig. passage of a frontier or line of battle: 'He's defected. He came across and that's that' (Seymour, 1980).

come again to resume your living physical state after death
An eagerly awaited expectation by some devout people, despite the manifest problems of space, etc.: 'He shall come again in His glory, to judge both the quick and the dead' (Common Prayer, 1662). 'Come back' in the same sense is ob.

come aloft *see* come

come around *see* come on (1)

come down etc. to cease to be under illicit narcotic influence
After the feeling of levitation: 'Floating. When she came down it was pretty grim' (Bogarde, 1981). Also of the unpleasantness and ill-temper which follow drug-taking. 'Come off', for such cessation, is now rare.

come home by Clapham *see* clap

come home feet first to be killed
Corpses are usu. carried that way round: 'Whoever came home feet first, it wasn't going to be him' (Fraser, 1977).

come in at the window etc. to be a bastard
The newcomer is fig. introduced into the household by any aperture other than the front door; following the window in popularity were the side door, the back door, the wicket or the hatch: 'In at the window or else o'er the hatch . . . I am I, howe'er I was begot' (Shakespeare, *King John*). A 'come o' will' was also a bastard – the will of God rather than the mother's: 'Little curlie Godfrey – that's the eldest, the come o' will' (W. Scott, 1815).

come into the public domain to cease being a secret
Of embarrassing or scandalous information which politicians or public employees wish to conceal: 'Naturally we are, all of us, in the Service, concerned that advice one has given could be misunderstood if it were to come into the public domain' (Lynn and Jay, 1986).

come off (1) *see* **come**

come off (2) *see* **come down** etc.

come on etc. (1) to menstruate
Obvious derivation and wide female use:
'Have you come on badly or something?' (P.
Scott, 1968 – one woman was asking another
about menstruation). The Am. 'come
around' is equally logically used in the same
way.

come on (2) a deceptive inducement to
enter into a long-term commitment
Advertising jargon for an offer intended to
tempt or trap the unwary: 'The electricity
bill, a come-on for *Time-Life* books . . .'
(Allbeury, 1980, listing the contents of mail).
A 'come-on' by a female is an act in a way
which implicitly invites a male to make a
sexual approach: '"Did she touch the young
guy? . . . . Stroke his hair. Put her hand on
his arm. Anything like that?" "You mean was
she coming on?"' (Sanders, 1981). Less
often of a male approach: 'He's come on to
me, you know. His own son's wife' (M.
Thomas, 1985).

come out to announce your availability as a
sexual partner
This was social jargon for the mainly
London parade of rich marriageable girls
before supposedly eligible bachelors: 'Girls
had to come out, I knew' (N. Mitford, 1949,
of that experience). Now widely used of
homosexual males revealing their tastes
publicly: 'The Bishops' group also says that
a homosexual who has "come out" should
offer his resignation to his bishop' (*Daily
Telegraph*, October 1979). Often in the fuller
form, 'come out of the closet' – *see* **closet**
(2): 'Lord Mountbatten was definitely Gay
himself though he never had the courage to
come out of the closet' (*Private Eye*, May
1981).

come over *see* **come**

come through to act under duress
From the meaning, to reach a goal. It is used
of paying a bribe, or responding in a desired
manner to such a payment; or of making any
payment or giving information under duress:
'They'll snatch your wife or take you out in
the woods and give you the works. And you'll
have to come through' (Chandler, 1939).

come to to copulate with
Particularly in marriage where the spouses
occupy separate beds: 'I have come very seldom to you in the last few years' (Bogarde,

1981, of a husband who seldom copulated
with his wife).

come to a sticky end (1) to fail disas-
trously but deservedly
The fate of an insect on fly paper. It may
describe an untimely death of a dissolute or
criminal person, the incarceration of a
rogue, an unwanted pregnancy of a flighty
girl, a woman's unhappy marriage especially
outside her social class, etc.

come to a sticky end (2) to masturbate
Of a male, from the ejaculation.

come to see to court
Properly, to visit, but a man who 'comes to
see' your sister is unlikely to content himself
merely with a visual inspection.

come to your resting place to die
The common likening of death to 'rest' in
the hope of resurrection, etc.: 'He drove me
direct to his bungalow and then to the resting place which she had come to just the day
before' (P. Scott, 1973). Some may prefer
the ob. Shetland Island 'come to yourself',
also to die, with it overtones of Buddhism: 'I
faer dis ane 'ill come ta himsel'' (*Shetland
News*, 1890, quoted in EDD).

come to your time to give birth to a child
Abbr. of 'time for birth'. SE but now perhaps ob.

come together *see* **come**

come up with the rations awarded for
no particular merit
Especially of Br. medals in wartime which
do not specify a specific act of gallantry, like
a DSO for a senior officer whose troops have
fought well. Now used of routine awards to
civil servants which excite resentment in the
less favoured sections of the population by
further debasing the discredited 'honours'
system.

come your mutton to masturbate
Of a male, from the sl. 'mutton', the penis.

comecon *see* **co-operate** (2)

comfort station a lavatory for public use
Of the same tendency as **comfortable** (1)
(q.v.): 'Ari habitually terminated the beach
section of his run by the comfort station
coyly labelled "Boys" and "Girls"' (L.
Thomas, 1979). In an Am. bus, where it lies
behind the back axle, it can be anything but
comfortable.

comfortable (1) having urinated
A genteel usage, often in the phrase 'make

yourself comfortable', sometimes shortened to 'comfy': 'She went in to make herself comfy; Sat on the seat and could not get her bum free' (Vulgar song – 'Three Old Ladies Locked in a Lavatory').

comfortable (2) drunk
From the feeling of well-being induced at some stage. Mainly Am.

comfortable (3) not in mortal danger
Hospital jargon, although a patient so described would seldom admit to being 'free from pain and trouble' (OED): '"Well, how is he?" "He is said to be comfortable." If so it must be the first occasion for weeks' (E. Waugh, 1955, of someone admitted to hospital). We can all sympathize with Mr Steve Wickwar, 27, who 'sustained severe cuts after being attacked by a two-year-old male leopard. . . . His condition at Northampton general hospital was said to be comfortable' (*Daily Telegraph*, April 1982 – but why not 'a leopard, 2'?).

commerce copulation
Properly, exchange or dealings between people but long used of copulation, especially if it is extra-marital. Explicitly as 'sexual commerce'; and 'sinful commerce' implies copulation with a whore: 'Jenny the tavern-girl was not alone in this world of sinful commerce' (Monsarrat, 1978, writing in archaic style). There is now also some homosexual use. A 'commercial gentleman' was a salesman or representative whose job entailed travel and absence from home, the mobility in the pre-motor age earning him and his job title a reputation for lechery. To avoid such stigma, the title changed over the years through 'traveller', 'agent' and 'representative' until they mostly came to call themselves 'managers'.

commission a bribe
Properly in this sense not the warrant to do something for another but a reward in percentage terms for doing it. Commercial jargon especially of dealing with corrupt or poor countries where you have to bribe officials to get orders but it is wise to throw a gloss of legality over the process: 'As for bribes . . . . this is a capitalist society, General. We prefer to talk about commissions and introducer's fees' (W. Smith, 1979).

commission agent a person who accepts bets for a living
He is neither an agent of those who place bets with him nor is he rewarded by the receipt of commission. The now SE use

seeks to mitigate the opprobrium which attaches to his work.

commit to consign to an institution for the insane
Properly, to give in charge, and clearly an abbr. of a longer phrase: 'Polly, you ought to commit your father' (McCarthy, 1963 – he was mad but at liberty).

commit a nuisance to urinate publicly other than in an urinal
Usu. of a male, where 'commit' means to perform and 'nuisance' is legal jargon for an offensive act: 'These are the same naughty young men who "Commit a Nuisance" . . . . Or it could be some old rustic twelve-pinter who is past caring' (Blythe, 1969). We now see the phrase on old signs, mainly in the negative, where we are abjured to 'commit no nuisance'.

committed dogmatic as to political or social views
Properly, devoted but you are often left to guess the object of the devotion: 'Committed to what? Abortion, Marxism or promiscuity? It's bound to be one of the three' (Sharpe, 1976). The word is used by bigots and enthusiasts of themselves but pejoratively of them by others.

Committee of State Security a Russian instrument of internal repression
The Komitat Gosudarstvenoi Bezopasnosti, or KGB. Sometimes abbr. to 'Committee': '"The Committee's involved," Suchko went on, using the standard euphemism for the KGB' (Moss, 1985). It is an indication of the confidence of the Russian autocracy that they have not recently seen a need to change the title as with the 'Cheka, Vcheka, GPU, OGPU, NKVD, MGB, several of which have been bywords for brutality' (FDMT). The Cuban 'Committee for the Protection of the Revolution' is a neighbourhood system of spying on local inhabitants, in the style of the Nazi 'Blockwächter'.

commode a portable lavatory
Properly, and until 18c. no more than a chest of drawers, which many of them were designed to look like: 'An ice-box built in a Marie-Antoinette commode' (Ustinov, 1971, shocked by the vulgarity). Dr Johnson, with Grose, says 'The head-dress of women'.

commodious too large
Properly, convenient but in real estate jargon, where we might have expected elegant

spaciousness, all we find is a place too big to heat or keep in repair.

common ground   a policy favoured by civil servants

Bureaucratic jargon, especially if a policy is being persisted in contrary to what the government wants or thinks is operative: 'In order to guide the Minister towards the common ground, key words should be inserted with a proposal to make it attractive' (Lynn and Jay, 1981).

common house   a lavatory

'Common' from the sharing. They were, and rarely still may be, used by the inhabitants of a row of terraced houses. In ob. use it was a brothel: 'Do nothing but use their abuses in common houses' (Shakespeare, *Measure for Measure*) and a 'common' customer, jack, maid, sewer, tart, etc. was a whore: 'I think thee now some common customer' (Shakespeare, *All's Well*). Shakespeare's 'commoner o' th' camp' was also a whore.

communicable disease   a venereal disease

The method of communication in lay use has to be sexual, which excludes measles, mumps, chickenpox, etc.

communication *see* **comprehension**

community affairs etc.   tension between Black and White people

Social service jargon seeking to avoid reference to skin pigmentation, which has come into common use. Used in various phrases associated with the distrust, jealousy, fear and antagonism which are present when Black and White people move into each other's territory. Thus a 'community affairs correspondent' exists because of and writes about discord between Black and White people. 'Community relations' has much the same use.

community alienation   lawlessness

Social service jargon to avoid blaming anti-social behaviour – it does not mean that the place is full of foreigners: 'The village now exhibits the signs of this community alienation with its smashed telephone kiosks, litter and graffiti painted on its mellow walls' (*Thatch*, March 1982). In Am. the vandals might be sent to a 'Community Treatment Centre', a prison and not a doctor's surgery.

companion   a paid partner for a homosexual

Of either sex, from the proper use of paying a person of your own sex to keep you company: 'I'm thinking of getting a new companion. There's a little actress on the train who would suit me' (G. Greene, 1932 – a female homosexual was speaking). But cf. **constant companion**.

companion spaces   adjoining lockers in a permanent store for corpses

Am. funeral jargon, especially when trying to sell graves to the living: 'Cosy "companion spaces" for occupancy by husband and wife' (J. Mitford, 1963).

company (1)   a person with whom you copulate extra-maritally

Properly, companionship. In Am. use, often of a transient relationship: 'And your wife on the outside, looking around for company' (Sanders, 1977).

company (2)   The main US organization for espionage and foreign subversion

A pun on the initial letters of 'Central Intelligence Agency' and the Spanish abbr. for company – 'c(ompagn)ia': 'Your outrageous statement that we intend to commit bodily harm tarnishes our friends in the Company' (Ludlum, 1979, of the organization).

comparable   equalling in strict monetary terms

The jargon of wage negotiations especially where the claimant enjoys the security of employment by the State. You try to obtain the level of wages paid to those in more demanding and less secure jobs (if not lower than your own) but do not agree to give credit for the various pension and holiday concessions special to government etc. service. Because Am. employers obliged by law to pay women at male rates sometimes presume to ask for the same performance from both sexes even where one may suffer physical disadvantage, negotiators on behalf of women may demand 'comparability' rather than equality.

completion   a sexual orgasm

Usu. of the female, whether final or not: 'In thanks, he summoned up a patient rigidity which brought her to six vast, grunting completions before she subsided into sleep' (M. Thomas, 1980).

complications   the swelling of an adult's testicles during mumps

This symptom, additional in some cases to a swelling of glands in the neck, is very painful and may lead to infertility: 'Measles without complications at nine and mumps when he was still too young for complications at ten' (Price, 1972).

complimentary included in the price
Often the usage seeks to mask an inconvenient substitution for a discontinued service, like a paper strip to clean your shoes in
place of a night porter. An irritating concept
but 'we will shortly take your beverage order.
The wine in your basket is complimentary'
(Republic Airlines Flight RC 207,
Greenville/New York, May 1981) was an
exception.

compound to copulate with
Properly, to mingle: 'My father compounded
with my mother under the dragon's tail'
(Shakespeare, *King Lear*). ob.

comprehension the abilty to read
Br. educational jargon, especially of children
who have not mastered (or 'missed'?) the
'three R's' after twelve years' schooling.
They may then be sent to other educational
establishments to be taught 'comprehension'
or reading; 'communication' or writing; and
'numeracy' or arithmetic. Or, as a variant:
'MID GLAMORGAN ADULT
LITERACY/NUMERACY SERVICE For
help with: READING SPELLING
ARITHMETIC' (Advertisement in
Rhymney Valley Express, noted in *Private Eye*,
October 1981).

comprehensive offering non-selective
entry
Of Br. schools which are not necessarily
'characterized by comprehension' or 'intensive' (SOD). Indeed '46 per cent of children
now leaving Mrs Williams' "comprehensive" secondary school system (are) unable
to read or write' (A. Waugh, *Private Eye*, July
1981 – however suspect Mr Waugh's statistics, many regret the destruction of the
selective entry to Grammar School and the
consequent polarization into those children
who receive adequate education in fee-
paying schools and those who don't in free
schools, a circumstance which has led to his
son and one of mine finding themselves in
the same class).

compromise (1) to involve in extra-
marital copulation
Of a man it formerly meant to be caught
acting dishonourably. Now usu. of a female:
'He began to fiddle with his clothes . . . . is
he going to do it here, in public, to compromise me?' (Bradbury, 1959).

compromise (2) to kill
The language of espionage and those who
fantasize about it: 'He was killed – and he
was killed – because whatever that woman

told him was so conclusive he had to be
compromised hours later' (Ludlum, 1984).

comrade a fellow Communist
From the sharing of a 'camera' or bed-
chamber, by Spanish soldiers. Grose gives it
as 'cambrade', of the same derivation, and
'generally used to signify companion'.

con to trick
Not relating to the path of a ship or 'set in a
notebook, learned, and conned by rote', but
an abbr. of 'confidence': 'Most of the people
you meet will be out to con you' (Sanders,
1980). 'Confidence' in this derogatory sense
was first used in 1866 of the advisers of the
Confederate President Davis. A 'con'-man
or -artist is a person who so tries to obtain by
deceit: 'Don't pull that con artist crap with
me, pal. I've seen you working this street for
three days' (Weverka, 1973).

concentration camp a place for arbitrary
imprisonment of political opponents, etc.
They were originally the areas in which
civilians were concentrated by the Spanish in
Cuba and the British in S. Africa to prevent
the feeding and hiding of men engaged in
fighting against them. The Nazis adopted
the tactic and the terminology (Konzen-
trationslager) but their prisons which started
as places for extortion, ransom and humiliation become depots for slave labour, starvation and extermination: 'There are not only
prisons now, there are concentration camps'
(Manning, 1962, of WW II). Also abbr. to
'camp': '. . . three-fifths of them had disappeared into camps that used the new
scientific methods . . . . They had an official
name – Vernichtungslager, extermination
camp' (Keneally, 1982, of Polish Jews in
WW II).

concentration problem (a) idleness
Educational jargon among those for whom
there are no lazy or stupid children: 'You
clearly have a concentration problem, "are
an idle bitch", and I was wondering . . .'
(Amis, 1978).

concern political dogmatism
Properly, care or interest: '. . . pressing agent
in the Claimants' Union, a focus of responsibility and concern' (Bradbury, 1975). In
the same sense 'concerned' means dogmatic:
'This kind of decent, modest radicalism . . . .
was a perpetuation of the concerned student
politics' (Bradbury, 1965). Much pejorative
use and cf. **committed**. The ob. Br. 'concerned' merely meant drunk, and was probably an abbr. of 'concerned in liquor': 'He

never call'd me worse than sweetheart, drunk or sober, Not that I knew his Reverence was ever concern'd' (Swift, 1723).

concert party the concerted buying of shares in a company in different names
Stock Exchange jargon where an attempt is made to build up a key or powerful holding without putting on notice the Board of the Company or the Stock Exchange.

concessional free or subsidized
The use tries to mask the granting of a privilege or charity both to individuals ('concessional' fares for old people) or to countries ('concessional' exports of food etc.).

concrete shoes murdered and hidden
A more accurate version of **cement shoes** (q.v.): '. . . it's tough to play golf in concrete shoes. *Comprende?*' (M. Thomas, 1980). Mainly Am.

condition (1) an illness
Properly, any prevailing circumstances but in matters of health any 'condition' is bad, be it of the heart, bladder, liver or whatever: 'Throughout the aircraft, the old, then those with pre-existing medical conditions, began to die' (Block, 1980).

condition (2) a pregnancy
This usage is not reserved for unwanted or difficult pregnancies and merely avoids direct reference to the taboo: 'Naturally, Melinda did not mention her condition' (Boyle, 1979 – Melinda Marling was pregnant by the spy Donald McLean before their marriage). In cases of pregnancy, 'conditions' are also described as 'certain', 'delicate' and 'interesting', these adjectives being descriptive of the woman's 'situation' or 'state of health'.

confederation a pressure group
Properly, any action jointly undertaken between states. The 'Confederation of British Industry' exists to further the interests of employers, managers and, to a much lesser extent, shareholders; the 'Confederation for the Advancement of State Education' strives not to improve the quality of teaching in state schools but to eradicate private schools; etc.

conference a period in which you wish to avoid callers
The excuse of businessmen and their secretaries, the evader being 'in conference': 'Ah'm afraid Miss Brimley is in conference. Can someone else answer your query?' (le Carré, 1962). The 'formal meeting for con-

sultation or discussion' (SOD) is where we go when we are 'at a conference'.

confinement the period of childbirth
Properly, no more than the fact of being shut up, as in prison: 'The women continue working down to the day of their confinement' (Mayhew, 1851, of childbirth). This SE development replaced 'bond', which used the same imagery. 'Confined' means the act of giving birth, having lost its 19c. meaning, constipated.

conflict a war
Properly, a strong disagreement or a single battle. But it sounds better than 'war', especially when the Korean 'conflict' burst upon us in 1950, so soon after WW II.

confrontation a war
Properly, a meeting face-to-face. Indonesia's 1963 attack on Malaysia was so described but limited to local armed raids and subversion. By the time of Vietnam, it meant that kind of war. Now also used by terrorists of their violence when war is waged indiscriminately against society: 'Well for one thing we haven't ruled out the possibility of confrontation' (Theroux, 1976 – terrorists were discussing tactics).

confused drunk
It certainly can take you that way: 'I gather our son was very confused *that* night; which is a mother's way of saying he was plastered' (Ludlum, 1979).

congress copulation
Properly, a coming together, as in the 'Congress System' established by the victors over Napoleon's France: 'I had heard precisely how that acrobatic quartet achieved congress' (Fowles, 1977 – four people were copulating). In modern use you normally find the prefixes 'sexual' or 'male': 'She's been repeatedly raped, both by male congress and by instruments' (West, 1979).

conjugal rights copulation with an unwilling wife
Legal jargon for marital copulation. 'Conjugal' means yoked together and in some societies the placing of a symbolic double yoke formed part of the marriage ceremony. A woman seldom seeks these 'rights' from her husband, except in satire: 'Wilt had enough troubles with his own virility without having Eva demand that her conjugal rights be supplemented oralwise' (Sharpe, 1976). A woman who applies to the Court for the 'restoration of the conjugal rights' seeks pecuniary rather than physical gratification.

conk (out) to die
From the unplanned stoppage of an engine
and the end of the movement: 'Jassy and
Victoria will scream with laughter when I
finally do conk out' (N. Mitford, 1949). The
Am. 'conk' is rarer: '. . . the paintings would
automatically increase in value once Maitland had conked' (Sanders, 1977 – Maitland
was an artist).

connect (1) to copulate
The imagery is from joining or fastening
together: '. . . two beautifully engraved
figures of man and woman who were con-
necting at every tick of the clock' (Richards,
1936). 'Connection' is usu. extra-marital
copulation: 'Privates in the Blues . . . . often
formed very reprehensible connections with
women of property, tradesmen's wives, and
even ladies' (Mayhew, 1862) and: 'Of
course, there had been no connection' (Harris, 1925, writing, unusually for him, of an
absence of copulation). To 'have connection
with' is to copulate with extra-maritally: '. . .
the gentleman had connection with me'
(ibid. – obviously no more a 'gentleman'
than were Mayhew's 'ladies' above).

connect (2) to find a source of illegal narcotics
The reference is probably to joining the
chain of distribution, or 'connection', which
in the jargon runs from manufacturer to
retailer.

connection see connect (1) (2)

connections people susceptible to bribery
Properly, people to whom you are related or
know well, with an inference that they are
influential: '. . . the redoubtable lady was
able first to defraud the public and then to
evade the consequences because she had
"connections"' (Shirer, 1984, and not of a
whore).

connubial pleasures copulation
Although 'connubial' means to do with marriage, the 'pleasures' can be taken by either
party within or without that institution: 'She
never married , but it didn't prevent her
from enjoying connubial pleasures'
(Ludlum, 1979).

conquer a bed to copulate extra-maritally
with its usual occupant
Of a male and see bed (2): 'When you have
conquer'd yet my maiden bed' (Shakespeare, All's Well). ob.

consenting adults male homosexuals
aged over 18 who engage in a physical sexual
act with each other

Br. legal jargon: 'Two consenting adults had
been ejected from the Gents' (Sharpe, 1975
– they were not 'consenting' to the ejection).
The former Br. stringent but largely unenforceable laws against overt expressions and
even private acts of male homosexuality have
been amended to permit almost any private
behaviour so long as minors are not involved.
The same laws never applied to female
homosexuality, reputedly because Queen
Victoria thought there was no such thing.

console to copulate with extra-maritally
Properly, to alleviate sorrow and it is used of
either sex, especially when a regular sexual
partner is absent: 'Another girl of similar
type, who had briefly consoled him in
France' (Boyle, 1979, of Philby). 'Consolation' is such copulation: 'Men whose wives
were sent out of harm's way were quick to
find consolation' (Manning, 1977, of
WW II).

consort with to copulate with extra-
maritally
A 'consort' is someone who keeps you company: 'Some of them consorted with – with
the worst type of native woman' (Fraser,
1975).

constant companion a person with
whom you are seen publicly and regularly
copulate extra-maritally
Journalistic jargon, when a public figure
might sue for defamation if the relationship
were spelt out: 'Miss Kristina Olsen, his
close friend and constant companion'
(Allbeury, 1975, of such an arrangement).
'Constant companions' means both parties
to such an arrangement, especially used
when both are public figures.

constructed brought to submission by
force or intimidation
The jargon of Vietnam: 'A "constructed"
hamlet meant not a newly built one but a
former Viet Cong hamlet that had been
worked over politically' (McCarthy, 1967). It
was 'reconstructed' if it had changed hands
three times, with intervening Viet Cong
control.

consultancy the humouring of a dismissed employee
A business practice for an unwanted senior
employee, to speed his departure, avoid
recrimination, ease his tax position, save his
face, protect trade secrets etc. A 'consultant'
is so treated.

consultant (1) see consultancy

consultant (2) A dispenser of bribes
Like medical doctors, many tradesmen
wanting to move up-market call themselves
'consultants' in whatever skill or product
they are trying to peddle. In the export of
arms, aircraft and expensive capital equipment to poor or corrupt countries, not
excluding Japan or Holland, prime ministers
or princes, the local 'consultant' protects the
vendor by arranging the bribery and paying it
out of his 'fee'. If a prince or prime minister
is among the bribed, he may call himself a
'consultant' too.

consulting Mrs Jones urinating
An Am. excuse, explaining the absence of a
third party. I have no clue as to the
etymology.

(consumer a buyer at retail has passed from
sociological jargon into general use and
avoids nasty capitalist notions of buying and
selling. You will remain a 'consumer', however much you waste or throw away.)

consummate to copulate with
Properly, to accomplish to the full. 'Con-
summation' is one of the essential
ingredients of a Christian marriage, in
default of which a Court will on request
grant an annulment. To 'consummate a
relationship' is to copulate extra-maritally: 'I
have had to learn (self-control). She has
refused to consummate our relationship'
(Townsend, 1982, of unmarried sweethearts). To 'consummate your desires'
implies less discrimination in the choice of
an extra-marital partner and is usu. of men,
but: '. . . there is a house in Regent Street, I
am told, where ladies, both married and
unmarried, go in order to . . . . consummate
their libidinous desires' (Mayhew 1862).

consumption pulmonary tuberculosis
Prior to penicillin, the dread and often fatal
disease which wasted away, or 'consumed'
the sufferer: 'The girl had died also since
then. Consumption devoured her'
(Keneally, 1979, of the 19c.). As 'consumption' became explicit, 'TB' – for tuber-
cule bacillus – became the favoured evasion
and so remained until the incidence of the
disease virtually vanished. Meanwhile N.
Europeans had evolved a defensive mechanism genetically, whereby an attacked lung
secreted moisture to isolate the tubercular
attack, and that today, unaware of the advent
of penicillin, makes them uniquely prone to
emphysema.

contact with to copulate with
From the touching but in this use the male is

the only one to do it, despite the mutuality of
the encounter: '. . . he would need . . . . to
augment his size and permanence by food,
booze, contact with a woman' (Keneally,
1982).

contagious and disgraceful disease a
venereal disease
Legal jargon in the Eng. law of slander. If
you wrongly imputed it in another, the plain-
tiff had no need to prove special damage.
Women had further protection which was
withheld from men; the Slander of Women
Act of 1891 made an imputation of unchastity by a woman actionable without proof of
special damage, but a man could not sue
successfully without such proof.

content kept involuntarily under heavy
sedation
Medical jargon: '. . . the few violent cases we
have are kept pretty, uh, content' (Sanders,
1979, of an institution for the insane).

content your desire to copulate
Normally of extra-marital copulation by
either sex: 'It was the Doctor who undertook
to content her desire' (Harris, 1925).

continent see **incontinent**

continuations trousers
They 'continued' a Victorian male's
waistcoat in a direction too delicate to mention. And see **unmentionables etc.** for more
of these quaint ob. uses.

contour a fat shape
Properly, the outline of any figure but jargon
for those who sell clothes, exercise equipment or dietary foods to the obese. To
'reduce your contour' is to slim or become
thinner.

contract (1) a bribe
Used of Am. payments to politicians, the
police, etc. in an attempt to put a gloss of
legality on the transaction.

contract (2) the hiring of a killer
Underworld jargon for a murder treated as a
commercial transaction: 'There's a contract
out on Billson and he's still alive' (Bagley,
1978 – the inference is that he should be
dead). To 'put out a contract' is to arrange a
specific murder. The 'contract' may also be
the potential victim: 'I want you to know that
you could become a contract' (Deighton,
1981).

contribution (1) a quantity of urine
Medical coyness when asking a patient to
urinate for analysis: '"The usual contribu-

tion, please," she said motioning towards the lavatory door' (Sanders, 1981).

contribution (2) a bribe
Paid, usu. from corporate funds, to secure either favours for an individual (e.g. a knighthood in BI) or privileged treatment for the corporation from government.

control unit a cell for solitary confinement
It is, I suppose, one way of 'controlling' a violent Am. prisoner.

controlled economy an oligarchic or bureaucratic tyranny
The jargon of Marxism where the work and earnings of all are decided by ministers and imposed by the bureaucracy. The resulting inefficiencies and relative poverty avoid the creation of an independent middle class, ever the cradle of effective revolt against despotism.

controlled substance a narcotic
So called because its legal manufacture and distribution is regulated and supervised. But the illegal market is uncontrollable.

(controller a senior accountant is an example of the arrogation to a lower function of the title to a higher. He used to be the person who checked on the person who kept the books.)

controversial politically damaging
Bureaucratic Whitehall jargon, mainly to be used when deflecting a politician from a course which a civil servant does not like: '"Controversial" only means "this will lose you votes". "Courageous" means "this will lose you the election"' (Lynn and Jay, 1981).

convalescent home *see* **rest home**

convenience (1) a lavatory for public use
Properly, anything which accommodates. Often specifically described as 'public', 'men's', 'ladies', etc. or merely in the plural: '. . . another tin outhouse with a sign saying Conveniences' (Theroux, 1983, of a lavatory on a camp site).

convenience (2) *see* **for your convenience**

convenient tiny
Real estate jargon, usu. when describing a garden manifestly inconvenient for drying washing, private subnbathing, lighting bonfires, growing vegetables, etc. In ob. Eng. use a 'convenient' was a whore who restricted her clientele, in some cases down to one regular customer.

conventional not involving nuclear or germ warfare
There is something bizarre in the notion that any weapons for killing or maiming are sanctioned by general agreement or established by social custom.

conversation *see* **criminal conversation**

convey steal
From the carrying off of the article taken: 'Conveyors are ye all, That rise thus nimbly by a true king's fall' (Shakespeare, *Richard II*). A 'conveyor' was a thief, 'conveyance' was theft and 'conveyancing' swindling, this usage long pre-dating the exorbitant fees charged by lawyers for the simple process of transferring title to real estate. ob.

convince to compel by force
Underworld and police sl.: 'He knew exactly what methods Willi Kleiber would use to "convince" Colonel Pitman to open the safe' (Deighton, 1981).

cook (1) to kill
I think not from culinary imagery, even as an abbr. of 'cook your goose', to cause to fail. Perhaps from execution by electricity: 'Those fucking sketches could cook him if we found the girl' (Sanders, 1977). Also of stock in a hot drought-ridden country: 'A drought . . . . would cook half the stock in the country' (Boldrewood, 1890).

cook (2) fraudulently to alter
Usu. as 'cook the books', dishonestly to revise accounts, from the culinary art of re-arranging ingredients to make a more acceptable dish. The phrase was first used of George Hudson, the Br. 19c. 'Railway King'. Trained as a draper, he founded a bank, promoted railway companies, introduced a 'clearing' system for shared services, became Chairman of the Midland Railway, was elected to parliament, had a hand in the construction of a fifth of the Br. rail system, overreached himself, falsified accounts to pay dividends out of capital, was sent to prison for debt and died in 1871 in comparative poverty.

cook (3) an opium addict
From the act of preparing opium over a flame. Now in Am. of anyone illegally preparing a narcotic for injection through the application of heat.

cooked drunk
The common Am. culinary imagery.

cookie *see* **new cookie**

cookie pusher a male employee who cur-
ries favour with his boss
From a man handing round the cakes at a
function largely attended by women and
owing nothing to the ob. 'cookie', cocaine:
'. . . do you see that furry-headed little
cookie-pusher Brittan is having the foun-
tains in Trafalgar Square drained for New
Year's Eve?' (*Private Eye*, December 1983, of
the Br. Home Secretary). Also used
generally of male homosexuals.

cool (1) to kill or to die
The common imagery of loss of body heat:
'. . . if the old lady hadn't been cool for a
month even, the will certainly wouldn't have
been proven' (Lyall, 1969).

cool (2) not carrying illegal narcotics when
searched
The reverse of **hot** (2) (q.v.) and perhaps
owing something to the meaning, poised and
unruffled.

cooler (1) a prison
Common imagery for the place where you
are sent to 'cool down': 'We could be put in
the cooler for these' (Theroux, 1973).

cooler (2) an intoxicant which is diluted
and served in a large glass.
Normally with ice in it. It is intended to cool
you down.

coop a prison
In this case, for humans and not for hens or
rabbits: '"No convictions, but prints on
file." "Been in the coop"' (Chandler, 1958).
Am. and perhaps ob.

(cop (1) to catch or seize is found in many
uses where it was interchangeable with those
words. Thus it meant to steal: 'I was taken by
two pals to an orchard to cop some fruit'
(Horsley, 1887) and in the same sense the
modern 'cop a cherry' is to copulate with a
female virgin. To 'cop it' is to die: 'I was
really really lucky. A lot of my mates copped
it' (Manning, 1977, of WW II). To 'cop a
packet' has the meaning of **catch a packet**
(q.v.). 'Cop the drop' is to accept a bribe;
'cop the bullet' is to be dismissed from
employment – *see* **bullet**; etc.)

cop (2) a policeman
He 'cops' or seizes you, and is also an abbr.
of **copper** (q.v.): 'The fuzz – that's what they
call them now, not cops any more' (Ustinov,
1971). A 'cop' shop or house is a police
station: 'I have to go to the cop house just
about now' (Chandler, 1958). I think 'cop', a

prison, is ob.: 'I saw a policeman taking two
men to cop' (EDD c.1900).

cop (3) to obtain illegal narcotics
Through buying, stealing or howsoever. Am.

cop a cherry *see* **cop** (1)

cop an elephant's *see* **elephant's**

cop it *see* **cop** (1)

cop out to plead guilty to a minor offence
among several
Part of the Am. process of plea-bargaining,
in return for which the prosecution does not
proceed with other serious charges. In rare
Br. use 'cop out' also means to die.

cop the drop *see* **cop** (1)

copper a policeman
It is always said, from the metal buttons on
their 19c. uniforms but see **cop** (2) for an
attractive alternative etymology: 'An' up
comes a bleedn' rozzer an' lumbers me. Wot
a life! Coppers' (Kersh, 1936).

copulate to fuck
Originally, to link together whence to
become joined together, from which the
common 'joined' imagery of fucking. As it is
explicit in SE and less jarring than 'fuck', I
use the word, along with 'copulation',
throughout this dictionary.

cordial (1) an intoxicant
Originally any food or drink which comforted the person who ingested it: '. . . make
invitation the one to the other for pipes and
foreign cordials' (Blackmore, 1869). In
modern use, the drink so described, like
'lime juice', is calculated to please but not
necessarily intoxicating.

cordial (2) cold and unfriendly
Diplomatic jargon which indicates the
opposite of the correct meaning, warm and
friendly.

cordless massager a masturbating
machine
It is shaped like a penis and used as a
vibrating dildo. A more explicit, and also
euphemistic, name for it is 'vibrator'.

corked drunk
Precisely what a 'corked' bottle of wine
should not be. The Am. imagery is unclear.

corn (1) low quality whisky
From the raw material, and often home-
made. In many compounds, as 'corn'-juice,
-mule, -waters, etc.: 'Various sorts of distilled spirits, particularly one named Corn-

waters' (Hibbert, 1822). 'Corned', drunk, may also come from drinking too much 'corn' although a more likely etymology is from the old meaning 'pickled', particularly as the use has recurred at various times since the 18c. in Am., Eng. and Sc.

corn (2) copulation with a woman
From the food a horse likes best and regularly. Usu. of extra-marital copulation. The ob. 'cornification', lust, comes from the Latin 'cornus', a horn.

corned *see* **corn** (1)

corner (1) to establish a monopoly in a product
Probably from driving cattle into the corner of a yard rather than from storing in a hidden place. The Br. criminal 'corner' means to sell shoddy goods at above their worth by persuading greedy buyers that they are stolen or in short supply.

corner (2) a urinal
Male use, from the facility to urinate in an open space so long as the penis is concealed: 'Oh, I'm so sorry, I was looking for a corner' (Olivier, 1982, quoting Churchill who entered a theatre dressing-room in 1951).

corner (3) a penis
Seen sexually, as in one phrase, 'get your corner in', to copulate: '. . . if he did get his corner into a nice mine wife' (Keneally, 1979, of the Chairman of a 19c. Am. miners' Benevolent Fund).

coronary inefficiency a weak heart
Medical jargon which borders on mere circumlocution or pomposity: 'A coronary inefficiency had made it necessary for Robert Winthrop to use a wheelchair' (Ludlum, 1979).

coroners the financial managers in film production
Properly, officers whose duty it is to guard the property of the Crown but better known for their inquests on corpses. Entertainment dysphemism, from their power to kill a production or, by cutting the budget, impair its artistic merit: 'The Coroners, whenever I met them, actually put their arms affectionately around my shoulders' (Bogarde, 1978, of film production).

corporal and four *see* **mount a corporal and four**

correct the unswerving acceptance of current party policy
Properly, adhering to high moral standards.

Nazi and Communist jargon: 'To ensure that political affairs would be handled correctly in an emergency' (Goebbels, 1945, in tr.) and: 'From the correct point of view there are no contradictions' (M.C. Smith, 1981, of Russian policy).

correction (1) a serious fall
Stock Exchange jargon of tumbling prices, which seeks to imply that they had previously risen too high: '. . . there were sufficient signs on the horizon to indicate that some major correction – for which read "collapse" – is called for ' (M. Thomas, 1982).

correction (2) *see* **house of correction** etc.

correctional prison
From the theory that convicts are there to be taught better ways. Thus the Am. 'correctional facility' is a prison, a 'correctional officer' is a gaoler, etc.

corrective training political imprisonment
The implication of this Communist jargon is that the prisoner is being taught the right way: 'Those who said that . . . . underwent corrective training that proved fatal in most cases' (Amis, 1980). Similarly, a Russian 'Correctional Labour Colony' – or 'Camp' – is a prison where the inmates are cowed by remoteness, poor food, overwork, the cold and generally inhumane treatment, the whole controlled by the Glavnoe Upravlenie Ispravi-telno-trudovikh lagerei, or 'Gulag'.

correspondent *see* **co-respondent**

corrupt to copulate with extra-maritally
Properly, to spoil, and in literary use it is the male who does this kind of spoiling: 'Angelo had never the purpose to corrupt her' (Shakespeare, *Othello*). The word is now rightly used of any conduct which leads another astray.

cosa nostra the Mafia
'Our thing' to the gangsters from Sicily and their adherents. Unhappily they too often share it with others. Whatever its other defects, Neaman & Silver (1982) include a comprehensive list of Mafia jargon, in their 'Thesaurus' (Am.) or 'Dictionary' (Br.) of Euphemisms.

costume wedding the marriage of a pregnant bride
Her physical indications rather than remorse at the pre-marital loss of virginity may inhibit the wearing of the traditional white gown. Cheshire.

cotton a female's pubic hair
From the fluffy appearance of the bush. It need not be white. Am.

cottonwood related to death by hanging
From the prevalence and convenience of the tree in those Am. areas which needed ad hoc gallows. Thus if you 'decorated a cotton-wood tree' or 'looked through cottonwood leaves', you were killed by hanging.

cough as a criminal to give information to the police
A common variant of the 'singing' theme, which includes making a confession of your own guilt: 'I could go up to Grosvenor Square and cough it all' (Theroux, 1976, of a threat so to give information). 'Cough syrup' is a bribe to prevent such revelations or like 'cough medicine', a humorous expression for a spirituous intoxicant.

counsellor a psychiatrist
Properly, anyone offering advice: '"I wish you'd take my advice and see a counsellor." "Everyone wants me to see a shrink!" she burst out' (Sanders, 1981). This Am. usage seeks to avoid an implication of mental instability, as most attorneys also call themselves 'counsellors'.

count (the) death
Boxing imagery and the 'long count', though rarer, shows greater knowledge of the sport. To 'put out for the count', again from boxing, is to make unconscious and usu. not to kill. The Am. 'count the daisies' is to be dead, the sums being done from the roots upwards.

counterattack an unprovoked aggression
There is no longer the prior requisite of an attack to counter: 'Thus did the Nazi dictator and his cohorts in Berlin see the German "counterattack" on Poland become a European war' (Shirer, 1984, of the invasion of Poland in 1939).

counter-force capability etc. the ability to hit both civilian and military targets with nuclear bombs
The language of the Pentagon; in a saner world it might mean how well you can push a loaded wheelbarrow up a slope. 'Counter-value capability' is the ability to hit civilian targets only, in either event using a 'counter-force weapon', or nuclear bomb.

counter-insurgency waging war in another country
The 'insurgents' are the native inhabitants who want to establish their own administra-tion in place of one imposed by those who use this phrase, like the French in Algeria, the Americans in Vietman and the British in various places: 'Kennedy men revealed the need for brand-new tactics with brand-new names: counter-insurgency, special warfare' (McCarthy, 1967).

counter-revolution any opposition to a Communist government
This Communist jargon is applied to the concept of free trade unions, secret suffrage, an absence of censorship, the availability of copying machines, private ownership of a typewriter, listening to foreign broadcasts, etc. The only authentic revolution is the one which brought power to the Communists.

country not reconstituted
The language of the coffee shop(pe): 'Your choice of three crisp slices of bacon . . . . served with one large country egg' (Am. Holiday Inn menu, May 1981 – in fact the short-order cook 'chose' the slices for me. The same menu offered an omelet with my 'favorite' filling, making two rash assump-tions – that I favour one particular filling and that they would be able to serve it if I decided to order it).

country club girls whores operating out of town
When the law closed the New Orleans brothels in 1917 as part of the war effort, many of the whores moved to country clubs out of town: 'The country-club girls are ruining my business' (Longstreet, 1956, of a city operator).

country Joe a local policeman
'Joe' is the name often given to someone considered simple. Am. CB sl.

country pay payment other than in cash
A travelling teacher or craftsman in 18c. New England might expect to be paid in goods and services in the primitive rural economy: 'My pay would be "country pay", that is, payment in kind' (Graves, 1941, writing of that period). ob.

(county snobbish, is pejorative rather than euphemistic. In 19c. Eng. it meant those inhabitants of a Shire of similar wealth and standing who formed its aristocracy based on landowning. Improved communications and the redistribution of wealth have destroyed the power base and the snobbery survives only among the more stupid of the sur-vivors.)

couple to copulate with extra-maritally
Its standard meaning is to marry of humans, to copulate of animals: 'Thou hast coupled this Hindoo slut' (Fraser, 1975). 'Couple with' is more common: 'Only ten minutes ago she had been coupling with me on the bed' (Fraser, 1969). In ob. use a 'coupling house' was a brothel.

courses menstruation
From the meaning, a period of time: 'I had my courses, my flowers' (Fowles, 1985, of a woman denying that she had been pregnant). ? ob.

courtesan a whore
In 15c. it referred to someone at court but the derivation is more likely from the Italian 'cortigiana', despite the morals and opportunities of Tudor courtiers: 'He regularly visited a famous courtesan in the Srinagar bazaar, and enjoyed other favours too' (Masters, 1976). SE.

courtesy included in the price
From the meaning, given freely; but the 'courtesy coach' takes you to an inaccessible hotel which you would not have used without it. cf. **complimentary**.

cousin cis a drunken carouse
Br. rh. sl. for 'piss' which, in the expression 'piss-up', has the same meaning. DRS says 'sis', I think wrongly.

cousin John *see* john (1)

Covent Garden ancillary to whoring
The London district, with the neighbouring Drury Lane, was a 17c. centre of prostitution. As 'Covent' is a corruption of convent, there were many ecclesiastical puns and witticisms. Thus a 'Covent Garden abbess' kept a brothel, or 'garden house', which contained 'Covent Garden goddesses'. They often infected their customers with 'Covent Garden ague' or 'garden gout', venereal disease, who were then said to have 'broken their shins against Covent Garden rails'. ob.

cover (1) to copulate with
SE of stallions, from the mounting of the mare, but rarely of humans: 'He'll ask you why you did it. "Because your overseer's covering 'em," you'll say, using a lady-like term' (Fraser, 1971 – the overseer was copulating with the Black slaves). In Coverdale and the Geneva Bible, to 'cover your feet' was to urinate, being a direct translation from the Hebrew.

cover (2) to dye
Mainly of men's hair. A 1983 advertisement for dye described it as 'covering grey hair'.

cover story a lie
Espionage jargon but also used by errant husbands etc. The story tries to 'cover' up the truth whence 'cover-up', an attempt wrongly to conceal by deceit.

covert act any illegal behaviour
Espionage jargon. 'Covert' means hidden or secret: '"Do you mean acts of sabotage?" "Er . . . could I just say 'covert acts'?"' (Lyall, 1985).

cow to kill in an open or sensational way
This may be a pun on 'cowboy' (which indicates a reckless or aggressive manner in any activity) and the proper meaning, to subdue by threats. The superb Am. 'cow brute', used by those who thought a bull too overtly sexual to mention, is unhappily ob.

crabs syphilis
Properly, an abbr. of 'crab-lice', which favour pubic hair, and therefore medically inexact. Am.

crack to rob
Either by forcible entry of a building or by opening a safe. The use far predates 'crack', the instantly addictive form of heroin. A 'cracksman' specializes in safe-breaking.

crack a bottle to drink intoxicants
Perhaps the very impatient may break the neck to get at the contents more quickly but the phrase is used of any wine drinking.

crack a Jane etc. to copulate extra-maritally wtih a female virgin
From **crack** (above), to rob, or from 'cracking' a problem? A Briton speaks of 'cracking' a 'doll' or 'Judy'. The ob. Br. phrases for the same achievement, to 'crack a pitcher' or 'pipkin' showed more imagination; both the pieces of pottery would remain serviceable after the 'cracking', but not as desirable as those without blemish.

crack your whip to copulate extra-maritally
Of a male, punning, I suppose, on the mastery of an animal trainer and the 'whip' or penis: 'She was crazy for me to get her that guy who wrote about cracking his whip all the time' (Sharpe, 1977).

cracked mad
The imagery is from having a flaw. In various phrases, like 'crack-brained' and the common sl. 'crackers'.

cracked in the ring *see* **ring** (1)

crackling a female viewed sexually by a male
Properly, the crisp and tasty outside of roast meat, especially pork. She is usu. described as a 'bit' or 'piece' of crackling.

cradle-snatcher an older person marrying one much younger
Properly, someone who steals a baby, and not its bed. The term is used of either sex, with disapproval if the elder is a woman or a much older man. To 'rob a cradle' is so to act. cf. **baby snatcher** etc.

cram down the reduction of a debt recoverable by a secured creditor
Am. legal jargon. The amount secured is reduced proportionately to the realization of the security as compared with its valuation when the security was granted. The ob. Br. 'cram' meant to copulate with, of a male, being of the same tendency as **stuff** (2) (q.v.). 'Cram it' is still an Am. variant of the vulgar injunction 'stuff it'.

cramps (the) menstruation
General female usage, from one of the symptoms. '"Just before your period?" "Yes," she said, "that's right. Before the cramps begin"' (Sanders, 1981).

crap to defecate
The word was defined as dregs until the 19c. although that was almost certainly a euphemism as the Old Dutch meaning was explicit. The *Slang Dictionary* of 1894 gives '*Crapping case*, or KEN, the water-closet. Generally called CRAPPING-CASTLE' and today a 'crapper' is rarely a person defecating but usu. a lavatory: 'He couldn't even take a little crap without two of his men checking out the crapper first' (Collins, 1981). The uses antedate the celebrated 19c. Eng. ironfounder called 'Crapper' who proudly incorporated his cast name in the elevated water tanks he manufactured for domestic lavatories, one of which is still in service near my home.

crash to return to normality after taking an illegal narcotic
The descent from the **high** (2) (q.v.); 'Brodie had said . . . . "I'm crashing." And she had gone to the mantelshelf . . . . and taken out a vial of powder' (Theroux, 1976). Also used by addicts of sleep following the ingestion of a narcotic.

crawl to copulate wtih extra-maritally
Of a male in rare spoken use – I suppose it is one way of approaching the encounter. To 'crawl in with' someone is specific, of male or female, being no more than an abbr. of 'crawl into bed with'.

cream to ejaculate semen
From the colour and texture, and in rare sl. 'cream' is semen: 'At the sight of his bride When he got her inside, He creamed all over the bedding' (*Playboy's Book of Limericks*). Thus the cliché 'cream your jeans' means male sexual excitement. 'Cream' is also used of the vaginal discharge of a sexually aroused female, whence the common 'cream for', to desire a male sexually: '"Honey," he said, "You're still creaming for me"' (Mailer, 1963). And a 'creamer' is a young female seeking extra-marital copulation: 'Plenty of young creamers ready to spread their pussies' (Sanders, 1982).

cream crackered exhausted
Rh. sl. on the vulgarism, **knackered** (q.v.). Used on BBC 21 September 1987 by a reporter of his exhaustion after a period of competitive rowing.

crease to kill by violence
Mainly in Am., I suppose from the collapse of the victim. In Br. use it also means to hit with a bullet without severely wounding.

creative fabricated or distorted
From the meaning, imaginatively artistic: '. . . some creative writing concerning Mal-ever's intrepid contribution to the Allied victory' (Deighton, 1981). 'Creative accounting' is commercial jargon for publishing false or misleading figures: 'The recent accounts . . . . provide one more educational insight into the creative accounting to which the Golden Wonder has been such a long-standing devotee' (*Private Eye*, January 1981).

creative conflict a bitter argument
The jargon of churchmen, who wish to give the impression that disagreement is anathema to them in their holy calling. You may also hear the phrase used of trespass, obstruction or other illegality organized to draw attention to a supposed wrong.

creature (the) spirituous intoxicating liquor
Properly, something created and perhaps only an abbr. of 'creature comforts': 'When he chanced to have taken an overdose of the creature' (W. Scott, 1815). The use survives in the Irish forms, 'cratur', 'crathur' or 'crater': 'Never a drop of the crater passed down Chancy Emm's lips' (Mayhew, 1862).

The ob. 'creature of sale' was a whore: 'The house you dwell in proclaims you to be a creature of sale' (Shakespeare, *Pericles*).

credibility gap the extent to which you are thought to be lying
Or, what is more honourable, reluctant to come to terms with unpalatable truth. The phrase comes from US strategic analysis in the 1950s and was used by Gerald Ford in this sense in 1966 when questioning President Johnson's statements about the extent of Am. involvement in Vietnam. 'We do not recognize them, helmeted, in a bomber aiming cans of napalm at a thatched village. We have a credibility gap' (McCarthy, 1967, of Vietnam). A 'serious credibility gap' means everyone thinks you are a liar.

creep joint a peripatetic gambling operation
It 'creeps' or moves, nightly, to avoid police interference. Am.

Cressida a whore
She was the lady who gave Troilus a hard time and Shakespeare a plot: 'The girl was born Cressida, a "daughter of the game"' (Manning, 1960).

crib a brothel
From the Am. dialect meaning, a house, and usu. implying meanness: 'Miserable naked girls in the twenty-five and fifty-cent cribs' (Longstreet, 1956). A 'crib man' is a thief who specializes in robbing private homes.

criminal assault the rape of a female
Properly, any force offered against another with intent is a crime, whether or not sexually inspired: '. . . leading a criminal assault by several Indians on an English girl' (P. Scott, 1975, of a rape). The woman may be said to have been 'criminally used': 'She was dragged from her bicycle into the derelict site . . . . where she was criminally used' (P. Scott, 1971, of the same event). If impregnated, she might be relieved of the foetus by a 'criminal operation' or induced abortion.

criminal connection extra-marital copulation
The 'connection' is as in **connect** (1) (q.v.) but it was never a crime to copulate in BI if the female were old enough and consented: 'These women seldom or never allow drunken men to have criminal connection with them' (Mayhew, 1862, of whores). The use is now perhaps ob.

criminal conversation adultery
Usu. of the woman and abbr. to 'crim. con.'

in legal jargon. 'Conversation' meaning copulation must always have been misleading and is now ob.: 'His conversation with Shore's wife' (Shakespeare, *Richard III*).

criminal operation *see* **criminal assault**

croak to die
From the death rattle of a dying person unable to clear mucus from his throat: 'They go mouching along as if they were croaking' (Mayhew, 1851). Less often 'croak' means to kill: '. . . the guy who had guts enough to croak "Tough Tony"' (Lavine, 1930). To 'croak yourself' is to commit suicide.

crock a drunkard
Properly, a bottle. The Am. 'crocked', drunk, puns on the meaning injured.

crook the elbow to be a drunkard
'Crook' means **bend** (q.v.). A Sc. variant of a common cliché.

cross to copulate with
Male usage, no doubt from the attitude assumed on the female: 'They found in the grass The marks of her ass And the knees of the man who had crossed her' (*Playboy's Book of Limericks*). The ob. Eng. 'cross girl' was a cheating whore, as a lawyer might observe accord without satisfaction, perhaps punning on the intention of the male and the thwarting, or 'crossing', by the female.

cross bar hotel a prison
Prisons are described as 'hotels' in various underworld euphemisms. In this punning Am. use, the bar must cross and secure the gate.

cross the floor to change political allegiance
The seating arrangements in the Br. House of Commons have the opponents facing each other across the floor of the House. If you change parties, you sit the other side. Sir Hartley Shawcross was known to be increasingly disenchanted with the socialist party of which he was a member and became known as 'Sir Shortly Floorcross'.

cross the road to flee
Of the terrorists in Rhodesia, who sought refuge in the bush when confronted with the better-equipped government troops. ob. since the establishment of Zimbabwe.

cross the Styx etc. to die
You were ferried to the other side of the Styx by Charon, so long as your relatives had remembered to put the fare in your mouth when they buried you. A dead Christian may

fig. 'cross the River Jordan' which is toll-free.

cross your palm to bribe
The derivation is probably from the gypsy request to have a palm 'crossed with silver' which pays for the fortune-telling, and as fortune-telling falls under the devil's sphere of influence, acts as a counter-spell by the use of a cross.

crown jewels *see* **jewels**

crud human shit
Properly, curdled milk, although the Am. army use may have other origins – *see* Jennings, 1965: '. . . "crud" has come into popular use as a euphemism for "shit"' (ibid.). Much fig. use, as a noun or adjective: 'This Reape apparently was a cruddy character' (Sanders, 1980). 'Cairo crud' is one of the many alliterative geographical terms for diarrhoea.

cruise (1) to seek a sexual partner at random
Usu. of a male, seeking someone of either sex according to his predeliction, on foot or in a car, on the street or at a party: 'I don't want to cruise any more. I'm afraid I won't be able to get it up' (Sanders, 1982). A 'cruise' is such a foray: 'A spell behind bars for a sexual misdemeanour and recent cruises around New York's gay clubs' (*Private Eye*, May 1981). In ob. London use a 'cruiser' was a whore who solicited custom from a hansom cab.

cruise (2) to be under narcotic influence
The imagery is from airline flight: 'Directors didn't seem to drink much. A little champagne or white wine. Although at least six of them were cruising at five thousand feet on something else' (Wambaugh, 1981).

cruise (3) programmed to hit a distant target
Of a radar-evading nuclear missile and very different from a sea-trip going from port to port.

crumpet a female viewed sexually by a male
Properly, a delicacy made of batter: 'Never short of crumpet. That's one thing about this job' (Deighton, 1972, of opportunities for extra-marital copulation). Usu. a 'bit' or 'piece' of crumpet.

crush a sexual attraction towards another person
From the wish to embrace the object of your affections? Am. 'crushes' are heterosexual in

the main while Br. schoolgirls in single-sex schools have 'crushes' homosexually, usu. on an older female: 'These are schoolgirl dreams. And why pick on me for your "crush"?' (Murdoch, 1977).

crypt a drawer in which dead bodies are stacked
The 'hidden place', whence the cellar of a church used for burial. Am. funeral jargon: 'The crypts facing the corridor are called "Mausoleum crypts" . . . . "Crypts" facing outside . . . . are now called "garden crypts" . . . . "It's all part of the trend towards outdoor living," explained the counsellor' (J. Mitford, 1963).

cube a lump of sugar with LSD on it
From 'cube sugar'. An addict is a 'cube head' and LSD 'cube juice'.

cuckoo (1) a male profligate
He does not necessarily cuckold another, although the word comes from 'cuckoo' which makes use of another's nest: 'The cuckoo that on every tree Mocks married men' (Shakespeare, *Love's Labour's Lost*). This ob. Eng. use is no great loss to the language but we could still use the colourful phrase, to 'cuckold the parson', which was not to copulate with his wife but with your betrothed before he married you.

cuckoo (2) insane
The cuckoo has the reputation for being a silly bird: 'Old defectors, old spies, they get a bit cuckoo' (le Carré, 1980).

cull to kill
Properly, to select, whence to select for rejection, as deer, seals, etc. The SE use is never of the killing of humans.

cult dated and of limited appeal
As in 'cult' movie. An editor told me that this work might turn out to be a 'cult book' – but not too soon, I hope.

cultural of unspecifiable characteristics
Properly, relating to good taste, manners, etc. but '"Cultural" . . . . is the sociologists' jargon for saying as Lewis Carroll once put it, "the word means just what I choose it to mean"' (Shankland, 1980). Thus, in social service jargon, to be 'culturally deprived' is to be poor. Mao's 'Cultural Revolution', supposedly against his own bureaucracy but soon threatening all social convention, was brought to its disastrous end only by the army in 1969.

(cumshaw a bribe is a word used in the Far East: 'The expression was originally "come ashore money", a sailor's tip to the launch boatman' (Jennings, 1965).)

cunning man a wizard
'Cunning' meant knowing and as most of them were in league with the devil, you had to speak kindly of them: 'A "cunning man" was long resident in Bodmin, to whom the people from all parts of the country went to be relieved of spells' (L. Hunt, 1865). (I give this ob. entry because I have given scant space to wizards in these pages, as against witches, and am not unaware of the laws governing these sexual matters. I find myself unable to protect myself by debauching the language to assuage the fanatics, as did the 1982 Editor of Roget's Thesaurus in her change of 'mankind' to 'humankind', of 'countryman' to 'countrydweller', etc.)

cup a protective shield for the male genitalia
A sporting use, from its shape, and more genteel than **box** (2) (q.v.).

cupcake a male homosexual
Not, I think, from **cup** (above), nor am I sure why the inoffensive confection should be so translated: '"Odd? Queer? Gay?" Audley raised an eyebrow. "A cupcake? I heard that word recently"' (Price, 1962).

cup too many *see* **in your cups**

cure (the) treatment for a taboo condition
From the regimen formerly available at spas to alleviate the pangs of rheumatism etc. Now of alcoholism, narcotic addiction or obesity: 'I haven't seen him for – well, since May. He was going to try the cure again' (Steinbeck, 1961, of an alcoholic). To have 'taken the cure' implies abstinence on the part of a former addict.

curious homosexual
From the meaning, unusual: 'He was my tutor. Surely you don't imagine I go to curious parties with Pinkrose' (Manning, 1965).

currency adjustment a devaluation
Political use, seeking to disguise the failure of the policy which led to the necessity. No politician hesitates to call a revaluation by its correct name. cf. **adjust**.

curse (the) menstruation
An abbr. of the 'curse of Eve', who thus burdened all females: 'You've probably got the curse or something' (Bogarde, 1978). Very common.

curtains death
Three derivations are suggested, each of which is plausible – from the end of a play in the theatre, from the screening of cells in a prison before an execution, or from the darkening of a room with a coffin in it. This Am. use is now universal but oddly not also as 'drapes'.

(**custodian** a caretaker is not euphemistic despite Jennings' story of the head of a research library who had to restyle himself 'director' to distinguish his office from that of the janitor.)

custody suite a prison cell
Usu. in a Br. police station: 'The police claimed that they had been instructed to refer to custody suites . . .' (*The Daily Telegraph*, April 1986, and not just for minors).

custom and practice a wasteful and inefficient method of working
Br. trade union jargon. Most industrial practices or working arrangements are not reduced to writing. Whatever processes have become habitual, particularly as to manning levels, bonus payments, breaks etc. become hallowed and cannot be unilaterally changed by managers even to increase competitiveness and so safeguard employment: 'We have the custom and practice of the shop floor behind us' (Price, 1978 – a trade union official was opposing a proposal for change).

cut (1) to render a male sexually impotent
Of domestic animals by castration: 'The bull calves are cut' (Marshall, 1818). Of humans by vasectomy.

cut (2) to dilute in order to cheat customers
Mainly of intoxicants and illegal narcotics, from the dividing and subsequent adulteration: 'The real thing. Pharmaceutical coke. Not the cut street stuff' (Robbins, 1981).

cut (3) drunk
From the dialect meaning, tacking or weaving? Often as 'half cut': 'On many a night we left the canteen half cut' (Richards, 1936).

cut (4) an illegal commission
Common criminal and commercial use, again from the dividing: 'Crap games were played in the corridor with the keeper "cutting" the game' (Lavine, 1930).

cut (5) a reduction in the size of the increase desired or expected by the recipient
Political use, of spending by government agencies etc. where decades of routine increases and consequenct profligacy lead to the expectation that anything in the public sector must keep growing and the wages of

those employed rise, whatever the state of the economy as a whole.

cut (6) to kill
Not necessarily with a knife: 'You Americans – you are so strange. You "put a man down", or you "cut him" or you "burn him", or you "put him away" or "take him for a ride". But you will never say you killed him. Why is that?' (Sanders, 1970 – the questioner had clearly not studied the language of taboo). Rarely too as 'cut down on': 'They want me to cut down on him . . . . I am to burn this man' (ibid. – the speaker was an assassin not a worker in a crematorium).

cut a cheese to fart
From the rich smell which may escape. Grose gives 'Cheeser. A strong smelling fart'. In Somerset you may still be said to 'cut a leg', in the same sense.

cut down on *see* cut (6)

cut off dead
Always of premature or untimely death, with imagery from the gathering of a flower in bloom: '. . . whose headstones record an early death, a cutting-off before the prime' (P. Scott, 1968).

cut out to steal
Said by sailors, from singling out a ship in the opposing fleet for concentrated attack and capture. The term is also used of displacing a female's partner, especially on the dance floor.

cut the mustard to copulate
Of a male; 'cut' means to share in but why 'mustard', unless from the German sl. 'Senf'? 'You can't cut the mustard but how about watching?' (Theroux, 1973). Abbr. to 'cut it': '"Are you married?" "Divorced." "Ha! Couldn't cut it, huh?"' (Collins, 1981). Some fig. use: 'None of this bailing out firms that can't cut the competitive mustard' (M. Thomas, 1982).

cut the painter etc. to die
Like a boat cast loose on the water and mainly of old seamen. 'Cut adrift', of the same tendency, is probably ob. 'Cut your cable' should indicate suicide but in fact is used of natural death in old age.

Cyprian a whore
Aphrodite, the Greek Venus, was revered in Cyprus: 'The Burlington Arcade, which is a well-known resort of Cyprians of the better sort' (Mayhew, 1862). Perhaps still some literary use but 'Cyprian sceptre', an erect penis, is ob.

Cythera related to extra-marital copulation
From the Cretan centre of the cult of Aphrodite, the Goddess of Love: '. . . nor indeed were we long before we finished our trip to Cythera' (Cleland, 1749, meaning they had copulated). 'Cytheromania' means nymphomania. ob. except perhaps in literary use.

D

D anything taboo beginning with the letter D
Usu. 'damn', 'damned', 'damnable' and the
like, which used to carry more weight than
they do today: 'And at last he flung out in his
violent way, and said, with a D, "Then do as
you like" (C. Dickens, 1861). The 'big D' is
death: 'The systematic encroachment of the
big D' (le Carré, 1980).

D and C the illegal abortion of a foetus
The medical abbr. for 'dilation and cur-
etage', otherwise known as a 'scrape': '. . .
going in for a d and c and coming out foetus-
free but permanently stained' (P. Scott,
1975).

DCM a notice of dismissal from
employment
The initial letters of 'Don't come Monday'
pun on the Distinguished Conduct Medal.
Mainly Am. – in Br. railway use, it meant
suspension for one day only.

dabble to use illegal narcotics irregularly
From the proper sense, to give casual or
intermittent attention to. The ob. Br. 'dab'
was a bawd: 'Their scrutinizing pow'r severe
Discerns a vestal from a dirty dab' (Pindar,
1816) and 'dab it up' meant to copulate, of a
male, from the meaning to thrust.

dad a mild oath
Mainly Am. use. DAS says it is a euphemism
for 'God'.

daddy a man who keeps a much younger
woman as a sexual mistress
Perhaps merely an abbr. of **sugar daddy**
(q.v.).

daisy (1) a grave
From the flowers on the turf, but this use is
ob. However the association of 'daisies' with
death continues. If you 'count' or 'push up'
daisies, you are dead.

daisy (2) a male homosexual taking the
female role
From the common female name, whence the
punning Am. 'daisy chain', a male homosexual orgy with heads threaded through
stems.

dally to copulate with extra-maritally
Properly, idly talking but men do it more
than women: 'On the night of the divorce he
was out with Australian harpie Lyndall
Hobbs with whom he dallied for a year or
two' (*Private Eye*, April 1981). 'Dalliance' is

so behaving: 'What time the gifted lady took
Away from pencil, pen, and book, She spent
in amorous dalliance (They do those things
so well in France)' (Parker, 1944, of George
Sand).

damaged (1) drunk
Mainly Am. use, from the temporary incap-
acitation.

damaged (2) having copulated before
marriage
Of a woman who at one time would thereby
have become less marriageable. Now perhaps ob.

damp down to increase saleable weight by
adding water
A usage mainly of the coal trade, where you
purport to lay dust before bagging and
weighing.

dance (1) to be killed by hanging
From the gyration and kicking of the victim:
'Spring's passage out was going to be at the
end of a rope, and unless I shifted I'd be
dancing alongside him' (Fraser, 1982).You
might also be said to 'dance' on air, at the
end of a rope, off, upon nothing, the Tyburn
jig, etc.: 'Matthew would be dancing on air
by next sun-down' (Monsarrat, 1978,
writing in archaic style). The 'dance-hall'
was the condemned cell and the 'dancing
master', the hangman. To 'dance a two-step
in another world' is to be dead, but not
necessarily by hanging: '. . . no good keeping
souvenirs of that sort when any moment we
may be dancing a two-step in another world'
(Richards, 1933, of WW I trench life).

dance (2) to be involuntarily under
another's control
You have to move as another tells you, and
not necessarily because a gunman is shooting at your feet. Much fig. use.

dance at to court heterosexually
Not, I think, from the activities of Salome
and suggesting greater decorum than our
present methods: 'I should have no opinion
of you, Biddy, if he danced at you with your
consent' (C. Dickens, 1861). ob.

dance barefoot to marry before an
unmarried elder sister
Of a girl and perhaps from the absence of a
dowry: 'I must dance barefoot on her wedding day' (Shakespeare, *Taming of the
Shrew*). The economic pressure on those
unwed females who were not allowed to
work to keep themselves made it socially
desirable that sisters should marry in

descending age order. If in Yorks. you remained a bachelor while your brother married, you might be said to 'dance in the half-peck', the derivation of which has eluded me. ob.

dance-hall hostess a whore
From her place of work and *see* **hostess**: 'A night-club or dance-hall hostess . . . . are the modern equivalents of the old-time disorderly house and of the street walker' (Lavine, 1930).

dance the mattress quadrille to copulate
The common 'bed' imagery: 'I could have had the buxom piece dancing the mattress quadrille within the hour' (Fraser, 1975). The ob. London 'dance a Haymarket hornpipe' was something of an in-joke meaning to copulate with a whore, as they frequented the Haymarket; it also includes two vulgar puns: 'Perhaps we'll dance another Haymarket hornpipe before long' (ibid. of copulation).

danger signal is up (the) I am menstruating
From the redness of the blood and the advice to stay clear. Quite common female use to husbands etc.

dangerous to women adept at persuading a female to copulate extra-maritally
You do not normally so describe a rapist: '"Is Morny dangerous to women?" "Don't be Victorian, old top. Women don't call it danger"' (Chandler, 1943). Lady Caroline Lamb inferred as much of Byron when she confided to her journal that he was 'Mad, bad, and dangerous to know'.

Darby and Joan a geriatric married couple living together
From the characters in Woodfall's 18c. ballad, who grew old together: 'Darby and Joaning it into the sunset' (Bogarde, 1981). Also used of paired homosexuals in the Br. Indian army: 'The attitude of other soldiers towards the "Darby and Joans" of the regiment was generally good-natured' (Allen, 1975).

dark (1) closed
Theatrical jargon, from the absence of advertising, footlights etc. when a play has flopped or a theatre management failed: 'The theatre is now "dark" – only the bars and a buffet are open to earn money' (*Sunday Telegraph*, November 1981).

dark (2) Black
The phrase 'dark gentleman' is used of a wealthy or cultured native of India or Africa by a White person trying to be respectful and avoid the offensive alternative allusions to skin pigmentation. 'Dark meat' is an Am. Negress seen sexually by an Am. White male: 'Bill, you better try some dark meat and change your luck' (Sanders, 1982, of a man unable to copulate with his White wife). 'Darky', a Black person, is now considered condescending and insulting although until two or three decades ago many White people saw no need to consider the sensitivities and pride of the poor or uneducated Black person: '"Why not go directly to Captain Anokye?" . . . . "but he's a darky," she said' (Sanders, 1977 – a White woman was speaking in a former African colony of a European power).

dark man the devil
A rare variant of the **black gentleman** (q.v.), the 'darkness' coming from his evil ways and from the soot which adhered to him as he made his way down the chimney: 'A drunk of really a noble class that brought you no nearer to the dark man' (Hardy, 1874).

dark meat (1) flesh of poultry other than the breast
The breast was the 'white meat' and twin evasions, which remain in common use, allowed our prudish ancestors to skate round two taboo parts of the body, breasts and legs. The use of 'drumstick' also avoids mention of legs but predates the 19c. Am. prudery which spawned 'lower limb' and 'trotter'. And *see* **game chicken** for more examples.

dark meat (2) *see* **dark (2)**

dark moon a wife's secret savings
A 19c. Eng. expression, when a wife was allowed no possessions and hid any savings away to provide for future disaster without telling her husband. ob.

darn a mild oath
An abbr. of the ob. 'tarnation' which 'was a blend of "damnation" and "by the 'tarnal" (eternal)' (Jennings, 1965). Still widely used for 'damn', which itself is now mild.

dash (1) to adulterate an intoxicant
Properly, to add flavour, as in a culinary recipe: 'This beer's dashed an' 'er aulus do dash it' (EDD – late 19c.). ?ob. but the practice of watering beer in BI is not.

dash (2)   a mild oath
From the literary convention of replacing a taboo word like 'damn' with a dash. I disagree with Partridge who says: 'Euphemistic only when used as an evasive for *damn*' (DSUE). The ob. Br. 'dasher' was not a lady who swore or sprinted, but a whore, perhaps punning on 'cutting a dash' and the time she accorded to each customer.

date   a social partner of the opposite sex
Obviously from specifying the meeting time and a survival from the period when courtship remained the subject of taboo: '. . . theories as to the girl's possible "date"' (Davidson, 1978). Men tend to 'date' girls – which is not to guess their age – rather than the reverse: 'If the Smiths hadn't been there I would have dated her myself' (Theroux, 1978). On a 'blind date' you take pot luck. The ob. Eng. 'dateless' meant not that you were leading a celibate life, but that you suffered from mental senility, unaware of the passage of time: 'We were like to be turned out on t'wide world, and poor mother dateless' (Gaskell, 1863).

daughter of the game   a whore
The 'game' is prostitution: 'The girl was a born Cressida, a "daughter of the game"' (Manning, 1960). Cressida was the lady who, by preferring Diomed to Troilus, gave Shakespeare a plot.

Davy Jones' locker   a grave at sea
Grose says 'David Jones. The devil, the spirit of the sea' and the first literary use was by Smollett in 1751, which may rule out derivation from the biblical Jonah, as is sometimes suggested. The 'locker' was his seaman's chest: 'All hands are snug enough in Davy Jones's locker' (Chamier, 1837 – they had died at sea). 'Davy Jones' natural children' were pirates, 'natural children' being bastards.

day of protest etc.   a politically motivated strike
Mainly trade union jargon for such an effort to influence opinion and coerce government by extra-parliamentary action and wide television publicity. Also, despite the cessation of work, as 'day of action', but cf. **industrial action**.

dead meat (1)   a human corpse
Criminal jargon beloved by writers of detective fiction. To 'make dead meat of' is to kill a human.

dead meat (2)   an older whore who still lives by prostitution
As different from 'fresh meat', which means a young whore new to the business, or rarely a sexually lax girl. 'Fresh and sweet' is used of a whore newly released from gaol.

dead soldier   an empty bottle of wine or spirits
Perhaps from the military appearance of a line of bottles: 'Or I'd take it to him if he had a dead soldier' (Sanders, 1980, of a bottle of brandy).

dead to propriety etc.   anxious to copulate extra-maritally
Of either sex, with 'dead to' meaning willing to ignore: 'I cannot suppose that he is altogether Dead to Propriety, though how long such Restraint will continue I cannot say' (Fraser, 1977 – a wife had been abducted). 'Dead to' honour, social behaviour, etc. meant the same thing. Probably ob.

deadhead   a successful scrounger
Because you can't include him when you count the takings. Of a non-paying spectator at a ball game, a fare-evader on a train, etc. Another Am. use is of a cadger at a bar who never buys others a drink.

deal   to supply illegal narcotics for payment
The Am. language of commerce is used to conceal criminality: '"A little grass now and then. Not from her." "But she deals?"' (Sanders, 1977, of marijuana).

dear friend *see* **chère amie**

dear John   the ending by a woman of an engagement or marriage
The WW II letter of dismissal which so many men serving abroad received started formally rather than by using the warmer appellations which indicate closer affection: 'The colonel confesses he should have got out on receipt of his first "Dear John" letter, particularly as this concided with the break-up of his regiment' (*Daily Telegraph*, January 1984).

death benefit   money paid by the State for burial expenses etc.
We are used to heirs profiting from death; indeed, we call them beneficiaries. But the pittance paid to a surviving Br. spouse might have avoided this particular juxtaposition of words and concepts.

debauch   to copulate with extra-maritally
Properly, to corrupt and today's 'debauches' refer only to drunkenness: 'Men so disorder'd, so debauch'd and bold, That this our court, infected with their manners, Shews like a riotous inn' (Shakespeare, *King Lear* – but

not of drunkenness). I have not decided what Dr Johnson meant when he wrote: 'A man may debauch his friend's wife genteely.'

debt of honour money lost at gambling and not paid
Under Eng. law gambling debts are not recoverable through the Courts, but a defaulter may lose his good name and his credit with his bookmaker – or get his teeth pushed in.

debt of nature *see* **pay nature's debt** etc.

decadent not conforming to accepted tastes
Properly, in a state of decline from past standards. Much used by autocrats of anything which they disapprove, from homosexuality to artistic style: 'Shetland had accepted eight "decadent" surrealist paintings that Göring had confiscated' (Deighton, 1978).

deceive to copulate extra-maritally
Of either sex. Properly it means to mislead as to the truth: 'Harper nodded and made a private vow that he would not deceive his wife' (Theroux, 1980, which does not mean that he would pretend only to drink one whisky a day).

decent wearing clothes which hide any suggestion of nakedness
You do not have to be fully clothed to be 'decent' but your attire must not suggest immodesty: '. . . since I could see she was clothed – "decent", as girls used to say' (Styron, 1976 – and they still do).

deck a packet of illicit narcotics
Usu. heroin, from being wrapped in paper like a pack of cards. To 'deck up' is to pack heroin for retail sale. Am.

decks awash drunk
Not just applied to Am. sailors but *see* **half-seas over**.

decline the fatal onset of pulmonary tuberculosis
A euphemism which became specific before being replaced with **consumption** (q.v.): 'She said one of his suitors was like to die of decline' (Hughes, 1856). ob. since WW II.

decontaminated temporarily embalmed
Properly, having a pollutant removed. This Am. funeral jargon for pumping some formalin into a corpse overlooks the fact that most dead bodies are aseptic: 'The incentive to select quality mechandise would be materially lessened if the body of the deceased were not decontaminated and

made presentable' (J. Mitford, 1963). In bureaucratic jargon, to 'decontaminate' a file is to remove embarrassing or incriminating papers from it.

decoy an unmarked police car
Properly, a lure, and you may be encouraged to keep pace with it and then be booked for speeding. Am. CB use.

(dedicated uncritically single-minded and enthusiastic is an overworked cliché of anyone you may admire for sticking to his job, even if he is not set aside for special use like a public highway or church.)

deed (the) copulation
Often extra-maritally, and always so if 'dirty' or 'vile': '. . . one that will do the deed Though Argus were her eunuch' (Shakespeare, *Love's Labour's Lost*, of Rosaline).

deep freeze a prison
The common Am. 'cooling' imagery: 'If the cops didn't grab him and toss him in the deep freeze' (Chandler, 1958).

deep interrogation *see* **interrogation (with prejudice)**

deep six to kill
Used normally of burial of a corpse, from the statutory minimum depth of a grave: 'How do you propose we deep-six that Straton' (Block, 1979 – they were trying to make an airliner crash). And of suicide: 'Barney would have expected his friend to deep-six it out of the window' (M. Thomas, 1980). So fig. of disposing of anything in Am. sl.: 'You can deepsix that crap. Eighty years old and still fucking. That I don't need' (Sharpe, 1977).

deep sleep an extended period of inactivity by a spy
To obtain a position of power in the society to be attacked, this **sleeper** (q.v.) is a long time awakening: 'Hard-picked subjects, with good career prospects, psychologically equipped for deep-sleeping' (Keneally, 1985).

(defecate the polite word for 'shit' which I have chosen to adopt, has no other SE meaning. It was however an early 19c. euphemism from the former meaning, to purify or cleanse. Thus Harvey could write 'The blood is not sufficiently defecated or clarified, but remains muddy' (on Consumptions). So also with 'defecation'.)

defence aggression
This is one of those opposites, like **health** and **life insurance** (q.v.). A 'Ministry of

Defence' is no less warlike than a Ministry of War. 'Active (air) defence' is military jargon for air raids and 'defence' budgets, debates, votes, procurement, strategy, etc. are all to do with fighting. The Br. 'D Notice' which is never called a 'defence notice' is an instruction to newspapers etc. to suppress news, ostensibly on the grounds that State security is involved.

defend your virtue to refuse to copulate extra-maritally
Usu. of a female and indeed: 'A male defending his virtue is always a farcical figure' (McCarthy, 1963). The phrase is also used for the rejection of homosexual approaches.

defensive victory the postponement of a defeat
Used to mask the reality of military disaster: 'On the Cowland front a complete defensive victory was scored yesterday' (Goebbels, 1945, in tr.).

defile to copulate with extra-maritally
Properly, to make filthy. Of a male, with a presumption of female reluctance: 'Children who only hours ago had been virgins, defiled by men they had never seen before' (Ludlum, 1979). In the same sense, to 'defile a bed' does not imply involuntary urination: 'My bed he hath defiled' (Shakespeare, *All's Well*). The male who thus copulates is a 'defiler': 'Thou bright defiler of Hymen's purest bed' (Shakespeare, *Pericles*).

deflower to copulate with a female virgin
OED gives a 14c. quotation from Wycliff in this sense as the first use and Shakespeare speaks of 'A deflower'd maid' (*Measure for Measure*) but the imagery is clearly from plucking a bloom. Also of loss of virginity other than by copulation: 'His female admirers had a model of it made in pure gold and organized a ceremony in which several virgins deflowered themselves on this object' (Manning, 1977). 'Defloration' is such copulation: '. . . the usual sanguinary symptoms of defloration' (Cleland, 1749). SE.

degraded copulated with extra-maritally
Of a woman. Properly, lowered in rank, which she may be if she is found out: ' "Do you suppose she has been . . . . degraded?" says he, in a hushed voice' (Fraser, 1971). Probably ob.

Delhi belly diarrhoea
An alliterative use not confined to India or its capital: 'Kind of a bowel thing. Up all night. Cramps. Delhi belly. Food goes right through you' (Theroux, 1975).

delicate condition etc. *see* condition (2)

deliver to drop on an enemy
Especially of bombs or 'ordnance'. The imagery makes the transaction more remote and guilt-free for the bombers, etc. In this jargon, a 'delivery vehicle' is not a milk float but a missile which carries a bomb.

demands of nature urination and defecation
You might think gravity came first, followed by breathing: '. . . walking with the sense of purpose proper to a man about to attend to the demands of nature' (Masters, 1976).

demi-mondaine a whore
Married people who 'went to the world' in the French Second Empire were the 'monde' and women on the fringes of that society unaccompanied by men were the 'demi-monde'. The ob. Eng. 'demi-rep', an abbr. of 'demi-reputation', meant the same thing.

democratic and **democracy** have always meant different things to different people and virtually never 'rule by the people'. At the best of times, the concept involves a modicum of social coercion or lack of choice; at the worst, the words are favoured by autocrats to gloss over their tyranny, as in the Russian satellite State which has the effrontery to call itself the 'German Democratic Republic'. But the words are convenient for all types of regime: ' "Vietnam's Democratic One-man Rule" – the Procustean subject was Diem. A democratic "dictator" or a "democratic" dictator?' (McCarthy, 1967). As an Am. politician you need money or influence to get anywhere in the 'Democratic' party, and both if you are to reach high office. Outside the Parish Meeting, where you can put up your own proposition instead of just saying yes or no to a series framed by someone else, the pure democratic concept is not workable without concessions to authority.

demographic strain too many people
'Demography' is the study of population statistics but this phrase does not mean your eyes ache from reading too many censuses. It is taboo to suggest that poor countries face starvation because ignorant people breed too fast and medical science allows too many to survive.

demonstration an attempt to coerce or influence by force
Properly, a showing, illustration or proof. The vocal and sometimes violent rally so styled is a useful device for protestors and agitators because any action or failure to react by Government assists in their cause: 'He never took part in demonstrations or marched in May Day parades' (McCarthy, 1963). The abbr. 'demo' has no non-euphemistic meaning.

demonstrator a car used by a motor trader and then sold as new
Motor trade jargon. The inference is that it has only been used for giving test drives to potential customers. It is the system through which the trader, his senior staff and his family obtain the constant use of new vehicles without having to meet the cost of purchase, depreciation or repair.

demote maximally to kill one of your associates
Espionage jargon, and your career as a spy certainly comes to an abrupt close: 'Jonathan smiled at the cryptic jargon . . . . in which "demote maximally" meant purge by killing' (Trevanian, 1972). A 'maximum demote' is such a killing: 'The assassinations are called "sanctions" if the target is someone outside the CII, and "maximum demotes" if the target is one of their own men' (Trevanian, 1973).

(dentures false teeth is not euphemistic even though there was an old meaning, dents. Dr Johnson gives neither word, but he does include the still current 'dentifrice'.)

departmental view the policy favoured by the senior civil servant
The jargon of the civil servant based in London. A 'ministerial view' is what the government thinks, but if that differs from the 'departmental view', the latter will in the medium term prevail.

depart this life to die
The inference is that you will arrive in another state of existence: 'Things went on smoothly for a dozen years, when the old Frenchman departed this life' (Mayhew, 1851). 'Take your departal' is ob.: 'When my father took his departal to a better world' (Galt, 1823). The 'departed' are the dead: 'Ground given over to the accommodation of the departed' (Amis, 1978) and the 'dear departed' either a dead individual or the dead generally. 'Departure' is death: 'This unsound mode of transport would have been

her only criticism of William's orchestration of her departure' (Archer, 1979, of a funeral). An 'unauthorized departure' in prison jargon is the escape of a prisoner.

dependency (1) a subject territory
Br. imperial use for those parts of the globe which were not Dominions, Colonies or Protectorates but ruled from London .

dependency (2) an addiction to narcotics or alcohol
The victim 'depends' on regular ingestion: 'It is estimated that at least two million women have dependancies – addiction would be a better word – on prescriptive drugs' (Sanders, 1981).

deprived poor
Properly, having lost something which you once had, which is not so for most paupers: 'A 1965 Jules Feiffer cartoon shows the progression from "poor" to "needy" to "deprived" etc.' (Pei, 1969, illustrating successive sociological jargon). In the same sense 'deprivation' is poverty. The Shakespearean sense, to kill, is ob.: ''Tis honour to deprive dishonour'd life' (*The Rape of Lucretia*). (How many meanings can be given to a *Daily Telegraph* headline of 4 October 1983: 'Deprived Families on Increase'? I offer a selection:

poor families are expressing views on a supplement of income
families subject to depredation are expressing views on a supplement of income
families have been denied the right to express views on an increase
families have been denied an increase offered to others
families have had an increase taken from them
the number of persons in each poor family is growing
there are more families subject to depredation
there are more poor families
It remains a fascinating language!)

derrière the buttocks
The French too have behinds and use the same euphemism.

deselect to reject and ultimately dismiss
Of an elected representative whom a caucus wishes to replace. The victim is often a socialist politician whose pragmatism has tempered his bigotry.

destabilize to overthrow
Properly, to introduce instability. Espionage

jargon when you are trying to introduce conditions under which a new government more to your liking might assume power.

destroy to kill has been a SE use since medieval times, but now has a special meaning, to put to death sick, old or unwanted pets or horses: 'If he makes another mess .... I'll have him destroyed' (N. Mitford, 1945, of a dog).)

detainee a political prisoner
Each of us becomes a detainee when our train is held up by the signals. Used of aliens in wartime and those opposed to Government in Ireland and S. Africa where subversives by official designation may be imprisoned without trial. Whence 'detention', such confinement.

developing poor and relatively uncivilized
Many of the countries so described have ceased spreading or becoming stronger for a variety of reasons since the withdrawal of a former colonial power: '... countries which have successively and with increasing euphemism been termed backward, underdeveloped, less-developed and developing' (FDMT – you could also add 'south', 'third world', 'emergent', 'emerging', 'nonaligned' etc. to bring the list up to 1983). Even in more fortunate or better-ordered societies 'development' may indicate a state of decay instead of the proper meaning, self-generating evolution; thus the Br. 'Development Areas' are those parts of the country which have fallen behind in the maintenance of economic standards. In educational jargon, a 'developmental course' is what we used to call cramming.

(deviation any political or artistic disagreement with what autocracy decrees is a correct Communist usage. An efficient tyranny has to nominate 'one way' if it is to survive, given the incurable individualism of humans. Whence 'deviationist', a dread accusation in those places.)

device any object the subject of a taboo
Properly, a mechanical contrivance. Of armament where, for a short while, 'nuclear device' may have sounded more acceptable than atomic bomb; of contraception: 'The pharmaceuticals don't agree with me. I had to go to a doctor and get a device' (Keneally, 1985); etc.

devil's mark (the) congenital idiocy
In Br. rural use. God and the devil seem to have caught the blame equally for the results of inbreeding and incest – see **God's**

child: 'That's where your village idiots come from. They call it the Devil's Mark, I call it incest' (le Carré, 1962). (Oddly, if there had been more incest, as over 70 generations for 15% of the population in S. India, the regressive genes would have been bred out.)

devotee of Bacchus see **bacchanalian**

diamond cutter an erection of the penis
From the hardness: 'Spermwhale watched and swallowed twice and developed a diamond cutter which delighted Foxy Farrell' (Wambaugh, 1975 – she was rubbing her naked body against him).

diaphragm a female contraceptive device
Properly, any dividing membrane. It is worn internally and usu. fitted medically: 'Having her fitted for a diaphragm by one more of Larry's associates' (Styron, 1976).

dick (1) a penis
Probably rh. sl. on **prick** (q.v.) but the penis is often given common male names – see **John Thomas, jock, willy** etc.: 'What she had said about things like his dick' (Amis, 1978, of a penis). The Am. 'dicked' means buggered: '... six bad (years) in San Quentin gettin' dicked by the residents' (Collins, 1981, of a male prisoner). 'Dick around' is a variant of 'fuck around' for promiscuous male copulation, and is also used fig.: 'Dicking around with his cows and windmills' (M. Thomas, 1982, of a painter). 'Dick's hatband', male homosexuality, referred to the effete Richard Cromwell and the crown he was unfit to wear in succession to his mighty father, Oliver: 'Hollo, thinks I, he ain't one of the Dick's hatband brigade, surely' (Fraser, 1977, writing in 19c. style). To 'wear Dick's hatband' was to be known as a male homosexual.

dick (2) a policeman
Usu. a dectective: 'One of the more ambitious would go to the Detective Bureau and become a dick' (Lavine, 1930).
Although 'Dick' is an abbr. of 'Richard' and Richard is rh. sl. for a turd (Richard the Third), I have no real idea of the etymology. An Am. 'dickless Tracy' is a policewoman, punning on her feminity and a cartoon character.

dickens the devil
On the common expression 'what the dickens ...' Partridge says 'In origin a euphemistic evasion for *devil* ' (DSUE) but the connection is not obvious.

dicky unwell
Rh. sl. for 'uncle Dick', sick. Widely used of

our own mild indispositions; of others usu. of a chronic state of ill-health, such as a 'dicky heart': '. . . sent me home. Said I had a dicky heart' (Theroux, 1974, of a retired former colonial resident).

dictatorship of the proletariat a self-perpetuating oligarchy
Marx used 'dictatorship' and 'rule' interchangeably, which gave Lenin, Mao and others the high authority for their systems which precision of speech might have denied them.

diddle (1) to urinate
Properly, to jerk from side to side, which a male may do to his penis when he has urinated; but 'Dicky Diddle' is also Br. rh. sl. for 'piddle'. Mainly nursery use.

diddle (2) to masturbate
Of both sexes, again from the jerking movement: '. . . she caught Leslie, then three, diddling herself and forced her to wear handspints' (Styron, 1976). 'Diddle' is also used of copulation, but I have not traced any literary example.

(diddle (3) to cheat, victimize or rarely to kill
is a word of 19c. origin which does not appear to have had a euphemistic source.)

die to achieve a sexual orgasm
Of a male: 'I will live in thy heart, die in thy lap, and be buried in thy eyes' (Shakespeare, *Much Ado*) or a female: 'These lovers cry – Oh! Oh! they die' (Shakespeare, *Troilus and Cressida*). And much subsequent poetic use but now ob. To 'die in a horse's nightcap' or 'die in your shoes' was to be killed by hanging. In ob. Kentish use, to 'die queer' was to kill yourself.

diet of worms the actuality of death
Modern science tells us that the process of corporal dissolution is fungal, with worms obtaining little sustenance. Happily Marvell knew better: 'then worms shall try That long preserved virginity, And your quaint honour turn to dust, And into ashes all my lust'. The 'Diet', or assembly, was held in the Rhineland city of Worms in 1521 and is remembered by generations of schoolchildren who have forgotten, if they were ever told, Martin Luther's great courage in attending.

difficult particularly objectionable
You may say this about other people's children, but it is wise to keep out of earshot of their parents if you do so.

ding-a-ling etc. a flaccid penis
From the pendant position of a bell clapper.

Mainly nursery use: 'The quads have been reporting progress on papa's dingaling daily' (Sharpe, 1979 – papa had damaged his penis on rose thorns). Wider Am. than Br. use which explains but does not excuse the naïvety of the BBC in permitting the repeated broadcast of a lyric in which a male singer invited his auditors to 'play' with his 'ding-a-ling'. Also in Am. as 'ding', 'ding-dong' or 'dong', with some adult use: 'His dong was never as all-fired important to Wally as yours is to you' (Hailey, 1979).

dip (1) to steal
Properly, to put into liquid, which necessarily involves a downward movement, and so specially of picking pockets: 'Dipping; lifting money out of a mug's pocket' (Kersh, 1936). A 'dip' or 'dipper' so acts: 'Twenty years of muggers and dips, safe men and junkies' (Mailer, 1965 – but don't rely on that kind of 'safe man' unless you wish him to break open a safe for you). In airline jargon, to 'dip' is to steal alcohol provided for passengers who have paid for it in the ticket price and sell it to 'tourist' or 'economy' passengers: 'During take-off . . . . the steward busily funnels liquor from the first-class bottles into miniatures. This is called "dipping"' (Moynahan, 1983). In ob. Br. derogatory use, a 'dipper' was an Anabaptist, from the total submersion of initiates during Christening.

dip (2) a drunkard
Perhaps just an abbr. of 'dypsomaniac' but the Am. 'dip your beak' or 'dip your bill' is also to drink intoxicants to excess.

dip your wick to copulate
Common male punning usage, from the immersion of a wick for lighting in oil, and *see* **wick**: 'Worms who had had an exhausting time dipping his wick, as he called it, all over Wimbledon' (Bogarde, 1978). Usu. of chance male extra-marital copulation.

diplomatic cold a polite excuse for non-attendance
Politer, in any event, than an unvarnished refusal. First contracted by Mr Gladstone but now caught generally.

direct action unlawful violence or trespass
Usu. in support of a political cause or a labour dispute. The essence is its illegality; there are various ways for those with a grievance to act directly through the courts, parliament, public meetings, etc.: '"I mean direct action," said Araba, ignoring Brodie. "In a word Susannah – violence"' (Theroux

1976). (You can often detect the bias of a specialist dictionary from its treatment of this kind of phrase. When Kay and Stevens (*Beyond the Dictionary in English*) talk about the use of direct action 'to draw attention to social injustice', they tell you more about themselves than about the language.)

direct mail unsolicited enquiries sent by post
It seeks an order, a subscription, a donation, political support, etc. but the delivery is not more or less direct than the rest of your mail, most of which you actually want to read. The Am. 'junk mail' is accurate but not euphemistic.

dirt/dirty anything harmful or damaging which may be the subject of a taboo
For example, to 'dirty your pants' is not to soil food on them but to urinate or defecate in them. A 'dirty' atomic bomb is going to go on killing more life for a longer period in a nastier way than a 'clean' one. A narcotics addict is 'dirty' not from failure to wash but from being caught carrying illicit narotics. A 'dirty' joke usu. involves copulation or homosexuality. The 'dirty deed' is extra-marital copulation by a male: '. . . my mind leaped to the conclusion that he meant he had taken her from me, and done the dirty deed on her' (Fraser, 1977). A 'dirty old man' seeks a sexual arrangement with a much younger woman, or, if he is a homo-sexual, with much younger males. A 'dirty weekend' may be fine and sunny but it is passed in overnight clandestine copulation: 'They've simply gone for a dirty weekend at the Spread Eagle' (Matthew, 1978). 'Dirt' is used as a noun in these and similar uses and has a criminal jargon meaning, information which is damaging to another. *See* too **clean**.

disadvantaged poor
Sociological jargon which would properly indicate that an 'advantage' had been taken away at some time, whereas those so des-cribed were not born into a wealthy home or subjected to better education or training; or, in a predominantly White society, them-selves White: 'I do want to help him – because he's black and probably grew up disadvantaged' (Theroux, 1982). 'A 1965 Jules Feiffer cartoon shows the progression from "poor" to "needy" to "deprived" to "disadvantaged"' (Pei, 1969).

disappear (1) to be murdered
The body is unlikely to be found. Jargon of the underworld and extremist autocracies.

disappear (2) to urinate
Mainly female use. They do not in fact van-ish after telling you that they are going to 'disappear', but pay a fleeting visit to a lavatory.

discharge to ejaculate semen
As in Pistol's gun: 'I will discharge upon her, Sir John, with two bullets' (Shakespeare, *2 Henry IV* – the 'bullets' were the testicles) or today: 'The executioner was the first to break away, for he had discharged between Erik's golden thighs' (Genet in 1969 tr.). 'Discharge' in the sense of leaving employ-ment is a SE use, from the meaning to free or rid but *see* **fire**.

discipline *see* **dominance**

discomfort agony
The supposedly comforting language of dentistry. However if your dentist, drill at the ready, informs you that you may feel a little 'discomfort', it is time to grip the arms of the chair and think pure thoughts.

discouraged drunk
This Am. use is odd because alcohol is sup-posed to make you brave.

disease of love a venereal infection
For many 'love' is synonymous with extra-marital copulation which often results in such disease: '. . . advertisements for doctors who cured "all the diseases of love"' (Man-ning, 1977).

disgrace to copulate with extra-maritally
But only if the news gets about, I suppose: 'So don't talk about people *making little* of other people, or of him *disgracing* me' (Bin-chy, 1985 – the speaker was pregnant and unmarried).

dish a sexually attractive woman
A male use, with the common culinary imagery.

disinfection mass killing
From the Nazi pretence that Jews, Gypsies and others killed by gassing were being put into a confined space for the purpose of eliminating lice etc.: 'The underground chambers were named "disinfection cellars", the above-ground chambers "bath-houses"' (Keneally, 1982, of Auschwitz).

disinvestment the disposal of shares, etc. as a political gesture
Not just any old sale. Those who use the term usu. want to denote disapproval of the government of S. Africa, although other

pressure groups may so act to publicize other issues. The rarer alternative, 'divestiture', has a clerical ring.

dismal trade the arranging of funerals for payment
'Dismal' means dreary and was used of the devil or a funeral mute (OED): 'There is no reason to believe the big-volume concerns will demonstrate a more tender regard for the pocket-books of their customers than has traditionally been the case in the Dismal Trade' (J. Mitford, 1963). A 'dismal trader' so arranges funerals but 'dismals', mourning clothes, is ob.

disorderly house a brothel
Originally 19c. legal jargon and still used, even of the most tidy and well-conducted brothel: 'If the neighbours chose to complain before a magistrate of a disorderly house' (Mayhew, 1862).

dispatch to kill
'Despatch' was the older spelling, and the only one recognized by Dr Johnson. From the meaning, send, it has long been used of the killing of both animals and humans: 'We are peremptory to dispatch This vigorous traitor' (Shakespeare, *Coriolanus*). Today it implies efficient and unspectacular killing: 'If custody was out of the question, employ all feasible measures for dispatch' (Ludlum, 1979).

dispense with assistance to dismiss from employment
Usu. peremptorily and with dishonour if not worse, of a senior official etc. although used humorously of lesser beings: 'The Führer will dispense with his assistance' (Goebbels, 1945, in tr. of such a dismissal). *cf.* **help** which has common imagery.

disport amorously to copulate
Properly, no more than frolicking with sexual overtones: 'Same old rut. A Richmond resident tells me that it is once again that time of the year when the deer in Richmond Park are disporting themselves amorously. Notices in the park are models of tact. They read demurely: "Warning, Excessive Deer Activity"' (*Daily Telegraph*, October 1987 – who was being warned, we must ask ourselves).

disposal a killing other than by process of law
Espionage and criminal jargon, from the need to get rid of the body: 'Disposals are not in our line of country' (Allbeury, 1981, of such a proposed killing). Thus 'disposal facilities', the ability to conceal the corpse:

'"Have you got disposal facilities if it's necessary?" "There's hundreds of acres of woods"' (ibid.).

dispute a strike
Abbr. of Br. 'industrial dispute', a variant of **industrial action** (q.v.). Used twice in three minutes by BBC Radio 4 on 15 June 1983: 'A dispute among Southern Region guards has led to the cancellation of trains' – they were not arguing about politics or soccer among themselves – and: 'A dispute among camera and technical staff has prevented the televising of sporting events'. In both cases the people concerned were striking without notice in breach of their contracts of employment and in defiance of their trade union. Purists will note and savour the use of 'among'.

dissolution (1) death
Properly, the splitting up into constituent parts, as the corpse into bones, or the body from the soul: 'A fetch .... comes to assure .... a happy longevity or immediate dissolution' (Banim, 1823).

dissolution (2) a persistent course of licentious behaviour
Of extra-marital copulation, homosexuality publicly flaunted, heavy gambling, drunkenness or the use of illicit narcotics. In each case normal restraint is 'dissolved'. He who so acts is 'dissolute'.

distinguished aged over forty
Of male politicians, entertainers and other public figures. Those who also have white hair may be 'very distinguished'.

distressed mad
Medical and sociological jargon. It properly means sorely troubled but today you call those people distraught.

distribute favours *see* **favours**

distribution the payment of a bribe
Usu. where there are several recipients, or where the organizer of a corrupt deal hands on bribes to others, which may then be called a 'secondary distribution': 'I also want acknowledgement from every recipient in the "secondary distribution", as you so nicely put it' (Erdman, 1981, of such a transaction).

disturbed (1) naughty or undisciplined
Educational and sociological use of children, by those who see infantile vice only as a product of a sick adult society: 'Boys and girls who steal or vandalize, or wet the bed,

or are found by their teachers or doctors disturbed . . .' (Bradbury, 1976).

disturbed (2) mad
Medical use – properly it means showing no more than unease: 'He had stopped looking for the hospital . . . . "Are you disturbed?" went on the lunatic' (Amis, 1978 – the lunatic was using the language officially used of himself).

ditch to crash an aircraft in water
From the drain dug to receive water whence the SE meaning to discard in such a drain, or elsewhere, any unwanted object. Originally WW II punning use but now of any aircraft so crashing.

dive (1) to pick pockets
From the movement of the hand: 'In using your nimbles, in diving in pockets' (Ben Jonson). Grose notes 'diver' as a pickpocket but the use is now perhaps ob.

dive (2) a place for the sale and drinking of intoxicants
Often low-class and from the Am. use of cellars, where the rent was lower. In the same sense Grose gives 'diver' as 'one who lives in a cellar'.

dive (3) to pretend to have been knocked down
Used of a boxer who goes of his own volition to the canvas: 'Some gamblers tried to scare him into a dive' (Chandler, 1939 – they wanted a boxer to throw a fight); and of a soccer player who tries to win an undeserved free kick.

divergence homosexuality
Moving away from the norm: 'Miles's divergence had been one of his most valuable assets' (Trevanian, 1972 – Miles was a homosexual).

do (1) to copulate with
Mainly male usage, from his supposed initiative: 'Doing a filthy pleasure is, and short' (Ben Jonson) or '"Where you might meet anyone and do anything." "Or meet anything and do anyone"' (Bradbury, 1975). Both sexes 'do it' – see it (2): 'Always wanted to do it outside, you know, ever since I read *Sons and Lovers*' (ibid.). To 'do a perpendicular' is to copulate while both parties are standing. 'Do what comes naturally' is of either sex: 'Their pimps would come round and collect, do what comes naturally, and cut out' (L. Armstrong, 1955). 'Do yourself' is to masturbate, usu. of a female as there are so many alternative

phrases for male masturbation: 'The thought of him inside her, made her squirm; for an instant she considered doing herself' (M. Thomas, 1980). Also as 'do it with yourself' again mainly of females: '"Have you ever done it with yourself?" Dottie shook her head violently' (McCarthy, 1963).

do (2) to kill
Usu. expanded to 'do for' or 'do in': 'Some of our chaps say that they had done their prisoners in whilst taking them back' (Richards, 1933). To 'do yourself in' is to commit suicide: 'He has written a letter to my parents. I might as well do myself in' (Townsend, 1982). In underworld sl. to 'do' or 'do over' also means to maim.

do (3) to cheat or rob
Perhaps only an abbr. of 'do the dirty' etc. Also as 'do over'.

do (4) a battle
Properly, a party or function. Usu. of a less successful and bloody encounter, such as the Br. 'Armhem do'.

do (5) to charge with an offence
Police use: 'She's been done twice for drunk in charge' (Allbeury, 1976). And a person charged, especially of a motoring offence, will refer to have having been 'done'.

do a brown see **brown-hatter**

do a bunk etc. to urinate
There are numerous sl. and dialect phrases meaning to urinate or to defecate which employ the verb 'to do' and I have listed many, 'slash' for example, under the noun because slashes, etc. are had, done or gone for, and the noun itself imparts the meaning of urination. 'Do a bunk' comes from the meaning, to depart quickly. The ob. Br. 'do a dike' was of urination or defecation, from the trench used in primitive arrangements. The punning 'do a job' is to defecate, as in **big jobs** (q.v.), mainly in adult use. To 'do a rural' is to defecate out of doors, and may be ob. To 'do a shift' uses the same imagery as 'do a bunk', etc.

do-gooder a self-righteous person who forces his concerns on others
Nearly always used derogatively: '. . . hated to . . . . make the other policeman think he was a do-gooder' (Wambaugh, 1975). 'Do-gooding' is so acting: 'What were her do-gooding parents but pious cheats?' (Theroux, 1976).

do-lally-tap mad
From the Indian transit camp at Deolali near
Bombay where time-expired Br. soldiers
were sent to await return to England. The
heat and the boredom were accentuated by
the vagaries of intercontinental transport. If
you arrived in the camp at the wrong season,
you could be stuck there for six months,
which would be additional to your contracted service in India: 'In India he had had a
touch of the sun, which we old soldiers
called "Deolalic Tap"' (Richards, 1933) but
the 'Old Soldier' also uses another spelling:
'Oh he's got the Doo-lally tap' (Richards,
1936).

do the right thing to marry the woman
you have impregnated
The initial extra-marital copulation was the
wrong thing: 'He Did The Right Thing, by a
girl who had only six months to live' (Lyall,
1982).

do your duty by to impregnate your wife
Referring to an obligation to produce an
heir, when it may also be used of a wife
having a son by her husband, with a side
glance perhaps at the ordinance in the marriage service concerning the procreation of
children: 'I regard it as my duty to have an
heir. If my husband refuses to do his duty by
me I shall find someone who will' (Sharpe,
1975).

do your paper work *see* **paper hanger**

dock to copulate with a female
It was at one time confined to copulation
with a virgin, using the imagery of pruning.
This is a convenient place to note a common
characteristic of etymologists and economists – they welcome any chance to disagree
with each other. Farmer and Henley trace
this meaning of 'dock' from the Romany
'dukker'. Partridge in DHS and DSUE looks
to 'the SE *dock* to curtail' which, in his judgment, 'is obviously operative'. Grose makes
no suggestion as to derivation but reports
'Docked smack smooth; one who has suffered an amputation of his penis for a
venereal complaint'. EDD correctly reports
that 'dock' meant to undress: 'mun dock this
gownd off'. OED does not give this use but
improves our knowledge by deriving the
'dock' in which a prisoner stands in Court
from the Dutch word for rabbit-hutch.
Having discovered that euphemisms may
have varied parentage, even to being reborn
after long disuse, my contribution to the
debate is to draw attention to a marine
'dock', a long, moist, narrow space into

which a ship moves and may fit snugly. I am
sorry that we will never know what Alfred
Holt thought.

doctor to change involuntarily or through
deception
Of adulterating intoxicants; administering
narcotics to race-horses to change their
form; falsely adjusting accounts or castrating
tomcats: 'One doctors a cat or a company's
accounts' (Howard, 1978); and now too of
vasectomy: 'Get her physician To make an
incision And be doctored before she is
mastered' (*Playboy's Book of Limericks*). All, I
suppose, from 'doctor', a medical practitioner, most of whom have earned and all of
whom use the honorific appellation unless
they are surgeons when, with inverted snobbery, they prefer to be styled 'Mister'.

doe a woman who goes to mixed parties on
her own
This Am. use involves the feminine of 'stag',
for males only. However much we legislate
to the contrary, males remain suspicious of
females who show that they need no male
protection. In 17c. Eng. a 'doe' was a whore,
and in later use any single woman at Oxford
University.

dole a payment by the state to the involuntarily unemployed
Properly, a portion, whence a gift made
regularly to the poor, as 'dole-bread' or
'dole-money' – and at funerals 'dole-meats'.
One of a succession of euphemisms – *see*
relief (1).

doll (1) a sexually attractive female
Dr Johnson reminds us that 'Doll' was a
contraction of Dorothy as well as being 'A
little girl's puppet or baby'. A female so described may be beautiful but slow-witted,
although 'real doll' implies beauty and brains.

doll (2) a narcotic in pill form
Usu. barbiturate or amphetamine. Susann's
punning 'Valley of the Dolls' started or sanctified this usage.

dollar shop a store for sale to privileged
customers
The chronic shortage of luxuries and hard
currency in Communist countries means
that certain goods are sold only to members
of the ruling autocracy, or to tourists who
can pay in US dsollars.

dolls *see* **guys**

dolly a whore
Perhaps from **doll** (1) (above) but also owing
something to her smart dress – 'dolled-up':

'It seemed rather steep of my father to keep his dolly at home with my wife there' (Fraser, 1969 writing in 19c. style). The 19c. 'dolly-common' or 'dolly mop' was a part-time whore: 'Maid-servants, all of whom are amateurs, as opposed to professionals, more commonly known as "Dollymops"' (Mayhew, 1862).

domestic a servant in the home
An Am. abbr. of 'domestic help' and *see* **help:** 'We used to call them servants. Now we call them domestic help' (Chandler, 1953).

dominance a sexual perversion in which a woman beats, etc. a man
Properly, authority or control over another. A male pervert is said to be 'into dominance' and may go to a specialist whore for 'discipline' or 'dominance training'.

don Juan a male philanderer
The successful practitioner in seduction inspired the music of Mozart and the words of Molière, Byron and Shaw, to mention but a few. Whence don Juanism, such behaviour: 'Etlin has great courage and charm, yet his Donjuanism somehow detracts from his authority' (Read, 1986).

done for subjected to a major misfortune
Of death – see **do** (2): '"They're both done for" .... George lay spread-eagled at my feet' (Fraser, 1971). Of serious wounding, especially in battle; of bankruptcy; of defeat; etc.

don't-name-'ems trousers
A 19c. example of the great trouser taboo – *see* too **unmentionables (1)** etc.

doorstep to abandon a baby
You left it on the step of a prosperous house and, if brave, rang the bell before you made off: 'When it became obvious .... from the hour of my conception, that my parents intended to doorstep me' (N. Mitford, 1945). This ob. use reminds us of the former stigmata of bastardy affecting both the mother and the child, and the lack of facilities for unmarried mothers and their children.

dope a narcotic
Properly, a thick liquid, the Dutch 'doop', whence prepared opium which looks like that at one stage: 'A younger sister whom she loved .... had taken to dope' (Harris, 1925). To 'dope' is to ingest illicit narcotics, or to give them to horses or greyhounds to alter form, whence 'the dope', inside infor-

mation about a race – which beast has been drugged? 'Dope', a simple person, comes from his opiate mien and behaviour.

dose a venereal infection
Usu. of gonorrhoea in a male. It is properly an amount of medicine and the use may allude to the attempted cure: 'And if I give that man a dose, that's my pleasure and he just gettin' what he's payin' for' (Simon, 1979, of a whore).

doss-house a brothel
'Doss' means sleep and a 'doss-house' is normally a sleeping place for the destitute. Am.

dotty mad
Properly, unsteady in gait (OED), whence feeble and so feeble-minded. It is used of eccentricity as much as of madness: 'There might be a basis of truth, but I felt she was pretty dotty' (Manning, 1965).

double (1) an alcoholic drink containing two standard portions
The volume of the standard portion seems to vary in relation to the Excise Duty of country concerned, so that one man's 'single' is another man's 'double': 'Scotty has really cashed in .... and was ordering doubles like a man possessed' (*Private Eye*, May 1981).

double (2) a spy working contemporaneously for two opposing parties
An abbr. of 'double agent': 'How else does anyone play a double?' (le Carré, 1980, of such a spy). In similar vein to 'double' is to pimp for two whores: 'In the meantime I'm going to "double" you (take a second woman)' (Londres, 1928, in tr.).

double depth the burial of corpses one above the other
Funeral jargon about a way of saving cemetery space: 'The companions will repose one above the other in a single grave space, dug "double depth", to use the trade expression' (J. Mitford, 1963). Am.

double entry dishonest
'Double-entry bookkeeping' is a self-balancing method of keeping simple accounts. This use puns on keeping two sets of account, of which one is intended to deceive: 'A double-entry man. Hong Kong's full of them. Twisters' (Theroux, 1982).

double-gaited having both homosexual and heterosexual tastes
DAS says 'An extension of the horse-pacing term' and I have no better suggestion:

'" . . . homosexuality isn't the handle it once was" . . . . "Pascoe's wife didn't know he was double-gaited"' (Bagley, 1982).

double-header copulation by a male with two females in each other's presence
Prostitutes' jargon, from the use of two locomotives to pull a train and perhaps punning on 'head', the glans penis: '. . . she wasn't interested in the hundred-dollar bag of bones who Juicy Lucy said was coming back at eight o'clock for a doubleheader' (Wambaugh, 1981).

double in stud to copulate with two people in each other's presence
Of either sex, despite the maleness of **stud** (q.v.): '. . . maybe there were some who doubled in stud' (Longstreet, 1956). Am.

double time extra-marital copulation
From the increased payment for overtime working and perhaps also alluding to 'two-time', to cheat: 'Your wife is standing right beside you and you are practically accusing her of a little double time' (Chandler, 1953). Am.

douceur a bribe
Properly a gratuity, in French and English: 'I bet he's had some little douceur slipped into his hand' (Manning, 1965). I prefer the 19c. spelling: 'Nobody is allowed to take dowzers' (EDD, from 1885).

douche a female contraceptive procedure
The French shower bath becomes a jet of liquid in a bidet and then a vaginal spray: 'Do you think I should take a douche . . . . *you* know . . . . birth control' (McCarthy, 1963).

dove an appeaser or pacifist
From the symbol of peace and the opposite of **hawk** (q.v.). The use is not necessarily pejorative and became hackneyed in the Kennedy and Johnson presidencies.

down coloured water
Am. night club jargon for a concoction sold to a man at the price of whisky for consumption by the employee sitting with him.

down among the dead men deep drunkenness
The 'dead men's are the skittles which have been knocked over in the W. Eng. inn game, whence too the rarer 'in the down-pins'.

down below the genitalia
Of either sex, despite the location of that part of the body above the legs. In nursery use a child or geriatric may be asked if he

has dried himself 'down below'. And sexually, where the logic is even less certain as the parties would probably be horizontal: 'We take it in turns to stroke and massage each other anywhere but what you used to call down below' (Amis, 1978).

down for good dead
The imagery is from boxing where it means knocked out unconscious.

down on *see* go down on

down the line (1) in prison
This may have come from the direction a WW I prisoner went after capture, although I suspect the usage antedates that conflict. The modern 'send down' is to sentence to imprisonment, owing something to the injunction of the Clerk of the Court to the gaolors after sentence: 'Send that man down' – to the cells.

down the line (2) the seedier parts of a city
Am. use for the location of brothels, gambling joints, etc. It may owe something to the linear arrangement of most Am. towns with a railroad as the axis, and the gravitation of such establishments to the periphery. The ob. Br. 'house in the suburbs' (q.v. under **house** (1)) employs the same idea.

down the road dismissal from employment
Used by employer and employee, for the direction you take when you quit your place of work.

Down's syndrome *see* **Hansen's disease**

downs depressant narcotics
The reverse of 'ups': '. . . took his pills by the fistful, downs from the left pocket of his tiger suit and ups from his right' (Herr, 1977). In Am. also as 'downers': 'He hoped there might be some downers left . . . . where his girlfriend left a small cache' (Wambaugh, 1975).

downstairs (1) the house servants
From their normal location in a semi-basement in a town house.

downstairs (2) the genitalia
A genteel use by male and female, so that a nurse may ask a patient if he has a problem 'downstairs'.

downward adjustment a devaluation or an economic depression
Economic or political jargon to avoid the panic which the truth might bring and imply that human agency still controlled events: '. . . the worst America has to endure is a

"downward adjustment of the economy"' (Jennings, 1965, noting the euphemism).

doxy a whore
Properly, a sweetheart, from the Dutch 'docke', a doll: 'A party taken on a cruise by wealthy degenerates, who had sold their doxies at various places in the Caribbean' (Fraser, 1971, writing in 19c. style). ob. except for literary use.

drag (1) the clothing of the other sex worn by a homosexual
From the theatrical use, a male actor (not usu. a homosexual) in female clothes, the long train being 'dragged' on the floor. A homosexual so attired is said to be 'in drag': 'A cop tried to intervene and was promptly felled by someone in drag' (Sharpe, 1977). A 'drag' is also an Am. male homosexual party.

drag (2) an illicit narcotic in cigarette form
In tobacco smoking, a 'drag' is a single puff at a cigarette being smoked by another. The imagery in each case is from the inhalation.

drain off to urinate
Usu. of a male, with obvious imagery: 'Weak bladders, old men . . . . Might as well drain off himself' (Grayson, 1975).

dram a spirituous intoxicant
You used to buy spirits from apothecaries, who used their own measurements, in this case 1/8th of a fluid ounce, the weight of a drachma, corrupted to 'dram': '"Come over for a dram," he urged them' (Boyle, 1979). The Sc. 'wee dram' is larger than the standard size.

draw a bead on to shoot at
The 'bead' is the foresight of the old style of rifle rather than the bullet. Also used fig. of anyone whose actions you watch closely: 'I am going to draw a bead on this gentleman. I am preparing an operation to liquidate him' (Goebbels, 1945, in tr. – he was particularly upset by the way in which the inhabitants of his home town had welcomed the Anglo-American invaders).

draw a blank to be very drunk
An Am. use, perhaps now ob., punning on the loss of awareness and an unsuccessful entry in a lottery: 'For after the funeral I drew a near-blank, as they said in those days about drunkenness in its most amnesic mode' (Styron, 1976).

draw the enemy into a trap to retreat involuntarily
Military use when you want to disguise your predicament in order to keep up morale: 'Of

course the officers knew, but they were telling us we were drawing the enemy into a trap' (Richards, 1933).

draw the king's picture to counterfeit money
Or the queen's, when Victoria ruled, or the president's, as the case may be, from forging the likeness on notes and coins.

draw the long bow to boast or exaggerate
The longer the bow, the further its potential range: '. . . draw the long bow better now than ever' (Byron, 1824, of boasting). In the same sense you might also 'pull' it: 'You will say, "Ah, here's Flashy pulling the long bow," but I'm not' (Fraser, 1973, writing in 19c. style). The ob. Sc. 'shoot among the doves' had the same meanings, which led to the kind of brick-dropping euphemisms bring about: 'A lady . . . . had heard her husband mention . . . . that such a gentleman . . . . was thought to shoot among the dows. She immediately took the alarm and said to him with great eagerness . . . . "My husband says ye shoot among the dows. Now as I am very fond of my pigeons. I beg you winna meddle wi' them"' (EDD).

draw too much water to outrank and require obedience
Naval use and imagery of someone who makes a decision which seems questionable but must be obeyed. Also some bureaucratic use, where the same conventions apply.

dream dust powdered illicit narcotics
Especially heroin. A 'dream stick' was opium. 'Dreams' are associated with the illegal ingestion of narcotics in many addict phrases.

dress for sale a whore
Apart from the fact that most women wear dresses, this CB Am. usage is doubly misleading. The 'dress' is not what's on offer and the transaction contemplated is of hire or licence, rather than sale. The ob. London 'dress lodger' was a whore clothed in suitable style by a pimp, working from a brothel called a 'dress-house': 'The dress-lodger probably lives some distance from the immoral house by whose owner she is employed' (Mayhew, 1862). Today an Am. pimp who decks out a whore is said to buy her 'bonds' or 'threads'.

dress on the left to be a male homosexual
Men usu. do up their jackets from the right: 'I wondered if the senator was attempting to discover whether I was "dressing on the

left" (as the London master tailors put it)'
(Behr, 1978).

drill to kill by shooting
From the boring of holes, which the bullets
are supposed to do: 'I could drill you and get
away with it' (Chandler, 1958).

drink an intoxicant or to drink intoxicants
The commonest euphemism for anything to
do with intoxicants and 'drunk' is so much
SE for intoxication that I use it as a definition, despite its euphemistic origins. Thus if
a friend offers you a drink, you do not expect
water. In many phrases, as 'drink taken',
slightly drunk, or 'in drink', drunk (but 'in
the drink' means involuntarily in any deep
water). To 'like a drink' is to be addicted to
alcohol. To 'drink too much' is to take intoxicants to excess, on a single occasion or
habitually: 'He sometimes drank too much'
(Harris, 1925, of an alcoholic). 'Given to the
drink', so addicted, is perhaps ob.: 'Some
say she cocks her wee finger. In short that
she's gien to the drink' (Barr, 1861). To
have a 'drink' or 'drinking' problem is to be
an alcoholic, not to have a restriction of the
throat: '. . . her father had had a drinking
problem' (Theroux, 1982). To 'drink at
Freeman's Quay' was to cadge intoxicants
from others. A 'non-drinker' takes no intoxicants and a 'drinker' too many: 'Aunt Estelle
was no "drinker" and her "wildness" was
the merest good spirits' (Murdoch, 1978). A
'drunk' may also be an habitual drunkard or
a carouse: 'He also had some glorious
drunks with the men he had met' (Richards,
1933), etc.

droit de seigneur copulation by a male
employer with a female employee
It means the right of the Lord (of the
Manor) but other dominant males, especially
in the entertainment industry, claim similar
privileges: 'The droit de seigneur died with
the Hollywood czars' (Deighton, 1972, of
such copulation). The rights of a Norman
Lord of the Manor were reputed, wrongly in
most cases, to include that of copulating with
each virgin in his territory. It is entirely pre-
dictable that this particular manorial right, or
perhaps duty, survives in our memory and
languages when other more important but
commonplace rights have been forgotten.
The feudal system functioned primarily on
the Lord's ability to demand free labour
from tenants or villeins, which they
euphemistically called 'boonwork', 'love-
boonwork' or 'bederipe' (reaping by request)
– just as the Tudor monarchs and their suc-

cessors called forced loans 'benevolences',
until the 1669 Bill of Rights brought that
practice to an end.

drop (1) to kill
By shooting, after which the victim falls. SE
of animals and underworld sl. of humans. In
the days of the Chicago mobs – those of the
1920's – 'drop down the shute' meant to
murder, from sliding the weighted corpse
into the lake: 'If he's alive, put him on ice
until tonight. Then drop him down the
shute' (Weverka, 1973).

drop (2) a quantity of intoxicant
This is a useful word as you do not have to
specify the quantity. Usu. of spirits: 'The
rum came up with the rations and was
handed over to the Company-Sergeant-
Major. If he liked his little drop, he took his
little drop' (Richards, 1933). 'Drop of blood'
is rarer: ' "Give me a drop of blood, will
you?" The bourbon tasted like linseed oil'
(Mailer, 1965). A 'drop on' means drunk:
'Two of our chaps with a drop on shot all the
bottles and glasses in a café' (Richards,
1933).

drop (3) to die
Usu. suddenly, of natural causes and perhaps only an abbr. of 'drop dead': 'Louie's
out mowing that lawn and he drops . . . .
Like that. The ticker' (Sanders, 1977). The
'long' or 'last' drop is death by hanging,
rarely tout court as 'drop': 'Unlike the festive
hangings of earlier times, the drop was performed in a church stillness' (Keneally,
1982). To 'drop off' is also to die of natural
causes, from either the fate of an old gate
which 'drops off the hooks' or from an avian
demise: 'The soo took the fever, the kye
drappit off (A. Armstrong, 1890). Thus the
fuller form: 'It's the dropping off the perches
. . . . Soon we shall all have gone' (N. Mitford, 1949). To 'drop in your tracks' is to die
suddenly, from racing imagery but not
necessarily of natural causes: '. . . if Kramer
had not been so inconsiderate as to drop in
his tracks. There was nothing like death for
spawning myths' (Francis, 1978). 'Drop your
leaf' refers to deciduous trees rather than
gate-leg tables, and is of natural death in old
age. To 'drop off' is also to fall asleep when
you should be keeping awake, etc.

drop (4) to give birth
Usu. of quadrupeds but to 'drop a bundle' is
to have an induced abortion in women: 'Ask
the girls who dropped their bundles' (W.
Smith, 1979, of such abortions).

drop (5) a place where stolen goods are left
Criminal and espionage use. A 'drop' may
also be the person who does the dropping.
('Drop' is a good illustration of the advantages of having a double-sourced language. I
have from time to time wondered how the
French have got by for so long without an
equivalent.)

drop acid *see* **acid**

drop anchor fraudulently to cause a horse
to run slowly in a race
The imagery is naval and the practice
associated with crooked gambling.

drop beads to identify yourself by the use
of jargon to another homosexual
The wearing of beads by a male denotes
effeminacy. If the string breaks, they distribute themselves over a wide area. Am.

drop-dead list the names of people to be
dismissed from employment
The offensive Am. expression 'drop dead'
expresses rejection.

drop off *see* **drop (3)**

drop the boom to refuse further credit to
a customer
Am. commercial use, from the defensive
obstruction to navigation. It avoids saying
directly that the other party is insolvent.

drop the hook on to arrest
The imagery has to be from fishing: 'The
buttons in the prowl car were about ready to
drop the hook on him' (Chandler, 1953).
Am.

drop your drawers etc. to copulate
extra-maritally
Of a female, with obvious imagery. '. . . those
pressed, permanented country-club types
. . . . would drop their drawers for a New
York Jew' (M. Thomas, 1980 – 'permanented' means having had their hair 'permanently waved'). A Br. female is more
likely, if so inclined, to 'drop her pants', the
equivalent of the Am. 'underpants'. The ob.
'drop your flag' was to surrender, of a ship
and not a female.

droppings the excreta of animals
SE in this use since the 16c.: 'There were
steaming piles of elephant droppings bang in
the middle of the road' (Allen, 1979).
Animals might also 'drop the crotte', from
the French 'crotte', dung – we hardly use the
Eng. 'crottels', horse dung: 'Buller splayed
out and dropped his crotte on the edge of the
path' (G. Greene, 1978). The ob. 'drop your
wax' was of humans.

drown your sorrows to drink intoxicants
to excess
Alcohol in sufficient volume is supposed to
bring solace to the unfortunate: 'If I didn't
know you better I'd have said you'd been
drowning your sorrows' (Amis, 1978). The
ob. Sc. 'drown the miller' meant either to be
made bankrupt or to add too much water to
whisky, both being derived from the proverb
'o'er muckle water drowned the miller'.

drumstick *see* **dark meat**

drunk *see* **drink**

Drury Lane ague venereal disease
Drury Lane, adjoining **Covent Garden**
(q.v.), was a notorious brothel area of pre-
20c. London. A 'Drury Lane vestal' was a
whore.

dry (1) prohibiting or not offering the sale of
intoxicants
It does not mean that nothing is available to
quench your thirst. The opposite of **wet (2)**
(q.v.).

dry (2) wanting an alcoholic drink
Usu. of beer with a pretence of temporary
dehydration: 'You dry, lad? S'm I, begod!
mouth like an ash pit' (Cookson, 1967).

dry (3) to forget your lines
Theatrical jargon, an abbr. of 'dry up', for
something which should not happen to a
professional actor: 'I delivered the previous
lines right on cue. But after the Yorick
speech I let them think I'd dried' (Deighton,
1972).

dry bob copulation without ejaculation
Partridge suggests 'ex dry bob, a blow that
leaves the skin intact' (DSUE) but I suspect
that is too intellectual an etymology if we are
familiar with the normal derivation of these
vulgarities. Consider rather 'dry', the
absence of semen, and 'bob', from the association with women's hair, both punning on
the schoolboy who eschews rowing. A 'dry
run', copulation during which the male
wears a contraceptive sheath, is a triple pun,
on the absence of a seminal free discharge,
on the feeling to the woman and on the
meaning, a practice. The ob. Br. 'dry pox'
was syphilis: 'The disease communicated by
the Malays, Lascars, and the Orientals
generally . . . . goes by the name of the
Dry —' (Mayhew, 1862 – he isn't always so
squeamish).

duck a urine bottle for males
Am. hospital jargon, from its shape. ('Duck', a zero, is generally thought to come from the shape of an egg just as 'love' in tennis comes from 'l'oeuf', although some still say it comes from playing for 'love', for nothing.)

duff *see* fluff your duff

dummy a lunatic
Properly a representation of the human form but common sl. use of an unthinking person: 'So don't get the idea all of Ellerbee's patients are dummies' (Sanders, 1985).

dump (1) to defecate
An obvious and rather distasteful Am. male usage: 'Everything hinged on that first dump of the day' (Theroux, 1971, of defecation). Also some fig. use: 'But maybe you also recall how your Service dumped all over us on that one?' (Lyall, 1985).

dump (2) to kill
Perhaps from **dump** (1) (above), or it might be from the dropping of the corpse: 'Now we've got to go back and check everyone . . . . to find out where they were when Dolly was dumped' (Sanders, 1986 – Dolly had been murdered). Am. sl.

dust (1) illicit narcotics in powdered form
From the visual similarity and in various compounds like **angel dust** or **dream dust** (q.v.). 'Dust' is also the supposed constitution of an old corpse, giving us the punning 'dust-bin', the grave, and 'dustman', a dead person.

dust (2) to kill
Probably wiping off rather than turning to dust, with the common blackboard imagery: 'The question is . . . . did she hate him enough to dust him' (Sanders, 1985).

Dutch appears in many offensive and often euphemistic expressions dating from the 17c. antagonism between England and the Low Countries. Thus anything described as 'Dutch' is likely to be bogus or inferior, as follow:

Dutch act (the) suicide

do the Dutch to kill yourself: 'You're not going to do the dutch, are you? . . . . Commit suicide?' (Sanders, 1980).

Dutch auction an auction in which the auctioneer drops the price until he gets a bid when he knocks down the article to the bidder.

Dutch bargain an unfair and unprofitable deal

Dutch cheer a spirituous intoxicant – the Dutch are gloomy otherwise.

Dutch comfort things canot be worse

Dutch concert music out of tune or a drunken carouse

Dutch consolation things could have been worse

Dutch courage bravery induced by intoxicants, inferring that a sober Dutchman is a coward

Dutch feast an occasion when the host becomes drunk before his guests

Dutch headache drunkenness or a hangover

Dutch reckoning an inflated bill without details, 'as brought at spunging or bawdy houses' (Grose – the tradition dies hard).

Dutch roll combined roll and yaw in an aircraft – it behaves like a drunken sailor. This phrase noted by Moynahan in 1983 as modern airline pilots' jargon shows how unforgiving of their historic enemies English-speakers can be.

Dutch treat entertainment or a meal to which you are invited, but where you have to pay for yourself, which is also called 'going Dutch': '"Here," Ardis Peacock said half-heartedly, "let's go Dutch." "No way . . . . I asked you to lunch"' (Sanders, 1980).

Dutch uncle someone who reproves you sharply, unlike the geniality of real uncles: 'I talked to him like a Dutch uncle. It doesn't seem to have done him any good' (Baron, 1948).

Dutch widow a whore

Dutch wife a bolster, the sole bedmate of many White bachelors serving in the Far East: '. . . he clutched tightly the bolster – sweat-absorbing bedfellow of sleepers in the East – known as a Dutch wife' (Burgess, 1959).

in Dutch in trouble: 'Got me in proper Dutch, you did' (B. Forbes, 1985 – a nurse had been exposed to criticism by a patient's action).
The exception is the **Dutch cap**, a contraceptive device worn internally, named for its shape and perhaps its country of origin. It was a male commentator of a hockey match between the ladies of Holland and England who described the goalkeeper of the visiting side as 'very experienced – she has thirty-two Dutch caps'.

duty defecation
Probably from the requirement placed daily
on children: 'Many an unwary person has
been knocked off his toes by a charging por-
ker before the completion of his duties'
(Simon, 1979, of open-air defecation in
India).

dyke a female homosexual playing the male
role
Perhaps not euphemistic as I can trace no
etymology: '"Good God, what was she, a
dyke?" asked the President. "No, a woman
in her middle forties, unmarried, sentimental"' (Ustinov, 1966).

dynamite a marijuana cigarette
There are two other Am. addict meanings, a
mixture of marijuana and heroin; and cocaine and heroin taken together by any
method.

dyslexic of below average reading ability
The condition involves a natural impediment which makes reading difficult. Many
parents however so describe their children to
explain literary shortcomings which may be
the result of heredity, environment, bad
eyesight, poor teaching or idleness.

E

EC *see* **earth closet**

ear a microphone used in secret surveillance
The jargon of espionage, or of spy fiction: 'If
they think you've got something to hide,
they'll plant another ear' (Francis, 1978).

early bath *see* **take an early bath**

early retirement dismissal from
employment
Not going to bed before 10 o'clock but
properly used of those who choose to give up
paid employment abnormally early: 'Paul
Bergmosen, in charge of purchasing, who
was given "early retirement" in 1977'
(Lacey, 1986 – he was dismissed).

earn to steal
A military use, seeking to show entitlement –
cf. **liberate** (2). In the Ottoman Empire, to
'earn a passport' was to be lent by the Sultan
from his harem to a minister whom you were
required to kill, by means other than assidu-
ous uxoriousness: 'Her task accomplished,
she was re-integrated into the Royal household and rewarded for her services. In the
argot of the Seraglio, this was known as
"earning a passport"' (Blanch, 1954).

earn the wages of sin *see* **wages of sin**

earth closet a non-flush lavatory
First used for those arrangements where
earth was used as an absorbent, and then for
any 'closet', or lavatory, which did not use a
water flush or chemical dispersion. Commonly abbr. to 'EC'.

ease springs etc. to urinate
Of a male, from the military action 'easing
springs' in which the rifle bolt is rapidly
moved up and down the breech, which has a
tenuous similarity to the stroking of the
penis to prevent a drip of urine. To 'ease
your bladder' applies to either sex: 'One man
I knew used to swear that he only eased his
(bladder) once a month' (Richards, 1936, of
service in India). To 'ease yourself' is to
urinate or defecate and to 'ease your bowels'
is to defecate: 'I had dismounted to .... try
to ease my wind-gripped bowels' (Fraser,
1973). A 'house of ease' is a lavatory, as is a
chapel of ease (q.v.) sometimes.

East to your death
From the direction in which Polish and
other Jews were sent by the Nazis to work in
the death camps: '"Where has Herr Hirsch-
mann gone?" I was able to ask. "The Germans sent him east"' (Keneally, 1985, of
WW II Belorussia – it meant he was dead).

East African activities extra-marital
copulation
A *Private Eye* refinement of the in-joke
'Ugandan affairs' (q.v. under **Uganda**): 'I
am distressed to see the old French word
"romance" used as a code name for East
African activities' (A. Waugh, *Private Eye*,
December 1980).

(East Asia All-one-Culture was the
name chosen for the anti-Western,
nationalist and Marxist society and university founded by Prince Konoye Atsumaro at
Shanghai in 1901. Its teachings, if not its
name, influenced and clearly confused Sun-
Yat-Sen, Gandhi, Chiang-Kai-shek, U Nu
and Mao, to name an eminent few.)

East Village a less fashionable area of New
York
Used to exploit the cachet of 'The Village' in
real estate dealings: 'Property speculators
tried to call the East Side of (10th Street)
"the East Village" but there were not many
takers' (Deighton, 1981). This is a sample
entry of common real estate misnomers,
rarely leavened by the humour of a Bristol
estate agent who sold one of my sons a flat
overlooking 'the dead centre of the City' –
the main cemetery.

Eastern substances illegal narcotics
From the association of China with opium or
from the source of much modern illicit
supply: 'The smell of exotic Eastern substances grown on the premises that wafts
gently across the square' (*Private Eye*, May
1981, of cannabis).

easy terms hire purchase
The use is so widespread that we no longer
address our minds to the reality that everything involved becomes more expensive and
difficult, except finding the initial down-
payment.

easy way out (the) suicide
Not an open door. The use implies a lack of
courage: '... they've told me it's cancer and
I'm taking the easy way out' (James, 1972,
from a suicide note).

easy woman a female with no reserve
about extra-marital copulation
'Easy' in the sense, compliant. They are not
necessarily whores: 'Whether we worked in a
Massage Parlour or were rich .... we were
still the same to you. Easy women' (Bogarde,

1978). And *see* 'lady of easy virtue' under lady.

eat to ingest illicit methedrine
Am. addict sl.

eat a gun to commit suicide with a firearm
The only sure way of killing yourself is to load it, point it upwards through your mouth and then pull the trigger: '. . . his back against the filthy tiled wall, and he was trying to eat his gun' (Sanders, 1977, of an attempted suicide).

eat flesh to copulate with a woman
More than Shakespeare's inventive mind at work: 'Suffering flesh to be eaten in thy house in contrary to the law' (2 *Henry IV*) because to 'eat' pussy, meat, or any other carnal names for the penis or vagina now means to stimulate such parts orally: 'Wouldn't you like to eat my pussy?' (Robbins, 1981, of a woman suggesting cunnilingus).

eat for two to be pregnant
The theory, unjustified in affluent families, is that a woman needs double rations during pregnancy: '"Do you ever remember me on a diet, Edie?" "No, I can eat for two." "You don't mean . . . ?" "Edie!" she laughed' (Deighton, 1972).

eat-in kitchen there is no separate dining-room
Am. real estate jargon when selling a small house or apartment.

eat stale dog to take a deserved reprimand
I think this is analogous to 'eat dirt', with 'dog' being an abbr. for 'dog shit': 'I can eat some stale dog and get by' (Chandler, 1939, of someone detected in wrongdoing).

eat the bible to perjure yourself
Under Eng. common law, merely telling lies is not an offence. False evidence given on oath, with the swearing usu. on a bible, constitutes the crime of perjury: '. . . told the lieutenant not to count on me to "eat the Bible"' (Lavine, 1930). Am.

eccentric mad
Properly, not moving on a centrally placed axis, whence, of human behaviour, whimsical or unusual in SE: 'The poor man is crazy; the rich man is eccentric' (Old Saw quoted in Sanders, 1977).

economic storm a slump
Perhaps no more than circumlocution, but stockbrokers, economists etc. go to great lengths to avoid any of the terms which might recall the events which happened between 1929 and 1935.

economical with the truth lying
The celebrated phrase of the Secretary of the Br. cabinet, Sir R. Armstrong, in an Australian trial in November 1986 when a former and indigent Br. secret agent sought dishonourably to publish confidential information, with the enthusiastic support of many Br. politicians. For the patriotic, or freedom-conscious, section of the population, their annoyance at the breach of faith was tempered by the sight of a pompous bureaucrat being subjected to stringent, if unfair, cross-examination.

economy cheap
Properly, the avoidance of waste, but does that mean airline travellers not in inferior seats are feckless? In supermarket jargon, 'economy' is meant to mean cheap but in fact means **large** (q.v.).

écouteur a person who obtains aural gratification from the sexual activity of others
Properly, from the French, a person who listens, but never a simple radio fan or even an eavesdropper: 'The shrieking bed springs were no accident. The manager's wife was an écouteuse' (Condon, 1966 – you will no doubt have already observed that I follow the literary convention of using the masculine case where either sex is imported).

edie a whore
Perhaps ob. London use of the cheaper type of whore, from the woman's name: 'The Edies of the East End, Piccadilly and the railway stations' (Gosling and Warner, 1960).

edged slightly drunk
The ob. Suffolk dialect use was probably not the direct parent of the modern Am., but both must have derived from being on the 'edge of drunkenness', or some such phrase: 'When he was nicely edged he was a pretty good sort' (Chandler, 1934).

educationally sub-normal imbecile
In fact the lower half of any grouping is sub-normal, but every child who attends ordinary classes is 'normal', however far below the norm his achievement may be. We are so used to this educational jargon that we never think what the words mean. Similarly the Am. 'educable' means moronic but with the possibility of just learning something.

effeminate a male homosexual
Properly, having the characteristics of a

woman: 'She wondered for a moment if he might be what people called effeminate' (Follett, 1978).

effing *see* F

effluent a noxious discharge
Of sewage or industrial waste, but it means anything which flows, including a trout stream. 'Sewage' itself started life in this sense as a euphemism, from its proper meaning, draining off water.

effusion an ejaculation of semen
Properly, a pouring forth, which is why the word is often used of wine: 'The mere effusions of thy proper loins' (Shakespeare, *Measure for Measure*). ob.

egg a bomb
'Laid' by WW II airmen, the word and imagery divorcing the perpetrator from the carnage.

elbow bender *see* bend

electric cure killing by electrocution
A sardonic Am. expression for death in the 'elecctric chair'.

electric methods torture
A refinement of Nazism but cf. **appropriate technology**: 'Bienecke used the "electric methods" pioneered by the SD in France – not the sort of scientific advance to crow about' (Keneally, 1985, of WW II German behaviour in Russia).

electrical fault an excuse for an embarrassing failure
This is the best kind of lie – simple in concept and difficult to disprove – which can be called in aid to explain a failure to operate a transport service or to provide any cover-up: 'There are bombs every day . . . . there was a fire which destroyed much of the new colour television studio which had been built for the World Cup broadcasts. This was called an "electrical fault"' (Theroux, 1979, quoting Borges – if your building is blown up it is at least part of the truth to say the electric system is faulty).

electrical surveillance *see* surveillance

electronic counter-measures spying
The phrase is used of both optical and electronic aids and the euphemism is in the 'counter-measures' because, far from 'countering' anything, you are invading another's privacy. If your operation remains undetected, you achieve 'electronic penetration'.

elephant and castle the anus
Rh. sl. for 'arsehole', from the area of S. London named after a public house which stood at the start of the old London to Brighton road.

elephant's drunk
Rh. sl. from 'elephant's trunk'. To 'cop an elephant's' is to become drunk and *see*, too, **jumbo**.

elevate to make drunk
Perhaps from the feeling of power or levitation experienced at some stage of inebriation. 'Elevated' and 'elevation' mean respectively drunk and drunkenness.

eliminate to kill
A variant of **liquidate** (q.v.) with the same etymology and connotations, usu. of political or espionage killings: 'We will just have to eliminate him. No time. No publicity' (G. Greene, 1978). An 'elimination' is such a killing: 'Elimination is rather a new line for us. More in the KGB line or the CIA's' (ibid.).

embalmed very drunk
The derivation is not from 'barm', froth, nor even from the punning 'embalming fluid', cheap whisky, but almost certainly from the lifeless condition of the subject.

embraces copulation
Properly, clasping in the arms affectionately, with familial or sexual fervour. Usu. of a female. '. . . solicited the gratification of their taste for variety in my embraces' (Cleland, 1749). A woman who 'shares her embraces' copulates regularly with two or more males contemporaneously. 'Illicit embraces' means extra-marital copulation: 'Harold and Noreen must have been surprised again in their illicit embraces' (McCarthy, 1963). You rarely see 'embrace' in the singular: 'When a girl's lips grow hot, her sex is hot first and she is ready to give herself and ripe for the embrace' (Harris, 1925).

embroider to exaggerate or invent
The derivation is from ornamental needlework and the use, to avoid direct accusation of lying. Raleigh accused the ancient Greek historians of 'embroidering and intermixing' fact and fiction although, as a historian himself, he should have known the way most history is written.

emergency a war confined to one country
The declaration of a State of Emergency in a country which is not an autocracy suspends those laws which may hamper the military

and the police in asserting their control. Thus a long and bitter struggle after WW II in Malaya between Chinese Communist forces and the Br. administration was described as the 'emergency'.

emergent poor and uncivilized
The use is mainly of former colonial territories in Africa, some of which, far from 'emerging', are retreating into greater proverty and the tribal divisions which their colonial masters had tried to break down: 'To avoid embarrassing its trading partners in emergent Africa, South African officials and trade organizations will not disclose the destination of its £800m. annual food exports' (*Daily Telegraph*, October 1981, which reported that 46 of the 49 member states of the 'Organization of African Unity', a body implacably opposed to the existence of South Africa, trade with and to a greater or lesser extent depend for food on their foe). 'Emerging' is used in the same sense: 'Except for King Paul of Greece . . . . they came from the emerging nations' (Manchester, 1968, of Mali, Yemen, Nigeria, etc.).

emotional drunk
Intoxication makes some people excitable or sentimental: 'Tired and emotional after a long flight from Australia . . .' (*Private Eye*, September 1981, of a drunken person).

employ to copulate with
In this ob. usage, the man is the employer: 'Your tale must be, how he employ'd my mother' (Shakespeare, *King John*).

employment unemployment
This is one of those evasive opposites like defence, health etc. (q.v.). Thus a 'Department of Employment' is concerned with finding jobs or providing for the unemployed.

empty your bladder to urinate
Perhaps circumlocution rather than euphemism, except that it could as well refer to letting air out of your football! 'Go to the bathroom, empty your bladder' (McCarthy, 1963).

enceinte pregnant
It means surrounded – and is also euphemistic – in French and so, when we use it, we are doubly evasive: 'The idea that Kay might be enceinte had stolen more than once into her quiet thoughts' (McCarthy, 1963).

encirclement a mutual defence pact among your neighbours
It is a delusion of tyrants that those whom they threaten are also threatening them. The Nazis and Communists seem especially prone to being 'encircled'.

end to kill
The common scepticism about your prospects of reincarnation: 'The sword hath ended him' (Shakespeare, I *Henry IV*). The Am. police 'end of watch' means death: 'Knuckles Garrity went End-of-Watch forever in the old police station parking lot' (Wambaugh, 1975). 'End', the buttocks, is probably ob. and was also inaccurate except as the proximate termination of the alimentary canal: '. . . settle their ends upon stools' (Tennyson, 1889).

Endlösung *see* final solution

endowed *see* well endowed etc.

energy release an accidental escape of radioactive material
An atomic power station should only release energy which is converted into electricity. This nuclear jargon seeks to play down the health hazards following the accidental release of radio-active materials. Am.

enforcer a criminal who terrorizes under orders
He may threaten or maim, to cow or punish for a gang leader, bookmaker, etc.: 'She was a freelance enforcer renowned for her skill in getting any job done quickly' (Collins, 1981 – but most 'enforcers' are male).

engine a penis
Viewed sexually and a variant of **machine** or **tool** (q.v.): '. . . too much desirability can freeze a man's engine' (Keneally, 1985).

(engineer is a valuable word for enhancing the status of any job, especially in Am. where it took one to drive a train. Now in many compounds, some accurate but most, pretentious.)

English connected with male sexual deviation
A usage not found in the BI. Of Am. bondage, masochism, etc. which may be known and advertised as 'English' arts, assistance, guidence, treatment, etc. – phrases which an innocent might think offered help in elocution or other investigation of the noblest and most versatile of tongues. In this regard at least, the French are kinder; the '*capôte anglaise*' is used in standard heterosexual encounters.

enhanced contouring cosmetic padding
Advertising use of female clothing to appeal
to women who think their breasts or hips are
too small but may not want others to think
that they think it: '. . . her bra comes with
"built-in emphasis" or "enhanced contouring"' (Jennings, 1965).

enhanced radiation weapon a neutron
bomb
We forget perhaps that a sun-lamp provides
us with 'enhanced radiation'.

enjoy to copulate with
Usu. of the male, from the days when the
pleasure was supposed to be his alone: 'You
shall, if you will, enjoy Ford's wife' (Shakespeare, *Merry Wives of Windsor*). But you need
not specify the woman: 'He felt entitled to
enjoy a woman' (Follett, 1978). To 'enjoy
favours' is more specific, and *see* **favours**:
'He regularly visited a famous courtesan in
the Srinagar bazaar, and enjoyed other
favours, too' (Masters, 1976). 'Enjoy her
person' is ob.: '. . . prostituted for some time
to old men, who paid a high price for the
enjoyment of her person' (Mayhew, 1862).
To 'enjoy hospitality' of a woman is to copulate with her extra-maritally: 'The scandal
mags said John Kennedy, quote, Enjoyed
her hospitality, unquote' (Sanders, 1977).
An 'enjoyed' woman is one who has copulated, whether or not the male found it
pleasurable: 'After Mrs Mayhew when I was
seventeen, no mature woman who had been
enjoyed ever attracted me physically' (Harris, 1925).

enjoy a drink to be a drunkard
You may also be said to 'enjoy' a glass, drop,
jug, nip, the bottle, etc.

enjoy Her Majesty's hospitality to be
in prison
In jail you do not have to pay for your keep.
The phrase is suitably adjusted for kings and
presidents.

enlist the aid of science to undergo cosmetic surgery
The 'scientist' removes wrinkles, causes
superfluous hair to vanish or implants it
where it is scarce, etc.: 'A few years ago
when my hair began to recede I enlisted the
aid of science' (Murdoch, 1978).

enter to copulate with
Of the male: 'She let out her breath in a long
quavering moan as he entered her' (Masters,
1976). The entry of a tongue into the mouth
of another is called 'French kissing'.

enter the next world etc. to die
In various forms, indicating devout belief or
scepticism: 'It was better to enter the next
world with a full belly' (Richards, 1933) or:
'within a month or so I shall have entered the
great "Perhaps", as Danton I think called
"the undiscovered country"' (Harris, 1925).

entertain (1) to beat a prisoner violently
The 'hospitality' is shown to coerce those in
police custody: 'The more they protested the
more they were *entertained*' (Lavine, 1930).
Am.

entertain (2) to copulate with extra-
maritally
Another way, I suppose, of keeping a man
interested or amused: 'She had "entertained" him before and each time he had
nearly ripped her in half' (Collins, 1981).

entertain (3) to bribe
Commercial use, of excessive prodigality,
like the Br. practice of paying for surgeons
and their wives to attend 'conferences' in
holiday playgrounds, so long as they continue to insist on the sole use of your product
in their operating theatre. 'Entertainment' is
such bribery.

equal pay inequitable remuneration
Properly, paying everyone who does precisely the same job the same money, from
the slogan 'Equal pay for equal work'. In
many jobs the work cannot be equal because,
apart from physical constraints, women are
barred by Statute from certain overtime,
nightwork, etc. A result is that the openings
for women may be fewer because they
become more expensive in real terms than
men. Happily they are better at many tasks
than men, and most of us prefer working at
what we do best anyway.

equipment is a word used to cover up and
evade in any matter the subject of a taboo.
Sexually it may refer to the breasts or vagina
of a female, the genitalia of a male; of illegal
narcotics it is a supply or the means of
introducing it into the body; in the airline
industry it is something which goes wrong
when your flight is delayed because of
'unserviceable equipment' – nobody must
suggest there is something wrong with the
flying machine; etc.

**equity equivalent contingent partici-
pation** a share of profit calculated by reference to equity growth
Not just Am. circumlocution because it is
used when the lending bank is forbidden by
law to enjoy profits of this kind: 'Our interest

wouldn't be in stock, of course Glass-Steagall rules that out. It'd be what they call "an equity equivalent contingent participation"' (M. Thomas, 1987).

erase to kill
A version of 'rub out', which uses the same imagery: 'I'd have hired a drunken lorry driver and had her erased on a zebra crossing' (Sharpe, 1977).

erection a sexual swelling of the penis
Properly, of anything, the condition of being upright and SE of buildings and penises: '. . . his toilet closet choc full of Japanese erection lozenges and love elixirs' (Ustinov, 1971). Whence 'erect', having such a swelling: 'He had woken erect himself' (P. Scott, 1975 – he had not been sleeping standing up).

errant engaged in extra-marital copulation
Properly, travelling, as knights-errant – knight-errants? – did, whence straying from accepted standards of behaviour: '. . . serving legal papers on reluctant defendants and following errant wives' (Deighton, 1981, of a private detective).

(escalate to wage war more fiercely takes its imagery from the moving stairway – presumably the one going up: 'Johnson, escalating, feigns to have no option in the war' (McCarthy, 1967, on Vietnam).)

escort a paid female companion to a man
Properly, a body of armed men, whence one person accompanying another. She is usu. also a whore, for a further fee: 'One was a persistent "escort" for Arabs' (*Private Eye*, July 1981, of a Bunny Girl – the quotation marks indicate that she was also a whore). An 'escort agency' hires out the women: 'But escort agency meant hookers for hire' (Theroux, 1982).

essence the male semen
From the meanings, the essential being and what is left after distillation: 'I want to drink your essence and I will' (Harris, 1925, of semen).

essentials the male reproductive organs
The brain, heart or liver assume less importance: '. . . once your essentials are properly trapped in the mangle there's nothing to do but holler' (Fraser, 1985).

estate a grave
The last property you occupy, in funeral jargon: '. . . the section of the cemetery, where your family estate is located' (J. Mitford, 1963).

eternal life death
A monumental favourite, although those who order the inscription are seldom anxious personally to put their faith to the test. The ob. 'eternity box', a coffin, represented a more pragmatic approach.

ethnic not of exclusively White ancestry
The commonest euphemism of the 1980s with 'ethnic minority' come to mean Black or Hispanic people according to where in Am. or BI you lived: 'The car had been stolen the previous night from outside a block of high-rise apartments in Brixton chosen because of its ethnic inhabitants' (B. Forbes, 1986 – Brixton has become a London ghetto). The word 'ethnic' means 'pertaining to nations not Christian or Jewish' (OED), from which anyone who wasn't a Christian or a Jew. As the practice of these religions was largely confined to Europe or those of European descent elsewhere, 'ethnic' came to mean those not of that skin pigmentation, and then of any particular pigmentation.

Eumenides the Furies
The Greeks called them the 'kindly ones' because they might get even more angry if their real names were used. Similarly they called the stormy and fearsome Black Sea the Euxine, the hospitable. Not so long ago we tried to appease the devil and the fairies in the same way – *see* **good man, good folk**, etc. – and some Christian prayers to an all-powerful and avenging God make strange reading.

evacuate to defecate
Medical jargon and an abbr. of 'evacuate your bowel'. Whence 'evacuation', defecation: '. . . supported the dysentery cases as they trembled and shuddered during their burning evacuations' (Boyd, 1982).

evacuation (1) *see* **evacuate**

evacuation (2) the mass murder of the Jews
The Nazi 'Aussiedlung'. The victims were 'evacuated' from their homes for forced labour or gassing.

evasion a lie
More than an avoidance of the truth: 'I should say she indulged in certain evasions' (Styron, 1976, of a liar).

Eve *see* **Adam**

eventide home an institution for geriatrics
An establishment so named lies just to the N of the city of Aberdeen but the imagery of comparing life to a day is common.

everlasting life death
Another trustful monumental favourite. The words are sometimes inverted in the verse of Hymns Ancient and Modern and in the poetry of Cranmer, lately rejected by the Church of England.

ewe mutton an older woman who affects the style of a younger
Derogatory female use of another. I include it to give the ob. Br. meaning, an elderly whore.

(exceptional stupid in educational jargon, may jar on those who think it synonymous with 'outstanding'. It is not euphemistic because the subject can as well be exceptionally bad as exceptionally good.)

excess to dismiss from employment
An Am. use when the employer wants to cut costs by getting rid of 'excess' labour.

exchange flesh to copulate
As different from swapping titbits of meat. This may again be no more than Shakespeare's vivid imagery: 'She would not exchange flesh with one that loved her' (*A Winter's Tale*).

exchange of views etc. a disagreement between rigidly opposed parties
Mainly diplomatic use. Qualifications like 'cordial' or 'helpful' do not indicate greater amity nor is an 'exchange of ideas' more propitious.

exchange this life for a better to die
A perhaps ob. monumental message: 'After a long illness which she bore without a murmur exchanged this life for a better on the 23rd day of March, 1815' (Monument in Bath Abbey).

execute to murder
Properly, to carry out any task, whence to effect the sentence of a court, especially of death. Because of the methods of the times, it became SE for beheading and today terrorists have adopted the word to try to cloak their killings with legality: '"The execution of hostages will begin then." "Execution." She was using the jargon of legality' (W. Smith, 1979, of a terrorist). In the same way 'executive action' is CIA jargon for an unlawful killing.

executive measure a political murder
Yet another of the WW II Nazi evasions: '"Lohse, I recommend that your office initiate an executive measure aimed at Oberführer Willi Ganz" .... *Executivmassnehme*, a classic "soft word" whose intent can be con-

vincingly denied long after the corpses are counted' (Keneally, 1985).

exercise your marital rights *see* **marital rights**

exhibit yourself to show your penis to a stranger in a public place
A persistent form of male sexual gratification, the erect penis being displayed to women or children: '... a wealthy old man charged .... with exhibiting himself to toddlers' (Sanders, 1973). To 'make an exhibition of yourself' is merely to behave stupidly.

exhibition a pornographic display
Properly a showing of anything, from fine art to kindergarten basketwork: 'The card had half a dozen choices on it: blue movies; girls; boys; exhibition; massage' (Theroux, 1973). The Spanish 'exhibición' is an Am. use for a trip into Mexico to see pornographic items which would be barred N. of the border.

expectant pregnant
An abbr. of 'expectant mother', who is said to be 'expecting'. We take for granted that what she 'expects' is the birth of a baby to herself, and not a birthday present or an increase in salary.

expedient demise a killing unlawfully by a government agency
The pretence is that the death was natural – a 'demise' – but timely: 'You had to give orders for the expedient demise of two men' (Deighton, 1981 – he called the book *XPD*).

expended killed
This use treats soldiers like ammunition: '"And what do you mean about me being 'expended'" .... "He has wanted to kill you"' (L. Thomas, 1978 – this is a rare non-military example). 'Expendable' is the number of soldiers you can afford to have killed or wounded in a battle: '"You're what they call "expendable". Clark nodded with sad honesty' (ibid.).

expenses an additional tax-free income
Properly, the amount incurred by an employee in the course of his work and reimbursed by the employer. Too often the disbursement has not been made as claimed, or at all. 'Expense account' living is the profligacy which results either from the payment in respect of fraudulent claims or from an employee's extravagance when he can charge what he spends to his employer's account.

experienced having copulated
Of either sex. Whereas, in most disciplines, to gain 'experience' you must practise often and become adept, in this activity a single essay may be enough: 'Stephanie too was "experienced". Whatever had it been like for her with all those men?' (Murdoch, 1977). Of an Am. motor vehicle, it means no more than it is not new.

expert a person who makes a living by professing knowledge
Others often find a claim of omniscience spurious: 'The directorate at ARCOS was topheavy with so-called "experts"' (Boyle, 1979). An 'expert witness' is a person with impressive qualifications who is paid to support on oath the case of a litigant.

expire to die
To breathe out, but for the last time: 'As to other euphemisms – of words which connote death . . . . "expire" for "die"' (J. Mitford, 1963). 'Expire' in an ob. doubly euphemistic use meant to reach a sexual orgasm – *see* **die** (above): 'When both press on, both murmur, both expire' (Dryden).

expose yourself to show your penis to a stranger in a public place
A Br. variant of **exhibit yourself** (above) but found in Am. also: 'He . . . . had rung the doorbell and introduced himself to Stacie, then had exposed himself' (Condon, 1966). 'Exposure' and the legal jargon 'indecent exposure' are such a display.

extended dull
This Am. educational jargon seems to be based on the premise that simple work which those so described find difficult 'extends' their faculties, as indeed it may.

exterminating engineer a rat-catcher
I give this Am. sample to illustrate the popular pastime of upgrading our job description to gratify our self-esteem, and that of our spouses. Logically, the **engineer** (q.v.) might be in the process of personal dissolution, and even if we accept that he is 'exterminating' something else, the choice is large. The Br. 'rodent operator' is no less pretentious and illogical – might he not provide performing shrews for a circus? Mencken

(*The American Language*) gives many examples of this restyling of jobs, some of which are ephemeral, some circumlocutary and a few euphemistic.

extra-curricular activity etc. extramarital copulation
Properly, anything to do with school which is done away from the classroom or campus. 'Extra-curricular sex' is more specific: 'An opportunity for extra-curricular sex occurred, and he hadn't fought it' (Hailey, 1979).

extra-marital excursion a single case of extra-marital copulation
It might be, but is not, a skittles tour with the lads or a day at the seaside with the Mothers' Union: '. . . similar situations – in reverse – when *he* returned from extra-marital excursions' (Hailey, 1979).

extras extra-marital sexual gratification
The service provided is usu. masturbation or copulation in a brothel which calls itself a 'massage parlour': 'Mr Bircher admitted giving the service with "extras" on request, consisting of acts of masturbation by him and his wife. Basic massage was £15. Erotic massage cost £20' (*Daily Telegraph*, January 1984, of a Cornish 'massage parlour').

extreme physical duress torture
Perhaps circumlocution rather than euphemism: 'Tell him he will be interrogated under extreme physical duress' (Hall, 1979).

extreme prejudice *see* **terminate** (1)

eye in the sky a police helicopter
The Am. CB expression is used to warn other truckers of possible speed assessment by police working from that vantage point.

eye-opener an intoxicant or narcotic taken on waking
Punning on the meaning, a surprise: 'A morning eye-opener (brandy, Scotch or whatever) would also be provided' (Sanders, 1980). The usage seems to have originated in France during WW I, especially but surprisingly among airmen. Now generally used by people addicted to alcohol or narcotics who need topping up before they can face another day.

F

F fuck
Nearly always for the verb. The common 'effing' is not used literally: 'It wasn't a case of where's my effing breakfast' (Allen, 1979).

facility (1) a lavatory
Properly, anything which makes performance easier: 'A small outdoor facility and the forest' (Poyer, 1980, describing a chalet on the edge of a village).

facility (2) an agreement to lend money by a bank
Banking jargon of the limit to which you may borrow. I suppose it makes life easier, for a while.

facts (of life) the human process of reproduction
Thus breathing, eating and growing old are not the 'facts of life', while conception, pregnancy, menstruation, birth, etc. are: 'I sometimes think your children are right and you don't know the facts of life' (N. Mitford, 1949). Sometimes abbr. to 'the facts': 'Linda's presentation of the facts had been so gruesome that . . . . their future chances of a sane and happy sex life (were) much reduced' (N. Mitford, 1945). A 'fact of life' is an unpalatable truth.

fade away to die
Especially of former soldiers: 'Frank wrote to me regularly until he faded away, in 1961' (Graves, in an introduction to a reprint of *Old Soldiers Never Die*). To 'fade' is underworld sl. for killing: '"You fade him?" "Not me. I just found him as he was' " (Lyall, 1965, of a corpse).

fag a male homosexual
Probably from the fact that male cigarette – or 'fag' – smokers were in the 1920s thought effemina.. by pipe and cigar smokers: 'An eager young fag, very pert in urchin cut and ear-rings, had accosted him' (Davidson, 1978). I think the longer form, 'faggot', comes from 'fag' in the way that 'pooftah'comes from 'pouff', and this despite the attractions or otherwise of 'faggot', a wretched old woman, from which came the ob. Br. use, to copulate with a whore.

faggot *see* fag

fair poor
A classification of scholastic performance,

the quality of goods or services, which is just above the bottom rating. It should mean favourable or even, in sl. use, mid-way between good and bad. Thus in BI a 'fair rent' is a statutory term for a rent controlled by law at less than an open-market rate: 'Their regulated rent (euphemistically called a "fair rent" by law) would buy dinner for one at a local restaurant' (Stevens, *Private Eye*, July 1981).

fair-haired boy someone being helped to win political office
He may be dark-haired or bald, even no longer young, but he must have a good chance of winning to let him repay the party managers who backed him. This Am. phrase is also used of a junior employee who seems destined for promotion, on his merits or otherwise.

(fair sex women is used in Milton's sense: 'The fairest of her Daughters, Eve'. The phrase therefore embraces some who are dark in complexion, or prejudiced, or not free from blemish, to take some of the other meanings of 'fair'. I give this short dissertation as an excuse for mentioning the ob. Cheshire 'fair lady', a sexual mistress; and the general 'fair trader', a smuggler, so called because, paying no excise duty, he asked none of his customers.)

fairy a male homosexual assuming the female role
From the modern Christmas pantomime concept of fairies: 'A mob of howling fairies, frenzied because the best part went to younger stars who didn't lisp' (Theroux, 1976). A 'fairy lady' is a female homosexual taking the female role.

faithful not copulating with other than your regular sexual partner
Usu. of such behaviour within marriage. Properly, true to your word or belief, but in this sense true to merely one of the marriage vows: 'He loved his beautiful wife and, so far as I know, was faithful to her' (Murdoch, 1978).

fall (1) to copulate with a man extramaritally
The imagery is from 'falling from grace': 'It is their husbands' fault, If wives do fall' (Shakespeare, *Othello*). In modern use to 'fall' is to become sexually attracted to a single person, as an abbr. of 'fall for': 'I didn't slip, I wasn't pushed, I fell, oh yes, right into the middle of a warm caress' (popular lyric).

fall (2)   to become pregnant
A common modern use, which may have
come from **fall** (1) (above). Of pregnancy
within or outside marriage: 'Annabel Birley
has fallen again and delivered another
(legitimate) Goldsmith into the world' (A.
Waugh, 1980). To 'fall for a child' or to 'fall
in the family way' both suggest pregnancy
outside marriage: 'The girl fell in the family
way and was sent out of the house' (Mayhew,
1862). 'Fall wrong to', of unmarried pregnancy only, is ob.: 'There was a lass . . . . who
fell wrong to a farmer's son where she had
been serving, and he wouldn't marry her'
(Saxon, 1878). To 'fall pregnant' is specific:
'. . . one of the Emalia girls fell pregnant,
pregnancy being, of course, an immediate
ticket to Auschwitz' (Keneally, 1982).

fall (3)   to die
On military service, if not in battle, from
being hit by a bullet, etc.: 'John Cornford
had fallen the day after his coming of age'
(Boyle, 1979). In Hitler's case, it covered
suicide but the intention was to show he died
fighting: 'Adolf Hitler fell in his command
post in the Reich Chancellery' (Official German announcement of Hitler's death, 1 May
1945, in tr.). Both soldiers and civilians 'fall
asleep': '. . . fell asleep in Jesus . . . . of
enteric fever in Mesopotamia' (memorial in
West Monkton church to WW I soldier).
You may 'fall off' the hooks or the perch as
easily as you may 'drop' – *see* **drop** (3): 'If the
excitement of sharing a bedroom with a
shapely lass should cause Fred to fall off the
perch' (*Sunday Express*, March 1980). The
Am. 'fall out' probably employs military
imagery. The 'fallen' are those who have
died on military service, unless they be
fallen women (q.v.). There was an ob. S.
Eng. use of 'fall' which conversely meant to
be born, of animals: 'The calf is lately fell'
(Ellis, 1750), and 'fall about', to be ready to
give birth, is still rarely used of humans.

fall (4)   to be sentenced to prison
I suppose from the reversal of fortune. An
Am. 'fall', apart from being the Br. autumn,
is an arrest and if you think that is likely, you
may keep your 'fall money' by you, to pay for
a lawyer, put up bail, bribe the police, etc.

fall among thieves   to admit to
drunkenness
Males use this biblical reference to explain
to their wives untypical behaviour attribut-
able to the wiles of others. Much humorous
use.

fall asleep *see* **fall** (3)

fall off the back of a lorry etc.   to be
stolen
Now specific of stolen goods sold below
market value in public houses etc.: 'You
wouldn't believe what I paid for them. Fell
off the back of a lorry' (Theroux, 1976 – and
even then it would be stealing by finding).
Valuables also 'fall off the back of' wagons,
trucks and even, in WW II, half-tracks:
'Scotch, which is said to have fallen off the
back of an American half-track' (Price,
1978, of WW II).

fall off the hooks etc. *see* **fall** (3)

fall off the roof   to start menstruating
Commonly in Am. female use, and as 'I fell
off' – I started menstruating, but the
etymology escapes me, unless it infers a
wound from falling.

fall out (1) *see* **fall** (3)

fall out (2)   radioactive matter introduced
into the atmosphere by human agency
Now SE and no longer used of seemingly
innocuous substances like volcanic ash, the
most likely proximate cause of the next Ice
Age.

fall out of bed   to fail commercially
This Am. phrase indicates failure after some
carelessness: 'But if Seaco fell out of bed, or
the bond market cracked' (M. Thomas,
1982, of a failing corporation).

fallaway   a sham victim of a motor accident
The accident is a sham too. The Am. pedestrian contrives to receive a blow from a
vehicle and claims damages for injuries
which may not have been sustained on that
occasion. He is so called because, if adept at
the fraud, he 'falls away' from the vehicle to
minimize his real injury.

fallen (the) *see* **fall** (3)

fallen woman   a female who has been
caught in extra-marital copulation
From **fall** (1) (above) and normally, but not
necessarily, of a whore: 'Let's face it dear,
we are nothing but two fallen women' (N.
Mitford, 1949 – they were not whores). You
must remember to choose your words with
care when a lady trips over her skis or her
shoelaces.

falling evil etc.   epilepsy
'Evil' in Eng., 'sickness' in Sc. but Webster
gives neither. The 'falling' is one of the
symptoms: 'To cure the falling sickness wi'
pills o' pouthered puddocks' (Service, 1887

– 'puddock' does not here have its normal meaning, a kite or buzzard, but is a corruption of 'paddock', a frog or toad).

false engaging in extra-marital copulation
The opposite of **true** (q.v.): 'False to his bed' (Shakespeare, *Cymbeline*). Of both sexes.

false market the improper rigging of share prices
Stock exchange jargon, especially where someone buys or sells on advance knowledge. If, however, the information reaches brokers or professional investors first to the detriment of the general public, the phenomenon is called 'normal market intelligence'.

falsies pads concealed in clothing to enhance a woman's breasts
Perhaps not euphemistic, and sometimes used too of padding elsewhere on female clothing. The padding of men's jackets to make the wearer look broad-shouldered is almost universal, but not the subject of euphemistic or derogatory comment.

familiar with copulating with extra-maritally
Properly, relating to your family, whence someone with whom you associate freely. Of either sex: 'The intimation is that you have been indecorously familiar with his sister' (Jennings, 1965 – was he bad-mannered in his copulation?). 'Over-familiar' usu. describes a male's rejected sexual approach to a female.

family (1) not pornographic
Not as modern as we might think – Bowdler called his emasculation of the Bard *Family Shakespeare*. Of entertainment with the assumption that an individual can see without being corrupted what the family should not. A 'family show' is one in which the vulgarity may be muted.

family (2) the Mafia
Again nothing is new – in 18c. Eng. a 'family' was an association of thieves: 'It ain't gonna be easy now, keeping the Feds and the Family from tumblin' on to me' (Diehl, 1978).

family jewels *see* **jewels**

family planning contraception
This SE use is in fact the reverse of planning a family for most people most of the time, and always for the unmarried. In many compounds like 'family planning requisites', contraceptives, etc.

family way *see* **in the family way**

fan club a group which clandestinely follows an individual
Espionage jargon, from those who adulate an entertainer: '. . . he chose a zigzag route to throw off any fan club' (Lyall, 1982). Also stock exchange jargon, cf. **concert party**.

fancy to desire sexually
An 18c. usage which predates the 19c. meaning, a girl's suitor: 'Crokey and lawn tennis for't young misses and their fancies' (*Weekly Telegraph*, 1894, quoted in EDD). Either sex may 'fancy' the other: 'You can't do it to an ordinary woman just because you fancied her at school' (Murdoch, 1978). In ante-bellum Am. a southern 'fancy' was a Black female slave with some White blood: 'These yellow wenches . . . . being graceful delicate creatures of the kind they called "fancy pieces", for use as domestic slaves' (Fraser, 1971 – they were also used in brothels). A 'fancy-man' is someone with whom a woman regularly copulates extra-maritally: 'I can only remember two of them that had regular fancy-men' (Richards, 1936, of soldiers' wives). Today a 'fancy' piece or bit is synonymous with 'fancy woman', a man's sexual mistress: 'They supposed that Donald must be keeping 'a fancy woman' in New York' (Boyle, 1979 – in fact Maclean was keeping a rendezvous with his Russian spymaster). A 'fancy seat cover' in Am. CB use is a sexually attractive woman spied in a car.

fanny the vagina or buttocks
Asexually of the buttocks, it can refer to male or female, as the cliché 'sitting on your fanny'. Sexually, it can refer to the vagina: 'She'd have your fanny for a dishcloth' (Sharpe, 1977) or to a woman who looks ready for copulation: 'Great fanny, the wife of the KGB Captain' (Seymour, 1982). Although derivation from an abbr. of 'fantail' has its advocates, it probably comes from Cleland's *Memoirs of a Woman of Pleasure*, which relates the adventures of Frances, or Fanny, Hill. The descriptions of her life as a whore in 18c. London are almost Shakespearean in the fertility of their sexual imagery. Cleland made his heroine live happily ever after, and that alone is worthy of note. He would rejoice to know that the Sybil Brand Institute, a women's prison on rising ground in Los Angeles, is popularly known as 'Fanny Hill.'

Fanny Adams nothing
She was murdered in 1810 but her memory

was kept alive in naval sl. for tinned meat. The meaning comes from the shared initials with 'fuck all'. (I have known two ladies called 'Fanny Adams', one who married a Mr Adams and the other with careless parents.)

fast ready to copulate extra-maritally
Of women, from the meaning, high-living: 'Anglo-Indians (regarded as "fast") swinging their bums' (Theroux, 1973).

fast buck (a) money obtained unscrupulously
The dollars come quickly and easily, but not necessarily dishonestly. An Am. use which has become general, even where the currency is something else.

fat cat a person who prospers through illegality or the exploitation of a senior position
Use. of politicians, professional men and civil servants. The ingredients are success, sleekness and self-satisfaction – actual purring is not expected: 'There's a fat cat called Rippon who used to be in very big with Heath and who now floats round the City' (*Private Eye*, November 1980, of a Br. politician).

fate worse than death unsought extra-marital copulation by a woman
A pre-WW II use, from the stigma of bastardy and the convention that women should be virgins when they married: 'So being rattled stupid by Solomon would be no fate worse than death to her' (Fraser, 1977). Still used humorously.

father of lies the devil
Dysphemism rather than euphemism, from Satan's being credited with the invention of lying: 'Terry Reeves believed this fantastical personage to be the Father of Lies himself' (Graves, 1941, writing in 18c. style).

fatigue (1) suffering from severe mental illness
In medical jargon, 'mental fatigue' has in places replaced **nervous breakdown** (q.v.) and 'shell-shocked' of WW I became 'battle-fatigued' in WW II.

fatigue (2) drunkenness
A rarer version of **tired** (2) (q.v.).

favour to copulate with extra-maritally
A form of Dr Johnson's 'regarding with kindness' I suppose, without some of the overtones of **favours** (below): 'He thanks our transport lady whom Mr Muspole claims to have favoured in the snooker room' (le

Carré, 1986 – he did not give her an easy break).

favours willing extra-marital copulation
The 'distributing', 'giving', granting', 'selling' etc. is done by whichever sex is in the subservient role, which is generally the woman: 'The small luxuries of life that plenty of women were prepared to exchange their favours for' (G. Greene, 1979). And of males: 'A fondness amounting to sexual mania for the favours of young men' (Sharpe, 1977).

feather-bed to grant excessive indulgence towards
From the warmth of bedding so stuffed. Holt, who is usu. right (or, like Fowler, I nearly always agree with him), suggests in *Phrase and Word Origins* that the derivation is from the Rock Island Railroad; when train crews complained of hard bunks, they were asked sarcastically if they wanted feather beds. Today it is also trade union jargon for forcing an employer to pay unnecessary labour, which may enable all to work less hard. 'Feather-bed' Evans was a Br. post WW II Labour minister who used the term of farmers, winning both immmortality and dismissal from office – if you are going to be outspoken in politics, you must also be wrong. In ob. Br. use a 'feather-bed' soldier was one who went whoring at lot.

feather plucker a term of abuse
Spoonerism and rh. sl. for 'fucker', used fig.

feather your nest to provide for yourself at the expense of others
Now SE from avian imagery. You can either do it by dishonesty: 'Mr Badman had well feathered his nest with other men's goods and money' (Bunyan, 1680) or through unprincipled self-enrichment: 'They have planned Germany's subjugation with an eye to feathering their own nest' (Goebbels, 1945, in tr. of the British). In ob. use a man who married a rich widow was also so described.

featuring having in the cast
A 'feature' player is properly one with a leading role. In the entertainment business, from which this comes, your billing may be more important than the money you receive, or the quality of your performance, and few laymen appreciate the niceties of 'starring', 'co-starring', 'guest-starring', 'also starring', 'introducing', 'featuring', etc.

Federal Hill organized crime and vice
From the mainly Italian district of Providence, RI out of which much of New England crime is controlled. This is a specimen entry – other cities and states, in Am. and elsewhere, have their allusions.

feed to suckle
You avoid mentioning the taboo breasts: 'Louisa was feeding her second baby in Scotland' (N. Mitford, 1945). 'Not to feed' a baby does not mean that you condemn it to death by starvation.

feed a dog etc. to urinate
A male expression, and he may also say he is going to feed a 'horse', 'parrot' or even a 'goldfish'.

feed a slug to kill by shooting
The 'slug' is a bullet: '. . . rubbing his greasy hair, and then feeding him a slug while he was still purring' (Chandler, 1943). The Am. 'feed the pills' is rarer, with 'pills' also meaning bullets: 'I want you to make certain that both you and your friend feed Danny Boy the pills' (Sanders, 1973 – two people were to be guilty of killing).

feed from home to copulate extra-maritally
Perhaps just another Shakespearean image, but it deserves its place: 'He breaks the pale, And feeds from home' (*Comedy of Errors*).

feed the bears to receive a ticket for a traffic offence
Am. CB use, with the 'bears' being the police, who are 'fed' by a fine which may get as far as the local municipality, and may not.

feed the fishes to be seasick
Old humorous use but never funny to the victim. You do not actually have to vomit over the rail.

feed the meter illegally to extend a period of parking
To prevent people hogging parking space, all coins should be inserted at the outset of the parking period which you buy.

feed your nose to inhale illicit narcotics through the nose
Usu. cocaine or heroin: 'A woman like that . . . . has got to be on. I'd be willing to bet she's feeding her nose' (Sanders, 1977).

feed your pussy to copulate
Rare and slightly offensive punning female use.

feel to excite sexually with the fingers
Either sex may 'feel' the other, or themselves: 'Blank reached inside his coat pocket to feel himself' (Sanders, 1981). A male who persuades a female to allow this activity is said to 'cop a feel': 'I . . . . with my beloved Maria did not even try to cop a feel' (Styron, 1976). To 'feel-up' is only done by a male to a female, for obvious reasons: 'He had probably been in the kitchen feeling Ella up' (Follett, 1979), and a 'feel-up' is what he does: 'How is this genital whatname different from a feel-up?' (Amis, 1978).

feel a draft to sense prejudice against Black people
From the discernible but invisible movement of air. Mainly Am. Black use.

feel no pain to be drunk
From the numbing effect of the intoxicant rather than unconsciousness: '"But they wasn't drunk." "Feeling no pain?" "Not even that"' (Sanders, 1981, and suggesting mild inebriation).

feel the need to want to defecate or urinate
A genteel usage which could mean almost anything: 'If she goes off to the bathroom when she feels the need, it's surely a good sign' (Francis, 1981, of someone in a state of shock).

feet first dead
This is the way corpses tend to be carried: 'Cut up rough and you'll go out feet first' (Deighton, 1981).

fell design a male attempt at extra-marital copulation
'Fell' means cruel or clever, this derivation being, I suppose, from the former: '"Are you a virgin?" he said suddenly, stopping right in the middle of his fell design' (McCarthy, 1963). Now only humorous use.

fellow commoner an empty bottle
Properly an 18c. student at Cambridge or Oxford universities who was wealthy and thus supposedly empty-headed as he did not need to work. Still heard in some Br. academic circles.

fellow traveller an undeclared Communist or an apologist for Communism
Trotsky's 'poputchik'. You followed the same ideological road, often professing membership of a less extreme political party as a power base: 'I know you had some Communist friends . . . . They thought you were a sentimental fellow-traveller, just as we did' (G. Greene, 1978). The phrase is less used now because open adherence to

Marxism is no longer a stigma, nor even a bar to becoming the Leader of the Greater London Council.

female (1) (2) *see* **male** (1) (2)

female domination a male sexual fetish
Not a realistic name for marriage. It involves obtaining sexual gratification from being assaulted or tied up by a female, who is usu. a whore: '"Big item in the FD market." "The what?" George asked. "Female domination. Whips and bonds"' (Lyall, 1982).

female oriented homosexual
Of a woman and Am. or it would be 'female orientated'. 'Female identified' means the same thing.

female physiology menstruation
Properly 'physiology' means a bodily function of which several are exclusive to women: 'I held her lightly, protectively, then murmured in her ear, "Beastly female physiology"' (Fowles, 1977, of a male wishing to copulate with a menstruating female).

feminine complaint an illness which affects only adult females
Not that her husband is out drinking again: '"Probably a feminine complaint," Scaduto's wife said. When I squinted she said, "Plumbing"' (Theroux, 1982).

feminine gender the vagina
Oddly, in languages where it is declined, it is usu. male like 'con' or 'cunnus': 'She went in to adjust her suspender. It got caught up in her feminine gender' (old vulgar song).

femme a female homosexual playing the female role
An Am. usage, from the French. Also rarely of a male homosexual playing the female role. A 'femme fatale' is a woman whom a man obsessively lusts after and an unexpected OED omission: 'I suppose such corny little manifestations of endearment were what she thought appropriate to her role as a femme fatale' (Deighton, 1985).

fence a dealer in stolen property
He provides a screen between the thief and the eventual buyer. To 'fence' is so to act: 'He used to take things home and "fence" them' (Mayhew, 1862, of stolen goods).

ferret to look for clandestine listening devices
A beloved word of the spy writers with its imagery of going down another's burrow, of chasing larger prey to the surface and of operating under the control of a remote and powerful master. A 'ferret' is a person who looks for such equipment or rarely an agent who intends to create a reaction from the opposition: 'A shadow executive for the Bureau is a ferret and they'd put me down the hole' (Hall, 1979, of such a spy).

fertilizer the excreta of cattle
It should mean anything which adds fertility to the soil, including compost and seaweed, and we differentiate factory-made chemical products as 'artificial fertilizers': 'Today's "fertilizer" was "manure" yesterday and "meadow dressing" the day before' (Jennings, 1965).

fetch to steal
Not usu. of humans: 'The fox fetched the last duck I had' (EDD). In ob. Br. use a 'fetch' was the ghost whose appearance presaged imminent death – 'fetching' you away – or long life. I suppose that those who did not die of fright made the alternative of longevity necessary, if the phantom were not to be discredited.

fiddle to steal by cheating
From playing the stringed instrument, whence acting irresponsibly and specially applied to manipulation of accounts. A 'fiddle' is any trick, even within the law, whereby someone may be cheated or overcharged. The ob. Sc. 'fiddle' was a child abandoned by gypsies, who favour the instrument.

fidelity copulation only with a regular sexual partner
It means faithfulness, in all its senses: '. . . expecting complete fidelity from Christine' (Green, 1979, of Rachman and Keeler – she must not copulate with anyone else).

fiend the devil
The dysphemism comes from the Old Teutonic, to hate, whence an enemy, and is a rare example of the devil getting his nominal due. 'Fiend' is also used of anyone obsessed with any activity, and especially if addicted to illegal narcotics, as 'dope-fiend'.

fifth column the traitors within your ranks
General Mola, investing Madrid in 1936 with four columns of soldiers, said that he had a fifth column already in the city, meaning covert Nationalist supporters. The use today usu. implies treachery: 'Their supporters here would know about it, and would be making preparations to join in, as a fifth column' (Masters, 1976).

fifty cards in the pack imbecile
You need fifty-two cards, except for tarot. Am.

fight in armour to copulate in a contraceptive sheath
Boswell used both the pun and the appliance, and had cause for regret when he omitted to do so. ob.

file a waste-paper basket
Perhaps jocular use by those who do not like storing documents and tend to make a fetish of their prejudice or idleness. An Am. would speak of 'file thirteen' or 'file seventeen'.

fill full of holes etc. to kill
The shooting may also fill you full of lead or of daylight. Rarely as 'fill in', which usu. means to assault violently. In ob. Br. use if you 'filled a pannier', you impregnated a woman, from the hooped framework which distended her skirt and concealed the swelling of pregnancy.

fill in the blank spaces in our history
to cease lying
Of a Russian tendency to allow some of the truth about the excesses of Stalin and Communism to be publicly revealed: 'In the past two weeks, the pace of the debate over "filling in the blank spaces of our history", to borrow Mr Gorbachev's own euphemism, has quickened' (*Daily Telegraph*, September 1987).

filler a cheaper substitute surreptitiously introduced to increase apparent weight or volume
The stratagem increases the profit on sale by weight or volume. Small coal and slack were used as a 'filler' in bags for large, but not today when all are equally dear. But chinaclay, inert, odourless, colourless and tasteless, goes into many things from 'cream' chocolates to latex thread. In the same sense a 'filler' is a trivial news item used to occupy space in a newspaper: 'We used to produce fillers, which is what the papers use to cement the real news to the adverts: "Sacked stripper organizes strike." You know the sort of thing' (Deighton, 1972).

fillet to steal
Properly, to remove flesh from the bone: 'We did think some spare parts might be filleted; but luckily nothing's gone' (*Sunday Telegraph*, October 1981 – a manager was talking about a factory in which employees had trespassed).

filly a woman viewed sexually by a male
Perhaps importing the common equine copulation imagery: 'We pre-war soldiers always made enquiries as to what sort of place it was for booze and fillies' (Richards, 1933). In ob. Br. use a woman who 'slipped her filly' had an abortion.

filthy any taboo sexual act
Of masturbation, attempted male fondling of an unwilling female or even attempted rape: '. . . that sailor tried to be filthy' (L. Thomas, 1977, of such an attempt). The ob. 'filth', a whore, came too from the dirt: 'Wisdom and goodness to the vile seem vile: Filths savour but themselves' (Shakespeare, *King Lear*). 'Filth' and 'filthy' are also used of talk or humour involving particularly copulation or homosexuality.

final solution the killing of all Jews
The Nazi 'Endlösung' which first emerged in 1938 when the hopes of deporting German Jews to colonize Madagascar vanished. After 1941 the system required Jews to be worked to death if possible, which relieved pressure on the gas chambers.

financial assistance state aid for the poor
True as far as it goes, but it could as well be a loan, gift or subsidy to the rich: '"You're on welfare?" "Financial assistance," she said haughtily' (Sanders, 1985). Am.

financial products forms of moneylending
Moneylenders like to use the word 'products' because it suggests their activities are beneficial: '. . . proliferation of new instruments and "financial products". Reshapings and reclothings of lending and borrowing packaged to the advantage of a now totally institutionalized market' (M. Thomas, 1987).

financial services money-lending
The language of those who offer credit or small loans at high rates of interest to the relatively poor. It should mean accounting, banking or money-changing.

finangler a cadger of meals
The Am. 'finangle' is to contrive a solution – to 'find an angle'? In this case you solve the problem of paying for your own food.

find to steal
From the pretence that the goods have been lost or abandoned, which is even barer when you 'find something before someone has lost it'. The imagery is as old as stealing, with the ob. Sc. phrase 'found a thing where the

Highlander found the tongs' – 'Spoken when boys have pick'd something and pretend they found it' (Kelly, 1721 – to Lowlanders the Highland Scots were remorseless thieves). A 19c. 'finder' was a thief: 'The "finders" and "stealers" of dogs were the most especial subject of a parliamentary enquiry' (Mayhew, 1851).

finger (1) to inform on or point out in a criminal context
The person who 'fingers', or betrays, another criminal to the police may do his pointing only fig.: 'Snyder had hoped to pick up a few hundred bucks by fingering Hooker to Amon Lorrimer' (Weverka, 1973, of pointing out a small-time crook to another gang boss). To 'put the finger on' is also to betray. To 'finger' a job is to draw the attention of criminals to an opportunity for crime: 'I figure he knew them, and they knew him. Maybe he fingered the job' (Sanders, 1977). 'Finger-man' has three meanings – he may identify either a victim to other criminals or a suspect to the police; or he may inspect the site of a potential crime; or he may be a killer, with his finger on the trigger: '. . . the finger man loiters ahead undetected till the target blunders into him' (le Carré, 1980). An Am. 'finger-mob' commits crimes without police intervention in return for information about other, more serious, criminals.

finger (2) to masturbate
Of a woman: '. . . her other hand fingering, all five fingers fingering like a team of maggots at her open heat' (Mailer, 1965, of a woman masturbating). A 'finger-artist' is a female homosexual.

finger-blight the reduction of an apple crop due to scrumping
This W. Eng. expression refers to a long tradition of depredations by boys from the widespread orchards, 'blight' being a natural phenomenon reducing yields. In my Somerset orchard today, we do not seriously look for a crop from the two apple trees nearest the lane. The ob. but picturesque 'fingers get close to the thumb' meant not stealing, from a clenched fist, but nepotism: 'Yes, sir, the fingers have got pretty close to the thumb' (Egerton, 1884, of nepotism).

finish (1) to kill
Of humans and animals. If they have been previously wounded or are sick, you 'finish them off'.

finish (2) to achieve a sexual orgasm
Very common use of both sexes. To 'finish yourself' is to masturbate to ejaculation or orgasm.

finish off (1) *see* finish (1)

finish off (2) to wipe dry your genitalia
Children or geriatrics are told to 'finish yourself off' after someone has helped dry them, which avoids having to refer to taboo organs.

fire to dismiss peremptorily from employment
Punning on discharge, which is SE for quitting, or being asked to quit, employment: '"Working?" "Nope, I got fired"' (Theroux, 1976). Although the dismissal is usu. peremptory, I do not think there is any derivation from 'fire', to shoot a projectile from a gun where the ignition of powder operates the 'fire-arm'.

fire a shot to ejaculate during copulation
An Am. use of obvious imagery. To 'fire blanks' of a male is to copulate without impregnation due to sexual impotence or other cause. To 'fire up' is to copulate with a woman extra-maritally on a single occasion, punning on the meaning to excite (from stoking a steam boiler) and the ejaculation.

fire has gone out the engine has stopped
WW II navy fliers' usage, with imagery from steam-driven ships. It described a crisis as the single-engine aircraft were often a long way from land or a carrier.

fireman a motorist exceeding the speed limit
Police humour, which is also used generally for anyone bustling about – 'Where's the fire?' The WW II Jewish camp police who helped the Nazis control other Jews were called 'firemen'. A 'visiting fireman' is a tourist who acts boisterously in a distant city, as firemen at conventions are said to; but the phrase is also used in a derogatory sense of a manager sent from a distant head office to a subsidiary to correct or analyse unsatisfactory trading results. Mainly Am.

firewater whisky
As well as burning your throat and guts, it is flammable: 'Would I be consultant in exchange for a generous consignment of firewater' (*Private Eye*, September 1981). 'Fired up' means drunk, probably from starting an engine and not necessarily after drinking whisky.

firk to copulate with
From the meaning to beat, using the common violent imagery: 'I'll fer him, and firk

him' (Shakespeare, *Henry V*, with beating only in mind). Partridge suggests 'partly a euphemistic pronunciation of *fuck*' and the present participle is often articulated thus.

firm (the) a spy organization
Much beloved by espionage writers, if none other, of both Am. and Br. organizations for spying and foreign subversion: 'Ever since he joined the firm as a young recruit' (G. Greene, 1978, of a Br. spy).

first strike unannounced aggression
A use when you attack before war has been declared; otherwise it would not be a euphemism. A 'first-strike capability' is an ability to attack the enemy with nuclear bombs without prior warning. And *see* **second strike.**

fish (1) a heterosexual woman
The word is used among Am. female homosexuals, for whom heterosexuality in women is taboo, and the imagery is from her being caught by a male. A 'fishwife' is the wife of a male homosexual. The Am. 'fish', a whore, is ob.

fish (2) a whore's customer
To be caught and cheated: 'You may sit and drink if you wish. I shall tell the girls that you are not a fish' (Trevanian, 1973 – he was in a brothel).

fish hook *see* **hook** (1)

fishing expedition (1) a foreign trip to seek a husband
Single girls were sent to Malta or India where they might meet naval or army officers whose prolonged absence from BI and the company of unmarried White women had lowered their standards when it came to assessing the qualities of a prospective bride. The annual excursion was known collectively as the 'fishing fleet'.

fishing expedition (2) an attempt to gain gratuitous information
Espionage jargon – you know not what you may catch: 'Oakes and Haig were Nolan's only hope for a fishing expedition' (Allbeury, 1980, of such an attempt).

fishmonger's daughter a whore
As with the ob. 'fish market', a brothel, the allusion is to the vaginal smell: 'Excellent well; you are a fishmonger' (Shakespeare, *Hamlet*) says Hamlet to Polonius, implying not that he was a pimp but that his daughter, Ophelia, was a whore. Polonius misses the point (along with many distinguished lexicographers), only to take another behind the arras in the Third Act.

fishwife *see* **fish**

fishy homosexual
Of a male, from the meaning queer or irregular: '. . . her only husband had been as fishy as Dick's hatband' (Fraser, 1975).

fistful *see* **handful** etc.

fit available for copulation
In male use, possibly because the female is not menstruating or perhaps merely prepared to copulate. Of a third party in male conversation 'she's fit' may mean that the woman is considered nubile.

five-fingered discount stolen
Am. CB use of stolen goods sold below their market value.

five-fingered widow male masturbation
Br. army use for those long absent from the company of White women: 'The red light districts . . . . were strictly out of bounds . . . . Many turned, as a last resort, to the "five-fingered widow"' (Allen, 1975, of service in India).

five fingers *see* **handful** etc.

five or seven drunk
The pre-WW II London use comes from the standard court sentence on conviction of being 'drunk and disorderly' or 'drunk and incapable' – five shillings fine or seven days in jail.

fix (1) to make an illegal arrangement
From the meaning, to mend or arrange anything. Often of a bribe: 'To a Metropolitan policeman fix could mean nothing other than a bribe' (Deighton, 1978). A 'fix' is anything illegally arranged, especially a horse race for a gambing coup: 'There's eight or nine races on a card and . . . . the fix can be in any time somebody says so' (Chandler, 1953).

fix (2) to castrate
Of domestic animals in Am., the arrangement or mending being less to their liking than that of their owners.

fix (3) an injection of illicit narcotics
Usu. heroin: 'Frank, had you had a fix?' (Davidson, 1978, asking about narcotic use and not navigational verification). A 'fix' is the quantity needed for one injection and to 'fix' is to supply with illegal narcotics.

fix up to hire a whore for another's use
Am. practice to influence visiting buyers etc. The operation of a flexible price structure, as everywhere else in the world, is forbidden by Federal Law, and the law, though widely

ignored, is often invoked when a disappointed competitor peaches to Washington. Thus you may be heavily fined or imprisoned for giving a good customer who pays quickly a discount, but not for 'fixing him up' – with a whore. Whatever the effect on normal business, it is all good for prostitution.

fixer an arranger of embarrassing, dubious or illegal business
In commercial jargon, he is the person who bribes where needed to secure a contract, isolating his principals from overt illegality by charging them excess commission to finance the bribery. The word is used of the various meanings of **fix** (above), except perhaps as a castrator of animals. A 'fixer' is also a person who deflects unwelcome publicity: 'He's a fixer, a smoother-out' (Price, 1970).

fizzer the accusation of a military offence
A Br. army pun on 'charge' and now met in civilian use.

flack out to die
Properly, to lose consciousness due to drunkenness or from lack of oxygen while skin-diving. Am.

flag is up etc. I am menstruating
Punning on the redness of the danger flag, the towel and the blood. Female use in a number of related expressions like 'flag of defiance', 'fly the (red) flag' and **baker flying** (q.v.). The ob. Br. 'flag of distress' was no more than a tactful warning in company that a man's shirt-tail was hanging out.

flake a lunatic
An abbr. of cornflake, perhaps, although I'm not sure where that takes us: '"What a character she is," he said. "A real flake"' (Sanders, 1986). Often used humorously of an eccentric. Am.

flap a military crisis
WW II usage, from the waving of arms or wings in agitation: 'I didn't know till I got there that there's a flap on' (Manning, 1977).

flapper a young woman who flouts convention
In N. Eng. dialect, a young whore; in W. Eng., a 19c. underpetticoat; in OED a young 'wild duck or partridge'; and in the 1920s, the 'flapper era': 'I was sure I would have enjoyed being a rich Canton flapper with a peacock called Bluey too' (Irvine, 1986, of a White expatriate). Now ob.

flash (1) to display your penis in public to a stranger
You open your raincoat 'in a flash' and thereby become a 'flasher': 'These men were rapists or Peeping Toms or flashers or child molesters' (Sanders, 1973). An Am. police officer who 'flashes tin' does no more than identify himself, the 'tin' being his badge of office: 'Chief, should Jason Two flash his tin or work undercover?' (Sanders, 1977). The ob. 'flash' girl, woman etc. was a whore who was especially ostentatious. '. . . keeping a cold eye on the more obvious thieves and flash-tails' (Fraser, 1977, writing in 19c. style). And Grose tells us that thieves and whores congregated in a 'flash panney'.

flash (2) to vomit
Am. use, usu. after drunkenness.

flat on your back copulating
Of a woman, from her probable posture: '. . . if I can't charm this one flat on her back, I've lost my way with women' (Fraser, 1971). The Am. 'flat-backer' in Black speech is a whore.

flatfoot a policeman
From the pounding the beat which is no longer necessary to earn the appellation. In Am. only abbr. to 'flat'.

flawed drunk
Perhaps a pun on 'floored' and on having an imperfection, as drunkards tend not to remain in pristine condition. Grose says 'flawd'.

fledgling nation a poor country
Said to have been coined by Eleanor Roosevelt, with avian imagery, of countries formerly administered as colonies in the days when we all hoped they would soar to new heights of prosperity and freedom.

fleece to defraud
By robbery or overcharging, from the shearing of sheep: '. . . all the petty cut-throat ways and means with which she used to fleece us' (Cleland, 1749, of a cheating bawd) or today: 'I knew I was being fleeced' (Theroux, 1983, of an excessive hotel bill).

flesh your will to copulate
Of a male: it is hard to say whether Shakespeare invented the imagery and whether he really meant the obscure vulgar pun: 'This night he fleshes his will in the spoil of her honour' (*All's Well*). ob.

fleshpot a brothel
Properly, the vessel in which meat was cooked, whence a source of luxury and

debauchery offering a variety of vicious attractions: '. . . found the "fleshpots" of Nairobi to be "insidious and most likely to corrupt"' (Allen, 1979).

fleshy part of the thigh the buttocks
It was here that a military bulletin said Lord Methuen had been wounded in the Boer War. Apart from late 19c. modesty, to be wounded in the buttocks might imply that you were not facing the enemy.

flexibility the abandonment of principles in pursuit of any object.
The object for bankers is profit; for soldiers, promotion; for politicians, power; etc.: 'Conservative MPs, impatient for the pre-election bribery to start, call for "flexibility"' (*Financial Times*, December 1981). Such conduct is described as being 'flexible': 'Pym is preparing . . . . a swift twitch of the rug from under the few remaining loyalist sheepshaggers. This is called being flexible' (*Private Eye*, May 1982 – Argentine impetuosity and stupidity prevented the Br. Foreign Secretary making any move to divest the Falkland Islands of Br. patronage).

flight *see* **fly** (2)

fling (a) extra-marital copulation.
From the meaning, indulgence in any unaccustomed excess: 'I had my fling with the Tanglin wife whom I reported as being "ever so nice"' (Theroux, 1973, of copulation).

flit (1) to leave accommodation without paying rent due.
Abbr. of **moonlight flit** (q.v.) perhaps: 'The family on the corner, two years in arrears on the rent, were doing another flit, all their furniture . . . . stacked up on creaking barrows' (Bradbury, 1976). In ob. Sc. and N. Eng. use, to 'flit' was to die: 'She canna flit in peace until she sees you' (W. Scott, 1816).

flit (2) a male homosexual usu. playing the female role.
He affects female mannerisms by 'flitting about': 'He assured me that he had a luscious ass . . . . Flits have always been attracted to me' (McCarthy, 1963). 'Flitty' or 'flit' is so acting.

float paper to issue cheques unsecured by bank deposits.
Pre-computer delays in the banking clearance system enabled a shrewd operator to generate credit balances during the four or five days it took to clear inter-bank cheques, by which time a fresh deposit in the paying bank would cover the initially uncovered cheque: 'He could probably stall (bankers)

for the necessary twenty-four hours. It wouldn't be the first time Lorrimer had floated paper for a day or two' (Weverka, 1973).

floater (1) an order to leave town.
From the Am. word for a vagrant or itinerant worker. To secure enforcement, the police or Court order may be backed up by a suspended jail sentence and the risk to the community of petty thieving or of having to support a vagrant is passed on to someone else.

floater (2) a corpse which has been a long time in water
Am. police and funeral jargon: 'Floaters . . . . are another matter; a person who has been in the Bay for a week or more . . .' (J. Mitford, 1963).

floating drunk or under narcotic influence
From the feeling of levitation or mental detachment. Am.

flog off etc. to masturbate
Of a male, using the common 'beating' imagery. He may also 'flog' the bishop, his dummy, his mutton, beef, donkey, etc.: '. . . dragged off to jail everytime he . . . . flogged his dummy on the porch' (Wambaugh, 1975).

flop to copulate extra-maritally
Of a woman, from the dropping readily to a prone position: 'Lois flops at the drop of a hat' (Chandler, 1943, of one such).

flower (1) the virginity of a woman
What you lose when you are deflowered: 'My affections in his charmed power, Reserved the stalk and gave him all my flower' (Shakespeare, *Lover's Complaint*). ob.

flower (2) a male homosexual
In this Am. use, he is said to take the female role, but I have not traced a literary example.

flowers the menstrual flow
Normally expanded to 'monthly flowers', from flowing rather than flowering, it might seem: 'I had my courses, my flowers' (Fowles, 1985, of a woman denying pregnancy).

flowery a prison cell
Br. rh. sl. for 'flowery dell' and sometimes used for the whole institution.

flowery language swearing
The embellishment unnecessarily added to normal speech. In the 19c. 'flowery language' was blasphemy.

fluff your duff to masturbate yourself
Of a male, from sl. 'duff', the buttocks or the suety dish. If the latter, merely a version of 'pull the pudding', to masturbate: 'What are you doing here in the dark – fluffing your duff?' (Sanders, 1982).

flush down the drain peremptorily to dismiss from employment
The imagery is from the lavatory: 'If I bounce him and ask Thorsen to get me another man, he'll flush Boone down the drain' (Sanders, 1977).

fluter a male homosexual
Probably punning on Am. 'flute', a penis, and the act of fellatio.

flutter (1) a wager
A 17c. use which is still current, from the excitement of gambling. Normally of a small bet placed by someone who is not an habitual gambler, but heavy punters so described their bets to minimize the extent of their addiction.

flutter (2) to copulate extra-maritally
Of either sex, and again from the excitement. The ob. Eng. 'flutter a skirt' meant to be a whore, from the method of advertising her wares.

flux menstruation
Properly, the condition of flowing or, as with solder, causing to flow: 'Even her body's flux, which she could feel in a gentle, almost controlled, flow, wasn't the inconvenient and disagreeable monthly discharge . . .' (James, 1980 – although that is what it was).

fly (1) in plain clothes
Of an Am. policeman, from the meaning knowing or cunning. It is especially used of a 'fly' ball, bob, bull, cop, dick, etc. assigned to duty away from his normal precinct to avoid criminal recognition.

fly (2) to be under illegal narcotic influence
Usu. the levitation from smoking marijuana: 'This is top-grade grass, the real stuff. We'll fly' (Sanders, 1982). 'Flight' or 'flying' is the state induced.

fly a kite (1) *see* **kite**

fly a kite (2) to write a begging letter
This was a considerable 19c. industry and art, especially in Mayhew's London, developed on the back of the penny post. Charities have taken over from rogues acting on their own account the business of begging by mail.

fly a kite (3) to smuggle a package into or out of prison
The trade inwards is usu. narcotics, and outwards, letters.

fly-blow a bastard
Punning on the deposit of eggs left in meat by flies, and the taint: 'She is still a bairn. And the flyblow of the system' (Cookson, 1969 – her autobiography was largely about her own bastardy).

fly-by-night (1) an absconding debtor
Hardy euphemistic in the original use of quitting your accommodation by night with all your goods and the rent unpaid, to stop distraint by your landlord. The term is still used of a trader whose credit is poor, before or after he absconds. Pre-20c. Eng. had two other types of 'fly-by-night': witches, on or off their broomsticks; and the ominous birds called night whistlers or gobbleratches, whose nocturnal flight presaged imminent death.

fly-by-night (2) drunk
Br. rh. sl. for 'tight', with perhaps a side-swipe at the unreliability of drunkards.

fly one wing low *see* **flying low**

fly the blue pigeon to steal lead
Usu. but not necessarily from the roof of a church. For a thief, 'blue' is lead: 'And there's the bluey . . . . the lead from the pipes, and the roofs like of churches' (L. Thomas, 1981). To 'pigeon' is to steal and the whole puns on bird fancying. (I had this vivid phrase marked as ob., and along with 10,000 or so others omitted from this book, until I heard it spoken in Musselburgh, Sc., in October, 1981.)

fly the red flag *see* **flag is up** etc.

flying handicap diarrhoea
This Eng. phrase puns on the celerity needed, the disability and a typical name for a horse race.

flying low inadvertently having a trouser zip undone
Used as an oblique warning to another male and punning on the trouser 'fly' and the dangerous operation of an aircraft. In WW II airforce sl., to 'fly one wing low' was to be drunk: '. . . half the officers in the club house were flying one wing low already' (Deighton, 1982).

flying picket a crowd from afar seeking to stop others working
They intimidate through numbers or

violence, to stop continued working by non-strikers or to prevent the distribution of stocks etc. The inability of the Br. police to counter mass harrassment and intimidation and to prevent violence led to controversial legislation which sought to define and restrict the right to picket.

fog to kill
Presumably from the disappearance of the victim. The Am. 'fog away', to kill by shooting, may also allude to the smoke from the gun.

foggy drunk
Your eyes may be and your memory becomes. Also as 'fogged'.

foil a small packet of illicit narcotics
From a normal way of packing tablets. Am.

foin to copulate
Properly, to make a thrust with a sharp weapon: 'When wilt thou leave fighting o' days and foining o' nights' (Shakespeare, *2 Henry IV*). ob.

fold to become bankrupt
Usu. of a business, from the collapse of a structure. This Am. use is now universal, but not in the rare Am. sense, to die.

folding camera *see* camera

follower a male who is courting a female
From the servant who 'followed' his master, it acquired the specific meaning of a man who courted a domestic servant girl: 'No, sir, missus don't permit no followers' (Mayhew, 1862). Then in upper-class use – those who had servants – of courting any girl: 'If she had no followers at all they would say she's a Lesbian' (N. Mitford, 1960). To 'follow', so to court, is ob.: 'He followed his wife ten year afore they were wed' (*Leeds Mercury*, 1893, quoted in EDD).

fondle to caress sexually
Properly, to handle fondly, usu. of a bird or pet mammal: '. . . she had learned to slide her hand into his slitted pocket and fondle him' (Sanders, 1973).

fool (about) with yourself to masturbate yourself
From the inconsequential action of 'fooling (about)': 'Honey . . . you don't care if I fool with myself a little' (M. Thomas, 1982, of a woman wishing to masturbate herself).

foot to levy an imposition on new employees to buy intoxicants
Perhaps an abbr. of 'foot the bill': 'When he wor lowse on his prentis-ship his shopmates

fooited him' (Treddlehoyle, 1875). A 'footing' was such a levy: 'I paid five shillin' for footin when I started' (Pinnock, 1895). This is a sample entry; many euphemisms were used of the common Br. 19c. practice of taking money by established workers from a new employee or apprentice.

footpad *see* highwayman

for the good of the cause we must accept inefficiency
The phrase is meant to imply that the muddle and suffering caused by the Russian Communist bureaucracy are temporary phenomena, to be replaced later by prosperity and efficiency. Solzhenitsyn used it as a title for a satirical novel.

for the high jump in deep trouble
Not participating in an athletics meeting. It originally meant sentenced to death by hanging, whence to die by any means: 'If I don't soon have a drop of hard, I'm for it' (Cookson, 1967 – 'it' is the 'high jump'). Now always fig. of peremptory dismissal or other disciplinary action: 'Satchthorpe and Frimston are for the high jump . . . . the Chief Constable's . . . . practically said as much' (Grayson, 1975).

for your convenience something provided which you have paid for
This slightly objectionable pretence of giving you something extra or special seems to have spread from Am.: 'The notice said they were sanitized under infra-red and ultra-violet light for Koolman's protection and convenience, but I suppose anybody would get the same kind of towel' (Deighton, 1972). However, all is forgiven when you meet an unconscious pun: 'For your convenience – Sanitor tissue seat covers' (a lavatory in Fall River, Mass., May 1981).

for your (own) comfort and safety to stop stampede to the exit
Airline jargon when taxiing to the ramp: 'For your own comfort and safety please keep your seatbelt fastened until the aircraft has come to a halt and the engines have been switched off' (every flight you go on). You will observe that the cabin staff moving about show no symptoms of discomfort or danger.

forage to steal
Mainly used by soldiers. Properly, it means food for cattle, which armies traditionally stole on the march for their horses, and then looking for any food to steal: '"Where the devil did you come by this?" "Foraged, sir"' (Fraser, 1969, of something stolen).

force-put job the marriage of a pregnant woman

'Force-put' is a matter of necessity in Devon dialect. Still heard in S. Hams despite the wide availability of contraception.

force your ardour upon to copulate with extra-maritally

The male 'forces his ardour' on the female, who is supposed to be unwilling: 'This was the evening when the conquerors of the Afrika Korps were to force their pent-up ardour on the ladies of Alexandria' (Manning, 1977 – she meant 'the conquerors who were in the Afrika Korps', and not the Br. 8th Army).

forced labour imprisonment under inhuman conditions

Not euphemistic in Nazi Germany during WW II because, despite the brutality and starvation, it was just that. In modern Siberian 'forced labour camps' the inmates are convicted criminals or dissidents and the economic function is subordinated to the penal.

(foreskin which is often used for a penis is properly the prepuce: 'At least the dusky women were beautiful and free – and be damned to the fiery foreskin' (Monsarrat, 1978).)

forget yourself to be guilty of a solecism

As by swearing where swearing is out of place; by making a sexual approach to a woman who has not signalled that she would welcome it; by urinating involuntarily, especially of a geriatric; etc. The use does not really indicate amnesia.

fork to copulate with

Of a male, punning on the 'pronging' and the place where the legs join the trunk. Referring to the latter, Shakespeare used the 'face between her forks' as a woman's frontal crotch: 'Behold yond simpering dame, Whose face between her forks presages snow' (*King Lear* – she is old because her pubic hair is going white). The ob. 'wear a fork' was to be a cuckold, from the proverbial horns, and the 'forked plague' was cuckoldry: 'This forked plague is fated to us' (Shakespeare, *Othello*).

form a criminal record

Police jargon probably from horse-racing, although there is usu. a special form on which these things are recorded: 'With regard to a police record, Artie Johnson is the only one with any form' (Davidson, 1978).

(fornicate to copulate extra-maritally is explicit in common use. It comes from the Latin 'fornix', an arch, whence a vaulted chamber and so a brothel. The Eng. dialect meaning, to tell lies, is ob.)

forspeak to call up evil spirits

This is the first recorded meaning, but it must have meant to deny originally. 'Forspoken' means bewitched. It also meant to speak ill of: 'We hae forespoke the Brownie. They say, if ye speak o' the deil, he'll appear' (Hogg, 1866). Sc. and ob.

(Fortress America is a recurring Am. belief that the United States are militarily and economically strong enough to avoid foreign treaties and involvements: 'If NATO begins to look like a really bad bet . . . . pull out completely and rely on Fortress America' (Crisp, 1982). 'Fortress Europe' – Festung Europa – was the Nazi-occupied continent as seen by themselves early in 1944: '. . . arguing about the strength and weakness of Fortress Europe' (Baron, 1948, of Br. WW II soldiers). 'Fortress Europe' proved to be assailable but 'Fortress America' has yet to be tested.)

forty-four a whore

I record this as an example of Am. rh. sl. which reached neither the BI or the thorough attention of Mr Franklyn.

forward drunk

An ob. Eng. use which may have come from the truculence of drunkenness or from making progress in that direction: 'Twer querish tack – beer and reubub weind an' bacca juice a-mixed, but I knowed we could get furrud on't' (Buckman, 1870 – a mixture of tobacco juice, beer and rhubarb wine is queerish tack indeed). The modern Am. 'forwards', amphetamine pills, might have the same derivation, if we could be sure what that was. The ob. N. Eng. 'forward at the knees' meant aged, from the way old people walk.

foul to defecate in an unaccustomed place

Usu. of dogs on carpets or sidewalks but rarely too of humans: 'Who had fouled his home?' (Boyd, 1982, of a house in which troops had defecated everywhere). To 'foul yourself' is to defecate into your clothing: 'They fouled themselves where they lay' (Fraser, 1971). It is also used of vomiting over your clothes, but not of falling into a patch of mud.

foul ane etc. the devil
Another common Sc. dysphemism and not all the abbr. uses are ob.: 'Our deacon wanda ca' a chair The foul ane durst him na-say' (Fergusson, 1773). Also as the 'foul thief': 'Seek the foul thief onie place' (Burns, 1785). The abbr. is to 'foul' in imprecations like 'foul skelp ye', the devil take you; 'foul may care', devil-may-care; and 'foul-fa'', the devil take.

foul desire etc. a wish to copulate
'Foul' meaning disgusting and it seems linguistically that only males are thus taken: 'If foul desire had not conducted you' (Shakespeare, *Titus Andronicus*). You may also have 'foul' lusts for or designs on a female who is not your wife and if you proceed to 'have your foul way with her', you copulate with her, although not necessarily against her inclination. Still used humorously.

foul play murder
Br. police jargon, and not merely the way professional footballers play football: '"He was shot." "Foul play . . . . Isn't that what you British call it?"' (Deighton, 1978).

foundation garment a corset
The imagery comes from building, although 'buttress' might seem more appropriate: '. . . she may be half-perishing in the clutch of a "foundation garment"' (Jennings, 1965, noting the euphemism).

fountain palace a public urinal
The 'fountain' was the running water and the 'palace' was the luxurious privacy in 19c. London after centuries of primitive arrangements. Probably now ob.

four-letter word an obscenity
Jennings (*Personalities of Language*) demonstrates that there are only eight among the catalogue of obscenities which contain four letters, and then, as always, enlightens and entertains the reader with an analysis of their use. However the most hackneyed obscenities do have only four letters. You may apply one of them to an unpleasant person – a 'four-letter man'.

four sheets in the wind *see* **sheet in the wind**

fourth a lavatory
The use seems to have originated in Cambridge University. The three 'Estates of the Realm' were the peers, the bishops and the commons. 19c. society delighted in nominating a 'fourth', with the press being the favourite: 'Just to make sure that the food and drink were equally up to the expectations of the fourth estate' (Deighton, 1982, of journalists). Carlyle says Burke first suggested the press, but Macaulay has a better claim.

fox hunting government monitoring of CB radio
The main Am. offence seems to be swearing. Giving warnings about the police seems quite acceptable and is a principal function of the radio link.

foxed drunk
Properly, deceived and so a variant of the ob. 'deceived in liquor', which implies that it was not your fault: '. . . poured drink into himself until he was completely foxed' (Fraser, 1970). As usu., the half is the same as the whole: 'Here I was, half-foxed and croaking to myself in a draughty shack' (Fraser, 1971). Both uses are now dated and 'catch a fox', to be drunk, is ob.

foxy eager for copulation
Properly, strong-smelling but that may be an uncharitable derivation, especially as the word is often used of a woman: 'Over forty and feeling foxy' (on a woman's apron, JFK Airport, 1979).

fractured drunk
Another Am. example of the 'broken' imagery.

frag to murder one of your officers in wartime
Unhappily no connection with the Yorks. dialect, to cram a room with furniture but an abbr. of 'fragmentation device', which is a long winded way of saying hand grenade: 'Molly Turner was important to me and you fragged her' (Sanders, 1984, of a later killing by a Vietnam veteran). This Vietnam use and practice indicated the low morale of many Am. soldiers, fighting an unpopular war in nasty conditions and with widespread narcotic addiction. The resentment of Black conscripts to mainly White officers added a further dimension.

fragile suffering from sub-acute alcoholic poisoning
Your head feels as though it could be easily broken.

frail (1) suffering from sub-acute alcoholic poisoning
A variant of 'fragile' above.

frail (2) a female viewed sexually by a male
Probably from, and as ob. as, the 'weaker sex' concept. A 'frail job' is a single act of extra-marital copulation by a male. The frailty of a 'frail sister', a whore, was moral rather than physical, her manner of life seeming to call for considerable stamina.

frame (1) falsely to incriminate
Like mounting a picture so that you can see it better: 'I take it you don't want your daughter-in-law framed' (Chandler, 1943, of such incrimination). The result is a 'frame-up': 'It's a frame-up as sure as ever I saw one' (Deighton, 1981).

frame (2) a male homosexual taking the female role
I suppose from the effeminacy of 'frame', a body. Am.

frank (1) copulating promiscuously
Dr Johnson gives licentious, from the proper meaning, liberal or generous: 'Chaste to her Husband, frank to all beside. A teeming Mistress but a barren Bride' (Pope, 1735). ob.

frank (2) unfriendly and without consensus
Of political talks between fundamentally opposed parties: 'Mr Mugabe had agreed on the need for urgent and "frank" talks' (*Daily Telegraph*, December 1980). 'Full and frank' in a communiqué tells you that the parties failed to agree on anything.

fraternize to copulate with civilians in militarily occupied countries
Strictly, to be friendly with the natives, but the frater was of less interest than his sister: 'Relics of the Great Fraternization Period, you remember' (Bogarde, 1981, of the many post WW II German bastards fathered by occupying soldiers). Mainly of activity in Austria and Germany after WW II.

freak (1) a male homosexual
From the concept of physical oddity: 'They wanted to go down to Greenwich Village and see the freaks' (Sanders, 1981). In prostitutes' jargon, a 'freak trick' is a man who ill-treats her or demands abnormal sexual treatment.

freak (2) an addict to illegal narcotics
Properly, an irrational event – it can hardly be derived from the meaning monster. To 'freak' is to take a hallucinogen, normally LSD. To 'freak out' is to be under any narcotic influence. A 'freak' used in a compound can indicate other areas of enthusiasm or addiction than to narcotics, as 'surf-freak' etc.

free (1) to steal
Often of horse theft, from the unhitching before driving or riding away. In WW II it became a common army variant of **liberate** (2) (q.v.) but the use *tout court* is rare. The modern use is 'free load', whence 'free loader' who is either a simple thief: 'Though gas meters were considered more difficult to tamper with, this had not deterred some ambitious free loaders' (Hailey, 1979) or a cadger at receptions etc.: 'Only 400 of the most abject freeloaders bothered to turn up' (*Private Eye*, March 1980). An occasion when 'free loaders' have ample chance to indulge their gluttony is known as a 'freebie'.

free (2) unmarried
The use deprecates the ties imposed by wedlock. Less often as 'in freedom': 'I've been alone all this time, I've stayed in freedom because of you' (Murdoch, 1978, explaining a reason for not having married). The ob. Eng. to be 'free of fumbler's hall' was to be unable to impregnate your wife.

free (3) an inducement to buy subject to taking on an obligation
Advertising jargon for an arrangement whereby the gullible subscribe to a magazine, buy a packet of cornflakes, take out insurance, etc. to get something which was costed in the original price.

(free a man for duty to replace a male soldier away from the battlefield by a female, is given by Mesdames Neaman and Silver as a euphemism and provides a useful signpost to their objectivity when they feel their sex is impugned: 'This military evasion of both truth and the responsibility for it implies, etc.' (Neaman and Silver, 1983). The term may be patronizing and offensive to some, but it acknowledges the reality that women in Western armies are not combatant troops.)

free from infection not suffering from venereal disease
In the army, a soldier can have measles and a heavy cold, but still be so described. Usu. abbr. to 'FFI'.

free-lance to copulate regularly with different men
A complex pun on 'lance', to copulate (though normally of the male), being 'free' from involvement with a pimp or not even demanding payment, and the 'free-lance' who works for more than one employer. Such a woman is called (among other things)

a 'free-lance' or 'free-lancer'. Rarely of males in the same sense.

free load *see* free (1)

free love unrestricted copulation outside marriage
The use implies an absence of concealment and disregard of convention for either sex: 'Dismal free love at a summer camp' (G. Greene, 1932).

free of your hips willing to copulate extra-maritally
Of a woman, whose hips may play some part in the action: 'Free of her lips, free of her hips' (Old Proverb).

free relationship a marriage in which a spouse is supposed to be able to copulate extra-maritally without recrimination
The phrase might suggest that a normal marriage involves sexual servility: 'Our marriage had broken up over my jealousy. Esther wanted a free relationship' (McCarthy, 1963).

free ride a whore
As different from a **ride** (q.v.) for which the male does not pay. Am. CB use.

free samples copulation with a woman prior to marriage
From a taster or trial quantity offered by a trader. The euphemism is used when there is a prospect of engagement, or of betrothed couples.

free trade etc. unrestricted or uncontrolled access to markets
The use implies more than the absence of duties or restrictions on import. Those for whom 'free' enterprise, trade, etc. are anathema can rightly complain of abuses and inequalities which result from human greed and that the price of an economic system which works better than the alternative is too high in social terms. A 'free-for-all' is not a Utopian society in which none pays but a derogatory term for the operation of an unregulated economy or labour market. The ob. SW Eng. and Sc. 'free trade' was smuggling, from the avoidance of Excise duty: 'My father let me have a horse from the stable and a ling-tow over my shoulder to go out to the free trade among the Manxmen' (Crockett, 1894).

free world the countries not under Communist control
Any other tyranny can be included, whatever the imperfections of its political arrangements: 'The Western countries call them-selves collectively the "Free World"' (Jennings, 1965).

freedom fighters terrorists
Even when opposing an autocratic regime, they normally seek to replace it with autocracy: 'We are not murderers . . . we are freedom fighters against international imperialism' (Sharpe, 1979).

freemans cadged cigarettes
Army use of an habitual cadger who is supposed to smoke this fictional brand, and *see* 'drink at Freeman's Quay' under **drink**. The ob. Br. 'freeman of Bucks' was a cuckold, punning on the county and the horns.

freeze an attempt to restrict pay increases by Statute
The imagery is from the immobility, if not the coldness, of ice. This is one of a series of Br. euphemisms used to try to hide the fact that, in a period of inflation, the absence of a pay increase means a reduction in real terms.

freeze off to kill
The common 'chilling' imagery: 'Frisky Lavon got froze off tonight' (Chandler, 1939).

freeze on to to steal
From the adhesive quality of ice. Of minor speculation and stealing by finding.

freeze out unfairly to eliminate minor shareholders
Commercial jargon, from the meaning arbitrarily to exclude. The majority holders of stock make life so unprofitable for the minority that they are induced to sell on unfavourable terms. In Australia, the 'freeze' is a wife's refusal to copulate with her husband, the use having as yet no Am. or Br. currency.

freezer a prison
The frequent Am. 'ice' imagery: 'You didn't spend three days in the freezer just because you're a sweetheart' (Chandler, 1953).

French (1) cunnilingus or fellatio
An Am. abbr. of 'French way', from supposed Gallic tastes: 'Only fooled around with him a little. I wasn't Frenching him' (Wambaugh, 1975). A 'French kiss' is heterosexual open-mouthed kissing, from which youths often contract glandular fever – the 'kissing disease' – because one female in five is a carrier.

French (2) an excuse for swearing
You pretend the taboo word is foreign:

'. . . not when some poor fucker . . . you'll excuse the French, Mr Carter' (Seymour, 1980).

French ache etc. syphilis
We all name bad things after our enemies – treachery for the Romans was 'Punic faith' and for the Cathaginians 'Roman faith'. Shakespeare refers to the baldness caused by this supposed import: 'Some of your French crowns have no hair at all' (*Midsummer Night's Dream*). In former times you might, if so unlucky, contract 'French' disease, fever, gout, measles or pox, and so become 'Frenchified', syphilitic.

French article etc. brandy
A euphemism of smuggling before passing into now ob. general use. Also as 'French' cream, elixir and lace, and a 'Frenchman' was a single bottle of brandy. I'm not sure why in Ire. 'French cream' was whiskey: 'Might he have the pleasure of helping her to a little more of that delicious French cream' (Kennedy, 1867, of whiskey).

French blue an illegal narcotic
Usu. amphetamine, from its colour and the country of manufacture.

French leave an unauthorized absence
Usu. of a soldier, implying a propensity in French troops for cowardice and desertion. Some civilian and fig. use: 'We could still, if we wished, take "French leave" of Vietnam' (McCarthy, 1967).

French letter a contraceptive sheath worn by a male
Perhaps the term comes from their being packed in small envelopes, coupled with the supposed Gallic penchant for frequent copulation: '. . . keep in their bags not even small change, only a powder-puff, a lipstick, a mirror, perhaps some French letters' (G. Greene, 1932). Abbr. to 'FL': 'Preyed on his mind, all those FLs did' (Sharpe, 1974). 'Frenchie' is rarer: 'You can't feel a thing with a Frenchie. You get more thrill with a pill' (Sharpe, 1976). 'French tickler' is ob.: '. . . you were screwing matron with a French tickler' (Sharpe, 1982). 'Froggie' is a naval corruption, from the derogatory name for a nation aware of the delicacy of frogs' legs. The 19c. 'French renovating pills' were taken in the hope of ending a pregnancy that ealier resort to a 'French letter' might have averted (Rawson, 1981).

French way *see* French

fresh drunk
Perhaps an abbr. of 'fresh in drink', with 'fresh' meaning lively, and so not far gone: 'He wa' to say drunk – on'y fresh a bit' (Pinnock, 1895). Inns stay open all day in Eng. market towns and drunken farmers used to return home 'market fresh': '. . . was already "market-fresh" when we started back' (*Cornhill Magazine*, 1896, quoted in EDD of a drunken farmer). More logically the 19c. Sc. 'fresh' referred to your sobriety before drinking intoxicants: 'There is our great Udaller is weel enough when he is fresh' (W. Scott, 1822).

fresh meat *see* dead meat (2)

freshen a drink to serve more alcohol
Formerly of adding more soda water to a partly drained glass but now you add whisky, etc.: '"Let me freshen your drink." Delaney said. He went over to the liquor cabinet, came back with new drinks for both of them' (Sanders, 1973).

freshen up to urinate
The standard Am. invitation to an arriving traveller, who may also change his shirt, defecate or take a shower: 'Why don't you just freshen up and then stroll on down the path, first right, to my lodge?' (M. Thomas, 1980 – the standard reply is 'Thank you, I'd be glad to wash my hands').

friar Tuck an act of copulation
Spoonerism and rh. sl. on Robin Hood's clerical companion: 'Friar Tuck at the Boar's Head with a soul full of hope' (old vulgarism illustrating three Spoonerisms). Also used for 'fuck' in expletives.

fricasseed drunk
The Am. culinary imagery.

fried drunk
Am. culinary imagery again.

friend an extra-marital sexual partner
Heterosexual: 'You got a friend that don't work and a husband that works, you're all set' (Chandler, 1943); or homosexual: 'I have a very nice friend. It's against the law of course' (G. Greene, 1973). *See* too **lady friend, woman friend** and 'man friend' under **man**. A 'rich friend' is always the male in such a relationship. 'Friends', 'close friends' or 'just good friends' are such partners: '. . . he mustn't say *good friends*, that was always taken as a euphemism for extreme intimacy' (Price, 1974); and: 'She managed to let me know . . . that Dylan Thomas had once been a "close friend"' (Fowles, 1977).

friend has come (my) I am menstruating
Punning on the arrival for a limited period

and perhaps the relief at not being pregnant. Females also have a '(little) friend to stay'.

friendly under military, political and economic control
Stalin's Yalta demand that E. European States should have governments 'friendly' to Russia was better understood by Churchill than by Roosevelt, and its implementation still oppresses Poles, Germans, Czechs, Slovaks, Hungarians, etc.

friendly fire being bombed or shelled by your own side
The use seeks to minimize the incompetence: '. . . strafed and bombed by American planes. (Afterwards the ghastly error was described in military double-talk as "friendly fire")' (Hailey, 1979).

frig to copulate
From 'frig', to rub, despite the etymological attractions of the Old Cornish 'freg', a married woman, and of 'Frigga', Odin's wife, the aptly-named Norse goddess of married love whom we commemorate each Friday: 'I kept on frigging her with my man-root' (Harris, 1925). It is also used of male masturbation, also from the rubbing: '. . . under a haystack in the country we gave ourselves to a bout of frigging' (ibid.). You now only hear it in the expletive 'frigging' for 'fucking'.

fringe insubstantial and fraudulent
Close to the edge of propriety and honesty. Commercial jargon, especially of financial institutions: 'The Bank of England's least favourite "fringe" banker' (*Private Eye*, March 1981, of an insubstantial Br. bank).

fringes extra payment in kind
Abbr. of 'fringe benefits' which some employees receive additional to the salary they reveal to the Revenue or their stockholders.

frog a policeman
From his manner of walking or from jumping on delinquents? It is childish and insulting to call a Frenchman a 'frog'.

froggie *see* **French letter**

front (1) an organization hiding its real objectives so as to appeal to the gullible and well-meaning
The method was first devised by Munzenberg, the Communist propagandist, and has been widely used by the Communists and others ever since: 'The World Committee for the Relief of Victims of German Fascism set the pattern for all future camouflaged "front" organizations' (Boyle,

1979). Today: 'We have Fronts for this and Fronts for that . . . . One should always ask what . . . . is behind a Front' (Francis, 1978).

front (2) a seemingly honest person or business shielding an illegal operation
Criminal jargon and practice, and also used of espionage: '. . . invested in a wide range of new enterprises one of which was a "front" for the Gehlen organization' (Allbeury, 1976). To 'front' is so to act: 'Where's the front money coming from? . . . . I think he's fronting for someone' (Deighton, 1981).

front door (the) copulation
As different from the 'back door', buggery: 'You'll be able to hand out radical deliverance to both of them now. One at the front door, and one at the back' (Bradbury, 1975 – advice from his wife to Howard, the trendy lecturer who offers advice and sexual service to all, on the break-up of a marriage). In rare use, the 'front' door or parlour can be the vagina, viewed sexually.

front loading the avoidance of risk through excessive down-payment
Commercial jargon of a common practice in international sale to an unreliable customer or a poor country. The surplus provides some hedge against cancellation or the inability of the buyer to complete the deal. It is facilitated by the eagerness of agents and those whom they are bribing to touch cash as soon as possible. Also as 'front money' or 'money up front'.

front office a police station
From the location of main offices in Am. factories etc. at the front of the building.

fruit a male homosexual
Which came first, the **raisin** (q.v.) or the 'fruit'? I suspect 'raisin', from the French meaning lipstick, but this conjecture is unsupported: 'Pastor was screwing that Mexican fruit' (Deighton, 1972). The punning 'fruit picker' is a male who occasionally seeks a homosexual partner. In Far Eastern use, a 'fruit fly' is a whore: '. . . sailing two fruit-flies as scrub-women (greasy overalls covering silk cheongsams)' (Theroux, 1973, of smuggling whores out to a freighter).

fruit machine a mechanical gambling device
From the symbols on the rotating discs in the early versions: 'As army-surplus dealer, a scrap-metal merchant, a fruit-machine importer – or a property man' (Green, 1979). The alternative name, 'one-armed bandit' from the actuating lever, is more fitting.

fruit salad a mixture of illegal narcotics
Supplies are pooled and each participant in
the 'fruit salad party' is meant to take a bit of
everything. A 'fruit salad' is also what you
end up with if you take one pill of each
narcotic from the family medicine store.

fruitcake a lunatic
From the cliché 'as nutty as a fruitcake':
'God knows they've got their share of armed
fruitcakes' (Lyall, 1985).

fry to be killed in an electric chair
One of the culinary evasions for a taboo
subject among violent criminals.

fuddled drunk
Properly, confused and descriptive of the
drunken state in which you think you can
drive but cannot find the keys of the car.

fudge (1) to deceive by making wrong
entries
Especially of falsification of accounts, being
a corruption of the SE 'fuddle', to confuse:
'Perhaps he had been fudging his tax
returns' (Chandler, 1958). To 'fudge an
issue' is a correct use, albeit something of a
cliché.

fudge (2) to masturbate a person of the
opposite sex
I suspect this Am. use comes from the
meaning 'devise as a substitute' (WNCD).

fulfilment copulation
Properly, the accomplishment of anything:
'In the corners couples embraced and
fondled, stopping just short of actual fulfilment' (Bradbury, 1959).

full drunk
It survives in the Sc. 'fou': 'The cup that
cheers, but maksna fou' (Tester, 1865 – he
means tea) and in various Am. clichés of
which the commonest (in every sense) is 'full
as a tick'.

full and frank *see* frank

full employment work is available for
most of the population
It does not mean that those who prefer not to
work are compelled to do so, nor that those
in employment have jobs which demand
their entire attention. Like many desirable
objectives, its achievement is not easily
reconcilable with individual freedom or economic efficiency.

full-figured fat
Of women rather than men. To be other
than 'full-figured' is not to be short of an
anatomical appendage. 'Full-bodied' is also

used in the same sense of women, but more
often of wine.

full in the belly pregnant
Not merely having eaten a hearty meal. In
various forms: 'He had run away from a girl
with a full belly and a father with a loaded
musket' (Monsarrat, 1978).

full treatment (the) copulation
The language of those heterosexual brothels
which operate under the cover of meassage
parlours etc.: 'Is it just your neck that's
giving you trouble, or do you require the full
treatment?' (Matthew, 1978).

fumble to copulate with
Properly, to use your hands awkwardly,
whence to caress: 'The dish you was trying
to fumble up the hall' (Chandler, 1958, and
not of a waiter). A 'fumble' is a single act of
extra-marital copulation by a male: 'I must
have carried twenty females to the barges
(and none of them worth even a quick
fumble)' (Fraser, 1975). An 18c. 'fumbler'
was a sexually impotent male, who could do
no more than caress a woman, whence 'free
of fumbler's hall' (q.v. under **free** (2)). If you
'fumble' for a check, you do not copulate for
payment but try to get out of paying for a
shared meal.

fun extra-marital copulation
Originally 'fun' meant a hoax or trick,
whence amusement: 'Country gentleman,
45, wealthy, tall, educated, is looking for an
attractive young mistress. For fun' (advertisement in *Private Eye*, April 1980). 'Fun
and games' is general sexual promiscuity:
'She was a bit of an all-rounder. Both sexes.
General fun and games' (Davidson, 1978).
'Fun loving' is promiscuous of either sex, or
addicted to alcohol, of a male: 'The
Washington Post had described him as "fun-
loving", which was journalese for a hearty
preference for alcohol or sex' (M. Thomas,
1980). 'Fun stick', the penis in punning rh.
sl., is happily rare. A 'fun-house' is a brothel:
'I'm exaggerating, but it *was* splendidly furnished, with more mirrors than a fun house'
(Sanders, 1986).

(funeral director an arranger of funerals is
pretentious rather than euphemistic,
although I hesitate before disagreeing with
Miss Mitford: 'Certain American
euphemisms – "funeral director" instead of
"undertaker"' (J. Mitford, 1963). Indeed
'undertaker' has a better claim – he might be
undertaking all sorts of things other than
burying corpses. The abbr. 'director' might

refer to any activity: 'The Director, Official publication of the National Funeral Directors Association' (ibid.).)

funny (1)   unwell
Tricked but not amused, usu. in the phrase 'feel funny'.

funny (2)   drunk
We hesitate to blame our indisposition on our intemperance.

funny (3)   homosexual
Of a male, from the meaning odd: 'And you said last night he was "that kind" . . . funny, kinky' (Bogarde, 1981).

funny (4)   mad
Again from the oddness and usu. in the phrases 'funny' farm, house or place, an institution for the insane: 'Wasn't that the first picture of Pound to appear after he was let out of the funny farm?' (Theroux, 1978), or: '. . . if Harold were really worried about joining his mother in the funny place, he should see a psychiatrist' (Wambaugh, 1975).

funny money   cash that cannot be spent openly
Of counterfeit notes or the proceeds of vice:

'As quick as he finds out that's funny money he'll put the finger on you' (Weverka, 1973).

furlough   the suspension of paid employment
Properly, paid leave of absence. Somewhat archaic until recent Am. jargon for cutting back on air crew.

furry thing   a rabbit
Br. seamen must not mention rabbits before putting to sea under an old taboo based on the substitution by fraudulent chandlers of rabbit meat, which did not keep, for salt pork, which did. In ob. Br. use a 'furry tail' was a worker who refused to join a trades union, a 'rat' to some.

fuzz   a policeman
Or the police generally. Probably an abbr. of 'fuzzy bear' and *see* **bear** (2): 'The fuzz – that's what they call them now, not cops any more' (Ustinov, 1971).

fuzzed   drunk
Properly, blurred, which things tend to become at a certain stage. Also in Am. use as 'fuzzy' or 'fuzzled'.

G

G anything taboo beginning with the letter 'G'
Either a mild expletive, usu. spelt 'gee', an abbr. of 'jeez' from 'Jesus'; or to rob, perhaps from the Am. 'gyp'; or the leader of a 'gang' of convicts; or a 'gallon' of whisky. The commonest, and non-euphemistic, use of 'G' is for a 'grand' – $1,000. 'Geed up', crippled, may just have arrived in Am. from the old Sc. dialect word 'jee', crooked: 'On a sair jee'd moss-grown stane' (Mucklebackit, 1885). The Am. 'G'-man' is a special kind of federal policeman, with 'G' for government. A motion picture graded 'G' can be shown generally.

gaff to cheat
From the Am. 'gaff', or fairground. Of the shortchanging and petty embezzlement for which fairs are notorious.

gage (1) cheap and unpalatable whisky
The Am. container so called holds a quart. Whence 'gaged', drunk but not necessarily on whisky.

gage (2) a marijuana cigarette
Is derivation from the token of defiance, the measurement of the quantity or merely an abbr. of 'engage'? None is convincing. To 'gage' is also to ingest illicit narcotics: 'The people who didn't smoke or gage, get razored in barrel-houses . . .' (Longstreet, 1956).

gain to steal
In the 15c. 'gain' was booty. Today it means to acquire something of small value without payment or detection.

gallant a woman's extra-marital sexual partner
Properly, polished or stately, which may be in contrast to her boring or boorish husband: 'Elspeth would be back in the saddle with one of her gallants by now' (Fraser, 1971, of a profligate wife). Today 'over-gallant' describes a male's unwanted sexual attention to a female: 'Sammy was . . . How shall I put it? I think the kindest way would be "over-gallant"' (Boyd, 1982). In ob. use 'gallant to' meant copulating with extra-maritally: 'Is it the case you had been gallant to her before marriage?' (Galt, 1826). 'Gallantry' was extra-marital copulation by either sex: 'She was not without a charge of gallantry' (Hutchinson, of an adulteress in mid. 17c).

(The Br. House of Commons requires certain forms of address for its members. In that world of make-believe, they are all 'honourable' and every ex-serviceman is 'gallant'.)

gallop to copulate with
Of males, using the common equine imagery: '. . . beaky, sharp-eyed old harridans whom I wouldn't have galloped for a pension' (Fraser, 1971). A 'gallop' is an act of copulation or the woman with whom you do it: 'She was a fine, rousing gallop, all sleek hard flesh' (ibid., of a woman). To 'gallop your maggot' is to masturbate, of a male.

game (1) wild animals killed primarily for human amusement
SE of those hunted in the wild, birds conserved so that they can be shot and certain large fish. 'Big game' describes large quadrupeds, mainly in Africa where they have not yet been hunted to extinction.

game (2) (the) prostitution
The same imagery as **sport** (q.v.) but a serious business if it is your livelihood: 'I'm old at the game' (Harris, 1925, quoting an old whore) and for Boswell the 'noble' game was copulation, with an actress whom he paid. A working whore is said to be 'on the game': 'Every girl in Bayswater bangs to him if she wants to stay on the game' (Turner, 1968). 'In the game' means no more than being a whore already: 'They don't take only women who are in the game already. They get hold of innocent women' (Londres, 1928 in tr., of pimps). In ob. use a 'game pullet' was a young whore and a 'gamester' any whore: 'She's impudent, my lord, and was a common gamester to the camp' (Shakespeare, *All's Well*). 'Game', of any female, indicates a supposed willingness to copulate extra-maritally and the jocular 'national indoor game' is copulation. At one time, if you were detected in adultery in Sc., the church demanded a 'game-fee': 'Niest ye maun pay down the game fee, An' nae mair we sal trouble thee' (Liddle, 1821).

game chicken a cock
You need to read Mencken's fascinating, exasperating and uneven *The American Language* to appreciate the length to which it was abused by the prudish to avoid saying 'cock' (the bird), 'leg' (the limb) and 'ass' (the animal). A popular alternative for 'cock', rooster, still survives but we have lost the joys of 'rooster roach', of drinking 'roostertails' and calling our helmsman a 'roosterswain'. *See* too **dark meat**.

gamester (1) *see* game (2)

gamester (2) a gambler
'Gaming' has meant gambling since the 16c.
because people have always wagered on the
outcome of games: 'The credit of a racehorse, a gamester, and a whore, lasteth but a
short time' (Torriano, 1642 – surely he
meant 'or a whore'). In the ABC used by
myself as a child and by my children: 'G was
a gamester who had but ill luck' (and we saw
no impropriety in 'U was an usher who loved
little boys').

gander-mooner a husband copulating
outside marriage
The month after the birth of a child was
known as the 'Gander Month' or 'Gander
Moon', from 'the month during which the
goose is sitting when the gander looks lost
and wanders vacantly about' (EDD). For this
period the Eng. father and husband was
supposedly given licence to copulate with
other than his unavailable wife. Both the use
and the giving of licence are ob.

(gang the Sc. form of 'go' has much the
same euphemistic uses. It has been generally
supplanted in SE, except in gangplank and
gangway.)

gang-bang *see* bang (1)

gap the vagina
From the opening between the thighs. Some
medical use. The ob. Lincs. 'gap-maker' was
a poacher, who might break through a hedge
to avoid detection.

gapping *see* take the gap

garconnière an apartment used by a married man for copulation with his sexual
mistress
Properly, in French, the establishment of a
bachelor: '. . . the distinguished brick-faced
town house in which he kept his garçon-
nière' (M. Thomas, 1982, of such a place).

garden (1) the vagina viewed sexually by a
male
If he is so vulgar as to use the expression, he
sees it as a place for cultivation, or pleasure,
or both. In rarer use as 'Garden of Eden' or
'Pleasure-garden'.

garden (2) to sow mines in water from the
air
It is important to adhere to a pattern and this
WW II imagery is from planting bulbs etc.
The use comforted the airmen by avoiding
explicit lethal terms and also reflected the
comparative safety of such an operation.

garden city a residential suburb
Ebenezer Howard's vision of idyllic houses
set among flowers and winding lanes was
first achieved at Letchworth in Eng., which
is still a delightful place, although the lack of
an inn may be vexing on a warm summer's
evening. It is now real estate jargon for a
major housing development not plagued by
excessive noise, smell, vibration, through
traffic or vandalism.

garden crypt a drawer facing outward in a
store for corpses
Funeral jargon, to persuade living customers
to pay more so that the dead may enjoy the
ambience: 'Crypts facing outside . . . are now
called "garden crypts" . . . "It's all part of
the trend to outdoor living," explained the
counsellor' (J. Mitford, 1963). Am.

garden gout / house *see* Covent Garden

garden of remembrance etc. the curtilage of a crematorium
Usu. a few seats, some roses, a path and a
lawn, all of which are soon forgotten: 'There
is something comfortlessly empty about a
"garden of remembrance" after the
loquacious populated feeling of a graveyard'
(Murdoch, 1978). A 'Garden of Honor' is
the part of an Am. cemetery in which you
can pay to put up a plate naming an ex-
soldier.

gargle to drink intoxicants
Properly, a liquid suspended in the throat
for medical purposes: '"Let's . . . . gargle."
He poured drinks' (Chandler, 1939). A
'gargle' is usu. whisky.

gas to kill in a sealed space by poison gas
Done on a mass scale by the Nazis, individually by the Am. penal system: 'He's not
around any more to be asked. They gassed
him' (Chandler, 1953). Rarely as 'get the gas
pipe': 'You may go down the toilet there,
Victor, but I get the gas pipe' (Diehl, 1978).
Properly speaking, we all live by inhaling gas
several times a minute, none of it immediately noxious or poisonous unless we smoke
tobacco or inhale narcotics. Those 'gassed'
in WW I were the victims of chemical warfare. I can just recall these prematurely aged
young men, often unmarried and unable to
work, with their incessant coughs, although
the one for whom I was given my middle
name died within a year of my birth.

gash a woman viewed as an object of extra-
marital copulation
Although 'gash' is a vulgarism for the vagina,
this use probably comes from the meaning,

something acquired for nothing or surplus to another's needs: 'Maybe there's some of that Swedish gash hanging around' (Sanders, 1977 – men were looking for women to pick up).

gassed drunk
From the Am. 'gas', very satisfying, perhaps punning on the meaning of an inferior substitute for potable alcohol. A 'gas-hound' drinks such fluid, but not in 'gas house', or beer saloon.

gastric flu diarrhoea
'Gastric' is of the stomach and influenza is a viral infection which most of us confuse with a common cold, but they don't add up to diarrhoea.

gate (1) to confine to college as a punishment
Originally of those colleges in Cambridge and Oxford which had formidable barriers to prevent unobserved access and formidable porters in the gatehouse.

gate (2) (the) peremptory dismissal from employment
The exit for the last time from the factory which you are 'given' in Am. and 'shown' in BI: 'Amtrack board facing the gate' (*New York Post*, September 1981, of their threatened dismissal en bloc). Like many of the 'dismissal' euphemisms, it can also mean the summary unilateral ending of courtship, almost always by the woman.

gathered to your fathers etc. dead
You do not necessarily have to be buried in a family vault. Less often we may be 'gathered to our ancestors' but not, as yet, to 'our mothers'. Legislation apart, this last is unlikely because the use is based on deep tribal concepts, and the human is rare among mammals in requiring the mature female rather than the male to leave the tribe. For those interested, this phenomenon is also reflected in most primitive conceptions of incest – the taboos are much stronger against marrying paternal relatives than maternal.

gay (1) enjoying or doing something the subject of a taboo
From the meaning, happy and pleasure-loving. Until quite recently 'gay' meant drunk or under narcotic influence, but no more – *see* **gay (2)** (below). In the 19c. the 'gay life' was prostitution, to 'gay' it was to go with whores, a 'gay house' was a brothel and there you might find whores known as 'gay' ladies or girls: 'I went through all the changes of a gay lady's life' (Mayhew, 1862, of a whore).

gay (2) homosexual
Now virtually SE from **gay (1)** (above): 'Investigations were proceeding with a gay club' (Davidson, 1978). 'Gay Liberation Front' has the distinction of combining three euphemisms – *see* **liberate** (3) and **front** (1): 'Now if this Piper was a gay liberationist Jew-baiter with a nigger boyfriend from Cuba called O'Hara' (Sharpe, 1977). 'Gay deceivers' are not worn to confuse homosexuals but are pads worn in the clothing to enhance a bust.

gazelles are in the garden you are flouting a minor social convention
Someone wants to tell you your nose is dripping, your trouser zip is undone, or as the case may be.

gear anything the subject of secrecy or taboo
Properly, equipment. In ob. Sc. use it meant smuggled spirits: 'There were . . . . two kinds of the lads who brought over the dutiless gear from Holland' (Crockett, 1894). In modern sexual use, the male or female genitalia. In narcotic addiction, the 'gear' is the apparatus you use to introduce the substance into your body. A burglar's 'gear' is his specialized tools. 'Gear', homosexual, may refer also to the indicative clothing worn, and in any case it is rh. sl. for 'queer'.

geared up drunk
Am. use, probably form **gear** (above). I have not seen it used of narcotic addiction.

gears have slipped mind is deranged
Motoring imagery – you still move but ineffectively: 'Her gears has slipped. Not a lot, but some' (Sanders, 1982). Similarly they may not mesh: 'It was just that the things she said and did were slightly askew. Her gears weren't quite meshing' (Sanders, 1986).

geezer an intoxicant or illegal narcotic
Perhaps from the Sc. 'guiser', a drunkard, which came from 'guised in liquor' – or perhaps not because it is also a term of derision (a 'silly geezer'); or, from the Icelandic, something which gushes, which drunkards do when they are sick. (Whence the 'geyser' which may gush hot water into the bath, if it does not explode first.) 'Geezed up' means drunk or under narcotic influence.

gender-bending the deliberate rejection of the characteristics of a sex
No longer a pupil's struggles with Latin

grammar. Usu. of flagrant homosexuality or bisexuality in dress, etc.

general discharge dishonourable dismissal from the US forces
Normal people get an 'honorable discharge'.

General Winter the harsh climate of Eastern Europe
The only soldier to have fought and beaten both Napoleon and Hilter: '"General Winter", whom Napoleon met in Russia' (McCarthy, 1967).

genital sensate focusing digital foreplay to copulation
Medical jargon which borders on circumlocution: 'He would have been at it anyway without having ever heard of genital sensate focusing' (Amis, 1978, of such activity).

gentle art (the) copulation
As Voltaire and others have pointed out, it does not especially bring to mind tameness or moderation: '. . . a fine, fat little rump she was . . . . but no great practitioner of the gentle art' (Fraser, 1985).

gentle people the fairies
'Fairies', prior to the Christmas pantomime, were nasty people and to assuage them, you attribute to them the major quality in which they are defective. In Ire. they are also known as the 'gentry' but I am not sure whether this was because the local gentry were worthy of respect, or because the gentry would be Anglo-Irish, and as nasty as the fairies themselves: 'Biddy was known, too, to have the powers of seeing the "gentry", beings who creep out from every mousehole and from behind every rafter the minute a family has gone to sleep' (Lawless, 1892). Hawthorns were called 'gentle thorns' despite their pricks, because the fairies put spells on them.

gentleman was once used of any occupation or state the subject of vilification or taboo
Thus in ob. Br. use he was without work in the days when that also meant without money, a grim joke on the wealthy who did not need to work: 'He is a gentleman now, without seeking the shelter of the workhouse' (O'Reilly, 1880). If a tramp, he was a 'gentleman at large'. The 'gentlemen' were smugglers: 'If the gentlemen come along don't you look out o' window' (Egerton, 1884). A 'gentleman of fortune' was a pirate and a 'gentleman of the road', a highway thief, who might also be called a 'gentleman's master', because gentlemen stood and delivered to him. A 'gentleman's gentleman' is a personal servant or valet. Then there were numerous oblique descriptions of work or taste, whereby you might be described as a 'gentleman' of the cloth, a tailor (not a parson); quill, a clerk; scalpel, a surgeon; of the back-door, a bugger; etc.

gentleman commoner an empty bottle of intoxicants
18c. wealthy students at Cambridge and Oxford were so called because they were thought to be empty-headed. Probably now ob.

gentleman friend an older man with whom a woman regularly copulates extra-maritally.
Mainly female use. He does not have to be 'of gentle birth' or behave chivalrously towards her or anyone else.

gentlemen a lavatory exclusively for male use
Less often in a compound by the addition of 'convenience' etc. than is the case with **ladies** (q.v.) but often abbr. to 'gents': 'I always thought wearing a kilt was a pretty daft idea, but they do save time in the Gents' (*Private Eye*, August 1980).

gentry *see* **gentle people**

geography the location of a lavatory
In genteel usage to a visitor, to avoid the need for exploration: 'Let me show you the GEOGRAPHY of the house' (Ross, 1956).

George to entice into copulation
I suppose this Am. male use comes from the meaning, enjoyable or exciting. In ob. Br. use 'George' meant a shit, being rh. sl. on George III, a turd.

Georgian old
Br. estate agents' jargon for a house usu. in poor repair. As the first four Georges ruled from 1714 to 1830, and the last two from 1910 to 1952, the net is spread quite wide.

German distorted to fit Nazi dogma
Everyone writes history from a nationalist viewpoint and excess of hindsight, although the Nazis and Communists bring to the task added ruthlessness and cynicism. The Nazis set themselves two further targets – moulding scientific facts to fit their often bizarre theories, and excising any Jewish contribution to learning. The resulting 'German' chemistry, mathematics, etc. would have been ludicrous had not the tragedy been so awful. 'Germanization', the adoption and adaptation by the Nazis of anything foreign,

led also to ridiculous and horrifying behaviour, such as the placing of fair-haired children from occupied countries in Nazi families to be brought up as Germans: 'It is believed they were the rejected ones from the Germanization program' (Styron, 1976, of mass killings of such children).

German Democratic Republic *see* **democratic**

Gestapo *see* **secret state police**

get a bullet to be killed violently
Usu. by being shot but it is also used of any method of killing: 'He will probably finally learn to understand the true nature of bolshevism only when he gets his bullet' (Goebbels, 1945, in tr. of Paarviki).

get a leg over etc. to copulate
This expression, and its variants 'get your leg across' and the ob. 'get your leg dressed' are of copulation by the male. Many of the 'copulation' phrases starting with 'get' are dealt with elsewhere and to avoid repetition and tedium this entry ignores them. For example, 'get stuffed' in all its meaning can be located under **stuff (2)**. The following expressions are not conveniently noted elsewhere:

get down to business to copulate, of either sex, usu. extra-maritally: '. . . going to bed with Lola in a great creaking four-poster which swayed and squealed when we got down to business' (Fraser, 1970).

get in her pants to copulate with a female extra-maritally does not imply that you are a transvestite: 'He'd tell a woman *anything* to get in her pants' (Sanders, 1977).

get into bed with to copulate extra-maritally on a single occasion: '. . . to get voluntarily into bed with a wanted murderess' (Sharpe, 1979).

get into her bloomers to copulate with a female extra-maritally is an Am. form of the (above) **get in her pants**: '. . . those motel units where you're planning to get into my bloomers' (Sanders, 1982).

get it in, on, off or **up** to copulate of a male and *see* **it (2)**: 'I know a pillar of the community who gets it off with alligators' (Sanders, 1982) and: 'He was too drunk to get it up even with the help of a crane, darling, but he paid his ten dollars' (Archer, 1979). 'Get it on' is also used of male homosexuality: '. . . an amusing set

of photographs of one man getting it on with a couple of sailors' (M. Thomas, 1980).

get laid to copulate or have copulated of a female, and usu. extra-maritally. This expression has totally supplanted the Eng. dialect 'get laid', to secure rest and quiet and a lady would be misunderstood today if she said 'I couldn't git mysel laid for the noise he mead' (EDD).

get off to achieve an orgasm of either sex: 'At my age, just getting off takes my breath away' (M. Thomas, 1980 – not referring to subsequent disengagement from the female).

get round to copulate with a female extra-maritally, from the meaning, to cajole.

get the upshoot to receive vaginally the male ejaculation is another of Shakespeare's lewd puns '"Then will she get the upshoot by cleaving the pin." "Come, come, you talk greasily; your lips grow foul"' (*Love's Labour's Lost*).

get there to copulate with a woman for the first time extra-maritally: 'Never seen her before tonight in my life. Bet I get there, though' (Bradbury, 1959).

get through to copulate extra-maritally of a male, punning on making a connection.

get up to copulate of a male. Common use since Sir Walter Raleigh's 'getting up one of the mayds of honour' (Aubrey, 1696) and probably long before that.

get with child to impregnate a female, within or outside marriage: 'At that time he got his wife with child' (Shakespeare, *All's Well*). It should mean literally, acquiring a step-child on marriage.

get your end away to copulate with a female.

get your end in to copulate with a female on a single occasion: 'We could both get our end in there' (Keneally, 1985 – two men were discussing copulating with a woman).

get your greens to copulate regularly, of either sex and often within marriage, probably from the supposed benefits of a diet regularly containing brassica: 'She's not getting what I believe is vulgarly called her greens' (G. Greene, 1967).

get your hook into to copulate with a woman; uses angling imagery: '"I'd like to get my hook into *her*," Davis said' (G. Greene, 1978).

get your muttons to copulate of either sex and *see* **mutton**: 'They couple like stoats, by the way, but only with men of proved bravery . . . you have to be blood-thirsty in order to get your muttons' (Fraser, 1977).

get your nuts off to copulate is usu. of the male, implying ejaculation.

get your rocks off to copulate is of either sex, despite the maleness of 'rocks', the testicles: '. . . thanks for coming over, we got our rocks off' (M. Thomas, 1980).

get your share to copulate frequently is usu. of a male, with more than one part-ner: '"Everyone talks about what a stud he was" . . . "He was getting more than his share even then"' (M. Thomas, 1980).

get your way with to copulate extra-maritally, of a male and again implying female reluctance.

get your will of to copulate of a male is rather dated and implies reluctant sub-mission by the female: 'When he had got his wills o' her' (Kinloch, 1827),

etc., etc.

get a marked tray to have contracted venereal disease
Am. hospital jargon. To avoid cross-infection, the crockery was not used by other patients. ? ob.

get along etc. to grow old
I suppose an abbr. for 'get along the road of life' or 'in years': 'He be gettin' along, and we can't expect him to be as nimble' (Hay-den, 1902). 'Get on' is SE for reaching old age: '. . .socialists conceding the excellence, which they could afford to do since there was only one of him and he was getting on' (N. Mitford, 1949). 'Up along' in Eng. dia-lect means elderly.

get away etc. to die
The soul departs from this tiresome place: 'The Laird, puir body, has gotten awa' (Thom, 1878). If a soldier 'gets it', he is killed: 'Richards got it in Danang' (Theroux, 1973, of a Vietnam death). A dying Christian may 'get the call' from a waiting deity.

get fitted to wear a contraceptive device
Abbr. of 'get fitted with the loop', etc. and

usu. of a female for the first time: '. . . asking them if they would like to come in and, as he puts it, get fitted' (Bradbury, 1976, of young women).

get off (1) to marry
Of a woman who might be anxious to find a husband. The phrase is also used when a mother wants to see marriageable daughters suitably married: 'You'd think she'd want to get her off all the quicker' (N. Mitford, 1949, of such a mother).

get off (2) *see* **get a leg over etc.**

get off (3) to take narcotics illegally
From the feeling of floating. To 'get on' is to start taking illicit narcotics regularly.

get off with to pair sexually with another
Of either sex, usu. of a person met socially on a single occasion.

get on (1) (2) (3) *see* **get along etc.; get a leg over etc.; get off** (3)

get on your bike to be dismissed from employment
From the days when the majority cycled to work, and cycled to find it: 'They'll still keep him on. There's no talk at all of telling him to get on his bike' (*Private Eye*, July 1980). The many other 'dismissal' phrases starting with 'get' are dealt with under **boot, kick,** etc.

get the shaft etc. to be killed
With many variations as to the weapon which may actually or fig. be used: 'Then you get the shaft' (Sanders, 1977, of such killing).

get the shorts to be insolvent
From the shortage of funds: 'Suddenly he's got the shorts . . . . he can't come up with the scratch and he's hurting' (Sanders, 1977).

ghost does not walk the cast will not be paid
Probably ob. theatrical jargon, the 'ghost' being the cashier. From the Hamlet of pre-union days, when only Marcellus spoke of striking, with his partisan.

G.I.s (the) diarrhoea
'GI' is for 'government issue' as marked on stores belonging to the US Army, whence private soldiers who are liable to intestinal disorders from a life of living rough and travelling.

gift of your body extra-marital copulation by a female
Usu. of a virgin, and anyway 'loan' would be more appropriate: 'He would not, but by gift of my chaste body To his concupiscible lust'

(Shakespeare, *Measure for Measure*). The use and the concept are dated.

(**gifted** clever, is educational jargon for a disciplined or attentive child. The use avoids your having to face up to other children being lazy, or stupid, or coming from unhelpful home backgrounds.)

giggle stick (1) the penis viewed sexually
Rh. sl. on 'prick' and punning on the stick for agitating a glass of sparkling wine, usu. champagne or 'giggle water'.

giggle stick (2) an illegal marijuana cigarette
From one of its effects. Am.

gild to tell a lie
Properly, to enhance the exterior appearance by the addition of a metallic coat and perhaps alluding to that misquoted cliché 'gild the lily' – Shakespeare wrote 'To gild refined gold, to paint the lily' (*King John*). Normally people 'gild' the facts, the truth, etc.: '"He lied to me about the security clearance." "It's a bad word to use in law. I'd agree he gilded the proposition"' (West, 1979).

ginger a male homosexual
Uncommon Br. rh. sl. on 'ginger beer', a queer. Less often written in full, as: 'I can usually detect anything that's ginger beer' (B. Forbes, 1986, of Donald Maclean).

gippy tummy diarrhoea
A corruption of Egyptian tummy, suffered by White visitors rather than the local inhabitants, who may also catch it anywhere in the world, it seems: 'She knew she was in for a further attack of "Gyppy tummy"' (Manning, 1977 – she was about to get diarrhoea again). Both spellings are common, as with 'gipsy' and 'gypsy'.

girl (1) a whore
I suppose from the meaning, a sweetheart: 'They turn the young Jewesses .... into what are generically known as "girls"' (Londres, 1928, in tr.). Often expanded to more explicit phrases like 'girl of the streets': 'The veritable girl of the streets is too "vicious"' (ibid.). To 'girl' is to seek after whores, and a 'girler' a womanizer: 'I hear this Frank Sinatra's a fearful girler' (Theroux, 1978). 'Girlie' often indicates that the women are being exploited for pornography or prostitution, as in 'girlie' bars, clubs, houses, parlours, etc. which are brothels: '... a front for the girlie house Billie ran upstairs' (Weverka, 1973) and '... direct traffic up to Billie's girlie

parlor' (ibid.). A 'girlie magazine' is an erotic publication and a 'girlie show' holds itself out as being a lewd live performance by females.

girl (2) any female of less than 50 years
Properly, a female child or servant. The use seeks to imply that the ageing process has been retarded: '... she was only a slip of a girl – what was she now – twenty-seven or eight' (Collins, 1981).

girl (3) cocaine obtained illegally
I have not traced the etymology.

give to copulate
Rare on its own, of male or female: 'Maybe Bill gives at the office' (Sanders, 1982 – not of charitable donations but of a man who did not copulate with his wife). In various compounds as follow:

> **give a little** to copulate rarely, of a female, usu. of a married or engaged pair: 'She still give you a little?' (Wambaugh, 1975, of an ex-wife).

> **give access to your body** to copulate of a female extra-maritally, perhaps for payment: 'She decided to .... give all soldiers who wished to take advantage of her free access to her body' (Richards, 1936).

> **give head** to copulate, of a male, from the glans penis. It also can mean to engage in fellatio: 'The old bastard had his son-in-law giving him head in the back seat' (Diehl, 1978).

> **give it to** to copulate of a male, despite the convention that the female is the generous party: 'You been giving it to her, have you?' (Allbeury, 1976, of copulation).

> **give out** to copulate of a female, although not the opposite of giving in: 'A guy buys gifts for his wife because he knows she won't give out if he don't' (Sanders, 1970).

> **give the time to** to copulate of either sex, but the etymology is obscure: 'I was personally acquainted with at least two girls he gave the time to' (Salinger, 1951).

> **give up your treasure** to copulate of a female, for the first time and extra-maritally: 'The summer solstice, when maids had given up their treasure to fructify the crops' (McCarthy, 1963).

> **give way** to copulate of a female, usu. after male urging and extra-maritally.

give your all to copulate extra-maritally Of a female, but not of a testatrix: 'Magill wasn't the first time I've given my Little All for my job' (Lyall, 1985).

give your body to copulate of a female extra-maritally: 'I loved a man, gave him my heart and, God help me, gave him my body' (Higgins, 1976 – it sounds almost like helping a transplant surgeon).

give yourself to copulate of a female, with implied extra-marital 'giving' by a virgin and the assumption that her virginity, once donated, cannot be returned: 'She was resolved not to give herself completely' (Harris, 1925) or, naming the donee: 'In small families the servants often give themselves to the sons' (Mayhew, 1862). Also some homosexual use: '... despite his decision to give himself to me, he was postponing the moment of going to bed' (Genet, in 1969, tr. of male homosexuals).

etc., etc.

give green stockings *see* **green gown**

give the air to dismiss from employment The many variants of this are dealt with under the noun, like **bag**, **boot**, **bullet**, etc.

give up the ghost to die The 'ghost' is the spirit which you surrender to heaven, or as the case may be, when your body dies: 'Man dieth, and wasteth away; yea, man giveth up the ghost' (Job xiv 10). There are many ob. dialect expressions indicating that the dead will make no further demand on terrestial resources, like the Lancs. 'give up the spoon' – you will eat no more: 'Johnny gan up his spoon one day beawt havin' any mooar warnin' nor other folk' (Brierley, 1865, of a sudden death).

given rig an uncultivated piece of ground left to placate the devil An ob. Sc. version of the practice noted elsewhere of trying to mollify the devil by leaving him some land of his own: '"The Gi'en Rig", which was set apart or given to the Diel, to obtain his good will' (Gordon, 1880).

given to the drink *see* **drink**

(**glamour** originally meant enchantment, from which to bewitch: 'Ye think I'm a witch and can cast the glaumour owre their een' (Cross, 1844). Happily few modern 'glamour girls' have retained the 'glamour-gift' – the power of casting malevolent spells.)

glass an intoxicant From the container out of which you drink: 'He, too, was happy to drink a glass before taking a quiet squint' (Kyle, 1978). Occasionally of intoxicants in general: 'The glass march'd pretty quick' (Cleland, 1749 – a lot of alcohol was drunk). A 'glass of something' is an intoxicant and a 'glass too many', drunkenness. In Ire. a 'glass' formerly equalled five measures of whisky.

glass house an army prison Br. army use from the glass roof of the one in Aldershot, and perhaps too the fig. 'heat' applied to the inmates.

glassy-eyed drunk From the vacant and watery gaze rather than the container which carried the damaging fluids.

glazed drunk An Am. version of **glassy-eyed** (above) using the same imagery.

glean to steal Properly, to pick up the ears of corn left by the reapers. Now a rare Br. use of pilfering small articles. At one time it also was applied to capturing stragglers from a losing army after a battle.

glove money a bribe By ancient custom, you gave gloves to anyone who had done you a favour, concealing any bribe inside. Sir Thomas More, when Lord Chancellor of England, kept the gloves which Mrs Croaker gave him but returned the hidden £40. We should not then be surprised that he was later beatified. ob.

glow to sweat Horses and women are said to 'glow', from the visual effect of moisture on the skin. Male sweat is quite a recent subject of taboo, fostered by misleading advertising on the part of manufacturers of deodorants. They persuade their customers that the smell of male sweat repels females sexually, although human biologists assure us that the converse is true.

glow on a state of mild drunkenness From the sweating which you experience: 'I didn't feel like getting a glow on. Either I would get really stiff or stay sober' (Chandler, 1953).

glue to steal Of Am. pilferage, the object sticking to you.

go (1) to die From the departure of the soul, or body, or both and in many phrases 'gang' is an alternative: '. . . he said "I think I'm going, Peters." He didn't speak again' (Manning, 1977). For this, and the following phrases meaning to die, read also 'gone', dead:

go again meant not to die but to reappear after death, perhaps from the second act of going afterwards: '. . . hes Vauther went agen, in shape of a gurt voul theng' (*Exmoor Courtship*, 1746, quoted in EDD).

go aloft is, for sailors, punning on the rigging and heaven.

go away is not common and can cause confusion: 'Not since my wife, Miriam . . . went away' (Diehl, 1978 – she could merely have left him).

go corbie came from the 'corbie-messenger' in ob. Sc. speech; he returned late or not at all: 'Hadna Pyotshaw grippit ma airm he was a gone corbie' (Gordon, 1885 – a 'corbie' is a crow).

go down was one of several ob. phrases for hanging, in odd contrast to **go up** (below). 'The lasses and lads stood on the walls, crying, "Hughie the Graeme, thou'se ne're gae down"' (W. Scott, 1803).

go down the nick is usu. of animals: 'Looks like they're all goin' to go down t'nick' (Herriot, 1981, of a herd of cattle).

go for a Burton alludes to the Br. habit of slipping out for a beer brewed in that Milwaukee of the Midlands. It also means the failure of any enterprise.

go forth in your cerements suggests that the corpse might in former times have been wrapped in waxed wrappings and is only used by a character like Stringer in Powell's *Dance to the Music of Time* novels.

go home should imply a return to heaven, but is also used of inanimate objects which are worn out, and the heavenly savour is lost in phrases like 'go home feet first' or 'go home in a box', the return of a corpse for burial.

go off the hooks from a falling gate is a rarer version of 'drop off the hooks'.

go on is common for the death of both humans and animals, giving both an implied option of a further stage of existence.

go out was used in WW I perhaps from the still current meaning, to lose consciousness. The modern cliché 'go out like a light' is to become unconscious or to go to sleep quickly.

go over is spiritualist and to a lesser extent Christian use, from the soul's passage to the 'other side' or another imprecisely defined destination.

go right was an ob. Eng. use, meaning to die and to go to heaven: 'I knowed 'e went right, far a says t'I, a says "I'a sin a angel"' (EDD).

go round land is both ob. and a contradiction, when you consider that in burial the land goes round the corpse: 'He went round land at las', an' was found dead in his bed' (Quiller-Couch, 1893).

go the wrong way is used after an illness, usu. of animals – to recover is the 'right way': '. . . a chronic state of diarrhoea under which the animal wastes away and dies. This is what is perfectly understood as going the wrong way' (EDD from W. Eng.).

go to a better place indicates only one among dozens of destinations of which many denote a heavenly reward – 'glory', 'life eternal', 'rest', etc.: 'I expect he's gone to his rest long since, poor man' (James, 1972) and others a continuation of a favoured occupation on earth: 'Now Sam's gone to the great massage parlor in the sky' (Sanders, 1977).

go to grass implied burial in the green Eng. churchyard, some going there 'with their teeth upwards'.

go to heaven in a string was the fate of 16c. Eng. Roman Catholics presumably from the death by hanging: 'Then may he boldly take his swing, and go to Heaven in a string' (T. Ward, 1708, quoted in ODEP).

go to the wall is also used of any failure.

go to your reward although I suspect most of us hope there will be no posthumous accountability: 'But it's a glory to know he has gone to his reward' (Sanders, 1980).

go to yourself was a Shetland Island use, and I give it for its overtones of Buddhism.

go under was not specifically for those who died of drowning, but from the common meaning, to fail.

go up was specifically to be killed by hanging, especially in 19c. Am. and rarely of a natural death: 'You'd better give it up if you don't want to go up' (Cookson, 1969 – she was being poisoned by working with lead paint). 'Go up the gate' referred to the entry to the churchyard, and not to the portal over which St Peter watches. The Nazi 'go up the chimney' referred to the burning of the corpses of their victims: 'The air stinks now but it might get better. A lot of Jews going up the chimney' (Styron, 1976).

go west represents a long tradition, based on the setting of the sun. The ancient Egyptians called their dead the 'west-erners'.

etc., etc.

go (2) to become bankrupt
As 'go' *tout court*, in the phrase 'on the go', and in many compounds. The ob. London 'go due north' was to the debtor prison in White Cross Street, to the north of the city. The picturesque 'go to staves' or 'fall at the staves' came from the collapse of a barrel when the hoops are removed. 'Go up Johnson's (or Jacksons's) end' was an ob. and inexplicable Eng. use but many still unfortunately 'go under', 'go for a Burton', 'go west', etc. The Am. 'go Chapter eleven' is to trade while insolvent under court protection, under the provisions of the Bankruptcy Reform Act of 1978 and the previous Act of 1898: 'The Lelands had first approached him in the summer of 1921, six months before they were driven to file Chapter Eleven' (Lacey, 1986). etc.

go (3) to urinate or defecate
Abbr. for 'go to the lavatory' etc.: '. . . especially Lally who was longing to "go" as much as we were' (Bogarde, 1978). In many compound uses 'go' and 'gang' were once more interchangeable than they are today; indeed, in ob. Br. use a 'gang' was a lavatory, probably from 'gang' or 'going', a drain, while 'geing or 'goung' was human excrement: 'No man shall bury any dung or goung within the liberties of this city' (Stowe, 1633, of London). There are probably hundreds of 'go' compound phrases for urination and defecation of which, to avoid tedium and save paper, I give the following only:

go about business to defecate refers to a common use of **business** (q.v.): 'They should go about their private business one hundred yards from the ordinary encampment' (Harris, 1925).

go for a walk with a spade is to defecate in the open air, burying the turds: 'I'd gone for a walk . . . You know, with a spade' (Manning, 1978).

go on the coal is to urinate, of blacksmiths, because urine serves both to damp the slack and to ammoniate it, making it better in the forge. By tradition, only a Br. working smith is allowed to 'go on the coal', the urine of others perhaps lacking certain desirable properties.

go over the heap to urinate of Br. colliery workers.

go places is to urinate or defecate, from leaving company to do so: 'What am I to do? I can't follow them when they go places' (Manning, 1977).

go round a corner to urinate, of a man, in the open air, may owe nothing to 'corner' (2) (q.v.), a urinal.

go to Cannes puns on 'can', a lavatory, but I imagine you have to write it before anyone sees the attempt at humour.

go to ground to defecate in the open is an ob. Br. use: '"Going to ground" is a phrase well known to the surgeons in the Birmingham hospitals' (EDD c. 1900).

go to the bathroom and other phrases using common euphemisms for lavatory are found under those respective headings.

go upstairs is to urinate or defecate, from the location of the lavatory where there is only one in the house, and for the lavatory reserved for female guests where there is more than one: '"Do you want to go upstairs, Emma?" she asked . . . . "I'll come too," said Louis . . . . "You can't come where she's going"' (Bradbury, 1959).

etc., etc.

go (4) (the) dismissal from employment
From finally leaving the place of work. Not common.

go all the way to copulate after a series of sexual familiarities
Teenage use. Other phrases relating to copulation and starting with 'go' are listed below:

go into to copulate of a male leaves little to the imagination. When Baroness Burdett-Coutts, a friend of Queen Victoria, married a man forty years her junior, the *Pink 'Un* published the following announcement: 'AN ARITHMETICAL PROBLEM: How many times does twenty-seven go into sixty-eight and what is there over?' (quoted by Harris, 1925).

go on to copulate, of the male, from a normal posture

go the length to copulate of a female extra-maritally, not from lying down but indicating the extent of her ardour: 'I had satisfied myself that his enthusiasm for Elspeth wasn't likely to go the length' (Fraser, 1977, writing in 19c. style).

go the whole way to copulate after pre-liminary fondling: 'If it had gone the whole way and the man had aroused her senses, the poor child was in a fix' (McCarthy, 1963).

go through to copulate by a male is rare and may be an abbr. of 'go through with it' or some such phrase.

go to bed with to copulate extra-maritally, of either sex, with the activity fig. taking place anywhere: 'Years ago she had gone to bed with him for a few weeks' (Amis, 1978 – you might suppose they were a pair of invalids). It is also used of homosexual activity: '"The idea of going to bed with Donald" he spluttered' (Boyle, 1979 – the splutterer was Burgess).

go to it to copulate of either sex was suf-ficiently ob. in 1940 for Herbert Morrison's wartime slogan in BI to be taken by most as an exhortation to work harder: 'The fitchew nor the soiled horse goes to't with a more riotous appetite' (Shakespeare, *King Lear*).

go with to copulate extra-maritally is more of women than of men: 'She hurt him terribly when she went with other men' (Green, 1979 – Keeler hurt Rachman).

go wrong to copulate with a man extra-maritally was doubly blameworthy if you were also impregnated: 'When I was six-teen," she said, "I went wrong"' (Mayhew, 1862).

etc., etc.

Many phrases starting with 'go' will be found under **go** (1) (2) and (3) (above). They are only cross-referred below when the phrase has another euphemistic use.

go case to work as a whore
Probably from **case** (1) rather than the client you take to yourself despite its prevalence among women working in night clubs etc.: 'I was green. It took me a week to realize that I was the only girl in the club not "going case"' (Irvine, 1986 – she was not sug-gesting that she and others were pregnant).

go down (1) *see* **go** (1)

go down (2) to be sent to prison
It probably refers to the descent from the dock to the cells but *see* too **down the line** (1): 'I often heard talk about criminals . . . . If they got you, then you went down' (Simon, 1979). 'Go up the river', to be sentenced to jail, come from the location of Am. penal institutions in New Orleans and elsewhere: 'The long-term prisoners waiting to go up the river' (L. Armstrong, 1955, of New Orleans).

go down on orally to stimulate another's genitalia
Heterosexual and homosexual use, with the active partner 'down on' the other: '"When I'm up, Barbara's down," says Howard . . . . "When you're up who, Barbara's down on whom?" asks Flora' (Bradbury, 1975).

go Dutch *see* **Dutch treat**

go into the streets to become a whore
From the open soliciting: 'While my boy lived, I couldn't go into the streets to save my life or his own' (Mayhew, 1862, of a whore).

go native as a politician to accept bureau-cratic attitudes and aspirations.
Whitehall jargon of Br. politicians, from the behaviour of a White person who when abroad adopts the indigenous Black life-style: 'When a Minister is so house-trained that he automatically sees everything from the Civil Service point-of-view, this is known in Westminster as the Minister having "gone native"' (Lynn and Jay, 1981).

go off (1) to die of pulmonary tuberculosis
From the gradual consuming nature of the disease: 'But he went off and was laid by soon after' (EDD c. 1900). ob. since WW II.

go off (2) to achieve a sexual orgasm
Of both sexes: 'There was an old whore in Montrose Who'd go off any time that she chose' (*Playboy's Book of Limericks*).

go on the box to be ill
Long before television, the 'box' was a sick club, from the weekly collection of sub-

scriptions in a place of work. If you were ill a long time and ran out of benefit, or if you recovered and went back to work, you went 'off the box'. To 'go on the club' in the same sense was specific, being an abbr. of 'sick club.'

go over (1) *see* **go** (1)

go over (2) to defect
Abbr. of 'go over to the other side' and today usu. to or from Communist allegiance. For the devout Anglican, to 'go over' was to join the Roman Catholic church, a fearsome treachery in the days when people worried about these things: 'Evangelical of course. No, I was glad that Wilfred didn't go over' (James, 1975, of an Anglican clergyman). 'Go over the wall' is used in the same sense, punning on the meaning, to escape from prison and the infamous 'wall' imprisoning the Germans under Russian domination: 'He didn't go over the wall until he had to' (Allbeury, 1981, of Philby). To 'go over the hill' is to escape from prison or to desert from the army: 'I guess he figured you'd gone over the hill' (Deighton, 1982, of an army absentee – it also means to have passed your peak). Sailors 'go over the side' if they desert their ship, or go ashore without a pass.

go over the top (1) *see* **over the top**

go over the top (2) to foul deliberately in soccer
The players are meant to kick the ball, and not each other. In a tackle, with the ball between the opponents, he who 'goes over the top' of it seeks to hurt or disable his adversary.

go short to copulate less often than you might wish
Properly, to lack a quantity of anything. This is a male usage though they may use it of a female if her denial might be construed as a defect in themselves: 'When I say she sometimes bored, don't think I mean she's goin' short . . . . I'm 'bout wore out pilin' inter that li'l darlin' (Fraser, 1971 – a man was speaking of his wife).

go slow deliberately to fail to do all the work for which you are being paid
A bargaining tactic which may in the short term cause an employer loss without corresponding hardship to his employees.

go to Denmark to have a sex-change operation
The pioneer work on this advance in surgery and the human condition was carried out in Denmark, a country long in the forefront of sexual licence and experimentation. This Am. phrase is also used of such surgery wherever undertaken.

go to Paul's for a wife to seek a whore for copulation
Prostitutes used to frequent the fashionable walks around London's St Paul's cathedral, whence Falstaff's allusion: 'I bought him in Paul's . . . . an I could get me a wife in the stews' (Shakespeare, 2 *Henry IV*). ob.

go up to be under illegal narcotic influence
From the feeling of levitation. Other phrases relating to illegal narcotics and starting with 'go' are dealt with, if at all, under the following word.

goat a male who habitually copulates extra-maritally
From the Grecian Pan and the general reputation of billy-goats. 'Play the goat' is so to act, although 'play the giddy goat' is merely to act stupidly. In ob. Br. use a 'goat-house' was a brothel and a 'goat-milker', a whore.

gobble pork etc. to practise fellatio
From eating meat: 'If he pays some chippie fifty to gobble his pork' (Diehl, 1978). 'Gobble your pecker' is more direct: 'I had her gobbling my pecker behind the lifeboats' (M. Thomas, 1980). In an Am. prison, a 'gobbler' is a male homosexual.

God's child an idiot
Another ob. Br. dialect phrase where the results of interbreeding were attributed to divine rather than parental agency: 'Such as him were called "God's Children"' (O'Reilly, 1880, of an idiot).

God's (own) medicine a narcotic
Of opium in the 19c., when it was freely available in nostrums for infant and adult use. Now of morphine, mainly used illegally and abbr. to 'gom'.

God's waiting room a resident institution for geriatrics
Making a charitable assumption about posthumous selection: 'In a private nursing home – one of those places they call God's waiting room' (B. Forbes, 1986).

gold *see* **silver**

gold-digger a woman who consorts with a man because he is rich.
Not necessarily confining her attentions to a single 'dig'. In ob. Eng. use a 'gold-digger' or 'gold-finder' emptied primitive lavatories of 'gold-dust', excrement, and an Am. 'gold-

brick' is still a turd, actually or fig.: 'Tarrant was the biggest goldbrick on the base' (Deighton, 1982).

golden bowler *see* **bowler hat**

golden handshake etc. the payment of lavish compensation for premature loss of employment
A 'handshake' is a token of depature: 'They have something called a "Golden Hand-shake". If they want to get rid of a foreigner they offer him a chunk of money as compensation for the loss of career' (Theroux, 1977). In commercial and industrial use, you pay the money to secure silence, preserve secrets and avoid litigation. The Am. 'golden parachute' is a beneficial service contract which a senior employee contrives to obtain to ease his fall if later dismissed from that job.

golden triangle the Siamese opium poppy district
From the geographical shape and the rewards of those who engage in the business: 'I was up in the north, where they grow poppies for opium and heroin. So-called "golden triangle"' (Theroux, 1975). Other dictionaries tell me that 'gold dust' is cocaine from any source, reflecting what it costs to buy illegally.

golden years (the) old age
Referring perhaps to ripened corn or your 'golden wedding' rather than the incipient setting of the sun – and certainly not to the prosperity of living on a pension: 'They are addressed as "senior citizens" and congratulated on their attainment of the "golden years"' (Jennings, 1965, of old people).

golly a mild oath
Perhaps the commonest corruption of 'God'. This 19c. use antedates by some forty years Florence Upton's Golliwogg books (of which I still have six of my father's). Other corruptions include goles, golles, gollin, golls, gull, goom, gomz, gom, goms, gommy and gum, as in 'by gum', etc.

gone (1) *see* **go** (1)

gone (2) pregnant
Usu. indicating the period since conception: 'What's he going to do about our Doreen who is six months gone?' (Tidy, *Private Eye*, March 1981). The rare and perhaps ob. Br. 'gone after the girls' meant infected with a venereal disease, the 'girls' being whores.

gone (3) drunk or under narcotic influence
You lose your faculties in either case, to a

greater or lesser extent: 'She was so "gone" by the time I finished clearing up . . .' (Bogarde, 1981 – she had ingested a narcotic). But to be 'gone on' anyone or anything is merely to be infatuated or obsessed.

goner a recently dead person
Pronounced, and sometimes spelt, 'gonner': 'Better say your prayers. If we crash, you're a gonner' (Manning, 1962).

good unwilling to copulate extra-maritally
Usu. of a female: 'If you can't be good, be careful' (Old saw). But a 19c. 'good-natured' Somerset woman was anything but 'good', her promiscuity coming from her willingness to please men in that regard.

good folk etc. the fairies
Another example of the fear and consequent evasiveness which these malevolent creatures inspired. In places as far apart as the Shetland Isles and Cornwall, they were the 'good folk': 'The guidfolk are not the best of archers, since the triangular flints with which the shafts of their arrows are barbed do not always take effect' (Hibbert, 1822). In Sc. they were the 'good neighbours': 'If ye ca's guid neighbours, guid neighbours we will be; But if ye ca's fairies, we'll fare you o'er the sea' (Ayrshire ballad, 1847 – note the derivative from the German 'fahren', which today persists only in 'farewell'). In Ire. they were the 'good people'.

good friends *see* **friend**

good man the devil
As with the **good folk** (above), you dare not suggest otherwise: 'The Guidman will catch you in his net' (Henderson, 1856). Farmers placated him by allocating to him an uncultivated piece of land which was known as the 'goodman's' craft, field, rig or taft: 'Bonny's the sod o' the Goodman's taft' (ibid.).

good time a single act of extra-marital copulation
A fairly conventional introduction by a whore: 'I'll try to give you a good time' (Harris, 1925) and a 'good time girl' is a whore. Men rarely offer women a 'good time', meaning copulation: 'The man was offering her a drink and a good time in Spanish' (Theroux, 1979).

goods (the) an illicit or damaging possession
Used of stolen property or illegal narcotics; and fig. of any information of a damaging or shameful nature, which can be used in extortion or as evidence of guilt: 'But what if

a twist exactly like her was a suspect, and you had to get the goods on her?' (Sanders, 1980).

goof a habitual user of illegal narcotics
Properly, stupid or eccentric, whence many meanings to do with unsophistication and incompetence. A 'goofball' may either be an addict: 'Clearest of all was that solitary *hoo* of the goofball in the crowd' (Theroux, 1978) or it may be an illicit narcotic: 'Goofballs are one of the barbiturates laced with benzadrine' (Chandler, 1953). 'Goofed' is under the influence of illegal narcotics.

goof up to kill
In Am. sl. use by any method. For a while 'gool' became something of an omnibus word, but this use is now probably ob.

goolies the testicles
We can, I think, reject derivation from 'gool', an outlet for water and Partridge's suggestion that it comes from 'gully', a game of marbles. The Hindi 'goli' meant a ball and this is another word brought into the language by Br. Indian troops: 'Then when he's off guard you give it to him in the goolies' (Sharpe, 1974).

goose (1) a whore
The common avian imagery and if she were a 'Winchester goose', she had syphilis, from the unsalubrious church-owned property in S. London where the poorer whores lived: 'But that my fear is this – some galled goose of Winchester would hiss' (Shakespeare, *Troilus and Cressida*). Compton Mackenzie reported that a 'goose girl' was a female homosexual, but nothing seems more innocuous than that Danish porcelain figure.

goose (2) to pinch a woman's buttocks
A male sexual approach as delicate as a nip from the bird's beak, or as indelicate: 'Leroy goosed the girl from behind, causing an alarmed but happy squeak to emerge from her lips' (Collins, 1981). Women rarely 'goose' men: 'They chivvied each other and laughed a lot. Once she goosed him' (Sanders, 1982). DAS says that a finger has to be poked into another's anus which, even with the intervention of clothing, brutalizes a fairly innocent activity.

goose (3) an act of copulation
Rare use from rh. sl. 'goose and duck', a fuck. Not used fig.

gooseberry (1) the devil
Usu. as 'old gooseberry': 'Th' match ther wur betwixt a tailior and owd gooseberry'

(Axon, 1870). The use survives in 'play gooseberry', to play the devil with a courting couple by keeping them company when they would far rather be left alone.

gooseberry (2) to steal clothes from a washing line
From the Am. meaning, a line with clothes on it, from which stealing is as easy as taking berries off a bush. Thus a 'gooseberry lay' is any crime easily carried out.

(goosberry bush *see* **parsley bed)**

Gordon Bennet(t) (1) a mild oath
You can use it for 'God'. From the Am. press proprietor who sponsored Stanley in his African travels and balloon races rather than the London stipendiary magistrate who came into prominence some decades later: '"Gordon Bennett!" Jack said, and in spite of myself I laughed out loud at the exclamation' (Theroux, 1982).

government inspected meat a soldier or sailor viewed homosexually
The 'inspection' meant they would be free from venereal disease and *see* **meat**. An Am. use of a known homosexual, or someone deemed worthy of an approach by another homosexual.

gow an erotic or salacious magazine cover
Properly, a narcotic, from the Cantonese word meaning sap, and now used in that sense mainly of illegal marijuana. I suppose the cover is intended to stupefy a browser into buying, especially as that kind of Am. publication is packaged in such a way as to prevent a prospective purchaser discovering the repetitious banality of the inside pages.

grab to steal
The common link between seizing and stealing: '"How are you going to get the money?" I asked. "Grab it. Steal it," he said' (L. Thomas, 1977). Aggressors also 'grab' territory from their victims.

gracious old and expensive
Of dwellings, in the language of estate agents. Other advertisers use 'gracious' when they tell us that if we buy their product, we can lead a life free of menial labour, giving sumptuous dinner parties to exciting people without having to shell the peas.

(graduate a medical practitioner is an ob. Sc. use which differs little today from our calling them all 'doctor', even those who qualified in the Apothecary's Hall: 'It's a' vera fine for you, Doctor Duguid of Kilwinning, a Gradawa o' Glesco' (Service, 1890).

'Graduate' was also once used in the same way in East Anglia.)

graft bribery
Properly, hard work, from the effort of digging, especially grave-digging. The euphemism may have come from the meaning, to insert a bud into other living stock to induce more profitable growth. The ob. Eng. 'graft', to cuckold, came from the fig. 'grafting', or implanting, the symbolic horns on the victim's head.

grand bounce *see* bounce (3)

grande horizontale *see* horizontal (1)

grandmother to stay menstruation
Another of the 'visitor' images, referring to an inconvenient but limited disruption of the normal tenor of your ways.

grandstand play accentuation of difficulty to win praise
From the location of the spectators, but not only of athletes, etc.: '. . . kept details to yourself. A real grandstand play' (Diehl, 1978, of a policeman who tried to solve a case on his own). In Am. pejorative use, to 'grandstand' is so to act: 'I relied on you to grandstand enough to let her get wise to you' (Chandler, 1958).

grape (the) wine
SE since 17c. The punning but perhaps ob. 'grape-shot' means drunk but a 'whiff of grapeshot' is not the bouquet – *see* whiff.

grass (1) to inform against
Probably rh. sl. from 'grass in the park', copper's nark: '"Favours. Grassing." Blamires said, "I've nobody to grass on"' (Kyle, 1975 – the police were trying to get information from a suspect about a third party). A 'grass' is an informer: 'There's a copper in that boy, you mark my words. He's a natural grass' (le Carré, 1986). In ob. Eng. use to 'grass' was also to kill, from the felling or the burying.

grass (2) marijuana
Abbr. of 'grass-weed' and perhaps the commonest addict use: 'Frank was restive about the marijuana. "You surely wouldn't make trouble about a scrap of grass"' (Davidson, 1978). Rarely as 'green grass': 'We are smoking too, man, you know? Grass. Green grass. You know what I mean?' (Simon, 1979).

grass (3) the female pubic hair
Am. use by both males and females.

grass bibi / bidi *see* bibi

grass-widow a woman of marriageable age divorced or separated from her husband
Properly, in modern use, a woman whose husband is absent for a long time because of his job. 'Grass' ought to be a corruption of grace but comparison with other Germanic sources would show that this 'grass' grows in the ground and the origin is to be found in the flora of the Indian hill-station to which a wife resorted while her husband sweated it out on the plains. In ob. Br. use there were three specific meanings; a woman who copulated extra-maritally (and many acquired that reputation, whether deservedly or not); a discarded sexual mistress; or a woman who became pregnant before marriage: 'Grass widows with their fatlings put to lie in and nurse here' (Hunt, 1896).

grasshopper a park policeman
Am. CB use, perhaps from his tendency to appear unexpectedly.

gratify *see* gratitude

gratify your passion etc. to copulate with a woman
A mainly 19c. usage in the days when such passions were officially confined to males: 'He cannot afford to employ professional women to gratify his passions' (Mayhew, 1862). Women may still 'gratify your desires', if so inclined, but 'gratify your amorous works' is ob.: 'She did gratify his amorous works' (Shakespeare, *Othello*). 'Gratification' was extra-marital copulation by a male: '. . . since the Roman Church regarded such errors as venal . . . . I had much gratification at little expense' (Graves, 1940, of a soldier's service in Ire.).

gratitude a bribe or payment for illicit services
To express thanks is not enough: 'Gratitude was a pay-off. Gratitude was drink and diamonds' (Keneally, 1982). In ob. Sc. use to 'gratify' meant to tip or to bribe: 'People were still obliged to gratify the keepers for any access they had to visit or minister to their friends' (Wodrow, 1721, of prisoners) and 'gratification' was a tip or a bribe.

grave (the) death
SE fig. use: 'There will be sleeping enough in the grave' (Franklin, 1758). In ob. Sc. use, the 'gravestone gentry' were the dead: 'My bed is owre amang yon gravestane gentry' (A. Murdoch, 1873).

gravy (1) an intoxicant
A variant of the Am. 'sauce', which is now much more common.

gravy (2) anything undeservedly awarded
The pleasant but unnecessary complement to the meat. To 'ride the gravy train' is to receive such benefits on a regular basis: 'The gravy train has not stopped entirely for Grub Street hacks' (*Private Eye*, July 1981).

graze to steal and eat food in a supermarket
Like cattle in a pasture, you eat what you take between the rows and pass the check-out desk with empty hands and a full stomach. The ob. Br. 'graze' on the plain or the common was to be dismissed from employment, presumably as a house servant, or merely to be evicted from your house: 'He turnde hir out at durs, to grase on the playne' (Heywood, 1546).

grease (1) to bribe
The usage predates **oil** (q.v.) but the concept of making something run easily is the same: 'With gold and grotes they grease my hands, In stede of ryght that wrong may stand' (Skelton, 1529) and today: 'He lacked the financial resources with which Oskar greased the system' (Keneally, 1982). As well as 'greasing' hands, we 'grease' palms, paws, etc. 'Grease' is bribery, a 'grease', a bribe but beware of ob. Br. 'grease the wheel', which was to copulate, of a male and punning on the lubricity.

grease (2) to kill
Perhaps from converting the body into a fatty substance, or merely a corruption of **crease** (q.v.): 'If .... he makes any threatening motion – anything at all – grease him' (Sanders, 1973). Am.

greased drunk
The common Am. culinary imagery and things may indeed seem to run more smoothly for a time: 'You come over early and we can get greased before the mob arrives' (Sanders, 1982 – the speaker was hosting a party).

(greasy spoon a cheap and inelegant Am. restaurant is descriptive but not euphemistic. They tend to use a lot of cooking fat but the washing of the cutlery is adequate, in my experience: '... he had wandered into a Forsythe Street greasy spoon and casually asked the Puerto Rican waitress ...' (Sanders, 1977).)

great pregnant
Abbr. of 'great with child': 'O silly lassie, what wilt thou do, if thou grow great they'll heez thee high' (Herd, 1771 – society would reward her not with weekly stipend and visits from sympathetic officials but with death by hanging).

great and the good (the) those comprising or approved by the Br. political establishment
An often derogatory description of the rich or powerful clique who seek to parcel out awards, rewards and places: 'Maynard, astute businessman ... Maynard, supporter of charity ... Maynard, the great and good' (Francis, 1985, of a rogue conspiring to be knighted).

great certainty etc. death
'Certain' that you will die in due course although uncertain for most of us as to what happens next: '"The Great Certainty looms," said Mr Flawse' (Sharpe, 1978). 'Now for the great secret', remarked the dying King Charles II, shortly before or after expressing concern about 'poor Nellie's' future. For others it is the 'great out' or the 'great leveller'.

great leap forward the reckless industrialization of a peasant country
The Chinese Communist government in 1958 so titled their plan to increase the productivity of agriculture and industry by a compound annual rate of 25%. By 1961 the vast country faced starvation and economic ruin.

great majority the dead
An abbr. of the 'great majority of souls' who are supposed to be in heaven or limbo: 'Life is the desert, life the solitude; Death joins us to the great majority' (Young, 1721).

Greater East-Asia Co-Prosperity Sphere the WW II Japanese empire
Founded on the divinity of the emperor, the extermination of Whites and the economic dominance of Japan, the 'sphere' included much of China, and all of Korea, the Philippines, Malaya, Indo-China, Burma and Indonesia. The subject peoples enjoyed less prosperity than their masters but, to be fair, the ratios haven't changed much today. This is an example of the many political euphemisms coined by the Japanese in WW II concerning their empire, much of which they had to rule in the English language.

Greek Calends (the) never
The Romans were meant to settle their taxes and other accounts on the calends of each month, but the Greek calendar had no

calends: 'The emergence of chaos in Germany .... would put off the pacification of Europe to the Greek Kalends' (Goebbels, 1945, in tr.).

Greek way (the) buggery
From the supposed practice of the Ancients, whence too the ob. 'Greek', to bugger. If you think our language is not even-handed between antagonists *see* **Turk**.

green goods counterfeit banknotes
'Goods' (q.v.) for the stolen element and 'green' for the colour of U.S. currency. A 'green goods' man is either an Am. forger or someone who passes forged banknotes: 'He was just in here looking for a green-goods man' (Weverka, 1973, of a passer of bills).

green gown an indication of female copulation
They are stained by being pressed on the grass: 'Then some greene gownes are by the lassies worne In chastest plaies' (Sidney, 1586). Much clothing was soiled on the eve of May Day, when convention allowed the lads and lasses to spend all night in the woods, ostensibly gathering flowers. A woman 'with a green gown' has copulated before marriage: '... she had had the salutation "with a greene gowne" ... as if the priest had been at our backs, to have married us' (G. A. Greene, 1599, quoted in ODEP). The 'green sickness' was 'The disease of maids occasioned by celibacy' (Grose) and to 'give green stockings' was to commit the solecism of getting married before your unmarried elder sister. All these useful phrases are ob.

green grass *see* **grass** (2)

green stamp collector a policeman with radar
'Green' from the colour of bills, 'collector' for the keenness of some Am. police in levying fines and the 'stamp' from the tokens given to shoppers which they may later exchange for goods.

greenmailer a corporate raider who seeks to get paid to go away
The green of the US dollar replaces the black of the **blackmail** (q.v.): '... the first place to which takeover artists and greenmailers and LBO peddlars came for cash and complicity' (M. Thomas, 1987 of a bank).

grief therapy spending money to alleviate bereavement
Am. funeral jargon for persuading the sur-

vivors to spend a lot making the corpse look like a healthy person and otherwise seeing it off in style: '"Grief therapy", the official name bestowed by the undertakers on this new aspect of their work' (J. Mitford, 1963). 'Grief therapist' thus becomes a new name for an arranger of funerals.

grim reaper *see* **reaper**

grind to copulate
Probably from the rotary pelvic pressing motion: '... a young person of Harwich, Tried to grind his betrothed in a carriage' (*Playboy's Book of Limericks*). A 'grind' is either an act of copulation, or a woman participant, and then always referred to in flattering terms – where do all the 'bad grinds' go? 'Grind' is also used less often of masturbation and a 'grinding-house' or 'grind-mill' is a brothel: 'It was a business in the grind-mills' (Longstreet, 1956, of New Orleans brothels). A 'grinding employer' was neither a miller nor one who copulated with his female staff, but a man who expected a lot of work for a little pay: '... grinding, or being compelled to do the same or a greater amount of work for less pay' (Mayhew, 1851). The ob. Br. 'grind the wind' was to be punished on a treadmill: 'The prisoners style the occupation "grinding the wind"' (Mayhew, 1862).

groceries bombs
WW II Air Force jargon for unordered deliveries on witless recipients.

groceries sundries intoxicants
Bought from the grocer and thus described on the delivery note so that the nature and extent of the purchases could be hidden from the servants and, very often, from the unknowing husband. ob. since WW II.

grog on board drunkenness
'Grog' was originally rum, from the nickname of the Br. Admiral Vernon (1684–1769) who instituted a ration for sailors and wore a grogram coat. It may now mean any spirituous intoxicant. 'Grogged' means drunk and a 'grog-hound' is a drunkard.

groin the genitalia
Properly, the place where the abdomen meets the thigh. In sporting jargon, he who is said to have received a nasty knock in the 'groin' has suffered a more telling and painful blow. Non-sporting use is uncommon: 'He was grabbed by a sensitive portion of his lower groin' (Lavine, 1930). To 'rub groins together' is to copulate: '... they should get

to know one another better . . . . by rubbing their groins together' (*Sun*, March 1981).

grope to fondle another person sexually
Properly, to use the hands for feeling anything. Usu. of a male whose activity may be inexpert and unwanted: 'You mean fornicating in the sauna or in a mop closet or underwater groping is okay?' (Sanders, 1973). Thus a 'groper' is an unattractive male suitor, replacing the two more realistic ob. meanings, a blind person, or a midwife.

gross height excursion a dangerous and unplanned loss of aircraft height
Civil aviation jargon in an environment where nothing must be acknowledged as dangerous or unplanned: '. . . a nose dive is never called a nose dive. It is a "gross height excursion"' (Moynahan, 1983).

gross indecency *see* **indecency**

ground rations copulation
Am. Black usage, from the place where the action may take place.

ground-sweat death
Properly in ob. use, the grave, whence the old proverb: 'A ground-sweat cures all disorders'. A 'ground lair' was a family burial place and 'ground-mail', a burial fee: '"Reasonable charges?" said the sexton; "ou, there's ground-mail – and bell-siller – and the kist – and my day's work"' (W. Scott, 1819 – a 'kist' is a coffin). I include these old Br. phrases because they represent a line of euphemism which has lapsed and because, as the quotation shows, nothing changes over the years when it comes to fixing charges in the funeral business.

grounded forbidden to fly an aircraft
Of a pilot who is unwell or subject to disciplinary action. Those of us who are not pilots are in this sense permanently grounded. A pilot who is 'grounded for good' is dead.

group sex a sexual orgy
It could mean no more than an outing to the Mothers Union, if the parson stays away, they being all females. It indicates a disregard for pair bonds and normal sexual practices: 'If God had meant us to have group sex, I guess he'd have given us all more organs' (Bradbury, 1976).

grow your greens to urinate outdoors
Br. male usage, combining the ridiculous with the notion of urine as a fertilizer.

growler-rushing drinking intoxicants at home

A 'growler' is a large pitcher which was taken to an Am. bar to be filled with cool beer which you took away, in the days before general domestic refrigeration. You had to rush to stop it warming up on the way. Still usu. of beer but occasionally of other intoxicants: 'Meanwhile my jug is getting low. How about rushing the growler for me?' (Sanders, 1980).

growth a carcinoma
Properly, something which has grown and, even of human tissue, not necessarily malignant. A common usage to avoid direct reference to the dread cancer.

grumble an act of copulation
From rh. sl. 'grumble and grunt', a cunt. Less often as 'gasp and grunt' despite the imagery that suggests.

grummet a vagina viewed sexually
Properly, a metal eyelet. Some Am. use and also of a single act of extra-marital copulation.

grunt to defecate
Am. nursery use, perhaps from the initial training in controlled defecation, where a grunt may accompany the muscular effort.

grunter a pig
Used to avoid speaking of something taboo among fishermen, the word 'pig' being sure to lead to a bad trip: 'When Kate referred to a pig she said grunter' (Cookson, 1969 – Kate was married to a mariner). Probably from the infections caused by rotten salted pork. *See*, too, **furry thing**.

guardhouse lawyer an opinionated know-all and trouble-maker
An Am. variant of **barrack-room lawyer** (q.v.). Guard duty involves long periods of boredom, providing the right environment for bores and agitators, as in other activities where people are paid to sit around waiting for something to do. Originally an army use but now general.

Guatemala the taking of illegal narcotics
The country is a favoured source of marijuana: '"Hey, where are we going?" Hood said, "Guatemala." Murf smiled. He understood the euphemism' (Theroux, 1976, – although written of London, Hood was an Am.). Br. allusion to Morocco might also be so understood: 'In all the smugglers landed a total of 30 tons of Moroccan Gold cannabis' (*Daily Telegraph*, November 1981).

guerillas terrorists
I give the normal spelling. In the Peninsular

War, they really did fight little wars – 'guerrillas' with two r's. Of Marxist guerillas there are three main types: Mao's operating in favourable conditions 'like fish in water'; Giap's using psychological and political weapons to destroy the resolution of a superior enemy; and Debray's, the commonest, using terror and intimidation in an unsympathetic or apathetic population, supported from abroad by mischievous or deluded foreign sympathizers, as with the IRA in Ire.

guest a prisoner
Usu. the jocular 'guest' of Uncle Sam, Her Majesty, etc.: 'To book a prisoner – I beg your pardon, "guest"' (Lavine, 1930). The ob. Sc. 'guest' was only a ghost, an unwelcome visitor or a linguistic corruption: 'Brownies, fays and fairies, And witches, guests' (Liddle, 1821).

guest-artist a paid performer making a single appearance
Entertainment jargon. Such a performer fills in the time allotted and helps to break the tedium.

guidance towards change a compromise under pressure
Under such compulsion a priest can afford to abandon principle: 'The Holy Spirit could guide the church towards that change' (BBC 2 September 1986 – a Cardinal was conceding that the shortage of bachelors in Latin America might lead to the waiving of the requirement that the clergy be celibate).

guide a propagandist and spy
Vistors to certain Communist countries are obliged to retain the service of a 'guide' who will prevent them seeing what the host nation wishes to hide or speaking to persons selected at random. The 'guide' will also try to indoctrinate the visitors and report on anything suspicious to the authorities.

guidelines an unenforceable government policy on pay
The word has the merit of being more tentative and less pretentious than the series of equally ineffective euphemisms introduced by government in a market economy which describes successive attempts to limit wage levels by decree – *see* **freeze, pause** (1), **restraint**, etc.

guinea-hen a whore
A pun on her fee and the common avian imagery: 'Ere I would say, I would drown myself for the love of a guinea-hen, I would

change my humanity for a baboon' (Shakespeare, *Othello*). ob.

gulag *see* **corrective training**

gull a whore who frequents naval bases
The common avian imagery, with a suitable choice of bird. Am.

gulls *see* **buoys**

gum-shoe a policeman in plain clothes
He walks quietly on rubber soles: 'Don't you call me "sister" you cheap gumshoe' (Chandler, 1958). Am.

gun (1) a criminal who carries a hand gun
Criminal jargon for someone who is also ready to use it: 'Especially if they're killers – guns for hire' (Bagley, 1978). But an Am. 'gun' can also be an unarmed professional thief, from the Yiddish 'gonif'. To 'gun down' is to kill or wound humans, singly or collectively. Animals are always 'shot'.

gun (2) a hypodermic syringe
Used illegally for a 'shot' of narcotics.

gun (3) a penis
Heard in Am. but ob. in Bl and the association of ideas is not new – *see* **pistol**.

gun down, *see* **gun** (1)

gunner's daughter a flogging
Properly, the barrel of a gun over which the victim was strapped, thus 'kissing' or 'marrying' her: 'I was made to kiss the wench that never speaks but when she scolds, and that's the gunner's daughter' (W. Scott, 1824). This is a sample entry from the days when both civil and military order were preserved by hanging, flogging and exile, the barbarities giving rise to numerous euphemisms.

guys a public lavatory for exclusive male use
With its counterpart 'dolls', perhaps from the musical play. Not common and relatively inoffensive, as these things go.

gyppy tummy *see* **gippy tummy**

gypsy's warning no warning at all
Only an Am. use in this sense. In ob. Irish use, a 'gypsy's warning' meant gin. The common meaning, the foretelling of a misfortune, stems from the predilection of gypsy ladies towards the telling of fortunes, after the precaution of crossing their palms with silver, not primarily as a payment but because it negates the power of the devil to interfere in something which usu. falls within his sphere of influence. Nonetheless, the ladies keep the money.

H

H anything taboo beginning with the letter H
Usu. 'hell' in the expression 'What the H?'.
In addict use, heroin: 'Daddy is fillin' the
gun full of beauteeeful H. Soon you will be
ridin' a wave' (Collins, 1981). 'H & C' is a
mixture of heroin and cocaine, punning on
the plumbing abbr. for 'hot & cold'.

habit an addiction to narcotics
Not used of the equally addictive alcohol or
tobacco, or of power. Your preference may
be indicated in a compound, like 'nose
habit', and the degree of addiction in a
phrase assessing the cost: '. . . $50-a-day
habit' (Lingeman, 1969). To 'kick the habit'
is to stop taking illegal narcotics.

had it dead
Of man, beast or worn out machinery:
'You've had it. You're snuffed. You're wiped
out' (Theroux, 1976).

hail Columbia an expression of
annoyance
Perhaps 'hail' is for hell and certainly 'Columbia' is the USA. To raise or get 'Columbia' is to express or to incur anger. Am.

hair of the dog a morning drink of an
intoxicant
Usu. after too many the previous evening.
Abbr. of the 'hair of the dog that bit you',
which is supposed to provide some protection against rabies: 'Do you feel like swilling
the hair of the dog with me?' (Francis, 1978).
In Am. use also as the 'horn of the ox':
'. . . three guys bellying up to the bar in an
adjoining room, starting their day with a
horn of the ox that gored them' (Sanders,
1979).

hair stylist a barber
To avoid anything so menial as washing,
cutting or dressing another's hair. You will
find 'hair sculpture' even more pretentious
and expensive.

haircut a financial collapse
All the locks are shorn: 'The total of the
Golden Grove haircut was less than $200
million in capital and reserves' (M. Thomas,
1982).

hairpiece a wig
It should be no more than a piece of hair, on
or off the scalp.

half a can a quantity of beer
The Am. volume is indicated by the container: '"Bring me half a can." A half-can
meant a nickel's worth of beer. A whole can
meant a dime's worth' (Longstreet, 1955).
The Br. 'half a pint' or 'pint' similarly
indicate quantities of beer: 'Pints were for
men and . . . . only boys drank halves'
(Sharpe, 1975 – today women seem to as
well). The ob. Br. 'half-pint' was to drink
beer to excess: 'Two miners "half-pinting"
in the public house' (Hunt, 1865).

half and half drunk
Usu. less than half sober: '"Were you drunk
at the time?" "Well, I'll tell you what it is,
gentlemen, I was half-an-half"' (Evesham
Journal, 1879, quoted in EDD). 'Half and
half' and 'top and bottom' also describe a
mixture of mild and bitter beers in the same
glass: 'He would not play except for a pint of
half-and-half' (Mayhew, 1862). In Am.
prostitutes' jargon 'half and half' is oral followed by vaginal sex (DAS).

half-baked bread a person of mixed
Indian and White ancestry
Br. Indian deprecatory use when there were
strong taboos among the Br. expatriates
about inter-breeding: 'They used to call us
Kutcha butcha, that is to say, half-baked
bread' (Allen, 1975, of such a person). ob.

half canned etc. drunk
As I note perhaps too frequently elsewhere,
in drunkenness the half is seldom less than
the whole and the attempt to minimize the
condition deceives nobody. Also as 'half'
cooked, corned, cut, foxed, gone, on,
screwed, shot, sprung, under, etc.

half deck a lunatic
From the partly open craft which is less
seaworthy than one fully decked: 'But all
those people on Doctor Diana's list sound
like half-decks' (Sanders, 1985, of a
psychiatrist's patients).

half inch to steal
Br. rh. sl. for 'pinch', mainly of pilfering:
'You used to 'arf inch suckers orf the barrers'
(Kersh, 1936, of stealing oranges from street
traders).

half-seas over drunk
Not the 'half' of 'seas-over' (see half-
canned etc.) nor even from a craft which is
awash, but from the Dutch 'op-zee zober',
or strong overseas beer. It is used either of
total drunkenness: 'I'm half-seas o'er to
death' (Dryden, 1692) or of a milder state:
'It was no longer the custom to get drunk,
but to get half-seas over was still fairly usual'
(Harris, 1925). And as 'half-sea': 'Hoarse

elder John sat at his knee, In proper trim –
more than half-sea' (Spence, 1898 – but we
must beware of forced rhymes).

(**hame** to copulate in Somerset dialect is not
euphemistic despite the attraction of
'hames', the curved twin pieces of wood
resting on the collar of a draughthorse and of
the female sexual shape. It is almost certainly
a survival of the Old Eng. 'haeman' (? have
man) to copulate.)

hammer to declare a defaulter
London stock exchange jargon, from the
hammering to obtain silence in which to
make the announcement amongst the hub-
bub on the crowded floor.

hammered drunk
Your head sometimes feels like it, especially
after poor red wine. Am.

hampton the penis
Only used literally, from rh. sl. 'Hampton
Wick', a district to the W. of London, and
prick: 'No worse off physically than for a
couple of smart tweaks of the hampton'
(Amis, 1978). Unusually, both words in the
phrase are used commonly for the rh. sl.
meaning, and 'wick' is met both literally and
fig.

hand-fast to cohabit and copulate extra-
maritally
I include this ob. Sc. entry to show that what
seems new in social behaviour may not be so:
'It was not until more than twenty years after
the Reformation that the custom of "hand-
fasting", which had come down from old
Celtic times, fell into disrepute, and consequent disuse. By this term was understood
cohabitation for a year, the couple being
then free to separate, unless they agreed to
make the union permanent' (Andrews,
1899). The custom survived until the 19c. in
Selkirk and Dumfriesshire, and now seems
once again to enjoy universal approbation,
except among those of us for whom the
change in convention came too late.

hand in your dinner pail to die
From the common image of needing no
more food. The phrase has survived the
introduction of crockery.

hand job the masturbation of a male
By himself or another: 'He declined her
offer of a compensating handjob' (M.
Thomas, 1980).

hand out (1) a payment by the State to the
poor
Originally of food etc. but now of cash pay-

ments. Much pejorative use among those in
work, whether or not they pay taxes.

hand-out (2) a bribe
Am. police etc. jargon: 'Six weeks' suspension and six weeks at reduced pay for taking
a handout' (Diehl, 1978, of a policeman).

hand-out (3) a written statement to the
press etc. containing inaccurate, incomplete
or misleading information
Properly, a summary in written form
intended to record or amplify verbal information: 'The question which has not been
raised in the Press here, force-fed as it is on
NASA hand-outs' (*Private Eye*, July 1983).

hand-tooled manufactured
The seller tries to imply that each article is
the result of individual skill rather than of
mass production although, in normal
engineering practice, the higher the level of
tooling, the lower the operator's involvement
and the better the product. It matters little
however as most buyers don't know what it
means anyway.

hand trouble unwelcome male attempts to
fondle a woman sexually
She, not he, has trouble with his hands:
'Bonnie had encountered men with hand
trouble' (Hynd, 1949). Mainly Am.

handbook a place away from a racetrack
where bets are placed illegally
Am. horse racing usage, from the recording
of the wagers. Sometimes the person who
accepts the bets is also called a 'handbook'.

handful a five-year prison sentence
Properly, what you can hold in your hand.
'Fistful' means the same thing, as does the
more expressive 'five fingers'.

handicap a physical or mental defect
Properly a disadvantage imposed on a con-
testant to make an equal contest: 'We fight
shy of abbreviations and euphemisms. They
rejoice in them. The blind and maimed are
called "handicapped", the destitute,
"underprivileged"' (E. Waugh, 1956 – 'they'
were the Americans, 'we', the British. Whatever would he say today?). In October 1983,
on a BBC programme a nearly blind woman
referred to her 'visible handicap', which was
not the barrel she had to crawl through in an
obstacle race.

handle (1) to embrace a woman sexually
Properly, to touch or hold with the hands: 'A
did in some sort, indeed, handle women'
(Shakespeare, *Henry V*). The ob. S. Eng.
dialect use was not euphemistic: 'In love

making, where the swain may not have the flow of language, he may sometimes attempt to put his arm around the girl's waist; this is called "handlin' on her"' (EDD – as ever Dr Wright uses 'lovemaking' for courtship). If you were said to 'handle a woman' today, you would be a pimp.

handle (2) the power over another to coerce or extort
From the leverage: 'In this permissive age homosexuality isn't the handle it once was' (Bagley, 1982).

handle the truth roughly to lie
Political use where a direct accusation of lying contravenes convention.

hang to kill by breaking the neck through suspension
Now the SE meaning, but it formerly meant death by crucifixion: '"No, Grace, we don't hang them any more." "Not even murderers?" "Specially not them"' (N. Mitford, 1960). The past participle is 'hanged' – except in sloppy speech only painters are 'hung': '"You'll probably be hung." "Not now I won't, get ten years"' (Murdoch, 1977, deliberately reflecting vulgar speech). A 'hang-fair' was an execution by hanging in public: 'The innkeeper supposed her some harum-skarum young woman who had come to attend the "hang-fair" next day' (Hardy, 1888). A 'hanging judge' readily sentenced convicted people to death: 'He'd got one or two unlikely convictions out of them. A hanging judge, some people said' (Christie, 1939). However the ob. Eng. 'hang in the bellropes' was merely to be jilted or to delay a wedding after the calling of banns, from denying the campanologists their fun and reward: '. . . the "deserted one" is said to be hung in the bell-ropes' (N&Q, 1867, quoted in EDD).

hang a few on to drink intoxicants to excess
Of an Am. male alone, or in company with other males: 'He had only hung a few on and was, for him, slightly sober' (Longstreet, 1956). Less often as 'hang one on', which means many more drinks than one. The ob. Br. 'hang it on with' was to copulate regularly with an extra-marital mistress.

hang a red light on to drive out of business
The imagery is from a closed road – for once 'red light' does not signal a brothel: 'I have enough influence around this town to hang a red light on you' (Chandler, 1958). Am.

hang in the bellropes *see* **hang**

hang on the bough to remain unmarried
Of a woman and *see* **without a head** for a dissertation on the economic problems of 19c. unmarried females. This ob. Sc. use takes its imagery from unplucked and wasted fruit: 'Ye impident woman! It's easy seen why ye were left hangin' on the bough' (Keith, 1896).

hang out the besom *see* **besom**

hang up your hat (1) to marry a woman wealthier than yourself
She provides the hall into which he walks to deposit his headgear, or the kitchen in which he used to 'hang up his ladle': 'Snelling "hung his hat up" – that is the local phrase – at the abode of Ephraim Shorthouse, whose daughter Cecilia was grown to a marriageable age' (D. Murray, 1890). I recall a certain childish confusion when I heard my father use the phrase of another member of the family.

hang up your hat (2) to die
Everyone wore hats when this was common. Those who rode, as most did, might also 'hang up' their harness or tackle. Today if you 'hang up your boots', you retire from playing a team game, although the imagery can be used for other sports: 'I'd always thought of thirty-five as approximately hanging-up-the-boots time' (Francis, 1985, of steeplechasing).

hangover the symptoms of prior sub-acute alcoholic poisoning
From the 'hanging over' of the ill effects until the next day: '"How's the hangover?" From the sound of it, on the mend. The hair of the dog had bitten' (Francis, 1978). 'Hung over' is so afflicted: 'He put down the receiver with all the gentleness of the badly hungover' (ibid.). Rarely abbr. to 'hung': '"Sweating out sour booze?" "You look hung yourself"' (Mailer, 1965).

hanky panky extra-marital copulation
Properly, trickery. Much favoured by mothers when telling daughters what not to get up to if spending an unchaperoned evening with a male.

Hansen's disease leprosy
After a short time, it will be equally feared, whatever you call it: 'The widely feared affliction now known as Hansen's disease' (*National Geographic Magazine*, August 1979, of leprosy). In similar fashion we seek to

hide the stigma of mongolism in 'Down's syndrome'.

happenings illicit narcotics
From the effects of ingestion and perhaps too after Kaprow's 'Pop Art'. There is some use too of any illegal or questionable events: 'If you only have a list of *happenings* – is that the latest Whitehall word?' (Lyall, 1985). The narcotic use is Am.

happy slightly drunk
The symptoms are the same for some, at some stage of drunkenness. The Am. 'happy hour' is the period – usu. over sixty minutes – during which bars sell intoxicants at reduced prices and give away food to encourage people to drop in on their way home from work; in theory to relax and relieve the tensions of the day, but you run into worse trouble when you arrive home drunk, broke and late: 'I bought two more: it was, after all, Happy Hour' (Theroux, 1979, of beer).

happy dust cocaine
Am. addict use: '. . . that happy dust gonna take you a real great snow ride' (Collins, 1981).

happy event the birth of a child
Of planned and unplanned, wanted and unwanted pregnancies alike.

happy hour *see* **happy**

happy release the death of a terminally ill patient
We use the phrase of others, although they may feel otherwise. Rarely in the same sense you may hear 'happy despatch', a translation of the Japanese 'hara-kiri' but not importing suicide. The 'happy hunting grounds' are the post-mortem destination of Am. Indians, and perhaps too of the scriptwriters who churn out the Westerns.

hard an extreme version of anything taboo or shameful
Thus 'hard core' is specific pornography, as different from 'soft', suggestive only; 'hard' drink, liquor, stuff, etc. is a spirituous intoxicant as against 'soft', or non-alcoholic, drinks: 'If I don't soon have a drop of hard I'm for it' (Cookson, 1967, of a man wanting whisky); a 'hard drinker' habitually drinks alcohol to excess and to 'harden a drink' is to add spirits to it: 'I carried it to the kitchen and hardened it up from the bottle' (Chandler, 1943, of a drink); a 'hard drug' is a potentially killing narcotic like heroin, compared with the less immediately dangerous

though addictive 'soft' drugs, especially cannabis; etc.

hard of hearing deaf
Deafness, unlike blindness, when so described is not understood to be an absolute condition, the sense being only partially impaired except where otherwise stated, as 'stone deaf': '"I'm hard of hearing, you know," she said. "Practically deaf"' (Sanders, 1980). A similar euphemistic form in French and German.

hard-on an erection of the penis
Of obvious derivation: '. . . getting a hard-on listening to a beautiful woman screwing another guy' (Diehl, 1978). To 'have a hard-on for' is to lust after a woman: 'And this Piper guy had a hard-on for old women' (Sharpe, 1977). (Neaman and Silver give 'get a HARD ON (reach for a pistol)' under 'BLOW JOB, A, Cracking a safe by using explosives'. We clearly move in different circles.)

hard room a prison cell
As different from those with soft furnishings: '. . . defacing the walls of some of the subterranean "hard-rooms" – a polite departmental euphemism for prison cells' (Deighton, 1985).

hard up poor
Usu. of a temporary shortage of funds and perhaps an abbr. of 'hard up against it'.

hardware (1) whisky
A 19c. Am. use revived during the Prohibition years, perhaps punning on 'hard' liquor but also seeking to conceal the nature of the purchase as in **groceries sundries** (q.v.).

hardware (2) any modern armaments
Military jargon for things made of metal like tanks, bombs, planes, guns and missiles: '"You're talking about hardware." . . . . "We don't buy mchine guns at the local ironmongers"' (Theroux, 1976).

harlot a whore
The word was used of a disreputable person of either sex before 'varlets' became male and 'harlots' female. Shakespeare writes of 'the harlot king' (*Winter's Tale*) and 'Portia is Brutus' harlot, not his wife' (*Julius Caesar*). It is a corruption of 'harlet', a small hiring, although Harlotte, the mother of the bastard William of Normandy, has had her share of unfair attributions down the ages.

harmful elements individualists
Communist dysphemism for anyone who questions the ways of autocracy.

harness bull a uniformed policeman
The 'harness' is the uniform, and 'bull', an Am. policeman.

Harpic *see* **round the bend**

Harry the devil
Usu. as the 'old', the 'Lord' or the 'living': 'By the livin' hairey, if I could win ower tae them' (Wardrop, 1881). Still used in exclamation and when we 'play old Harry' about something which upsets us.

hash marijuana
A punning abbr. of 'hashish', and a 'hash-head' is an addict.

hat and cap gonorrhoea
Am. rh. sl. for 'clap'.

hatch the birth of a child
Emergence from an egg is clearly less taboo than the method of mammalian delivery: 'The female mind . . . . takes an interest in the "Hatch, Match and Despatch" of its fellow creatures' (Payn, 1878).

hatchet man someone entrusted with a job requiring ruthlessness
Not he who chops the kindling in the back yard. Of a professional killer: '. . . regular hatchetmen on their payrolls who were available to kill at a moment's notice' (Lavine, 1930); of an employee entrusted with a difficult or unethical transaction: '1981 is not exactly turning out to be a vintage year for Eric Levene, Sir James Goldsmith's hatchet man' (*Private Eye*, April 1981); of a writer who attacks unfairly: 'This series is going to be very sympathetic to the police . . . . I'm not out to do a hatchet job' (Sanders, 1973); of a manager entrusted with the peremptory dismissal of staff; etc.

haul a quantity of stolen property
Properly, the sum gained from any transaction in fig. use. For the police, to 'haul in' is to arrest. In ob. Br. use, to 'haul ashore' was to retire from employment, from the beaching of an old boat.

haul your ashes to copulate with a female
'Haul' has a meaning, to harm another physically, which is a common image where male copulation is concerned; and 'ashes' are 'hauled' or pulled out from the small door at the foot of the furnace, which is red and glowing within. But I don't find either of these clues to the etymology convincing. A male may 'get his ashes hauled': 'I pop in a red, get a little shot, you get your ashes hauled. Same dif' (Diehl, 1978, or in translation 'I like self-induced narcosis, you pre-fer promiscuous copulation'). Whence 'hauled', having copulated, usu. extra-maritally.

haute cuisine expensive food
Properly, high quality cooking: 'When I'm away I live in hotels, where I get junk tricked out as haute cousine' (Follett, 1979). Away from France, the 'high' thing is usu. the price.

Havana rider a passenger who seeks to take control of an airliner in flight
Am. airline use, from the preferred destination of many such pirates: 'Research in America has come up with a fair picture of the "Havana riders", as airline staff call them' (Moynahan, 1983).

have to copulate with
The word is used of either sex. Of an individual act: 'I was so impatient I had her without getting out of my chair' (Fraser, 1969) or of copulation generally: 'You must have had a lot of men? . . . . Have you enjoyed it?' (Amis, 1978). And in phrases as follow:

have a man/woman to copulate extra-maritally, with the action being more important than the choice of partner.

have at to copulate of a male, from the meaning to attack: 'I woke up and had at her again' (Fraser, 1970).

have it to copulate of either sex is often expanded to 'have it away' or 'have it off': 'The true test of love is when you can watch your wife having it off with someone else and still love her' (Sharpe, 1976). 'Have it off' is also used of homosexual activity: 'Khaliq will insist on having it off with the other ranks' (M. Thomas, 1980).

have relations to copulate is a genteel usage: 'You perhaps ought to have relations once to make sure of happy adjustment' (McCarthy, 1963) and to 'have sexual relations' is more explicit: 'I'm not "very highly sexed". I can live perfectly well without sexual relations' (Murdoch, 1978).

have sex to copulate, within or outside marriage. It is also used of homosexual activity.

have something to do with to copulate, usu. of a male: 'The euphemistic modern to have (something) to do with a woman' (Partridge, 1947).

have your end off to copulate, of a male, the 'end' being the penis: 'He has been having his end away' (P. Scott, 1977) is a variant.

have your way with to copulate, of a male extra-maritally, with a suggestion of duress: 'Piper prowled the dark streets in search of innocent victims and had his way with them' (Sharpe, 1977). To 'have your filthy way' denotes no lesser degree of male cleanliness.

have your will of to copulate, again usu. of the male, especially if the will is 'wicked': '. . . sweeping her off at his saddlebow and having his wicked will of her' (Fraser, 1982).

Most of these uses are part of daily talk and literature to the extent that we forget their intrinsic stupidity. Only hermaphrodites do not 'have sex'; even orphans 'have relations'; and we 'have something to do with' every person of the opposite sex whom we meet in our daily lives.

have drink (taken) *see* drink

have the painters in to be menstruating
Common female usage, from the staining and colour, the protective sheeting, the temporary dislocation and the inconvenience.

hawk a person who advocates aggression as a way of defence
The idea comes from Calhoun's 'War Hawks' political party of 1812 and was revived in the confrontation post WW II between the USA and Russia. The ob. Eng. 'hawk' was only a policeman, watching and seizing his victims.

hawk your mutton etc. to be a whore
'Hawk' is to offer for general sale and *see* mutton (below). In rarer form, she might 'hawk her pearly', the oyster being a bivalve to which the vagina is coarsely likened: 'I told her to hawk her pearly somewhere else' (Sharpe, 1976). The ob. Eng. to 'hawk your meat' was to display an immodest amount of bosom as an allurement to males.

hay marijuana
An Am. use older, perhaps, than the now fashionable 'grass'.

hazard of the town the contraction of venereal disease
The 'town' implied enjoyment of its debauched pleasures: '. . . in his fears of the hazard of the town, he had been some time looking out for a girl to take into keeping' (Cleland, 1749). The phrase is ob. but the hazards persist.

hazy drunk
Things may seem a little misty to the drunkard, and his memory defective.

he-biddy a cock
Another example of 19c. Am. prudery. Similarly a 'he-cow' was a bull.

head (1) to kill by beheading
As in the modern use, where we 'head' gooseberries etc., taking the top off: 'Has not heading and publickly affixing the head been thought sufficient for the most atrocious state crimes?' (Maidment, 1868). A 'heading' was such an execution, carried out by a 'heading-man', often upon a 'heading-hill', for the convenience of onlookers. Many seem not to have been deterred from crime by the severity of the penalty.

head (2) a lavatory on a ship
Originally in a warship, but now general: 'There was a small head off the little cabin' (Sanders, 1977). Usu. in the plural: 'He heard the liquid pour in the bowl of the heads' (W. Smith, 1979). Occasionally used in affectation by yachtsmen ashore.

head (3) the incidence of sub-acute alcoholic poisoning
Abbr. of headache which you are likely to get if you have been drunk. Women too may say they have a headache when they wish to signal an unwillingness to copulate: 'You were glad you found out about the headache before you invested too much time and money and hope in her' (Chandler, 1953).

head (4) *see* give head *under* give

head (5) a narcotics addict
Perhaps from the effect on alertness. Usu. in combination, like 'snow-head', addicted to cocaine. A 'head-kit' is the apparatus used for illegal administration of narcotics.

head-case an idiot
A 'case' of weakness in the head, referring to a single aberration or general deficiency: 'His teachers at school didnae think he was very bright. They thought he was a head case' (Theroux, 1983).

head-count reduction the dismissal of numbers of employees
Not a diminution in the frequency of counting them. Industrial jargon where a policy decision is made to reduce the payroll either systematically or by a single major reduction.

head-hunter (1) a recruiting agent who entices employees to change jobs

Punning on the seeking out a person with special talents and the neighbourhood sport of Papuans. The object is to obtain for the new employer, who pays a large fee, the knowledge, contacts, skills and experience which the employee has acquired serving a competitor.

head-hunter (2) a police internal disciplinary inspector
Am. police jargon. He is looking for dishonest policemen who will have no future in the police service if discovered: 'Headhunters made rank consistently better than other investigators' (Wambaugh, 1975).

head job (a) fellatio
Prostitutes' jargon, from the 'head', or glans penis: '. . . receiving a listless headjob from an ageing black prostitute' (Wambaugh, 1975). A 'head chick' is a whore who offers such a service.

head-shrinker a psychiatrist
Punning on the cerebral centre of their investigation and the practices of primitive tribes apropos their enemies: 'One day I may need some headshrinking work done' (Ustinov, 1971). Also abbr. to 'shrink': '. . . ending up on some shrink's couch twice a week' (Hailey, 1979). The evasion is needed because the need to see a psychiatrist, though a status symbol for some, is a shameful matter for most normal people.

headache *see* **head (3)**

headache-wine a narcotic made from the petals of Eng. poppies
In ob. Eng./Ire. use, common corn poppies were called 'headaches' and unmarried girls had a fetish against touching them, perhaps because they were prey to seduction in a drugged state: 'Corn-poppies, that in crimson dwell, Call'd head-aches from their sickly smell' (Clare, 1827). (I include this entry to show that the narcotic problem is not new, and to provide an excuse for my single quotation from John Clare.)

health illness
Here, as with 'defence' or 'life insurance', you avoid mentioning the taboo by stating the converse. Thus the medicine industry refers to its commercial activity as 'health care', selling its products to the sick; the Br. 'National Health Service' provides for the ill and dying, without however neglecting the well-being and security of its administrative staff; and we refer constantly to 'health clinics', 'health insurance', etc.

hearing-impaired partly deaf
To impair is an active verb, indicating a positive weakening in quality or strength but those so described may have suffered a similar degree of deafness since birth.

heart condition a malfunction of the heart
Medical jargon, in which all 'conditions' are bad: 'He had suffered from a heart condition for several years' (*Daily Telegraph*, November 1980). Sometimes abbr. to 'having a heart', but who doesn't ?

hearts penurious
Br. rh. sl. for 'hearts of oak', broke, and punning on an affluent building society of the same name. Sometimes in the full form: 'It left me 'earts-of-oak' (Kersh, 1936).

heat (1) the alarm caused by a concentrated official investigation
Of concerted police activity against specific crime; or army attacks on terrorists or rebels; of a government inquiry into bureaucratic scandal or administrative malpractice; etc. Perhaps from the rise in body temperature when we are alarmed.

heat (2) a hand gun
From the warmth of the barrel and perhaps punning on 'firing': '"Ahh, I'm carrying," Boon said. "Someone will spot the heat"' (Sanders, 1977). Also as 'heater': '"All right, Dad. Shed the heater." . . . . He put his enormous frontier Colt on the floor' (Chandler, 1939). To 'pack' heat is to carry such a gun.

heaven dust cocaine
An addict use. 'Heaven and hell' is phenocyclidine, which involves painful withdrawal symptoms. 'Heavenly blue' or 'blue heaven' are other narcotics used illegally, perhaps punning on the colour of the tablet.

heavies gangster hoodlums
They intimidate by their physical size and use violence on behalf of their boss.

heavy date an important tryst for courtship
'Heavy' means important, and *see* **date**: 'Thought you had a heavy date tonight, Molly?' (Deighton, 1981). 'Heavy necking' or 'heavy petting' indicates sexual activity just short of copulation. A 'heavy involvement' indicates an extra-marital arrangement which includes copulation, often where marriage cannot be contracted. The ob. Sc. 'heavy' was an abbr. of 'heavy of foot', meaning in a late stage of pregnancy: 'James cam to me ae morning when she was heavy o' fit' (Service, 1887).

heavy landing an aircraft crash on the runway
Aviation jargon for mishaps where nobody is injured: '. . . a DC10 of the big American carrier Overseas National careered off the runway at Istanbul after a heavy landing' (Moynahan, 1983). The phrase avoids words like mistake or crash.

heel-tap a small volume of alcohol left in the glass
The 'tap' was the sole of a shoe in cobblers' jargon although Holt identifies it as 'the layers of the leather heel' (*Phrase and Word Origins*, 1936 – and he is usu. right). Whichever the case, it lay at the bottom of the shoe: 'Seize the bottle and push it about; Don't fill on a heel-tap, it is not decorous' (A. Boswell, 1803). Today the admonition 'no heel-taps' means that the glass must be drained before replenishment.

heeled (1) drunk
Probably from being tilted over. Am.

heeled (2) carrying a gun
Properly, possessed of goods appropriate to your condition: 'I noticed Collins's hand stray under his jacket, and wished I'd thought to come heeled myself' (Fraser, 1982). 'Well heeled' means wealthy.

heels foremost dead
From the normal direction in which corpses are carried.

(hegemony comes from the Greek meaning ruler whence, in Marxist jargon, the dominance of one social class. For the Chinese Communists it also means the threat to China from the surrounding Russian-controlled frontiers.)

height of connubial bliss copulation
'Scaled' within marriage, although the cliché plumbs the depth of banality.

heist to steal
A variant of **hoist** (1) (q.v.) or from German via Yiddish, as a form of asking. It refers normally to taking a truckload of goods or to an armed robbery. A 'heist' is such a robbery: '"This is a heist!" Frisky yelled. "Out of there and line up"' (Chandler, 1939). Mainly Am.

help a domestic servant
Abbr. of the Am. 'hired help' and implying voluntary assistance rather than servitude: 'I don't want my help to know or guess' (Harris, 1925 – he claimed to be copulating with an Am. housewife). 'Help' is also used of any Am. employee.

help yourself to steal
Properly, not to await service by another. Now used of unpremeditated pilfering, especially where the goods are unguarded.

help the police (with their inquiries) to be in custody and presumed guilty of an offence for which you have not been charged
This Br. phrase seeks not to pre-judge guilt, to avoid the possibility of a subsequent conviction being quashed: 'When someone is helping the police with their inquiries into a murder it may not be proven that he is a murderer but the suggestion is there' (Sharpe, 1976). To 'assist the police', etc. means the same thing. In Am. police jargon and practice, 'helping with inquiries' means something quite different: '"He is helping us with our inquiries." "What a pompous phrase for torture"' (Theroux, 1977). A transatlantic visitor, reading Br. newspaper reports, might be led to judge the suspects so described a very accommodating and gentlemanly crowd.

hemp marijuana
An abbr. of 'Indian hemp': 'Reefers, grefa, musta, the hemp' (Longstreet, 1956). In the 1920s when we still used the 16c. Arabic 'hashish', leaving 'marijuana' to the Spaniards, 'hemp' indicated death by hanging, by a 'hemp-string', or hangman's noose: 'In a' probability he wad form a bonnie tossil at the end of a hemp string' (Willock, 1886 – a 'tossil' was a tangle). 'Hemp strung' was death by hanging, or by the 'hempen fever'; a 'hempen widow' had seen her husband so killed; and a 'hempshire gentleman' was a criminal, who would be hanged if he were caught, punning on the Eng. county which has long been abbr. from Southamptonshire to Hampshire.

hen-silver etc. extortion at the church door before a wedding
In a refined form, firearms were used: 'Formerly a gun was fired over the house of a newly married couple, to secure a plentiful issue of the marriage (probably to dispel the evil spirits that bring bad luck). The firing party had a present given them . . . . and this was termed hen-silver' (*Penrith Observer*, September 1896). Money collected generally for intoxicants at a wedding, or 'hen-drinking', was called 'hen-brass'. This ob. N. Eng. entry shows that marriage was an occasion for drunkenness and expense for our ancestors too, and for refined extortion long before the days of the wedding photographer.

herb (the) marijuana
An Am. variant of the commoner 'grass'.

hereafter (the) death
Religious use, anticipating the life to come, or as the case may be: 'The contents of that box were all that held off the Hereafter' (Francis, 1978).

(hetaerism means prostitution, from the Greek word for concubine. It is also anthropological jargon for the tribal custom in which women copulate openly and freely with any of the men in the community, but it is not yet so used in universities or the entertainment industry.)

hick a corpse
Properly, an unsophisticated country dweller. It is said that this ob. Am. use came from his availability in the anatomical dissection industry, if he ventured alone into town, an understandable concern about the risk of resurrection of an incomplete body giving rise to a cadaver shortage on both sides of the Atlantic. The 19c. 'hic jacet' was a tombstone, punning on the coat and the Latin 'here lies': 'By the cold Hic Jacets of the dead' (Tennyson, 1859).

high (1) infected with venereal disease
This ob. Br. imagery came from rotten meat.

high (2) drunk or under narcotic influence
From the feeling of elevation, but you do not use it for those lapsed into torpidity or unconsciousness. Of drunkenness: 'We'd had some people in for cocktails, and we all got quite high' (McCarthy, 1963) and of illegal narcotics: 'The user smokes them in big puffs getting high' (Longstreet, 1956). Whence a few clichés, like 'high as a kite'. An adverse reaction to narcotic ingestation is a 'low'. To 'live on the high-fly' in 19c. Eng. was to rely on the proceeds of begging letters, a career made possible by the introduction of the penny postage.

high forehead (a) baldness
We comment on this only in other men: '"And the receding hairline?" "Receding what?" .... Godfrey swung round. "High forehead," he said' (Lynn and Jay, 1986, of a politician being groomed for a television broadcast).

high in the belly in an advanced state of pregnancy
Pregnancy was the subject of many Br. old wives' tales and to be 'carrying high' meant different things in various parts of the country, few of them according with medical science.

high jinks extra-marital copulation
Properly, a carouse which you had if you played the game involving dice, the repetition of verses and forfeits; the more you drank, the more mistakes you made, the more forfeits you paid, the more you drank, and so on. Daughters today are still advised by anxious mothers not to get up to any 'high jinks'.

high jump see for the high jump

high-yellow girl see yellow (2)

highball a measure of whisky with ice etc. in a tall glass
'High' from the glass and was the 'ball' a bowl? 'Aren't you coming up with me to have a highball for the road?' (Ustinov, 1971). For Am. railroad engineers it meant a clear track, which has no bearing, I think, on the etymology.

highgrade to steal
From the useful Am. phrase meaning to take the easiest pickings, of timber from a forest, ore from a mine, etc. Thus a 'highgrader' is a discriminating and selective thief.

highjack see hijack

Highlandman's burial a funeral lasting more than a day
I include this ob. Sc. expression to justify the following quotation: 'Whaever wished for a pouchfu' o' drink might tak' it .... Whan we got tae the kirkyard .... we put the coffin twice in the grave wrang .... We got it to fit at last, and in wi' the moulds on't. The grave-digger we made a beast o'. Sic a funeral I was ne'er at afore; surely I ay think that it was na unlike a Hielan'-man's burial' (MacTaggart, 1824).

highwayman a thief on the highway
Not just any wayfarer. So described, he was usu. on horseback, when he was properly a 'high pad', as different from a 'footpad', who robbed on the 'pad', or path, on foot. Such robbery was called the 'high law', and the thief the 'high lawyer'.

hijack to take illegal possession of a vehicle
Doubtfully euphemistic and now SE. Originally Am. Prohibition use, when it became easier to steal from smugglers than to smuggle on your own account. The command to put up your hands was a laconic 'High, Jack': 'No one's saying your dad had anything to do with the hijack' (Deighton, 1981, using the

now standard spelling). A 'highjacker' so operated: 'Highjackers stopped cargoes at interurban boulevards' (Longstreet, 1956, of the Prohibition days). While lorries and their cargoes are still thus stolen, a post-1970 refinement has been the seizure of commercial aircraft in flight to extort political or financial concessions.

hike to forge an increase in value on a negotiable bill
From the proper meaning, to hoist or raise. In commercial jargon, a 'price-hike' is an unwarranted increase in a selling price due to the strength of demand. The ob. N. Eng. 'hike' was to dismiss peremptorily from employment, hooking the employee out of work and sending him on a long walk: 'Another minute an' he'll hyke me aff' (Proudlock, 1896, of such dismissal).

hinterland the territory in from the coast over which empire was claimed
If you conquered a coastal strip in late 19c. Africa, the rest of the continent leading inland from that coast belonged to you rather than to another colonial power, the indigenous population having no rights. Eventually you would squabble with your European competitor when the accidents of geography threw you together, as at Fashoda.

historic old
A usage of estate agents which sometimes traps them in tautology: 'Historic Saxon barn' (*Sunday Telegraph*, May 1981, implying construction before 1066).

hit (1) drunk
Rh. sl. from 'hit and missed', pissed, and punning on what you sometimes feel like.

hit (2) to kill
Usu. of assassination, which is also called a 'hit': 'This is some kind of Mafia hit?' (Diehl, 1978, of such a killing). A 'hit man' is a professional killer: 'You've narrowed the field down to a couple thousand hitmen' (ibid.). Criminals apart, you are also 'hit' when you are struck by a bullet, etc. In ob. Br. rh. sl. to 'hit' was to kiss, from 'hit and miss', and earlier still, to copulate, with the common violent imagery: 'She'll find a white that shall her blackness hit' (Shakespeare, *Othello*).

hit (3) to steal
There are two distinct Am. meanings; of street robbery, which may have developed from the hobo jargon 'hit', to beg with

threats; and of a planned major theft, in which a bank or warehouse may be 'hit'.

hit (4) to administer an illegal narcotic
To another or yourself, and usu. in cigarette form: 'I want another hit before you bring him in. I want to be really up for what I have to do' (Robbins, 1981). To 'hit the pipe' is so to smoke opium or marijuana.

hit the bottle etc. to drink intoxicants to excess
The commonest alternative is 'hit the hooch'. Of a single debauch: 'We were kind of hitting the bottle a little. I guess we were pretty noisy' (Chandler, 1943) or of sustained excesses: '. . . hitting the hooch like you birds been' (ibid.). Less often as 'hit it': '. . . poor old Carlisle, who between you and me had been hitting it a bit of late' (*Private Eye*, September 1981).

hit the bricks to go on strike
From the Am. sidewalk on which the strikers may congregate. If a prisoner escapes, he is also said to 'hit the bricks'. To 'hit the hump' is also to escape from prison, or to desert from the army, from the fig. hill over which the fugitive disappears.

hit the sack with to copulate with extramaritally
Of either sex and not interchangeable with 'sleep with', because that euphemism covers marital copulation too: '. . . blame a Colonel for hitting the sack with a hooker' (Ustinov, 1971).

hit the silk *see* bale out (2)

Ho Chi-minh diarrhoea
Named for the Moscow-trained Communist who successively and generally successfully took on the Japanese, the Anglo-French-Chinese army of occupation, the French, the United States, and perhaps half his fellow-countrymen and neighbours, bequeathing to his successors a new name for Saigon, militarism, tyranny and poverty. An Am. Vietnam army usage.

hoary-eyed drunk
From the look of frost over them. A cockney editor would have advised DAS not to give a separate entry for London's 'oryide'.

hobby-horse a whore
The article in Morris dancing which became a children's toy. This ob. use puns too on 'hobby', a wanton and the common equine copulation imagery: 'My wife's a hobby-horse' (Shakespeare, *Winter's Tale*).

hochle to copulate extra-maritally and openly
Properly, to sprawl about. Dr Wright defines this perhaps ob. Sc. use as 'To tumble lewdly with women in open day' (EDD – a fine example of his Cleland-like definitions where he has to define any impropriety. Do not be misled into thinking that there was once an 'open day' for tumbling lewdly with women).

hoist (1) to steal
The common lifting concept. In 19c. Eng. specifically of pilferage from retail shops, whence 'on the hoist', so engaged. Today it applies to any theft and a 'hoister' is a thief.

hoist (2) to drink intoxicants
From lifting the vessel to the mouth, in phrases like 'hoist' one or a few: 'The pub was full of hollering men . . . . Murf said, "I think I should split." "Forget it. Let's hoist a few"' (Theroux, 1976).

hoist (3) peremptorily to dismiss from employment
An Am. use, perhaps from the sudden 'lifting' out of a job.

hoist (4) to kill by hanging
Normally of an impromptu performance rather than death on the gallows.

hoist your skirt to copulate extra-maritally
Of a female, and implying an element of spontaneity: 'Every girl in the reseau would hoist her skirt for *you*' (Allbeury, 1978).

hold illegally to possess narcotics
Whether for your own use or resale, on your person or elsewhere: 'Never hold when you can stash' (addict proverb).

hold-door trade (the) prostitution
From the whores who seek customers when lounging against a partly-open door: 'Brethren and sisters of the hold-door trade' (Shakespeare, *Trolius and Cressida*). The phrase is ob. but the practice persists.

hold-up a robbery
Properly, a delay of any kind and I suppose a considerate thief may 'hold-up' his hand to stop you, before taking your valuables: 'You'll hold me up now, I suppose!' (Chandler, 1939). Formerly of stage coaches but now of any robbery, especially where violence is threatened.

hold your liquor to drink a lot of alcohol without appearing drunk
Without vomiting either, but intermediate urination does not disqualify you: 'He can't drive, he can't cook, he can't hold his liquor' (Theroux, 1978). Strictly each of us with a charged glass in his hand holds his liquor.

hole (1) to kill
From the entry of the bullet or the excavation for the grave – I suspect the latter: 'Keep yourself from being holed as they holed Muster Bingham the other day' (Trollope, 1885). The modern cliché 'a hole in the head' is not your mouth but death from a bullet.

hole (2) the vagina viewed sexually by a male
Thus a woman who copulates, especially promiscuously, may be described as a 'good bit of hole', ignoring the other bodily orifices which are vulgarly so described: the ear (earhole); the mouth (mouth-hole); and anus (arsehole); but not the nostrils. In ob. use expanded to the 'hole of contentment' or the 'holy of holies' which puns on a quiet and secret place: 'I want to see the Holy of Holies, the shrine of my idolatry' (Harris, 1925).

hole (3) *see* **black hole**

holiday a term in prison
A sometimes jocular explanation of absence: 'Not since I took that little state-financed holiday' (Lyall, 1969, of a prison sentence).

hollow legs the ability to drink a lot of liquor without getting drunk
The volume has to be stored somewhere, it seems: 'Born with hollow legs! I watched with fascination while the gold liquid disappeared like beer' (Francis, 1978). This common cliché is also used of a glutton.

Holy Alliance (the) a pact for mutual protection and conquest
After Napoleon's departure, the Austrian, Prussian and Russian despots claimed this title for their treaty which they said was 'to regulate the affairs of Europe by the principles of Christian charity' – or to hang on to their thrones and what they had managed to grab at Vienna, picking up more territory from third parties opportunistically. The thieves did not fall out for several years.

holy of holies (1) *see* **hole (2)**

holy of holies (2) a lavatory
There are several puns here, apart from the allusion to the quiet and secret place. The Latin 'sanctum sanctorum' is rarer and loses all in translation.

Holy Roman Empire a loose confederation of central European autocracies
It has been fashionable, as it is facile, to say it was not holy, not Roman, not an empire. Certainly it was only Roman in the sense that Byzantium was Roman, the intended successor of a great tradition. Yet we who have struggled since WW II for a militarily and politically united Western Europe through economic development should not denigrate the ideal of a similar grouping in which church and member states tried to keep the peace. When early in the 17c. the political mould was broken, it was religion which made the sequel so bloody and prolonged, and that at least is unlikely to happen again.

holy wars the expansion into the Middle East by western adventurers
We know them better as the Crusades. The prime cause was probably not religious – although that was the excuse – but the overpopulation of western Europe prior to the fortuitous onset of the Black Death. After culling humanity for over a century, the problem was starting to recur when the Age of Discovery revealed softer victims in the Americas, Africa and the East.

holy week the period of menstruation
Not the week before Easter but punning on the proscription of copulation, the duration of the disability and perhaps too on 'hole', the vagina.

home an institution
For orphans, chronic invalids, young criminals, geriatrics, etc. We play down the formal and alien nature of such places by stealing the most basic and emotive of our familiar concepts. But compare a 'rest home', such an institution, and a 'home of rest', a morgue. The builder or estate agent who tries to sell you a 'home' when he is offering a house seeks to appeal to the same concepts.

home equity loan a second mortgage
Usu. to fund consumer extravagance and on onerous terms: '"Home equity loan" sounded ever so much more palatable than "second mortgage", palatable to the extent of seventy-five billion dollars already on the banking system's books' (M. Thomas, 1987).

homelands the areas in S. Africa where Black Africans can subsist in normal family groups
Political jargon of the Whites, as part of the policy of **separate development** (q.v.). The pretence is that urban workers migrated from such territories, which lack the resources to support the populations assigned to them. Thus the urban worker lives apart from his family in many cases, with a responsibility of sending funds for its survival to the 'homeland'.

homely plain
The 'unaffected naturalness' (WNCD) becomes plainness in a woman, and even downright ugliness: 'It was the homeliest members of your class who became teachers' (McCarthy, 1963).

homework (1) a woman with whom a man copulates extra-maritally
Properly, a task undertaken additional to and outside your normal duty or curriculum, like a school exercise which has been done in the evening at home. In this use, the activity can hardly be classed as work and it is never done at home. A secondary Am. meaning is sexual excitement prior to copulation, perhaps punning on the 'preparation' aspect of 'homework'.

homework (2) preparation before a discussion
In the cliché 'doing your homework', whether of research done for you by others or of a quick glance at the papers before the meeting starts. The use seeks to imply virtuous zeal and efficiency.

(homo which is an abbr. of 'homosexual' is nearly always used of a male despite its derivation from the Greek 'homos', the same, and not from the Latin 'homo' a man: 'I'll never understand women. Sometimes I think these goddamned homos have got something' (Deighton, 1982, implying that all 'homos' are males). The Cambridge-recruited WW II spies for Russia were known as the 'homintern', from 'homo' and 'comintern', because of their homosexuality: '. . . bound to him intellectually, emotionally and sometimes physically as active members of what has since been aptly nicknamed the "Homintern"'(Boyle, 1979).)

honest not copulating extra-maritally
Not necessarily truthful or trustworthy in other respects: 'I do not think but Desdemona's honest' (Shakespeare, *Othello*). And we may still 'make an honest woman of' someone, under appropriate circumstances.

honey human excrement
Am. use referring no doubt to the colour and texture rather than the smell or sweetness. The army might fill, and then empty, a 'honey bucket': '"I emptied the

honeybucket!" shouted an American voice'
(L. Thomas, 1981) the aggregate being carried away in a 'honey wagon' or, in the navy,
a 'honey barge'. In airline jargon, a 'honey
cart' empties the lavatories after each long
flight: '. . . the sanitary servicing vehicle
("honey cart" to the crews)' (Moynahan,
1983). A 'honey-dipper' is not a bee but a
lavatory cleaner: 'The V.C. get work inside
all camps as shoeshine boys and laundresses
and honey-dippers' (Herr, 1977, of
Vietnam).

honey man a person with whom a female
regularly copulates extra-maritally
From giving 'sweeteners' rather than getting
sweetness. Am.

Hong Kong dog diarrhoea
Only of the affliction if contracted in Hong
Kong. Because it 'dogs' the sufferer? I doubt
it.

honk to feel the genitals of a male
Prostitutes' and police jargon of a sexual
approach, usu. in a public place, where the
action resembles squeezing a bulb horn:
'Sabrina . . . . gave his genitals a squeeze
. . . . He knew he had been "honked" as the
vice cops called it' (Wambaugh, 1975).

honked drunk
Probably from the Am. 'honk', to vomit, but
it may be used of drunkenness even if you
don't throw up.

(honky a White person is a pejorative Black
use adverting to the relative size of White
noses vis-à-vis their own.)

honour the avoidance of extra-marital copulation
Of female integrity in this respect, if none
other: 'You sitting there with your legs
crossed and a hole in the head and me trying
to explain how I shot you to defend my
honour' (Chandler, 1958). Of a male it
meant the avoidance of being cuckolded:
'You're a sneekin' varmint to take advantage
of a man's hospitality to try and steal his
honour' (Fraser, 1971, writing in 19c. style –
Flashman had copulated with the wife, as
usu.).

(hooch – also spelt 'hootch' – is any low-
grade intoxicant other than beer. It comes
from the Alaskan 'hoochinoo', which was a
compound of yeast, flour and molasses or
sugar favoured by the native inhabitants.)

hoof (the) peremptory dismissal from
employment
A Br. variant of **kick** (2) (q.v.).

hook (1) to steal
Normally by using bent metal on a pole
through a window, like the modern E.
African 'fish hook', but without the Kenyan
refinement of razor blades let into the pole to
deter you from grasping it as you see your
valuables vanishing through the shutters: 'I
guessed he had hooked it from the Miskito
Indian on the Rio Sico, after his showerbath'
(Theroux, 1981, of pilfered soap). In ob. Br.
use a 'hooker' was such a thief, working 'on
the hook'.

hook (2) a threat used to influence conduct
The imagery is from angling: 'He had a hook
of some sort into her' (Chandler, 1958, of
such coercion).

hook (3) an enticement leading to trickery
Again angling imagery: '"Let's hear what
the guy has to say." The hook was in'
(Weverka, 1973).

hook (4) a hypodermic needle
From the usu. shape of a needle used in
surgery. The word is also sometimes used of
the illegal narcotic, punning on your addiction to it.

hooked under an addictive compulsion
Angling imagery again. Of addictions to golf,
surfing, an author or anything, and especially
to narcotics: 'The kid never did get hooked
on the hard stuff' (Sanders, 1977).

hooker (1) *see* **hook** (1)

hooker (2) a whore
The derivation is from catching a customer:
'Some nights we go about and don't hook a
soul' (Mayhew, 1862, of a whore and not a
Salvationist). General Hooker's exploits in
Washington brothels came later and the
abundance of whores in Corlears Hook or
the Caesar's Hook districts of New York
served to keep the usage alive: 'Even the
hookers had done no more than cast an eye'
(Mailer, 1965, of whores). 'Hook-shop', a
low brothel, is ob.

hooky human excrement
Perhaps from the shape it sometimes takes.
It is used for 'shit' in the literal, allusive, fig.
and expletive senses of that over-worked
word.

hooligan an inhabitant of a Communist
state who actively dissents from national
policy
A Communist dysphemism, from the 19c.
Patrick Hooligan who gave his name to
young London ruffians engaged in non-
political rowdyism. If your norm is unthink-

ing acquiescence, a dissentient must be branded as mad, criminal or guilty of rowdyism.

(hoosegow a prison comes from the Spanish 'husgado' or 'juzgado', which meant a court, an association of ideas which you find also in **chokey** (q.v.): 'In that case, stew in a French hoosegow for the rest of your natural' (Sharpe, 1982).)

hop a narcotic
Originally opium and I think from the twisting vine rather than a corruption of some Chinese script, as is sometimes suggested: 'They take him over to the hospital ward and shoot him full of hop' (Chandler, 1943). A 'hop-head' is an addict: 'Frank wasn't just a deviant and not just a hop-head' (Davidson, 1978). A 'hop-joint' is where you can buy and ingest illegal narcotics and become 'hopped', under narcotic influence: '"Coked" or "hopped up" gunmen' (Lavine, 1930).

hop into bed to copulate extra-maritally
Usu. on a first or single occasion and not propelling yourself on one leg only: '"How about hopping into bed?" "At half-past four on a Sunday afternoon?"' (Francis, 1978). The Am. 'whore-hopping' is not brothel leap-frog but copulation with prostitutes: 'Red-necks who had come down for the beer-drinking and the whore-hopping' (Theroux, 1979). The ob. Br. 'hop-pole marriage' was living together unwed, or a marriage hastily contracted to avoid the bastardy of a child, in which case the arrangements might be signified by actually jumping together over a stick, or hop-pole.

hop off etc. to die
This and 'hop the twig' employ avian imagery to denote departure. After passing into disuse, the phrase was taken up by WWII fliers and is still used: 'It's not often multi-millionaires hop their twig' (Bagley, 1982 – and even they do it only once).

hop toad a large portion of whisky
From the iron bar used by Am. railmen for derailing wagons. Such a draught overturns the person who drinks it.

hopper a lavatory
Properly, an inverted cone through which solids are discharged into a container, which explains the imagery: 'Mom on the hopper with her knees pressed together' (Theroux, 1973). Am.

(hopping-Giles a cripple came from St Giles, their patron saint. Many ob. dialect expressions referred to the uneven or 'hopping' gait of cripples in the days before they had acquired a **handicap** (q.v.) and any cripple would respond to the name of 'Hopkins'.)

horizontal (1) pertaining to copulation
From the normal attitude of the parties. A 'horizontal life' was living as a whore: '. . . through this horizontal life I have risen from being a homeless waif to become a famous lady' (L. Thomas, 1977). A 'horizontal conquest' is an act of extra-marital copulation, the victor usu. but not necessarily being the male: '. . . diamonds and rubies . . . . and the other battle honours of her horizontal conquests' (Ustinov, 1966). The 'grande horizontale' was a famous whore: 'Lola Montez, the grande horizontale, began her whoring in Simla' (Theroux, 1975). In Am. 'horizontal jogging' is copulation, perhaps also alluding to the beneficial effects on the heart which both forms of activity are said to induce: '. . . women didn't go in for all this casual, take-it-or-leave-it horizontal jogging that seems to lie at the very root of our society today' (Matthew, 1983).

horizontal (2) drunk
A rare Br. usage, probably from actually or fig. lying on the ground.

horn (1) an erect penis
Common enough in the 16c. for Shakespeare's punning vulgarism: 'I can find no rime to "lady" but "baby", – an innocent rime; for "scorn", "horn", – a hard rime' (*Much Ado*). To 'have a horn' is to be thus sexually aroused. The 'horn of fidelity' was a drinking cup, doubtless with sexual overtones, which Morgan la Faye sent King Arthur to enable him to test the chastity of the ladies of his court. History sadly records that only four out of the hundred examinees managed to 'drinke cleane', thus preserving the liquid and their honour.

horn (2) to cuckold
The traditional 'horns' of cuckoldry, with their male sexual insinuations, were fig. placed on the head of the deceived husband: '. . . by those that do their neighbours horn' (Colvil, 1796) and today: '. . . evidence of Julie and Ronnie putting horns on the head of (her husband)' (Sanders, 1979). To 'wind the horn', or blow it, was to acknowledge that you had been cuckolded, by a 'horn-maker': 'Virtue is no horn-maker' (Shakespeare, *As You Like It*). He who was 'horned'

was cuckolded: 'Our horn'd master (waes me for him). Believes that sly boots does adore him' (Morison, 1790 – but not sly enough to deceive the servants too). This field of literary ingenuity of which I here only explore the headlands is no longer cultivated. Perhaps we have ceased to care about cuckoldry.

horn of the ox *see* **hair of the dog**

horner a sniffer of cocaine
From the nose which becomes sore and runny as the narcotic damages the mucous membranes, along with much else.

horny (1) the devil
He has them on his head. Usu. 'old' and in various spellings: 'Should Hornie, as in ancient days, 'Mang sons o' God present him' (Burns, 1785). To many of the 19c. Irish population, 'horny' was a policeman.

horny (2) anxious for copulation
Improbably – *see* **horn** (1) – used of either sex. Of a male: 'Even if they did put bromide in the tea he still felt horny every morning and woke up with an erection like a tent pole' (Bogarde, 1978) and a female: 'The stewardesses were plain and presumably horny' (M. Thomas, 1980).

horse (1) gonorrhoea
Rare Br. rh. sl. for 'horse and trap', clap.

horse (2) to defecate
Again Br. rh. sl., this time on 'horse and trap' for crap.

horse (3) a corrupt prison warder
He carries loads of contraband in and out of Am. prisons.

horse (4) heroin
Probably a corruption of 'heroin', despite the attractions etymologically of 'riding' under its influence. Widely used, as in Deighton's punning title for a novel, *Horse under Water*. 'Horsed' is under narcotic influence.

horse apples the turds dropped by a horse
Especially in a street, where they may pile up like apples on a fruiterer's shelf: '. . . "horse apples", "cowpats", "prairie chips", "muck", "dung", etc.' (Jennings, 1965, listing words commonly used as euphemisms for animal shit; but he missed 'manure', from 'main-d'œuvre' or manual labour).

horse collar etc. an expression of disgust
An Am. may select some part of the animal or its accoutrement when it is not appropriate to say 'horse shit'. The ob Br. 'horse-leech' was an extortioner, after the blood-sucking worm of the order hirudinea; he was usu. a male but, if female, demanded payment for sexual services or for silence about past sexual encounters.

hospital (1) an institution for the insane
An Am. use which glosses over the shameful nature of the affliction both for the patient and for his family: 'American insane asylums are now simple *hospitals*' (Mencken, 1940). Much of the taboo associated with madness came from the fact that a majority of the lunatics were alcoholics or syphilitic.

hospital (2) an unauthorized prison
Jargon of the Am. Central Intelligence Agency for a place where suspects may be illegally held.

hospital job a contract which can be loaded with excess charges
In normal manufacturing use, a job you can work on when you have nothing else to do, delivery not being urgent. The dishonesty starts when you start loading such a contract with waiting-time and scrap because your customer, usu. the government, is too inefficient to detect malpractice.

hospitality free intoxicants
Properly, the provision of a welcome and entertainment to a visitor: 'The landlord . . . . was happy to stay open as long as Seddon Arms wanted a drink. Maxim was beginning to guess at the scale of "hospitality" which the arms business could afford' (Lyall, 1980). Whence the television 'hospitality room' in which the tongues of amateurs are lossened and to which the staff repair for free supplies: 'In the hospitality room George Foster stood with his clipboard in one hand' (Allbeury, 1982).

hostess a whore
Of those places where arrangements for extra-marital copulation are made as an adjunct to the provision of food etc.: 'Once a hostess, always a hostess. You always were a bit of a whore' (Kersh, 1936). This explains why 'air hostesses' prefer to be called 'cabin flight attendants'.

hostile class elements citizens opposed to Communism
Communist dysphemism – 'element' is a pejorative word. The inference is that there exists a 'class' hostile to the 'masses' rather than to a self-perpetuating tyranny.

hot (1) eager for copulation
From the increased bodily temperature and flushing caused by sexual excitment and also

properly used of other emotions, like anger, which give rise to the same symptoms: 'I have never in my life seen so many ladies so hot in such a small place' (Green, 1979, of lustful females). The 'hots' indicates lust for a specific person: 'Now he's got the hots for this young chick' (Sanders, 1973). Certain compounds have special meanings as follow:

>   **hot back** lust: 'When gods have hot backs, what shall poor men do?' (Shakespeare, *Merry Wives of Windsor*). ob.

>   **hot for** lusting after, of either sex.

>   **hot-house** a brothel, punning on the horticultural use: 'She professes a hothouse, which, I think, is a very ill house too' (Shakespeare, *Measure for Measure*). ob.

>   **hot pants** an urge to copulate, normally of a female: 'If she ever got hot pants, it wasn't for her husband' (Chandler, 1953) and rarely of a male: 'I've still got hot pants for her, if you want to call that love' (McCarthy, 1963).

>   **hot stuff** a female who copulates enthusiastically and extra-maritally, usu. without payment or much encouragement.

>   **hot-tailing** extra-marital copulation on a regular basis, punning on a rapid pursuit: 'She's going to be hot-tailing it with every . . .' (Price, 1982 – a man with a broken spine was speaking of his wife).

>   **hot time (a)** frequent and animated copulation, within or outside marriage: 'Reggie gives me a hot time in bed' (overheard at a ladies' bridge table in 1948).

etc., etc.

hot (2) obtained or retained illegally
Usu. of stolen goods, which may fig. 'burn' you if you touch them: 'Boudreau sold cheap liquor and handed fixes downtown and sometimes sold hot goods' (Weverka, 1973). You dispose of stolen goods in a 'hot market': 'Not rich enough for the hot market' (Price, 1979, of stolen property), etc.

hot (3) infected with venereal disease
Normally of a male, from the burning sensation when urinating but perhaps also from the risk of infecting another.

hot (4) radioactive
Nuclear jargon, probably taken from the 'hot spot' on a bearing, where heat indicates danger or trouble.

hot (5) drunk
It often makes you perspire at one stage. Am.

hot pillow motel a place which lets rooms for extra-marital copulation
The pillows have little time to cool down: 'That notorious hot-pillow hotel on the far side of San Jorge. God knows, Stone had never been fastidious about where he'd take his girls for a quickie' (Deighton, 1972). Likewise the 'sheets': 'The hotel was noted for its hot-sheet business' (M. Thomas, 1980).

hot seat an uncomfortable position of authority
Usu. in circumstances where something has gone wrong and others are jumping for dry land. From the electric chair used for execution: 'The killers who end up in the gas chamber or the hot seat' (Chandler, 1953). In criminal use, the 'hot squat' is always the electric chair but the ob. Eng. 'hot place' was hell.

hot shot a fatal dose of illegal narcotics
The impurities of illegal narcotics, often adulterated along the distribution chain, constitute an additional addict risk. Am.

hot wire to steal a car by by-passing the ignition switch
Punning perhaps on 'hot' (2) (above) and the modification of the circuitry: '. . . faking a left to land a right, hot-wiring a car, and finding a place to dispose of the body' (Theroux, 1976).

hourly hotel a place which lets rooms for extra-marital copulation
Day or night, you are charged for a short period of occupation, often with a whore: '. . . bustin' the massage parlours, movie pits, hourly hotels' (Diehl, 1978).

house (1) a brothel
'House' is properly used of a dwelling or any other building given over to a special purpose, such as a theatre or debating chamber. The use *tout court* for a brothel is ob.: 'Some of the girls about here live in houses' (Mayhew, 1862, but not chastely with their parents). There is usu. amplification as follows:

>   **house of accommodation** was a place which let rooms to whores: 'They enter houses of accommodation, which they prefer to going with them to their lodgings' (ibid.).

house of assignation was rather like an **hourly hotel** (above): '. . . keepers of houses of assignation, where the last-mentioned class might carry on their amours with secrecy' (ibid. of 'ladies of intrigue'). ob.

house of ill-fame was a brothel, which might at the same time have a reputation for excellence: 'There is in Exeter Street, Strand, a very old established and notorious house of ill-fame' (ibid.).

house of ill-repute was a brothel, again often with a good reputation for its whores and decor, if not decorum: 'A girl who had been forced into a house of ill-repute' (Lavine, 1930).

house in the suburbs was a 16c. brothel, when they tended to be located on the edge of a town.

house of profession was a brothel: 'I am as well acquainted here as I was in our house of profession' (Shakespeare, *Measure for Measure*).

house of resort was a brothel: 'Shall all our houses of resort in the suburbs be pulled down?' (ibid.).

house of sale was a brothel, not an auction room: 'I saw him enter such a house of sale – Videlicet, a brothel' (Shakespeare, *Hamlet*).

You might also find 'houses' of civil reception, evil repute, pleasure, sin, tolerance, etc. or, inverted, a 'scalding house', where you might be venereally infected, a 'common house' or an 'ill-famed house': 'Lord Euston was said to have gone in an ill-famed house' (Harris, 1925)

etc., etc.

house (2) a lavatory
Again the building given over to a particular purpose. Although Dr Johnson defines lavatories as 'houses', he does not so define a 'house'. In various compounds like 'house' of office, of ease, of commons, of lords, etc. most of which are ob.

house (3) an institution for the homeless
An abbr. of the dread 'workhouse': 'Many old people . . . . have to enter the "house", as it is nick-named, like humble suppliants' (Gordon, 1885). A workhouse was also known as a 'house of industry': 'The House of Industry for the reception of the poor of eleven of our fourteen parishes' (Peshall, 1773). ob.

house-cleaning a re-organization which leads to dismissals
An Am. phrase for an infrequent investigation in the police or bureaucracy when inefficiency or corruption have reached levels which can no longer be ignored. The imagery is from the annual major assault made domestically in the spring on curtains, carpets, etc.

house man a security guard
Police jargon: 'I'm the house man here. Spill it' (Chandler, 1939). Am.

house of correction a prison
Named in the hope that there will be no recidivism: 'Lyburn . . . . is unlike any other house of correction in the world' (Ustinov, 1971). The modern Am. 'correctional facility' uses the same imagery and 'house of detention' is explicit: 'Incarceration in the House of Detention means loss of wages and a job' (Lavine, 1930).

house proud obsessed with domestic cleanliness and tidiness
This tedious affliction, normally of childless wives, has little to do with pride in the family residence. In many rural districts the Br. 'housekeeper' is expected to do more than keep house when ministering to a single male: 'Several housekeepers . . . . chosen for their willingness to endure the bed and board of old Mr. Flawse' (Sharpe, 1978). Let me at once add that many respectable ladies follow this occupation and who is to blame them if, living with widowers, they change their status and their testamentary expectations.

house-trained not subject to involuntary urination or defecation
Usu. of pet animals and sometimes too of young children. Thus of any person induced to perform a subservient or unusual pattern of behaviour, like a working husband who also undertakes an undue portion of the domestic chores, or a politician who goes along with bureaucratic practices and abuses: 'The Civil Service phrase for making a new Minister see things their way is "house-training"' (Lynn and Jay, 1981).

housekeeper *see* **house-proud**

how's your father extra-marital copulation
A male expression, perhaps from an opening conversational gambit and also used of unmarried pregnancy: 'The girl was in the club, knocked up, a bun in the oven – 'ow's yer father' (Lyall, 1982).

hulk a prison
Properly, a ship and then the hull of a ship which is no longer seaworthy but good enough to keep convicts in. Still used fig., usu. in the plural.

human intelligence the use of spies
Not the 'sapiens' of homo sapiens but the acquisition of 'intelligence', or information, by human rather than other agencies such as interception of radio, satellite photography, etc.

human relations copulation
I deal with 'have relations' under **have** (above) but this absurd phrase deserves its own entry. Our family in the narrow sense comprises our 'human relations' while in the broader view we have 'human relations' with everyone we come into contact with: 'She had no idea of elementary human relations' (Fraser, 1969, meaning she knew nothing about procreation).

human rights individual licence beyond that permitted by existing institutions
The phrase comes from the 1948 United Nations' 'Universal Declaration of Human Rights', a concept to which no exception can be taken by those who consider mankind to be paramount on earth. In practice 'human rights' can provide a slogan for those who wish to overturn an established form of social living acceptable to a majority, using violence if necessary.

hummingbird an instrument of death by electrocution
The 'chair' gives a noise when the current is switched on. Am.

hump to copulate
Dr Johnson gives only a 'pretuberance', and such is certainly involved in the transaction which makes derivation from the meaning, 'to carry a load', less likely. Grose says 'once a fashionable word for copulation' and it is back in fashion: 'His trouble was seducin'. Story is he humped the faculty wives in alphabetical order' (Bradbury, 1965). In the 19c. you might 'hump the mutton', punning on porterage: 'She completed her undressing while we were positively humping the mutton all the way to the couch' (Fraser, 1977, writing in 19c. style). The ob. Br. 'hump it' meant to die, probably from the departure of a porter after taking up his load (and you can still see a stand on which porters rested their loads without taking them off their backs on the S. side of London's Picadilly near Hyde Park Corner).

hung like claiming the fabled sexual prowess of
Of the male in various clichés. Thus 'hung like' a bull or stallion implies large genitalia – not just the testicles – or obsession with their sexual function: 'I hear he's hung like a horse' (Sanders, 1986, of an Italian male). 'Hung like a rabbit' suggests a penchant for frequent copulation; etc.

hunt to seek a homosexual partner
Of a male, and often in urinals: 'Gilbert's given up "hunting", he says all he ever wanted was love and he's got mine' (Murdoch, 1978).

hunt the brass rail to frequent bars selling intoxicants
There used to be a brass rail in many bars which you could rest a foot upon: 'Virgins, reporters, house-wives, kept-wenches, customer's men hunt the brass rail' (Longstreet, 1956). Am. and perhaps ob.

hunt the fox down the red lane to become drunk
The 'red lane' is the throat: 'I am sorry, kind sir, that your glass is no fuller . . . . So merrily hunt the fox down the red lane' (Dixon, 1846). Br. and perhaps ob.

husband (1) a pimp
Of his relationship to the senior of the women in his stable: '. . . to denounce a woman to her "husband" if the creature makes advances to you' (Londres, 1928 in tr.). In ob. Eng. use a 'husband' was also a whore's regular customer: 'I know very many sailors – six, eight, ten, oh! more than that. These are my husbands. I am not married, of course not' (Mayhew, 1862).

husband (2) a homosexual taking the male role
Male or female, if they co-habit sexually with another homosexual: 'The "husband" he tripped with a heel behind her ankle' (Sanders, 1982, describing a fight with a pair of female homosexuals).

hush money a bribe to ensure silence
The payment is made to an extortioner or to a former employee who may possess potentially damaging information. The ob. Br. 'hush' meant to kill, again from the silence which follows. A 19c. Eng. 'hush-shop' was an unlicensed inn which continued trading after licences became mandatory: '"Hush" signifying that the company frequenting such places were expected to conduct themselves as orderly as possible

that no alarm might be given to parties in authority' (Brierley, 1865).

hussy a woman who habitually copulates extra-maritally
A corruption of 'housewife', from the days when only the marital bargain granted the right, or duty, of copulation. Soldiers still call their small sewing pack, or housewife, a 'hussif'.

hustle (1) to steal
Properly in this sense, to beg, from the forwardness of an experienced mendicant. The words 'hustle', a theft and 'hustler', a thief, are now mainly used of Am. addicts seeking cash by any means so as to buy a supply of illegal narcotics.

hustle (2) to engage in prostitution
Again from the vigorous importuning in a public place: 'I hustled at a dead run until the streets were empty and the bars closed' (Theroux, 1973). In very common use a 'hustler' is a whore: 'I don't think she's an out-and-out hustler' (Allbeury, 1975). The 19c. Br. meaning, to copulate, has lapsed.

Hyde Park case a person who spies on courting couples
The large central London park is much used for courtship and al fresco copulation because it is not closed after nightfall: 'The public will like it . . . . still better when he's a

Hyde Park case' (G. Greene, 1932, of such a voyeur). ? ob.

hygiene the disposal of pads etc. dirtied by menstrual discharge
Properly, health, which Hygeia was the goddess of. A common evasion of advertisers and in hotel lavatories.

hygienic treatment the temporary preservation of a corpse
Am. funeral jargon, which ignores the fact that newly dead meat is aseptic; we are conditioned to hang parts of a pig – a side of bacon – in our kitchens or pheasants in our larder, but we regard with distaste the corpses of those formerly near and dear to us: 'Although some funeral directors boldly speak of "embalming", the majority consider it preferable to describe the treatment by some other term as . . . . "Hygienic Treatment"' (J. Mitford, 1963).

hymenal sweets copulation by a male
A pedantic and probably ob. phrase, alluding to the hymenal membrane, although not necessarily to the female's first essay in copulation. If you do find anyone using this expression, he is likely also to refer to the vagina, if at all, as a 'hypogastric cranny', from the lower part of the abdomen or 'hypogastrium' and not rh. sl. with the coarse 'fanny'.

I

I am listening I have already made up my mind
Used by anyone who is not interested in the proposal being put to him, 'listening' not importing considering or paying attention.

I hear what you say you are mistaken
A convenient form of words, especially for bureaucrats, as it obviates the need to enter into discussion or argument.

I must have notice of that question I am not going to answer you
This response is best used in an interview broadcast live where you wish to hide facts or ignorance. Radio and television are too ephemeral for there to be a risk of your bluff being called.

ice (1) a bribe
Not from the sl. meaning, diamonds but from the stickiness of frozen water. However DAS suggests derivation from the initials of 'Incidental Campaign Expenses', which is at least ingenious. Am.

ice (2) to kill
Probably from the permanent lowering of body temperature rather than the ice in pre-refrigeration morgues: 'I heard what The Bat did to you for icing High Ball Mary' (Diehl, 1978). To 'put someone on ice' is to kill: 'Somebody put this Domino on ice about four hours ago .... it wasn't no amateur hit' (ibid.). Am.

ice box (1) a prison
Originally a cell used for solitary confinement, where you were sent to cool down: 'A prisoner sent to the "ice-box" or solitary' (Lavine, 1930) but later any place of confinement: 'He has so far stayed out of the icebox' (Chandler, 1953, of a criminal who had escaped prison). 'On ice' usu. means solitary confinement, which may be spent in the 'icehouse': '... three days in the icehouse' (ibid.). The 'iceman' who used to deliver it to your home before refrigerators were common had a reputation for copulating with housewives, whence O'Neill's punning *The Iceman Cometh*. Am.

ice box (2) a mortuary
The ice was to stop the corpses decomposing prematurely. This Am. use has survived refrigeration: 'He's got seven stiffs down there in the icebox' (Diehl, 1978).

ice cream illicit narcotics in crystalline form
From the appearance and the vanilla colour. The 'ice cream man' supplies addicts, but an 'ice creamer' with the 'ice cream habit' is only moderately addicted. Am.

ideal for modernization dilapidated
In this estate agents' newspeak, 'ideal' means only fit for: 'Stone-built semi-detached cottage. Ideal for modernization' (*W. Daily Press*, May 1981).

identification the ability to pay
In an Am. hotel, a passport will not suffice. The desk staff will want cash or the imprint of a credit card before they hand over the key to your room. Whence the greeting, 'May I see your identification, please'.

ill (1) menstrual
Common female usage and imagery: '"When were you ill last?" "About a fortnight ago," she replied' (Harris, 1925).

ill (2) suffering from venereal disease
Usu. of a whore and in prostitutes' jargon: 'The poor girl may not even have known she was ill (syphilitic)' (Harris, 1925).

ill (3) in the custody of an espionage agency
The natural state of one in a CIA hospital (2) (q.v.). And the Russians said that Taraki, the Afghan President shot in 1979, died 'of a serious illness', which means the KGB caused him to be killed.

ill-adjusted mad
But no tinkering with the mechanism will put things right: 'We aren't here to provide a haven for the ill-adjusted' (Bradbury, 1959).

ill-famed house *see* house (1)

ill man the devil
A dysphemism not about his health but his character, who might take you away to the 'ill place' or the 'ill bit', hell: 'The devil .... took him awa' to the ill bit' (A. Armstrong, 1890). Whence the ob. Br. 'ill', bewitched: '... the child had been ill-wished and .... would never be better until "the spell was taken off her"' (R. Hunt, 1865).

ill-used having copulated extra-maritally
Of a female, supposedly against her will and regardless of the tenderness which the male may have displayed: 'I cannot believe that she will be ... ill-used, in any way, if you follow me' (Fraser, 1977, writing in 19c. style). The use and concept are now probably ob.

illegal operation an induced abortion
Before the days when such became legal:
'What about you, doctor – and your little
professional mistake? Illegal operation, was
it?' (Christie, 1939). To jump the red light at
an intersection is also an illegal operation.

(illegitimate a bastard is said by OED to be
'the earliest sense in Eng.' and we must
accept that it is the earliest recorded sense. It
must however have come from the proper
meaning, unlawful: 'A yearly average of
1,141 illegitimate children thrown back on
their wretched mothers' (Mayhew, 1862).)

illicit pertaining to extra-marital copulation
Properly, unlawful although Eng. Common
Law, perhaps wisely, saw no criminality in
adultery, leaving jurisdiction to the church.
Usu. in compounds like 'illicit' embraces,
connection, commerce, intercourse, etc.

illuminated drunk
A less common version of **lit** (q.v.).

imaginative journalism sensationalist
invention
It is unwise to call a journalist a liar because
he will have many more chances of damaging you than you will of hurting him, as
Goldsmith found out during his feud with
Private Eye: '... a piece of imaginative
journalism was being perpetrated by one of
its own reporters' (*Private Eye*, June 1981).

imbibe to drink intoxicants
Usu. to excess, if someone says you 'imbibe'.
It really means to drink anything.

immaculate in fair decorative order.
No used residence is ever 'free from spot or
stain' (SOD). This is real estate puffing for a
house which you can move straight into, if
you can stand the wallpaper.

immediate need on death
Am. funeral jargon, of those whom they consider improvident because they do not pay
their burial expenses several years in
advance: 'The American Cemetery reports a
discussion on "Immediate-need selling"'
(J. Mitford, 1963).

immigrant a Black person living in Britain
Any White, such as a person of mixed Greek
and German ancestry born in Argentina, can
make his home with due consent in BI and
not be classed in popular speech as an
'immigrant'. Conversely: 'Most "immigrants" have been here for many years, and
two of every five of them were born in the
United Kingdom' (Howard, 1977, of
Blacks).

immoral associated with prostitution
Properly, contrary to virtue but confined to
sexual misbehaviour in various legal jargon
phrases. Thus 'immoral earnings' are what a
whore gets paid and a pimp takes from her:
'It would mean my arrest on a charge of
living off immoral earnings' (Theroux,
1973). 'Immoral girls' are whores: 'Though
they'd twice given him the boat fare home he
had spent it on drink and probably on
immoral girls' (Bradbury, 1976). An
'immoral house' was a brothel: 'The dress-
lodger probably lives some distance from the
immoral house' (Mayhew, 1862) and to-day
a building used for 'immoral purposes' is
either a brothel or where whores take their
customers: '... full of brothels, almost every
house being used for an immoral purpose'
(ibid.), etc. The Am. Mann Act, known as
the Immorality Act, makes it unlawful to
transport a female across a State line with
intent to 'induce, entice or compel her to
give herself up to the practice of prostitution,
or to give herself up to debauchery, or any
other immoral purpose'. It is happily a
defence to plead that the seduction came as
an afterthought.

impale to copulate with
Of a male. Properly, to surround with a
fence, whence to thrust a stake into a body:
'Before she could turn round I had impaled
her, and was subsiding into a chair with her
on my lap' (Fraser, 1971).

implement a penis
In its sexual role: '... he was such a big man
and could nigh-on dig post holes with that
there implement of his' (Keneally, 1979, of a
libertine).

impotent sexually infertile
Properly, powerless in any regard but used
in this sense of either sex, and also of males
who cannot achieve an erection of the penis:
'... advertisements for doctors who cured
"all the diseases of love" and promised the
impotent "horse-like vigour"' (Manning,
1977).

improper involving extra-marital sexual
behaviour
Either heterosexual or homosexual, being in
either case a deviation from propriety in this
limited area of behaviour. Thus the ob.
'improper house' was not badly constructed,
but a brothel: 'Neither are the magistracy or
the police allowed to enter improper or disorderly houses, unless to suppress disturbances' (Mayhew, 1862 – he seems to
discount the possibility of their being custo-

mers). An 'improper suggestion' is a homo-sexual approach or an invitation by either sex to copulate extra-maritally: '. . . one of the tarts plucked at Kavanagh's sleeve and made an improper suggestion' (Fraser, 1975). etc.

improvement (1) a forcible depopulation
The Sc. Highland Clearances replaced people with sheep to increase rents and give the Clan Chiefs more spending money in Edinburgh and London: 'The necessity for reducing the population in order to intro-duce valuable improvements' (MacKenzie of Coul, who goes on to advise his evicted clansmen to 'find happiness as the servants of servants'). Many of the dispossessed found their way to America where they remained staunch royalists in the sub-sequent war with a majority of the colonists who, with some help from France, Spain and Holland, achieved independence.

improvement (2) a reduction in quality or service
Any statement that a change in procedures is to 'improve service to customers' should be viewed with as much scepticism as an asser-tion by a civil servant which is prefaced by 'of course'. It usu. conceals the intention of improving profitability by selling less for the same money: 'Improvement means deterior-ation' (Hutber's Law).

improver an underpaid worker
A 19c. device under which prospects were set off against a living wage. The practice continued up to WW II after which juveniles became entitled to adult wages. This had two unplanned results: those in work and living at home found themselves with higher disposable incomes than their elders and, because they lack training and dedication, many uneducated young people are too expensive to employ and so face permanent unemployment. I leave social comment on these phenomena to the sociologists.

in (1) imprisoned
Criminal abbr. of 'in prison': 'She was in the first time for robbing a public' (Mayhew, 1851).

in (2) copulating with
Of a male, with obvious derivation: 'Climb-ing into bed with . . . . Lady Fleur, when that noble lord was not only in it but in her' (Sharpe, 1978).

in a certain etc. condition *see* condition (2)

in Abraham's bosom dead
Where Dives reputedly saw Lazarus, although it seems poor recompense for a lifetime of penury and abuse: 'The sons of Edward sleep in Abraham's bosom' (Shakespeare, *Richard III*). Literary use only.

in bed *see* bed (2)

in calf etc. pregnant
It is usu. male practice to describe preg-nancy in females by the SE terms for farm and other domestic animals. Farmers tend to use 'in calf'. 'In foal' is more general: 'She had just discovered . . . that she was in foal for the ninth time' (Fraser, 1975, of Queen Victoria). 'In kindle' is properly of rabbits, and now rare of women. 'In pig' is quite common: '"I'm in pig, what d'you think of that?" "A most hideous expression, Linda dear"' (N. Mitford, 1945). 'In pup' is widely used, not only of bitches or by dog-lovers. 'In pod' is from the fruit of a leg-uminous vine, although a 'pod' was also a protuberant stomach: 'I've 'ad seven girls i' pod and wor going wi' a married woman' (Bradbury, 1976). I have never seen the common Br. 'in for it' in print.

in care *see* care

in Carey street bankrupt
From the location of the Bankruptcy Court in London. You might have thought that 'in the Crown Office' meant the same thing, and would have been wrong – it meant drunk, punning on the head and a govern-ment building in London.

in circulation ready to copulate
There are two distinct uses of females; of a normal sexual partner, to indicate that she is not menstruating or incapacitated by partur-ition; and of a female earning her living by prostitution: '. . . cannot conceive that a grown-up girl can earn her living in any other way. At twelve she is in secret circula-tion' (Londres, 1928, in tr.).

in conference *see* conference

in-depth study industrial espionage
Properly a pretentious and often tautological phrase for an investigation or survey. Busi-ness jargon for the illegal acquisition of information, drawings, etc. which you pay a third party to obtain to avoid overt crimi-nality.

in drink *see* drink

in flagrante delicto in the act of extra-marital copulation

Legal jargon for those detected in the non-crime of adultery. Also used of detection in other wrong-doing, which is being caught 'red-handed', the victim's blood being fig. upon you.

in foal *see* **in calf** etc.

in for it *see* **in calf** etc.

in freedom *see* **free** (2)

in full fig having an erect penis
Properly, dressed in full uniform or in the height of fashion. ? ob.

in full fling engaged in regular extra-marital copulation with one partner.
A 'fling' is a temporary bout of uncharacter-istic hedonism: 'It seems she's in full fling with Valhubert' (N. Mitford, 1960). ? ob.

in heat *see* **on heat**

in heaven etc. dead
Mainly tombstone usage among Christians, or monumental masons, along with 'in the arms of' Jesus, his Maker, the Lord, etc. These uses soften or mask the reality of death, especially to children who may be told a deceased relative is 'in heaven' etc. rather than in the graveyard.

in kindle *see* **in calf** etc.

in left field mad
From Am. football, I suppose, with perhaps a hint of the normal sinister connection: 'Sometimes they make sense and sometimes they're way out in left field' (Sanders, 1985).

in liquor *see* **liquor**

in name only without copulation
Of marriage, especially where the parties have continued to live together: 'My hus-band was . . . in name only' (Ludlum, 1979).

in need of supervision criminal
Police and prison jargon of convicted child-ren and juveniles who have to be locked away. It might suggest that well-behaved children do not need the supervision of adults.

in oestrus *see* **oestrus**

in pig *see* **in calf** etc.

in place of strife strife
A Br. Labour government consultancy document of the late 1960s outlining measures to curb the immunities from law of trade unions and strikers and sponsored by Mrs Castle was so entitled. The opposition by union chiefs led to capitulation by the government and indirectly to Mrs Thatcher.

in pod *see* **in calf** etc.

in protection *see* **protection**

in pup *see* **in calf** etc.

in rut copulating
Properly the sexual excitement of a stag dur-ing the appropriate season: 'I could hear Deborah in rut, burning rubber and a wild boar' (Mailer, 1965). Am. rather than Br. use.

in season able to conceive
Of mammals other than humans, which are also said then to be 'in use': 'That bitch director marched through the offices like a gorilla in season' (Ludlum, 1979). Unlike other mammals, a woman conceives when not bleeding after ovulation and the phrase has the wider meaning of available for cop-ulation: 'The point of women being in sea-son all the time with only brief interruptions . . .' (Amis, 1978).

in the altogether naked
From the biblical passage: 'Thou wast altogether born in sins' (John, ix 34) with the association of nudity; or perhaps merely an abbr. of 'altogether without clothes'.

in the arms of Jesus etc. *see* **in heaven** etc.

in the arms of Morpheus asleep
The expression is used by and of those who should have kept awake. Morpheus, the God of Dreams, was the son of Hypnos, the God of Sleep, but those unversed in Greek myth-ology use father and son interchangeably.

in the bag taken a prisoner of war
Sporting imagery, from what the hunter shoots and so carries: 'Tell him if he tries to stick it out, he'll only end in the bag' (Man-ning, 1977, of WW II).

in the barrel about to be dismissed from employment
Or 'fired', which makes it twice-removed from the SE 'discharged'. Am.

in the black *see* **black market**

in the box copulating
Of a male, from **box** (3) (q.v.) the vagina. When there was more piety and less overt obsession with copulation, a 'good man in the box' was a rousing preacher, the 'box' being the pulpit.

in the business *see* **business**

in the cart in serious difficulty
You could only ride in the cart in Medieval Europe if you were a female, a child, or an old, sick or wounded male. Thus a fit adult male only found himself 'in the cart' on his way to execution, where the method of conveyance both degraded the victim and facilitated the hanging, as the cart could be driven off once the noose was secured.

in the club pregnant
Abbr. for 'pudding club', which is itself an abbr. of the punning 'plum(p) pudding club': 'Chaps having it off get taken aback when young women are put in the club' (Davidson, 1978). Whence 'join the club', to become pregnant.

in the family way pregnant
Probably a corruption of 'in the way of having a family' although only used of a mother and there is often an overtone of unwanted pregnancy: 'But she's not so fucking happy when she's in the family way' (Manning, 1977).

in the hay copulating
Properly, in bed, from the stuffing of a mattress with hay: 'Tell me friend, what's she like in the hay?' (Fraser, 1971).

in the mood ready to copulate
Female usage, especially in the negative when she wishes to avoid copulation with a regular partner: '"I'm not in the mood tonight," Saroya told Robin' (*Daily Mirror*, February 1980).

in the rats suffering from delirium tremens
Army usage. Pink elephants, snakes and rats are the reputed visitors to the delusions of those so afflicted: 'Seeing the pool of sacred snakes . . . . sent him "in the rats"' (Richards, 1936).

in the raw *see* **in the skin etc.**

in the ring engaged professionally in cheating or thieving
A 'ring' is a cartel, from people meeting in a circle and *see* **ring** (2). In modern use of fraudulent antique dealers who combine to buy cheaply at auction and of manufacturers exploiting a joint monopoly. In the 19c. it was used for stealing: 'These parties are connected with the thieves, and are what is termed "in the ring", that is, in the ring of thieves' (Mayhew, 1862).

in the sack copulating
Properly, in a bed and usu. of extra-marital copulation: 'A medical examiner took a smear. The German girl has been in the sack tonight' (Mailer, 1965). But cf. **into the sack**.

in the saddle copulating
Of either sex, using the common equine imagery: 'Elspeth would be back in the saddle with one of her gallants by now' (Fraser, 1971).

in the skin etc. naked
Particularly of nudity in public and breach of convention: 'She must sunbathe in the skin' (L. Thomas, 1979 – from the absence of strap marks). The common 'in the buff' comes from 'buff' as an abbr. of 'buffalo', whence hides, whence leather, whence again skin. 'In the raw' is also of nakedness where you might be reasonably expected to be wearing clothes: 'I know what you were doing in the middle of the bay in the raw' (Sharpe, 1977).

in the sun(shine) *see* **sun has been hot today**

in the tank drunk
The Am. etymology escapes me: 'Spermwhale was almost in the tank, a fifth of bourbon or Scotch in the huge red hand' (Wambaugh, 1975).

in the trade earning a living from prostitution
The phrase covers anyone, pimp, bawd or whore, who makes money out of extra-marital copulation. But the Br. 'in trade' is used derogatively of those who manufacture or distribute goods, by landed or professional people, being an interesting combination of jealousy and snobbery.

in trouble *see* **trouble**

in your cups drunk
You need only one 'cup', if it is large enough, or refilled sufficiently often: '. . . in his cups, could do an admirable soft shoe clog' (Sanders, 1973). Also as a 'cup too many', again without necessarily changing your drinking vessel. In ob. use a 'cup-man' was a drunkard.

incapable drunk
From the Br. legal offence 'drunk and incapable', of a drunkard who had lost physical control, as against 'drunk and disorderly', a rowdy drunkard: 'She was so drunk. Incapable – isn't that the word they use?' (Theroux, 1976).

incident a battle in peacetime
Properly, an occurrence: 'The Phantom dived past, pulling up sharply, with another thunderclap of sound. "We're going to end up with another 'incident'," Kit said grimly' (Masters, 1976). In a 'border incident' opposing soldiers start shooting at each other.

income maintenance State aid to the poor
Am. social service jargon. The recipients do not have to maintain their incomes by working.

income protection arranging your affairs to avoid tax
Although legal, it is looked upon with disfavour, especially by those who have no opportunity to do it themselves: 'Tax avoidance, or as Mr Treyer preferred to call it, Income Protection' (Sharpe, 1978).

incompatible with status spying
In phrase like 'activities', 'behaviour' etc. 'incompatible with status' when a diplomat is caught spying in a host country and declared *persona non grata*.

inconstancy regular extra-marital copulation
Properly, a propensity for change: 'Inconstancy was so much the rule among the British residents in Cairo, the place, she thought, was like a bureau of sexual exchange' (Manning, 1978).

incontinent (1) copulating extra-maritally
Of either sex. Properly, without an interval or delay which would imply a certain robustness. 'Continent' is copulation only within marriage, if at all: 'He had rekindled her . . . . she had never been particularly continent' (le Carré, 1980). 'Continency' is so behaving: 'In her chamber, Making a sermon of continency to her' (Shakespeare, *Taming of the Shrew*).

incontinent (2) urinating or defecating involuntarily
Again from the proper meaning, without interval, and the opposite in this sense too of 'continent'. Medical jargon for a common manifestation of extreme age or sickness, but not used of babies before they have learned the requisite control: 'The geriatric ward, where . . . he found himself surrounded by the senile and incontinent' (G. Greene, 1979). 'Incontinence' is so afflicted: '. . . embarrassed at the incontinence which had overtaken him' (M. Thomas, 1980).

inconvenienced crippled
Am. use as in 'The National Inconvenienced Sportsmen's League' (quoted in Rawson, 1981).

incurable bone-ache syphilis
Not rheumatism or arthritis. Until Fleming's discovery of penicillin, the condition might be arrested but not cured, and mental institutions were full of patients suffering from neurosyphilis, or general paralysis of the insane: 'Now the rotten diseases of the south . . . . incurable bone-ache' (Shakespeare, *Troilus and Cressida*). ob.

incursion an unprovoked attack
Properly, a running into but used in this military sense since 15c.: 'The White House, describing the invasion (or, as it preferred, "incursion") of Grenada' (*The Story of English*, 1986).

indecency an illegal male sexual act
Properly, unseemliness of any kind and used of homosexual and heterosexual behaviour. 'Gross indecency' is buggery or bestiality: '. . . he was arrested by members of the Metropolitan vice squad for an act of gross indecency in Hyde Park' (B. Forbes, 1986). An 'indecent offence' is usu. an illegal homosexual act: 'Accused by fellow officers of an indecent offence with a local youth' (*Private Eye*, July 1980). An 'indecent assault' is nearly always against a woman, with the man seeking sexual gratification, by force if need be, and pinching her buttocks may qualify, if she objects. For 'indecent exposure' *see* **expose yourself**. In the 19c. 'indecency' also covered extra-marital copulation: 'Numbers sleep on the kichen floor, all huddled together, men and women (when indecencies are common enough)' (Mayhew, 1851).

indescribables trousers
From the vintage years of 19c. prudery and *see* **unmentionables** etc. ob.

(Indian hemp and **Indian hay** are common names for Canabis Indica.)

Indian National Army a force formed by the Japanese in WW II from captured Indian soldiers
It was not national, it was not allowed to operate as an army and it never got into India. Nicknamed by Br. Indian troops the 'Jiffs', those induced to join by ill-treatment in camps or other persuasion were despised by most of the three million Indians serving with the Indian Army because of their breach of faith, having eaten the salt of those

whom they deserted. The INA as reconstituted was largely the creation of Subhas Chandra Bose, who visited Hitler in 1941 to win support for Indian independence. He was sent by submarine to Japan, where he formed a 'Provisional Government of Free India'. His 1945 death in a plane crash came as a relief to his former colleagues in Congress, who sought freedom after a Br. victory and not fresh subjugation under the Japanese, although recent attempts have been made in India to re-establish his reputation as a patriot. Wisely the victors, Indian and British alike, dealt leniently with INA captives after the war.

indiscretion a bastard
From a want of care on the mother's part, the father being blameless, it seems. The ob. Eng. 'indiscretions' meant involuntary vomiting, urination or defecation: 'Nurse's vails, *obs.*, a nurse's clothes when penetrated by nepial indiscretions' (EDD – 'nepial' means childish).

indisposed (1) menstruating
Properly, unwell, with common allusion to sickness: '*Flag* 3. A sanitary pad or towel. Hence, *the flag (or danger signal) is up:* she is "indisposed"' (Partridge, DSUE).

indisposed (2) drunk
Again from feeling unwell later and perhaps excusing an absence: 'When a rich man gets drunk, he is indisposed' (Sanders, 1977). Hudson points out that public performers are never 'ill' when they fail to appear, they are 'indisposed' (DDE).

indoctrination camp a political prison
These were the special prisons to which the Chinese Communists sent those who had worked closely with Russians between 1947 and 1959, from which contact they had to be decontaminated.

indulge to drink intoxicants
Properly, to humour or gratify and used normally of those who say they won't or don't: '"Drinks, Chester," she said. "The usual for the Reverend and me. Mr Bigg isn't indulging"' (Sanders, 1980). If you 'over-indulge', you get drunk.

industrial action industrial inaction
Trade union jargon in BI for a strike which has almost become SE. Not used in the plural of more than one strike: 'Khafiq's fight was delayed, successively by industrial actions involving baggage handlers at Heathrow and air controllers in France' (M. Thomas, 1980 – an Am. wrong use of Br.

English). 'Industrial relations' is not the interplay between supplier and customer but the dialogue, or lack of it, between employer and employee.

industrial logic greed
A bid to take over another corporation is often justified on this nebulous ground. The true motives are usu. megalomania, the elimination of competition or a chance of asset-stripping, especially where the victim has been careless about its use of working capital.

inexpressables *see* **unmentionables etc.**

infidelity clandestine extra-marital copulation
Properly, an absence of faith, whence acting dishonestly in any respect: 'In conducting these amours they perpetrate infidelity with impunity' (Mayhew, 1862). 'Infidelities' are a consistent pattern of such conduct with different partners: 'Mavis had seized the opportunity to catalogue his latest infidelities' (Sharpe, 1979).

informal acting illegally or without required permission
Properly, casual or easy-going, which is not one of the properties of a receiver of stolen property, or 'informal dealer': 'No action would be taken against "informal" dealers who came forward, and nor would the money be confiscated' (Davidson, 1978). A street market in BI which is not shut down despite its lack of official licence is called an 'informal market'. etc.

information lies and a selection or suppression of the truth
What is normal in a totalitarian state at all times is also a wartime practice of others. A 'Ministry of Information' controls the issue of, edits, distorts, invents, selects and suppresses news. 'Disinformation' is the publication of rumours and untruths to confuse and mislead.

initiation the first act of copulation
Properly, becoming the member of a club, etc. usu. with due ceremony. Of either sex and 'initiation into womanhood' is specific, as well as being ridiculous when applied to an adult: 'She thought vaguely about the morning and her "initiation into womanhood"' (Boyd, 1982, of a bride on her honeymoon).

initiative a belated reaction
Properly, a first step. It is often used when you try to head off a disaster, such as a 'wage initiative' taken by government which is

trying to check a sequence of inflationary wage settlements; or to describe bureaucratic machinations: '. . . there was a top-level conspiracy – no, wrong word . . . *initiative* . . . a top-level initiative among the Joint Chiefs' (Block, 1979).

inner city slum
Used of derelict housing, abandoned shops etc. which remain when those who can afford to have escaped to the suburbs to avoid noise, taxes, smell and mugging.

inoperative lying
Properly, in this sense, invalid. Part of the language of Watergate where lies were 'inoperative' statements and the current version of the truth was 'operative'.

inquisition torture
It went a lot further than mere questioning when 16c. Spanish priests got their hands on heretics: '. . . the priests who worked for the Inquisition three hundred years ago, and who could prove from the Bible that God *wanted* people racked and tortured' (Keneally, 1979).

insatiable having a wish for frequent copulation
Properly, not capable of satisfaction in any particular respect and of either sex, within or outside marriage: 'Her mother had warned her that men were insatiable, especially in heating climates' (P. Scott, 1977).

inside in prison
Mainly criminal use: '. . . an unfortunate habit to be inside, those who treat H.M.'s prisons as hotels' (Ustinov, 1971).

inside track an unfair or illegal advantage
19c. oval racetracks were operated without staggered starts and the animal on the inside had less far to run than the competition.

insider a person using confidential information to his own advantage
Properly, any person with such knowledge, usu. of a financial deal, whether or not he abuses the confidentiality: 'As an insider, I'll get my arse in a sling if I wheel and deal' (Sanders, 1977). 'Insider-dealing' is dishonestly using the information.

instant bestseller *see* **bestseller**

institutionalize to confine involuntarily
Especially if you are mad: 'Nathan is *insane*, Sophie! He's got to be . . . *institutionalized* ' (Styron, 1976).

instrument the penis
Viewed sexually and with common imagery,

mainly in female use: '. . . he could just touch the cloven inlet with the tip of his instrument' (Cleland, 1749) and Maupassant boasted: 'I can make my instrument stand whenever I please' (Harris, 1925). In my reading only Chaucer's Wife of Bath uses 'instrument' of the vagina.

intelligence spying
The ability to comprehend has been thus debased since the 16c.

intemperance regular drunkenness
The converse of 'temperance', moderation, which is SE for refusal to drink any intoxicants at all: '. . . had, through intemperance, been reduced to utter want' (Mayhew, 1851).

intentions a resolve by a male to marry a specific female
As against intending to continue to enjoy the pleasures and rewards of courtship. Although a girl's father may no longer dare ask a young man what his 'intentions' are, for fear of being told the truth, the concept survives in the rather dated 'my intended', the person whom you have arranged to marry, English having no convenient equivalent for 'fiancé(e)'.

intercourse copulation
Properly, any verbal or other exchange between people and an abbr. of 'sexual intercourse', which could apply to holding hands or kissing, but doesn't: 'Have you ever had intercourse, Dorothy?' (McCarthy, 1963).

interesting condition (an) pregnancy
The condition certainly interests gossips.

interfere with to assault sexually
Journalistic and forensic jargon for extra-marital male physical acts against boys and non-consenting females: 'They are quite alive and nobody has interfered with them, not yet' (N. Mitford, 1960, of boys who had absconded from boarding school).

intermission a period of television advertisements
The temporary cessation becomes a constant interruption on Am. television.

internal affairs the investigation by policemen of allegations against the police
Most police forces are reluctant to wash dirty linen in public, or at all, and complaints against them, often maliciously inspired, are the subject of taboos: 'In Internal Affairs in his sneakers and sweatshirts, investigating complaints against his fellow officers'

(Diehl, 1978). The Russian 'Ministry for Internal Affairs' is the fearsome MVD.

internal security the repression of anti-government action
In a totalitarian state, where the 'internal security' is good, the tyrant dies in office and in bed.

international bestseller *see* **bestseller**

interrogation torture
When a Communist responsible for **internal affairs** (q.v.) does the asking. The KGB 'interrogation with prejudice' uses the same imagery as the CIA 'terminate with extreme prejudice', to kill: '"Interrogation with prejudice" left Viskov crippled and his wife mute (a suicide attempt with lye)' (M.C. Smith, 1981, of Russian prisoners). The Br. 'deep interrogation' in N. Ireland, which involved prolonged discomfort for the victims, was later held to be 'in contravention of human rights'.

intervention a military invasion
Properly, placing yourself between two other parties. The continued use of 'intervention' by the BBC when speaking of the Russian occupation of Afghanistan in 1979 and 1980 caused offence to other than etymologists, even if the events occasioned only muted protests at the time from the usu. vociferous western liberals.

intimacy copulation
The SOD says 'Close familiarity; euphem. for illicit sexual intercourse 1676' – and in every year since then, of both marital and extra-marital copulation: 'A social escort who .... would amateurishly offer "intimacy", as they called it' (Theroux, 1973). So too 'intimate', copulating with: 'You also need a bath and a change. Especially if you propose to be intimate with anyone other than myself' (Bradbury, 1975).

(into deeply interested in is applied alike to respectable and taboo activities. Thus to be 'into etymology' indicates a proper, if eccentric, love of words, while to be 'into leather' shows an improper and socially unacceptable addiction to kinky sexual practices.)

into the sack copulating
From the sl. meaning, into bed, but there is less immediacy than with **in the sack** (q.v.), just as 'into' implies more time for contemplation of what is to come than 'in bed': '"Would you get into the sack with a phallic symbol?" "I go to bed with you, don't I?" she said lightly' (Theroux, 1976).

intrauterine device a female contraceptive worn internally
As with atomic bombs, 'device' always indicates a desire to avoid a direct statement.

intrigue (an) extra-marital copulation
In this sense, an 'intrigue' is a plot, whence something done surreptitiously. Usu. in the plural: '. . . only stipulating for the preservation of secrecy in their intrigues' (Mayhew, 1862, of extra-marital copulation).

introducer's fee a bribe
From the sum paid to the agent who brings contracting parties together: 'As for bribes . . . . this is a capitalist society, General. We prefer to talk about commissions and introducer's fees' (W. Smith, 1979). In ob. London use, an 'introducing house' was a brothel for daytime use, where whores introduced themselves to potential customers: 'Introducing houses, where the women do not reside, but merely use the house as a place of resort in the daytime' (Mayhew, 1862).

invade to copulate with
The male 'invades' the female, on however temporary a basis. Partridge says: 'A literary euphemism' (DSUE) and the OED agrees with him, but only in the sense, to attack personally.

invalid coach a hearse
An invalid description, even if it takes its Am. cargo to a 'slumber room'.

inventory leakage stealing
Not an imperfectly corked bottle in the stores. Used of regular stock losses due to pilferage by customers and employees in large stores.

invert a male homosexual
Fig. turned upside-down, if you are heterosexual: '"We don't call anyone a queer, homo, pouf, nancy or faggot." "What in hell do you call them then?" . . . . "Inverts"' (Bogarde, 1978). Whence 'inverted', homosexual, and 'inversion', homosexuality.

investigate to create, exaggerate, exploit or distort a scandal
But you describe it as enquiry: '"What d'you mean – smear?" "Have it your way – 'investigate', if you prefer. Just so you keep on digging until something starts to smell. Choose your own euphemism"' (Price, 1979). Whence, 'investigative' journalism, reporting, etc.: '"I do investigative reporting

when I think it's needed." "Yeah, investigative, meaning one-eyed, slanted"' (Hailey,
1979).

investment a short-term speculation
This sort of gambling has been facilitated in
London by the two-weekly account system
on the stock market, the aim of fund managers to perform quarterly miracles and the
legal price-ramping which follows: '. . . the
king of the takeover business and his many
satellites and lieutenants were in the regular
habit of making such "investments"' (*Financial Times*, September 1987, of Slater). For
Shakespeare, an 'investment' was what you
wore, and not just beneath your skirt;
whence the 17c. buying goods for trade and
then putting money into any property from
which you look for future benefit. The 19c.
military development, a siege, is not far from
what Slater and others have in mind.

investor a gambler
The usage seeks to delude punters into
thinking that they are not losing their money.

invigorating cold
Of water for swimming, weather for walking,
etc. Anyone who says that participation in
the activity to which they are committed
would be 'invigorating' wants you to suffer
with them.

involved actively and uncritically supporting extreme policy
Mainly sociological jargon: 'Charming girl,
very committed, very involved. You must
have read about her campaign . . .' (Theroux, 1976). Although 'involved' should mean
complex, the people so described are usu.
simple and unthinking. 'Involvement' is such
devotion to extremism.

(Irish is an abbr. for Irish whiskey.)

Irish hoist a kick in the pants
An Am. usage despite which it seems that
the Irish were generally the recipients.

Irish pennant a loose end
In both literal and fig. senses, based on an
Am. patronizing view of the Irish: 'Always
loose ends. You know what they call them in
the Navy? Irish pennants' (Sanders, 1985).

Irish promotion a reduction in wages
The English need constant reassurance
about the supposed lower status and intelligence of the Irish. An 'Irish(man's) rise'
means the same thing.

Irish toothache a pregnancy
Adverting perhaps to the supposed con-

fusion of the Irish, in Eng. eyes, and the
dental troubles of undernourished pregnant
women. In the male, it means an erection of
the penis, and although this condition is not
unconnected with pregnancy, the etymology
escapes me.

Irish(man's) rise *see* Irish promotion

iron (1) a handgun
The metal is inexactly specified, but a 'steel'
has long been a sword or a bayonet: 'He
punched Malvern with the muzzle of the gun
. . . . "Keep your iron next to your own
belly"' (Chandler, 1939).

iron (2) a male homosexual
Rare rh. sl. on 'iron hoof', a pouf.

Iron Curtain the European frontiers of the
Russian subject states
Churchill never acknowledged his debt to
Goebbels for the imagery, nor Goebbels to
Schwerin von Krosigk: 'As soon as the
Soviets have occupied a country, they let fall
an iron curtain' (Goebbels, 1945 in tr.). We
forget too that the Russian *Literary Gazette*
used the same expression in 1930 for what
was seen as a western policy to isolate Russia
from the rest of Europe.

iron out to kill
I suspect not from the Am. 'iron', a gun, but
from the flattening of the victim. Rarely too
as 'iron off'.

irregular *see* **regular (1)**

irregular situation a Roman Catholic
priest who lives and copulates regularly with
a woman
Church jargon. Celibacy of the clergy is
another relic of St Paul's sexual inhibitions,
although they managed without it for the
first 400 years or so.

irregularity (1) *see* **regular (1)**

irregularity (2) dishonesty or fraud
Properly, anything which deviates from the
norm: 'These "irregularities" had allegedly
taken the form of loans she had not repaid
(sic)' (*Private Eye*, April 1981).

it (1) the sexual attraction of the female for
the male
From the 1930s prudery about sex: '"It is
not beauty that makes every head (except
one) turn on the beach to look at her." "It's
IT, my boy," said the Major' (Christie,
1940).

it (2) copulation
A usage without any previous reference to

the subject matter: 'I would have asked you anyway . . . . you see, I like it with you' (Bradbury, 1975, of an invitation to copulate).

it's a big firm my depredations will pass unnoticed
Originally army use, of waste or pilfering and now used in the same senses by those working for a public employer.

itch a wish to copulate
Usu. of a woman, from the supposed aphrodisiac properties of cantherides which, by inducing vaginal itch, is said to stimulate sexual desire: 'A tailor might scratch her where'er she did itch' (Shakespeare, *The Tempest* with another of his obscure sexual puns). Rarely of men in the same sense: 'I was beginning to itch for her considerably' (Fraser, 1969). 'Itchy feet' is the propensity, especially of women, to leave a regular sexual partner for another, without any reference to fungal or other infection – unless you are a prisoner when it denotes an intention to try to escape. *See*, too, **seven-year-itch**.

J

J a marijuana cigarette
From the 'J' in Mary Jane – *see* **Mary** (2) and explicitly as 'J stick' or 'J smoke'. Am.

J Arthur masturbation
Br. rh. sl. on J. Arthur Rank, wank: '. . . having to slip into the bog at the office and give yourself a quick J. Arthur into this little bottle' (Matthew, 1983). The Br. miller and lay reader rather improbably found himself during WWII chairing a company dominating the Br. film business, acquired from the financially versatile Oscar Deutsch, from whom we inherit the Odeon.

jab a vein to inject an illicit narcotic
Addict use: '. . . smoke marijuana or opium, or sniff snow or jab a vein' (Longstreet, 1956). Rarely too as 'jab off'.

jack (1) a penis
One of the male names often used, whence the Am. 'jack off', to masturbate of a male: 'The schmuck hasn't done anything but indict homos and jack-off artists for two years' (Diehl, 1978). Rarely 'jack' can also be semen. The ob. 'jack of both sides' was a male homosexual, perhaps indicating too heterosexuality: 'A Godly and necessary Admonition concerning Neutres, such as deserve the grosse name of Jack of both sydes' (Title of Broadsheet, 1562, quoted in ODEP). 'Jack in the orchard' was copulation and 'jack in the box' was syphilis, being punning rh. sl. on 'pox'.

jack (2) a policeman
Most 'Johns' are also 'Jacks' in familiar speech – see **john** (4): '. . . a uniformed cop was using a small walkie-talkie . . . . Another jack was sitting and writing in a notebook' (Lyall, 1972). Also in Am. CB use as 'jack rabbit'.

jack it in to die
From the meaning, to give up an attempt or enterprise. Rarely too as 'jack it'.

jack off *see* **jack** (1)

jacket a criminal record
From the file cover: '. . . you don't think people like that have jackets, do you?' (Sanders, 1985, of people working in learned professions). Am.

jag house a brothel
A 'jag' was a load, and used of drunkenness just as 'load' is today: 'A man with a "fairish jag on" would be one with rather more intoxicants than he could "carry streck"' (*Yorkshire Weekly Post*, 1899, quoted in EDD). Thus a 'jag house' was an inn where you could get drunk, whence a brothel which today tends to cater mainly for male homosexuals.

jagged drunk
From visiting a 'jag house' or merely feeling rough? Am.

jail bait a sexually mature female below the legal age of copulation
Laws change but human physiology doesn't and we forget that our twelve-year-old girls were thought ready for marriage in the 1920s. The Am. 'jail bait', or CB 'San Quentin jail bait', tempts men to risk imprisonment by copulating with her illegally: 'Two chickies, delicious little morsels of jail bait' (Collins, 1981).

jakes a lavatory
Just as in the modern Am. 'john', you visited 'Jake's place'. Dr Johnson's examples from Shakespeare, Swift and Dryden are all lavatorial, although he defines the word as a house or office, giving two euphemisms for one: 'I will . . . . daub the walls of a jakes with him' (Shakespeare, *King Lear*). Cleland in 1749 uses the singular: '. . . breath like a jake's' but his punctuation is sometimes imperfect. Wits, especially in the 19c., also used 'Ajax', punning on the King of Salamis.

jam to copulate
From the pressing tightly together: '"He had a good grip on her and she closed her eyes and they did it." "Did what?" he said hoarsely. "Jammed"' (Theroux, 1978).

jam tart a whore
Rh. sl. for 'sweetheart' but now almost always abbr. to 'tart': 'Young lady, indeed. She's a tart' (G. Greene, 1932).

jane (1) a whore
In Eng. the derivation was from rh. sl. on 'Jane Shore', the sexual mistress of King Edward IV: 'Louis Quatorze kept about him, in scores, what the Noblesse, in courtesy, term'd his Jane Shores' (Barham, 1840). I suspect Am. has eschewed the monarchic etymology in favour of derivation from the Hungarian 'jany', a girl: 'He happened to bring a couple of beautiful janes along' (Condon, 1966).

jane (2) a lavatory for the exclusive use of women.
A feminine, or feminist, **john** (1) (q.v.).

jar an intoxicant
Usu. beer, from the container: '"Have you been drinking?" "A jar or two," I admitted. "But nothing noticeable"' (Lyall, 1975). If you 'enjoy a jar', the inference is that you are a drunkard.

Jasper a female homosexual
After pondering on the English, Greek, French, Hebrew and Latin meanings, which are all the same and of no relevance, I tracked a rare meaning, variegated. But I suspect the derivation is merely from 'john', a male homosexual playing the male role. Am.

jawbone on credit
You talk the seller into parting with the goods without paying him. Usu. in the Am. phrase, 'buy jawbone', to buy on credit: '. . . men who have more complaints than dollars – individuals who, in digger's parlance, live on JAWBONE (credit)' (London *Times*, October 1862, of inhabitants of San Francisco, not Australia).

jazz to copulate
From the frenzy of the tempo or the ecstatic abandonment? And which came first? To 'jazz yourself' is to masturbate: '. . . thought it the apex of bliss To jazz herself silly' (*Playboy's Book of Limericks*). Am.

jelly roll appertaining to copulation
In Am. Black use it has a variety of meanings examined, along with its African derivation, in *The Story of English* (1986).

jerk off (1) to masturbate yourself
Of a male, from the sharp movement of the hand: 'He's jerking off thirty times a day, that fuckin' guy, and they's all set to give him a medical' (Herr, 1977 – the 'fucking' has to be fig.). You may also be said, if a male, to 'jerk' your maggot or turkey. A 'jerk', someone who so acts, is now quite a mild insult: 'Look, you think this is some penny-ante organization I'm running, you stupid jerk' (Poyer, 1978). Some fig. use: 'I've got the feeling someone is jerking me around, and I don't like it' (Sanders, 1980). The ob. Br. 'jerker' was a whore.

jerk off (2) illegally to inject heroin slowly
You allow the narcotic to mingle with blood in the phial so that eventually you inject a mixture.

jerry a pot for urine
Dr Wright says it is an abbr. of 'Jeremiah, a chamber utensil' (EDD) but for the more ambitious it might have been an abbr. of 'Jeroboam', a bowl or bottle which contains 10 to 12 quarts. No connection probably with the ob. Br. 'Jericho', a lavatory, which was merely one of those unlikely places to which people said they were going. The German soldier, or 'Jerry', wore a helmet of much the same shape but that too is probably only an abbr. of German.

jet-lag sub-acute alcoholic poisoning
Properly, disruption of the biological clock through time change. On long flights many people drink too much alcohol at what seems to be a bargain price, to which you can add tiredness, dehydration from high-altitude flying, lack of exercise and excitement: 'I am still under the weather due to jet lag et al.' (*Private Eye*, March 1981 – he had a massive hangover).

jewels the male genitalia
Am. rather than Br. use, from their pendulate proclivity: 'If I'd given him a bright, "Good morning, Sam!" he'd have kicked me in the jewels' (Sanders, 1979). Sometimes as 'crown jewels' or 'family jewels': '. . . draw up the knees to protect the family jewels' (ibid.).

Jezebel a whore
She was the naughty wife of Ahab: '"But that's . . ." She was about to say "a mortal sin" but desisted. "It makes me a Jezebel, doesn't it?"' (Read, 1986). Long ago you qualified as a 'Jezebel' merely by wearing make-up. Although a stand-by for the vituperative oratory of John Knox and Titus Oates, Dr Johnson missed it but as he intermingles his 'I's' and 'J's' as a single letter, we can overlook this rare lapse.

jig-a-jig etc. extra-marital copulation
From the movement and mainly Far Eastern use: '"Dated her," I said. "You mean a little boom-boom." "Jig-jig," he said. "But it comes to the same thing"' (Theroux, 1978). 'Jiggy-jig' is the next most common form: '. . . the familar cry of "jiggy-jig, Sahib." Very small boys did the soliciting for these native girls' (Richards, 1936, of India). Then come 'jig', 'jiggle', 'zig-zig', etc. The Am. 'jing jang' or 'yin-yang' comes from Eastern symbolism of the male and female genitalia: 'Then I have them by the ying-yang' (Steinbeck, 1961).

jiggle to masturbate
Of a male on his own, from the meaning, to move back and forth: '"Nothing of the sort, he lay there jiggling like." ("I guessed what she meant . . . . frigging himself")' (Harris,

1925, of Carlyle's behaviour on his wedding night. Evidently Mrs Carlyle had more to put up with than the celebrated cup of tea, or less).

Jim Crow the unfair treatment of Black people by Whites
Properly in Am. any poor man. The character came from a song in the Negro minstrel show written by Tom Price (1808–1860): 'It was my first experience with Jim Crow. I was just five, and I had never ridden on a street car before' (L. Armstrong, 1955). Rarely as 'Jane Crow' for such behaviour to Black women in Am.

Jimmy urination
Rh. sl. from 'Jimmy Riddle', to piddle, which is also used by males. Dictionaries tell me there is a punning 'Jerry riddle' too.

job an act the subject of a taboo
Of defecation, mainly in nursery use, and also as **big jobs** (q.v.); of robbery, especially if planned in advance or with forcible entry, as in the film title *The Italian Job*; of copulation, as in **on the job** (q.v.); etc.

job action job inaction
The Am. equivalent of the Br. 'industrial action', the procedure through which employees in concert seek to bring pressure to bear on their employer by failing to do their work properly, or at all, while retaining an entitlement to be paid.

job turning reducing the responsibility and pay associated with an appointment
An Am. phenomenon created by the imposition of **equal pay** (q.v.) and 'equal opportunity', a measure restricting the appointment of a fit White male if there is any other applicant. 'Job turning' occurs when an employer is obliged by law to put a woman in a job for which he thinks a man more suitable and of which the previous incumbent was a male. A feminist will tell you that this is merely another example of males wanting to retain domination over females. A manager will tell you that the change in status reflects the fitness for the post of the new incumbent and he has to find a way round a stupid law to keep his business running. In varying degrees, both are right.

jock a penis
Vulgar on its own: 'He washes his jock in public and he's shy?' (Sharpe, 1977) but almost SE in 'jock-strap', the support worn over the male genitals: '. . . some joker wearing a coconut mask and a feathered jock-strap' (Sanders, 1977). In ob. use to

'jock' was to copulate with a woman and 'jockum', an abbr. of 'jockum gage', a pot for urine.

jocker a male homosexual
From **jock** (above). Sometimes too as 'jockey'.

joe a ponce
Rh. sl. for 'Joe Ronce' whose exploits have not merited an entry in the DNB. The other Br. rh. sl. 'joe' is from 'Joe Hunt', 'cunt' being used perjoratively and not anatomically. In ob. Am. use, a 'joe' was a lavatory.

john (1) a lavatory
From the 'cousin John' Am. men and women were wont to visit: 'Running back and forth, practically living in the john' (Theroux, 1975). In 1983 I was working for a Welsh company operating also in Eng. with a glazing subsidiary called 'Jonwindows'. Apparently I was the only person ever to have asked whether that indicated a rather limited involvement in the market.

john (2) a woman's regular extra-marital sexual partner
He need not necessarily be married to a third party. Am.

john (3) a male homosexual playing the male role
He often lives with another homosexual. There is probably a direct derivation from the ob. Eng. 'John and Joan', a male homosexual in the days when all homosexual males were thought also to be heterosexual, and there were no homosexual females.

john (4) a policeman
An Am. abbr. of 'John Law': 'So the Johns came for him' (Chandler, 1939) and, of the Am. police generally: 'I'd have no trouble with John Law' (Sanders, 1982).

john (5) a possible customer for a whore
Am. prostitutes' jargon: 'Our hustlers sat on their steps and called to the "Johns" as they passed by' (L. Armstrong, 1955).

John Barleycorn *see* **barley cap**

John Thomas etc. a penis
The common use of masculine names and without necessarily sexual inference: 'John Thomas doesn't even have a chance to lift his head' (G. Greene, 1978). I never cease to wonder at the thoughtlessness of Mr and Mrs Standing of my former acquaintance who gave their son these Christian names. 'John Willie' is rarer: 'What I call your penis

and what you prefer to regard as your John Willie' (Sharpe, 1978) – whence perhaps **Willy** (q.v.). The Am. 'Johnnie's out of jail' is an oblique warning of an undone trouser zip.

join to copulate
Of the same tendency as the common 'couple': 'Lovers passed the virulent lice to each other when they joined, fast and secret in some hidden corner' (Keneally, 1982). ? ob.

join hands with to marry
No game of ring-a-roses when marriage too was the subject of reticence and evasion: '. . . the day before his Highness the Prince of Wales was to join hands with the Princess of Saxe-Gotha' (Fowles, 1985, writing in archaic style). ob.

join the club *see* **in the club**

join your dear husband etc. to die
For widows, naturally, in that case but the sentiment appears in all religions which predicate continued physical existence after death, or some form of spiritual continuation or renewal. Thus you may 'join' dead relatives: 'He was about to join his ancestors' (Sharpe, 1978); or wartime comrades: 'It would not be so terrible to join them once again' (Deighton, 1981, of a former German soldier whose friends had been killed in Russia); or all humanity which has predeceased you, when you 'join' the many, the immortals or the great majority: '. . . he was really doing no more than joining that majority' (Price, 1985, of someone dying). The devout even aspire to 'join their Maker'; etc.

joiner a person who seeks popularity or business by attaching himself to associations, etc. in which he has no special interest
Am. pejorative use, but not of someone who works with wood: 'He appeared to be a genial greeter and joiner, an intellectual lightweight' (Sanders, 1977).

joint (1) a marijuana cigarette
Formerly, the equipment of an opium user and I see no clear connection with 'joint', the place where you take part in any communal activity, including the illegal ingestion of narcotics: 'Two or three people can get high on one joint (marijuana cigarette)' (Longstreet, 1956 – he would not need the brackets today).

joint (2) a penis
I imagine from the meaning, a piece of meat

cut ready for cooking: '. . . drawings of a man's joint, a woman's cooze' (Sanders, 1982). To 'unlimber your joint' is to urinate, of a male: '. . . graffiti . . . . where males unlimbered their joints' (Styron, 1976). Am.

jolly (1) drunk
A rarer use than **merry** (q.v.). Today a 'jolly' is a drunken occasion to which usu. only men are asked; or an enjoyable but unnecessary trip at another's expense by politicians, union officials, etc. ostensibly in the line of duty. The ob. Eng. 'jolly' of a bitch meant able to conceive: 'Nine days jolly, Nine weeks in belly, Nine days blind, That's a dog kind' (Old proverb).

jolly (2) fraudulently to inflate bidding at an auction
When the auctioneer 'jollies things along'.

jolly (3) an act of extra-marital sexual behaviour
Homosexual or heterosexual, from the business meaning, an enjoyable though unnecessary trip, paid for by another, or from **jolly** (1) (above): '. . . found the names of Thomas J. Kealy and Constance Underwood, and what they had been paying for their jollies' (Sanders, 1984 – the names were in a prostitute's notebook).

jolt anything taboo which gives you a shock or impetus
For narcotic addicts, an injection of heroin; for criminals, a term in prison; for drinkers, an intoxicant, usu. whisky: 'I think maybe I'll get a jolt too' (Sanders, 1982) or specifically: 'I went out to the kitchenette and poured a stiff jolt of whisky' (Chandler, 1939); etc.

Jordan a pot for urine
Dr Johnson spells it 'jorden' and suggests derivation from Greek. ODEE says: 'Early forms with u do not support the conjecture of deriv. from the River Jordan' but I am less sanguine where pre-1850 spelling is concerned and the synonym 'chamber' has 19 different ways of being spelt in EDD, which makes a redundant 'u' small beer: 'Thou will allow us ne'er a jordan, and then we leak in the chimney' (Shakespeare, 1 *Henry IV*). 'Jordeloo' was the warning in Edinburgh after 10pm that urine was about to be thrown into the street from an upper room, a compound of 'jordan' and 'below' or 'l'eau', just as 'gardyloo' – gardez l'eau – heralded the descent of other liquids.

joy (1) pertaining to extra-marital copulation
For male or female, as in 'mutual joy':

'. . . the woman . . . . seeking mutual joys courts him to run the complete race of love' (Lucretius in tr.). A 'joy' girl or sister is a whore: 'The gambling casino on the lake, and the fifty-dollar joy girls' (Chandler, 1953) who may work in a 'joy house' or brothel: 'I ain't been in a joy house in twenty years' (Chandler, 1940). The punning 'joy ride' is a single act of copulation: 'I feel no fatigue, indeed, I feel the better for our joy ride' (Harris, 1925 – he never wasted time by taking a girl for a spin in the park). 'Joy stick', a penis, is punning if tasteless rh. sl. on 'prick' and the aircraft control column. The 'joy bag' is not the scrotum but a contraceptive sheath; etc.

joy (2) relating to the illicit use of narcotics
In many compounds, like 'joy popper', an occasional user; 'joy powder', morphine; 'joy flakes', cocaine; 'joy rider', a person who takes narcotics on a single occasion; 'joy smoke', marijuana; 'joy stick', an opium pipe; etc.

joy ride to take and drive away a motor vehicle without consent
Under the old Br. larceny rules, this was not a criminal offence unless there was proof of intention 'permanently to deprive the owner thereof', and it was usu. impossible to establish a theft of fuel. Still an addictive activity of some young criminals.

Judy a whore
Probably from the common girl's name, which became a name for common girls. In ob. Br. use, it also meant a sexual mistress: 'He went tul his wife at Wortley, an his judy went to Rotherham' (*Dewsbro Olm*. 1866, quoted in EDD).

jug a prison
Although probably from the Sc. 'joug', a pillary, as 'He set an old woman in the jougs' (W. Scott, 1814), this 19c. development may also owe something to the confining nature of a stone vessel. To 'jug' is to imprison: 'He is arrested. He is jugged' (Manning, 1960).

jugged drunk
The common culinary imagery, although today we only 'jug' hares, or from the vessel which held the damaging fluids.

juggle to copulate
If Shakespeare was running true to form, punning on the play with balls: 'She and the Dauphin have been juggling' (1 *Henry VI*). ob.

jugs a woman's breasts
Probably from the visual resemblance of pendant breasts, with an allusion to milk: 'Blue eyes. Peaches-and-cream complexion. Big jugs' (Sanders, 1971). Grose tells us that a 'double jug' was 'a man's backside'.

juice (1) an intoxicant
The common modern use probably came from the proper meaning, liquid of fruit etc., rather than from the Sc. 'juice of the bear', whisky. 'Juniper juice' was gin but 'the juice' means any intoxicant: 'The cops will probably want you so stay off the juice' (Deighton, 1972). To 'juice' is to drink spirits: '. . . would gather after a long day in the IO shop to juice a little' (Herr, 1977 – in fact they gathered in the IO shop after a long day elsewhere). Whence too 'juiced', drunk; 'juice head', a drunkard; 'juice joint', a bar; etc.

juice (2) a payment demanded or made illegally
What comes in Am. if you **squeeze** (q.v.). Of extortionate rates of interest, made by a 'juice dealer', or loan shark, and collected by a hoodlum or 'juice man'; of the proceeds of organized vice; of bribes: 'The bookie was a big operator and sent his juice money directly to City Hall' (Weverka, 1973 – he actually sent it 'direct' without an intermediary but not necessarily promptly).

juiced up desiring immediate copulation
Of a female, from the vaginal secretion: '. . . he knew how to get a girl juiced up better than anyone she'd ever known' (M. Thomas, 1982, of a philanderer).

juju a marijuana cigarette
Probably an Am. abbr. of 'marijuana' but referring to the Black African connection: 'I knew a guy once who smokes jujus' (Chandler, 1940).

(juke house was a brothel from Gullah, before achieving comparative respectability from the automatic musical devices placed there for the further delectation or otherwise of visitors.)

jumbo drunk
Br. rh. sl. from 'jumbo's trunk'. In supermarket language 'jumbo' means big.

jump (1) to rob
From the pouncing. An Eng. 18c. use since revived in Am.: 'Instead of "jumping" those stores for an average of forty dollars' (Lavine, 1930).

jump (2) to abscond without paying
Of the same tendency as the SE 'jump bail':
'She jumped her bill' (Chandler, 1939). ? ob.

jump (3) a single act of copulation
A male usage but he does not have to leap on
to the female: 'You've never had a quick
jump in the hay in your life' (Steinbeck,
1961). To 'jump' is to copulate extra-
maritally and a 'junior jumper' is a youthful
rapist. The ob. Br. 'jump the besom' meant
to cohabit and copulate after banns but
before marriage, the'besom' being a whore
as well as a type of broom. 'Jumping'
brooms implied extra-marital copulation in
various parts of BI and a 'broomstick match'
was a Common Law marriage: 'I never had a
wife but I have had two or three broomstick
matches' (Mayhew, 1851).

jump ship to desert
It should be the opposite of keelhauling. SE
of seafarers and rarely used of others:
'Moscow Centre officers who were thinking
of jumping ship' (le Carré, 1980).

jump the last hurdle to die
With steeplechasing in mind.

junk illegal narcotics
Properly, old rope, whence hemp, whence
narcotics generally. A 'junkie' is an addict:
'A cheap junkie's arms and legs are covered
with unhealed scabs' (Longstreet, 1956). A
'junker' in this world is not a Prussian aristo-
crat but a peddler in narcotics, as is a
'junkman': 'I just retired a junkman' (Diehl,
1978, of killing one such). 'Junked up' is
under narcotic influence: 'Will you go out
now, before he gets junked up for the
evening?' (Chandler, 1939).

just good friends *see* friends

(**justify** is an interesting illustration of the
misunderstanding or confusion which can
arise from the use of euphemism. From the
old Sc. sense, to bring to justice, it came to
mean either to acquit or to kill by execution.
When Sir Walter Scott wrote in 1817 'Our
great grand uncle that was justified at Dum-
barton' we have to read on to learn uncle's
fate.)

K

KGB *see* **Committee of State Security**

(Kaffir a Black African is an insulting usage by White residents in South and East Africa: 'The South African troops had loudly vowed to sort out any "bleddy kaffirs" they found' (Boyd, 1982). It should apply to a member of the Bantu tribe, or to a native of Kafiristan in Asia.)

kangaroo court an ad hoc investigation in which the issues are prejudged
Prison and trade union usage and practice for summarily disciplining those who fail to comply with unenforceable instructions. The offender has fig. to 'jump to it', like the marsupial. A prison 'kangaroo club' is a body of long-serving inmates: 'He was president of the Kangaroo Club and would hold court to instruct them in their duties' (Lavine, 1930, of new inmates).

kayo to kill
From the boxing 'KO', or knock-out: '. . . this stiff got kayoed around the end of October' (Diehl, 1978).

keel over to die
From the capsizing of a boat: 'He told me he might keel over at any time' (A. Waugh, *Private Eye*, August 1980).

keelhauled drunk
It was Dutch practice to drag defaulters under the keel of a boat for punishment and we still use the word of a verbal reprimand. If you were dead drunk, you might look and later feel like a victim of 'keelhauling': 'They wad fuddle an' drink till they were keelhaul'd' (W. Anderson, 1867). Probably ob.

keep to maintain a sexual mistress
This 16c. euphemism implies both provision for her upkeep and keeping her sexual activities for yourself: 'One officer offered to keep me if I would come and live with him' (Mayhew, 1862). A 'kept woman' is not one who receives housekeeping money from her husband: 'Most kept women have several lovers . . . . and in ninety-nine cases out of a hundred escape detection' (ibid.). 'Kept mistress' is explicit: 'It is a mistake to suppose that kept mistresses are without friends and without society' (ibid. – in the same passage Mayhew had alleged that most of them have 'several lovers'). 'Kept wench' is rarer: 'Virgins, reporters, housewives, kept wenches' (Longstreet, 1956 – but which was

the oddity in that class?). The male was a 'keeper', which we now reserve for a custodian of animals in a zoo: '. . . amongst the kept mistresses . . . . I hardly knew one that did not perfectly detest her keeper' (Cleland, 1749).

keep company with to copulate with extra-maritally
Properly, to accompany, whence, in SE to court: 'Their sweethearts or husbands have been keepin' company with some one else' (Emerson, 1890). And *see* **company** (1).

keep sheep by moonlight to be killed by hanging
You watch over them from the gallows. I include this ob. Eng. entry as an excuse for quoting: '. . . that shepherded the moonlit sheep a hundred years ago' (Housman, 1890).

keep up with the Jones's to live beyond your means
The 'Jones's' are your mythical neighbours who always seem to be able to afford the new curtains your wife coveted or the garden tractor your husband has been collecting brochures about.

keep your legs crossed to refuse to copulate
Of a female, of extra-marital copulation, and often in the negative: 'I don't think she keeps her legs crossed all the time' (Price, 1972). Less often as 'keep your legs together': '. . . had kept her legs tightly together' (Price, 1975, of a woman who had not copulated).

kerb crawling looking for a whore
Usu. of a man who drives slowly in part of a town frequented by whores. He may also, but rarely, be a pedestrian, and the phrase is used too of whores soliciting male pedestrians while travelling slowly in a car.

key the penis
From the manner of its entry into a lock, whence 'keyhole', the vagina viewed sexually. A 'key party' is a sexual orgy in which females pair with males after the supposedly chance selection of a key from those thrown into a central pile

Khyber the anus
Br. rh. sl. for 'Khyber Pass', the arse. You hear it most, but not very often at that, in the vulgar riposte 'up your Khyber', whence a punning Br. title 'Carry on up the Khyber' for a film which contrived to live down to it in vulgarity and banality.

kick (1) to die
Probably from the involuntary spasms of a killed animal. Usu. as 'kick' in, it, off or up: 'Thou'se no kick up, till thou's right aul' (Picken, 1813). The common 'kick the bucket' – from which 'kick it' probably comes – is supposed by OED and others to derive from the 'bucket' or beam from which you tied a Norfolk pig to facilitate slitting its throat and which it then kicked in its death throes. Lexicographers are plagiarists, and that kind of etymology tends to have special appeal for them. I suspect 'kick the bucket' merely comes from a preferred method of those who kill themselves, or others, by stringing the victim up to a beam, and then kicking away the upturned bucket on which he was standing: 'It all went. So he kicked the bucket, literally' (Sanders, 1977, of a suicide). The ob. 'kick the wind' was to be killed by hanging, from the death movement and the subsequent tenure of the gallows by the corpse. The rare 'kick your heels' puns on idleness: 'In a few moments most of them would be kicking their heels in a different world from this one' (Richards, 1933).

kick (2) the peremptory dismissal from employment
Usu. of a single employee, who 'gets the kick', but the violence is only fig.

kick stick a marijuana cigarette
From the 'kick', or thrill, smoked alone or at a 'kick party'. To 'kick the gong around', to smoke narcotics illegally, puns on the excitement and the symbolic oriental gong.

kick the habit *see* habit

kickback a clandestine illegal payment
The derivation must be from the vicious habits of starting handles in the days before cars had electric starters. Of hidden commissions, percentages or the proceeds of vice or bribes: 'It's the job if I get a kickback' (Chandler, 1939).

kid an adult
A child since the 16c., before which it was only the young of a goat. Untypically missed by Dr Johnson and his team. Now used to minimize age: 'He was still a kid, no more than thirty, thirty-two' (M. Thomas, 1980). In ob. Eng. use to 'kid' also meant to impregnate, or to give birth, of both women and goats.

kidnapper an elderly male marrying a young female
Pejorative rather than jocular use, and no subsequent demands for ransom. Rarely too

of an older woman marrying or seeking the companionship of a much younger man.

kife whores
In Am. circus jargon, it means to swindle. MBD also gives 'male homosexuals' but I have not seen that elsewhere and I suspect that Mrs Byrne is wrong.

killed while trying to escape *see* **trying to escape**

kilo connection a dealer in illegal narcotics
In this business, a kilo is a large amount, and *see* **connect** (2). It is at this stage that the narcotics are usu. adulterated before being passed down the distribution chain. Am.

kind copulating without payment
From the meaning, friendly or considerate and of a female extra-maritally – within marriage males tend to think they copulate as of right. Of a male, it means exercising tenderness or restraint in copulation: '"Your highness", he said at last, "will you be kind to our treasure" .... It's a polite way of suggesting you don't make too much of a beast of yourself on the honeymoon' (Fraser, 1970).

king Lear a male homosexual
Br. rh. sl. for 'queer' with perhaps a passing thought to the monarch's madness.

king over the water a Stuart pretender in exile
Possibly used of Charles II and James II during their 17c. absences from the throne and certainly much in vogue after the Hanoverian kings took over after Queen Anne died in 1714: 'He so far compromised his loyalty, as to announce merely "The King", as his first toast .... Our guest .... added, "Over the water"' (W. Scott, 1824). You normally passed your wine glass over your glass of water without venturing verbal amplification. In retrospect, it all seems a little childish but loyalty to the Stuarts also implied adherence to Roman Catholicism, which in turn involved civil disabilities if not persecution.

king-sized the biggest
It also means the fattest in Am. Puff perhaps more than euphemism and the royal frame is not necessarily outsize.

kingdom-come death
Despite our generally unsatisfactory experience with theocracies, we do not demur at the plea in the Lord's Prayer: 'Piper being

blown to Kingdom Come in the company of Mrs Hutchmeyer' (Sharpe, 1977).

kinky displaying bizarre sexual tastes
A 'kink' is a bend, as in a hosepipe, and 'kinky' implies a number of deviations. Formerly only of male homosexuality: 'And you said last night he was "that kind" .... funny, kinky' (Bogarde, 1981). Now used of any perverted extravagance.

(kip sleep, comes from the Danish 'kippe', a small inn. In ob. Eng. use, it meant a brothel.)

kiss to copulate with
This dates from the era when you only kissed within the family. If you got that far with someone of the opposite sex to whom you were not related, there was no stopping further progress. Whence the euphemistic definition of Dr Wright: 'Obs. To lie with a woman' (EDD). If you 'kissed St Giles' cup', you were killed by hanging, from the practice of offering the victim a cup of water of St Giles in the Fields on his final journey from Newgate to Tyburn. To 'kiss the cap' was to drink intoxicants to excess, 'cap' meaning cup, and a 'kiss the cap' was a drunkard. To 'kiss the counter' or 'kiss the clink' was to go to prison. To 'kiss the ground' was to die: 'I will not yield to kiss the ground before young Malcolm's feet' (Shakespeare, *Macbeth* – although here it could mean to pay homage). All these Br. uses are ob.

kiss-off (1) the summary dismissal from employment
From the gesture of parting On the Am. west coast, you may call it a 'New York kiss-off', in New England a 'California kiss-off', which shows we still impute bad habits or behaviour to our rivals. Some fig. use, as when you bring a conversation to a polite close: '"Yes. Sure. Fine," Delaney said heavily, feeling this was just a polite kiss-off' (Sanders, 1973).

kiss-off (2) to die
An Am. use, again from the gesture of parting.

kiss-off (3) to engage in fellatio
From the use of the mouth. Rarely too, without much logic, of buggery.

Kit has come I am menstruating
'Kit' is an abbr. of Charles and *see* **Charlie** (1). BI.

kite to issue a negotiable instrument uncovered by the drawer
Abbr. of the 19c. 'fly a kite', which had the same meaning, from launching something without support: '"Just don't start kiting checks," Delaney warned' (Sanders, 1985). The device was widely used to obtain credit through the banking system while a cheque was being cleared but the advent of computers has stopped it being done with safety on a regular basis. A 'kiteman' still tries, however.

kitty the vagina viewed sexually
A variant of **pussy** (q.v.), whence the double-punning saw: 'A thrifty tom-cat puts something in the kitty every day'. In ob. Eng. use a 'kitty' was a prison or lock-up, from which we probably get the central pool in a game of cards.

knackered *see* **knackers**

knackers the testicles
A knack was a toy or small object and he who made it was a knacker, whence a saddler and then someone who brought old horses for their hides. The use may have come simply from the 'small object' meaning. Partridge says, 'Prob. ex dial knacker, a castanet or other "striker".' (DSUE – the imagery of the small Spanish chestnut is persuasive) but as usu. I prefer Dr Wright's 'Two flat pieces of wood or bone' especially when he adds 'Of unequal length' (EDD). To be (k)nackered is to be exhausted, usu. of a male and almost certainly with copulation imagery where it is synonymous with being 'fucked'.

knee-trembler a whore who copulates while standing up
Of obvious derivation. Both parties are said to be 'knee-trembling', if so engaged.

knees up copulating
Of a female, from a common attitude: '... he's had more hot dinners in my house than I've had nights with my knees up' (Lyall, 1972).

knight a person associated with any illegal, taboo or despised occupation was a source of much Br. wit. A 'knight of Hornsey' was a cuckold, punning on the London borough and the horn of cuckoldry; a 'knight of the road' was a mounted thief; my favourite is the 'knight of the Golden Fleece', for a lawyer; etc.

knock it back to drink intoxicants to excess
Once, or many times, perhaps from angling the glass as you drink: '... he'd begun to knock it back at half-past ten in the morning' (P. Scott, 1977).

knock off etc. (1) to kill

As a bird from a branch but an Am. use of humans too: 'So you wouldn't knock him off . . . but you might throw a scare into him' (Chandler, 1939). 'Knock on the head' comes from the slaughtering of cattle for meat, but is also used of killing humans by any method. To 'knock down' is to kill animals by shooting: 'She knocked down squirrels with exquisite faces' (Mailer, 1965).

knock off (2) to copulate with extra-maritally

The male 'knocks off' the female, usu. in a casual relationship in which he is careful not also to knock her up. A 'knock' is such an event: 'Throw her away and she'll always come back for another weekend of cheap knock' (Fowles, 1977). And *see* **knocking shop etc.**

knock off (3) to steal

Of minor thefts, from the concept of dislodging something from a counter or barrow.

knock off (4) to drink intoxicants

Usu. beer, and specifying in pints the amount consumed. And *see* **knock it back.**

(All these meanings of 'knock off' seem to owe nothing to the principal sl. use, to stop doing something, or to cease work.)

knock out a fraudulent auction

There is usu. a conspiracy between the auctioneer and some of the bidders. Auctioneers' jargon which puns on 'knock down', to register a sale by the fall of the hammer, and the boxing term, to render unconscious.

knock over to kill

By shooting, from hunting jargon: 'I heard . . . . he had been knocked over in the last month of the war . . . . the rumour proved false . . . . he is alive and kicking' (Richards, 1933).

knock up to impregnate a female

Usu. of unwanted pregnancy in an unmar-ried woman: '. . . they told me that seven of the girls were knocked up – well, pregnant' (N. Mitford, 1960). This use has now virtually displaced the former meanings, to wake by knocking or, as 'knocked up', exhausted.

knocker a penis

From the shape of a door knocker, and punning on its sexual function – *see* **knock off** (2): 'Susie was a perfect fool for any chap with a big knocker' (Fraser, 1982). ? ob.

knockers a woman's breasts

Probably, as with **knocker** (above), from the shape of old door knockers and their movement in a vertical plane when activated.

knocking shop etc. a brothel

From the ob. 'knock', to copulate: 'At the fifth knocking-shop, I struck pure gold' (Fraser, 1971 – the gold was fig. He found a bawd to hide him). Formerly as a 'knocking' house or joint also.

knot to copulate

From the meaning, to unite: 'A cistern for foul toads To knot and gender in' (Shakespeare, *Othello*). I am not sure about: '. . . young people knotting together, and crying out "Porridge"' (Pepys, 1662). ob.

know to copulate with

It was a euphemism in Hebrew, Greek and Latin which explains why the translators for King James I (of England) found it so useful: 'And he knew her not till she had brought forth her first-born son' (Matthew: 25, of Joseph and Mary). We still use 'knowledge' for copulation.

know the score *see* **score** (1)

knuckle sandwich a punch in the face

Not meat from near the joint of a pig placed between slices of bread: 'First the velvet glove, then the knuckle sandwich' (Sanders, 1977). Am.

(Kojak a policeman in Am. CB sl. comes from a television detective.)

L

labour (1) childbirth
Properly, physical toil but so long SE that we do not think about it.

labour (2) unemployment
The former Br. Ministry of Labour existed to try to place the involuntarily unemployed in work, operating through a series of 'Labour Exchanges', which also gave State aid to the needy. Thus to be 'on the labour' was both to be without work and in receipt of such funds.

labour education arbitrary imprisonment on political grounds
A Chinese prison regime of work and harangues. A Chinese woman who wished to marry a French diplomat was in 1981 accused of 'illegally living together with a foreigner' and sentenced to two years 'Re-education through labour' (*Daily Telegraph*, November 1981).

lack of moral fibre cowardice
Mainly Br. WWII military use, often as 'LMF': '. . . stamped on the record of failed officers. *Lack of moral fibre*. If Second-Lieutenant Audley suffered from LMF . . .' (Price, 1978).

ladies a lavatory exclusively for female use
Often as 'ladies' convenience, room, toilet, etc.: 'I tapped a kidney in the ladies room' (Theroux, 1978). Men use 'gentlemen'.

lad an exclusive male extra-marital sexual partner
Mainly a N. Eng. use: 'But when I was nineteen he sought me out and he became my lad' (Cookson, 1969). So too with **lass** (q.v.).

lads a lavatory exclusively for male use
You may see this in a trendy restaurant, which will then have a corresponding 'lassies', for females. Unhappily this usage is not confined to Scotland.

lady a whore
As in the oldest of jokes: '"Who was that lady I saw you with last night?" "That was no lady; that was my wife"'. In ob. use a 'ladies' college' was a brothel where you might contract 'ladies' fever', or syphilis. In many compounds as follows:

    lady boarder a whore who worked in a brothel: '. . . played for the lady-boarders and their friends' (Longstreet, 1956).

    lady of a certain description a whore: 'There are two kinds of person who supply the police with all the information they want; one, that of unmarried ladies of a certain description . . .' (James, 1816).

    lady of easy virtue a whore, with 'easy' meaning compliant.

    lady of intrigue a woman who sought to conceal extra-marital copulation: 'By ladies of intrigue we must understand married women who have connection with other men than their husbands and unmarried women who gratify their passions secretly' (Mayhew, 1862). ob.

    lady of no virtue a whore, although no less adept at the job than other whores: 'So when he visited ladies of no virtue, it might be for purposes of fornication . . .' (Masters, 1976).

    lady of pleasure a whore, not to be confused with a 'lady of leisure'. A 'pleasure house' is brothel.

    lady of the night a whore, but no more nocturnal than her colleagues: 'The lady of the night studied Abel carefully' (Archer, 1979).

etc., etc.

lady bear *see* **bear** (2)

lady dog a bitch
The very fastidious want to avoid any hint of confusing the inoffensive quadruped with the spiteful and domineering biped.

lady friend a female with whom a male regularly copulates extra-maritally
She does not have to be a woman of breeding or distinction, but the use implies slightly more acceptability than **woman friend** (q.v.): 'It's my lady friend. I've reason to suspect that she's getting a bit on the side' (James, 1972).

lady in waiting a pregnant woman
Mainly humorous use, punning on the Court official. The ob. Eng. 'lady in the straw' was in process of being delivered of a baby.

ladybird a whore
Apart from the insect, it meant 'sweetheart': 'What, lamb! What, ladybird! God forbid' (Shakespeare, *Romeo and Juliet*). ob.

Lahore house a brothel
Punning on the Indian city, although I never heard it used in India: '"Bad girls here," said the tonga driver . . . . but I saw none, and

nothing resembling a Lahore house' (Theroux, 1975 – perhaps it was just his pun).

laid to rest dead and buried
A monumental favourite. The ob. 'laid in the lockers' meant death at sea, from the storage of the corpse for subsequent burial on land. But if you died at sea beyond the Thames estuary town of 'Gravesend', you were burried at sea.

lame duck (1) the holder of an office who has failed to secure re-election
His successor will have been elected on a different platform and until the handover he lacks effective power. I suspect Peter Pindar was merely being rude when he described Pitt as 'A duck confounded lame Not unattended waddling' because that may well precede the 19c. use, 'a stockjobber who speculates beyond his capital, and cannot pay his losses. Upon retiring from the Exchange he is said to "waddle out of the alley"' (*The Slang Dictionary*, 1874).

lame duck (2) a failing business
Especially in a declining industry where overmanning, change of trade or chronic lack of investment make unaided survival unlikely. The politically inexperienced Minister John Davies used the phrase of Br. firms seeking State aid, and later wished he had chosen his words better.

lamp habit *see* chef

lance to copulate with
Properly, to pierce, with the common male thrusting imagery: 'She would fall in a faint, And only revive when lanced freely' (*Playboy's Book of Limericks*).

land of Nod sleep
A pun on Cain's travels when he 'dwelt in the land of Nod' (Genesis iv 16). Formerly of sleep generally: 'There's queer things chanced since ye hae been in the land of Nod' (W. Scott, 1818) but now only nursery use for coaxing children to bed in the frightening dark.

(landing officer a prison warder.
Br. prison jargon, and perhaps more pomposity than euphemism. He looks after rows of cells, or 'landings'.)

landscaped tidied up
Properly, made to look scenically attractive. Real estate agents and builders use it of any housing development where most of the rubble has been removed from the site or covered with an inch or two of earth. In either case the topsoil will have disappeared.

language swearwords
An abbr. of 'foul-language': 'I'll have no man usin' language i' my house' (D. Murray, 1886 – he was not a Trappist abbot).

language arts the ability to speak coherently
Sociological and educational jargon. You must never imply that any child comes from an environment or has a defect which prevents it speaking normally. Am.

lard dishonestly to increase a claim for repayment
You enrich the mix by adding too much fat: 'The housekeeper at Twin Beeches regularly larded her books with non-existent bills' (Deighton, 1972).

large (1) pregnant
Rare female use: 'It was when I was large with our Lizbeth' (EDD).

large (2) small
Well, smaller than 'family' or 'jumbo' in supermarketspeak: 'The smallest tube of toothpaste you can buy is the "large size"' (Jennings, 1965). *See also* economy.

lass *see* lad

lassies *see* lads

last call etc. death
In various combinations reflecting the finality of death, and sometimes referring to the dead person's job. Thus the 'last curtain' falls on actors who may take their 'last bow', while cowboys head for the 'last round-up'. To pay our 'last debt' does not imply comment on the solvency of our estate, and the 'last trump' is not for card players but for all those who hear the call to the seat of judgement. The 'last end' and 'last resting place' are specific, at least until the resurrection. The 'last rattler' is not for the commuter who will take the train no more and set out on his 'last voyage', but from the noise of congested breathing which may precede death. If you are 'at your last', death is near: '. . . which he sent me when he was at his last' (Mayhew, 1962, and not of a cobbler). etc.

last favour (the) extra-marital copulation
Granted by the female after prior familiarities. However the ob. Br. 'last shame' was a term of imprisonment.

last waltz to walk to execution by electrocution
A waltz traditionally ends the ball. Am.

latchkey subject to parental neglect
Of children who have nobody to greet them
when they return home from school, etc.:
'"In a world of latchkey children," he said,
"children whose only companion is the television set . . ."' (M. Thomas, 1985). The
incidence in any area of juvenile deliquency
correlates precisely with what bureaucrats
choose to call the female activity rate, the
percentage of women who work outside the
home. Women are not alone in seeing the
achievement of 'liberation' accompanied by
unwanted consequences.

late (1) newly dead
Venerable enough to have been used by
Caxton in 1490 but still often confused with
unpunctuality. The ob. 'latter end' meant
death.

late (2) failing to menstruate when expected
With fears of unwanted pregnancy: 'He
thought of her telling him she was late, had
never been late before, and was he going to
walk out on her' (Seymour, 1980).

late developer a poor scholar
Used by parents who have hope rather than
by teachers who have experience: 'She was a
late developer and a bit of a slow-coach'
(Murdoch, 1977).

late disturbances etc. a recent war
'Late' means former: 'The year of 1688
brought to England the worst turmoil since
the "late disturbances", as Mr Pepys had
once described a brutal civil war and a royal
beheading' (Monsarrat, 1978). In the same
way 'late unpleasantness' was used in the
south of the Am. Civil War and widely by the
protagonists in WWI.

latrine a lavatory
Like 'lavatory' itself, descended from the
Latin 'lavare', to wash. Usu. of primitive and
communal structures, as in the army: 'Latrines . . . . often consisted of no more than a
small mud hut with an open door' (Allen,
1979).

latter end the buttocks
'Latter' means final. Also as 'latter part'.

laughing academy an institution for
lunatics
Not a school for comedians but from a
symptom of insanity: 'The way you're going
in to bat to get the old man back in the
laughing academy' (Wambaugh, 1975).

launder to bring tainted cash into open circulation in apparent legality
You are 'washing' money which has been

stolen, is the proceeds of vice or undeclared
income: '. . . accused of "laundering" some
of the marked banknotes used to pay the
Schild ransom' (*Daily Telegraph*, July 1980).
Also of public funds secretly diverted from
the purpose for which they were voted:
'Cash from various Ministries is "laun-
dered" and diverted to the secret service'
(*Daily Mirror*, February 1980). A 'laundry' is
a bank or seemingly legal trading concern
through which such money passes.

lavabo a lavatory
'I will wash', from the Latin and Psalm xxvi,
and still used interchangeably with 'lavatory',
but not very often: 'They follow me even to
the lavabo' (Theroux, 1975).

lavatory a place set apart for urination and
defecation
Properly, a vessel for washing in, and then
the place where you went to wash: 'Remember that our "lavatory" is really a
euphemism' (E. Waugh, 1956, but I use it
passim to define others).

lavender related to male homosexuality
Scent is made from the plant and the use of
perfume by males used to indicate homosexuality. An Am. 'lavender convention' is a
meeting of male homosexuals, or 'lavender
boys'.

law and order brutal repression of the
poor
Properly, adequate police protection for person and property. The phrase has overtones
of excessive police or para-military zeal,
especially against Blacks in a society with a
majority of Whites, or in ghettos.

lay to copulate with
The male usu. 'lays' the female, from his
superior attitude perhaps, or from assisting
her to a prone position: 'Laying me's part of
your terms of service?' (Bradbury, 1975).
Shakespeare used 'lay down': 'The sly
whoresons have got a speeding trick to lay
down ladies' (*Henry VIII*). A male may 'lay a
leg' across, on or over a female: 'Whar was a'
his noble equals when he bute to lay a leg un
my poor lassie?' (Graham, 1883). Shakespeare also uses 'lay it' for a woman's
restoring a penis from an erect to a flaccid
state by copulation: 'To raise a spirit in his
mistress' circle Of some strange nature, letting it there stand Till she had laid it and
conjured it down' (*Romeo and Juliet*). 'Laid',
meaning copulated with, usu. refers to the
less experienced party, whether male of
female: 'A place where even the most dif-

fident foreigner can get laid' (Theroux, 1975). A 'lay' is a woman who copulates extra-maritally, usu. with male laudatory adjectival embellishment – the 'bad lays' are not talked about, if there are any. A 'lay' is also an act of extra-marital copulation: 'He smiled to himself, watching her, thinking about the high cost of a free lay' (Weverka, 1973). The ob. Eng. to 'lay a child' was not to be a paedophile but to attempt to cure it of rickets by taking it to a smithy where three smiths of the same name worked and there subjecting it to a number of experiences which are detailed in the EDD, none of which we would view with confidence today.

lay down your life etc.　to be killed in wartime
There are overtones of voluntary sacrifice: 'David Haden-Guest . . . . also laid down his life' (Boyle, 1979). You also die if you 'lay down' your burden, knife and fork, etc. The Sc. 'lay down the clay' is ob., the 'clay' being the human body: 'I'll soon lay down the clay, yet ere I go away I'd like to see the brig across to Torry' (Ogg, 1873).

lay hands on　to beat
Someone who expresses a wish to 'lay hands on' you is seldom a faith-healer or a bishop seeking to achieve your confirmation. Rarely too it means to kill, especially of suicide where you may 'lay (violent) hands on yourself'.

lay in *see* lie in

lay off　to dismiss from employment
Formerly for a short period only, until business picked up, but now of permanent dismissal: 'I didn't know my old man had been laid off' (Theroux, 1977, of lost employment).

lay out　to prepare a corpse for burial
You straighten the limbs before the onset of rigor mortis might make it hard to accommodate the body in a standard coffin. 'Laid out', meaning drunk, probably comes from the sl. meaning, knocked unconscious, although some drunkards look like cadavers.

lay paper　to pass worthless cheques
Perhaps from the old-style paper-chase. In Am. it also means to put forged banknotes into circulation.

lay pipes　to seek votes through bribery
From the engagement of unemployed labourers on public works in return for their votes. Am.

lead　a bullet used for killing
The victim has a 'bellyful of lead' or is 'filled full of lead'. The rarer 'lead ballast' is a bullet wound: 'You won't float long if I put lead ballast into you' (Fraser, 1970). 'Lead buttons' end up inside your flesh and not outside your coat: 'Talk to me like that . . . . and you are liable to be wearing lead buttons on your vest' (Chandler, 1943). If you are fed a 'lead pill', you may end up by dying of 'leaden fever' or the punning 'lead poisoning'; etc.

lead apes in hell　to die without having copulated
Of a woman, who has refused to accommodate sexually the fig. monkeys on earth, perhaps alluding to simian vigour: 'I must dance barefoot on her wedding day, and, for your love of her, lead apes in hell' (Shakespeare, *Taming of the Shrew*). ob.

lead in your pencil　sexual potency
Almost always of the male, with the 'pencil' being the penis in nursery use, and likening the ejaculation to the core of graphite (not lead) which is used for writing: 'Wally shook some drops of Angostura into the gin. "That'll put lead in your pencil," I said' (Theroux, 1973).

leaf (the)　illicit cocaine
Because it comes from the leaf of the coca plant. Am.

leak (1)　urination
Of obvious derivation. 'Leaks' may be had, done, needed, sprung, taken, etc. by either sex, in mildly vulgar use: 'Shuffling through the house in carpet slippers to take a leak' (Theroux, 1978). To 'leak' is to urinate: ' . . . we were allowed out for twenty minutes drinking and leaking' (Lyall, 1972).

leak (2)　to release information furtively
Either of a politician who wishes to sound out public opinion about future policy; or, more commonly, the unauthorized disclosure of confidential information by an employee for financial or political purposes: 'Someone in that group was leaking. Newspapers were getting rumours' (Sanders, 1973). A 'leak' can either be such confidential information, or the source from which it escapes. 'Leaky' describes a body prone to such disclosures. 'Leakage' is now ob.: 'We discussed leakages. Lady S. said that the surest way of making people repeat things was to say "Don't quote me"' (Colville, 1985).

leaky　menstruating
Rarely now used of involuntary urination:

'As leaky as an unstaunch'd wench' (Shakespeare, *Tempest*).

lean on to extract a benefit from
Silence from a witness, money from a victim, etc. from actual or threatened violence: 'I know his victims. I know who he leaned on' (Theroux, 1976).

leap to copulate with
In humans now replaced by 'jump', which is of the same tendency – *see* **jump** (3): 'I should quickly leap into a wife' (Shakespeare, *Henry V*). A 'leaping-house' or 'leaping-academy' was a brothel: 'Dials the signs of leaping-houses' (Shakespeare, 1 *Henry IV*) and: '. . . teaching 'em Latin in the environs of a leaping-academy' (Fraser, 1982). To 'leap on' suggests an excess of zeal in the male: 'You can't take a vow of celibacy . . . . you'll end up leaping on somebody and then feeling guilty' (Murdoch, 1985). Still SE of farm animals: 'His bulls leap at 5s a cow' (Marshall, 1811). To 'leap the broom' was to cohabit and copulate extra-maritally. The ob. 'leap in the dark' was death by hanging, punning on the cliché Hobbes is said to have used on his deathbed.

learn on the pillow to acquire proficiency in a foreign language from a native sexual mistress
Those who use the expression want to draw attention to the extra-marital copulation rather than to any linguistic achievement.

leave to desert a spouse
When we use this word, we ignore the fact that married couples part company daily, to come together again in the evening: 'He shocked Victorian society even more by leaving her' (Howard, 1978).

leave before the gospel to withdraw from the vagina before ejaculation
From attending church but forgoing the most important part of the service. Especially Roman Catholic use and practice, mechanical and chemical forms of contraception being eschewed.

leave of absence suspension from employment during investigation of a supposed offence
Properly no more than a vacation but used by an employer to avoid a defamation charge until the offence is proved: '"But not canned; just on leave of absence." "Without pay," I said bitterly' (Sanders, 1986 – an employee had been accused of theft).

leave shoes under the bed to copulate extra-maritally
Not merely staying in an hotel on business: 'Haven't you been leaving your shoes under a strange bed' (Sanders, 1979).

leave the building etc. to die
The 'building' is the body to which the soul is attached while you are living: 'I could quietly die – or as Papa said, "leave the building"'(Theroux, 1978). If you affect clichés, you are more likely to 'leave the land of the living': 'Let us cut him off from the land of the living, that his name be no more remembered' (Jeremiah). Those who 'leave the minority' rely on the assumption that the majority are already dead. The Am. 'left town' means dead. Rarely as 'leave' *tout court*: '"I think," the maid replied, "Mr Ford will be leaving us"' (Lacey, 1986: Henry Ford was dying).

leave the class etc. to urinate
'Please may I leave the class?' echoed through all our schooldays, unless it were 'Please may I leave the room?'.

leave your pillow unpressed not to copulate within marriage
Of a male, from sleeping in other, presumably pillowless, beds: 'Have I left my pillow unprest in Rome, Forborne the getting of a lawful race?' (Shakespeare, *Antony and Cleopatra*). ob.

lebensraum *see* **living space**

led astray having voluntarily done something of which you profess later regret or shame
Men most use it as an excuse when they come home drunk, women of eating fattening food and both of extra-marital copulation: 'She had been led astray before I met her . . . . and was a common prostitute' (Mayhew, 1862).

left supporting Marxist theory and practice
Abbr. of 'left-wing', from the seating plan of the French Estates General, where the Third Estate sat on the king's left. In the 1930s 'left' described a fawning and uncritical admiration of Stalinist Russia, as in the 'Left Book Club'. Today a person of the 'left' may hold more extreme views than the policy of the party to which for political convenience he adheres. In ob. Br. use a 'left twin' was not the one with extreme political convictions, nor even the left-handed one, but the survivor and much in demand medically, having 'the power of curing the thrush' (Henderson, 1879).

left-handed (1) bastard
From the bar sinister on the coat of arms. A 'left-handed alliance' was cohabitation and copulation by an unmarried couple. If there had been a ceremony, the man would have taken the woman's left hand, instead of her right, she becoming a 'left-handed wife'.

left-handed (2) homosexual
From the perhaps sinister deviation from the normal. Am.

left-wing *see* left

leg-over copulation
Usu. extra-marital, when the male is said to get or have his 'leg over': 'Bert asked me if I'd had my "leg over" yet' (Townsend, 1982). A 'leg-over' situation is thought to describe an unmarried couple known to copulate regularly.

leg-sliding extra-marital copulation
Of either sex, from a movement involved: 'Everyone's allowed a bit of leg-sliding these days' (le Carré, 1980).

legal resident a spy accredited as a diplomat
As different from an 'illegal resident', a spy who works in another country under cover: '... he should never have been appointed to the vital position of legal resident in the USA' (Deighton, 1981, of a Russian spy with diplomatic status).

legless drunk
From your inability to walk steadily, or at all: 'Bagley getting legless on Southern Comfort' (*Private Eye*, June 1981).

lend to give
If you ask someone to 'lend' you a match, you do not contemplate repaying him, and in any event 'He that lends, gives' (17c. proverb, meaning you won't be repaid, or see your adjustable spanner again). In 1941 the US Congress agreed to lease arms to Britain under the fiction that the 'loan' would be repaid after WW II, a measure which was helpful to the penurious combatants, the Am. armament manufacturers and the US economy. Truman wisely and abruptly ended 'Lend-Lease' in 1945.

length a term of imprisonment
A rare version of the common **stretch** (q.v.).

lesbian a female homosexual
Originally you referred to the poetess herself – *see* 'Sappho' under **sapphic** – rather than to her island home: 'It was commonly rumoured that Tanya was a Lesbian' (Brad-

bury, 1959). Abbr. to 'les' or 'lez': 'She-would-not-screw. I often wondered if she was a closet lez' (Sanders, 1977) and corrupted to 'lizzie': 'To get into Mortimer's outfit you have to be a lizzie or a drunk or an Irishwoman' (Manning, 1978, writing of the Br. First Aid Nursing Yeomanry, abbr. to FANY and the members being generally known to WW II soldiers as 'fannies', to some more intimately than to others). 'Lesbianism' is female homosexuality: 'I practiced Lesbianism, which was certainly sterile' (Harris, 1925). 'Lesbic' is an adjective form: '... this perverse intertwining of two figures in lesbic passion' (ibid.).

less academic etc. stupid or unteachable
A group of expressions prefixed 'less' glosses over the deficiencies of certain children about which educationalists choose to speak allusively. Such a child may also be 'less' able, gifted, prepared, talented etc. This entry and those which follow are no more than samples of a common euphemistic use of 'less' in phrases covering a range of taboo subjects.

less attractive repulsive
Those who insist that Cinderella's slipper should be of fur, in a correct translation from the Dutch, are likely also to refer to her two 'less attractive' sisters.

less developed poor
Of a country which may combine a seat in the United Nations with poverty and maladministration. 'Lesser developed' indicates no worse a state: '... loans to lesser developed countries such as Zaire and Jamaica' (M. Thomas, 1980).

less enjoyable boring
Of books, plays, etc. especially when the speaker wishes to cover himself against passing a judgment which might indicate a lack of taste or discernment. Normally the full comparison is not made, so that you never learn with what it compares unfavourably.

less prepared of inferior attainment
The usage seeks to gloss over deficiencies or difficulties arising from heredity, environment, education, etc.: '... the selection of the best-qualified black applicants .... in preference to less gifted or less prepared blacks' (Pei, 1969).

let go to dismiss from employment
The Am. employer seems to imply that in dismissing a worker, he does him a favour: 'It wore the sheriff down after a while and he

let George go' (Chandler, 1943, of a dismissed deputy). Very common.

let in to permit a male to copulate with you extra-maritally
From the physical penetration rather than the prior entry into an apartment: 'I still thought it good policy not to let him in yet a while. I answered then only to his importunities in sighs and moans' (Cleland, 1749).

let me I will persist without interruption
In the forms 'let me finish', 'let me say at once', etc. when politicians are being interviewed and are determined to deliver a prepared statement and avoid answering embarrassing questions.

let off etc. to fart
An abbr. of 'let off wind' rather than from the firing of a gun: '"He keeps letting off," she repeated in a whisper .... "I think it's because he's scared"' (L. Thomas, 1986, of farting). The rarer 'let fly' implies a more violent, noisier, release.

let out to dismiss from employment.
An Am. version of **let go** (above) but woe betide the employer who forcibly confines his employees after hours, or indeed at any time: 'Jay Allen, the most brilliant among us younger men, would soon be let out' (Shirer, 1984, of a journalist about to be dismissed).

letter box a place where a spy may leave a message
But not for the postman to collect. Espionage jargon, or of those who write the stories: 'The rulebook said Kleiber should be provided with a "drop" and "letter box".' (Deighton, 1981).

leverage borrowing
Am. rather than Br. use but in both societies a 'leveraged' bid or purchase is one in which a predator borrows excessively in the expectation of repaying his loan from the victim's assets: 'Anyway, this investment banker specializes in "leveraged buyouts"; it's the new thing in Wall Street fashion' (M. Thomas, 1987, who is worth reading for an informed account of how the combination of dishonest corporate officers and greedy bankers robs investors).

levy male masturbation
Br. rh. sl. on **wank** (q.v.) from a firm of London caterers, 'Levy and Franks'. ? ob.

liaison the repeated clandestine extra-marital copulation with the same person
Properly, the culinary thickening of a sauce, whence a close relationship: '... striking up occasional liaisons which she alluded to by saying .... "He's an old boyfriend of mine"' (Theroux, 1976). In espionage jargon a 'liaison officer' is a controller of spies. Semenov of the KGB was so described, his career spanning Montevideo in 1944, where he met Agee, and service in Cuba with the 'General Directorate of Intelligence'.

libation an intoxicant
Properly, the ceremonial offering of a drink: '"... this may be a good time for a drink. Do you concur, Senator?" "A small libation would not be inappropriate," he said in a wry manner' (Sanders, 1984).

liberal intolerant
Properly, free-thinking and objective but appropriated by some so sure of their own rightness that they brook no contradiction: 'He is, on the surface, the perfect 24-carat knee-jerk liberal sap' (*Daily Telegraph*, February 1980, of Edward Kennedy). In pejorative use by extremists, 'liberal' may mean supine or indecisive: 'I'm beset by a good liberal ambivalence' (Bradbury, 1976). In ob. use a 'liberal' woman was willing to copulate extra-maritally: 'It's sign she hath been liberal and free' (Shakespeare, 1 *Henry VI*).

liberate (1) to conquer
Properly, to free: 'Egypt would be liberated and Rommel and his men would keep their assignation with the ladies of Alexandria' (Manning, 1977).

liberate (2) to steal
Originally WW II army use when freeing, occupying and looting tended to go hand in hand: 'It's a gold watch – a *liberated* gold watch' (Price, 1978, of WW II). Now in general use: '"Are you going to be warm enough in that jacket?" "I'm all right, I liberated it from a second-hand shop"' (Theroux, 1976).

liberate (3) to permit or encourage to flout social convention
Again the concept of setting free: '... her immersion in the pop scene, and how it had liberated her' (Bradbury, 1976, of a woman so behaving). 'Liberation' is such flouting of convention or denial of manners, of minority dissident groups etc. In prostitutes' jargon a whore working without a pimp is also said to be 'liberated', but that must be distinguished from **women's liberation** (q.v.).

lick of the tarbrush *see* **tarbrush**

lick the dust to die
Usu. after being killed, from the attitude of a

corpse in a dry terrain: 'His enemies shall lick the dust' (Psalm 72). 'Bite the dust' is a common usage, especially for Redskins in cowboy films.

lid an ounce of marijuana
It is the quantity which fits into the lid of a tobacco tin and makes about 40 cigarettes: 'Tommy smoked a couple of lids a week' (Wambaugh, 1981). Am.

lie in to await the imminent birth of a baby
Greek, Latin and Teutonic roots of 'lie' all mean bed where, in the language of euphemism, you only give birth or copulate: 'Within ten days she'll be lying in' (Graves, 1940, of a pregnant woman). Formerly to 'lay in' was synonymous: 'When the gal is in the family way, the lads mostly sends them to the workhouse to lay in' (Mayhew, 1851). A 'lying-in' is a childbirth, formerly attended by the 'lying-in wife', or midwife: 'As well as can be expected. That's the answer of a lying-in wife' (Wilson, 1836).

lie together *see* lie with etc.

lie with etc. to copulate with
It has long been assumed that the adult male and female cannot 'lie' in each other's company without copulating, within or outside marriage: 'To tell thee plain, I aim to lie with thee' (Shakespeare, *3 Henry VI*). 'Lie on' might be more accurate, but is less used: 'Lie with her, lie on her' (Shakespeare, *Othello*). To 'lie together' implies extramarital copulation: 'Foreign students were positively encouraged to lie together, he said sardonically, so that they didn't go out and pursue the natives' (Francis, 1978, of Moscow University). The ob. Br. 'lie backwards and let out your forerooms' meant to be a whore, being a rather complex vulgar pun on the female posture in copulation and on letting the more desirable rooms in a house while you remain in the back quarters.

life (the) any taboo way of earning your keep or existing
Whores' jargon of prostitution, thieves' for stealing and of narcotic addiction, especially when you alternate between scheming to get money to buy narcotics and periods under narcotic sedation.

life everlasting *see* everlasting life

life insurance etc. contracting for a sum to be paid on death
Living is a more saleable commodity than dying. The 'life' is the person whose death triggers the payment, 'life cover' is such

assurance, a 'life office' is a company which trades in such contracts, etc.

life of infamy etc. being engaged as a whore
How the righteous profess to see it: '. . . she may have been a servant out of a place . . . . and betaken herself here to a life of infamy' (Mayhew, 1862 – 'here' was a brothel). We still talk of a 'life of shame' but the concept has tended to go out of fashion.

life preserver a cosh
It is not intended to preserve the victim: 'Macarthur was hit with a life preserver . . . . on the back of the head' (Christie, 1939 – it killed him).

Liffey water Guinness' stout
After the river which flows through Dublin, and sometimes even if your particular potion was brewed at Park Royal in London: 'Let's do it the Irish way, with a jar of Liffey Water' (Theroux, 1976). 'Stout' is an abbr. for 'stout beer', meaning strong.

lift (1) to steal
Usu. of pilfering, from the casual taking: 'Billy can lift your jock strap, and you wouldn't feel a thing' (Weverka, 1973). Specially too of plagarism in 20c. Am., of picking pockets in 19c. Eng. and of digging up corpses from graves in 18c. Sc.: 'Resurrectionists . . . who were as ready to lay their murdering hands on the living, as to lift the dead' (Whitehead, 1876). A 'lifter' is a thief, usu. by picking pockets. 'Shoplifter', a thief from a store, has been in use since the 16c.: 'I know it's bloody for them, but thousands of people shoplift' (Francis, 1981). The ob. Sc. 'lift the books' was to withdraw from regular service in a church in the days when church membership was a social necessity, apart from any moral benefits: 'He saved a public scandal by lifting his books . . . . resigning his membership' (Johnston, 1891, of a churchgoer).

lift (2) an ingestion of illegal narcotics
From the feeling sometimes induced: ' "Want a lift?" "I can use something," Janette said. She took a small vial from the bag' (Robbins, 1981).

lift (3) to arrest
Mainly police jargon: 'The lift and then the interrogation, the interrogation and then the imprisonment' (Seymour, 1982).

lift a leg (1) to copulate
Of a male, from getting himself into a convenient attitude: 'I'll ne'er lift a lawless leg

Again upon her' (Burns). cf. **get a leg over** etc.

lift a leg (2) to urinate
Properly of a dog, from the action, and rarely of a male human: 'She opened the front door, and watched him go over to the hedge where he lifted a leg' (Ustinov, 1966, of a dog). The ob. Eng. 'lift a gam' was to fart; a 'gam' was a leg, and also a school of whales, but their propensity for 'blowing' does not seem to have contributed to the etymology.

lift your elbow etc. to drink intoxicants
On a single occasion, from the conveyance of the glass to your mouth, or more often of a drunkard. In the same sense you may also 'lift' your arm, little finger or wrist: 'Liquors a bit, don't you know; lifts his little finger' (Peacock, 1890).

lift your hand to to hit
A man who has never 'lifted his hand' to his wife has not been deliquent in waving greeting to her – indeed, the contrary is likely to be the case.

light (1) sexually promiscuous
Of no moral weight: 'Light wenches will burn. Come not near her' (Shakespeare, *Comedy of Errors* – they were not condemned to the stake but would give you venereal disease).

light (2) a male homosexual recognition signal
The universal password, usu. in the question 'Can you give me a light?': '. . . it was not granted to me to live a moment of happiness, because a sailor's face in front of me went blank when I asked him for a light' (Genet, in 1969 tr., of a homosexual).

light fingered thieving
From the propensity to lift small objects: '. . . . Rose and Crown public house, resorted to by all classes of light-fingered gentry' (Mayhew, 1862). An old superstition has passed into oblivion: 'The baby's nails must not be cut till he is a year old, for fear he should grow up a thief, or . . . . "light-fingered"' (Henderson, 1879). The ob. Sc. 'light footed' or 'light-heeled' meant promiscuous, of a woman; and the modern Am. 'light footed' means homosexual, of a male. An ob. Eng. 'light-skirts' was a whore.

light-footed *see* **light-fingered**

light in the head of low intelligence
Not a turnip on Hallowe'en: 'The kid's a little light in the head. His brother takes care of him' (Sanders, 1970).

light the lamp to copulate
Probably punning on the whore's trademark of a red lamp, and the sexual stimulation: 'She confided to me that she had lit the lamp four hundred and two times, in one week, in her Casita' (Londres, 1928, in tr. of a whore). A man may use the phrase of extramarital copulation on a single occasion, usu. with a woman who is not a whore.

lightning a low quality spirituous intoxicant
From the effect when it strikes you. Usu. of whisky in Am. and of gin in Eng. The Am. 'Jews' lightning', is arson, from the phenomenon of business premises being burnt down after being struck by lightning from a cloudless sky when trade is bad, but not so bad that you have neglected paying your fire insurance premiums.

like a drink *see* **drink**

like that *see* **that way**

lily a male homosexual
I suppose from the woman's name and the pale colouring, although the flower is an emblem of chastity and innocence. Am.

limb (1) a leg
A classic of 19c. Am. prudery. Even your dining table had 'limbs'.

limb (2) a policeman
Abbr. of 'limb of the law', which used to mean a sheriff's officer: 'Be't priest, or laird, or limb o' law' (Nicholson, 1814). There is no etymological connection with the ob. 'limbo', a prison, from the place where unbaptized infants dwell along with those who predeceased Christ and various others: 'I have some of them in limbo patrum' (Shakespeare, *Henry VIII*).

limejuice an attack carried out from the air on a limited target
WW II description of attacks by rocket-firing Typhoon aircraft called up by Am. and Br. infantry, probably from the astringence and squirting of the juice of the fruit: 'He was also aware that the drone of limejuice was building up into a roar' (Price, 1978, of WW II fighting).

limit (the) extra-marital copulation
Usu. after a series of lesser sexual encounters with the same person.

limited stupid or incompetent
Of children, educational jargon to avoid precision as to idleness or stupidity; of adults, lacking in ability or intelligence. One of the sillier euphemisms, as we are all confined

within limits, of memory, knowledge, experience, common sense, physical power, etc.

limited action a war
The stronger participant so describes it when he wants his adversary to get no help, and to keep his own domestic population inviolate: 'The black magic of violence; and even then the language of the mad foments it .... "bushfire war", "limited actions"' (West, 1979).

limp very drunk
From the inert posture of the drunkard. Am.

limpwrist a male homosexual
From the action of masturbating yourself: 'He looked like a peroxided limpwrist' (Wambaugh, 1983). Adjectively as 'limp-wristed': 'His limp-wristed nancy-boy of a son' (*Private Eye*, January 1980).

line to copulate with
Properly, of a wolf or a dog and ob. of humans: 'Winter garments must be lined, so must gentle Rosalind' (Shakespeare, *As You Like It*). 'Lined', pregnant, is also ob.: '. . . she got lined by a big black buck' (Graves, 1941, writing in archaic style of a pregnant woman).

line your pocket etc. wrongfully to enrich yourself
The money provides the 'lining': '. . . adept in the field of corruption and lining his own pocket' (Goebbels, 1945, in tr.). The older form was to 'line your coat: 'Throwing but shows of service on their lords, Do well thrive by them, and when they have lin'd their coats, Do themselves homage' (Shakespeare, *Othello*).

link prices to arrange an illegal cartel
Manufacturers either divide markets on a geographical basis or agree to quote the same prices in each market.

liquid an intoxicant
It could be anything logically from water to sulphuric acid. Usu. in compounds. A 'liquid refreshment' is an intoxicant and not a cooling soft drink. A 'liquid restaurant' is one which also sells intoxicants, especially if such sale is forbidden: '. . . indebted .... to the owner of a "liquid" restaurant' (Lavine, 1930, writing during Prohibition). A 'liquid lunch' is the drinking of excessive intoxicants at midday, with little or no food: 'Following our liquid lunch, he agreed to totter round the greens with me' (*Private Eye*, August 1981).

liquidate to kill other than by process of law
Properly, to clear away, whence the inference of ruthless efficiency: 'The silent liquidation of many friends in the Soviet Union without a single bleat of protest from the freedom-loving West' (Boyle, 1979). Despite a Russian penchant for thus clearing away opponents, I do not think we have to follow SOD into 'Likvadirovat' for the etymology. In legal jargon, a 'liquidator' also kills off failed companies.

liquidity crisis an inability to pay your debts as they fall due
Commercial jargon for an insolvency which has not yet been declared, and less often used of personal penury. 'Liquid' funds are those at your immediate disposal, unlike 'fixed' assets in the form of machinery, buildings, work-in-progress and other investments often incapable of immediate realisation.

liquor a spirituous intoxicant
Properly, any liquid. In various spellings: 'Lecker makes her drunk as David's sow' (*Gentleman's Magazine*, 1742, quoted in EDD) and 'Some said it was the likker' (Longstreet, 1956). 'Liquored' means partly drunk and 'full of liquor' or 'in liquor', drunk: 'He was in liquor when he made his first appearance' (Monsarrat, 1978).

lit drunk
From the generally exhilarated state rather than the redness of the nose: 'An old con like me don't make good prints – not even when he's lit' (Chandler, 1939). Also of being under narcotic influence.

little bears the local police
See **bear** (2). Most Am. towns have a local police force who can be zealous about imposing on-the-spot fines for traffic violations, with the money going towards local taxes, if it gets that far. CB.

little bit a whore
See **bit**. The adjective does not define the lady's girth or height: 'There's always a little bit at that truck 'em up stop' (CBSLD). CB sl. Am.

little boys' room a lavatory for exclusive male use
Fairly common adult male usage, despite its cloying imagery. 'Little girls' room' for females is equally nauseous but happily less common: 'She slid out of her chair, "Just goin' to the little girls room, hon"' (Collins, 1981).

little finger the penis

As in the delphic claim: 'My little finger is thicker than my father's loins' (1 Kings). Partridge said in 1947 'Still current, among women, as a euphemism', but we must have moved in different circles.

little gentleman in black velvet the death of King William II

The king, hated by the Jacobites, was riding a horse which stumbled on a molehill. He fell off, broke his collar bone and died from complications which ensued. So the Jacobites toasted the mole: 'The little gentleman in black velvet who did such service in 1702' (W. Scott, 1814). They also toasted the **king over the water** (q.v.) and 'limp' – Louis, James, Mary, Prince of Wales – which was hardly a rousing call to arms even without its modern overtones.

little girls' room *see* **little boys' room**

little house a lavatory

It was often a small detached shed. In ob. use a 'petty house'.

little jobs *see* **big jobs**

little Mary the stomach

This 19c. euphemism can still be heard, reminding us that the stomach was the subject of taboo because of its sexual, child-bearing and defecatory functions. As trousers and legs came under the same types of taboo, we may wonder how so reticent and sheltered a society managed so effectively to reproduce itself.

little people etc. the fairies

You had to speak allusively of malevolent people who could do you so much harm. Also as the 'little folk' and *see* **wee folk** etc.

little school *see* **big school** *under* **house** etc.

little something an intoxicant

Of the substance on its own, or added to a non-alcoholic drink with which you have already been served.

little stranger an unborn child

Nursery usage to avoid truthfulness about pregnancy.

little visitor menstruation

In female use interchangeable with **visitor** (q.v.), the affliction being equally severe in either case.

live as man and wife etc. to cohabit and copulate extra-maritally

From the supposed regular copulation of married couples: 'Irene and I lived together as man and wife' (L. Armstrong, 1955 of his sexual mistress). Indeed a married couple who do not copulate with each other may be said not to 'live as man and wife' regardless of their sharing a house. To 'live in sin' means the same thing, the 'sin' being the mortal sin of adultery, and is often used of a couple who so conduct themselves before marrying each other: 'But the first year we lived in sin' (Sanders, 1973, of such a couple) and 'But then aren't you living in mortal sin?' (N. Mitford, 1945). The ob. N. Eng. 'live tally' was more picturesque, a 'tally' being a corresponding piece which exactly fits the other: 'Aw'd advise thi t' live tally if theaw con mak it reet wi some owd damsel' (Brierley, c. 1880 – most men would prefer some young damsel, I suspect). To 'live together' always implies extra-marital copulation, but not necessarily cohabitation: 'If parties is married, they ought to bend to each other; and won't, for sartain, if they're only living together' (Mayhew, 1851). 'Live with' is perhaps the commonest use, of either sex: 'You lived with women. You lived with that old actress' (Murdoch, 1978). 'Live together' and 'live with' are also used of homosexual arrangements. To 'live on' or 'live off' another may mean, for a man, to be a pimp and for a woman, a sexual mistress: 'In this life I have known, loved, lived for, lived on, lived off.... many men' (L. Thomas, 1977, of a whore). For 'live by trading' *see* **trade**. A 'live-in' girlfriend, etc. is a sexual mistress with whom the male also cohabits: '. . . attending Hollywood high society affairs as his live-in girlfriend rather than as his wife' (*Daily Telegraph*, September 1981).

lived in untidy

Of another's house, sometimes with an implication of dirtiness. A 'lived-in' face indicates premature and incipient decay through excesses.

livener an intoxicant taken early in the day by a drunkard

Either by a person drunk on a single occasion, or by an habitual drunkard: 'Your Lordship has heard of people having "liveners" in the morning' (*Birmingham Daily Post*, 1897, quoted in EDD). The sufferer is supposed to be stimulated by the fresh infusion.

living space the territory to be taken by German from Poland and Russia

Nazi jargon for part of the policy of aggression 'to obtain by the German sword sod for the German plough'. The German word 'lebensraum' is now as notorious: '*Lebensraum* which should have meant living-room but actually signified the occupation of Europe and as much of Russia as Hitler had been able to lay his hands on' (Sharpe, 1979). Even more sinister was the lesser known Nazi policy of 'Lebensborn' under which fair Polish or Czech children were taken from home and placed with German families to be raised as Germans and thus augment the Teutonic stock.

Lizzie *see* **lesbian**

load (1) the quantity of intoxicants which has made someone drunk
You usu. have, carry or get on a 'load': 'Sure, I seen him drunk. Lots of times. He's have a load on' (Sanders, 1977). 'Loaded' is drunk: 'I'm not loaded, as they haven't told me when the bars around here open up' (Ustinov, 1971). Also of being under the influence of illicit narcotics.

load (2) the genitalia of a male
Am. male homosexual use: 'The long-haired youth entered, came close to Firenza's side, pressed his nylon-sheathed load against the doctor's arm' (Sanders, 1977).

loaded (1) *see* **load** (1)

loaded (2) fraudulently increased
The account is made heavier with fictitious or inflated entries.

loaded (3) laced with intoxicants
Of any non-alcoholic drink: 'We sipped our loaded coffee' (Chandler, 1939).

loan a gift
See **lend**. In ob. use it meant a gift from a superior (OED) before it came to import an obligation to return or make restitution. 'Loan-soup', fresh milk given to passers-by, came from the 'loan', or cowshed.

local bear etc. a policeman attached to a small force
See **bear** (2) and as different from a state trooper. In Am. CB also as 'local' boy, yokel etc.

lock out a refusal by an employer to allow employees access to their place of work
Trade union jargon and perhaps not euphemistic except that it is often rhetorically used under circumstances when an employer has closed his factory until obtaining guarantees about normal working during a quarrel: 'We have been given two days . . . . to carry on production or we should be locked out' (Allbeury, 1982).

loco mad
From the narcotic 'loco weed', which deranges cattle: 'The average square would say those animals were all loco' (L. Armstrong, 1955).

log-roller a person who gives selfish and insincere support
The first 'log-rollers' were the neighbours who helped each other manhandle heavy tree branches for winter domestic burning, from which came the meaning, political support in return for another favour: 'The members (of Congress) . . . . make a compact by which each aids the other. This is called log-rolling' (Bryce, 1888). The modern Am. use covers any insincere commendation, as in literature; and any reward for sycophancy: 'If either were appointed . . . . it would be a piece of disgraceful log-rolling' (Manning, 1965 – both candidates had flattered the patron).

loins the male genitalia and their reproductive role
Properly, the region of your body between your ribs and your hips: 'A tongueless man may pass through his loins his unsung music' (Kersh, 1936). Much biblical and some literary use.

long-arm inspection a medical inspection of the penis
DAS says the inspection is 'of the erect penis' and *see* **short-arm inspection**. To 'long-arm' is to hitch-hike. Am.

long home etc. death
Really the grave: 'Horn sent her off to her long hame to lie' (Burns, 1785). Those who die also go on their 'long journey': 'I expect this is our last time around, Dick, but I hope to take a few of them on the long journey with us' (Richards, 1933, of going back into the WW I trenches after leave). The 'long day' is the Christian day of judgement, when a considerable catalogue of offences comes up for hearing; whence the admonition: 'Between you and the lang day be it' (Pegge, 1803). A 'long walk off a short pier' is murder by drowning: '. . . such topics as hanging, cyanide, and a long walk off a short pier' (Sanders, 1979).

long illness (a) cancer
The language of the obituary notice, often adding with what fortitude the ordeal was borne. The Am. 'short illness' may indicate suicide.

long in the tooth old
From ageing a horse by the recession of its gums: '. . . he wanted to link up with some nice little bit less long in the tooth' (Christie, 1939).

loo a lavatory
Probably a corruption of 'l'eau', and not from the card game at which you might be subject to a forfeit: 'She sat in the loo on the pink tufted candlewick of the seat cover' (Bradbury, 1976). Mailer spells it 'lou', unless I have a misprint: '. . . like a three-year-old who's got to go to the lou' (Mailer, 1965). The Br. railway 'superloo' is a station lavatory which might actually be clean, though you pay highly for it.

look after see **take care of** (1) & (2)

look at the garden etc. to urinate out of doors
Males say that they are going to do it, usu. on a dark evening. They may also 'look at' the compost heap, crops, flowers, lawn, roses, vegetable garden, etc.

look in a cup a foretell the future
For some, the tealeaves reveal all: 'I'm just broucht a si o' tea wi' me, an' I wis just wantin' you to luik in a cup fir me' (Stewart, 1892). The practice is now rare, and not just because of the introduction of teabags.

looking glass a pot for urine
This Irish use is now ob., which is just as well. I draw your attention to the obvious joke involving the traveller and the waitress in EDD Vol. III p. 635.

loop (1) to kill by hanging
From the noose: 'Like moussie thrappl't in a fa', Or loon that's loopit by the law' (Ainslie, 1892 – the mouse was throttled and a loon is a person of low rank, whence of a woman, a whore: 'If she has been a loon, it was your son made her sae, and he can make her an honest woman again' (W. Scott, 1822)).

loop (2) a contraceptive used internally by a female
From its shape. To be 'on the loop' is to be using such a method.

loose (1) willing to copulate extra-maritally
Used of women rather than men from the 16c., from the relaxation of normal, tighter, standards: 'There were 8,600 prostitutes known to the police, but this was far from . . . . the number of loose women in the metropolis' (Mayhew, 1862). 'On the loose' was living as a whore: 'When I lived with S. he allowed me £10 a week, but when I went

on the loose I did not get so much' (ibid.). The ob. Eng. 'loose in the hilts' punned on a dagger unfit for use: 'A sister damned: she's loose i' the hilts; Grown a notorious strum-pet' (Webster, 1623, quoted in ODEP). A 'loose house' was a brothel: 'You'd think she had started a loose house dead centre of the village' (Cookson, 1967). A 'loose fish' is a male profligate who has escaped the matri-monial net; etc.

loose (2) suffering from diarrhoea
Originally diarrhoea was the 'loose disease'. Of both humans and animals. To 'loosen the bowels' is to cause to defecate: 'It was fit to loosen the bowels of a bronze statue' (Fraser, 1975). 'Looseness' is mild diarrhoea.

loose in the attic etc. mad
'Attic' is sl. for head: 'He's a goddam loony bird. He's just uh . . . a little loose in the attic' (Diehl, 1978). You may also be 'loose in the' head or any of the other sl. words for head.

lord Harry see **Harry**

Lord has him (the) he is dead
A Christian use, in expectation of joining Jesus in heaven. The Lord may also 'send for you': 'A woman like me doesn't part with pearls and diamonds until the good Lord sends for her' (Sharpe, 1977).

Lord of the flies the devil
Beelzebub, 'fly-lord' in Hebrew, was the Prince of the Flies in Syrian mythology.

lose to destroy
Of embarrassing files, documents and, recently, tapes although Nixon had too good a retrieval system for the last-mentioned.

lose the vital signs to die
Perhaps medical circumlocution rather than euphemism. The ob. 'lose your wind' was not to recover from a bout of indigestion but to die, from the cessation of breathing. In ob. Br. army usage you might also 'lose the number of the mess'.

lose your cherry etc. to copulate for the first time
Of a female, the 'cherry' being the maiden-head: 'In thirty years you can get born, grow up, go to college, get married, lose your cherry, have a couple of kids' (Diehl, 1978). The ob. Sc. 'lose your snood' meant the same thing, the silken snood being worn as a symbol of virginity: 'A' body kens it's lang syne you tynd your snood' (Hamilton, 1897 – 'tyne' means lose) and 'snooded folk' were

unmarried females. To 'lose your innocence' is to copulate for the first time, of either sex: 'In less than no time I had lost my senses and also my innocence' (Richards, 1936, of himself). To 'lose your virtue' is to copulate outside marriage, of a woman: 'Every woman who yields to her passions and loses her virtue is a prostitute' (Mayhew, 1862). To 'lose your character' is either to be guilty of a crime, of either sex, or to copulate extra-maritally, of a woman: 'I might not lose, with my character, the prospect of getting a good husband' (Cleland, 1749). To 'lose your reputation' is to be known either as a whore or as a woman who has copulated extra-maritally: 'We cannot go there. The night watchman will see us. You will lose your reputation' (Bradbury, 1976). 'Lost', of females, does not imply being unaware of their bearings but engaged in prostitution: 'They weren't by any means all lost women when they came' (Londres, 1928, in tr. of whores in Argentina); etc.

lose your lunch etc. to vomit
Usu. when drunk or on a boat. You may also 'lose' your breakfast, dinner, doughnuts or whatever else you may have eaten.

loss (1) a bereavement
You do not necessarily miss the person who has died: 'But she told her other gentlemen she could feel he had had a *loss*' (le Carré, 1980).

loss (2) *see* night loss

lost (1) *see* lose your cherry etc.

lost (2) killed
Usu. through violence: 'My . . . my wife and son, sir . . . lost in the uprising . . . murdered' (Fraser, 1975). 'Lost at sea' means drowned.

lot a battle in which there were many casualities
A WW I usage which sought to play down the horror of the carnage: 'I was in the last lot, sir. In Flanders' (Kyle, 1968).

lothario a male who constantly makes sexual proposals to women
After the character in a play of 1630, *The Cruel Brother*, by Davenport: 'He pointed out the office lothario and the office seductress' (Sanders, 1981).

lotion an intoxicant
Properly, the action of washing, whence any liquid applied externally to the body: 'I suggested to our noble friend that a lotion might not come amiss' (*Private Eye*, March 1980 – he was offering an intoxicant).

love to copulate with
The supposition that people copulate only with those they have great affection for is laudable and in 'make love' we find the commonest euphemism for copulation: 'He should make love to her, or, in the parlance, screw her' (Masters, 1976). Now used too of physical homosexual relationships, whether female: 'The shy girl she had loved the night before' (Theroux, 1976) or male: 'The allegation that he had ever made love to Maclean' (Boyle, 1979, of Burgess). To 'make love to yourself' is to masturbate: 'She sometimes made love to herself, on the bath mat' (McCarthy, 1963). 'Love-making' is copulation: 'Rachman's love-making was clinical and joyless' (Green, 1979). 'Love-juice' is the vaginal secretion of a sexually excited female: 'I felt her warm love-juice gush' (Harris, 1925). The 19c. 'love that dare not speak its name' was male homosexuality – Queen Victoria did not allow for female homosexuals.

love affair a relationship which involves extra-marital copulation
A debasement of the proper meaning, a courtship between unmarried persons. Now used too of a single act of extra-marital copulation: 'Do you want me to drop in for a short love affair?' (Murdoch, 1978). As with **love** (above), also used of homosexual activity.

love child etc. a bastard
This use predates the modern assumption that copulation and love go together and might even suggest that children born in wedlock are unwanted: '. . . little to dispute save the paternity of "love children"' (Bartram, 1897). In many similar forms, like 'love-bairn', 'love bird', 'love begotten', 'lover child', etc.

love nest the place where a sexual mistress is housed
See **love** (above): 'As a love-nest, the place had its points' (Chandler, 1943).

loved one the corpse
Am. funeral jargon, which makes an unwarranted assumption in many cases: 'As for the Loved One, poor fellow, he wanders like a sad ghost through the funeral men's pronouncements' (J. Mitford, 1963). Evelyn Waugh entitled his 1948 novel about the Californian funeral industry *The Loved One* but it is otherwise almost entirely free from euphemism, like most of his writing, and the dedication turned out to be the wrong Mitford sister, Nancy instead of Jessica.

lover a woman's regular extra-marital partner in copulation
It is remarkable that the language has evolved no specific word for so common a need, and this use invites us almost to assume that husbands do not love their wives: 'In a marriage, if the lover begins to be bored by the complaisant husband, he can always provoke a scandal' (G. Greene, 1978). 'Lovers' means both partners in unmarried heterosexual copulation on a regular basis; 'Soon, however, everybody knew that they were lovers' (Harris, 1925, of Parnell and Mrs O' Shea). Today 'lovers' can also be homosexual partners in a physical relationship: '"Are you and she lovers?" asked Treece. "No; she's never done *anything* to me," said Viola' (Bradbury, 1959).

low *see* **high** (2)

low budget etc. cheap
A cheap or skimpy film or television show is called 'low-budget'. 'Low cost', of an article offered for sale, seeks to avoid the association of cheapness with nastiness or poor quality. 'Low key' of advertising, etc. implies being done on the cheap, with musical imagery. 'Low income' implies poverty of people, houses or district. 'Low girls' are whores of the meaner kind: 'The most of the low girls in this locality do not go out till late in the evening, and chiefly devote their attention to drunken men' (Mayhew, 1862). etc.

Low countries *see* **Netherlands**

low flying far exceeding a speed limit in a motor vehicle
As different from **flying low** (q.v.), which is having a trouser zip inadvertently undone. The two are not used interchangeably.

low profile the avoidance of publicity
The imagery is from tank warfare, where you try to keep your hull down to reduce the target. A usage of politicians, corporations, etc. doing nothing when they should be acting, or hiding what they are doing.

lower abdomen etc. the genitalia
Of males, it is a useful evasion for sports commentators when a player has suffered a disabling blow. 'Lower stomach' is used of both sexes: '. . . caressed the hair of her lower stomach affectionately' (Bradbury, 1976).

lower the boom on to arrest
The assumption has to be that the victim is already in harbour which suggests inverted imagery: 'We lowered the boom on Ross Minchen. He's behind bars right now, with his lawyer fighting to get him out' (Sanders, 1986). Also commercially of putting a customer on the stop list for non-payment.

lubricate to bribe
A rare variant of **oil** (q.v.). But when James Boswell 'lubricated' a female, he referred to his seminal discharge.

lubricated drunk
A variation of **oiled** (q.v.). It can also mean being maliciously plied with intoxicants by others.

Lucy in the sky with diamonds lysergic acid diethylamide
The initial letters of LSD. Many adults who affected admiration for pop music, especially of the Beatles, tended to miss the references to illicit narcotics and the implicit sanctioning of drug abuse. This was a title of a Lennon/McCartney song of 1967.

lulu a sum fraudulently claimed as expenses by an employee
Probably punning on the Am. sl. 'lulu', something exceptional, and a payment 'in lieu'.

lumber to copulate
It has the air of Br. rh. sl. – say 'lumber and lump', hump or thump – but that is speculation: 'Zoë lumbers for a fiver' (Kersh, 1936). ? ob.

lump a corpse
Am. criminal jargon which is probably an abbr. of a 'lump of meat': 'The lump is on the way down now. The big problem . . . . is whether to do a cut 'em-up before lunch or after' (Sanders, 1973, of a medical post-mortem examination). In ob. Br. use 'lumpy' was either drunk or pregnant or, I suppose, both.

lunchtime engineering bribery through excessive hospitality
Especially in the aircraft industry where buyers and sub-contract managers are known to habituate certain bars and restaurants at midday, and like vendors to pick up the tabs. Indeed, where the selection is on engineering grounds rather than price or delivery, the lavish entertainer usu. turns out to have the technical edge on the competition.

lungs a woman's breasts
Viewed sexually by a male: '" . . . it's not a bad piece." "Good lungs," Eddie admitted' (Sanders, 1982, and not of a singer).

lush an intoxicant

Properly, succulent or tender, whence luxurious and in sufficient funds to afford luxuries, as '. . . moving back there when a bit more lush' (Manning, 1965, of returning to the best hotel). OED tends to support this etymology but Brewer thinks the celebrated Alderman Lushington came first, although I suspect the reverse: 'We gets in some lush, and 'as some frens, and goes in for a regular blow-hout' (Mayhew, 1862). In modern use, a 'lush' is a regular drunkard: 'He was a lush. He got the sack' (Theroux, 1973 – I'm sure the pun was unintentional). 'Lushy' or 'lushed' meant drunk: '. . . on a bench by a railing of the boat, lushed to the gills' (L. Armstrong, 1955). 'Lush' house, crib, ken, etc. for a place serving intoxicants are all ob.

but you may still meet a 'lush-roller' who steals from drunkards. 'Alderman Lushington' means either drunk or the intoxicant; etc.

Lydford law arbitrary punishment

This is a sample entry of the many local geographical euphemisms which have now largely been lost except to students of local history or, in the BI, to those who trawl through the EDD. In this example, special courts in the tin-mining districts of Devon and Cornwall, known as the Stannary, held jurisdiction under which a judge at the small Devon border town of Lydford caused a tin-miner to be hanged in the morning and then sat in judgment on him during the same afternoon.

M

M anything taboo beginning with the letter
M
Especially marijuana in addict use.

machine an erect penis
An old but rare variant of **tool** (q.v.): '. . .
that machine whose touch has something so
exquisitely singular in it, to make its way into
me' (Cleland, 1749).

mackerel a pimp
The French 'maquereau' is more widely
used. Abbr. in Am. to 'mac', 'mack' or
'macko'.

mad money the cash being carried by a
woman entertained by a male
Not inflation under socialism. The Am.
female can use it to make her own way home
if she gets 'mad', angry.

madam the female keeper of a brothel
Rather a come-down for 'my lady' but the
honorary title of any bawd from Shakespeare's 'Madam Mitigation' (*Measure for
Measure*) to Madam Mitchell who kept a
noted WW II brothel in Madras: '"What can
I do for you Madam?" "Miss," she said. "In
my country a lady doesn't like being mistaken for a madam"' (Deighton, 1978). For
the French 'madame' was also the guillotine.

made at one heat stolen
This is a sample entry from the days when
the smithy was more essential to society than
the garage today. In forge-work, you only
make an article by reheating it and rewor-
king it many times. If there were only one
operation, it had to be thievery. Somerset.

Magdalene a whore
Christ's disciple, Mary, was supposed to
have been a whore who repented and she
gave her name, mainly in the 19c., to others
who had yet to renounce their way of life:
'After that our Magdalenes were left alone'
(Fraser, 1982, writing in 19c. style of
whores).

mail a letter to urinate
A common and transparent Am. male excuse
for leaving others. But cf. **post a letter**.

mail cover the interception and unauthorized reading of letters
It should mean no more than an envelope.
The term was used by the US Post Department for its clandestine post-WW II perusal

of letters from Am. citizens to Communist
countries (Jennings, 1965).

mainline illegally to inject a narcotic
intravenously
The 'main line' is the blood vessel in the
arm, from railroad imagery, and the effect is
almost immediate: 'A high-wire performer
who hit the main line in his own office'
(Chandler, 1953).

majority rule the assumption of power by
Blacks in a colony
The formula inevitably led to a transfer of
power where Black residents outnumbered
White settlers, as in Rhodesia. However
decades of maladministration in N. Ireland
led to a suspension of delegated power to the
Protestant majority.

make (1) to copulate with extra-maritally
Normally the male 'makes' the female: 'The
team made eight hits And a girl in the blea-
chers called Alice' (*Playboy's Book of Limericks*). However either sex can 'make it with'
the other, a male: 'Georges Simenon, who
says he made it with ten thousand different
women' (Hailey, 1979) or a female: 'This old
meat made it with Bernard Shaw' (Bradbury,
1976). 'Make out' is Am.: 'I know you were
making out with that German maid' (Mailer,
1965). 'Make whoopee' is perhaps ob: 'I
heard two people in the next room making
whoopee – the old man's archaic term for
fornication' (Styron, 1976). A 'make' can be
a single act of copulation and the woman
described as an 'easy make'. A place where
individuals habitually go looking for this kind
of relationship is a 'make-out joint': '. . . the
bar was the best make-out joint in Fort
Lauderdale' (Sanders, 1982). (Etymologists
will observe that **make** and **do** (1) (q.v.)
carry their subtle distinctions into
euphemism also.)

make (2) to steal
Army usage whence any fraudulent act,
especially robbery, in criminal jargon: '"It's
not a make," I said. "You're in trouble"'
(Chandler, 1939 – the intruder was not just a
thief).

make a call to urinate
Perhaps punning on a visit to the lavatory
and the **call of nature** (q.v.): '"I just want to
make a call," said Willoughby, and he disappeared into the toilet' (Bradbury, 1959).
Common use by both sexes, but rarely of
defecation.

make a hole in the water to kill yourself
by drowning

I suppose you have to jump from a height: 'Why I don't go and make a hole in the water I don't know' (C. Dickens, 1853). ? ob.

make a mess to urinate or defecate involuntarily
Nursery, sickroom and geriatric use of humans and generally of domestic animals, especially indoors: 'If he makes another mess .... I'll have him destroyed' (N. Mitford, 1945, of a dog).

make a suggestion to propose extra-marital copulation
It is what men 'suggest' to women generally, or whores to men: '. . . if anybody had made a suggestion to her then, she would have slapped his face . . . . But look at her: she'd sleep with any Tom, Dick or Harry for two or three pounds' (Kersh, 1936). To 'make an improper suggestion' is more explicit and also used of homosexual approaches.

make an honest woman of to marry a woman you have impregnated
Honest (q.v.) used to mean not ready to copulate outside marriage and this phrase was once used seriously: 'It was your son made her sae, and he can make her an honest woman again' (W. Scott, 1822, of a pregnant woman). Now only used humorously: 'But if you're really so old-fashioned .... it's called "making an honest woman of me"' (Price, 1970, of a man proposing to marry his sexual mistress).

make away with (1) to kill
Usu. of domestic animals, if unwanted or ill. Of humans usu. of suicide: 'Ready to make away with themselves' (Burton, 1621). To 'make an end of' is explicit.

make away with (2) to steal
From the act of physical removal.

make babies together to copulate
Usu. within marriage and not really anticipating a multiple birth. It is perhaps my least favourite euphemism. To 'make a child', slightly less cloying, means to become a parent: 'Aren't you ever sad .... that we haven't made a child' (G. Greene, 1973).

make little of to copulate with extra-maritally
Usu. of the woman after she has been made large by impregnation: 'You let *David Power*, the doctor's son, make little of you, and get you into trouble?' (Binchy, 1985). Also perhaps of either party: 'So don't talk about people *making little* of other people, or of him

disgracing me. I was just as eager, all the time, as he was' (ibid.).

make love *see* love

make off with to steal
A commoner variant of **make away with** (2). It is never your own property that you take with you. In ob. Eng. use it also meant to kill.

make old bones to live long
Euphemistic in the negative in which it is normally used: 'I feel I shall never make old bones' (N. Mitford, 1945).

make out *see* make (1)

make room for tea etc. to urinate
A common, almost genteel usage which I have never seen in print. Not generally used by or of a person drinking intoxicants but note '"Knock that back and have another." "I'll make room for it first if you don't mind"' (Amis, 1986, of drinking intoxicants).

make sheep's eyes to show sexual interest in another
From the unintelligent staring of the wide-eyed beast. In former times you might 'cast sheep's eyes': 'I swear I have often seen him cast a sheep's eye out of a calf's head at you' (Swift, 1738 – 'calf' too implies youthful longing, as in 'calf love').

make the beast with two backs *see* beast with two backs

make the (bed) springs creak to copulate
The usu. 'bed' imagery, within or outside marriage: 'We'd been married a long time and made the springs creak times without number' (Fraser, 1971). The springs may also 'squeak' under the same provocation: '"It would improve everyone present if the bedsprings squeaked a bit more often." "Let's leave sex until after tea," said Treece' (Bradbury, 1976).

make the chick scene to copulate with a woman
Of an Am. male homosexual, for whom heterosexuality is taboo: '. . . that roaring faggot .... He makes the chick scene from time to time' (Mailer, 1965).

make the supreme sacrifice to be killed
On war service but not necessarily in action: 'Fellow members who had made the supreme sacrifice . . .' (Boyle, 1979, of war dead).

make time with to copulate with extra-maritally
The male is usu. the maker: 'It doesn't help when they go into the bar and find a couple of guys trying to make time with them' (Sanders, 1983, of a club for women). Am.

make up to to attempt to court
Of either sex to the other: '. . . me mother would have a fit if she thought I was making up to you' (Cookson, 1967).

make water to urinate
'Discharge' it, would be slightly more accurate and *see* water: 'Heave up my leg, and make water against a lady's farthingale?' (Shakespeare, *Two Gentlemen of Verona*).

make yourself available to be ready to copulate with outside marriage
The woman indicates the 'availability', usu. without payment: 'He . . . . would have toyed with her and cast her aside . . . . if she had been callow enough to make herself immediately available to him' (W. Smith, 1979). However the politician who 'makes himself available ' for nomination or re-selection thinks to gain votes from a show of reluctance.

maladjusted naughty or stupid
Properly, and sometimes used of, a child who has emotional imbalance or suffers from bad home influences. But mainly educational or 'social worker' jargon in a world where there are no bad or simple-minded children, only a sick society. Whence maladjustment, mental illness in children or adults: 'I was good at diverting myself, and others, from the deeper causes of my "maladjustment"' (Irvine, 1986 – she was in an institution for the insane).

malady of France syphilis
The **French ache** etc. (q.v.): 'My Moll is dead i' th' spital of malady of France' (Shakespeare, *Henry V*). ob.

Malayan Peoples' Anti-Japanese Army bands of Chinese Communists in Malaya
The people who so styled themselves were not Malays, not noticeably active against the Japanese and not an army, except insofar as the Br. 'Force 136' incorporated them by proxy in the Br. 14th Army. Their intention of seizing power in September 1945 was thwarted by the invading Br./Indian troops who, being ignorant of any far-off declarations of human rights, summarily imprisoned the leaders, disarming and disbanding the rest. In December, against the advice of the soldiers, the leaders were released and thus was born the Malayan **Emergency** (q.v.).

male (1) a lavatory for the exclusive use of males
In factories or office blocks, with its 'female' counterpart.

male (2) homosexual
As in 'male' movies for those who are 'male' identified or orient(at)ed. 'Female' can be, but isn't usu., a similar signal for women homosexuals.

(malt beer comes from the grain prepared for brewing and gave rise to many euphemisms like 'malty', drunk; 'malt-worm', a drunkard; 'troubled with a malt sucker inside', having a craving for beer; and the Sc. 'malt above the water' or 'malt above the meal', drunkenness: 'When he was riding dovering hame (wi' the malt rather abune the meal)' (W. Scott, 1814). 'Malt' today is used mainly as an abbr. for 'malt whisky'.)

Malta dog diarrhoea
Caught, and spoken of, by Br. servicemen on the island. The etymology is as obscure as that of the **Hong Kong dog** (q.v.).

man (1) a male with whom a female regularly copulates extra-maritally
Properly, her husband but in this use always with the possessive article: 'He is not my man, he is my husband' (*Evesham Journal*, 1899, quoted in EDD which corresponds with the oldest joke – 'That's no lady, that's my wife'). In modern use he is likely to be a 'man friend'.

man (2) a policeman or warder
The Am. CB 'man with a gun' is a patrolman with radar. 'The Man' is an Am. prison governor: 'If he went to The Man to complain about it, you got him alone someplace, more places to ambush a man in prison' (McBain, 1981, of buggery in gaol).

man (3) a personal valet
Rather more than merely an abbr. of 'man-servant'. The Black 'man' as a method of male address comes from the rejection of the servile 'boy' used by generations of Whites.

man-root *see* root (1)

managerial privileges extra-marital copulation with a female entertainer
Producers and directors are supposed to be the particular objects of favour: 'Tammy gave what we call "managerial privileges" to

agents, impresarios and the rest of the gang' (Allbeury, 1980). Also as 'management privileges': 'On the bed upstairs, Julie had let him enjoy what are known in show business as "management privileges"' (Allbeury, 1981).

manhole cover a towel worn during menstruation
A rare jocular, if unfunny, pun on the metal cover for a hole in the street.

manhood the male genitalia
Properly, the state of being an adult male: '. . . tying a handkerchief round the remains of his once-proud manhood' (Sharpe, 1979 – he had snagged his penis on a rosebush). Much fig. use for male copulation: 'I was oblig'd to endure one more trial of his manhood' (Cleland, 1749, of a whore). To 'eliminate manhood' is to castrate: 'I know what you mean about eliminating manhood – even in animals' (Hailey, 1979).

manual exercise masturbation by a male of himself
Punning on the phrase 'manual work'.

manure *see* **horse apples**

marbles the testicles
From the glass spheres beloved by schoolboys, which were once made of marble. To 'lose your marbles' is to be mentally unstable: '. . . now openly saying that Sir Ian has lost his marbles' (*Private Eye*, August 1980). The Am. 'marble orchard' is a cemetery, from the crop of tombstones.

marge a female homosexual taking the female role
In 19c. Eng. it meant an effeminate youth, either from an abbr. of the name 'Margery', or from the meaning 'edge', or punning on both. Still in Am. use.

Maria Monk the male semen
Br. rh. sl. for **spunk** (q.v.). It is a long way back to the poetess Mary Monck or Monk, who died in 1715, but I know of no other eminent lady of the same name.

marine residence a dwelling near the sea
Real estate jargon, but not a houseboat.

marital aid an instrument to use in seeking sexual pleasure
In fact, the object is unlikely to feature in any exchange within wedlock, often merely adding zest to masturbation or other solitary activity: '. . . in their bedroom drawers I would find what the dirty shops called "marital aids"' (Theroux, 1983).

marital rights copulation by a man with his wife
They were demanded from a reluctant wife in an age when both lay and ecclesiastical law held that it was a woman's duty to copulate with her husband on request, even at the cost of debilitating, dangerous and unwanted pregnancies. Today used only by husbands with willing wives and a dated sense of humour. To 'exercise marital rights' with other than your wife is to copulate extramaritally.

mark a swindler's victim
'Marked' or watched, for his suitability, whence the ob. punning 'walk penniless in Mark Lane', to have been swindled but not necessarily in that London street. The ob. Sc. 'mark' was an invulnerable spot on the body of a wizard or witch, which played an important role in detecting them as such: '. . . through which mark, when a large brass pin was thrust till it was bowed, both men and women, neither felt a pain, nor did it bleed' (Ritchie, 1883, describing how you might unmask a witch or wizard).

marriage joys copulation
But what of shared children, companionship, warmed slippers or a cooked meal? Shakespeare meant none of these in 'The sweetest silent hours of marriage joys' (*Richard III*). Now too of extra-marital copulation.

martyr to (a) suffering from
The death or persecution is only fig. The *Daily Telegraph* of 7 September 1978 hesitated to call the Br. Prime Minister a liar, a 'martyr to selective amnesia' being a more telling and memorable indictment.

Mary (1) a homosexual playing the female role
Either male or female, from the name.

Mary (2) marijuana
An abbr. much used in pop songs for oblique narcotic reference. Because English speakers tend to pronounce the 'J' in marijuana, sometimes as 'Mary Jane' or 'MJ'. 'Mary Anne' is rare.

massage (1) to bribe
Properly, the application of friction to free muscles.

massage (2) to assault violently
Am. police jargon for the use of force to obtain information: '"Shellacking", "massaging" . . . . and numerous other phrases are employed by the police . . . . as

euphemisms to express how they compel reluctant prisoners to refresh their memories' (Lavine, 1930).

massage (3) copulation
Again the application of friction, where it can also mean masturbation of a male by a whore (or 'hand relief' in the jargon) apart from vaginal prostitution: '"You want a massage?" she says. I says forget it. They don't mean massage' (Theroux, 1975). Whence 'massage parlour', a brothel: 'Whether we worked in a Massage Parlour or were rich .... we were still the same to you. Easy women' (Bogarde, 1978, of Indonesia in 1946). The whores are called 'masseuses': 'Accompanied by my personal assistant-cum-masseuse Miss Rita Chevrolet (*Private Eye*, February 1980).

massage (4) deliberately to inflate the price of a quoted security
Brokers' jargon for stimulating interest in a stock without overt fraud. Similarly used by accountants for presenting figures in a way which gives an unduly favourable impression.

masses (the) those ruled by Communist autocrats
Marxist jargon for the great body of humanity whose communal will is revealed to those who have won power over them: '"Look at Lenin," she said. "Did he think about himself?" "He thought about the masses."' (McCarthy, 1963).

masseuse *see* **massage** (3)

masterpiece a competent piece of artistic work
Properly, the article submitted by the apprentice to show that he has acquired the skill of the master. An advertising cliché, used especially for quite banal work where the author may previously have turned out something of merit.

masters the politicians in government
A sarcastic and resentful use by senior civil servants who consider themselves better fitted to govern by virtue of their intellect and experience than the elected amateurs who head their ministries: '... the very archetype of everything our masters have told us to avoid' (le Carré, 1980, of a civil service gaffe).

mate to copulate
Of animals this is a proper, non-euphemistic, use: 'Mating pythons are a very rare and a very strange sight' (Richards, 1936). In humans 'mating' properly means

marriage but is used of copulation within or outside marriage: 'He'll never be able to mate with a woman again' (West, 1979 – but with what, if not with a woman?) and a 'mating' is an act of copulation: '... half a dozen mamas enjoyed unexpectedly vigorous matings later that evening' (Erdman, 1974).

matron an old woman
Properly, any married woman, with a presumption of sobriety and godliness.

mattress relating to copulation
The common association of beds and copulating in a variety of compounds like 'mattress drill' or 'beating the mattress', copulation and rare uses such as 'mattress extortion', sexual blackmail by a female: 'So you con him into moving to sunny Florida. Maybe a little mattress extortion there' (Sanders, 1982).

mature (1) old
Properly, fully developed: '... the high payers at the front wind up with some of the more mature girls' (Moynahan, 1983 – older stewardesses work the 1st class in aircraft). In educational jargon, a 'mature student' is someone who returns to class after years outside the educational system.

mature (2) fat
The language of those who seek to sell clothes to obese women. The 'maturer' figure is no more mature than the 'mature'.

Maud a male homosexual
Usu. paid for his services. From the girl's name and not the Sc. striped shepherd's plaid.

maul to caress a reluctant female
Properly, to handle roughly but to an unwilling partner, any fondling is excessive: 'Because you give me the occasional meal .... doesn't mean you have the right to maul me' (Archer, 1979). Female use.

mausoleum crypt a drawer for a corpse facing on to a corridor
Funeral jargon for the slots facing into the building which are harder to sell, due to the absence of a view: 'The crypts facing the corridor are called mausoleum crypts' (J. Mitford, 1963). A far cry from the mausoleum of Mausolos' widow who, with the help of a few thousand slaves, ran up the famous sepulchre at Halicarnassos around 353 B.C. to keep his memory alive.

me-too slavishly copying
Commercial use where a product is

launched similar to that of a competitor to attempt to exploit a market he has developed: 'Everybody knows there are "me-too" drugs . . . . But they sometimes lead to new discoveries' (Hailey, 1984).

meat a person or the genitalia of a person viewed sexually
If a female by a male, usu. all of her: 'Away, you mouldy rogue, away. I am meat for your master' (Shakespeare, 2 *Henry IV*). If a male by a female, his erect penis: 'A lot of them look like they need . . . a hot meat injection' (Styron, 1976, of young women). If of a male homosexual, the patient in buggery: 'Together, he and Jimmy had shared some of the choicest meat inside the prison' (McBain, 1981). Whence many compounds – 'fresh meat', a young whore; 'stale meat', an experienced or older whore: '. . . since to the accustomed rake the most prized flesh is the newest, some now counted her stale meat' (Fowles, 1985, of an experienced whore); 'meat and two veg.', the penis and testicles; the ob. Br. 'meat-house', a brothel and the modern Am. 'meat-rack', a meeting place for male homosexuals: 'The meat racks, the quick sex, the beatings' (Collins, 1981, of a male homosexual's life); 'a bit of meat', an extra-marital sexual partner: 'I don't want you coming round here after my little bit of meat' (Richards, 1933, of a sexual mistress); 'tube of meat', an erect penis: 'All because of that lousy tube of meat. I want to hump every woman I see' (Sanders, 1982). 'Meat' is also Am. underworld sl. for the corpse of someone killed violently, with the 'meat wagon' an ambulance or a hearse: 'They have the meat wagon following him around to follow up on the business he finds' (Chandler, 1943, of Marlowe, his corpse-prone private eye).

meathead a fool
All of us have meat of sorts in our heads, if you think about it: 'Rev, in this town, with this Administration? Don't be a meathead' (M. Thomas, 1987). sl.

medal showing a visible undone trouser fly-button
Pre-zip usage to warn another male without undue embarrassment. DSUE says 'jocular c.p. carrying on euphemistic S.E.' but hardly a catch phrase by any normal definition.

medical representative a drug salesman
This is what drug company representatives who visit doctors and hospitals call themselves. The business makes high profits from high-pressure selling and any veneer of altruism helps, even in a name.

medicine a spirituous intoxicant
This substance is seldom ingested to treat disease: '. . . fond of taking their medicine' (Mayhew, 1851, of drunkards). The pretence that you drink spirits for your health is not new, nor does it take anybody in.

medium small
Properly, between big and little, but not in the grocery business.

meet with an accident to be murdered
From the Am. underworld, or those who write about it: '"He met with an accident. He's dead." . . . . "Yeah, he's dead. You shot him"' (Chandler, 1939).

meet your Maker etc. to die
Some Christians who use this and similar expressions have serious doubts about whether the rendez-vous will be kept. Similarly, a Moslem might, if so favoured, 'meet the Prophet': 'He intended to meet the Prophet shod, smiling, and at peace' (M. Thomas, 1980).

meeting where you claim to be when you do not wish to talk to someone
The standard rebuff to an intruder by telephone or in person.

mellow slightly drunk
Properly, ripe but a euphemism since 17c.: 'Two being "half-drunk", and the third "just comfortably mellow"' (Bartram, 1897).

melt to ejaculate semen
The imagery is from liquefying under heat: '. . . made me soon sensible of his melting period' (Cleland, 1749). ? ob.

member (1) a penis
Properly, any limb of the body: 'Affection and the erect male member tend to go hand in hand, if you'll pardon the expression' (Amis, 1978). The *membrum virile* is the erect penis, with a Latin gloss: 'And not a bad label for his membrum virile either' (Sanders, 1980). The ob. Br. 'member for Horncastle', a cuckold, was a complex vulgar pun on the Lincs. parliamentary constituency.

member (2) *see* **club** (3)

memorial relating to death
Properly, maintaining the memory of anything. An Am. 'memorial' association or society is a rather grander version of the burial club: '"Funeral societies" or "Mem-

orial Associations"' (J. Mitford, 1963) and
'Memorial societies .... constitute one of
the greatest threats to the American ideas of
memorialisation' (ibid. – 'memorialisation' is
funeral jargon for spending as much money
as can be extracted from the bereaved on
smartening up the corpse, a fancy casket,
etc.). An Am. 'memorial counsellor' is a
salesman of plots in a cemetery: 'A cemetery
salesman (identified on his card as a "memorial counsellor")' (ibid.) and a 'memorial
park' is a cemetery: '. . .not in a graveyard or
cemetery, but rather in a "memorial park"'
(ibid.). A 'memorial home' is a structure on
the walls of which you can pay to have a
tablet fixed recording the death, and a
'memory garden' is an open space within the
confines of a cemetery or crematorium.
Mainly Am.

men a lavatory for male use only
Usu. in a place where nobody is trying to sell
you anything, such as a government office.
Often expanded to 'men's toilet' and in Am.
to 'men's room', which latter could just as
well be a dormitory, but isn't: 'His first destination, the men's toilet' (Bradbury, 1976)
and 'I went into the men's room, just to look
in the mirror' (Theroux, 1973). The sexual
counterpart is **women** (q.v.).

ınen in blue *see* **blue** (1)

ménage à trois three people living
together in a sexual relationship
Literally, domestic arrangements for three
and *see* **à trois**. To 'maintain a clandestine
ménage' is to keep a sexual mistress:
'Although he was indeed married, he also
maintained a clandestine ménage' (R.V.
Jones, 1978).

men's room *see* **men**

mense(s) (the) menstruation
Properly, month(s) but long SE: 'He would
say .... "I'se glad to see ye after yer mense",
before beginning the churching' (Linton,
1866 – the 'churching' was a rite of supposedly cleansing a woman after childbirth).
Nearly always in the plural: 'A woman does
not get gout unless her menses are stopped'
(Condon, 1966).

mental mad
Properly, pertaining to the mind: 'Non-U
mental/U mad' (Ross, 1956, who here and
elsewhere reminds us that greater security or
better education tend to reduce or eliminate
the use of euphemism in speech). 'Mental' is
used to describe any condition from mild
eccentricity to lunacy. Thus those treated

under the Br. 'Mental Deficiency Act' of
1913 with a mild condition might find themselves locked up among madmen, the company and the treatment only making their
illness worse; and conversely, the reluctance
to describe a lunatic other than by
euphemism cannot have helped him or those
responsible for his treatment. Today
'mentally handicapped' lumps together those
of widely varying degrees of affliction.
'Mentally retarded', of low intelligence, mis-
leadingly implies a wilful holding back – *see*
retard.

merchandise any illicit possession
Often narcotics, but otherwise synonymous
with the commoner **goods** (q.v.).

mercy a mild oath
Am. CB radio use for illegal profanities. The
ob. Sc. 'mercy' whisky, brought warmth and
comfort: 'The Bailie requires neither precept nor example wi' his tumbler when the
mercy's afore him' (Galt, 1826).

(mercy killing, the failure to keep alive by
artificial means, is also a journalistic cliché
for the murder of an incurable patient by
doctor or near relative. In either case it is not
euphemistic. However the Nazi 'mercy
death' was less merciful: '. . . the Gestapo is
now systematically bumping off the mentally
deficient people . . . . the Nazis call them
"mercy deaths"' (Shirer, 1984).)

merry drunk
Cheerful, but not offensive. The ob. 'merry-
begot' or 'merry-begotten' was a bastard,
conceived I suppose in pleasure rather than
in drink: 'That Joe Garth is a merry-begot'
(Caine, 1885) and 'A love or merry-begotten
child, a bastard' (Grose).

mess (1) to copulate extra-maritally
Probably an abbr. of 'mess about', to act in a
sloppy, unconventional or disorganized way:
'I got a decent wife. I don't go messing any
longer. I just don't have the energy' (Sharpe,
1977). A 'messer' is a part-time whore, with
the same etymology and a reputation for
spoiling the market for fulltime workers.

mess (2) turds or urine in an unwanted
place
On the carpet of household pets but also of
humans and other animals: '. . . the goat
which was for ever trotting in and making a
mess on the fireplace' (W.S. Moss, 1950).

message an advertisement
Am. television jargon: 'We'll return after

these messages' (ABC announcer, September 1983).

Mexican brown etc. marijuana
From the country of origin and the colour: 'That's what speed and Mexican brown does to ya. A hardballer' (Wambaugh, 1983). It can also be 'Mexican' green or red. A 'Mexican mushroom' is the hallucinogenic Psilocybe Mexicana. Am.

Mexican raise etc a promotion with no increase in pay
Many Mexicans working in the USA without permits are subject to exploitation. A 'Mexican promotion' means the same thing.

Mexican toothache etc. *see* Montezuma's revenge

(mezz a marijuana cigarette comes from the jazz clarinettist Mezz Mezzrow, known for his addiction: 'A reefer five foot long The mighty mezz, but not too strong' (Longstreet, 1956). Am.)

Michigan roll a sham bundle of currency
It usu. has a good note or two on the outside. Am. underworld sl.

Micky *see* Mike Bliss

Micky Finn a drugged intoxicant given to an unsuspecting victim
From a late 19c. Chicago innkeeper of evil reputation. The additive was often chlorine which reacts with alcohol to form chloral hydrate in water, with hypnotic or anaesthetic effects on him who drinks it. Today a 'Micky Finn' is any drink mixed so as to ensnare or immobilize the victim.

microwave club a place where married women may meet men for extra-marital copulation
Usu. an Am. dancehall or bar. The microwave oven allows a wife to serve her husband with hot food despite an afternoon's dalliance.

mid-job *see* on the job

middle-aged old
Halfway to three score years and ten is thirty five but no man under forty-five or woman under fifty would admit to having reached middle age: '. . . in that advanced stage of life that we optimistically call middle age' (Deighton, 1982). 'Middle-age spread' is obesity around the waist: 'Middle-aged spread is a genuine fact of life . . . . The flesh can resist the pull of gravity for so long' (Matthew, 1983).

(middle class means different things to different people. In Am. it may be a synonym for having European ancestry. Despite pseudo-intellectual sneers at generally accepted or 'middle-class' morals, most Br. people, if asked, say that they belong to this classification and that kind of comfortable morality, based on the home and family, has a greater appeal than the alternatives which pass in and out of fashion.)

middle leg *see* third leg

middle passage the west-bound transatlantic voyage of a ship carrying slaves
The 'passage' was the sea voyage from Africa to the Americas in the **triangular trade** (q.v.).

midnight baby a bastard
From the mysterious time of conception rather than of birth: 'I never knew who my daddy was. I was what they called a "midnight baby"' (Sanders, 1984). Am.

migraine a sub-acute alcoholic poisoning
It is the same word as 'megrim' which meant depression or a fad as well as a bad headache. This medical condition is much called in aid by women who do not wish to acknowledge having been drunk, the taboo against female drunkenness being greater than against male: 'She had stayed at home with a hangover that she called a migraine' (Manning, 1978). The affliction may also be contracted at short notice by a female who does not want to copulate with her regular sexual partner.

Mike Bliss urination
Rh. sl. for 'piss' and found usu. in fig. use, to take the 'Micky', 'Michael', 'Mick' or 'Mike', to taunt, imitate or humiliate: 'Look at Bill wobbling his belly . . . mickying her, he is' (Cookson, 1967).

military intelligence spying
It could mean no more than knowing how to fire a gun: 'Foreigners have spies; Britain has Military Intelligence' (Follett, 1978). But nearly everybody has 'military attachés', whose main function is to uncover the military secrets of the country to which they are accredited.

militia an armed body operating outside normal military regulations
Properly, a body supplementing and under the control of regular forces. It is usu. raised to support an autocracy, or, like the notorious 'milice' in WW II, to assist the suppression by a conqueror: 'He more than anyone

else knew that the Militia existed in order to betray' (Genet, in 1969 tr.) and '. . . the *Service de l'Ordre Légionnaire* – which is now the Milice – the scum of the scum' (Price, 1978).

milk (1) regularly to defraud
By taking small amounts from a till, persistent pilfering, etc. Now especially of illegally syphoning fuel from motor vehicles.

milk (2) to masturbate
Of a male, from 'milk', the semen. Rarely, too, of ejaculation during copulation.

milk run a comparatively safe wartime flight
WW II flier's jargon, usu. of a mission over enemy territory taken regularly or an a single occasion: 'We'll be over the sea most of the way . . . . Another lousy milk run' (Deighton, 1982). From the daily doorstep delivery common in BI.

mingle bodies to copulate
A purist might say that only a limited portion of each does the mingling. Usu. of extramarital copulation: '. . . in the eight times their "bodies had mingled" since that first evening' (Boyd, 1982).

Ministry of Defence etc. *see under* **defence, health, internal affairs**

minor function (the) urination
As different from defecation, which I have yet to see called the 'major function': '. . . going to the W.C. (Generally for the minor function)' (Franklin, DRS).

minority group a community of non-Whites living in a predominantly White-occupied country
A usage which skirts round reference to skin pigmentation. Thus the Chinese in San Francisco can be a 'minority group' despite a world preponderance of Chinamen: 'I used to be coloured, right? Then I was a Negro. And then I turned into an Afro-American. After that I was just a member of a Minority Group. Now, I'm black' (Theroux, 1982). 'Minorities' tends to include also those with less common religious or sexual views: '. . . the minorities ran the risk of losing others' sympathy and support' (Jennings, 1965).

minstrel a Black person in a predominantly White-occupied country
From 'nigger minstrel', a performer who blacked his skin to emulate or caricature a negroid appearance: '. . . he was responsible for admitting the Minstrels in such numbers in the first place' (*Private Eye*, 1981, of

Enoch Powell). Especially in derogatory use by Br. Whites of immigrants from W. Indies.

misfortune a bastard
Properly, ill-luck, which it certainly was for mother and child: '. . . had "had a misfortune" – in the shape of a bouncing boy' (Bartram, 1897) and 'To light of a misfortune is the ordinary euphemism' (EDD c.1900). A 'misbegot' or 'mishap' was also a bastard. A 'mishap' was also premature delivery of a foetus, in which case an animal or woman was said to 'misgo': ''Tis a thousand pities her should'a miswent' (EDD).

miss (1) *see* mistress

miss (2) to fail to menstruate at due time
Abbr. of 'miss a period' and often with overtones of unwanted pregnancy: '"Has 'er missed then?" "No, but us've 'ad some worryin' times"' (conversation in S. Devon between two males in 1948). 'Mis(s)' is a common abbr. too for miscarriage.

miss Nancy *see* nancy

missionary position copulation where the male lies atop the female
European missionaries brought this fashion to Polynesians who had preferred the quadripedal approach: '"The guy's on top and the girl's on the bottom, and they're – well, you know, screwing?" . . . . "Not the missionary position"' (Theroux, 1973 – but it was). Sanders (1982) probably invented the 'Ms-sionary position' – the female astride the male.

mis-speak to lie
Properly, to speak evil or to speak incorrectly: '. . . do they bar him for his "mis-speakings", or do they just take over and appoint someone else as candidate?' (*Private Eye*, October, 1986). This is one of Richard Nixon's contributions to the language from the days of Watergate.

mistake an unwanted pregnancy
Usu. within marriage. The word is also used of the resulting child.

mistress a man's extra-marital regular sexual partner
Properly, the female head of the household, but now always used improperly except when abbr. to 'Mrs' or in girls' schools: 'My mistress is my mistress' (Shakespeare, *Titus Andronicus*). 'Kept mistress' is explicit: 'It's not fair to the girl, this life as a kept mistress' (Harris, 1925). 'Miss' was formerly used in the same sense: 'Priests, lawyers, keen physicians, kept misses' (Galloway, 1810).

misuse to copulate with extra-maritally
But not the opposite of **use** (1) (q.v.): 'Did you ever misuse my Ephie .... Did you ever have her?' (Keneally, 1979). ? ob.

mixer a whore who finds customers in bars
Properly, a fluid added to a spirituous intoxicant to make it more palatable. Am.

mob an association of criminals
The 19c. Eng. use came from *mobile vulgus*, the rabble, and a 'mob' might also be a whore. Now mainly of an Am. criminal gang: 'Wasn't it enough he had to pay protection on his place to the mob' (Collins, 1981). A member of such a gang is a 'mobster': 'A mobster newly acquitted from a charge of swindling the city' (Ustinov, 1971).

model a whore
Abbr. of 'model girl', a mannequin and before the complaints start thundering in let me assert that doubtless many lead wholesome lives of sexual rectitude. However prostitutes who advertise their availability by defacing telephone booths etc. profess to being so employed, as do high-class whores who have no need for promotional activities: 'Miss Keeler, a freelance model, was visiting Miss Marilyn Rice-Davies, an actress' (*Daily Telegraph*, December 1962, quoted by Green, 1979).

modern convenience a lavatory indoors
This does not imply that a public **convenience** (1) (q.v.) is necessarily ancient. Br. real estate jargon, abbr. in small advertisements to 'mod cons'. In similar code 'all mod cons' means you can expect hot and cold running water and a bath as well as an indoor lavatory.

mole a conspirator or spy within an organization
Espionage and labour union jargon, from the burrowing habits of the mammal and perhaps its blackness, but not its blindness: 'There were no "moles" at large in Washington: "Indifference, not treachery, was at the root of America's attitude"' (Boyle, 1979). The ob. Eng. 'mole country', death, came from the prevalence of molehills in churchyards.

molecular roulette the unbridled use of medical narcotics
A derivative of Russian roulette and **Vatican roulette** (q.v.): '... describing "me-too" drugs and "molecular roulette"' (Hailey, 1984). Am.

molest to attempt to copulate with an unwilling female
Properly, to inconvenience. Legal jargon and common Am. usage: 'I revived her by threatening to carry her into the bushes and molest her' (Fraser, 1975). So pervasive is the euphemistic use that a female may be said to have been brutally attacked, but not 'molested', unless her assailant's motives are sexual as well as predatory. 'Molest' is also used of any sexual assault by an adult upon a child.

moll a whore
Probably from the common girl's name and in ob. use a 'moll-shop' was a brothel. Previously, a 'moll' was merely a sweetheart, as she remains when the female companion of the Am. gangster. The ob. Br. 'Moll Thompson's mark' was nothing more than emptiness of a bottle of intoxicant, punning on the initials 'MT'.

Molotov cocktail a simple petrol bomb
Molotov was the Russian foreign minister in WW II whose name has thus been not inappropriately perpetuated. He it was who concluded Stalin's peace pact with Hitler in 1939, among other perfidious acts in a long and often sinister career. But even this claim to fame was wrongly acquired, the device having been invented by the Finns for use against their Russian aggressors.

mom-and-pop staid and old-fashioned
Like your aged parents: '... a small-time mom-and-pop dope store would be allowed to flourish unmolested' (McBain, 1981). Am.

momentary trick (the) copulation
The duration of a casual encounter: 'For the momentary trick Be perdurably fined' (Shakespeare, *Measure for Measure*). ob.

Monday man a stealer of clothes from washing lines
Clothes were traditionally washed and hung out to dry on Mondays. As modern appliances have released Am. women from the drudgery of the old copper boiler, so the washing may be done, and stolen, any day. A 'Monday man' does not ride in a 'Monday car', which, like the 'Friday car', is likely to have been sloppily assembled by inattentive workers, nor would he be welcome in the Br. 'Monday Club', an association of hard-line conservatives.

Monday-morning quarter-back a fantasist who judges by hindsight
The Am. spectator who watches a weekend

game may take his criticism to work with him on Monday: '. . . the Monday morning quarterback who could have won the ball game if he had been on the team. But he never is. He's high up in the stands with a flask on his hip' (Chandler, 1958).

monkey (1) *see* **suck the monkey**

monkey (2) an addiction to illicit narcotics
Probably from the image of 'having a monkey on your back', which you cannot shake off. Am.

monkey business extra-marital copulation
Properly, any mischief which a monkey might get up to. Used sometimes as a warning from a girl to her suitor but more often from her mother to them both: '"No monkey business," he agreed. "Shit, I won't touch her"' (Sanders, 1977, of an artist to a young model's mother).

monosyllable the vagina
The taboo 'cunt', viewed sexually by a male. Grose says 'A woman's commodity' and *see* also DSUE for a learned disquisition.

Montezuma's revenge diarrhoea
Usu. but not necessarily contracted in Mexico by US visitors. Montezuma II was the Aztec emperor when Cortes invaded and was killed by his own people in 1520 when he told them to submit to the invader. Also as the **Aztec two-step** (q.v.), 'Mexican toothache', Mexican two-step', 'Mexican fox-trot', etc.

monthlies *see* **monthly period etc.**

monthly period etc. menstruation
From its regularity and incidence: '. . . her monthly period. We call it menstruation' (Sharpe, 1978). Abbr. to 'monthlies': 'Molly was easily excited, especially about the eighth day after her monthlies had ceased' (Harris, 1925). Rarely as 'monthly courses'.

mooch to pilfer
Properly, to hang about, whence to beg and so to steal: 'I don't mean to say that if I see anything laying about handy that I don't mooch it' (Mayhew, 1851). I include this ob. Br. entry as a rare example of a word which has reverted from its euphemistic to its proper use in modern speech.

moonlight (1) smuggled spirits
ob. smugglers' usage, from the time when the business was best done and an habitual smuggler was said to have been 'bred in the moonlight': 'Thirty "crack" hands, who had been bred in the "moonlight" from boyhood' (Vedder, 1832). In many other uses 'moonlight' was synonymous with smuggling and a 'moonraker' was a smuggler, from the practice of throwing contraband into a pool if detected, recovering it later: 'Getting ready for the moonrakers at the great pool' (Verney, 1870).

moonlight (2) to wound
The agrarian disturbances of 19c. Ireland took place at night, some notices about threatened arson being signed 'Captain Moonlight'. Apart from arson and pillage, those in or loyal to Br. authority were maimed: 'He had deposed to his experience of being moonlighted in the thigh' (*Daily Telegraph*, November 1888, quoted in EDD). Ire. ob. (It is easy now to forget that such famous anti-British Irishmen as Burke, Gratton, Swift, Emmet, Parnell, Wolfe Tone and Thomas Davis were Protestants. Resentment of the Br. tie was not a Roman Catholic monopoly.)

moonlight (3) to work at a second job without paying taxes etc.
The work is usu. done in the evening: 'A joiner who "moonlights" at weekends for his mates' (Shankland, 1980). A worker who continues to draw unemployment monies from the state is also said to be 'moonlighting'.

moonlight flit etc. the clandestine departure of a tenant in arrears with his rent
As distress could be levied on household chattels in the premises for arrears of rent, but not on the same chattels if moved elsewhere, you had to take all with you when you vacated the property, and this was best done at night: 'He has e'en made a moonlight flitting' (W. Scott, 1822). You might also have made a 'moonlight' flight, march, touch or walk; or you might 'bolt' or 'shoot' the moon: 'Nobody was allowed to shoot the moon' (Besant and Rice, 1872). The phrase was also, and rarely still is, used of a debtor fleeing his creditors: 'He was fain to make a moonlight flitting, leaving his wife for a time to manage his affairs' (Galt, 1821). And *see* flit (1).

moonraker *see* **moonlight** (1)

moonshine whisky
From an illicit still, which is operated at night to avoid detection: '. . . made their living by odd ends of trade, from moonshine, from cutting lumber . . .' (Keneally, 1979).

moose a whore
Neither a corruption of 'mouse' nor punning
on the deer but an Am. Korean war usage
from the Japanese 'musume', a girl (DAS).

mop up to kill or capture surviving
opponents
Military jargon. The imagery is from
cleaning up spillage: 'Franco ruled. It was all
over bar the mopping up' (Boyle, 1979).

moral immoral
Another of the opposites, like **defence**
(q.v.). 'Moral danger' is not to be at risk from
an excess of goodness and the police 'Morals
Squad' is after vice, whatever the rectitude
of its members.

more than a good friend a person with
whom you regularly copulate extra-maritally
Another kind of **friend** (q.v.): 'It would have
taken no special investigation to establish
that they were more than good friends'
(Price, 1971).

Morocco *see* **Guatemala**

most precious part the male genitalia
Valued for copulation rather than urination:
'Corporal Brownlee was hit in the most
precious part of his body' (Farran, 1948).

moth in your wallet (a) stinginess
The Tineola bisselliella doesn't normally go
for leather, although it favours an undis-
turbed site for its eggs: 'Symington would
pick up the tab . . . . there were no moths in
his wallet' (Sanders, 1985).

mother an elderly male homosexual
A modern Am. use which replaced the ob.
Br. meaning, a bawd.

mother five fingers male masturbation
Of the same imagery as **five-fingered
widow** (q.v.): 'Always looking for something
better. Know what I mean? Then I end up
with Mother Five-fingers' (Sanders, 1981).

mother's blessing a narcotic administered to a baby
The 'blessing' was the peace which came
from silencing a crying child: 'Give the
babies a dose of "Mother's Blessing" (that's
laudanum, sir, or some sich stuff) to sleep
'em when they's squally' (Mayhew, 1862).
The usage and practice survived to WWII
but are now ob.

mother's ruin etc. gin
Its 19c. cheapness led to wide female addiction and consequent demoralization. Now
only humorous use: '. . . struggling to get his
arms around a Europack of litre-sized

Mother's Ruin' (*Private Eye*, April, 1980).
Franklyn in DRS says it is rh. sl., adding 'the
phonetics are poor' – too poor, I suspect,
when another etymological explanantion is
simpler. Rarely as the punning 'mother's
milk'.

motion (a) defecation
Medical jargon, from the movement of the
bowels and generally in the plural, where
'motions' means faeces: 'She had dreams of
cooking by perpetual motion, or rather by
perpetual motions' (Sharpe, 1971, of Mrs
Wilt's 'biological' lavatory that was supposed
to generate heat for domestic purposes).

motion discomfort airsickness
Airline jargon, in support of the pretence
that any passenger actually enjoys air travel:
'"I am still suffering from motion discomfort" . . . . "It means air sickness"' (N. Mitford, 1960). The 'motion discomfort bag'
you may find on an Am. airline is for you to
be sick in.

motivate to encourage employees to do the
work for which they are being paid
Properly, to show the reason for acting. This
management jargon tries to imbue routine
work with a purpose other than pay.

mount to copulate with
SE of animals and for humans the common
equine imagery: 'Like a full-acorn'd boar, a
German one, Cried "O!" and mounted'
(Shakespeare, *Cymbeline*). A male may describe his complaisant sexual partner as a
good 'mount' – it remains a mystery where
the 'bad mounts' get to.

mount a corporal and four to masturbate
Of a male, punning on the constitution of a
Br. army guard and the thumb and four
fingers.

mountain dew whisky
In modern use synonymous with
moonshine (above), from the process of
distillation and the place where it is done: 'A
"greybeard" jar of the real Glengillodram
mountain dew' (Alexander, 1882).

mousehole a vagina
Not necessarily viewed sexually: 'Scissored
her legs open – and pulled a length of mag-
ician's scarves, knotted end to end, out of
her mousehole' (Theroux, 1978). Perhaps
also punning on 'mouse', a sexually attractive
female: 'Tempt you again to bed; Pinch
wanton on your cheek; call you his mouse'
(Shakespeare, *Hamlet*).

mouth to kiss lecherously
Properly, to utter: 'He would mouth with a beggar, though she smelt brown bread and garlick' (Shakespeare, *Measure for Measure*). ob.

move to steal
Mainly Am., with the common imagery of shifting the stolen article.

move your bowels to defecate
Medical jargon and perhaps circumlocution rather than euphemism as in many cases we are merely recording cause and effect: 'He lay in bed, reading nothing; he moved his bowels' (Bradbury. 1959, writing of a stay in hospital). Whence 'bowels' as an absence of constipation: 'Good bowels were beyond price' (Keneally, 1979, of military service) and 'movement' as an act of defecation: 'Observe the time of day when he has his movement' (McCarthy, 1963).

movement (1) *see* **move your bowels**

movement (2) an ossified institution or association of institutions
Those who affect this title are often remarkable for their rigid and unchanging attitudes and behaviour, although to be fair the Br. Building Society 'movement' appears to have moved from its former deep conservatism in recent years.

Mozart drunk
Br. rh. sl. from 'Mozart and Liszt', pissed. **Brahms** (q.v.) is more common.

Mrs Chant a lavatory
Br. rh. sl. for **aunt** (2) (q.v.). Female use.

Mrs Duckett a mild oath
Br. rh. sl. for 'fuck it': 'A comment rather than an expletive: the workman who hits his thumb with a hammer uses no euphemism' (Franklin, DRS).

muck a mild oath
Used for 'fuck' fig. in all declensions. DAS says that 'muck up', to make a mess of '= fuck up, a euphem.' but I'm not so sure.

mud opium
From its texture and colour

mud-kicker a whore
Of poor quality, lying down al fresco, and liable to bilk or rob her customer in Am. use. The ob. Eng. 'mudlark' was a thief of coal etc. from ships grounded by the tide on the London foreshore and picking up what an accomplice tossed over the side: 'The mudlarks are generally known as thieves' (Mayhew, 1862).

muff the female pubic hair
But not used for keeping the hands warm: 'I had a photograph of that sanctimonious prick Merriman with his nose in some call-girl's muff' (M. Thomas, 1980). A 'muff diver' indulges in cunnilingus.

mug to rob by violence in a public place
In ob. Br. use it was to bribe with an intoxicant, from the container: 'Having .... mugged as we say in England, our pilot' (Ingelo, 1830). Specifically in 19c. London of robbery by garrotting but today any violence suffices for a 'mugger', who so robs, from 'mug', a dupe and not from 'mugger', 'an intinerant dealer in earthenwear vessels' (EDD) or 'the broad-nosed crocodile of India' (SOD).

mug-shot a frontal photograph taken by the police for identification
From sl. 'mug', the face. The subject seldom sits voluntarily.

muggy drunk
Properly, moist and usu. of the weather: 'They're rayther muggy oft' (Clark, 1839, of drunkards). 'Muggy' also means stupid.

mule (1) whisky
Usu. from an illicit Am. still and with a strong kick.

mule (2) a carrier of illegal narcotics in bulk
From the smuggling on rough mountain tracks in Central Am.: 'Some smuggle for their own use, but most are "mules", paid $1,500 or so a trip' (Moynahan, 1983, of airline narcotic smuggling).

multi-cultural mixing Blacks and Whites
'Multi-coloured' would be offensive and euphemistically inaccurate – *see* **coloured**: 'All-black schools in multi-cultural Brent would be a form of apartheid' (*Daily Telegraph*, October 1983). This apparent assumption that your culture is determined by your skin pigmentation is only made by those who favour an 'integrated society'.

multiple an orgy with more than two participants
And usu. more than three: 'One woman paid a grand for a "multiple": four men in a scene that lasted all afternoon' (Sanders, 1983). 'Multiple diplomatosis' is not sexually acquired but describes derogatively the unnecessary acquisition of successive degrees by adults reluctant to quit institutional life.

municipal farm a prison
As different from the funny farm (q.v. under

funny (2)): 'A striker caught with a slingshot was sentenced to the municipal farm' (Lacey, 1986).

Murphy as a whore to cheat a customer
An Am. and not an Irish trick, but perhaps from the simplest of 'Murphy's laws', if something can go wrong, it will. The intended customer, having reached an accord with the whore or her pimp, is afforded no satisfaction.

muscle to assault criminally
From the force used: 'You couldn't muscle anyone, Peter. You're a softy' (Sanders, 1983). Whence a 'muscleman', who is no keep-fit enthusiast but employed to carry out criminal acts of violence: '. . . kind of muscleman for a big protection gang in Tokyo' (West, 1979). 'Muscleman' is also abbr. to muscle: 'Not so much between the ears, but he was a good muscle' (Sanders, 1980). Am.

mush to rob householders while professing an itinerant trade
Abbr. of sl. 'mushroom', an umbrella. Umbrella-men went from house to house, itinerant crooks found it good cover and the trade got a bad name. 'Mush' is still a Br. mode of male address, importing no ill-will or accusation of dishonesty.

muslin a female viewed sexually by a male
She used to wear it in her dress or skirt although the whole was described usu. as a 'bit' or 'piece' of muslin. ? ob.

muster your bag to be ill
Br. naval usage, from having to take your kit to the sick bay if you reported sick. However in the WW II Br. army you were too weak to carry your kit bag if you dared to report sick.

mutate to dye
Of women's hair and certainly not to change genetically and permanently through natural processes: 'She "mutates" or "colour-corrects" her hair' (Jennings, 1965).

mutt deaf
Rh. sl. of 'Mutt and Jeff', better known as the Br. WWI service and victory medals than for the comic cartoon characters, but no longer well-known as either. ? ob.

mutton a person viewed sexually by another
As you may expect, it is normally the man who so views the woman: 'The duke . . . . would eat mutton on Fridays. He's past it now' (Shakespeare, *Measure for Measure*). 'Mutton', a whore, is ob. but 'in her mutton' still means copulating, and not necessarily for payment by the male. 'Mutton-monger', a male profligate, is ob. To 'come your mutton' is to masturbate, of a male. 'Mutton dressed as lamb' is a derogatory description of a woman affecting the dress or style of someone much younger: '"Youthful excess is one thing," said the Dean, "but mutton dressed as lamb is another"' (Sharpe, 1974).

mutual abuse/pleasuring *see* **abuse** and **pleasure**

muzzy drunk
Properly, dull and overcast of the weather. Quite common female use of themselves when slightly drunk.

my word a turd
Br. rh. sl., mainly of canine deposits on pavements etc.

N

nab to steal
Properly, to catch or arrest: 'They ha'
nabb'd my gold' (Clark, 1839). 'Nab' is
found in many 18c. compounds such as 'nab
the stoop', to stand in the pillory; 'nab the
snow', to steal linen from a line; etc. Often
corrupted to 'nap' in which form it was used
of venereal disease, from the 'catching' of it.
The WWI 'napoo', death, may have been
punning on 'nap' and a corruption of 'n'y a
plus', but I suspect it was merely from the
French.

nameless crime (the) sodomy or
buggery
A perhaps ob. usage but fashionable when
homosexuality was an intellectual fetish of
Keynes and others who thought it
demeaning to lavish their affection and sexual energies on mere women.

nancy a male homosexual
From the female name – her surname seems
to have been Dawson. Originally as 'Miss
Nancy' and then as 'nancy boy': 'He looked a
bit of a nancy boy to me' (Matthew, 1978).
Also abbr. to 'nance'.

nanny a whore
The female partner of **goat** (q.v.) rather than
from the nursery form of 'nurse'. A 'nanny-
house' was a brothel: '. . . speech smacking
of grogshop or nanny-house' (Graves, 1940,
writing in archaic style). ob.

napoo *see* **nab**

nappy an infant's towel to contain excreta
Probably merely an abbr. of 'napkin', a small
'nap' or piece of linen but it might also pun
on the catching function – *see* **nab**. The ob.
Sc./N. Eng. 'nappy', drunk, came from the
dialect word for froth on the ale: 'While
nappy, he's happy' (Gray, 1811).

**narrow passageway to the unknown
(the)** death
You are given no chance to turn aside: 'The
narrow passageway to the unknown which
everyone must cross' (J. Mitford, 1963). The
ob. Br. 'narrow bed' was a grave.

nasty (stuff) a spirituous intoxicant
Unpleasant to the teetotaller but now
humorous use only: '"What you need is a
wee bit of the old nasty." I uncorked the
Armagnac' (Sanders, 1983) and 'How about
a bit of the old nasty stuff before we turn in?'

(Sanders, 1977). In ob. use to 'nasty' was to
befoul with excrement: 'If any person shall
be convicted before the session of nastying
within the walls of the churchyard, he or she
so offending shall be liable in the sum of one
mark' (Keith Kirk sessions, 1749, quoted in
EDD – the mark was worth 13s 4d. Scots or
13⅓d. English).

national assistance *see* **assistance**

National Front a chauvinist Br.
totalitarian political group
A fringe imitation of Fascism which provides
its Marxist counterparts with a pretext for
displays of equally bigoted violence. Those
who assume the style 'national' seldom speak
for the nation and may try to stop others
from speaking at all.

national indoor game *see* **game** (2)

national security guard an instrument
of civil repression
A phenomenon of any totalitarian state
because autocracy can brook no overt
opposition: 'The shark pool . . . . was established by Nassir's feared henchmen from the
National Security Guard' (*Daily Telegraph*,
August 1980). And *see* **security service**.

national service compulsory conscription
into the armed forces
Civil servants, politicians even, may consider
their service to the nation no less meritorious
than spending a limited period on and off
the barrack square. The usage conceals the
military nature of the engagement, although
some pacifists in BI were given the alternatives of going down the mines, felling trees
or attending the sick.

National Socialist chauvinistic and
totalitarian
The 'National Socialist German Workers'
Party' was better known as Nazi: '. . . we
shall settle accounts with them in the manner to which we National Socialists are
accustomed' (Hitler, speech of 20 July 1944
in tr. of the Jews).

nationalize to expropriate
In theory to prevent exploitation by foreign
owners, to safeguard services required by
the community or to prevent monopoly; in
practice to perpetuate monopoly, to safeguard overmanning and to prevent efficient
business development. Compensation may
be paid to the former owners in varying
degrees. 'Nationalization', such appropri-
ation, now has overtones of protecting
employees at the expense of customers and

therefore meets insurmountable difficulties when the customers have an alternative source of supply.

native a Black
Properly, as Dr Johnson, an 'original inhabitant' but extended in the colonial era to all non-Whites: '"He admits to having abandoned twenty men to their deaths." Vera said: "They were only natives"' (Christie, 1939). A White expatriate's Black mistress was known as his 'native comfort'.

natural (1) an idiot
Probably an abbr. of 'natural' (born) fool, an expression which antedated this use by a century (OED): 'We had oor naiteral. He was known as Daft Jamie' (Inglis, 1895). ? ob.

natural (2) bastard
Properly, sired by, of any child and although a 'natural son' is always a bastard, we cannot assume that children born within wedlock were conceived by unnatural or supernatural means. A 'natural father' sires the bastard: 'Edward VII, a most wide-ranging man in his attraction to ladies, was his natural father' (Condon, 1966).

natural break the intervention of advertisements in a television broadcast
The Br. licensing authority stipulates that the intervention of advertisements should not unduly interrupt the continuity of a programme.

natural functions (the) urination and defecation
Eating, sweating and breathing are equally natural, to name a few: '. . . reaching peaks of embarrassment whenever he wished to fulfil one of his natural functions' (R. V. Jones, 1978). Rarely as 'natural purposes'. The ob. 'naturals', an abbr. of 'natural parts', meant the genitalia of humans and animals and to 'be in your naturals' was to be naked.

natural vigours copulation
Of a male in the days when it was thought to come less naturally to females: 'I have my natural vigours, like any man' (Fowles, 1985, of a man excusing a sexual approach to a woman).

nature's garb nudity
No clothes at all, as worn by a 'naturist', in pursuit of 'naturism', a penchant for individual or communal nakedness.

nature's needs urination or defecation
A rare variant of **natural functions** (above): 'For another of nature's needs I also inserted a large rubber bag' (Theroux, 1975).

naughty copulating extra-maritally
Usu. of a female as it was not considered wickedness in a male: 'She had been naughty as a girl, she said, especially with one boy' (Harris, 1925). In modern nursery use, the 'naughty bits' are the male or female genitalia, the usage making a number of perhaps unmerited assumptions. The ob. 'naughty-house' was a brothel: 'This house, if it be not a bawd's house, it is pity of her life, for it is a naughty house' (Shakespeare, *Measure for Measure*).

nautch girl a whore
Properly, a professional Indian dancing girl: 'She kept a troupe of nautch-girls who were also prostitutes' (Richards, 1936, of India). A 'nautch', a vagina, might just have come from the Hindi but I favour derivation from the 18c. Am. 'notch', a 'narrow pass or defile between mountains' (SOD); and a bad etymological third is 'notch-gears – an iron cock with notches' (EDD).

Neapolitan bone-ache syphilis
The disease you caught from the Italians, if not the French or the Spanish: 'Vengeance on the whole camp! or, rather, the Neapolitan bone-ache! for that, methinks is the curse . . .' (Shakespeare, *Troilus and Cressida*). Syphilis was also known sarcastically as the 'Neapolitan favour'. ob.

near (1) stingy
From the proper meaning, 'close', itself an abbr. of 'close-fisted': 'Some were beginning to consider Oak a near man' (Hardy, 1874).

near (2) imitation
Mencken gives: 'near-silk, near antique, near-leather, near mahogany, near-silver and near-porcelain' (1941). Consumer protection legislation has thinned the list, but the Br. 'near-beer', served in an unlicensed den called a 'near-beer club', survives to avoid breaking liquor licensing laws: 'Near-beer costs two shillings a glass: call it just beer – forget the "near"' (Kersh, 1936).

necessary a lavatory
The Italian 'necessario' or the French 'nécessaire', which latter survives in literary use: '. . . this unlucky medicine chest having played the same part that Marie Antoinette's nécessaire did in the escape to Varennes' (N. Mitford, 1945). Also in ob. use as 'necessary house': 'A contrivance for emptying every Necessary House in the City of London' (Monsarrat, 1978, writing in archaic style). Whence the 'necessary woman' who was not the mandatory female member of any com-

mittee but the lavatory emptier: 'Trott the Necassary Woman, who stalked the house at all hours . . . . to empty and then clean the several privies' (ibid.).

necessities urination or defecation
Perhaps a survival from **necessary** (above): 'Only let him out in the garden for necessities' (Herriot, 1981, of a dog).

neck to indulge in physical courtship
Short of copulation, from the placing of an arm around the other's neck at some stage: 'To copulate or at least neck, in the relative comfort of a parked sedan' (Ustinov, 1971). The ob. 'neck' meant to kill, of rabbits etc. by breaking the neck and of humans by hanging or decapitation: 'Mony a ane they necked after the battle' (MacTaggart, 1824).

neck-oil an intoxicant
Army use of beer: '. . . we were fond of a drop of "neck-oil", which like "purge" was a nickname for beer' (Richards, 1936).

necktie party a lynching
The 'necktie' was the noose: 'Its solitary bent branch enough to tell any Western fan that it would eventually be used for a necktie party' (Deighton, 1972). A 'necktie sociable' is also a lynching. The victim was 'measured for a necktie': '. . . then he knew he was being measured for a necktie' (Price, 1985, of someone facing death by killing). Am.

need a desire to urinate or defecate
Abbr. for 'need to urinate' etc.: 'Mostyn . . . . had flitted from the room to cope with a nervous need' (Price, 1970). The ob. to 'need parsley' was to be dead, from the practice of the Ancient Greeks who covered their tombs with this slow-dying herb.

needle to strengthen an intoxicant by adulteration
Originally by introducing an electric current through the rod shaped like a needle, whence any form of lacing: 'The smell of needled beer' (Longstreet, 1956). 'Needle park', in New York City, is a haunt of narcotic addicts with their hypodermic syringes.

negative contribution a sale at a loss
Manufacturers' and commercial jargon. The 'contribution' is that part of the price left over after deducting the cost of labour and materials. A 'positive contribution' indicates that some or all overhead and selling costs have been recovered. A 'negative profit contribution' means that you have lost money after deducting all your costs.

negative growth a decline
Politicians so speak of the national product, businessmen of turnover or profits: 'With International Leisure somewhat becalmed at 112p having shown no negative growth in two years . . .' (*Private Eye*, September 1986). It is taboo to use words which expose recession or failure.

negative (income-) tax state payment to the poor
The proposition seems to have been first expounded by Milton Friedman under the title 'negative tax'. The object is to give the rich less to spend (as at present through income tax) and the poor more, cutting out the present cumbersome channels of individual assessment and distribution.

negative stock holding orders which cannot be delivered
This is how your computer describes empty shelves in the warehouse when you have overdue orders and clamant customers. Generally computers are programmed to deduct orders from unallocated stocks and to throw up re-order or remanufacture schedules.

negatively privileged poor
Sociological jargon and a correct statement only of those who have elected to lead a life of monastic asceticism. *See* also **privileged** and **underprivileged**.

negotiable we do not expect to receive the asking price
Estate agents' jargon, often abbr. to 'neg.' in small advertisements. Of an overseas commercial sale to a corrupt buyer, a 'negotiable' price means that it can be inflated by the amount of bribery needed to win the order.

negotiation an illegal act in espionage
Properly, a business transaction involving haggling: 'He was an extraordinary asset to the American intelligence community, a veteran of twenty-two years of the most complicated "negotiations"' (Ludlum, 1979). Whence 'negotiator': 'The State Department's small band of "negotiators" . . .' (ibid.).

(negro or negress persons of East, central, West or South African descent with or without some White ancestry is not euphemistic but is today considered offensive and therefore should not be used. Those formerly so described prefer 'Black' which is inaccurate, as is 'White': but by the use of a capital letter, we can meet our linguistic susceptibilities, and theirs. Rawson

(1981) has a learned note on this subject, and draws attention to the ob. euphemistic use of 'negro' for slave.)

neighbourhood connection a receiver of stolen property
Am. thieves' jargon.

Nelson's blood rum
Rum was used as a preservative of the Admiral's corpse on its return from Trafalgar for burial in 1805. Tradition has it that much of the preservative was syphoned off and drunk by sailors on the way.

neoplasm a cancer
Properly, a fresh growth. Mainly medical jargon.

nerve agent a noxious gas
Br. military jargon. It could mean anything which excites one of the senses and so stimulates a nerve, not excluding a woman's perfume.

nervous breakdown a severe mental illness
Not paralysis, where some of the nerves really do break down: 'The man before him had similarly had a nervous breakdown and had had to be brought South by an Indian sub-assistant surgeon' (Allen, 1979). The expression may describe any condition from depression to madness, temporary or permanent.

nest the vagina
I suppose the imagery is visual: 'In your daughter's womb I'll bury them: Where, in that nest of spicery, they shall breed' (Shakespeare, *Richard III*). Partridge says: 'Low coll. when not euphemistic S.E.' (DSUE). ob.

Netherlands (the) the male and female genitalia
Probably punning on the Low Countries, itself a convoluted punning 16c. joke: 'The Netherlands? – O, sir, I did not look so low' (Shakespeare, *Comedy of Errors*). 'Netherlands' is ob. but 'nether' parts or regions in the same sense persist.

neutralize to kill
Much more than rendering neutral or inert: 'It means they don't know he's been . . . neutralized' (Follett, 1978, of a killing).

never-never a contract for hire-purchase
A relic of the pre-WW II, and pre-inflation, ethic that you should 'never' enter into a contract for something you could not pay cash for, and you would 'never' finish

paying. As hire-purchase has become respectable, and better regulated by statute, so the euphemism has fallen into disuse.

New Commonwealth non-White
After WW II 'Empire' had too many overtones of conquest and White superiority and the Br. adopted 'Commonwealth' as the collective noun of those former colonies which wished to stay in the club. Whatever the relative length of your association with Britain, you belong to the 'New Commonwealth' if your citizens are Black.

new cookie a younger female for whom a man abandons his wife
A 'cookie' is a promiscuous female likely to be found in an Am. bar: '. . . you might come clean about that blonde cookie you've parked on big-hearted Mrs Swallow. Rumour has it that she's pregnant' (Lodge, 1975), or the female genitalia viewed sexually by a male. This phrase puns on the warmth and freshness of a newly-baked cake.

new economic zones the barren places to which you exile your opponents
They are too busy trying to stay alive to cause trouble, or they die. Thus the victorious Communist Vietnamese eliminated those who were unable to get hold of a boat: 'Vietnam's "New Economic zones" (in fact areas of internal exile where many starve and perish)' (*Daily Telegraph*, February 1980).

New Order a chauvinist tyrannical autocracy
The rule of the Nazis: '. . . told them there was a new order in Europe' (Keneally, 1982, of Nazis in WW II Poland). But 'order' for some was disorder for most. The Philippine variant was called the 'New Society' and a great many Filipinos looked back with regret to the old.

Newgate a prison
Of other Br. prisons than the notorious one in London. There were many compounds to do with jail, hanging, etc. like 'Newgate bird', a thief; 'Newgate solicitor', a corrupt lawyer; etc. Now ob. except in literature.

news management the official suppression of information
For Am. military or political purposes. The 'management' embraces delay and manipulation rather than attempts to get lies published.

nibble an act of extra-marital copulation
Properly, a small bite: '"She makes a damn pretty widow" . . . . "Wouldn't mind a nibble

myself"' (Lyall, 1972). Rarely too used within marriage by a husband.

nice time a single act of copulation with a whore
Prostitutes' jargon often used when soliciting: 'You've given me the ticket, and I've given you a nice time' (G. Greene, 1932). 'Nice-nice' is copulation: 'I should have made nice-nice with Martha' (Sanders, 1983).

nick (1) the devil
After one of the Nordic evil spirits or monsters: 'O thou! Whatever title suit thee, Auld Hornie, Satan, Nick, or Clootie' (Burns, 1785). Today usu. as 'old Nick' but also as 'Nickie', 'Nicker', etc.

nick (2) to pilfer
Properly, cutting or catching unawares, whence originally only of pilfering: 'We dinna steal. We only nick things whiles' (Crockett, 1896). Today of any stealing: 'He was caught nicking shavers' (N. Mitford, 1960). The ob. 'nicks' meant stolen property.

nick (3) a police station or prison
Where you are taken when you are 'nicked', detected in crime and arrested.

nick (4) to castrate
From the cutting: 'Through mist or fog to nick a sturdy hog' (Dickinson, 1866). Now used also of vasectomy.

nickel and dime to shortchange or cheat
From the pre-WW II stores like Woolworth, which offered goods to the value of 5c and 10c: 'The kind of guy who'll nickel-and-dime his own mother' (M. Thomas, 1987). Am.

night bucket a pot for urine
Usu. in communal male sleeping quarters where it can avoid the ingress of cold air through repeated opening of a door in winter.

night club etc. a place in which to meet whores
Properly, a restaurant open to the public for entertainment until late at night, and some of them are indeed properly conducted, but: 'A night-club or dance-hall hostess .... are the modern equivalent of the old time disorderly house and of the street-walker' (Lavine, 1930). The ob. Br. 'night house' also had no facilities for copulation on the premises so that whores took their customers elsewhere but it provided no entertainment other than eyeing the females: 'These

generally resort to night-houses, where they have a greater chance of meeting customers' (Mayhew, 1862, of whores).

night crawlers active traffic police patrolling at night
Not to be confused with nocturnal insects or reptiles. Am. CB sl.

night job devoting the entire night as a whore to a single customer
Interchangeable with **all-nighter** (q.v.): 'They ran to wake up mama, who was sleeping after a night job' (L. Armstrong, 1955). The ob. 'night man' was a fairy and, if on horseback, a 'night rider', both of whom you did well to steer clear of. A 'night-whistler' was a bird which flew overhead in the dark as an omen of death.

night loss the involuntary ejaculation of semen during sleep
Female usage, usu. referring to the soiled bedlinen.

night physic etc. copulation
The 'medical' treatment taken by the male at night. Less often as 'night exercise' or 'nocturnal exercise', perhaps punning on military manoeuvres: '... if I'm not down to twelve stone by the time we reach Calcutta, it won't be for want of nocturnal exercise' (Fraser, 1975). The Am. 'night baseball' usu. means extra-marital copulation, a pun on **ball** (q.v.) and the male habit of leaving home to watch a game.

night stool a portable lavatory
Sickroom use. It looks like a square seat.

nightcap an intoxicant
You don't place it on your head but drink it before retiring to an unheated bedroom: 'A "nightcap", which consisted of a stoup of mulled claret, well spiced and fortified with a glass of brandy' (Lowson, 1890). Now of any intoxicant drunk in the evening: 'May I please offer you a nightcap?' (M. Thomas, 1980 – the offerer was trying to pick up a stranger).

nightingale a police informer
From the 'singing' properties of man and bird. In ob. Br. use a 'nightingale' was also a whore, from her hours of work; or a soldier who cried out while being flogged, to avoid which a victim would chew, or bite, a bullet, thus further enriching the language.

nightsoil human faeces
'Soil' has meant excrement since the 16c. and primitive lavatories were cleaned at night, sometimes by a 'nightman' in an

operation called, in London at least, a wedding: '. . . thrust our ragged clothes, with a stick deep into the night soil at the necessary house' (Graves, 1940, writing in archaic style). Now only jocular fig. use as a variant of 'in the shit'. 'Night water', of urine, is ob.: 'You try to tell us that the might of this great army rests upon goddam night water?' (Keneally, 1979, of a Confederate Army forbidden to make noise at night).

nightwork copulation
Punning on nocturnal labour: 'Ha, 'twas a merry night. And is Jane Nightwork alive? . . . She was then a bona-roba' (Shakespeare, 2 *Henry IV*). Probably ob.

nineteenth the bar at a golf club
Abbr. of humorous 'nineteenth hole'; the first eighteen involve striking a ball and walking after it.

Nimrod a penis
Viewed sexually and punning on the renowned hunter from Genesis 10:8/9: '. . . 'tis whispered she requires such Stabbing there as more often leaves Sir Nimrod dead than she' (Fowles, 1985, writing in archaic style). ? ob.

nip (1) to steal
A variant of **pinch** (1) (q.v.) and much rarer. It used to appear in many compounds to do with pilfering, cutting purses, etc. and also meant to give short measure: 'Ye was set aff frae oon for nipping the pyes' (Ramsay, 1737). A 'nipper' was a thief.

nip (2) a spirituous intoxicant
Properly a 'nipperkin', the eighth part of a pint: 'Down to the bar to snatch a furtive "nip"' (Doherty, 1884).

nip (3) to castrate
From the action of the tool employed: 'It was to "nip" some calves . . . or more correctly to emasculate them by means of the Burdizzo bloodless castrator' (Herriot, 1981).

no better than she ought to be sexually promiscuous
Usu. of a younger woman by an older. DAS says: 'One of the oldest euphem. terms in the lang.' 'No better than she should be' means the same thing.

no chicken old
A 'chicken' is properly the young of a domestic fowl, whence a child. Almost always of a woman and venerable enough to have been used by Swift in 1720: 'And Caroline is twenty-seven. No chicken' (Bogarde, 1981).

no comment I admit nothing
Much political and business use in reply to journalists. It is the only defence of those who know that, when scandal is in the air, to be quoted is to be misquoted, and selectively.

no longer with us etc. dead
Especially used of a former associate: 'None of us could believe that the charming Deborah . . . . was no longer with us' (Mailer, 1965). 'No more' is used of any dead person: 'Poor Johnny is no more. For what he thought was H_2O was H_2SO_4' (Children's rhyme).

no-man's-land a lavatory for exclusive female use
A rare pun used only by females.

no right to correspondence dead
Russian Communist usage in various similar forms – the dead cannot read letters: '"No right to correspondence" – and that almost for certain means: "He's been shot"' (Solzhenitsyn, 1974, in tr.).

no scholar dull
Parental description of a child who may then be said to have other talents as 'good with his hands' and, if you are a manufacturer, be recommended to you as a potential industrial manager, being unsuited for more intellectual callings. (This is a sample entry, of many expressions starting with 'no', which seek to soften or understate a weakness or infirmity.)

no show the fraudulent entry of a name on a pay sheet
The use covers two types of fraud: that of a person who fails to report for work but still collects his pay, sometimes by arrangement with a superior; and the case where the named employee does not exist and the pay is drawn by another. 'No show' now describes a passenger with a confirmed booking on a flight who fails to appear.

no-tell used for extra-marital copulation
It is the manager who keeps quiet: 'He was found in one of those no-tell motels' (Wambaugh, 1983). Am.

nobble to kill
Properly, to tamper with a horse illegally, whence to do a lot of other evil deeds like bribing and stealing in the 19c.: 'Ah thowt ah'd tak a wauk an nobble a few specimens foe me-sen' (Treddlehoyle, 1892). Whence the modern meaning: '"I saw a bloke nobbled here," she said. "I mean killed"' (Theroux, 1976).

nocturnal emission an involuntary ejaculation of semen
Spitting, vomiting or ejaculation during copulation are not so described. A rather grander version of **night loss** (above) with a suggestion of erotic dreaming: 'He got a great deal of pleasure from nocturnal emissions' (Sharpe, 1978).

nocturnal exercise *see* **night physic**

nocturne a whore
Properly, a night scene in a painting or a dreamy musical compositon. I give this ob. Br. use to allow me to quote Georges Sand's apocryphal pun to Chopin: 'One nocturne deserves another'.

noggin an intoxicating drink
Properly, an eighth of a pint of any liquid: 'Only share of two noggins wid my brother' (Carleton, 1836). Now used of any type of beer or spirits, but not usu. of wine.

nominal extortionate
Merchant bankers etc. so describe fees, given in round sums, which are breathtaking to their provincial customers, the inference being that a full charge would amount to much more. (A London estate agent who came to view a property in the country for two hours with a view to obtaining disposal instructions once asked me for a 'nominal' fee of £750 for his time. He lost the job, and his firm lost all the lucrative property work for a national company of which I happened also to be chairman.)

non-aligned vacillating between Am. and Russian influence
The expression comes from a conference held in Belgrade in 1961 of small countries which so described themselves, because they claimed to support or be supported by neither of the superpowers. Some, like Cuba, are subservient and others switch sides according to the inducements currently on offer, whence Jennings' description of them as 'no more than potential parasites' (1965).

non-Aryan Jewish
The Nazis adopted de Gobineau's theories of 'racial purity', which classes Slavs and gypsies with Jews under this heading. As Himmler had limited numbers of gypsies and no Slavs to persecute before 1941, Poles apart, 'non-Aryan' became generally associated with Jewishness, as dysphemism rather than euphemism.

non-dairy not made of milk
But implying affinity with the cow, with such tradenames as 'Non-dairy Creamer'. The contents of a substance given to passengers by airlines to put in their tea or coffee under the name 'Coffee-mate®' are as follow: 'Ingredients corn syrup solids, partially hydrogenated coconut oil, sodium calcinate, mono-acid diglycerides, di-potassium phosphate, sodium aluminosilicate, artificial flavor, artificial colors'.

non-person an outlaw
Communist jargon used of those whose former fame or achievements embarrass the present rulers: 'Krupsky was banished twenty years ago. He became a non-person' (Ludlum, 1979).

non-profit avoiding taxation
Not any old loss-making enterprise. An Am. business device whereby the eventual beneficiary passes the profit through a tax-exempt charity: 'The profits that are now routinely extracted by the promoters on "non-profit" cemeteries are spectacular' (J. Mitford, 1963).

non-white a person whose ancestry is not entirely White
Particularly of those with any Black ancestry: 'Non-whites are even more overwhelming in their desire for work' (Pei, 1969). Howard writes of 'non-white': 'the latest silly extremity into which we have been forced by euphemism' (1977) but this taboo about skin pigmentation will go on spawning euphemisms until a person with only one White great-grandparent is described as 'non-black', or found unworthy by society of separate notice.

nonsense extra-marital sexual activity outside normal courtship
Properly, an absurdity: 'He was a calm, down-to-earth creature who brooked no kind of "nonsense"' (Bogarde, 1981, of the proprietor of an erotic photographic studio). Genteel and perhaps ob. usage.

nookie copulation
A 'nook' is a small orifice or corner, whence the vagina viewed sexually: 'You might even have enough free time to get you a little nooky' (Styron, 1976). Now very common, within or outside marriage, in popular speech.

North Britain Scotland
Quite common when many Scots were ashamed of the relative backwardness of their country: 'Near to this Marble are

deposited the Remains of Hugh Campbell Esqre of Mayfield in the County of Ayr North Britain 5 Jan 1824' (Memorial in Bath Abbey). Whence 'North Briton', a Scot, although John Wilkes who used the nom-de-plume was a Londoner. It is perhaps not surprising that the 1979 edition of Collins English Dictionary, compiled in Scotland, omits this entry but the use is not long dead. A WW II colleague, later to command the garrison at Edinburgh Castle, had that august postal address; he once received a letter redirected and marked 'Not SS Edinburgh Castle. Try Edinburgh NB'.

nose open eager for copulation
Bulls and stallions flare their nostrils when sexually excited. Of humans the phrase is used of the male or female although the physical symptoms are different from those of animals: '"I seen her mooching around upstairs." Murf licked his lips. "She's got your nose open?"' (Theroux, 1976).

not a great reader illiterate
You still hear this among country folk in SW Eng., and no doubt elsewhere. This is a sample entry of many phrases prefixed 'not' which seek to minimize or conceal a weakness or infirmity.

not all there imbecile
Of a mental state and not the amputation of a limb: 'That poor creature who's not quite all there' (Christie, 1940). Atypically, 'all there' means keenly intelligent.

not as young as I was old
None of us is as young as we were, even as the eye crosses the page. We use this expression as an excuse for our own failing powers, but of another might say that he 'was not in his first youth'.

not at home at home but unwilling to speak to a caller
The converse of 'At home', a specific invitation to visit at a set time: '"Want to see Mrs Morny." "She's not at home." "Didn't you know that when I gave you the card?".... "I only knew when she told me"' (Chandler, 1943). Also as 'not in': 'Weren't you told she was not in?' (ibid.).

not available to comment unwilling to risk being compromised
This is how journalists describe a victim who has denied them the chance of confronting him with an accusation or scandal.

not dead but gone before dead
Christian usage, implying both that the dead

person will be reunited with a spouse still alive, and that meanwhile he is enjoying eternity in a state not dissimilar to life on earth. Less often as 'not lost but gone before', with 'before' meaning ahead.

not in *see* **not at home**

not inconsolable ready to copulate with other than your usual but absent sexual partner
For 'consolation' *see* **console**: 'It is feared she waited for him in vain. Not that the Lady Frances, a creature of some resilience, proved inconsolable' (Boyle, 1979 – the 'him' was Philby).

not interested in the opposite sex a homosexual
A genteel usage of adult males.

not invented here we reject and denigrate all ideas other than our own
The main defensive mechanism of the employees in any establishment whose duty it is to think or innovate. Your existence is not longer justifiable if outsiders discover or invent something which you have been paid to discover or invent: 'They didn't think of it, so they'll piss all over it. *Not invented here!*' (M. Thomas, 1980). Often abbr. to 'NIH'.

not sixteen annas to the rupee imbecile
Br. Indian army use, for the old currency in which 4 pice = 1 anna, 16 annas = 1 rupee. And the Br. 'not sixteen ounces in the pound' meant the same thing. But cf. **twelve annas in the rupee.**

not very well ill
Hospital and valetudinarian jargon which forgets that 'very well' ought to imply excellent health. If the patient is geriatric, 'not at all well' or 'not doing well' indicates that he is dying.

notice dismissal from employment
Abbr. of 'notice of dismissal', which is given or received. 'Notice' as a verb is ob.: 'Notice me as much as ever ye like, I'll not clean them pigs out' (Francis, 1901).

nouvelle cuisine small portions of food sold at high prices
The presentation on the plate is often tasteful, but there is plenty of room for an elaborate lay-out. cf. **haute cuisine.**

nuisance *see* **commit a nuisance**

number is up about to be killed
WW I usage. from the game of 'house' where each player has a numbered card, and perhaps referring to each soldier's individual

army number. It indicates the fatalism of the trenches, with a deity selecting his faithful or victims on a chance basis: 'It's all right, you laughing, but I know my number is up' (Richards, 1933, of WW I).

number nine a laxative
The standard Br. army purgative. Some fig. use as when a sluggard might be told he needed a 'dose of number nines'.

number one urination
Mainly nursery usage.

number one, London menstruation
Any etymological link with the town house of the Iron Duke, which is now a museum overlooking Hyde Park Corner, is obscure. Eng. ? ob.

number two(s) defecation
Mainly nursery usage: 'Stand over him and, as he put it "do number two – oh lots of it – all over me"' (Theroux, 1973).

numeracy *see* **comprehension**

(**numerate** to be able to understand accounts is quite a modern invention. It also means the ability to add and in Eng. dialect used to mean to grow or spread: 'Them primroses numerates fast' (EDD).)

nun a whore
The religious orders provided many allusive words for sexual subjects before and immediately after the dissolution of the Eng. monasteries, partly because of the supposed dissolution of their members and partly because the economic power of the Church had engendered that mixture of envy and outrage in 16c. England without which Henry VIII's Reformation would have failed. Thus when Hamlet says to Ophelia 'Get thee to a nunnery' (Shakespeare, *Hamlet*) he is telling her he thinks she is a whore, a 'nunnery' being a brothel. ob.

Nuremberg trials the legalistic vengeance of the winners of WW II
The rules had to be invented as the game was being played, the Emperor of Japan being a favoured absentee.

nurse to suckle a baby
Probably from the name given to a woman who was paid to suckle another's child: 'Priss . . . . was nursing her baby . . . . "I never expected a breast-fed grandson," said Priss's mother' (McCarthy, 1963). The ob. Eng. 'nurse-child' was a bastard, because it was raised away from its mother.

nursing home an institution for geriatrics
Properly, a hospital for any sick person, in which sense it is still widely used in BI.

nut a lunatic
'Nut' is sl. for the human head and this must be an abbr. of 'gone in the nut' or some such expression: 'It was the laugh of a nut' (Chandler, 1940). A 'nut' college, farm, hutch or house is an institution for the insane: '. . . round up of nut-houses, likely nutters on parole' (Davidson, 1978). The FBI list of mad or unstable people likely to attack a public figure is called the 'nut-box'. A 'nutter' is a lunatic, who may be 'nutty', 'nuts' or 'off his nut', mad.

nuts testicles
Also as, and perhaps even an abbr. of, 'nutmegs' but *see* 'cobs' *under* **cobblers** for the same imagery: '. . . the new government . . . . will cut our nuts off' (M. Thomas, 1980 – the threat was fig. only).

nymph a whore
Properly, a mythical semi-divine and beautiful maiden. More explicitly as 'nymph' of darkness, of delight, of the pavement, etc.

NYR lost in action
WWII aircraft usage, as an abbr. of 'not yet returned' from a mission over enemy territory: '"We've got a lot of NYRs, Lester." "Not Yet Returned doesn't mean dead"' (Deighton, 1982 – but it meant shot down or crashed, with death a probability).

O

O opium
In addict use.

oats copulation
Usu. by a male, within or outside marriage, with an inference of regular need: 'I have to go out later, so you'll have to wait even longer before you get your oats' (B. Forbes, 1986 – a woman was refusing to copulate immediately with a man). From the food the horse likes to get daily rather than 'sowing wild oats'.

obligatory female a woman occupying a position beside men other than on the basis of her suitability or qualification
Also known as the 'statutory woman', she eases the consciences of the men and may appease the feminists: '... she's my recommendation .... for our obligatory female' (Price, 1985, of such an appointee).

oblige to copulate with
Properly, to gratify. The woman 'obliges' the man, usu. extra-maritally but not necessarily for payment.

obstacle detachments units placed behind the front line to stop desertion or retreat
A Russian phrase to describe a feature of both German and Russian armies in WW II where cowardice, desertion or flight were summarily and ferociously punished. Goebbels' diaries give a clear account of the horrendous practices of the SS behind the Eastern Front in 1945.

obtain to acquire illegally
Usu. of stealing but also of forbidden or other embargoed goods: '... "many small pleasures ... not the least of which is obtaining Cuban cigars." "Obtaining," was the Director's favourite euphemism' (Van Lustbader, 1983, of an Am. espionage agency).

occupied defeated and annexed
Not all conquerors depart: 'Bohnen had never liked California ... that soft-living, slow-moving region that Easterners called "occupied Mexico"' (Deighton, 1982). But in E. Europe 40 years after WW II it is not a joke.

occupy to copulate with a female
From the physical entry: 'These villains will make the word as odious as the word "occupy"; which was an excellent good word before it was ill sorted' (Shakespeare, 2 *Henry IV*). An 'occupying house' was a brothel. The rare modern use seems to come rather from 'occupied', or engaged, with: 'Karl was not ready, having been occupied with a Negro girl in his tent' (Harris, 1925).

octopus a male eagerly caressing a female
He seems to have more than two hands: '"What's he like?" "Oh, well, octopuses, wow!" Brenda said' (Davidson, 1978).

odd homosexual
Usu. of a male, from the meaning, out of the ordinary but as more people find nothing out of the ordinary in male homosexuality, so this euphemism is falling into disuse.

oestrus copulation
Of cattle, from the gadfly which induces frenzy, and 'in oestrus' means ready to conceive: 'The required cow in oestrus was in a large loose box' (Herriot, 1981). Of humans in rare use it means a sexual orgasm and the ob. Eng. 'on the gad' was to be engaged in prostitution.

of mature years old
We do not mean a female of nineteen or a male of twenty-one. It is not full development we see, but incipient decline.

off (1) to kill
Perhaps an abbr. of 'bump off' and hardly from the meaning, in a state of decay: 'Maybe he stiffed the waiter and the guy followed him down here and offed him' (Sanders, 1973). DSUE also gives to die as a WW I usage and today to 'off yourself' is to commit suicide: 'I just don't wanna off myself like so many cops do' (Wambaugh, 1975).

off (2) to copulate with
Am. male use, perhaps from the sl. 'have it off'.

off at the side etc. mad
'Off', with its implications of departure and decay, precedes many phrases describing stages of mental illness: 'Not "all there" – "off at the side"' (Linton, 1867, of a mild condition). 'Off your head', with variations of 'head' by sl. alternatives like 'chump', 'gourd', 'nut', 'turnip', etc. indicates a more serious state: 'He feared she had gone off her gourd, and he was scared' (Sanders, 1982) and 'Unless he'd gone off his turnip, I suppose' (le Carré, 1980). 'Off your trolley' came from the vehicle which ran on an electric overhead power supply, with the imagery, but not the euphemistic meaning,

of **off the rails** (below): 'If you're not drunk, you're off your trolley' (Ludlum, 1979). 'Off the wall' is rare: '. . . it was a crazy cackle, and maybe she really was off the wall' (Sanders, 1982), etc.

off duty menstruating
A female use, to explain why she cannot copulate.

off games menstruating
A variant of **off duty** (above) punning on 'fun and games' and a schoolgirl's minor indisposition: '. . . errant husbands who have looked to her for corrective therapy during periods when their wives have been in the country/abroad/off games' (*Private Eye*, December 1983).

off the payroll dismissed from employment
Joining the rest of humanity which was never on that particular payroll in the first place: 'So the old boy hadn't known I was "off the payroll"!' (Shirer, 1984 – an Am. publisher had contacted a journalist who had been dismissed from the newspaper).

off the rails being detected in reprehensible conduct
Criminal or sexual, of a person hitherto considered above reproach, and implying a continued pattern of such behaviour.

off the voting list dead
Voting lists containing the name of every adult are regularly updated but the dead do not enjoy the franchise, except in N. Ireland.

off the wagon *see* **on the wagon**

off-white wedding the marriage of a pregnant bride
She may or may not eschew the pleasure of a virginal white dress: 'I married Pauline hastily – a quiet off-white wedding at her parish church' (Lodge, 1962 – Pauline was pregnant).

offer yourself to ask a man to copulate with you
Usu. extra-maritally and free of charge: 'She tracked me down to my rooms in Oxford and offered herself to me' (Amis, 1978). In ob. use either sex might, it seems, 'offer kindness' to the other in the same sense: 'Offred her such Kindnes, as sticks by her ribs a good while after' (Wilson, 1603, quoted in ODEP).

oil to bribe
Less common than **grease** (above) but more venerable as a euphemism. Usu. of con-tinued or large-scale corruption when it may be expanded to 'oil the wheels'.

oiled drunk
Things may for a time seem to run more smoothly: 'Phipps, described by Yakimov as "a trifle oiled", had attacked the Major' (Manning, 1965). The ob. Br. 'oil the wig' meant to become drunk and the ob. Sc. 'oil of malt' was whisky.

old a' ill thing etc. the devil
Our ancestors really believed that if you talked of the devil, he might appear, but with a certain naivety assumed that he could be fooled by allusive references. Many of these 'nicknames' and evasions were preceded by 'auld' or 'old', and include bendy, blazes, bog(e)y, boots, boy, chap, child, cloutie, dad, davy, driver, gentleman, gooseberry, Harry, hornie, lad, mahoon, man, Nick, one, poger, poker, Roger, ruffin, Sandy, scratch, serpent, smoker, sooty, thief, toast, etc. Only a few are euphemistic; others were dysphemisms and some downright insulting. If nothing else did, the variety must have confused him. Elsewhere I have dealt with the various names, ignoring the prefix 'old'. And I have referred to the rather sad practice of farmers who left a patch of ground untilled for the devil's use, in the hope that it would placate him and he would leave the rest of the farm alone: 'The old man's fold, where the druid sacrificed to the demon' (EDD – I wonder if the farmer had to pay tithe on it too). To 'talk to the old gentleman' was to die: 'I reckon thar be a few Pawnees talkin' to th' old gennelman 'fore long' (Fraser, 1982).

old Adam (the) a man's lust
From the unregenerate character of our common ancestor before life became complicated for him and he passed on to us, with St Paul's help, our sexual complexes: 'I felt the old Adam stir at the sight of her' (Fraser, 1973).

old bill *see* **bill**

old boots a sexual mistress who has been discarded by another
Your predecessor had enjoyed the best use of her. Less often as 'old shoes'. The later incumbent was said to 'keep' or 'ride in' such footwear. (My children, of whose feet such tender care has been taken, find it hard to credit that I had my first pair of new boots at the age of eleven.)

old faithful menstruation
By coming back regularly, anxiety about
pregnancy is lifted.

old-fashioned derelict
Real estate jargon: 'When applied to houses
old-fashioned means a draughty ruin. When
applied to clubs it means bad food and no
women' (Theroux, 1982).

old Joe venereal disease
Stalin was so known in a brief period of
WW II popular enthusiasm, which seems to
have no relavance at all to this Am. usage.

old maid an unmarried woman who is
unlikely to marry
A 'maid' was an unmarried girl and, after the
17c. in the normal progression of these
things, an unmarried female of any age:
'There will the devil meet me, like an old
cuckold, with horns on his head, and say,
"Get you to heaven, Beatrice, get you to
heaven; here's no place for you maids:" so
deliver up my apes, and away to St Peter'
(Shakespeare, *Much Ado About Nothing – see*
lead apes in hell for the simian allusion;
there was no place for virgins in hell). I refer
elsewhere to the problems and stigma facing
single women who were denied the right by
society properly to support themselves.

old man (1) *see* **old a' ill thing etc.**

old man (2) the penis
Male usage, usu. of your own, possibly from
'old man', the devil with his evil and unres-
trained sexual conduct, although normally
used to describe a penis in its flaccid state:
'His old man needed to set it trying to haul
itself up into his abdomen' (Amis, 1978 – he
had difficulty in getting an erection).

old man (3) a man with whom a woman
cohabits and copulates extra-maritally.
The phrase is widely used of a husband in
speech: 'She had an "Old Man" – the name
we used to have for a common-law husband'
(L. Armstrong, 1955).

old man's friend pneumonia
It was the illness which allowed the elderly to
die quite quickly without much pain. Penicillin now preserves them for more lingering,
painful and degrading deaths.

old soldier a pretence of hardship or
physical incapacity
Acted, or 'come', by beggars seeking alms
and sympathy in the days when wounded
soldiers were returned to society without
pensions or other relief. We still use the
phrase of a child who seeks consolation
without special apparent cause.

older woman (the) a geriatric female
Advertising jargon which omits to state what
her age is compared with. Similarly the
advertisers' 'larger woman' is not merely
bigger than a midget, but raw-boned and
very tall, or very fat.

oldest profession *see* **profession**

on (1) drunk
Of a mild state: 'I shouldn't like to zay how
he was drunk . . . . he was a little bit on like'
(EDD). That use is ob. but we still hear 'half
on', which as usual is no less drunk than the
whole.

on (2) pregnant
The ob. usage differs from the modern: 'I
doubt she's on again, poor lass' (EDD) meant
'I think she's pregnant again' whereas we
might take it as no worse a circumstance
than perhaps missing a train to work. But we
have no doubt about the status of a lady who
is 'four months on'. EDD also gives 'Of a
female "Maris appetans"' but, exceptionally, without an example and it may just
have been an abbr. of 'on heat'.

on (3) habitually using illegal narcotics
An Am. abbr. of 'on drugs': 'But a woman
like that living a life like that, has *got* to be
on' (Sanders, 1977).

on a cloud under narcotic influence
From the floating feeling, but I don't know
why the cloud is sometimes numbered
'nine'.

on heat able to conceive
Of female animals, from the increased tem-
perature associated with sexual excitement.
Of a woman, it means promiscuous: 'Those
bloody women! Like a lot of randy she-cats.
And there's that bitch back again, on heat, as
usual' (Manning, 1962, of Princess
Teodorescu). 'In heat' is less common:
'"I'm no bitch in heat," she said between
tight teeth, "take your paws off me"'
(Chandler, 1958). 'In the heat' means cop-
ulating: '. . . make love to her afterwards.
Would you like to hear tapes (of) Mike
Santos in the heat?' (West, 1979).

**on the bash/beach/bend/bottle/
chisel** *see* **bash/beach/bend/bottle** (1)/
chisel

on the club etc. ill and absent from work
The Br. 'club' was an association of workers
paying money weekly into a communal fund

from which they received help when ill. 'On the panel' meant the same thing, from the 'panel', or list, of doctors willing to treat patients unable to pay their fees (although the Sc. 'on the panel' meant being accused in court: 'Mr James Mitchel was upon the panell at the criminal court for shutting at the Archbishop of St Andrews' (Kirkton, 1817)). The Sc. 'on the board', indigent, came from the parochial 'board' which dealt locally with paupers (EDD). 'On the box' formerly meant destitute, being helped from the donations made in church: 'Fifteen got assistance from the Poor's Fund; or as it was generally expressed . . . . fifteen . . . . were on the box' (Pennecuik, 1715) but latterly 'on the box' was synonymous with 'on the club', the weekly contributions being collected in a box.

on the coal *see* **go** (3)

on the couch engaged in extra-marital copulation
The same imagery as the **casting couch** (above) although offices are seldom so furnished: 'My wife thinks I have endless lines of big-titted girls trying to get me on the couch' (Deighton, 1972).

on the end of a shovel *see* **play your harp**

on the game *see* **game** (2)

on the grind engaged in prostitution
Whores' jargon, punning on 'grind', to copulate and the 'grind' of daily toil.

on the Hill engaged in bribery
The 'Hill' is the Capitol Hill in Washington where lobbyists may offer more than verbal persuasion to legislators and their staffs.

on the hoist *see* **hoist** (1)

on the job copulating
A common pun on being engaged in work: '"We told him you'd been on the job continuously" . . . He paused fractionally as the implications of that statement flashed through his mind' (Price, 1970). Whence 'in mid-job', so engaged: 'If he could snap his fingers and boof, there he was in mid-job, very pleasant' (Amis, 1978).

on the labour/loose *see* **labour** (3)/**loose** (1)

on the make seeking an extra-marital sexual relationship
Properly, overly ambitious or greedy in an impatient way. The Am. euphemism is used of both sexes: 'Once in a while . . . . a man and

a woman talk without dragging bedrooms into it. This could be it, or she could just think I was on the make' (Chandler, 1953).

on the needle addicted to illegal narcotics taken by self-injection
The 'needle' is the hypodermic syringe. Rarely of narcosis.

on the nest pregnant
From the sedentary behaviour of a broody hen. Am.

on the pad in receipt of regular bribes
Am. police jargon, from the written list of those participating in such payments.

on the panel *see* **on the club**

on the parish destitute
Until quite recently each Eng. or Welsh parish had to provide for the needy poor within its boundaries, either on its own or in a 'union' with another parish or other parishes. The poor might be housed in the 'parish-house' and the cost was met by a levy on property called a 'parochial rate', so that to be 'on the parochial' was to be a pauper anywhere in the BI: 'They did their very best to get him tae gang on the "parochial" ' (*Aberdeen Weekly Free Press*, March 1901, quoted in EDD). These phrases are still heard in country districts among the old despite the post-WW II elimination of such local arrangements.

on the peg/pill *see* **on the shelf/pill** (2)

on the piss engaged on a drunken carouse
Usu. drinking beer, where the bulk induces frequent urination. It does not mean, like the former Indian premier Desai, you drink your urine for medicinal purposes.

on the ribs indigent
I suppose because of the protrusion of the ribs of an undernourished person: ' "How's life, Duke?" "On the ribs." "You skint?" "Dead skint" ' (Kersh, 1936). ? ob.

on the road to Buenos Ayres becoming a whore
Argentina is the only Am. state in which all the indigenous inhabitants were exterminated by immigrants from Europe (which makes their criticisms of the Falkland Islanders as not being indigenous inhabitants unpersuasive). As a result, unlike elsewhere in Am. male-orientated early societies, they could not use native women as whores. Whence the 'white slave' trade which recruited or enticed White females from Europe. Londres chose *The Road to Buenos*

Ayres as the title for his 1928 study of this phenomenon.

on the road to reform harsh treatment for a political prisoner
Russan Communist usage. 'Reform', the destruction of the prisoner's individualism, is achieved by a combination of starvation, banishment to a remote region, brutality and long hours of manual work. This silences all but the most obdurate and discourages them from reflecting aloud about the Helsinki, or any other, agreement on human rights to which Russia may have been a public signatory.

on the rockpile in prison
From the breaking of stones as a convict's chore rather than a reference to the Br. prison at Portland, where the famous stone is quarried: 'Anyone who's fool enough to invite ten years on the rock-pile for his superstitions deserves all he gets' (Fraser, 1975, writing in 19c. style).? ob.

on the roof *see* **on the tiles**

on the shelf unmarried and unlikely to marry
Usu. but not always of females and derogatory in modern use. The imagery is from retailing. Rarely, of women only, as 'on the peg', where an unused garment may stay.

on the side a benefit which you enjoy illegally or immorally
Such as a bribe; undeclared and untaxed income; extra-marital copulation, especially where a man keeps a sexual mistress, or 'bit on the side'; etc. The imagery is from the additional food on a separate plate but served with the main dish.

on the skids failing
Of a commercial enterprise. A 'skid' is a piece of wood on which an object is placed to facilitate unstoppable movement, such as the launching of a ship: 'Its current affairs flagship World in Action is on the skids' (*Private Eye*, May 1981).

on the square living honestly
Criminal jargon in a society where it is reprehensible to be law-abiding: 'Going on the square is so dreadfully confining' (Mayhew, 1862). The members of the Freemasons' secret society so describe their participation among themselves, not because they lead honest lives but from the set-square used in building.

on the street(s) *see* **street (the)**

on the stroll engaged in prostitution
From the leisurely walk while seeking custom: 'Hello, Mayann. What in the world are you doing out on the stroll tonight?' (L. Armstrong, 1955 – I don't think Mayann bothered to elaborate).

on the take *see* **take** (1)

on the tiles etc. engaged in a carouse
In the nocturnal company of the tomcats, of any leisure activity outside the home, usu. of a male, and involving a late return: 'I saw you sneaking up the stairs. Been having a night on the tiles, have you?' (Sharpe, 1975). The Am. 'on the roof' is rarer: 'I was on the roof last night and I've got a hangover' (Chandler, 1944).

on the town (1) engaged in a carouse
Properly, a rare visit to a city's theatres, etc. without much thought of expense and used of both sexes without any implication of the debauchery imported by **on the tiles** (above). The ob. Br. 'on the town' meant being engaged in prostitution as a regular way of life: 'She had been on the town for fifteen years' (Mayhew, 1862, of a whore).

on the town (2) indigent
An Am. version of **on the parish** (q.v.) with the same etymology.

on the trot (1) a fugitive from prison
From the running: 'I'm looking for someone, and if he's here, he's probably told you he's on the trot' (Follett, 1978).

on the trot (2) *see* **trots (the)**

on the wagon refraining from drinking intoxicants
Abbr. of 'water wagon', in which potable supplies may be distributed. Of a single case of abstinence, as someone about to drive a car; or of a former addict to alcohol who is trying to cure himself: 'On the wagon now, of course, and what he drunk was with a wink and shake of the head' (Longstreet, 1956). 'Off the wagon' indicates backsliding by a former addict: 'When a man like that goes off the wagon, he bites dust' (Kersh, 1936).

on the way pregnant
The destination is unstated: 'She is two months on her way' (Shakespeare, *Love's Labour's Lost*). Now rare.

on top of copulating with
Of a male, from the common posture and inferring a single act extra-maritally: 'Isn't there anything else to interest you, except

twenty minutes on top of a girl?' (Kersh, 1936).

on your bones indigent
Starvation has consumed the flesh: 'Give us a chance, constable; I'm right on my bones' (Galsworthy, 1924).? ob.

on your shield dead
The shield doubled for a stretcher if you were killed in battle: '. . . the only way out was on your shield' (Keneally, 1982, of trying to resist the Nazi police).

on your way out dying
A common version of **leave the building** (above): 'A pretty little nurse to special him on his way out' (Price, 1979, of a dying patient).

onanism male masturbation
Onan spilled his seed on the ground, for which he was slain by the Lord (Genesis, 38): 'One night I got thinking of E. . . . and for the first time in months practised onanism' (Harris, 1925). The biblical evidence points rather to the 'withdrawal' method of contraception, of which Harris was naturally aware: 'Very soon I played Onan and like that Biblical hero "spilt my seed upon the ground"' (ibid.).

one foot in the grave near death
Through old age or terminal illness, the other foot supposedly functioning normally. Some fig. use of an ineffective person and in both cases dysphemism rather than euphemism.

one for the road an extra intoxicant before leaving company
From the warming, or stirrup, cup taken before cold winter journeys on horseback or in an unheated coach.

one night stand overnight copulation with a chance partner
Punning on the travelling show which plays a single performance before moving on but not also punning, I think, on 'stand', an erection of the penis or the copulation of a stallion: 'An opportunity for extracurricular sex occurred . . . . Afterwards there had been still more opportunities – some the usual one-night stands' (Hailey, 1979). Also as 'one-nighter': 'This little lady is a born one-nighter' (Francis, 1982).

one o'clock at the waterworks your trouser zip is undone
An Am. warning from one male to another. From the hour when an employee might leave his office and go for lunch?

one of those a male homosexual
Used by those who are not homosexuals, but for male homosexuals 'one of us': 'When you asked him whether he knew any girls – the shadow of homosexuality, is he one of those?' (le Carré, 1986). Less often, sober and godly matrons may refer to a whore as 'one of those', for whom 'one of us' would mean a social equal, usu. in the negative and derogatively: '. . . he's not what Aunt Fenny calls one of us' (P. Scott, 1968, of a policeman commissioned into the army).

one of us *see* one of those

one over the eight a quantity of intoxicants which has made drunk
There are eight pints in the gallon, which was considered a sufficient amount of beer for a regular drinker: '"Had one over the eight" diagnosed Mr Blore accurately' (Christie, 1939, of a person who was drunk).

one-parent family a parent living alone with dependent offspring
Social service jargon now becoming SE. Usu. divorce is involved, there being no suggestion that the mother was artificially inseminated or that there are fewer than two parents. The absent parent indeed, with the tacit and financial approval of society, may have created and assumed new familial burdens: 'The one-parent family is going to be the big social problem of the 1980s, with the present rate of divorce' (Price, 1979).

one thing copulation
There can be few wives who have not, at least once in their marriage, expressed the view that a male's interest in a female is solely sexual: 'I'd really – only – wanted – one – thing. She told me so this morning' (Amis, 1978).

one too many an intoxicant taken to excess
Whence 'had one too many', drunk: '. . . had one too many in a bar somewhere' (McCarthy, 1963).

one way ride a murder by criminals
Where you go if you are 'taken for a ride': 'Charlie Luciano – now nicknamed Lucky Luciano on account of a one way ride that he came back from' (Collins, 1981).

one wing low *see* flying low

open access needing no qualification
Of entry to a university course without passing previous examinations: 'But both courses are "open access"' (*Daily Telegraph*, October 1983, of degree courses in two London

Polytechnic Colleges with Marxist bias, in 'social sciences'; the intention was to make it easy for Blacks to enrol, and students could have **remedial** (q.v.) lessons in the English language before embarking on their further studies).

open housing having no restriction on new residents in a district
Am. White Christians are compelled to allow non-Whites and non-Christians (especially Blacks and Jews) to set up homes in the locality which they have kept to themselves. The objection, apart from snobbery and prejudice, is usu. economic because 'open housing' may drive down values of real estate.

open-legged inviting extra-marital copulation
Of a promiscuous woman who is not normally a practising whore: '. . . the risks to my health, in being so open-legg'd and free' (Cleland, 1749).

open marriage a marriage in which neither party hides extra-marital copulation
The 'openness' consists of neither lying to the other about lying with others: 'A groovy couple with an open marriage' (Bradbury, 1976).

open season the police are out in strength
Properly, the season during which the law allows hunting. CB sl. Am.

open your bowel(s) to defecate
A 'bowel' is properly an intestine, whence any internal organ, and was so used by Cromwell: 'The enemy in all probability will be in our bowels in ten days' (letter, 1643). The euphemism is medical jargon: '"Have you had your bowel open?" he had asked Carfax' (Bradbury, 1959).

open your legs to copulate with a male
And be **open-legged** (above): 'I'll teach her not to open her legs for bloody Germans' (Allbeury, 1978, of a WW II French-woman).

opening medicine a laxative
Not the first dose in a series, but 'opening bowels': 'Any pukka old soldier would have much preferred a dose of opening medicine' (Richards, 1933 – to compulsory Church Parade).

operant conditioning payment by results
Am. management jargon, with 'operant' meaning having an effect or capable of being measured. In some circles 'piece-work' has undesired overtones.

operational difficulties your flight is going to be late again
Airline jargon for soothing the travelling public: 'The Aeroflot flight was eight minutes late. For "operational reasons," the girl at Information explained' (Seymour, 1982). There are many problems associated with loading and moving complex machines under congested conditions through an unnatural and often hostile environment, which the travelling layman should not be told about.

operator a swindler
Properly, anyone who carries out an operation but, whatever his fee-structure, do not so describe a surgeon in his hearing: '"What does that mean – operator?" "Well, I've done a bit of villainy"' (L. Thomas, 1978). Of politicians, businessmen, etc., an 'operator' may use unconventional or questionable tactics to achieve his ends; of illegal narcotics, he is a dealer.

oral sex cunnilingus or fellatio
Passionate kissing is not so described: 'He preferred oral sex, something that obviated the need for a bed' (Green, 1979, of Rachman).

orchestras the testicles
Br. rh. sl. from 'orchestra stalls', balls; '. . . catching one a direct bullseye in the orchestras, thus putting one completely *hors de combat* for at least a week' (Matthew, 1983).

order of the boot etc. summary dismissal from employment
After the ancient 'orders' of chivalry. There is no actual kicking, nor shoving if you get the 'order of the push'.

orderly marketing price fixing between competitors
The customers are all quoted much the same price, or the markets are shared out on a geographical basis between the fixers. 'Orderly progress' means either price fixing or the retention of a monopolistic position, both being dear to the hearts of those managing Br. state industries: 'Last week he sang of "orderly progress" as "preferable to the dangers of unbridled competition"' (*Sunday Express*, May 1981).

ordure excreta
Properly, filth. Of faeces: 'Barbarians! The place is covered in . . . human ordure' (Boyd, 1982 – troops had defecated in every room) and of vomit: 'But it's hard enough . . . without havin' that ordure there atop ye' (Keneally, 1979 – soldiers were being sick).

organ the penis or vagina
Abbr. of 'sexual organ' or 'organ of sex'.
Usu. of the penis: 'He displayed the organ,
the secondary function of which is the relief
of the bladder' (Manning, 1965) with
'organs' meaning the penis and testicles:
'You've got to have a healthy view of your
organs' (Bradbury, 1976 – you do it with
mirrors?). Rarely of the vagina: '... that
organ of bliss in me, dedicated to its reception' (Cleland, 1749).

organize to induce to join a trade union
Trade union jargon, from the 'organization'
of a branch etc. Of those who wish to participate and those who have to be coerced. In
this language a company without a union,
however well run, is said not to be
'organized'.

ossified drunk
Instead of being **stoned** (q.v.), you are
turned into bone. Am.

other side (the) death
In spiritualist jargon, across the barrier
between this world and the next. For others,
the far bank of the Styx or Jordan on the way
to the Elysian Fields or to life eternal. For a
spy it is the enemy: 'He thought the Other
Side was maybe savouring the tourist attractions ...' (Price, 1985).

other side of the tracks the poor section
of town
When the Am. railroad arrived, it was often
located on the edge of town where property
was cheaper and it could be placed down-
wind of houses to avoid smoke, noise and
fire hazards. Eventually the town would
develop around the station, with the richer
inhabitants staying in the cleaner area and
the poorer on 'the other side of the tracks'.
Now some fig. use too.

other way (the) homosexual
Of either sex and a departure from the normal. 'He wouldn't look at his servants. His
inclinations, if she knew it, are all the other
way' (G. Greene, 1932 – the servants were
female).

other woman (the) a husband's sexual
mistress
Legal jargon ignoring the fact that all
womankind is 'other' than the wife: 'If Polly
were not the "other woman", she would
advise Gus to go back to her' (McCarthy,
1963).

ounce man an illicit dealer in narcotics
He buys in bulk and sells, often after adul-
tering the product, in small lots. Am.

out *see* **come out**

out of circulation menstruating
Female usage, often to a male, with imagery
from the lending library.

out of context something said inadvisedly
A use by politicians when they have forgotten what exactly they said, wish they had
never said it or were unaware that anyone
was recording it. As journalists are known to
select unfairly, if it improves the story, this
defensive manoeuvre is often effective.

out of town in prison
Suggesting perhaps that the convict might
be away on business. Some humorous use.
Am.

out of your mind etc. mad
The phrase also means temporarily forgotten and is so used of our own lapses of
memory. Also, of madness, 'out of' your senses, skull, head, etc.: 'He's out of his skull
.... ready for certifying' (Bogarde, 1981).

out to grass dismissed from employment
or in retirement
Equine imagery, from the life of an old horse
which has escaped the knacker. (A 'knacker'
was somebody who dealt in small goods –
'knick-knacks' – and Dr Johnson has no
other meaning. Does the weary sportsman
who profess himself to be 'knackered' mean
he has been dealt with as a trifle, or killed as
a horse too old to work?)

out to lunch mentally unstable
The Am. imagery is of a short absence from
home, whence a mild and perhaps temporary
mental affliction: 'His wife died about two
years ago and he's been somewhat out to
lunch ever since' (Diehl, 1978).

outhouse a lavatory
From its separation from the dwellinghouse,
across a court or down the garden. Whence
to go 'out the back', to the lavatory. 'Outdoor plumbing' is an Am. humorous use for
a lavatory which is no more than a shed, a
seat and a hole in the ground.

outrage to copulate with a woman extra-
maritally
Properly, you have given offence to her and
an 'outraged' female is likely to suggest
unenthusiastic participation, if not rape:
'She complained to him that .... some
British soldiers had assaulted and outraged
her .... She could have identified at least
forty men who had outraged her' (Richards,
1933, of a WW I French village whore).

outstanding expensive
Estate agents' puffing, from the meaning
'exceptional.' Literally, all construction is
outstanding, with exception of in-ground
swimming pools, crypts, subways and fall-
out shelters.

over-civilized decadent
Nazi dysphemism in a culture where to
appreciate beauty was to be effete: 'They are
nearer to France, Europe's most over-
civilised country' (Goebbels, 1945, in tr. of
the Rhinelanders whose supine reception of
the Anglo-American invaders contrasted
with the fanatical defence on the Eastern
Front. There was a simpler explanation for
the contrast, of which those facing capture
by the Russians were keenly aware).

over-gallant *see* **gallant**

over-geared insolvent
'Gearing' is the ratio of borrowings to assets.
An 'over-geared' company is too deeply in
debt but, to maintain confidence and avoid a
writ for defamation, it is taboo to talk of
insolvency.

over-invoicing the payment of a bribe in a
place selected by the recipient
In some markets, where corruption is
endemic but to be caught is to have your
hands or your head cut off, the selling price
of goods may be inflated by an amount which
will in due course be placed to the credit of
the person bribed somewhere beyond the
jurisdiction of his masters. The invoice sent
with the goods is the sum of the true cost
plus the bribe. cf. **under-invoicing**.

over Jordan etc. dead
Those who have reached the **other side**
(q.v.). Whence the punning film title
'Johnson over Jordan'. Rarely as 'over the
creek'.

over-refreshed etc. drunk
There are several phrases prefixed by 'over'
which, sometimes humorously, seek to attribute drunkenness to a socially acceptable
cause. Some may have taken a **refresher**
(q.v.) too many: '. . . post-prandial euphoria
that Harry Woods euphemistically termed
"over-refreshed"' (Deighton, 1978). Or
may have 'over-indulged': '. . . thought for a
moment I might have been over-indulging'
(*Private Eye*, July 1981). Politicians especially
seem to be prone to 'over-tiredness': 'He
turned up to the first production meeting –
in the morning – in an advanced state of
over-tiredness' (*Private Eye*, 1980). Others
become 'over-excited'. 'Overcome' may be

no more than an abbr. of 'overcome by
drink', etc. For 'over the bat' *see* **bat** (2).

over the broomstick cohabiting and copulating outside marriage
This common 19c. imagery is examined in
jump (3) (above): '. . .this woman in Garrad-
street here, had been married very young,
over the broomstick (as we say), to a tram-
ping man' (C. Dickens, 1861).

over the top achieving sexual orgasm
Usu. of a female: 'She made love to herself
on the bath mat . . . . She always felt awful
afterwards . . . . especially when she took herself . . . . "Over the Top"' (McCarthy,
1963). I suspect no link with attacking from a
trench in WWI: 'Darling, you can't really
imagine ONE going over the top?' (N. Mitford, 1960 – the homosexual Cedric is
explaining why he declined to participate in
WWII and I suspect the delightful Miss
Mitford knew both meanings).

over your time late in menstruating
Female use, with an implication of unwanted
pregnancy. It may also refer to a delayed
birth.

overcome *see* **over-refreshed** etc.

overdo the Dionysian rites to become
drunk
Dionysus discovered the art of wine-making
and travelled widely to pass on his important
knowledge. Being of catholic tastes, his rites
included sexual orgies, plays, human sacrifice and flagellation, in addition to drinking
wine. The ob. 'overdone', drunk, probably
owes nothing to this classical libertine.

overdue (1) pregnant
From failing to menstruate at the expected
time but not necessarily of an unwanted
pregnancy.

overdue (2) in difficulty or crashed
Aviation jargon, of an aircraft which has
failed to report by radio as required during
flight, or not landed as expected: '*Overdue*
connoted something quite different from *late*
in airline parlance' (Block, 1979).

overfly to spy from an aircraft over enemy
territory
Properly, to cross a country in the course of
a commercial flight by a recognized and
agreed path. The Am. government in May
1960 described Gary Powers' shooting down
in a U2 aircraft over Russia as an 'overflight'.
In 1962 they exchanged Powers for the
Russian spy Rudolf Abel.

oversee etc. to bewitch
 To 'oversee' is to inspect or supervise, but
one glance was enough for a true witch: 'It
have brought all kind of disaster along with
it. I must have been overseen when I took it'
(Gissing, 1890). To 'overlook' was just as
dangerous: 'Wha kens what ill it may bring
to the bairn, if ye overlook it in that gate?'
(W. Scott, 1819). And as 'overshadow': 'The
last witness said deceased had been "over-
shadowed" by someone' (*North Devon
Herald*, 1896, quoted in EDD). In Sc. friends
and relatives at the bedside giving comfort
were said to 'oversee' a dying person. ob.

(OVRA the Italian Fascists' political police
deserves a mention for honesty if not
humanity. Alone among such bodies, it was
an 'Organizzazione' which acknowledged its
function of 'Repressione' as well as 'Vig-
ilanza'.)

P

P anything taboo beginning with the letter P
Usu. 'piss' and spelt **pee** (below). Used fig.
in the common 'P off', go away.

pacify to conquer
Properly, to bring peace to: '. . . the
unsettled areas where we are still engaged in
pacifying the Tajicks, Uzbecks and Khokan-
dians' (Fraser, 1973, of 19c. Russian
imperial expansionism). Whence 'pacification', conquest, which Nixon favoured in the
Vietnam war: 'Pacification, for example, was
hardly anything more than a swollen, com-
puterized tit being forced upon an already
violated population' (Herr, 1977). For the
British, their colonial rule in Africa was the
'era of pacification' (Allen, 1979).

pack it in to die
Properly, to desist: 'That's where Jack's
mate from Hong Kong packed it in' (Theroux, 1973, of a death). In WW I to 'pack up'
was to be killed in battle, from the meaning,
to cease to function.

package on (a) drunkenness
The **load** (1) (q.v.) which you have taken
aboard and not of the ob. 'pack', a rum-like
liquor named for the unfortunate Eng.
General Pakenham who was killed in the
Battle of New Orleans which was fought two
months after the signing in Europe of a
peace treaty between the combatants.

package store a place which sells intoxicants
The Am. shopkeeper will hand them to you
in a sealed container which you may not
break open on the premises.

packet (1) a serious wound or death
Properly, a small pack, whence an article
sent by post, as in the 'packet-boat' which
carried the mails. In WW I this particular
missive was despatched at you by the enemy
and the recipient 'copped' or 'caught' it.

packet (2) venereal disease
The article 'copped' or 'caught' by careless
or unwary servicemen in WW II. But today
to 'catch a packet' may mean no more than
having a number of bills descend on you at
once.

pad (1) a whore's bedroom
In Am. sl., any room, from the sleeping mat,
with overtones of illicit narcotics: 'Women

walking the streets for tricks to take to their
"pads"' (L. Armstrong, 1955).

pad (2) dishonestly to inflate a claim
From 'padding' clothing, etc., to cause an
apparent increase in size: 'The surcharges,
padding and fictitious costs that were an
inevitable part of every account' (Deighton,
1972). There is no etymological link with the
ob. 'pad', to rob, as in 'footpad' who robbed
on foot, which was from a 'pad', a path.

pad (3) a cloth worn by a menstruating
woman
Euphemistic only as 'wearing a pad', which
does not indicate preparedness to play
hockey or baseball. In ob. Eng. use, such a
towel was a 'padlock', punning on 'pad' and
on 'padlocking the gentleman's pleasure
garden' – the vagina.

paddy wagon a police vehicle
From the preponderance of Irishmen in
New England police departments and not
from the national origins of those incarcerated.

pagan a whore
Properly, one who does not worship God,
and prostitution was no occupation for the
upright: '*Prince Henry* What pagan may that
be? *Page* A proper gentlewoman' (Shakespeare, 2 *Henry IV*). ob.

painted woman a whore
Not an artist's model but one who painted
her face before the practice became in succession permitted, normal and then obligatory. Now perhaps ob.

painters are in (the) I am menstruating
From the disruption and discoloration.
Common female use.

palm (1) an indication of bribery
From the upturned hand, palms and venality
have long gone together: 'You yourself Are
much condemned to have an itching palm'
(Shakespeare, *Julius Caesar*). Whence many
punning terms for bribery – 'palmistry',
'palm soap', 'palm oil', 'palm grease', etc.: 'It
would be hard to dispute that a little such
palm-grease must, upon occasion, have
found a compliant hand' (Monsarrat, 1978).
To 'anoint a palm' is to bribe.

palm (2) to cheat by prestidigitation
You conceal cards in the palm of the hand.
Also used fig. of other forms of cheating or
sharp practice, as in the phrase to 'palm off
with', to give something of lesser value than
agreed.

pan a pedestal type lavatory
Properly, any bowl but a 'bedpan' is not used for cooking or washing. Whence 'down the pan', irretrievably lost. A 'pancake', a round, flat pile of cow shit, comes from its appearance.

panel (the) see on the club etc.

panel-house a brothel
I would like to think this Am. use came from the ob. E. Eng. dialect 'panel', a whore: 'Panels march by two and three, Saying, Sweetheart, come with me' (Old ballad quoted in EDD). However the more likely derivation is merely a description of a place where there are cubicles divided by panels. Rarely too as 'panel-joint'.

pansy a male homosexual
From the delicate flower, viola tricolor: 'You're just a filthy pansy! No wonder your marriage has failed' (Masters, 1976).

panther sweat whisky
DAS suggests: 'May have originally been a euphem. for "panther piss"': '"Ran alky through here," he said, "in a beatup truck, white lightning, panther piss – whatever you want to call it"' (Sanders, 1980). But where did 'panther piss' come from, in the absence of panthers? Am.

paper a house to fill a theatre by giving tickets away
Punning theatrical jargon, the 'house' being the audience.

paper hanger a policeman giving a ticket for speeding
With similar punning humour, he may also be said to be 'doing his paperwork'. For a criminal 'paperhanging' is not household decoration or catching motorists but forging or passing bad cheques: 'I've been stung too many times by the summer people. Paper-hangers I call them' (Theroux, 1974 – an innkeeper was complaining about losses on bad cheques he had cashed).

paper out on a commercial agreement to murder
Another Am. form of **contract** (2) (above): '"It wasn't no amateur hit." "Are you tellin' me there was paper out on her?"' (Diehl, 1978).

Paphian a whore
Paphos, or Cyprus, was sacred to Venus, the goddess of love: 'Cyprians of the better sort . . . . well acquainted with its Paphian intricacies' (Mayhew, 1862, of London whores). ? ob.

parallel parking extra-marital copulation
The car illegally left beside the permitted one at the kerb. A colourful Am. use. And see **park**.

parallel pricing the operation of a cartel
The quotations or sale prices of competing manufacturers are held in an agreed relationship. Common commercial use.

paralyzed very drunk
And immobile: 'Dead drunk, paralysed, spifflicated' (Chandler, 1953).

paralytic very drunk
Immobile, but not from paralysis or palsy: 'We had a marvellous wedding, Jerry and me. I was paralytic' (Theroux, 1983 – but what did Jerry think about it?).

paramour a person with whom you regularly copulate extra-maritally
Properly, a suitor, acting 'through love', and of both sexes although women seem to have more paramours than men: 'Married women go there with their paramours, for they are sure of secrecy' (Mayhew, 1862).

parboiled drunk
The common culinary imagery. This time, thoroughly boiled, whence overheated.

parity the achievement of the best in any aspect of conditions of employment
Trade union jargon. The equality you seek is only with the best, whether in terms of wages, hours of work, holidays, pensions, sick pay etc.

park to copulate extra-maritally
The Am. use, supposedly from parking your car in a secluded spot. There is no etymological link with the 19c. London whores or: 'Park women, properly so called, are those degraded creatures, who wander about the paths most frequented after nightfall in the Parks, and consent to any species of humiliation for the sake of acquiring a few shillings' (Mayhew, 1862).

parliament a lavatory
Punning on 'sitting'. The ob. Br. 'parliament', whisky on which excise duty had not been paid, reflected the widespread smuggling of spirits before the Railway Age: 'It's as good parliament as ever a gentleman tasted' (Crocker, 1862).

parlor house a brothel
The Am. parlor, with the kitchen and bedroom, was where you expected to meet a woman. ? ob.

(parsley bed, the mythical place from which girls came at birth, is defined by EDD as 'A euphemism for the uterus'. Boys favoured gooseberry bushes as pre-natal abodes, perhaps because the gooseberry bush, needing no cultivation or protection from weeds, was usu. to be found at the bottom of a cottager's garden. Parsley beds can be overgrown too.)

part furnished without security of occupation
The provisions of the Br. Rent Acts give extensive rights of tenure to tenants of unfurnished premises. A few worthless items of furniture may be left in the accommodation by a landlord in the hope that a new tenant may not acquire such rights. Perhaps becoming ob. as successive legislation to protect tenants drives all rented property off the market – which is indeed an effective way of protecting them.

part with child to abort involuntarily
Or, in the Sc. dialect, to 'part with Patrick': 'Or he wan back she parted wi' patrick' (Graham, 1883).

partially sighted nearly blind
If baldness were a subject of pity instead of humour, we would talk of the 'partially haired'.

participate in to work for
The usage seeks to play down the tedium of menial employment: 'Secretaries who are seen to participate in the fast-moving oil business' (*London Times*, May 1976, quoted in DDE).

parts *see* private parts

party (1) a battle
Usu. of short unsuccessful or violent fights: 'Dutch civilians weeping . . . . for the few returning guests departing from what someone on the staff had chosen to call "a party"' (Bogarde, 1978, on the Battle of Arnhem).

party (2) an act of extra-marital copulation
Not, I think, from the social meeting for pleasure but because 'party' is sl. for a person, whence rarely for a person who is sexually promiscuous: 'A smart little party of sixteen or so' (overhead in Connecticut, 1982). A 'party girl' is a whore, presumably from her attending social events where she can meet customers: 'There were some snide references to what had befallen her, including a mention that she was known as a "party girl"' (Sanders, 1986). Am.

party member a Communist
The usage dates from the pre-WW II time when you kept quiet about being a Communist because many would consider you to be a traitor with revolutionary tendencies: 'That's why people convert to Catholicism, or become party members' (Bradbury, 1959). With our present choice of extreme political groupings, being a Communist is a fairly conservative thing to admit to.

pass (1) to die
The passage is from this world to the next: 'Harriet laughed. "You have only to let them pass and they lose their importance." "You may pass with them, of course" David said with a wry, sombre smile' (Manning, 1962 – Harriet was speaking of events). More often in a compound, like 'pass away': 'Flora must have felt she was going to die, for just before she passed away . . .' (L. Armstrong, 1955); 'pass into the next world': 'He was the first to pass into the next world' (Richards, 1933); 'pass on': 'She murmured something sensitive just before she passed on' (Bradbury, 1976); 'pass off' the earth, etc.: 'I haven't got the wind up, but some strong healthy men have been unlucky enough to pass off this Ball of Clay in double-quick time since we have been at this station' (Richards, 1936, of India). Christians and Spiritualists may 'pass over', arriving on the far bank of the Styx, the Jordan, the Great Divide, etc. To 'pass in your checks' is a rarer variant of **cash in your checks** (above). To 'pass out' is rare of dying, meaning usu. to faint. A 'passing' commonly describes a death.

pass (2) an unsolicited sexual approach
Usu. by a male to a female whom he does not know well, perhaps from the attack fleetingly made by an aircraft: 'Too many passes had been made at it and it had grown a little too smart in dodging them' (Chandler, 1943, of a woman's face). But also of homosexuals: 'Burgess sought Rees out later earning a mild rebuff for "making a tentative pass" at him' (Boyle, 1979).

pass water to urinate
The phrase is so common that we give it no thought but *see* **water**: 'The nurse took him into a little cubicle and asked him to pass water into a bottle' (Bradbury, 1959).

passing *see* pass (1)

passion a homosexual attachment
Properly, any strong emotion and so used, especially in the plural, of heterosexual lust. The dated abbr. 'pash' usu. refers to

unreciprocated female homosexual desire: 'Are you getting a pash for that little thing?' (G. Greene, 1932, the question being asked by one women of another about a third). Rarely of one-sided heterosexual desire: 'Janet seems to be getting a pash for this Savory man' (ibid. – but people normally have pashes 'on' rather than 'for').

past (your) anything shameful or secret about your past life
Of criminal activities, or failure in business and especially of extra-marital copulation, in which case your 'past' can be your general promiscuous conduct or an attachment to a single person: '"Part of your past, I presume?" "No. At least, not as you mean it"' (Manning, 1965).

pastie a waitress bare above the waist except that her nipples are covered
From the small decorative patches which are 'pasted' to the skin to comply with the law in districts where **topless** (q.v.) service is forbidden. The Am. establishment where serving-girls are thus attired may also be called a 'pastie'.

pasture to copulate with
Of a male, grazing as it were: 'Fielding thought of Hecht pasturing in that thick body' (le Carré, 1962).

patient see **agent**

patriotic front an organization of terrorists
They metamorphose if they win power.

patron (1) a man who keeps a sexual mistress
Properly, he who stands in the relationship of a father, whence the concept of protecting: 'An impotent and unkind man will produce a woman predisposed to fall in love instantly with her succeeding patron' (Chandler, 1966).

patron (2) a customer
The 'pater' has here moved from being a protector to being a supporter, as of the arts. The shopkeeper who so describes his customers seeks to put a finer gloss on a commercial relationship.

pause (1) the natural permanent cessation of menstruation
Abbr. of 'menopause'. Properly, a 'pause' is a cessation for a short time of something that will be resumed.

pause (2) a statutory restriction on increases in pay

One of a series of terms aimed at disguising Br. political attempts to hold down wage increases on a national basis: 'In 1961 . . . . Selwyn Lloyd introduced what he euphemistically described as the Pause, to combat growing inflationary problems' (Green, 1979). The inference was that increases would be resumed after a brief delay.

pavement artist an expert at clandestinely following another
Espionage jargon, punning on the beggar who chalks on paving stones: 'Rostov had commandeered all Petrov's best pavement artists and most of his cars' (Follett, 1979).

pavement princess a whore
Found at the roadside where the trucks pull up. Am.

paw to fondle a woman sexually
With an inference of undue vigour, as an impatient horse strikes the ground with his hoof, and punning on 'paw', a hand: 'When you ask any of the men here, they just want to paw you' (Chandler, 1953). I have unsuccessfully sought the *mot* about the profligate King Edward VII: 'He never reigns but he paws'.

pax Britannica the British colonial rule
Unlike the golden years of the Pax Romana, its injustices clouded by time, the two centuries of British empire, which petered out in apathy and the 1960s, saw continuous fighting somewhere or other. The Romans enjoyed the advantage that their subjects saw no acceptable alternative to the Imperial system. We should not however be too dismissive: 'The Pax Britannica gave both British and Indians a quite remarkable degree of safety in their daily lives' (Allen, 1975).

pay a visit to urinate
Abbr. of 'pay a visit to the lavatory' and punning on a social call. Sometimes expanded, as 'pay a visit to the old soldiers' home', but seldom used of defecation.

pay for your dinner to copulate extra-maritally on a single occasion
The male pays for the meal, and 'repay' would be more accurate: '"You mean I don't have to pay for my dinner?" "I ought to slap your face for that crack"' (Chandler, 1958 – the male had declined casual sex).

pay off (1) a bribe or illicit reward
The action is clothed with commercial propriety: 'Ezra is still in the saddle, even after that payoff business in Malawi' (M. Thomas, 1980).

pay off (2) to kill
Probably from the SE 'paying off' a ship's
crew at the end of a voyage, their service
being concluded. Am.

pay nature's debt etc. to die
From the necessity of death in the natural
order. This, and to 'pay nature's last debt',
infer natural death. To 'pay' the extreme,
final or supreme penalty is to die violently,
whether by being murdered, executed or
killed in war. To 'pay your debt to society' is
to be killed judicially, usu. for murder. A Br.
soldier who 'paid with the roll of a drum' did
no more than fail to pay his debts. It was
forbidden to arrest a soldier for debt when
he was on the march.

peace a device, stratagem or policy designed
to disarm or weaken your opponents
Those preparing for or practising aggression
often profess their peaceful intentions, as
did Hitler in his notorious 'Peace Speech' of
17 May 1933. The Communists were not
slow to learn from their fellow totalitarians
and sponsor 'peace' councils, campaigns,
offensives, initiatives, etc. while continuing
to occupy, attack, undermine and threaten
non-Communist states. The Br. 'peace
women' too use violence in their pacifist
support of unilateral nuclear disarmament.
Whence also a 'peace-keeping action', the
military occupation of another country, by a
'peace-keeping force': 'First they call the
army a peace-keeping force' (Sharpe, 1979).

peace at last death
A tombstone and obituary favourite, referring to the dead person and not the sur-
vivors.

pecker a penis
Properly, an instrument for making a hole by
pecking. Common Am. use: '. . . caution a
feller about despairing of his poor engine
and perhaps hitting his pecker with a hammer' (Theroux, 1973). The Br. 'pecker' was
the nose, whence the expression 'keep your
pecker up' – keep cheerful, an exhortation
which an Am. might find impracticable as
well as impertinent.

peculiar homosexual
A variant of **queer** (q.v.): 'The idea came to
her that Dick was, well, *peculiar*' (McCarthy,
1963). For Webster in 1833 the 'peculiar
members' were the testicles and in ob. Br.
use, a 'peculiar' was a sexual mistress, being
something for your exclusive use.

peddle arse to be a whore
From 'peddle', to offer for sale, and *see* **arse**:

'I'm too old to peddle my ass' (Sanders,
1981, of a female). Some homosexual use
also.

pee to urinate
The usu. spelling of **P** (above): 'The
Brigadier on his way back from a quick pee
in the bushes' (Bogarde, 1978).

peel a banana to copulate
Of a male, perhaps from the movement of
the prepuce. A Black man who 'peels a fine
green banana' copulates with a pretty light-
skinned Black woman. Am.

peeler a policeman
After the original **bobby** (q.v.), Sir Robert
Peel. Whence perhaps the Am. 'peel', to
arrest.

peg a spirituous intoxicant
Br. Indian usage which appears (above) in
chota peg. N. Eng. communal drinking
bowls had 'pegs' which marked each person's share, but the Indian use is probably
from a 'peg in your coffin', which each
brandy or whisky in that climate probably
was: 'We had our pegs on the verandah'
(Fraser, 1977). To 'peg' is to drink intoxicants to excess: 'What with rum and pepper –
and pepper and rum – I should think his
pegging must be nearly over' (C. Dickens,
1861 – punning on to 'peg', to knock on the
floor for attention).

peg out to die
From the scoring at cribbage, where the first
to finish moves his peg to the end of a row of
holes on a board.

pencil a penis
From the shape and construction rather than
the shared Latin ancestry. Partridge gives
'pencil and tassel, a (little) boy's penis and
scrotum: lower-class euphemism' (DSUE –
'tassel' being Br. rh. sl. for 'arsehole').

penetrate to copulate with
Again sharing its etymological stem with
'penis'. It has overtones of lack of (female)
consent, just as the espionage jargon 'penetrate' does, meaning to enter a building
without permission.

penman a forger
Properly, a skilled writer with a pen. Underworld use.

penny a policeman
A pun on **copper** (q.v.) from the US cent
which is called a 'penny'. Although pre-
decimal Br. coins of low value were called

'coppers', the pun failed to bridge the Atlantic. ? ob.

people's imposed by autocracy
The language of totalitarianism in various compounds as follow:

people's army an army pledged to the support of a regime when the former non-political and professional army has been disbanded.

people's car a device for financing Nazi re-armament. In 1938 a German who had paid 750 marks at a rate of not less than 5 marks a week received an order number, but none received a car. Today 'Volkswagen' has long shaken off its dubious beginnings.

people's court a tribunal supporting the regime without trained judges, juries, justice or mercy. There is however a certain irony in the fact that the three Communists acquitted before the courts in 1934 of involvement in the Reichstag Fire should have been the first victims of the Nazi *Volksgerichtshof*.

people's democracy a Communist tyranny. Newspeak at its best.

people's justice summary killing without trial. Not even the legalistic routine of a 'people's court' to delay the process: 'Spare them after all? When they should be punished according to the people's justice!' (Kyle, 1983, of the Czar and his family).

people's militia an armed force supporting those who have recently seized power. It may be institutionalized to keep a watch over and counterbalance the remains of a professional army.

people's republic a Communist tyranny. Slightly less offensive than a 'people's democracy' although the 'people' are unlikely to notice the difference: '... fatuous violation of language that in our day terms the grotesque dictatorship a "People's Republic"' (Theroux, 1979).

People's War WW II after the Germans attacked them in 1941 for the leaders of Russian Communism. It certainly wasn't a 'Generals' War', as Stalin had killed 90% of them, and it took months of Nazi brutality and stupidity to unite the attacked fully against the attackers: 'The twenty million dead in the People's War'

(Allbeury, 1982, writing from the Russian viewpoint).

Percy *see* **person**

perform (1) to defecate or urinate when required
Nursery usage when a child is being taught to avoid doing so involuntarily: 'On the rare occasions when – by pure chance . . . . – he "performed", she moderated her pantomime of approval' (McCarthy, 1963). To 'perform a natural function' is more specific: 'Temple felt an urge to perform a natural function' (Boyd, 1982). Used too of domestic pets.

perform (2) to copulate
Chiefly of a male: 'You see . . . he can perform, or he wants to, anyway he does' (Amis, 1978, of copulation). Whence 'performer' as someone who so 'performs': '. . . the writer or artist . . . . is a better performer in love's lists than the navvy' (Harris, 1925) or as someone who engages in sexual activity in public for a payment: 'He's the performer. In return, he'll get it for nothing' (Manning, 1978, of a couple copulating before an audience). 'Perform' is also used of homosexual activity or sexual deviation.

period (1) the time of menstruation
Abbr. of 'monthly period' of menstrual flow: '"Next Monday?" asks Howard. "No good," says Flora. "That's my period"' (Bradbury, 1975 – they were planning copulation).

period (2) old and dilapidated
Properly, a passage of time but perhaps no more than an abbr. of 'colonial period', etc. Estate agents so describe a residence when decay and disrepair are so apparent that they cannot be glossed over: 'Impressive stone-built period house (available for the first time for 50 years). Ideal for renovation' (*W. Daily Press*, May 1981).

periodic rest a term in prison
Usu. of an habitual criminal. I particularly recall it being used of the incarceration of Hoffa, the former boss of the Teamsters' Union, whose stay in jail was not accompanied by great physical hardship. He had the distinction of going inside through the efforts of Robert Kennedy and coming out in 1971 through the clemency of Richard Nixon.

permissive opposed to accepted convention
Properly, done under consent. The 1970s usage implied that society should accept

selfish and hedonistic attitudes to sex, pornography, parenthood, etc. in a 'permissive society', where such behaviour should be the norm. Now some pejorative use.

perpetual care fund a supplemental burial charge
Am. funeral jargon. The customer is persuaded to pay a capital sum which will supposedly keep the grave in good order for ever: 'Another idea used by virtually all cemeteries is the "perpetual care fund" .... a surcharge of ten to twenty per cent for future care' (J. Mitford, 1963).

person the male genitalia
Probably abbr. from 'personal parts', which also describes the vagina, as though your nose or ears are not equally personal to you. Abbr. to 'Percy', punning on the male name.

personal assistant a shorthand typist
The usage inflates the vanity of the employer and the salary of the employee.

personal hygiene the disposal of soiled menstrual towels
The containers for such towels are so labelled in hotels. 'Hygiene' means relating to health.

personal hygiene station a lavatory in a spacecraft
Astronauts' jargon in a male world. But where will a female astronaut dispose of her soiled menstrual towel?

personal parts *see* person

personal relations copulation
Often in the phrase 'have personal relations with', which you do with anyone you meet, of either sex, by shaking hands with or talking to them: 'Personal relations, as they used to say. But what's personal about relations? .... Two victims sharing groins' (Bradbury, 1965). 'Personal relations' is similarly used for homosexual encounters: 'Burgess had ample opportunity to indulge his fetish for "personal relations" under cover of the rigidly enforced nightly blackout' (Boyle, 1979).

personal representatives those who administer the estate of a person who dies intestate
Or who appoints no living executor. But the 'person' they 'represent' is dead.

personal services extra-marital sexual activity
Usu. copulation by a female for payment: 'Recruiting "a lady of my acquaintance" for

personal and espionage services' (Boyle, 1979). 'Personalized messages', delivered over the telephone or by cassette, are usu. pornographic aids to self-masturbation.

personality a nonentity
Properly, the fact of being a person with individual characteristics. Entertainment jargon, in a milieu where the article on sale is individuality: 'He wouldn't allow the *TV Times* to describe him as a TV personality. That's just for jokeless comics who wished they could sing and dance' (Deighton, 1972).

persuade to compel through violence or threats
Properly, to convince by argument: 'No less than 260 of our illustrious legislators were vulnerable to KGB "persuasion"' (*Private Eye*, April 1981, suggesting that membership of the House of Commons does not immunize from adultery, homosexuality, pederasty, chicanery, extravagance, etc.). Police, criminal and espionage use and for some villains a 'persuader' is a handgun or other violent weapon: '... pistols, whips, blackjacks, lengths of rubber hose called "persuaders"' (Lacey, 1986).

pessary a female contraceptive
Properly, an oval counter, whence any medical plug worn internally: 'Get yourself a pessary .... a female contraceptive' (McCarthy, 1963).

pet (1) to caress physically during courtship
Probably from the stroking of the domestic animal: '... held in his gentle brutal mitts for a petting session' (Ustinov, 1971). There is unhappily no etymological link with the ob. N. Eng. 'petting-stone', a rock which a bride had to negotiate at her wedding, to leave all her 'pets', or ill-humours, behind her.

pet (2) a sexual mistress
The Am. imagery is of the domestic animal kept for its owner's pleasure, or pleasuring: 'Cynical as a Park Avenue pet after her butter and egg man goes home' (Chandler, 1958).

peter a penis
Apart from the common use of male names for the penis, the etymology is obscure and I don't think much of the suggestion that it comes from a 'petard', a mine: ''Twas the peter of Paul the Apostle' (*Playboy's Book of Limericks*). Mainly Am.

Peter Funk an auctioneer's stooge
Probably from the automatic repeating

device, or 'peter', used in telegraphy. It has the sound too of rh. sl. but the available rhymes are not appropriate. Am.

petite amie etc. a sexual mistress
The little female friend, but not normally French. Less often as 'petite femme': 'Time the *petite femme* got herself into a *negligée*' (N. Mitford, 1945). 'Petit ami' as the partner for a male homosexual is even rarer: 'Your *petit ami* was calling me a horrid baggy little man' (Sharpe, 1977).

petrified drunk
Showing no sign of movement, as if turned into stone. Mainly Am. In BI it still normally means no more than frightened.

petty house *see* **little house**

phantom a person paid while not working or a non-existent employee whose wage is drawn by another
The Am. victim is usu. a large public employer. Either the person on the payroll exists but as a friend of the foreman or a politician gets paid without working; or the payroll numbers are inflated by a person who does not exist, with the foreman stealing the wages.

pharmaceuticals illicit narcotics carried personally
Along with your aspirins and toothpaste: '. . . whom Caryn still saw, but now only as a matter of form and pharmaceuticals' (M. Thomas, 1982 – she got her supply from him).

pharmacy a private store of illegal narcotics
Properly, a place where drugs are dispensed: 'Barney convoying personal pharmacies through airports' (M. Thomas, 1980).

pheasant plucker a term of abuse
Spoonerism rather than mere rh. sl. No connection with ob. Br. 'pheasant', a whore or 'pheasantry', a brothel.

physic a laxative
Properly, any medical treatment: 'The physic will clean him out real good' (L. Armstrong, 1955). I have not met the further meaning of copulation, given by DSUE, except as **night physic** (above).

physical involvement extra-marital copulation
Not just shaking hands, which is all the words imply, except of a team game where there would be overtones of unsporting play: 'Her solicitors have been instructed to sue

any hack who dares to suggest a physical involvement' (*Private Eye*, March 1981).

piccolo player a male homosexual
Usu. in Am. of fellatio, from the mouthing of the instrument.

pick to steal
OED notes a use in 1300, which makes it one of the oldest euphemisms in the language, and in regular use since then: 'A charge of picking and unlawfully intromitting with his neighbour's goods' (Hector, 1876). The ob. forms of 'pickle', and Sc. 'pike' meant the same: 'Ye pykit your mother's pouch o' twalpennies' (W. Scott, 1818). An animal which 'picked' gave premature birth, from the dialect meaning to throw: '. . . produces a calf prematurely – in local phrase, "picks her cau'f"' (Atkinson, 1891).

pick a daisy etc. to urinate
A punning female use, perhaps from the bending down and the 'daisy' or chamber pot, with the common floral motif around its rim. To 'pick a pea' punned with less subtlety whereas to 'pick a rose' brought to mind a nozzle producing a fine spray. These, and other, flowers might be also gathered, plucked or pulled.

pick-me-up an intoxicant
Properly of a medicine taken as a tonic, whence jokingly of spirits: 'If I had any more of these pick-me-ups I'd be under the table' (Theroux, 1979).

pick off to kill
Choosing whom you aim at: 'Go ahead.You can pick him off' (Genet, in 1969 tr., of a killing).

pick up a casually met sexual partner
Males will 'pick up' anyone, but the female who does it is likely to be a whore: 'You don't think they make me look like a tart? . . . . I'll go up the Broadway looking for pick-ups' (Theroux, 1976) and: 'Rachman continued to pick up other girls' (Green, 1979).

pick up a nail to contract gonorrhoea
The discomfort felt by the male when urinating or undergoing a pre-penicillin cure was akin to lameness in a horse. The ob. 'pick up a knife' was to fall off a horse in the days when to be a bad rider was like being a bad driver today, it being jokingly suggested that the faller left the saddle on purpose.

pickled drunk
The common culinary imagery but this time with a reference to the preservation of anatomical specimens in alcohol.

pie-eyed drunk
Unable to focus rather than with eyes like pies: 'Brother Yank doesn't believe in getting his nose in the trough before 10 p.m., by which time one and all are absolutely pie-eyed' (*Private Eye*, April 1981).

piece (1) a female viewed sexually by a male
Properly, a part of something and a synonym of **bit** (above): 'The greatest little piece in the business, and for half a page in your rag – she'd do it' (Deighton, 1972). More often as a 'piece of' arse or ass, buttered bun, crackling, crumpet, goods, muslin, rump, skirt, etc., most of which are dealt with under those headings: 'I was day after day closeted with this choice piece of rump, and not so much as touching her, let alone squeezing or grappling' (Fraser, 1975). A 'piece of trade', a whore and a 'piece on a fork', copulation are both ob.

piece (2) a handgun
Perhaps an abbr. from 'fowling-piece' but so used of both cannons and pistols since the 16c., and of cross-bows before that:'"You carry a piece?" her asked suddenly . . . . "Oh no," I said. "I don't believe in violence"' (Sanders, 1980).

piece (3) a small quantity of illicit narcotics
Insofar as there are standards in this business, a 'piece' is an ounce. Am.

piece of paper a speeding ticket
Apart from the nuisance of having to pay a fine, this Am. CB usage minimizes the indignity of having been caught.

piece of the action *see* action (1)

piece off to bribe
In general use, to buy silence or favours, from the actual or fig. peeling bills off a bankroll. Specifically it refers to bribing a foreman etc. to give you a job, in return for handing over a part of your wages. Am.

(pig a police officer is no new concept of abuse, being noted by Grose. The variation 'pig-feet' is new: '. . . they'd tell the pig-feet if they came asking around' (Lyall, 1982). There is no etymological link, I suggest, with the ob. Sc. 'pig', a pot for urine: 'Into my putrid channel At night each wifie tooms her pig' (Ogg, 1873 – to 'toom' is to empty).

pigeon (1) the dupe of a criminal
Old enough for Grose but still modern criminal use. In a 'pigeon-drop' the victim pays money to thieves for a share in a bogus bank-roll which they profess to have found. But cf. **fly the blue pigeon.**

pigeon (2) a vehicle caught speeding
From the speed of the bird: 'The Smokey at milepost 116 has a pigeon' (CBSLD). CB sl. Am.

piggyback to use another's reputation for your financial or social ends
Properly, a ride given to a child on the back of an adult: 'You're doing me the very same way. You're piggybacking' (Theroux, 1978).

pile into to copulate with
Of a male, with the common violent and penetrating imagery: 'I'm 'bout worn out pilin' inter that li'l darlin'' (Fraser, 1971 – a husband was speaking of his wife's sexual desires).

piled with French velvet infected with syphilis
A complex pun on the 'pile' of shorn cloth, 'velvet' a vagina and the **malady of France** (q.v.): 'Thou art piled, for a French velvet' (Shakespeare, *Measure for Measure*). ob.

pill (1) a penis
This ob. Sc./N. Eng. use, from Norwegian dialect, survives in the diminutive 'pillock', which is commnly used fig. as a mild insult.

pill (2) a contraceptive taken orally by women
Not just any medicament prepared for swallowing: 'In the pre-Pill world of our youth . . .' (Bradbury, 1976). Whence 'on the pill', taking such contraceptives regularly and by inference able to copulate without impregnation.

pill (3) an illicit narcotic tablet
Originally of opium or nembutal, but now anything goes: 'A friend of mine had killed himself . . . . He had done it with pills' (Herr, 1977). A 'pillhead' is specifically addicted to amphetamines or barbiturates.

pillow partner a person with whom you often copulate extra-maritally
Of either sex, but not a spouse: 'I can usually make use of a native pillow partner' (Fraser, 1971).

pills the testicles
Probably from 'pill', a ball rather than the medical tablets but unlike **balls** (above) rarely used fig. or as an oath.

pin the penis
Of the same tendency as **prick** (below) but much less common.

pin-money the receipts from casual prostitution
From the SE meaning, funds which a

woman can spend on personal needs, this income being earned without her husband's exertions, and perhaps also punning on **pin** (above).

pin-up an erotic picture of a female
In WW II titillating and often crude photographs, etc., of women were displayed in barrack-rooms, etc. secured by drawing-pins. A woman so depicted, or considered worthy of having that distinction, was also known as a 'pin-up'.

pinch (1) to steal
Properly, to nip between the fingers: 'He had spent most of his life in clink for pinching anything from a roll of linoleum to a hurricane lamp' (Bogarde, 1972).

pinch (2) to arrest
From the grasping of the suspect: 'He got acquitted for that there note after he had me "pinched"' (Mayhew, 1851). In modern Am. use too as an arrest: 'Maybe he knows something that could hang a pinch on her' (Chandler, 1958).

pine overcoat a coffin
'Worn' if you are killed but not if you die in bed. For other examples of this type of macabre humour, *see* **wooden box etc.**

ping-ponging passing a rich patient from one specialist to another
A medical version of the long rallies in table tennis. Am.

pink panther an unmarked police car
Perhaps from the plain-clothes detective in the television cartoon. CB sl. Am.

pink slip a notice of dismissal
If that is the message, it is 'pink', whatever the colour. Rarely too of normal retirement: 'I'm forty-seven hours and fifty-five minutes from owning my own pink slip' (Wambaugh, 1983, of a policeman about to retire). Am.

pioneer a soldier sent to intervene in a foreign war
Properly, a soldier who clears the way for his own following troops: 'China had sent several fresh brigades of "volunteers" and "pioneers" into the fray' (Ustinov, 1966).

piped drunk
Probably not from the ob. 'pipe', to put liquor into a cask or to drink it and perhaps from the notion that any vessel overfilled needs plumbing. The Br. 'pipe', to weep, is rh. sl. for 'pipe your eye', to cry.

piran drunk
This entry is for my Eng. W. Country readers: 'St Piran is the patron saint of tinners, popularly supposed to have died drunk' (EDD). Cornwall. ? ob.

piss pins and needles to be infected with gonorrhoea
Of a male, from the sensation while urinating. In rarer usage, to 'piss pure cream'. The ob. 'piss your tallow' was to ejaculate before vaginal entry: 'Send me a cool rut-time, Jove, or who can blame me to piss my tallow?' (Shakespeare, *Merry Wives of Windsor*).

pissed drunk
From the need to dispose of beer drunk to excess: 'I am not introspectively drunk. I am merely pissed' (Sharpe, 1977). But you can equally become 'pissed' on wine or spirits. The fig. 'pissed off' means no more than disaffected, drunk or sober. Rarely abbr. to 'P.O.'d': 'I think the president was very angry .... In fact royally P.O.'d might be a very good word for it' (*Washington Post*, March 1987, quoting Maureen Reagan).

pistol a penis
Of obvious imagery. Whence Shakespeare's punning character. ob.

pitcher to demand money from a suitor coming from another village
The tribute was paid to the local lads for access to one of their females and he who refused to pay was 'pitchered': 'W.M. was "pitchered" at Smithy-place, near Honley; he was, in fact, thrown into a sump hole, where he was almost suffocated' (*Leeds Mercury Supplement*, March 1896, quoted in EDD – the miscreants were fined £4). This ob. Yorks entry is a sample chosen from the many phrases which illustrate the parochial nature of society until recent times, and the tribal practices which such parochialism fosters. Whence the modern phenomenon of the football hooligan.

place a lavatory
Probably the location given over to a special use rather than an abbr. of a 'place to urinate'. You may often hear a male enquiry: 'Where's the place?'

place-man a spy
Properly, someone who holds a responsible place in government service but in this use, punning on having been 'placed' as a spy by his masters: 'Soviet officials had access to a variety of French political and military secrets through experienced "place men" such as Burgess's associate' (Boyle, 1979).

place of safety an inhumane prison
Himmler's favoured term for his concentration camps. The ob. Br. 'place of correction',
a common jail, was at least named in honest,
albeit usu. unfulfilled, expectation: 'Your
places of correction would be as quiet as
Chelsea Hospital' (Ustinov, 1971).

plain brown wrapper an unmarked
police car
Like a parcel packed without anything to
advertise its contents. CB sl. Am.

planned community a housing estate
Real estate jargon, describing a conglomer-
ation of very similar dwellings built to a high
density. Once the houses are sold, the community goes its several, unplanned, ways.

planned termination suicide
A popular use, from **terminate** (1) (below).
Also of induced abortions.

planned withdrawal a defeat
A common military and journalistic excuse
on the losing side: 'Surprise and mobility,
coupled with an overwhelming air support,
turned "planned withdrawals" into creeping
rout' (Boyle, 1979). Anything said to be
'planned' is likely to have been an unfortunate accident. Watch especially for 'as
planned' in a Chairman's statement,
indicating an unexpected set-back.

planner an official who discourages the
development of real estate
The function is of necessity negative
because the only sanction is to say 'no'. In
rare cases such a 'planner' may initiate a
comprehensive design or reconstruction,
perhaps adopting the style of 'town planner',
often with unfortunate results. 'Planning' is
the operation of such a system of restraint.
As with the Am. 'zoning', the benefits of
stopping ugly and unsuitable development
are paid for by the creation of famine in
development land.

plant (1) to bury a corpse
The imagery of horticulture, without the
crop: 'Y'wouldn't want to be planted without
ceremony.Why not put Baptist?' (Manning,
1962). 'Planted' means dead and buried.
The ob. 'plant a man' was to copulate, again
using horticultural imagery but this time
anticipating that the seed might bear fruit.

plant (2) falsely to place incriminating
material on another
Again with horticultural imagery: 'With the
evidence you'd arranged for him to find . . . .
Or to put it bluntly, planted' (Crisp, 1982). A

'plant' can also be a story introduced into a
periodical for the purpose of advertising or
promotion, and not necessarily false.

plant the books *see* **book**

plasma an intoxicant
Properly the substance in the blood in which
other elements are suspended: 'And
speaking of the old nasty – it's past noon,
and you could use some plasma' (Sanders,
1985).

plastered very drunk
Properly, covered with a substance that
sticks to you, as does the smell of intoxicants,
but perhaps only from the immobility of a
limb in plaster: ' You could tell by his eyes
that he was plastered to the hairline' (Chandler, 1953).

plater a person who engages in fellatio for
payment
From the concept of eating presumably ham,
as fellatio is also known as a 'plate of ham'.

play to copulate or masturbate
The imagery of **sport** (q.v.): 'As well a
woman with an eunuch play'd As with a
woman' (Shakespeare, *Antony and Cleopatra*). There are many specialist variants as
follows:

> **play around** to copulate extra-maritally,
> usu. with more than one person contem-
> poraneously: 'Not with the chauffeur . . . .
> I don't have to dig down that far if I want
> to play around' (Chandler, 1939).

> **play at hot cockles** to masturbate of a
> female, the 'cockles' being the vulva.

> **play games** to copulate extra-maritally,
> usu. of a woman and perhaps with a single
> partner: 'She was playing games with
> Vannier' (Chandler, 1943).

> **play hookie** to copulate extra-maritally
> with one partner, of either sex, with the
> imagery of staying away from school: 'The
> safest racket in the world is to rob a mar-
> ried man or woman who is playing hookie'
> (Lavine, 1930).

> **play in the hay** to copulate extra-
> maritally and casually but not necessarily
> al fresco, and *see* **in the hay** (above): 'If
> every girl who's ready to play in the hay
> was to get married, we'd have damned few
> spinsters' (Fraser, 1969).

> **play mothers and fathers** to cop-
> ulate, usu. extra-maritally, with a Br. ver-
> sion 'play mums and dads': 'And at a

moment like this my wife has to play mothers and fathers with that bastard' (C. Forbes, 1985).

play on your back to copulate, of women: 'Lulls him while she playeth on her back' (Shakespeare, *Titus Andronicus*).

play the ace against the jack to copulate, of a woman, punning on a game of cards and **ace of spades** and **jack** (q.v.), but not necessarily of a brunette.

play the beast with two backs *see* **beast with two backs**

play the field to be sexually promiscuous, of either sex, from betting on several or all the runners.

play the goat to be sexually promiscuous, of a male. But 'play the giddy goat' means merely to act stupidly.

play the organ to copulate or masturbate, of either sex, punning on the musical instrument and *see* **organ**.

play the skin flute to bugger
The imagery is as in **fluter** (above): 'He looks like a guy who plays the skin flute' (Sanders, 1984).

play tricks to copulate extra-maritally, usu. of a female and often in the past tense where a single woman becomes pregnant, but not, I think, punning on the prostitutes' jargon **trick** (q.v.).

play with to masturbate or sexually excite, heterosexually or homosexually, often as 'play with yourself': 'All the time we were playing with ourselves, I kept thinking of Mary's hot slit' (Harris, 1925).

make a play for to seek to copulate with extra-maritally, usu. by a male: '"Don't make a play for me, Peter." "I wasn't planning to"' (Sanders, 1983).

A 'playmate' or 'playfellow' is someone of either sex with whom you copulate extra-maritally: 'To seek her as a bed-fellow, In marriage-pleasures play-fellow' (Shakespeare, *Pericles*). A 'playboy', apart from being a wealthy hedonist, can be any promiscuous male, although not to be confused with the ob. Eng./Ire. 'playboy', the devil: 'The divil sitting cheek be jowl with him in his own chimbley corner . . . . an' himself an' the playboy sloughed out o' the same pipe' (MacManus, 1898).

etc., etc.

play your harp to be dead
A jocular usage because those who believe in a posthumous harp-playing heaven tend not to be sacrilegious. In similar vein a dead rascal may be said to be 'stoking Lucifer's fires' or 'on the end of a shovel'.

please yourself on to copulate with
Of a male in the days when females were not meant to take much pleasure in it: 'They will please themselves upon her' (Shakespeare, *Pericles*). ob.

pleasure to copulate with
Normally of the male: 'Not the most joyous pleasuring I have taken part in' (Fraser, 1969) but sometimes of the female: 'Three doe-eyed, heavy hipped women pleasuring one man' (Masters, 1976). In modern use 'have' or 'take' pleasure with: '. . . she oft-times embraced my body round about, and had her pleasure with me' (Apuleius, in tr.) and : 'Later, stirred by the curry, he took pleasure with his second wife' (Sanders, 1977). An Am. 'pleasure-house' is a brothel: 'It was a pleasure house, where those rich ofay (white) business men and planters would come' (L. Armstrong, 1955). The ob. 'pleasure-garden' was the vagina viewed sexually by a male, with its 'pleasure-garden padlock', the towel worn during menstruation. 'Mutual pleasuring' can also be masturbation of each other by any combination of males and females.

plot to rob
Properly, to plunge in boiling water, whence to scald before plucking of a fowl, and then the plucking of the fowl: 'When old John Knox and others some Began to plott the bags of Rome' (Henderson, 1856). The devil's name 'plotcock' came from the symbolic 'cock' and his penchant for flaying people alive: 'Seven times does her prayers backwards pray, Till Plotcock comes with lumps of Lapland clay' (Ramsey, 1800 – all genuine witches pray backwards and Lapland was their fabled homeland).

plough to copulate with
Of a male, punning on the entry of the share into the furrow and the chance of issue: 'He plough'd her and she cropt' (Shakespeare, *Antony and Cleopatra*). ob.

plough under needlessly to cause the death of
From the way a farmer disposed of an unsaleable crop. In 1940 Wendell Wilkie, opposing Roosevelt's third term as President, appealed to isolationists and pacifists by saying that his opponent was determined to 'plough under

every fourth American boy'. Because Wilkie lost, we forget how close he came to winning.

pluck to copulate with
Of a male. DAS says: 'Rhyming euphem. for the taboo "fuck".' But to 'pluck a rose' is to copulate with a female virgin and the imagery may merely be from the gathering of a flower.

pluck a daisy etc. *see* pick a daisy etc.

plucked from us unexpectedly or prematurely dead
In floral imagery, the deity being credited with choosing the choicest blooms: 'The most heavenly girl in the whole glorious world has been plucked from us' (Mailer, 1965). In Br. universities, 'plucked' formerly meant failing to graduate; an unpaid tradesman had the right to pluck the gown of the Chancellor when the name of his debtor was read out at a degree congregation, and the degree was not conferred until the debt had been settled.

plug (1) to kill or wound by shooting
Properly, to stop a hole, which a bullet may do, after first making it: 'I'd plug you as soon as I'd strike a match' (Chandler, 1943).

plug (2) to copulate with
Of a male, again from the hole-filling. Mailer uses 'plug' also of buggery: 'There was a high private pleasure in plugging a Nazi . . . . she was loose . . . . as if this was finally her natural act' (1943).

plum pudding club *see* in the club

plumb to copulate with
Properly, to sound a depth. Being also euphemistic in French and German, we have what I believe to be the only limerick which can be rendered equally in each language, the Eng. version being: 'There once was a plumber of Leigh/Who was plumbing a girl by the sea/In the midst of his plumbing/ She said "Someone's coming."/ "I know," said the plumber, "It's me."'

plumber an irregular and illegal presidential agent
His function, after the Ellsberg disclosures in 1971, was to stop 'leaks' (q.v. under **leak** (2)). Non-Am. observers were struck less by the methods employed – lying, robbery, defamation – than by the incompetence. However the language was enriched by 'characterization omitted' and 'expletive deleted' as well as the rich use of euphemism when the participants came to explain and try to justify what they were up to.

plumbing (1) a lavatory
From the ancillary piping: 'Unless you've shifted the plumbing around here, I can find it' (M. Thomas, 1980 – he was looking for a lavatory).

plumbing (2) the parts of the body concerned with urination and defecation
A genteel and rather coy use, likening the body mainly internally with that aspect of domestic construction: 'Helena had known about sex from a very early age but treated it as a joke like what she called her plumbing' (McCarthy, 1963).

(plumbioscillosis shirking is a dog-Latin phrase for **swinging the lead** (below). The doctor thus tries to hide his diagnosis from the patient in the hope that the employer, to whom the chit may be shown to justify absence from work, may have had a classical education.)

plunge away to copulate
Of the male, from the movement: 'Flashy is plunging away on top of the landlord's daughter in the long grass' (Fraser, 1977).

pocket to steal
Usu. of money or trifles, small enough to go into it and without premeditation.

pocket pool etc. male masturbation
From the cue and balls used in the game: 'You're playing with yourself. Lay off the pocket pool' (Theroux, 1978). The more common Br. form is 'pocket billards'. A 'pocket job' implies ejaculation: '. . . reduced to performing pocket jobs' (Styron, 1976). The ob. Br. 'pocket the red' meant copulation by a male, with punning imagery from snooker or billiards.

poetic truth lies
A Nazi concept now exploited, like so many others, by the Communists: 'Convenient lies ("poetic truth") as he once called them' (Trevor Roper, 1977 – the 'he' was Goebbels, the master of mass communication).

point Percy at the porcelain to urinate
Of a male. The 'porcelain' is the stall or bowl in an urinal and *see* 'Percy' *under* person.

poison an intoxicant
A jocular reference to the possible harmful effects: '"What's your poison?" Dundridge said he'd have a gin and tonic' (Sharpe, 1975).

poison the blood of a nation as a whore to transmit venereal disease
An insight into 19c. Br. morality with its

implication that the woman was the only guilty party: 'A woman . . . . only yesterday had two buboes lanced . . . . and yet she was . . . . poisoning the blood of the nation with the most audacious recklessness' (Mayhew, 1862).

poison pill the deliberate assumption of corporate liabilities to deter or repel an unwanted predator
A tactic of the defended bid, with success leaving a sour taste in the mouth, or worse: '"Poison pill" meant that AbCom would issue a dilutive new stock . . . . and that would double or triple the cost of AbCom to an unfriendly enquirer' (M. Thomas, 1985).

poke (1) **(the)** summary dismissal from employment
Punning on the meaning, to push but a 'poke' is also a sack, as the phrase 'a pig in a poke': 'He's gi'en him t'poake' (*Leeds Mercury Supplement*, April 1896, quoted in EDD) would mean the same thing today, but the passive might convey a different meaning to modern ears: 'I wor poked afore eleven o'clock t'next morning' (Burnley, 1880, of a dismissal).

poke (2) to copulate with
Of a male, with common imagery: 'Don't get to poke too many women too often' (Bradbury, 1976). A 'poke' is either a single act of copulation: 'Nice trouble-free way of victualling your girl-friend between pokes' (Amis, 1978) or the female participant as seen by the male as in the cliché 'a rattling good poke'; in male gallantry or conceit there are no bad 'pokes'. Also some homosexual use of buggery, whence the Am. 'pogey bait', candy, from the 'inducement held out by old sailors for the favours of fair-cheeked, smooth-bottomed young cabin boys' (Styron, 1976). The ob. Br. 'pole' merely meant to copulate without these other refinements.

poke (3) a prison
I suggest from the sack – *see* **poke** (1) – rather than being thrust or 'poked' inside: 'He just got out of poke a few months ago' (Sanders, 1970). sl.

polar bear a policeman
A rare but not necessarily wintry elaboration of **bear** (2) (above). CB sl. Am.

police action a war
Used by Harry Truman of the Korean War, because Congress never declared it to be one, and now common when a participant wants to play down the conflict. Dean Rusk

called the Korean War, a 'limited war' although Douglas MacArthur considered that there was 'no substitute for victory', even if that meant starting WWIII. For the Russians the lesson was never to walk out, but stay and use your veto if you want to avoid your puppets fighting the 'United Nations'.

political and social order internal repression
The Brazilian version of a familiar autocratic device: 'The Department of Political and Social Order, a bland title for the administration of terror and thumbscrews' (Simon, 1979, of Brazil).

political change a humiliating defeat
Kissinger's contemporary description of the final conquest of South Vietnam by the Communists and the humiliating Am. withdrawal. It turned out to be quite a change.

political education the arbitrary imprisonment of critics
Communist jargon from the pretence or belief that opponents of the system are deluded and may learn their errors in the Gulag camps. Also as 'political re-education'.

polluted drunk
Rendered impure by alcohol, I suppose. Am.

pom-pom copulation
WW II Am. army use, from the quick-firing gun or by association with **boom-boom** (2) (q.v.).

pony an act of defecation
Br. rh. sl. from 'pony and trap', crap and usu. as 'have a pony', to defecate.

poof *see* **pouff**

(poontang copulation by a White male with a non-White female might suggest that she would be Chinese but the word arrived through New Orleans rather than San Francisco, and the female is usu. Black: 'A growin' Southern boy's got to have his poontang' (Styron, 1976). As with so many other similar words, it has now also been borrowed for acts of male homosexuality.)

poop to defecate
Am. nursery usage, and also of domestic pets, whence the 'pooper scooper' for removing your dog's shit from the sidewalk. The derivation is probably onomatopoeic. In limited use to 'poop' is also to fart.

pooped drunk
Properly, flooded by the sea coming over the

stern, but not only of sailors: '... seldom sober by seven and almost always pooped by eight' (Sharpe, 1978).

poorly (1) very seriously ill
Hospital jargon, replacing the normal meaning, mildly unwell. The patient described as 'very poorly' is unlikely to survive.

poorly (2) menstruating
From the meaning, unwell and often in the female phrase, 'my poorly time'.

pop (1) to do any exciting, unconventional or illegal act
The various uses have different derivations. Taking narcotics illegally comes from 'popping' them into your mouth, whence 'popper', such a narcotic: 'The ammoniac aftersmell of poppers hung in the air' (M. Thomas, 1982). In the meaning to copulate, of either sex, the allusion is to the sensation of orgasm: 'Azalo figured she'd be lucky to get twenty bucks a pop' (Sanders, 1985, of a whore). A 'pop-artist', who uses common objects to create a work, is probably from an abbr. of 'popular' as is the tuneless thumping noise called 'pop music'. Also to pawn in the 'pop shop': 'I had to pop the silver; you know what I mean' (Guinness, 1985).

pop (2) to kill
Causing another to **pop off**? 'We don't pop people any more. We've learned from the Argentines. People just disappear' (Sanders, 1984).

pop off to die
The imagery of a cork leaving a bottle gives the sl. meaning, to depart, whence to die of natural causes: 'Look here, Hugh, I'm afraid Percy has popped off' (Matthew, 1978). Rarely as an active verb, to kill.

Pope's telephone number (the) Vat 69 whisky
The London telephone system formerly used the first three letters of a place name as part of the telephone code for subscribers in that district. Thus 'Vatican' would have been reached by dialling VAT followed by an individual number. ? ob.

popping up the daisies dead
The corpse is supposed to provide sustenance for the common churchyard wild flower. Some jocular use, even of those cremated.

popsy a whore
Properly, and still used as, a term of endearment to a girl, whence an attractive young female. The euphemistic use is usu. generic:

'... enough popsy to satisfy an army' (Fraser, 1977). The variant 'poppet' implies a less sexually-charged regard.

Popular Front a Communist-controlled alliance including non-Communists
Russian hostility to German Social Democrats and other non-Communists before 1932 was an important factor in bringing the Nazis to power through apparently legal means. By 1935 Russian policy was changed to fostering political coalitions in which domestic Communist parties under Russian direction appeared to make common cause with socialists and others opposed to Fascism: 'The Comintern's strident anti-Fascist and pro-Popular Front campaigning' (Boyle, 1979). The ploy succeeded and 'Popular Front' governments won power in Spain, France and Chile, each of which in a different way having to pay dearly for its thus being manipulated and deceived.

population transfer the forcible deportation of a minority
Natural movements involving the transfer of population on a surprising scale take place in a civilized society as a result of individual choice. A totalitarian state needs to break up or isolate a cohesive minority ethnic group, especially where the language or culture differs from that of the regime, and the same ruthlessness may be observed in Nazi Germany, Communist Russia and in S. Africa.

porch climber a thief from houses
A convenient mode of access to an upstairs window: 'He was a two-bit porch climber with a few small terms on him' (Chandler, 1939 – a 'term' is a prison sentence).

pork (1) a Federal benefit diverted to local political purposes
From the richness of the meat, it can come in the form of funds, jobs or patronage. A 'pork barrel' is a scheme funded Federally with pickings for local politicians: 'America's production of space centres .... symbolise an ancient discipline which lies at the heart of politics here: pork-barrelling' (*Private Eye*, July 1983). A 'pork chopper' gets a job as a sinecure in return for past favours. Am.

pork (2) a person or the genitalia of a person viewed sexually
Of the same tendency as **beef, meat** and **mutton** (q.v.): 'I've known greater beauties, and a few that were just as partial to pork' (Fraser, 1982). Specifically of the penis: '... he's one a these pissy pork pullers. Takes a leak and beats off' (Wambaugh, 1975).

porridge prison
Partridge suggests a pun on **stir** (q.v.) but it is also a staple item of breakfast fare in Br. prisons.

Port Said garters a male contraceptive sheath
WW II usage of Br. troops in Egypt. Was this how they kept their socks and spirits up? ob.

possess to copulate with
Historically the male 'possessed' the female, despite the physical contradiction: 'I have bought the mansion of love, but not possesst it' (Shakespeare, *Romeo and Juliet*). If used at all today, 'possess' would imply extra-marital chance copulation as our culture now rejects the concept of the wife as a chattel.

post a letter to defecate
Punning on an excuse for absenting yourself from company and the process of defecation, a letter being commonly pushed through a small aperture to fall in a receptacle below.

posterior(s) the buttocks
Properly, later in time, from which behind, and after that the etymological progression is obvious: 'Her posteriors, plump, smooth, and prominent' (Cleland, 1749).

pot (1) to kill by shooting
From hunting for the cooking pot but also used of attempts to kill or wound: '... wasn't anything much else to shoot at so I took to potting them' (Sharpe, 1978). A 'pot' is such a shot, usu. taken without premeditation.

pot (2) a habitual drunkard
From the drinking vessel rather than the sl. term for belly and to 'pot' is to drink intoxicants to excess. 'Pot-walloper' had two meanings, a drunkard, and someone entitled to vote under the Br. Reform Act of 1832, because he had boiled, or 'walloped', his own pot in the parish for the previous six months and was therefore a bona fide householder. **Potted** (q.v.) is drunk and 'pot-valour' is drunken courage, etc.

pot (3) a receptacle for urine
Properly, any container for liquids: 'I had taught him to use a pot' (N. Mitford, 1960, of a child's urination). To 'pot' is to sit a child on such a vessel in the hope that it will urinate or defecate. You also hear the abbr. 'po' and the diminutive 'potty', whence the Am. CB. sl. 'potty mouth' who uses foul language on the air.

pot (4) marijuana
Either from the Am. Indian 'potaguaya' or from the container in which the leaves and stalks are brewed – the abbr. of 'pot liquor' to 'pot' favours the latter: '... to graduate to student parties to smoke pot' (Bradbury, 1976).

potboiler a repetitive or facile work by an established artist or author
Originally of the person who perpetrated it but now of the product: 'Then, when I got in the swing of things and began turning out four potboilers a year' (Sanders, 1980).

Potomac fever a desire to be elected to Federal office
And specifically to the Presidency, from the river flowing through Washington DC: 'Baxter contracted a terminal case of Potomac Fever. He started to dream of the White House' (M. Thomas, 1980).

Potsdam a prison for captured Br. soldiers
In WW I you might talk of 'dining with the Kaiser in Potsdam' if captured: '... so this was "Potsdam", this moist foul-smelling cell' (Grinnell-Milne, 1933). ob.

potted (1) dead
Punning perhaps on being shot by a **pot** (1) (above) and on the imagery of **plant** (q.v.). Br. rather than Am.

potted (2) drunk
Put into a container for preservation, in which the agent may be alcohol. Am.

potty mad
Usu. in a harmless or eccentric way: 'It was only a question of time before the Goat-Major would go stone potty' (Richards, 1936). Perhaps from sl. 'gone to pot', destroyed.

pouff a male homosexual
Not from the Eng. dialect meaning 'a big stupid person' (EDD) but probably in both cases from the exclamation, implying a lack of substance or value: 'Don't tie the tapes under your chin ... or they'll think you're a pouff' (Francis, 1978). The meaning, a round footstool, is almost ob.: '... sitting animatedly forward on what used to be called a pouf or pouffe but obviously couldn't be these days' (Amis, 1978). Also as 'pooftah': 'If Prince Charles shows no interest, he *must* be a pooftah' (A. Waugh, *Private Eye,* July 1980).

pound to copulate with
Male usage, with the common violent imagery, although of chance extra-marital occasions rather than those involving coercion or roughness. Whence the punning 'pound the keys': '... hoped the little

bubblegummer had been well pounded by the piano-tuner so she could get . . . . to the home for unwed mothers' (Wambaugh, 1975).

pound salt go away and leave me alone
An abbr. of the vulgar Am. invitation to 'go pound salt up your arse' and owing nothing, I think, to **pound** (above) which is not normally used fig. or abusively. DAS says: 'This euphem. much more common than the full term'. Also, but less often, as 'pound sand'.

powder room a lavatory for the exclusive use of females
It used to be that part of a warship adjacent to the guns where the powder was stored. You used children to pass thence to the gun-deck so that the size of the passage could be restricted and danger from enemy fire or flashbacks minimized. Today the 'powder' is the scented talc which women put on their faces. To 'powder your nose', to urinate, is usu. of women: 'Back in the Long Gallery some of the women went upstairs to "powder their noses"' (N. Mitford, 1949) and rarely, jocularly, of men: 'Peter laughed, "I've had enough of the bloody sun. I'm going to powder m'nose"' (Manning, 1978). To say you are going to 'powder your nose' is genteel, but the rarer 'powder your puff' is not, punning on the powder puff and the pubic hair. For a male to 'powder your hair' in the 19c. was to become drunk, wigs then being commonly powdered.

powder your nose *see* **powder room**

pox (the) syphilis
Properly, any disease which brings up pustules on the skin but, as Dr Johnson reminds us, 'This is the sense when it has no epithet': 'I couldn't be sure she hadn't got the pox' (Archer, 1979). 'Poxed' is so infected and 'poxy' a dated term of abuse.

practice development advertising and marketing
The rules on overt advertising being relaxed, Br. lawyers and accountants, conditioned by decades of covert touting for clients, still feel a need to conceal their hypocrisy: 'Professions cringe at the word (marketing). A more acceptable term . . . . is "practice development"' (*Financial Times*, November 1987). (As a young practising solicitor I was pressed by my partners to take on criminal cases at uneconomic fees because the constant repetition of the firm's name in the local press was the only permitted form of advertising. A disadvantage was that the new clients ten-

ded to be unwilling to be distributed around the practice.)

prairie oyster (1) the testicle of a calf
Eaten in Am. as a delicacy. Calves' testicles are also eaten in BI but described as 'sweetbreads', properly the term for the pancreas.

prairie oyster (2) a pungent alcoholic drink with raw egg in it
Not to be confused with the Am. 'prairie dew', an illegally distilled drink.

Pravda a selection of the truth mixed with lies and distortion
This Russian newspaper, whose title translates as 'Truth', was also legally published under the Czar from 1912 to 1914. It followed the Orwellian precept of calling itself precisely what it was not but changes with the times. It is still fairly hard going.

pre-arrangement etc. the payment for a funeral before death
Am. funeral jargon for selling burials and their trappings in advance to the morbid and lonely: 'The cemetery industry has found an answer to high cost through pre-arrangement' (J. Mitford, 1963). Also as 'pre-need': 'A "pre-need memorial estate"; in other words, a grave for future occupancy' (ibid.).

pre-dawn vertical insertion an invasion by armed parachutists
Neither clocking on for the first shift nor starting the day with copulation, but how the heroic invaders of Grenada described their exploits.

pre-emptive strike an unprovoked military attack without warning
'Pre-emptive' is buying first, whence keeping others out. The term is used by Israelis and others to excuse this type of aggression.

pre-owned not new
Advertising jargon: 'the modern euphemism for "second-hand"' (Pei, 1969 – or third-, fourth- or fifth-hand). Perhaps an evasion more than a euphemism.

precautions contraception
Abbr. of 'precautions against pregnancy', usu. 'taken' or 'neglected': 'She hoped she might be pregnant, since she had taken no precautions' (McCarthy, 1963).

precocious spoilt and ill-mannered
Properly, developing early. Used of children other than your own, out of earshot of their parents.

predilection homosexuality
Properly, a tendency or preference for anything, even for heterosexual encounters:
'"Predilection?" he said, giggling. "What a
sensitive way of putting it!"' (Sanders,
1986).

pregnancy interruption an induced
abortion
An 'interruption' is properly a disturbance
with an assumption of resumption. This
medical jargon is sometimes enlarged to
'voluntary pregnancy interruption' or VPI.

preliterate uncivilized
Anthropological and social science jargon of
societies which remain illiterate. The usage
denotes a touchiness on behalf of savages
who can't read what they would be touchy
about.

premature conceived before marriage
Used of babies, in all respects like those
carried a full term, born within seven or
eight months of their parents' wedding.

premium costing more
Properly, an award or prize, whence worth
more than its face value. Advertising jargon
and much loved by estate agents.

preparation room a mortuary
Am. funeral jargon and not referring to an
annexe of the kitchen: 'He suggests a rather
thorough overhauling of the language . . . .
"preparation room not morgue"' (N. Mitford, 1963).

preparedness the military help given to
the British in WW II prior to Pearl Harbour
Am. isolationism was so widely supported
even by those who were not pro-Nazi like
Lindbergh that support for the embattled
Br. Empire had to be disguised by
euphemism: '. . . he had financed an expensive advertising campaign in the country's
largest newspapers, savagely attacking "preparedness" . . .' (Lacey, 1986 of Henry Ford
whose anti-Jewish paranoia cannot have
failed to see attractive features in Nazism).
Am. ob.

present arms to have an erect penis
Punning on the military drill in which the
rifle is held vertically in front of the body:
'. . . by the time she was done I would be
esctatically ruined, and certain sure I'd never
be able to present arms again' (Fraser,
1971). The ob. Eng. 'presenter' was a
whore, who 'presented' herself to you, but
you still had to pay.

preserved drunk
An Am. variant of the more common
pickled (q.v.) with alcohol the agent of preservation.

pressure cooker bar a rendez-vous for
housewives seeking extra-marital copulation
And of course for men seeking such housewives. The pressure cooker cooks a hot meal
quickly if you are late getting home. Am.

pressure of work an excuse for any neglect, inefficiency or discourtesy
Those who use it are normally lazy or disorganized.

prestigious expensive
Properly, concerned with juggling, or prestidigitation, but latterly commonly used as
conferring prestige. Estate agents love it:
'City of London's most prestigious fully-
serviced apartment block' (*The Times*, May
1981, but not Buckingham Palace.) Also,
unhappily, in other commercial puffs.

preventative a contraceptive sheath
Army usage and in Am. syphilis and gonorrhoea were the 'preventable diseases'. The
ob. Br. 'preventative man' neither sold nor
wore such articles, but was a coastguard.

preventive detention arbitrary
imprisonment
In a totalitarian state, without process of law.
In the BI it means a long sentence for a
dangerous or hardened criminal.

preventive war an unprovoked attack
without warning
The theory is that you are 'preventing' your
opponent getting the drop on you. Today it
is thought slightly effete for a nation to
declare war formally and in this respect, as in
so many others, the Nazis set a pattern of
conduct which has been widely emulated,
not least by those who were once their
victims.

previously owned second hand
And not just owned by the manufacturer or
dealer: 'Buyers looking for a "previously
owned" motor car (to use the current trade
euphemism) tend to be very selective' (*Daily
Telegraph*, October 1987).

prey to (a) suffering from
The victimization is only fig. as with those
who describe themselves as a 'prey to dys-
pepsia'. Not so the ob. Br. 'prey to the
bicorn', a cuckold. The 'bicorn' was a mythical two-horned beast which devoured men
whose wives dominated or deceived them.
Its counterpart, the 'chichevache', which ate

obedient wives, was reputed to feed but rarely.

priapism an erection of the penis
From Priapus, the Pan of Mysia, who was born with 'the extraordinary deformity to which he owes his name' (*New Larousse Encyclopedia of Mythology*). Mainly medical use.

price adjustment etc. an increase in price
In retail trading, all 'adjustments' and 'revisions' are upwards – a reduction needs no euphemism.

price crowding a price increase not authorized by the proprietor
Mainly supermarket jargon. The device is normally used by a manager to create a reserve which can be used to make good losses or shortages for which he might be held responsible.

prick a penis
Once SE but now common sl., of obvious origin: 'What did in for him Was a prick in the skin, When the prick should have been in Ophelia' (*Playboy's Book of Limericks*, of Hamlet). Also used fig. as a term of mild abuse or rebuke among males.

pride an erect penis
Abbr. of 'pride of the morning', an erection of the penis upon waking which comes from the proper meaning, mist or a shower heralding a fine day: 'Said a just-wed professor named Ted, To a redhead coed in his bed .... Won't you swallow my pride dear instead?' (*Playboy's Book of Limericks*).

prime saleable
Properly, first, whence implying of first quality. Commonly used of perishable food-stuffs, especially meat.

prime the pump deliberately to cause inflation
Of government spending when the political consequences of higher unemployment etc. outweigh the damage caused by short-term inflation – few politicians concern themselves with the consequences longer term caused by inflation because that will be somebody else's problem: 'The new administration coming into power in just two weeks would have no choice but to "prime the pump" through massively increased government expenditure' (Erdman, 1986).

primed drunk
Like a pump, and perhaps also alluding to an explosive charge: 'When he was "primed",

was Nathan's wont to pass, No licensed house without another glass' (Doherty, 1884). Sc./Eng.

princess an expensive whore
From the meaning, a classy type of female or one who affects airs: 'Willy goggled at a couple of painted princesses swaying by in all their finery .... "Whores" says I' (Fraser, 1973, writing in 19c. style). The use seemed to be a synonym of 'prima donna': 'By lorettes I mean those I have touched on before as prima donnas' (Mayhew, 1862) but survives in modern speech, as the Am. **pavement princess** (above).

private enterprise illegal trading by an employee
Properly, trade or industry not financed by or under the control of the State, but some pejorative use by socialists, etc. The euphemism is of government servants who exploit their position for personal gain, of smuggling by transport workers, etc: 'But there was a great deal of what you might call private enterprise on that run' (Price, 1970, of smuggling by airline staff).

private office *see* **privy**

private parts the human genitalia
Those not ordinarily exposed to the public gaze: '"No more private selves, no more private corners in society, no more private properties, no more private acts." "No more private parts," says Barbara' (Bradbury, 1975). Less often of domestic animals, where there is no concealment: 'Buller was licking his private parts with the gusto of an alderman drinking soup' (G. Greene, 1978). Abbr. either to 'privates': 'He had not let Oliver in until his privates were covered over with water' (Bradbury, 1979) or to 'parts': '"You find the model ugly?" "No not at all. I mean her ... parts"' (Amis, 1978). In ob. use as 'privy parts': 'He moved their privy parts to the front' (Plato in tr. – Zeus was the mover) or as 'privities': '... felt great pain in her privities, as if her swooning had not spared her and some rude forcing had taken place' (Fowles, 1985, writing in archaic style).

privateer a whore
She works on her own, usu. part-time like the pirate who combined 'private man of war' and 'volunteer'. BI ? ob.

privates *see* **private parts**

privileged rich
Sociological jargon and not really implying

that they have honourable distinctions. Indeed in the eyes of those who use this dysphemism the opposite is true. The converse is **underprivileged** (q.v.).

privy a lavatory
From the privacy: 'Hadjimoscos, sick in a privy, had spewed out his false teeth' (Manning, 1960). 'Private office' is now ob. in this sense, having been adopted as a rather grand social distinction for those whose status demands individual secretarial arrangements. The ob. 'privy stool' was a portable combination of lavatory seat and bucket: '... chairs and privy-stools necessary for a royal visit' (Monsarrat, 1978, writing in archaic style – I hope the two puns were unintentional). For 'privy parts' *see* **private parts**.

pro a whore
An abbr. of professional or of prostitute – or both: 'You the bloke that floated them pros out to the *Everett*?' (Theroux, 1973 – some whores had been sent out to a ship). I suppose the WW II military 'pro-pack', a soldier's contraceptive kit, came from this abbr. or from **prophylactic** (below).

probe to copulate with
Of a male, but not with a blunt-ended exploratory surgical instrument: 'Says Barbara frankly "I was probed." "That's true," says Howard. "At the purely external level you got screwed"' (Bradbury, 1975).

problem an unwanted and often irreversible condition
The word is used to conceal truth or inadequacy in many compounds. Thus a 'cash problem' in an individual is a shortage of money, and not a lack of pockets in which to keep it. In a company, a 'cash flow problem' means it is overtrading or insolvent. A 'communication problem' means that nobody understands us or we don't understand them. A 'crossword problem' means we cannot do the crossword (a 'problem problem'?) although a problem crossword is one we should be able to solve. A 'drink problem' is alcoholic addiction for a 'problem drinker': '... the fact that she was a "problem drinker"' (Styron, 1976), although a 'drinks problem' at a party would indicate that you are running out of supplies. A 'heart problem' is a malfunction or failure of that organ, with other organs or bodily zones being similarly identified according to your disability. A 'husband' or 'wife' problem indicates that the 'problem' husband or wife is a drunkard, takes illicit drugs, copulates extra-maritally, spends too much or lacks

some common marital virtue. In addition a 'woman's problem' may be the onset of menstruation, which she may describe as her 'problem days', or it may be a disorder of the womb. Hitler referred to the 'so-called Austrian problem' when looking for justification of his 1938 invasion. To have a 'pigmentation problem' is to be Black in a mainly White country: '... wants to send anyone with a pigmentation problem back to Islamabad' (Sharpe, 1979). A 'weight problem' is obesity, and not starvation: 'If you are destined to be fat, food makes you fat. But I have never had a weight problem' (Murdoch, 1978). etc. etc.

procedure any taboo or unpleasant act
Properly, a method of acting. In the language of doctors and dentists, it is anything which will cause pain. For police and lawyers, it is a civil or criminal legal action. For pregnant women, it may be an induced abortion. For the Nazis, it was mass murder: 'Schindler heard rumours that "procedures in the ghetto" were growing more intense' (Keneally, 1983, of WW II Poland), etc.

process a penis
Properly, anything which sticks out: '... washing my process and asking me if I've got the clap' (Theroux, 1979).

procure to arrange prostitution on behalf of another
Properly, no more than to obtain, of anything, but legal jargon in this sense: '... she had never heard of my sister, but she would undertake to procure her for me for seventy-five dollars' (Fraser, 1971). Formerly a 'procurer' did nothing more harmful than to arrange affairs or collect taxes for another but today he and a 'procuress' are pimps: 'A middle-aged man doing the same thing was a dull dirty procurer' (Theroux, 1973).

prod to copulate with
Of a male, but I have yet to see it outside specialist dictionaries.

productivity deal an unwarranted general increase in pay
Properly, more pay for increased productivity. The phrase covers a stratagem whereby, to avoid creating a precedent or infringing a regulation, employees formally undertake to carry out duties ostensibly additional to those previously contracted for, in return for an increase in wages beyond the norm.

profession (the) prostitution by females
Prostitutes' jargon: '... containing some bit-

ter observations by an old member of the Profession' (Londres, 1928, in tr.) and the 'oldest profession' with its Biblical references is a cliché: 'It was maybe the oldest profession . . . . but New Orleans was proud *and* ashamed of its cathouses' (Longstreet, 1958). A 'professional' or 'professional woman' is a whore, the latter perhaps punning on the propriety of the learned professions: 'He cannot afford to pay professional women to gratify his passions' (Mayhew, 1862). And *see* **pro** (above).

professional car a hearse
Am. funeral jargon. 'Processional' would be more appropriate.

professional foul a deliberate infringement
Soccer jargon for unsporting and often dangerous violence against an opponent to deny him an advantage – the foul of one who 'plays' as a professional. BI

progressive opposed to restraints on behaviour
Properly, moving towards improvement but socialist etc. jargon for those whose conduct is not restrained, on occasions, by the law, morality or good manners: 'Day Release Apprentices had to have their weekly hour of progressive opinions' (Sharpe, 1979). For a Communist, 'progressive' means Communist.

proletarian Communist
The 'proletariat', from the Latin 'proletarius the lowest class in the Servian arrangement' (Smith), first indicated those in feudal service and then anyone who worked for a wage, among whom middle-class revolutionaries traditionally seek support. Whence a 'proletarian democracy', a Communist autocracy; 'proletarian internationalism', Russian imperialism; etc.

promoted to Glory dead
A usage of the Salvation Army, whose members live as closely as any may get to the Christian ethic, and deserve any glory that may be going.

promotion bribery
As with the 'promotional' competitions among dealers arranged by oil companies, with prizes of holidays for two in far off places which are often awarded ahead of the event; or of the excessive expenditure devoted by drug and medical supply firms to the Br. National Health Service to ensure the wasteful selection of branded products in preference to cheaper equivalents.

prong to copulate with
Of a male, with the common 'forking' imagery: 'I hear she's some kind of guru to the old man . . . . Think he's pronging her?' (M. Thomas, 1985).

propaganda the publication of matter to support a cause without regard to objectivity or truth
Originally, the propagation of Roman Catholicism and when a body of Cardinals was set up in 1622 by Pope Gregory XV for that purpose, it took the same name. The Nazis refined the concept: 'This newsreel contains pictures of which we can make really good use for propaganda purposes' (Goebbels, 1945, in tr.). Now mainly pejorative use.

prophylactic a contraceptive sheath
Properly, the prevention of any disease but widely used in WWII of any process to reduce venereal disease.

proposition to suggest extra-marital copulation to
Mainly the male 'propositions' the female, but not always: 'I didn't take her up on a proposition she made to me . . . . a bodily proposition' (Masters, 1976). Also some homosexual use: 'He might feel like hitting the first one who propositioned him' (Davidson, 1978, of homosexuals).

protection extortion
The practice of selling immunity from your own depredations is well documented from Anglo-Saxon Danegeld in England to 20c. Mafia activity in Am.: 'He was supplying Rachman's clubs with protection' (Green, 1979). Just as being 'in the rag-trade' is making money in the clothing business, so being 'in protection' is living by such extortion: 'I'm going into protection . . . . scare the shopkeepers silly' (Murdoch, 1977).

protective custody arbitrary imprisonment
The Nazi 'Schutzhaft' of February 1933, the subject of much imitation by Communists and others: '*Schutzhaft* (Protective Custody) a catch-all word whereby men, women and children disappeared and were never seen again' (Deighton, 1978). The pretence is that the victims are incarcerated to prevent ill befalling them.

protector (1) a man keeping a sexual mistress
From the 19c. convention that an unmarried woman living alone should have a male to look after her: 'They are dismissed . . . . and

set once more adrift. They do not remain long . . . . without finding another protector' (Mayhew, 1862, of such women). ? ob.

protector (2) a contraceptive sheath
It 'protects' against venereal disease and unwanted impregnation – and against the sensation induced by 'unprotected' contact.

protectorate a conquered territory
Widely used by the European colonizers of Africa who were anxious to 'protect' themselves against seeing a rival grab the territory ahead of them, although they did not use the word in that sense. More recently of Bohemia and Moravia under Nazi Germany: 'The Anglo-Americans intend to reach the Protectorate before the Soviets' (Goebbels, 1945, in tr. Unhappily for the Czechs, and for Europe, his political judgment was superior to his forecasting; the Western powers held back their armies and so condemned Czechoslovakia to prolonged Russian domination). Thus for the Nazis and others to 'protect' was to incorporate and rule by force: 'He had warned that Germany would know how to "protect" the ten million Germans living on its borders . . . . Everyone knew what Hitler meant by "protect"' (Shirer, 1984).

(proud able to conceive is SE of female quadrupeds whence of sows the punning 'proud in the pen', where 'pen' also means vagina.)

provision an arbitrary adjustment in figures to be publicly reported
'Provisions' properly are reserves made against contingencies, to avoid a misleading statement of assets or profits. Reserves and deductions made on a subjective basis to satisfy a client by reducing taxable income or otherwise understating the financial position are also called 'provisions'. Public accountants have to be flexible because they lose audits if they upset clients.

provocation the statement of a contrary or independent view
Properly, a hostile act calculated to excite a reaction. Hitler so described any intimation by his neighbours that they might defend themselves if attacked and the Communists have adopted the euphemism. Br. trade unions also describe as 'provocative' any management which takes a resolute line during a dispute, especially if it communicates directly with the workers involved.

prune-juice a spirituous intoxicant
From the colour and the laxative effect? Am.

'pruned', drunk, may come from 'prune-juice' but a more likely derivation is from feeling like a tree which has lost its appendages and extremities.

pruned *see* **prune-juice**

psycho a lunatic
From the Greek, it means relating to the breath, whence of the soul or mind. This Am. use is probably no more than an abbr. of 'psychopath': '"Keep that psycho away from me," Wade yelled, showing fear for the first time' (Chandler, 1953).

public assistance *see* **assistance**

public convenience *see* **convenience** (1)

public feeling the obsessions of a politican
Much called in aid by demagogues who seek to clothe their own views with the ostensible endorsement of the general public. On certain issues 'public feeling' may run so high that spontaneous demonstrations have to be arranged.

public house an establishment where intoxicants may be sold and drunk
Not a Br. version of the 'long house' of the inhabitants of Borneo. Now commonly and internationally abbr. to 'pub', the 19c. 'public' being ob.: 'Being also a public, it was two stories high' (W. Scott, 1814).

public relations the presentation of yourself or your client in a favourable light
Properly, making relevant facts or opinions known to the public. The commercial or political euphemism refers to conscious distortion or selection of truth. A 'public relations officer' is paid to do this for others. Abbr. respectively to 'PR' and 'PRO': 'We're in the same racket . . . . and you're the kind of PRO I like' (Deighton, 1982).

(public school a fee-paying school for children of 13 years and older is a Br. historical misnomer.)

public sector borrowing requirement government overspending
The 'public sector', that part of a mixed economy which is directly controlled by government, has no sanction of bankruptcy to inhibit proligacy: 'A series of heavy expensive settlements has piled up that debt, euphemistically called the Public Sector Borrowing Requirement' (*Daily Telegraph*, December 1980).

public tranquillity internal repression
In China internal political control is the function of the Department of Public Tran-

quillity, one of the softer terms for that necessary totalitarian function.

pudding club *see* **in the club**

puddle involuntary urination
From the shallow and temporary pool of rainwater. Usu. 'made' by small children or domestic animals.

(pudendum the vagina comes from the Latin word meaning 'shame' and in ob. use referred equally to the penis and testicles. Despite modern relaxation of Pauline sexual guilt, the use attracts etymologists, not least Eric Partridge in DSUE.)

puff *see* **powder room**

pull (1) to cause a horse to lose a race fraudulently
Racing jargon, from the jockey's handling of the reins. To 'pull up' is also used in the same sense, although it properly means, to bring to a halt.

pull (2) to copulate extra-maritally
From drawing the object of your lust towards you, perhaps, although it sounds a bit thin: 'If someone does recognize me, word will go back that the brigadier's pulling outside duty' (Ludlum, 1984 – he was meeting a woman in a truck stop).

pull a train to copulate in immediate succession with a number of males
The imagery is from coaches behind an engine: '. . . trying to persuade her to pull the train for a few of the choirboys' (Wambaugh, 1975 – the 'choirboys' were off-duty policemen). The male participants successively 'board the train': 'I just can't board the train like horny old Spencer' (ibid.). Am.

pull in to arrest
Police jargon, often expanded to 'pull in for a chat' etc.: 'What do you say to a man from SAVAK when he says . . . . "We'd like you to replace Barnheni as office manager, because we'll be pulling him in for a chat very soon"' (West, 1979).

pull off (1) etc. to masturbate
Of a male. Also as 'pull the pudding', 'pull the wire', 'pull yourself', etc.

pull off (2) to refrain improperly from prosecuting a criminal
From the meaning, to draw away from: 'The detectives who were offered all kinds of inducements to pull off' (Lavine, 1930). Am.

pull out of the air etc. fraudulently to invent

Usu. of figures in prospectuses and other published accounts. To 'pull figures out of a hat', meaning the same thing, takes its imagery from conjuring: 'The *Veterinary Record* said he "pulled figures out of a hat to fit his arguments"' (*Private Eye*, May 1981).

pull rank to use seniority to secure an unfair advantage
Of those in hierarchical employment like sailors or civil servants and euphemistic only when not used of normal commands or orders. SE.

pull the long bow *see* **draw the long bow**

pull the pin (1) to desert your wife
The male imagery is from the uncoupling of rolling stock on a railroad with the engine running free, and not from activating the primer on a hand grenade, although for many husbands the latter might seem more appropriate.

pull the pin (2) to retire
With the same imagery: '. . . he wondered if he could afford to pull the pin when he got twenty-five years in' (Wambaugh, 1983).

pull the plug to kill by withdrawing mechanical life support
Punning on the electrical connection to life support machinery and the flushing of a lavatory. Also of killing: 'Hubby Luther pulled the plug on her' (Sanders, 1986, of a wife murderer).

pull the rug to render bankrupt
From causing a person standing on a rug to fall when you jerk it. Normally used of a banker or creditor who refuses to give further time to pay, thereby crystallizing other indebtedness.

pull the trigger to cause to ejaculate
Of obvious punning imagery: 'I know how to pull his trigger. His wife doesn't' (Sanders, 1981).

pump ship etc. to urinate
Of a male, from the jet of water going over the side. Also rarely as 'pump bilges'.

pump your pickle etc. to masturbate
Of a male. the 'pickle' in this case is a gherkin, whence a penis. Also as 'pump your shaft': 'So there he stood, pumping his turgid shaft' (Sanders, 1973).

punch to copulate with
Of a male, with the common violent imagery: 'Danny introduces Angel to this broad which Danny has been punchin' since high school' (Diehl, 1978). Am.

punter an inexperienced visitor who can be overcharged or robbed
Properly, someone who bets on horses, whence an habitual loser: 'Many airport taxi-drivers strongly object to driving their fellow-countrymen, motivated . . . . by the prospect of picking up a "punter", someone who can safely be overcharged' (Moynahan, 1983). Eng.

pup to impregnate a woman
Canine imagery, although there need be no suggestion of bitchiness: 'I want all these wenches pupped' (Fraser, 1971). In coarse speech, to 'pup' may also mean to be delivered of a child, and *see* 'in pup' *under* **in calf** etc.

purge (1) beer
Probably from its laxative effect: 'We were fond of a drop of "neck oil", which like "purge" was a nickname for beer' (Richards, 1936). ? ob.

purge (2) to attack violently
Properly, to cleanse from some kind of defilement: 'The next day what they euphemistically call a "purging operation" was effected. In this instance they purged Fatah' (Price, 1971).

purification of the race the systematic killing of Gypsies, Jews and Slavs by the Nazis
Those living in Germany had to conform to the Teutonic ideal. We sometimes forget mad, crippled or deformed Germans were also killed by the Nazis with the same justification.

purple heart a narcotic in pill form
Usu. morphine or barbiturate of that colour and punning on the Am. medal for the wounded: '. . . the notorious so-called Purple Heart tablets which were a source of drug addiction in teenagers in Britain from the early 'sixties' (Foster, 1968).

purse the vagina
From the appearance and ob. except in the punning vulgarism: 'Every woman sits on her purse', a variant of 'sitting on her bank' or she can make money as a whore. Rarely too in ob. use of the scrotum.

push (1) an act of copulation
From the male ingress and also from the rh. sl. 'push in the truck', a fuck, but not, I think, from 'push-over', an object easily accomplished: 'Sing, dance, cook, plenty push' (Sanders, 1977 – a female servant was being extolled to a bachelor). To 'push' is to

copulate of a male: '"You pushing her?" . . . . "Every chance I get"' (Sanders, 1970 – the lady was not confined to a wheelchair). The ob. Br. 'pushing' school or shop was a brothel, punning on the proper meaning, a fencing school: 'I mean he spent an hour a day at the pushing shop down near the railway, rooting himself stupid' (Keneally, 1985).

push (2) **the** peremptory dismissal from employment
Common use by employees and also of a courtship ended unilaterally. The violence in each case is only fig.

push (3) a sustained attack
WWII military jargon: 'The gen is that the jerries are preparing a push on Alam Halfa' (Manning, 1977).

push (4) to distribute narcotics illegally
Properly, to sell energetically. A 'pusher' is any dealer in illegal narcotics, especially by retail: 'He was on the weed. I pretended to be a pusher' (Chandler, 1958). A 'share-pusher' fraudulently sells bogus or over-valued securities.

push up the daisies to be dead
If buried, you may nourish the common churchyard flower: 'If I'd been born fifty years sooner I'd have been pushing up the daisies by now' (N. Mitford, 1960).

pussy the vagina
A commoner version of **cat** (2) (above): 'She could not even get her forefinger into her pussy' (Harris, 1925). 'Pussy-whipped' means besotted with a female who takes advantage of the infatuation, punning on 'horse-whipped': 'An old man like that. Our father. Pussy-whipped' (Sanders, 1980). An Am. 'pussy lift' is an operation to tighten the vagina and so enhance sexual enjoyment: '. . . Piper with the happy illusion that pussy lifts were things cats went up and down in' (Sharpe, 1977). 'Pussy' is also an act of copulation viewed by a male: 'Brancussi, Unafraid of black pussy, Walked under the ladder and had her' (*Playboy's Book of Limericks* – the painter was using a Black model).

put an act of copulation
In common speech, 'had' or 'done' by the male, from the meaning to push or thrust. In Am. use also as to copulate: '. . . you been put-putting with blondie here, my wife' (Mailer, 1965). 'Put and take' is the joint act by male and female. To 'put a man in your belly', to copulate of a female, puns on the male ingress and the conception: 'So you

may put a man in your belly' (Shakespeare, *Winter's Tale*). To 'put it about' is to copulate promiscuously, usu. of a female: 'Certainly not some blonde tart who undoubtedly put it about if the mood took her' (C. Forbes, 1987). 'Put it in' and 'put it up' are explicit in male use: 'They thought it would save their kids or their daddies, letting me put it up them' (Allbeury, 1980, of a German prison guard). To 'put out' is to copulate extra-maritally, of a female, from the meaning to act in an extroverted way: 'Any girl . . . . is caught in a sexual trap. If she won't put out the men will accuse her of being bourgeois' (Lodge, 1975). To 'put to' is to copulate, of women or men, from the proper meaning, to start work: 'As rank as any flax-wench that puts-to, Before her troth-plight' (Shakespeare, *Winter's Tale*). The Am. 'put a move on' is also to copulate extra-maritally: '. . . too sore and shaken to put a move on her' (Wambaugh, 1983). etc.

put away (1) to kill
Of old, diseased or unwanted domestic animals: 'I have left instructions for Buller to be put away – as painlessly as possible' (G. Greene, 1978, of a dog). In ob. use. 'put away' might mean dead, from the burial of the corpse: 'Some poor comrades undertook to see her put away' (Hartley, 1870). To 'put yourself away' is to commit suicide or, in ob. use to 'put hands in (or on) yourself': 'Belus . . . . put hand in himself and became his own executioner' (Brand, 1721) and: 'Who being to be tryed, put hands on himself at the devil's instigation' (Maidment, 1844).

put away (2) to confine to a lunatic asylum or prison
From the involuntary removal from society: 'He was a bit "tropo" . . . . They put him away in the end' (Simon, 1979).

put away (3) to consume intoxicants
Not putting the bottle back in its rack: '. . . it was astounding to see (her) put away the booze' (Styron, 1976, of an alcoholic). If you 'put it away', you regularly drink intoxicants to excess: '. . . the walking wounded of the day watch *really* put it away' (Wambaugh, 1983).

put daylight through to kill by shooting
Mainly WW I usage from fig. making a hole through the body: 'He wouldn't have given him that chance, but soon put daylight through him' (Richards, 1933).

put down etc. to kill
In ob. use of execution: 'The most . . . .

accomplished lady . . . . was suffered to be put down as a common criminal' (Hogg, 1822); of modern murder: 'I am going to be forced to put down the first hostage' (W. Smith, 1979); but usu. of killing old, ill or unwanted domestic animals: '. . . an old smelly Border Terrier which Uncle Matthew had had put down' (N. Mitford, 1945). To 'put off', to kill an animal, is now rare: 'Ir ye gaun to pit aff da auld koo?' (*Shetland News*, 1900, quoted in EDD). To 'put out', of humans, is ob. as is 'put in a bag', killed in battle in the days when military corpses were buried in sacking.

put horns on *see* horn (2)

put in the schwartzes to de-stat to intimidate protected tenants into vacating accommodation
'Schwartzes', Blacks, were West Indian immigrants to Br. in the early 1960s and the 'stat' was the 'statutory', or protected, tenancy, usu. at an uneconomic rent. Native Londoners found the noisy and alien neighbours unacceptable: 'Rachman, of course, did "put in the Schwartzes to de-stat" ' (Green, 1979, of a slum landlord who bequeathed his name to the language).

put in your ticket to die
A ship's officer gives up his current licence, or 'ticket', on retirement. Mainly marine use.

put on the spot to kill
Am. underworld jargon, the 'spot' being a place of danger: 'Youthful killers on the East Side can be hired to "knock off" or "put a guy on the spot"' (Lavine, 1930).

put out (1) *see* put down etc.

put out (2) *see* put

put out a contract *see* contract (2)

put out to grass to retire prematurely
Usu. for early senility, inefficiency, etc. with imagery from a horse which escapes the knacker: 'If you think you are going to be put out to grass, you are mistaken' (Price, 1970, of a man being moved from his job prior to normal retiring age).

put the arm on etc. to extort by threats or violence
The imagery, and of 'put the scissors on', is from wrestling: 'Other guys roll over and lie still the moment you put the arm on them' (le Carré, 1980) and: '. . . if I don't get it then in one-pound notes, I'll put the scissors on you' (Kersh, 1936). Also as 'put the black on', where 'black' is an abbr. of **blackmail**

(q.v.) and as 'put the burn on' for which *see* too **burn** (3).

put the bite on *see* bite

put the clock back fraudulently to alter the reading of a mileometer
Punning car trade jargon to cheat buyers of used cars, with the 'clock' being the mileometer. Today done circumspectly although no less frequently as a Br. criminal offence. Also as 'turn the clock back', or, of the operation, to 'clock' a vehicle.

put the file in order to conceal a mistake or omission
Bureaucratic jargon with the file-mentality cocooning the civil servant. So long as the documentation is in order, all are above criticism.

put the finger on *see* finger (1)

put the skids under wilfully to cause to fail
From the method of launching a ship or getting treetrunks to a mill. Once on the 'skids', the motion cannot be voluntarily arrested.

put to to mate with
Of mares etc.: 'We put her to Sandcastle yesterday morning' (Francis, 1982, of a mare). And *see* also **put**.

put to bed with a shovel etc. dead
Or with a 'mattock' or a 'spade', of natural death or a killing. To 'put underground' is to kill, usu. leaving the burial to others: 'If you don't keep quiet for ten minutes, I'll put you underground too' (G. Greene, 1932). 'Put under the sod' means no more than dead and buried: 'Charlie, who was put under the sod, poor chep, a year come Michaelmas' (Pease, 1894).

put to rest dead
The corpse does not necessarily have also to be buried: '. . . didn't expect things to change much until she was put to rest' (Sanders, 1986). And *see* at **rest** etc.

put to sleep to kill a domestic animal
Commonly of old, ill or unwanted pets: '"I'll have it put to sleep!" he shouted . . . . "Oh, darling," she pleaded, "he's only a puppy"' (Ustinov, 1966).

put to the sword to kill
Usu. of a large number of helpless victims, by any form of violence: '. . . took Siakat by storm and put not only the Egyptian garrison, but every man, woman and child in the place to the sword' (Harris, 1925).

put your lights out to kill
'Lights' means eyes but the phrase also puns on extinguishing a lamp: 'All men who were lucky at gambling very soon had their lights put out' (Richards, 1933, of WWI trench life).

put yourself away *see* put away (1).

Q

quail a whore
Not from the Celtic 'caile', a young girl, but the common avian imagery, this time from the reputedly amorous game bird: 'Agamemnon, an honest enough fellow, and one that loves quails' (Shakespeare, *Troilus and Cressida*). ob.

quaker's burial ground *see* **bury a quaker**

qualify accounts to throw doubt on published figures
Properly, to modify in some respect and there are indeed some technical 'qualifications' which do not indicate that the directors are a bunch of crooks and the company is headed for receivership. The 'qualification' is a modification of the standard form of words in an auditor's report.

quarantine a military blockade
Properly, the period of forty (*quarante*) days in which a widow might stay in her deceased husband's house, whence any period of isolation against disease, etc. Kennedy used the phrase of his 1962 blockade of Cuba.

queen a male homosexual
Usu. an older man playing the female role or affecting effeminate manners or dress: 'He won't hold your hand and ask for your autograph like that old Harley Street queen you normally see' (Deighton, 1972). An ob. form was 'cotqueen', which really meant the wife of a manual labourer: 'You cotqueen, you' (Harris, 1925). The ob. 'queen' or 'quean', a whore came from its meaning any female animal, especially a cat – which may 'look at a queen' – and S. Devon crabs, which you will hear as 'coin': 'To call an honest woman slut or queen' (W. Scott, 1820). A 'queen-house' was a brothel.

queer (1) drunk
Properly, not in your normal state of health and still rarely used of a drunkard, with a suggestion that his condition may have been caused by something else. The meaning, to make drunk, is ob.: 'Queered in the drinking of a penny pot of malmsey' (W. Scott, 1822).

queer (2) of unsound mind
Perhaps an abbr. of 'queer in the head'. In this usage, people tend to be a 'bit queer', implying a harmless and mild condition.

queer (3) homosexual
Almost always of males and equally common as an adjective: 'I'm not, um, queer. Well, you know, I don't like boys' (Theroux, 1975). 'Queerdom' is a tendency towards male homosexuality.

question to arrest
Br. police jargon much used when publicizing particulars of a suspect. If the police announce that they would like to 'question' someone corresponding with your description, you should take an overnight case to the interview.

questionable immoral or illegal
Properly, something which should be inquired into but now almost always in a derogatory or euphemistic sense. A 'questionable' motive is concealed or dishonest; a 'questionable' act offends the law or propriety; a 'questionable' payment is a bribe; etc.

quick pregnant
From its first SE meaning, animate, and used of pregnancy after the foetus has started kicking: 'She's quick; the child brags in her belly' (Shakespeare, *Love's Labour's Lost*). ? ob.

quick one an intoxicant
Usu. drunk by an addict: 'His short sharp nose looked as if it had hung over a lot of quick ones in its time' (Chandler, 1943). Less often as a 'quickie': 'And maybe we'd better break open the bottle for a quickie' (Sanders, 1980).

quick time a single act of copulation with a whore
The jargon of prostitutes who have a time-based tariff: 'Want a quick time, long time, companionship, black leather bondage?' (graffito quoted in Rees, 1980). The common 'quickie' can be with any female: 'Stone had never been fastidious about where he'd take his girls for a quickie' (Deighton, 1972).

quickie *see* **quick one** and **quick time**

quiet it to die
An Am. use, from the ensuing silence, but I know of no literary example.

quietus death
Properly, a legal discharge from an obligation, whence removal from an office: 'When he himself might his quietus make With a bare bodkin' (Shakespeare, *Hamlet*) and in modern use: 'It looks as if Armstrong has got his quietus' (Christie, 1939).

quit to die

From the leaving and specifically as the Am. 'quit the scene'. To 'quit cold' is to die by violence, although those who die naturally also lose body heat: 'Quit cold – with a slug in his head' (Chandler, 1939).

quod a prison

It was formerly spelt 'quad', an abbr. of 'quadrangle', the area in which students were confined as a punishment: 'He has got two years now. I went to see him once in quod' (Mayhew, 1862). To 'quod', to send to prison, is ob.: '. . . been quodded no end of times! She knew every beak as sat on the cheer' (ibid. – the 'beak', or magistrate, sat on the chair).

R

RD *see* **refer to drawer**

racial displaying prejudice against or hostility to an ethnic group
No longer distinguishing between people of different races, nor referring to the human race in its entirety, as when Marie Stopes was the President of the 'Society for Constructive Birth Control and Racial Progress'. The Nazis seem to have been the first to use 'racial' as indicating a human species. For them 'racial science' concerned itself with demonstrating that Germans were better than anyone else – the 'master race' – and 'racial purity' denoted that you had no Gypsy, Jew or Slav among your ancestors since 1750, which qualified you to apply to join the SS who, by 1940, 'had already done sterling work in matters of racial purification' (Keneally, 1982 – they had killed lots of cripples, Gypsies, Jews and Slavs). Today a 'race relations officer' concerns himself with discord between ethnic groups in the same community; the Br. 'Race Relations Board' bullies, cajoles and prosecutes those who do not look with favour on non-Whites; 'racial discrimination' is no longer the anthropological ability to tell one group from another; 'racial' is a term of abuse, often abbr. to 'racist' for the convenience of sub-editors, demagogues and the writers of graffiti; etc.

racy prepared to copulate extra-maritally
A variant of **fast** (above) and a 'racy girl' is not a sprinter or jockey but a whore: 'The Eden Hotel . . . . where the racy girls hung out, was entirely rubble' (Shirer, 1984).

radical supporting extreme political or social change
Properly, going back to the roots, from which ignoring accepted mores. In ob. Eng. dialect a 'radical' was 'an impudent, idle, dissipated fellow' (EDD) – readers of Bradbury's *The History Man* may think little has changed. For the Nazis, to be 'radical' was ruthlessly and fanatically to disregard the conventions of civilized conduct: 'Had we proceeded in a more radical fashion in our treatment of prisoners of war the numbers of German soldiers . . . . surrendering . . . . would have been smaller' (Goebbels, 1945, in tr. He repeatedly returns in his diary to his failure to secure German secession from the Geneva Convention). Today 'radical' is often used pejoratively: '. . . avid, punitive, radical ladies . . . . enlisting my support for experimental sex-play in the nursery schools' (Bradbury, 1976). And pre-WW II the New York police had a 'Radical Squad' whose duties were mainly breaking up Communist rallies.

rag (the) a brothel
Br. Indian Army use, perhaps from the sl. name for the London Army and Navy Club: 'In this brothel, or Rag as it was called by the troops' (Richards, 1936). The ob. 'rag water' was gin, because those who became addicted ended up dressed in rags.

rag(s) on menstruating
Common female use, of obvious imagery.

rail (the) syphilis
DAS says 'Orig. "ral"; "rail" is a variant' which might just carry us back across the Atlantic to the ob. Eng. 'rale', to stray.

railroad to treat in a ruthless and unfair way
The imagery is from the track which you cannot leave. Usu. of wrongful imprisonment: '. . . railroaded to jail in an incredibly short time' (Lavine, 1930), or of summary dismissal from employment: 'His father, in real life, had been framed and railroaded out of his position' (McCarthy, 1963). Am.

rainmaker a person paid primarily for his contacts
He brings in to an Am. financial house what his African counterpart brings down from the skies, both activities intended to generate growth without subsequent effort: 'Thanks to his mother and the Wallenberg connection, young Paul Mayer could bring in big business. In the United States they would have called him a "rainmaker"' (Erdman, 1966 – Mayer was operating in Europe).

raise a beat etc. to have an erect penis
Also as having 'a beat on', from the observable pulse. Commonly used fig. in the negative, when an exhausted male will claim that he 'cannot raise a beat'. To 'raise a gallop', with its equine imagery punning on **gallop** (above), is rarer.

raise the wind to secure funds to meet an obligation or need
The imagery is from setting in motion a becalmed sailing boat. Still widely used, especially where you have no resources of your own and the funds are hard to obtain.

raisin a male homosexual
I suspect from the French meaning, lipstick

and that **fruit** (above) is a later variant: 'He had more wrinkles than Auden, that other amazing raisin' (Theroux, 1978, of Maugham).

rake-off a payment made under bribery or extortion
Usu. on a regular basis from an illegal operation, like gambling. The imagery is from removing with a rake, with perhaps the roulette table in mind: 'I'll give you a third, as I gave Curtis. The "rake-off" don't hurt anyone' (Harris, 1925 – the inverted commas show the then novelty of the usage).

ram to copulate with
Of a male, from the fecund animal and perhaps too the common violent imagery: 'Flirting and ramming with white women' (Fraser, 1975). A 'ram' is also a promiscuous male: 'Must 'ave been quite a ram in 'is day' (Ustinov, 1971). The ob. Cornish 'ram-riding' was a public ordeal to which adulterous women were subjected, if caught, but without literally having to straddle a sheep: 'They had seized the woman . . . . and were hauling her along in a Ram Riding' (Quiller-Couch, 1891).

ramp to cheat
Properly, to snatch. Commonly of robbing, tricking, overcharging, giving wrong change, etc. A 'ramp' is anything which causes you to be cheated, deceived or overcharged. In ob. Br. army use, the 'ramps' was a brothel, perhaps because you often paid dearly for your pleasures, then or later.

ranch hands flyers engaged in military defoliation
Vietnam usage for an activity most Am. servicemen undertook with a reluctance which would have been even greater if they had known the latent effects of the chemicals involved upon themselves: 'There was a special Air Force outfit that flew defoliation missions. They were called the Ranch Hands' (Herr, 1977).

randy eager for copulation
A 'ran-dan' was a carouse: 'Is the laird on the ran-dan the night?' (Tweeddale, 1896) and this is a corruption. In the late 19c. 'A randy sort o' a 'ooman' (EDD) was one who enjoyed a good party but the association with intoxicants has now gone: 'I want you just as you are. Final. Got it? I'm randy now' (Bogarde, 1981). A Br. use which makes both sexes look with disfavour on the Am. abbr. of the name Randolph.

Rangoon itch a fungal infection of the penis
Burmese whores were notoriously disease-ridden: 'The houses you come away from with the fungus on your pecker known as "Rangoon itch"' (Theroux, 1973).

Rangoon runs diarrhoea
Not journeys to and from the city. One of the geographical alliterations inspired by cities where disease is commoner than cleanliness, and *see* 'runs' *under* run (4).

rank capable of impregnation
Properly, lush or strong-smelling. The use of women is ob.: 'The ewes, being rank, In the end of autumn turn'd to the rams' (Shakespeare, *Merchant of Venice*).

rap the accusation of a criminal offence
Properly, a rebuke or slap: 'I'd rather be under a murder rap – which I can beat' (Chandler, 1951).

rap club a brothel
To 'rap' is to talk or chatter, especially to another Am. narcotics addict. 'Rap' club, parlors, studios, etc. also tend to cater for male sexual deviation.

raspberry (1) a fart
Rh. sl. from 'raspberry tart' but almost always used fig. of a mild admonition or reproach. Oddly, people understand the association and vulgarity of 'blowing a raspberry', making a sound like a fart through pursed lips.

raspberry (2) a cripple
Br. rh. sl. from 'raspberry ripple', a type of ice cream.

rat a mild oath
Abbr. of 'drat': 'Rat the town, I say' (Fielding, 1729) but today used, if at all, in the plural. 'Rabbit' was once used in the same way but not, I think, euphemistically.

rather exceedingly
Many expressions introduced by 'rather' are on the borderline of understatement and euphemism, so that a 'rather naughty' child is a badly behaved brat. Similarly 'rather a handful' denotes worse trouble with a spouse, child or horse than a 'handful', as much as you can handle; and 'rather poorly' in hospital jargon means that the patient is very ill.

rationalize to dismiss employees
Properly, to think in a rational manner, whence to deal sensibly with a problem. Often a manager who 'rationalizes' does no

more than cover up multiple dismissals. On a large scale, such a 'rationalizer' may buy up and close competing factories, strip assets, eliminate domestic competition and encourage imports, reduce employment, generate large sums of cash and, if Br., end up in the House of Lords.

ratten to damage tools as a way of enforcing trade union membership
'Ratten' means rat, and this 19c. example is a timely reminder that, then as now, men can behave in just as unsavoury a way as masters: 'To maim a man is not to ratten him, but to take away his wheelbands is' (*Sheffield Independent*, 1874, quoted in EDD, q.v. for a fearsome account of what went on under this practice). Yorks ob.

rattle (1) to copulate with
Of a male normally, from the shaking about which may be involved: 'All I'd done was rattle Mandeville's wife' (Fraser, 1971). A 'rattle' can also be the woman involved, always with a laudatory adjective; or a single act of copulation: 'It was her thinking she was the thinking man's rattle' (Amis, 1978).

rattle (2) to urinate
Am. rh. sl. from 'rattle and hiss', with probably something of the common serpentine imagery.

raunchy lustful or pornographic
It originally meant sloppy whence, with unusual rapidity of progression, poor, then cheap, then drunk and now the sexual uses: '. . . importuning me with words delectably raunchy and lewd' (Styron, 1976). And you still meet it of any wild behaviour: 'But then things got a little raunchy. They wanted to go down to Greenwich Village and see the freaks' (Sanders, 1981). Still mainly Am.

ravish to copulate with a woman under duress
Properly, to seize or carry off anything: 'The ravisht Helen, Menelaus' wife, With wanton Paris sleeps' (Shakespeare, *Troilus and Cressida*) and, in modern use: 'I don't know why, but that ravishing of Lily made her dear to me' (Harris, 1925). The slightly ob. female expression of delight 'How ravishing!' came from the meaning, ecstatic, and not from any Freudian fantasies.

raw naked
The undressed state: 'But screw the pyjamas; I sleep raw' (Sanders, 1983). Usu. as **in the raw** (above).

razor to wound or kill by cutting
The cut-throat razor is not here used for shaving: '. . . razored in barrelhouses and end up being shot in a saloon' (Longstreet, 1956).

re-educate to extinguish a former political allegiance
The Communists, who use harsh imprisonment, are better at it than the Americans who relied on logic and bribes: '. . . turn every deserter into a defector by "re-educating" him in a camp' (McCarthy, 1967, of Vietnam).

re-entry recovery from an illegal narcotic ingestion
With the common 'flying' imagery. Especially used after LSD.

re-introduced to society freed from political imprisonment
Communist jargon, much used in the 1978 upheavals in Afghanistan.

reading Geneva print drunk
This is a sample entry of several ob. literary puns on the city renowned for its piety and its printing, and on gin which is also called 'Geneva' from the French *genièvre*, the juniper berry: 'You have been reading Geneva print this morning already' (W. Scott, 1816).

realistic not inflated
Of prices generally, but especially used by estate agents when they wish to signal that a house is being offered for sale at something near its true value.

Realpolitik a policy of ruthless chauvinist militarism
Bismark's *Policy of Realism* led the cultured, pacific but too disciplined Germans to the wars of 1864, 1866 and 1870 directly; indirectly to 1914 and 1939; and for those in the East, to prolonged subjugation.

ream to bugger
Properly to enlarge a hole by inserting a metal tool: '. . . maybe a night in the slammer where the boogies will ream you' (Sanders, 1985 – a policeman was threatening a male homosexual).

reaper (the) death
Father Time carries a scythe as well as an hourglass. A 'grim' was a death's head or skeleton in N. Eng. dialect, and the more common 'grim reaper' may come from this as well as the figure's remorseless mien: 'The goal was to outmanoeuvre the Grim Reaper' (N. Mitford, 1963).

rear (1) the buttocks
Not the heels or shoulderblades. Females, especially in Am., may be said to have a 'rear end': '... her sumptuous rear end' (Styron, 1976).

rear (2) to defecate
The etymology suggested by DHS of soldiers falling out to the rear seems unnecessarily complex. Br. 'rears', lavatories, were so named from their location behind and away from houses, and the usages are probably linked.

receding nearly bald
An abbr. of 'receding hairline' although, when the expression is used, that is usu. only one symptom of incipient baldness. Men use 'receding' of themselves, or of those whom they wish to flatter. In others, male baldness is a subject for frankness and humour.

receiver a dealer in stolen property
From his willingness to 'receive anything brought' (Mayhew, 1862) and SE. The ob. Br. 'receiver-general' was a whore, punning on the office of a senior official and her 'reception' of men generally.

rectification of frontiers the annexation of territory by force
Nazi and Communist usage. If you go far enough back, you can establish hundreds of States of Israel, although one has brought problems enough.

red devil etc. an illegal narcotic
In many compounds, from the colour of the pill. A 'red devil' is a barbiturate or seconal. The two exceptions are 'red dirt marjuana', the wild plant, from the Southern Am. deserts where it grows; and 'red cross', morphine, because it may be stolen from a first aid kit.

red eye bad whisky
From its effects on the drinker, and also of other inferior Am. concoctions. However the 'red-eye' or 'red-eye special' is any overnight flight from the west coast to the east of the USA, or less often of a night flight to Europe: 'I'm on the redeye back to the Big Apple' (M. Thomas, 1980, of a return to New York City).

red-hot poker an erect penis
A triple pun on the Kniphofia. I have traced no literary use.

red lamp etc. a brothel
From the traditional sign: 'There was a Red Lamp in Bethune situated about five yards off the main street' (Richards, 1933). Rarely

as 'red-lighted number': '... also featured at the red-lighted number of the brothel area of a town' (Longstreet, 1956). A 'red-light' area, precinct, district, etc. is a brothel quarter: 'They paid for promotion or detail to the red-light precinct' (Lavine, 1930 – a New York policeman would expect regular bribes from bawds).

red rag (the) menstruation
A variant of **rag(s) on** (above) and punning on the cliché, a 'red rag to a bull'. In speech either 'waved' or 'worn'. The 'red flag is up' puns on the danger signal rather than the Communist emblem.

Red Sea is in I am menstruating
Alluding perhaps to the adventures of Moses and others recorded in Exodus.

red-squad (the) police concerned with subversion
An Am. use, from fear of Communist influence: 'The New York Police Department has a Red Squad. They change the name every two years or so – Radical Bureau, Public Relations, Public Security. Right now they call it the Security Investigation' (M. C. Smith, 1981).

redhaired visitor (a) menstruation
A rare version of the common 'visitor' theme.

redistribution of property looting
Mainly WW II use of soldiers in Europe: 'He didn't call it stealing though, "redistribution of property" he called it' (Price, 1978, of WW II).

redistribution of wealth exceptional taxation of the rich
Taxation is used to deplete privately-held capital and severely restrict the level of any tax-paid income in the professed belief that resources will be available to satisfy the increased spending power of the beneficiaries: '... wilful and cruel disruption of the economic fabric that was called the redistribution of wealth' (Allbeury, 1976). The device works in the short term not so much by improving the position of the poor as by fuelling inflation and thereby eroding the savings and earnings of rich and poor alike. Persistence, with continuing high inflation, causes savings to dry up and the introduction of wage, price, import, exchange and other controls associated with socialist government.

redlining refusing credit solely because of the place of residence of the applicant

You highlight the address in a list, fig. or in fact: '. . . entire areas of the city, poor areas, humble areas, were beyond the credit . . . . the inhabitants of those districts were exiled from creditworthiness. That foul practice was called redlining' (M. Thomas, 1987). Am.

reds (the) menstruation
A common female use of obvious derivation.

redundant dismissed from employment
Properly, in superabundance which an individual, 'made redundant', can hardly be: '"And now they've turned you out?" he asked. "Who said they had?" . . . . "I thought you said something about being made redundant"' (Sharpe, 1974). The Am. 'reduction in force' means what it says, that less people have work, the leavers being 'riffed'.

reefer a marijuana cigarette
The etymology is uncertain, although some suggest it comes from the method of hand-rolling the cigarettes: 'A two-time loser sneaking home from a reefer party' (Chandler, 1943).

refer to drawer this cheque is unpaid through lack of funds
Banks use this phrase because it is dangerous to dishonour a cheque by mistake and thereby imply that the drawer has written it fraudulently. Commonly abbr. to 'RD'.

referred failed
Properly, put back. Eng. university jargon.

refresh your memory to extract information through violence
Police and criminal usage, and quite different from an aide memoire: 'They compel reluctant prisoners to refresh their memories' (Lavine, 1930, of the New York police).

refresher an intoxicant
From the supposed bracing effect: 'He marches out, with his hat on one side of his head, to take another "refresher"' (Jefferies, 1880).

refreshment an intoxicant
If offered on a Sunday school outing, a 'refreshment' is likely to be tea or lemonade but on most other male social occasions, you would expect beer or spirits.

regular (1) in the habit of daily defecation or monthly menstruation
Laxative advertisements enshrined the defecatory use: 'I've always been regular as clockwork, all my life, and then, bingo' (Ustinov, 1971, of defecation). 'Irregular' is used as the converse in both senses: 'Irregularity was one of my problems these days, so I was unusually prepared' (P. Scott, 1975, of menstruation).

regular (2) small
In the jargon of packet sizes – 'jumbo', 'family', 'economy', etc. – 'regular' is the little one and often the worst value.

regularize (1) to make good a bureaucratic omission or mistake
Civil service etc. jargon. So long as the impersonal file has been amended to comply with regulations, it matters little what delays and blemishes it hides.

regularize (2) to invade
The intended inference is that things are being restored to normal. It took one Polish, one East German and twelve Russian divisions to 'regularize' the position in Czechoslovakia in 1968.

(rehabilitate to release a political prisoner or restore the reputation of someone who has been traduced is not Communist jargon but 16c. SE. 'De-rehabilitation', to change your mind about them and put them back in prison or your black books, is new and a useful word in the arbitrary U-turns of Russian and Chinese Communist lore.)

relate to copulate with
Properly, to be connected in any way: '"Can't you just say 'fuck' once in a while?" But Piper wouldn't. "Relating" was an approved term' (Sharpe, 1977). In sociological jargon, someone who 'fails to relate' to another just doesn't get on with him.

relations see **have relations** under **have**

relations have come (my) I am menstruating
From the limited duration and inconvenience of the visitation, or in some cases, the relief at seeing them. The visitors are sometimes 'country cousins', from their ruddy complexions.

relationship a connection which involves extra-marital copulation
In fact we have a 'relationship' with anyone we deal with, as buyer or seller, friend or enemy: 'For just over three months Jeanie has had a relationship with a Russian' (Allbeury, 1982 – he was copulating with her). Used alone or with adjectival embellishment, where the 'relationship' may be

close, long-term, special, or as the case may be. Now too some homosexual use.

relative deprivation the fact that some people are richer than others
Sociological jargon which avoids any reference to poverty. *See* too **deprived**.

release (1) to dismiss from employment
The employee has not in fact been held against his will: '. . . since released (not surprisingly) to pursue "other business interests", the banking euphemism for goodbye' (*Private Eye*, April 1988) and: 'The pilot's release from the team is a result of an administrative action' (*Daily Telegraph*, January 1987 – it could hardly have been implemented without an administrative action, you might suppose, whatever the causation. It appears the pilot was dismissed from an aerobatic team because he had crashed an aeroplane). Of single and multiple dismissals.

release (2) a death
The soul has left the body for more congenial climes. Much used after a painful terminal illness in the cliché 'happy release'. 'Released' means dead, usu. of those killed by violence: 'Let these serve as a sacrifice to those dead innocent spirits so cruelly released at Jhanoi' (Fraser, 1975, writing in 19c. style).

release (3) the ejaculation of semen
By whatever means, under the theory that unrelieved sexual tension in a male is bad for him: '. . . indulged in this pastime night after night as much to give him some "release" (she actually uses the odious word)' (Styron, 1976, of masturbation).

released *see* **release** (2)

relevance an area of enquiry or thought which interests a dogmatic idealist
Properly, appertaining to the matter in hand: 'Colette, indulged with every possibility of happiness and improvement, was whining about relevance' (Murdoch, 1977). In the same sense 'relevant' has to do with any obsession of a dogmatist.

relief (1) public aid given to the indigent
Originally a feudal payment to an overlord on coming into an estate: 'The parish granted no relief and even if it had done so it is very doubtful whether the strikers or their wives would have accepted it' (Richards, 1936). This is an early, but still current, example of the string of euphemisms which

we use to conceal the charitable nature of state aid to the poor.

relief (2) urination
You usu. 'need' or 'obtain' it: 'Archie had needed immediate relief in the bathroom' (Davidson, 1978). And *see* **relieve yourself**. Rarely of defecation or vomiting.

relief (3) copulation
With the male's tensions subsequently quietened, I suppose: '. . . the Euphoric Spring has heated your blood to the extent that you're prepared to fly me six thousand miles to obtain relief' (Lodge, 1975).

relieve to dismiss from employment
This Am. use is of the same tendency as **let go** (q.v.), as though the dismissal were a kindness to the employee by letting him get on with something else. The SE 'relieve of duties' is usu. of an official for misbehaviour or dereliction of duty.

relieve of virginity to copulate with a female virgin
Usu. extra-maritally and perhaps no more than circumlocution: 'Dottie had wanted to be "relieved" of her virginity' (McCarthy, 1963).

relieve yourself to urinate
You obtain **relief** (2) (above): 'He felt a sudden urge to relieve himself' (Diehl, 1978, of urination). Rarely of defecation, except in a fuller form like 'relieve your bowels': 'They went in the dawn, brass lotah in hand, to relieve their bowels in the spaces between the houses' (Masters, 1976).

relocation killing
A Nazi use for the despatch of Jews etc. to the death camps: 'In Berlin, they wrote "relocation" and believed themselves excused' (Keneally, 1982, of orders for the rounding up of Jews for murder).

relocation camp a place for the imprisonment of enemy aliens
Am. WWII usage when the presence of Japanese-Americans on the possibly threatened West coast posed a considerable dilemma: '. . . most of them were interned at the time in "relocation camps"' (Jennings, 1965, of Japanese-Americans).

remain above ground not to die
The presumption is that the dead are buried. The following quotation shows what can happen when a euphemism is interpreted literally: 'Mrs Van Butchell's marriage settlement stipulated that her husband should have control of her fortune "as long

as she remained above ground". The embalming was a great success' (J. Mitford, 1963 – Mr Van Butchell showed more enterprise than taste).

remains a corpse
Funeral jargon and 'mortal remains' is specific: 'Today, though, "body" is Out and "remains" or "Mr Jones" is In' (J. Mitford, 1963).

remedial applicable to the dull and the lazy
Properly, helping to cure something, as 'remedial education' should be short-term special instruction to overcome a specific weakness in an otherwise normal child. In educational jargon, 'remedial' is used to avoid mentioning any fundamental inadequacy of which mention would be taboo: '. . . the staff even have to lay on a remedial English course for students with a "less than adequate mastery of the English language"' (*Daily Telegraph*, October 1983, of a London Polytechnic more given to politics than education). As with lunacy, the blurring of levels of disability is no kindness for those who require long-term help.

remittance man an unsuccessful, embarrassing or improvident member of a wealthy family sent to reside in a distant country
He is sent enough to live on so long as he stays there: 'Remittance man – a form of Kenya settler said to depend on remittance from UK to stop him returning' (Allen, 1979). (Post-empire, there is nowhere to send a Br. ne'er-do-well, unless into politics.)

remount a girl recruited for prostitution
Pimps' jargon, punning on the cavalry term for a fresh horse and the common riding imagery: '"To come for remounts" means to come back to France to find women for export' (Londres, 1928, in tr.).

remove to kill
But not necessarily making off with the body. DSUE says of 'removal': 'Ex a witness's euphemism in the Phoenix Park assassination case', but Dr Johnson gives both dismissal from a post and going away, both of which are common 'death' images. The Sc. 'removed', dead, probably came in those pious times from the separation of the soul from the body: 'When a person has just expired, the Scotch people commonly say, he is removed' (*Monthly Magazine*, 1800, quoted in EDD).

rent a payment extorted illegally or for an illicit transaction

Not necessarily on more than one occasion, as from a tenant to a landlord. In ob. use., of cash paid to a highway robber. Also of regular extortion and, in homosexual jargon, money paid to a male by another, the recipient being a 'rent boy': 'Moreover, when the *Sunday People* published its front-page "caring" shocker about Harvey and the ex-public school rent boy' (*Private Eye*, October 1986). A 'renter' is a prostitute, male or female, who works on a part-time basis.

repose to be dead and buried
An Am. extension of the common 'resting' imagery: 'The companions will repose one above the other in a single grave space' (J. Mitford, 1963). A 'reposing room' is a morgue: 'Reposing room or slumber room, not laying-out room' (ibid.).

resettlement mass murder
Properly, voluntary or involuntary movement of residence. The Nazi *Unsiedlung* took Jews from ghettos to their death: '. . . the huge "resettlements" from the Warsaw ghetto . . . . were coincident with the establishment of . . . Treblinka and its gas chambers' (Styron, 1976).

residential provision a place in a boarding institution
This Br. usage is more than inelegance or circumlocution, because in sociological jargon you must use words which avoid the taboo 'board school', a prison for young criminals, or 'boarding school' to which the rich send their children for a more thorough and intensive education than that provided free by the State. A 'resident' may be a homeless geriatric, a lunatic, a chronic invalid or a prisoner.

resign to be dismissed from employment
Usu. said of and by senior employees, to avoid losing face: 'I worked as a personal secretary in London until I was fi . . . until I resigned' (Bradbury, 1976).

resign your spirit to die
An ob. use which seems to discount the prospect of reincarnation: 'Resigned her Spirit to Him who gave it on the 13th day of March 1818' (Memorial in Bath Abbey).

resistance (the) the organization in France between 1940 and 1945 opposing the German occupation to which in retrospect every Frenchman says he belonged
Properly, those few who continued actively, at great peril and with infinite courage, to oppose the Germans and their French allies,

which included the *milice*, Vichy and all those who sought a quiet life: 'All the world will claim to have been in the Resistance then. You won't find a collaborator in all France' (Allbeury, 1978). (It may take another generation before the shame of those days – of the grovelling, not of the defeat – ceases to mould French attitudes, just as it took generations to forget that Joan was sentenced and burnt by her fellow-countrymen.)

resisting arrest in custody
Police etc. usage for the wrongful wounding or killing of a prisoner: 'I like it better you get a slug in the guts resisting arrest' (Chandler, 1939). Of the same tendency as **trying to escape** (below).

resources control the destruction of crops
Am. Vietnam usage. It should mean no more than rationing: '. . . bombing, defoliation, crop-spraying, destruction of rice supplies, and what is known as "Resources Control"' (McCarthy, 1969).

rest home an institution for geriatrics
Not punning on the fact that most of them will stay there for the rest of their lives: 'A ninety-two-year-old who died in a rest home' (J. Mitford, 1963). The 'Convalescent Home' in East Haddam, Ct, masks its purpose with a less accurate title.

rest room a lavatory
Wide Am. use by both sexes, usu. of those in public use and not excluding the positively unrestful cubicles on long-distance buses: '. . . asked where the bathroom was. The restroom was filthy' (Diehl, 1978). The attempt by the Am. funeral industry to use 'restroom' for morgue not surprisingly found few takers.

resting unemployed
Theatrical jargon which seeks to infer that the idleness is voluntary: 'The demoralization of so many of my out-of-work companions. "Resting" is one of the least restful periods of an actor's life' (Murdoch, 1978).

restorative an intoxicant
Now more common than the **refresher** (q.v.) which uses the same imagery.

restorative art the cosmetic facial treatment of corpses
Am. funeral jargon: '. . . transferred from a common corpse into a Beautiful Memory Picture. This process is known in the trade as embalming and restorative art' (J. Mit-

ford, 1963). A 'restorative artist' is a beautician to the dead: '. . . features remoulded by the hand of a Restorative Artist into unfamiliar expressions of benign sweetness' (ibid.). The 19c. London 'restorer' dealt not with corpses but with negotiating the ransoms for stolen dogs which was big business and not illegal, as dogs were incapable of being stolen under Common Law: 'A restorer, who undertook "to restore the dog if terms could be come to"' (Mayhew, 1851). And *see* **transported** for the story of the Duke of Beaufort's dog's collar.

restraint a policy intended to restrict increases in pay
One of a series of euphemisms by which government seeks to mask an intervention to wage bargaining which is usu. ineffective in the short-term and counter-productive in the longer-term. If you are looking for self-denial in the employed population, you will be disappointed.

restricted growth dwarfishness
'Restriction' should mean a deliberate holding back. A BBC programme broadcast on 15 January 1987, was devoted to 'people of restricted growth'.

restructured presented in a dishonest or misleading way
Of financial reports, where the method of presentation introduces falsehoods or hides truth: 'When the Saudis take a look at some of these "restructured" balance sheets, they're going to need about ten seconds to figure out what pushing oil back down to ten bucks a barrel would do to a twenty-to-one debt to equity ratio at Texaco' (M. Thomas, 1987 – and did, as it turned out, although other factors came into play too).

resurrection man etc. a stealer of corpses
When it was widely supposed that those who died in Christian belief would in due course undergo a resurrection of the body, few wished to risk having their corpses dissected in pursuit of medical knowledge for fear of a dismembered or partial return to earth. The market had therefore to be supplied, especially in Sc., by raiding churchyards. This punning usage may first have been applied in 1829 to Burke and Hare, who carried the business a stage further by murdering future supplies when a paucity of natural deaths caused fresh corpses to be in short availability. Also as 'resurrection cove' or 'resurrectionist'. ob.

retainer a series of payments made regularly to an extortioner
Properly, a sum paid to book the services of
a lawyer etc.: 'I can afford a substantial
retainer. That's what you call it, I've heard.
A much nicer word than blackmail' (Chandler, 1958).

retard a simpleton
Properly, anything delayed or held back:
'How long is the old girl going to take? No
one said she was a fucken ree-tard' (Theroux, 1978). 'Retarded' is educational jargon
for a congenital etc. inability to learn.

retire to kill
The victim certainly stops working: 'I just
retired a junkman' (Diehl, 1978). (The
French *en retraite*, retired, led a Belgian
friend, kindly talking to me in English, to
refer to an old soldier as a 'general in
retreat'.)

retiring room a lavatory
Br. usage at a function where its duration
demands a presence longer than a normal
interval between urination. On such
occasions a monarch who 'retires' does not
abdicate.

retreat a lavatory
Punning on the solitary religious activity. In
various forms such as the doubly punning
'beat a retreat'.

retrenched dismissed from employment
Properly, reduced in the interest of economy
but used of those who have to go rather than
those who form the continuing workforce.
Am.

returned empty A woman returning to
Britain after a visit to India neither married
nor engaged to be married
Thus were described the unsuccessful
members of those who had been on the
fishing expedition (1) (q.v.). The imagery
would be familiar in the days when affluent
families were accustomed regularly to return
used soda syphons etc. to a supplier and may
just have punned on the unimpregnated
condition of the young marriageable women
involved. ob.

returned to unit failed
Br. army jargon often abbr. to 'RTU' for
those who fail to complete a special course to
qualify for an elite corps, as an officer, etc.:
'They would be conditionally accepted or
RTU'd. Returned to their original units'
(Allbeury, 1982).

reverse a defeat
Properly, the opposite of anything but used
in this sense since 16c., especially if it is your
side which loses. Similarly too of a pecuniary
or business misfortune.

reverse engineering unauthorized
copying
Not the gear which propels backwards. You
obtain your competitor's product, take it
apart and then use the technological
improvements, suitably disguised, in your
own.

revision of prices *see* **price adjustment**

revisionist anybody who questions the
current policy of an autocracy
A Communist dysphemism, with much
pejorative use: '. . . illegal cheap hotels that
seem to have a collectively revisionist
attitude regarding official papers' (Ludlum,
1979).

reviver an intoxicant
From its supposed ability to liven up the
drinker, but not used only, as you might
suppose, of the first potation.

revolutionary organs of power a
Communist government
It sounds like motorized wheels. If you
stipulate that the revolution which brought
you to power is of indefinite duration, you
automatically preclude the need for any
fresh revolutions: 'Mikoyan concludes the
revolutionaries should establish "revolutionary organs of power" (a euphemism for
Communist dictatorship)' (*Daily Telegraph*,
June 1980). Should internal disorder surface, you meet it with 'revolutionary
firmness': 'Western governments wouldn't
be capable of handling them with "Revolutionary firmness". Meaning eight armoured
divisions and a couple of MVD special
brigades . . . . And a thousand cattle trucks
for the lucky survivors' (Price, 1972).

rib joint a brothel
Probably from the ob. 'rib', a woman, after
the manner of Eve's creation. DAS says
'from "tenderloin" reinforced by "crib
joint"', which might be right although I
favour less complex etymologies. Am.

rich friend *see* **friend**

Richard a turd
Br. rh. sl. for 'Richard the Third', who had a
bad press from the Tudors and Shakespeare, which is why he is commonly considered more of a shit than Edward, William,

Henry or George, of whom there were also three or more.

ride to copulate with
Usu. of a man, with the common equine imagery: 'You rode, like a kern of Ireland, your French hose off' (Shakespeare, *Henry V*). But also of a woman, especially if above the man: 'Gabby groaned as she rode him at a little under a canter. He lay easing himself up to her' (L. Thomas, 1979). A 'ride' is either a female viewed for copulation, or the act: 'Reckon you'll count it a pretty dear ride you had, friend. Was she good?' (Fraser, 1971 – Flashman had copulated with his master's wife). To 'ride St George' was 'The woman uppermost in the amorous congress, that is, the dragon upon St George' (Grose – it was said to be the way to beget a bishop). However to 'ride abroad with St George but at home with St Michael' imported neither sexual variety nor custom at Marks and Spencers but that the man was a braggart away from home but henpecked indoors. A 'riding master' was a woman's extra-marital sexual partner: 'I was the Queen's current favourite and riding-master' (Fraser, 1977, writing in 19c. style) and 'riding time' was the season for impregnation, properly of sheep and vulgarly of women: 'Warn him ay at ridin time To stay content wi' yowes at hame' (Burns, 1786 – 'yowes' means ewes). etc.

ride the red horse to menstruate
Of obvious derivation.

ride the wooden horse to be flogged
From the 'horse', or stool', over which the victim was strapped. ob.

ride up Holborn Hill etc. to be killed by hanging
Holborn Hill was on the road between Newgate Prison and the Tyburn gallows in London: 'I shall live to see you ride up Holborn Hill' (Congreve, 1695). This is a sample entry, many cities making similar use of a geographical feature which the condemned man passed between prison and the scaffold. Of general use was 'ride backwards', because they sat you that way in the cart for the journey. To 'ride the mare' was less common, and I have not traced the etymology. To 'ride out' was to be a thief, particularly on the borders of Eng. and Sc., where riding and robbery were almost synonymous: 'Ride, Rowlie, hough's i' the pot' (Nicholson and Burn, 1777 – 'hough' was the last remaining piece of beef, and it was time to rustle some more). ob.

(**rif** to dismiss from employment comes from the US Federal 'reduction in force'. It may also describe an Am. military demotion.)

rifle to copulate with
Of a male. You have a choice of three etymologies – from the technical term for the copulation of hawks; from the plundering of booty; or from the concept of screwing. BI ? ob.

right thing *see* **do the right thing**

right-wing chauvinist and totalitarian
A euphemism for some of those extremists who so describe themselves, but much derogatory use by Communists etc. of those holding more moderate socialist views than themselves.

ring (1) a vagina
Viewed sexually, from its supposed shape: 'I'll fear no other thing, So sure as keeping safe Nerissa's ring' (Shakespeare, *Merchant of Venice*). A woman who had copulated before marriage was said, with punning vulgarity, to be 'cracked in the ring'. Now also used of the anus of either sex, especially in male homosexual use.

ring (2) a cartel
From the concept of meeting in, and making completely, a circle. Wide commercial use and in particular of dealers who combine to buy cheaply at auction. (Those interested in cartels and their euphemisms can do no better than read Jones and Marriott's *Anatomy of a Merger*, which deals with the electric lamp manufacturers – the Am. 'Incandescent Lamp Manufacturers Association' of 1896; the German 'Filament Trust' or *Draht-konzern* of 1911; and the Br. 'Electric Lamp Manufacturers Association' of 1919.)

ring (3) a female contraceptive worn internally
From its shape, whence the punning: 'Wedded, as it were, by proxy, with the "ring" or diphragm pessary' (McCarthy, 1963).

ring the bell to impregnate a woman
From the fairground trial of strength which involves a sledge-hammer and a moving object in a vertical column. The use implies intent.

ringer a racehorse etc. fraudulently substituted for another
In early 20c. sl., a 'ringer' was a person who closely resembled someone else, often in the cliché 'a dead ringer'. There may be some connection with 'ringing the changes' in campanology.

rinse the application of dye to hair
Properly, a cleaning by water. Mainly female
hairdressing jargon: '. . . married the Buick
dealer on the adjacent lot, and got a blue
rinse' (Bradbury, 1976). Old women with
white hair have 'blue rinses'.

rip off to cheat by stealing or overcharging
Perhaps from tearing paper off a pad, or
notes from a roll: 'We get ripped off for half
a million, and we respond with free psychiatric treatment and maintenance for the villain's family' (West, 1979). And of
plagiarism: 'Such rip-offs of their material
are strictly banned by the GTV hierarchy'
(*Private Eye*, May 1981). To 'rip off a piece
of arse' is to copulate with a woman extra-
maritally, to **cheat** (q.v.) on your normal
partner but not by avoiding payment: '. . .
picks up a hooker and rips off a bit of ass'
(Theroux, 1973). A 'rip-off' is any example
of such cheating and a 'rip-off merchant' an
habitual swindler: '. . . there are plenty of
ripoff merchants around in this game'
(*Private Eye*, September 1981).

ripe drunk
And ready to fall? This Am. use has, I fear,
no connection with the picturesque ob. Eng.
'ripples on': '"'E 'ad the ripples on," –
drunk he was not, though he had exceeded
his rightful allowance' (EDD – 'ripples' are
the attachments to the sides of a cart to
enable it to carry more than its normal load).

ripped drunk
Feeling torn ? Am.

ripple a succession of orgasms
In a female, presumably from the succession
of waves, but what male will ever know? '. . .
sometimes a whole series of orgasms followed (wasn't "rippling" the word used ?)'
(Hailey, 1984).

rise an erection of the penis
In Am. you call an increase in pay a 'raise', to
avoid misunderstanding.

river (the) an intoxicant
Br. rh. sl. of 'River Ouse', booze.

rivet to copulate with
Of a male, usu. extra-maritally on a single
occasion, from the metal fastener passed
through a hole in engineering: 'When I was an
undergraduate you got sent down if you were
caught riveting a dolly' (Sharpe, 1974). ? ob.

roach the butt of a marijuana cigarette
Perhaps it looks like a beetle. Used either as
a synonym of butt: 'The marijuana cigarette
which he smoked down to the roach'

(Longstreet, 1956) or as the entire object:
'The waitress took the roach, sniffed it, and
said, "Thank you, dear. Just what I need"'
(Saunders, 1986).

road apples horse shit in the street
From the way it may be piled naturally and its
value as free manure. Am.

road is up for repair (the) I am menstruating
A multiple pun on the red warning light, the
closing of the passage and the temporary
nature of the affliction.

rock *see* **roll** (1)

rock crusher a convict
From the activity in which prisoners were
traditionally engaged. Am.

rocks the testicles
A variant of the SE **stones** (q.v.) and *see* 'get
your rocks off' *under* **get a leg over** etc.

rocky (1) mad
Unstable, like an unbalanced chair: 'I guess
you're a bit rocky. You haven't escaped from
anywhere, have you?' (G. Greene, 1932).

rocky (2) drunk
Again from the lack of balance. Am.

rod (1) to copulate with
Of a male, from the insertion of a rigid probe
as when cleaning a chimney.

rod (2) a handgun
Properly, a straight bit of wood: 'I don't never
let Frisky carry a loaded rod' (Chandler, 1939
– a craftsman who at least knew when he was
writing incorrect English). 'Rodded' is so
armed: 'The derby hat saw if I was rodded.
He took the Lüger' (ibid.).

rod (3) a penis
From its propensity to rigidity: 'The liveliest
parts of his body became spiritualized, and
his rod itself' (Genet, in 1969 tr.).

roger (1) to copulate with
Of a male, usu. naming the female. Most
authorities trace the derivation from a name
commonly given to a bull but as we have a
recorded 18c. use, it may have come from the
ob. SE meaning, a ram: '. . . find oneself
being rogered by one of his libidinous hereos'
(Bradbury, 1976). Also spelt 'rodger'.

roger (2) a penis
I suspect not from its role in 'rogering'
(above) but from the 'Jolly Roger', or pirate
flag. Rare.

roll (1)   to copulate with

Of either sex, from the movement: 'A beautiful blonde virgin from Boulder Swore no man on earth had yet rolled her' (*Playboy's Book of Limericks*). A 'roll' is an act of copulation: '. . . our last meeting had been the monumental roll in her pavilion' (Fraser, 1975). The cliché a 'roll in the hay' is of extra-marital copulation, but not necessarily in an agrarian setting: 'A hotel room rented . . . . for a roll in the hay' (Chandler, 1953). The ob. 'roll the linen' punned on the ironing of sheets: '. . . in my absence she'd been rolling the linen with any chap who'd come handy' (Fraser, 1977, writing in 19c. style). In rare use, to 'rock', to copulate, probably comes from the association of 'rock' and 'roll'.

roll (2)   to rob violently

Often applied to an Am. drunkard who is knocked, or 'rolled', over before being robbed and in general use of street theft: '. . . rolled by a tough hackie and dumped out on a vacant lot' (Chandler, 1953).

Roman   sexually orgiastic

From the fabled orgies of the ancient Romans, which involved intoxicants and general abandon, rather than the depravities of the modern city or its church. It is an abbr. of 'Roman culture' or 'Roman way' in Am. advertisements offering access to sexual depravity. A 'Roman spring' is lust in the elderly.

Roman candle   a failure of a parachute

Failing to open fully, it resembles the firework: '. . . we were all well acquainted with details of a Roman candle' (Farran, 1948, of parachuting).

romance   extra-marital copulation with one person

Properly, a courtship, from the tale of chivalry which was set down in vernacular French rather than in Latin: 'I am distressed to see the old French word "romance" used as a code name for East African activities' (A. Waugh, *Private Eye*, December 1980).

romp   to copulate with

Properly, to frolic: 'What these Indians don't know about the refinements of romping isn't worth knowing' (Fraser, 1975). A 'romp' is also an act of copulation, or a partner in such an act: 'I'd rather think of her as the finest romp that ever pressed a pillow' (Fraser, 1970).

room and board with Uncle Sam   imprisonment

An Am. refinement of **guest** (above): 'Using narcotics without a licence can get you room and board with Uncle Sam' (Chandler, 1953).

rooster *see* **game-chicken**

root (1)   an erect penis

From the source of procreation or from the shape of 'root' vegetables? '. . . a thicket of curling hair that spread from the root all round thighs and navel' (Cleland, 1749). 'Man-root' is explicit: '. . . moving her pussy the while up and down harshly against my man-root' (Harris, 1925).

root (2)   a marijuana cigarette

Perhaps from its shape. Am.

root about   to copulate energetically

The imagery is porcine rather than punning on **root** (1) (above): 'Where did you ever learn to root about like that? Didn't know such things went on outside a Mexican whorehouse' (Mailer, 1965). Rarely abbr. to 'root': 'I mean he spent an hour a day at the pushing shop down near the railway, rooting himself stupid' (Keneally, 1985).

rootle   to copulate

A rare variant of **root about** (above) using the same imagery.

rope (1) **(the)**   death by hanging

Noose and all: 'We're dealing with big violent organized gangs. Comes of scrapping the rope' (Kyle, 1979).

rope (2)   a marijuana cigarette

From the association with **hemp** (q.v.). Am.

roses (the)   menstruation

From the colour of blood: 'Such a bad headache. Had her roses probably' (Joyce, 1922). The ob. 'rose-coloured' was a euphemism for 'bloody' as a mild form of swearing.

rosy   drunk

From the facial glow. The meaning, wine, may have been merely the anglicizing of 'rosé': '. . . finished the rosy, and applied himself to . . . . another glassful' (Dickens, 1840).

rough trade   an uncouth male in a sexual role

Aggressive and often badly-dressed or dirty, he is either a homosexual taking the male part: 'I don't do chickenhawks and I don't do rough trade and I don't work men's rooms' (M. Thomas, 1980) or he is an uncouth but virile man consorting and copulating extra-maritally with a wealthy or cultured woman: '. . . being admonished . . . . for her public

Ugandan activities with her "rough trade" boyfriend' (*Private Eye*, April 1981).

round the bend mad
Mentally going out of sight: '"Keitel also is going round the bend," Jodl observed' (C. Forbes, 1983). In BI 'Harpic' means the same thing, from the brand name of the substance claimed to clean lavatories 'right round the bend'.

round objects you are wrong
A derisive riposte, punning on **balls** (q.v.) but not used of the testicles medically.

roundheels a sexually promiscuous woman
From the unsuccessful boxer who spends much of his time in the ring on his back, the shape of his heels facilitating his frequent falls: 'Little roundheels over there . . . . she's a blonde' (Chandler, 1951). Am.

routine (nursing) care only allow to die
Hospital jargon where extra medical care would only prolong suffering. In Am. 'no mayday' has the same implication, particularly of a patient who falls into a coma.

roving eye (a) a tendency towards extra-marital sexual activity
Usu. of males but recently also of women, and not referring to the ceaseless vigilance of a naval officer on watch: 'This was a predator, a huntress. Artemis for pants. Old Cap'n Hawley called it a "roving eye"' (Steinbeck, 1961).

rub off etc. to masturbate
Usu. of a male. Also as 'rub up': 'Lucy was standing between his legs and rubbing him up' (Sanders, 1982) and as 'rub yourself': '. . . he rubbed himself and the orgasm came' (Harris, 1925). In ob. use a 'rub off' was a single act of copulation.

rub out to kill
The act of erasing: 'Somebody rubbed him out this afternoon with a twenty-two' (Chandler, 1939).

rub the bacon etc. to copulate
One of the common 'meat' images: 'If (they) really did have the hots for each other, maybe Scoggins walked in on them while they were rubbing the bacon' (Sanders, 1979). Also as 'rub the pork': 'As long as you and I keep rubbing the pork' (Sanders, 1982, of a man and his sexual mistress).

rubber a male contraceptive sheath
The Am. word for what in BI is an inoffensive article of stationery. The word comes from the material and not from the 'rubbing'

of copulation: 'Inside my valise Are some rubbers and grease' (*Playboy's Book of Limericks*). Whence the advertisers' 'rubber goods': 'A druggist with a *Rubber Goods* sign taped to his window' (Theoroux, 1973). The Am. 'rubber cookies' is rare.

rubber heel a police detective
Also too of Am. private detectives, from the walking around quietly.

rubber tire *see* **spare tyre**

ruddy a mild oath
For 'bloody'. Properly, glowing with a pink hue: 'You ask for the impossible. You ask for the ruddy impossible' (Hemingway, 1941).

rude noise a belch or fart
Which a child may say it has made, or be reprimanded for making.

rug a wig worn by a male
The covering over a bare area: 'Your hair. It's beautiful. Is it a rug?' (Sanders, 1973). Whence the Am. fig. 'pull your rug' in handfuls etc., to be exasperated, but cf. **pull the rug**.

ruin to copulate with a female extra-maritally
The inference was that her marriageable worth had been lowered by the experience. 'I've often heard the boys boasting of having ruined girls' (Mayhew, 1851). Whence 'ruined (in character)', a woman known to have so copulated: '. . . seduced by shopmen, or gentlemen of the town, and after being ruined in character . . .' (Mayhew, 1862).

rumble to steal
Probably from the improvised seat at the back of a carriage from which servants might toss purloined goods to an associate on foot, and certainly a 'running rumbler' was 'A carriage-thief's confederate' (DSUE). Modern airline jargon too for the stealing of consumable stores by cabin staff: 'Methodically, the stewards first "rumble" the dry stores' (Moynahan, 1983).

run (1) to smuggle
As in the current 'gunrunning'. The OED devotes over 14 pages to 'run', which gives the etymologist a wide choice of derivations for any euphemism; this seems to have developed from the single voyage or excursion: 'You can lay aground by accident and run your goods' (Slick, 1836). A 'runner' was a smuggler and a 'run' is still an attempt to smuggle: 'A fine clear run . . . . all the goods snugly stowed away' (Ainslie, 1892).

run (2) to flee in defeat from a battlefield
The motion is away from the enemy, not towards him, and the usage is by the winners: 'What? do they run already? Then I die happy' (Wolfe, 1759, of his victory of Quebec – his eternal repose was no doubt disturbed two centuries later when the mean-minded descendants of the vanquished stooped to removing the stone which commemorated the place where he fell).

run (3) an unexpected and sustained series of demands on a bank for repayment
The phenomenon occurs when depositors lose confidence in a bank which has borrowed 'short' and lent 'long': '. . . if the run persisted, cash reserves would be exhausted and FMA obliged to close its doors' (Hailey, 1975).

run (4) to urinate or defecate
Usu. with urgency, needing to move fast. The 'runs', diarrhoea, is of the repeated urgency and perhaps the composition of the faeces: '. . . don't eat any of those goddamn grapes – they'll give you the runs' (Price, 1978). In genteel use, a 'runny tummy' is diarrhoea.

run (5) (the) peremptory dismissal from employment
From the supposed speed of your final departure. A mordant wit may give you your 'running shoes'.

run around with to copulate with extra-maritally and regularly
Properly no more than to consort with socially: 'Gus had walked out on her because she had been "running around" with a Party organiser' (McCarthy, 1963).

run away etc. permanently to leave the matrimonial home
Usu. of a wife but not always with or for another male: 'The fact that she did not even take her handbag with her is proof . . . . that she was not "running away"' (Murdoch, 1978). To 'run off' means the same thing, but is used of either sex, usu. when going to a new sexual partner: 'Rita's third husband had run off with a male dancer' (ibid.).

run into a bullet to be killed
Often used where there is a pretence that the killing was accidental: 'If it develops that a rival ran into a spare bullet while someone was practising target-shooting, that's just too bad' (Lavine, 1930).

run off the bathwater to urinate
As emptying a tub. A 'run-off' is urination.

run on (a) menstruation
Common female use of obvious imagery.

run out of steam to be sexually impotent
Of a male, with a suggestion of previous virility. The imagery is of an engine improperly fired: '. . . normal except they've run out of steam and can't make it with a woman any more' (Hailey, 1979).

run round the Horn repeatedly to mislead or deceive
Usu. of prolix evasion, from the fluctuating winds of the Cape which might frustrate the progress of a sailing ship: '"I won't run you around the Horn," Sandecker spoke quickly, "but I can't tell you any more than I already have"' (Cussler, 1984). Also of the movement of a newly-arrested person from one police cell to another to prevent access to a lawyer: 'By the time the lawyer finds out, we've moved him again. We waltz him "around the horn". It's an old routine' (Sanders, 1973). Am.

runner a policeman
Not merely in Bow Street or London, where many Victorian 'runners' were remarkable for their old age and immobility. Both they and the criminal classes took unkindly to Peel's transfer of his successful innovations in Dublin to the streets of London. (As with **run** (above) there are many euphemistic meanings for 'runner' – smuggler, fugitive, conveyer of illegal bets, journalist who makes irregular contributions, etc.).

running bear a mobile highway policeman
A CB amplification of **bear** (2) (above). Am.

runny tummy *see* **run** (4)

runs *see* **run** (4)

rural construction etc. the policing of conquered territory
An Am. Vietnam usage, and not of cottages in the countryside: 'Rural Construction is the old name for Revolutionary Development – the "workers" are paramilitary elements' (McCarthy, 1967). Similarly 'rural development' was the establishment of a community which you hoped did not support the Communists, often abbr. to 'RD': 'We sterilize the area prior to the insertion of the R.D. teams' (ibid.).

rush a growler *see* **growler-rushing**

rush job the marriage of a pregnant woman
The hastily arranged wedding is often to the putative father.

Russian duck a single act of copulation
Br. rh. sl. for 'fuck' and, in the way of these
things, probably punning on an element of
haste.

rusty rifle (a) syphilis
Br. army usage, likening an impediment in
the urethra to rust in the barrel. A soldier
found to have either was likely to be severely
disciplined. ? ob.

S

S and M a sexual deviation involving violence
The initials of 'sadism and masochism': 'The chap was into S and M. Well, "S" really. Very keen on spanking' (Theroux, 1982).

sack (the) dismissal from employment
A workman who had to provide his own tools kept them in a bag or sack at his employer's workshop. To be given it by the master was a token of dismissal: 'Sacked by a British bank for interfering with a woman in Fixed Deposits' (Theroux, 1973). An unsatisfactory member of the Sultan of Turkey's harem who 'got the sack' received more peremptory and drastic treatment; she was stitched up in one and thrown into the Bosphorus.

sad homosexual
Of males who are presumably no longer **gay** (q.v.): '... a giveaway, this time specially directed at the "Sad" community' (*Private Eye*, February 1984).

saddle to copulate
Of a male, with the common equine imagery: 'He had been saddling up with all the wenches on his estate and breeding bastards like a buck rabbit' (Fraser, 1970). In modern use perhaps more as 'get in the saddle': 'Just before they get in the saddle they say, "Okay, put your clothes on – you're under arrest"' (Theroux, 1973). A 'saddle-broken' woman is used to copulation: '... too bad she had a husband, of course, but at least she'd been saddle-broken' (Fraser, 1973). Specialist dictionaries tell us that a 'saddle' is a vagina but I have seen no literary use.

safe *see* **safety**

safe house a refuge for spies
Not merely a dwelling which is unlikely to collapse: 'The Russian spy master had a "safe house" for a time at 3 Rosary Gardens' (Boyle, 1979). In espionage jargon, 'secure house' is a synonym.

safety a male contraceptive sheath
Protecting from venereal disease and a paternity suit. Less often as a 'safe' although: 'Whether this is a covert invitation to "safe" sexual relations is unknown' (Pei, 1961). Am.

St Colman's girdle has lost its virtue
there has been extra-marital copulation
The mythical but magical garment encircled fully only those who were chaste. I include this ob. entry because it was the euphemism used in 1890 of the Irish Protestant patriot Parnell when he had formed an adulterous association with Mrs O'Shea. In the subsequent divorce case, he unwisely appeared without counsel – and was publicly disgraced. Thus was lost a unique influence and bridge in Anglo-Irish politics.

salami tactics
the elimination of non-Communists from a coalition
Communist jargon and specifically of the slicing away of non-Communists from the post-WWII Hungarian coalition government formed under Russian occupation.

saloon a place where intoxicants are drunk after purchase
Properly, it is no more than a hall. An Am. 'saloon' is almost any bar but the Br. 'saloon bar' is a better furnished, dearer and often drearier room than the public bar.

salt (1) to cheat by improper addition
From adding to food, to improve or disguise taste. Of a mine, where valuable minerals are introduced to misrepresent the worth; of an account, where wrong items are charged for; etc.

salt (2) powdered heroin
From its crystalline appearance. Am.

salt and pepper (1) adulterated marijuana
Of obvious derivation. Rarely too of other narcotics. Am.

sat and pepper (2) the police
From the chequered pattern of some uniforms or patrol cars. CB sl. Am.

salt and pepper (3) a Black consorting heterosexually with a White
From the contrasting pigmentation. In this Am. use, the male is usu. Black.

salute upon the lips a sexual kiss
19c. reticence when those who were 'free of their lips' were said also to be 'free of their hips': '... he repeatedly subjected me to the *assault* of his *salutes* upon my lips' (Fraser, 1977, writing in 19c. style).

salvage to steal
Properly, to save from fire, shipwreck or other disaster. In WW I and II 'salvage' became synonymous with looting, from

bombed or deserted buildings. Today it covers any stolen articles, particularly if they are later offered for sale in a market ouvert, where a buyer always acquires a good title even against the rightful owner in the BI.

Sam (1) a policeman
Especially if he is on counter-narcotic duties for 'Uncle Sam'.

Sam (2) a Black male who is submissive to Whites
Am. Black sl., from 'Little Black Sambo' and the common slave servant name.

samizdat *see* **self-publication**

sample urine
Medical jargon and an abbr. of 'sample of urine' which is needed for analysis.

San Quentin jail bait *see* **jail bait**

sanction an assassination
Properly no more than a penalty: '. . . he had performed a half-dozen counter-assassinations ("sanctions"in the crepuscular bureaucratese)' (Trevanian, 1973). Espionage jargon.

sanctum sanctorum *see* **holy of holies (2)**

sand rat a cheap whore
Br. Indian army use, from the squirrel-like mammal which infested *bashas*, or sleeping huts: 'The few cases that were contracted were with the Burmese and Chinese sand-rats' (Richards, 1936, of venereal disease).

sanguinary a mild oath
A rather laboured form of **bloody** (q.v.).

sanitary man a cleaner of lavatories
'Sanitary' means pertaining to health but to avoid confusion and loss of face the once properly styled Br. 'sanitary inspector' now calls himself a 'public health inspector': '. . . latrine buckets introduced which the sanitary men emptied every night' (Richards, 1933). The Am. 'sanitation man' remains a 'dustman' in BI.

sanitary napkin etc. a cloth worn during menstruation
Once again health and cleanliness are confused: 'Don't block the toilet with sanitary napkins' (Bradbury, 1959). 'Sanitary towel' is more common: 'She sold sanitary towels to the younger women in the pension, passing them over, wrapped in plain paper, with a secrecy that suggested a conspiracy' (Manning, 1977).

sanitary treatment embalming a corpse
Am. funeral jargon which ignores the fact that fresh corpses are aseptic: 'The use of the word "embalming" is best avoided. . . . other terms as "Temporary Preservation", "Sanitary Treatment", or "Hygienic Treatment"' (J. Mitford, 1963).

sanitized (1) cleaned
You read it on the irritating paper strips across lavatory bowls and tooth mugs in certain types of hotel which need to convince you that they tidy rooms between customers.

sanitized (2) destroyed
Espionage jargon, of evidence 'cleaned' out of the way.

sapphic a female homosexual
Sappho was the poetess who lived in Lesbos: 'I never picked you for a sapphic . . . . were you always that way?' (McCarthy, 1963). A 'Sappho' is a female homosexual, 'sapphism' is female homesexuality and a 'sapphic attachment' is such a relationship: 'A lady gym teacher with whom she had formed a Sapphic attachment' (Theroux, 1979) and: 'One of the fillies started an affair with a lady passenger . . . . I had to make up to an emigrant to tempt my Sappho back to me' (Londres, 1928, in tr.).

satin gin
From the supposed smoothness and the colour. Now rare except in brand names.

saturated drunk
Thoroughly soaked in intoxicants. Am.

sauce (the) an intoxicant
Usu. whisky and of excessive drinking and someone 'on the sauce' is an alcoholic: 'I had been on the sauce and behaving badly' (Theroux, 1978). A mainly Am. version of **gravy (1)** (above).

sauna parlour a brothel
Public wash-houses have catered for other masculine needs than cleanliness since antiquity but you are more likely to get a genuine sauna in a 'sauna parlour' than a massage in a massage parlour.

sausage a penis
Mainly nursery use, without sexual connotations. In the same society also a turd.

save spend
A commercial inducement to buy something you do not need because of a price reduction.

save it to refuse to copulate
Of a oman who permits passionate

embraces before marriage, but no more: 'A wet tongue kiss, a few minutes in their arms .... but – she was saving it for her husband' (Longstreet, 1951).

say a few words　to make a speech
Of indefinite duration. The pretence of an impromptu performance is often belied by the furtive production of notes.

scald　to infect with venereal disease
From the burning sensation, especially in the male, and you were likely to be so infected in the ob. Br. 'scalding-house' or brothel.

scalp　to kill
Originally the skull, and then the skin and hair covering it which Am. Indians removed as evidence and trophies.

scalp dolly　a wig
The 'dolly' is probably from the child's toy, rather than the spreading of the head of a rivet or a corruption of 'doily'. You use this Am. term only if someone else is wearing the wig.

scandal sheet　an expense claim
From the newspaper which is also likely to contain exaggerated or fictional episodes.

scare (the)　criminal extortion
From the intimidation of the victim and usu. as 'put the scare into'.

scarlet fever　lust for soldiers
I cannot exclude this rare treble pun, on the disease, the colour of the uniform and the activities of the 'scarlet woman': 'Nursemaids are always ready to succumb to the "scarlet fever". A red coat is all powerful with this class, who prefer a soldier to a servant' (Mayhew, 1862). London ob.

scarlet woman　a whore
From the woman 'arrayed in purple and scarlet colour .... THE MOTHER OF HARLOTS' (*Revelations* xvii) but any adulteress will do: 'The Colonel evidently objected to its presence in the house at the same time as his Scarlet Woman' (Sharpe, 1978). Our Protestant ancestors found it an abusive and useful epithet for the Roman Catholic church.

scatters (the)　diarrhoea
Of humans and animals. It probably comes from 'scate', 'a dysenterical disease in sheep' (EDD) although to 'scatter' was to urinate in ob. Br. dialect.

schmear *see* **smear** (1)

school　a prison
The Am. 'big school' is for men, the 'little school' for women and children.

scivvie　a whore
Properly, a female domestic servant and 'skivvy' in Br. spelling. The Am. 'skivvie-house' is a brothel: 'Little chickie workin' the skivvie houses' (Herr, 1977).

score (1)　to copulate with a woman extra-maritally
Usu. of a single episode and without payment: 'Brunton was all set to score with a Moral Philosophy student in his rooms – a female student' (Price, 1979). The punning 'know the score' is to be sexually experienced, of men and women.

score (2)　a successful crime
Both the act of robbing, cheating, pimping, etc. and the proceeds: 'At first .... we thought it was a junkie looking to score' (Sanders, 1985, of a murder – many crimes are committed by narcotic addicts desperate to obtain cash with which to buy illegal drugs).

Scotch mist　drunk
Br. rh. sl. for **pissed** (q.v.) from the drizzling cloud which blots out the landscape.

scour　to administer a laxative
Properly, to clean thoroughly the inside of anything. A beast with 'scour' has diarrhoea, which you also caught from a bad beer, or 'scour-the-gate': 'There's first guid ale, And second ale and some, Hink-skink and ploughman's drink, And scour-the-gate and trim' (Chambers, 1870).

(scrag　to kill or to assault comes from the meaning, a thin person whence a thin neck, whence hanging by the neck or garotting. A 19c. 'scragger' was a hangman.)

scratch (1)　the devil
Because of his propensity to 'seize rapaciously' (OED). Usu. as 'Old Scratch': 'Give over action to like old Scratch' (Slick, 1836).

scratch (2)　a wound
A brave soldier sought to minimize the extent of his injury: 'She gave a little scream. "You are wounded! Your arm!" "It's a scratch, nothing more"' (Fraser, 1970).

scratch (3)　to kill
In Am. to 'scratch' is to eliminate the name of a candidate from a list and there is a general meaning, to withdraw from a contest: 'I scratch the colonel in Hong Kong,

Corrigon shows up. I scratch Corrigon, there's the dame' (Diehl, 1978). Am.

screw (1) to copulate with
Of a male, from the entry into a fitting aperture: '"Well you, Howard," says Flora, "who did you screw last night?"' (Bradbury, 1975). But either sex may be said to 'screw around', to copulate indiscriminately: 'Blokes who screw girls who screw around a lot are usually blokes who screw around a lot' (Amis, 1978). A 'screw' is a male's sexual partner, always with a laudatory adjective – as I note elsewhere, in male vanity or fantasy, there are no 'bad screws'. 'Screwing' means copulation: 'Everyone gets laid, too, but that doesn't eliminate screwing as a subject' (Theroux, 1975). Also much fig. use as a synonym for 'fuck': 'She was drowned out by a chorus of "Screw the profiteers"' (Hailey, 1979).

screw (2) a prison warder
He turns the key: '. . . known as a hard-boiled "screw"' (Lavine, 1930). The Br. derivation is probably from the tightening of the screw on an apparatus on which a prisoner underwent forced exercise, or 'hard labour', in his cell.

screw loose (a) idiocy
Usu. of someone subject to insane delusions but not mad: 'He clearly had more screws loose than a drunk sapper' (Fraser, 1977). 'Screwy' implies a less serious condition: '"The girl is screwy," I said. "Leave her out of it"' (Chandler, 1958). The Am. 'screw factory' is an institution for the insane: '. . . had to be taken to the screw factory' (Wambaugh, 1975, of a lunatic).

screwed drunk
Probably a pun on **tight** (below): '. . . a glance sufficed to show even Philippa . . . . that he was undeniably screwed' (Somerville and Ross, 1897, of a drunkard). To be 'half-screwed' is to be no more sober.

screwed down dead
As the coffin is sealed after the last peep at the corpse: 'Then don't talk as if I'd been screwed down' (Cookson, 1967).

scrub to remove hesitation or error
Cleaning the tape of a pre-recorded speech so that the broadcast version does not say too much, or tell all the truth. Am.

scrubber a whore
Of the meaner sort and perhaps from the posture of the floor cleaner: 'Not all of them were scrubbers. Jane Wentworth wasn't . . . .

Marilyn would have fitted into that list of likely pick-ups' (Price, 1979). A London *Times* 1972 headline 'Heath's Whitehall Scrubbers' party' was changed in the second edition, before the office cleaners had time to instruct their lawyers, to 'Celebrating a whiter Whitehall'.

scrump to steal
Properly, to collect windfalls or other small apples to make 'scrumpy', rough cider. And in Somerset today we understand 'To goa a scrumpin, that is fetchin' apples off someboddy's trees' (Hallam, 1866).

sculpted manufactured
Advertisers' pretentiousness, seeking to imply that a forged, cast, turned, moulded or other machine-manufactured article has been produced through a sculptor's individual skill: 'Each is sculpted in a classic traditional pattern' (*Aspect*, October 1983, making an 'offer' of 'FREE! Solid Brass Candlesticks').

scupper a whore
Am. naval use, and it sometimes embraces amateurs. Properly, that part of the ship through which waste water is washed.

scuppered killed in battle
The etymology seems inappropriate because those so killed die involuntarily, while the essence of a 'scupper' is its planned egress.

sea food whisky
An Am. Prohibition use 'to mislead the police or strangers' (DAS). Most of it came by sea or via the Great Lakes. 'Sea food' today is snob catering jargon to avoid the downmarket connotations of 'fish and chips'. You may expect to order fish, molluscs and marine crustaceans, but not plankton or seaweed.

sea gull a whore
She follows the Am. fleet from port to port. Also used of similarly peripatetic wives and sweethearts.

sea lawyer *see* **barrack room lawyer etc.**

season the fixed period in which marriageable girls were publicly displayed
When a Br. girl with rich parents had to **come out** (q.v.): '"The Season" being a sort of ritual marriage market to which every parent then subscribed anxiously' (Blanch, 1954).

seat the buttocks
A transference from the thing you sit upon to the part on which you sit. With **bottom** (above) a very familiar coy evasion.

seat cover a nubile female in a car
Punning Am. CB sl.: 'Lay an eyeball on that
seat cover comin' up in that show-off lane'
(CBSLD).

secluded inconveniently isolated
Estate agents' jargon for a house with no
access to public transport, utilities, shops, etc.

seclusion involuntary solitary confinement
The subject does not seek his privacy. Jargon of violent criminals and lunatics.

second eye the anus
Am. homosexual use. For French homosexuals, the 'bronze eye'.

(second front the sea-borne invasion of N.
Europe in 1944 was a misnomer rather than
a euphemism. It reminds us of the extent to
which the Russians succeeded in persuading
their western allies to see things from their
perspective and conform to their designs.
Thus we discounted in our reckoning the
Burmese, Italian and other fronts, some of
which had been claiming Br. lives at a time
when Stalin and Hitler were dividing their
gains in E. Europe.)

second-strike retaliation
Nuclear jargon, and not a further blow from
the party making the **first strike** (q.v.). A
'second strike capability' is your theoretical
power to respond despite the devastation of
an attack.

secret parts the human genitalia
Those not normally revealed in company:
'*Hamlet*. Then you live about her waist, or in
the middle of her favours? *Guildenstern*
Faith, her privates we. *Hamlet*. In the secret
parts of Fortune? O, must true; she is a
strumpet' (Shakespeare, *Hamlet*). And *see*
private parts for Guildenstern's contribution to the ribald pun-swapping.

secret (state) police an instrument of
civil repression
The full phrase is a literal translation of
Geheime Staatspolizei, usu. abbr. to Gestapo.
Today a 'secret police' is a necessary adjunct
to any tyranny.

secret vice etc. self masturbation
Of either sex, although normally of a male:
'. . . the various lubricants I had used while
practicing the Secret Vice' (Styron, 1976).
Also as the 'secret' sin or indulgence.

secretary the sexual mistress of an
employer
Often a proximity relationship but it is also a
favoured title, especially where the parties

are travelling together: 'Wives, daughters
and mistresses too – documented as secretaries' (Deighton, 1978). To avert criticism,
I must explain that the majority of 'secretaries' do not perform for their employer the
dual role which was alluded to in the following exchange on a BBC 'Today' programme:
'*Editor of Cosmopolitan Magazine* (who had
advertised for a male secretary and was
being gently teased). It is said that a secretary is everything to a man that his wife is,
apart from sex. *Robert Robinson*. You think
so?'

section eight a military discharge for
mental instability
From US WW II Regulations: 'You hold on
. . . . Or you get shipped home on a Section
Eight' (Deighton, 1982, of WWII airmen).

secure house *see* **safe house**

security risk anyone you disagree with
Espionage jargon. The expression was
coined by the unbalanced US Senator
Joseph McCarthy to describe anyone politically to his left in public life – in practice just
about everybody.

security service a department for internal
espionage and repression
Properly, it should provide national protection against treachery, commercial protection against fraud and theft. For
Communists, it becomes a body concerned
more with the security of the rulers than of
the ruled.

seduce to copulate with a woman extra-
maritally
Properly, to persuade a vassal to break vows
of loyalty and, in the days of chaperoning,
seductions were mainly limited to wives: 'By
long and vehement suit I was seduced To
make room for him in my husband's bed'
(Shakespeare, *King John*). The word is now
used even if the woman consents without
'long and vehement suit'.

see (1) to copulate with extra-maritally
Of either sex, from the sense to visit: '. . . it
was true, yes, she *was* seeing another man.
She *was* in love with another man' (McBain,
1981). Also as prostitutes' jargon, where it is
no more remarkable than a lawyer 'seeing' a
client or a dentist 'seeing' a patient. To 'see
company' is explicit.

see (2) to satisfy by bribery
Usu. as the Am. 'see' the doorman, the cops,
etc.: '. . . doing business without "seeing the
cops"' (Lavine, 1930). Lavine also uses 'see'

for passing part of a bribe to a superior:
'Woe to the cop who collects anything . . . .
and doesn't "see the sergeant" ' (ibid.).

see a man about a dog to go to any place
the subject of taboo
Probably from dog fancying. Your destination depends on the company you are with
– a lavatory in mixed company; an inn, in the
presence of your family at home; home, if
parting from friends who are staying
together drinking; etc.

see the rosebed etc. to urinate out of
doors
Of a male at night, usu. in mixed company
when the lavatory is reserved for females.
Others may 'see' the compost heap, the view,
the vegetable garden, or whatever. But to
'see your aunt' is to defecate, in female use,
punning on **aunt** (2) (above).

seed the male semen
That which is sown: 'She that sets seeds and
roots of shame and iniquity' (Shakespeare,
Pericles, with his penchant for vulgar puns)
and in modern use: 'I felt my seed coming'
(Harris, 1925).

seen better days poor
Usu. of those commanding sympathy
because their poverty has succeeded
affluence. Of machinery it means worn out.

seepage the amount stolen from a retail
store
Properly, the liquid which has slowly
escaped from a container. Now the jargon of
supermarkets.

segregation the availability of inferior
facilities for a minority ethnic group
Properly, no more than separating one thing
from another. A dysphemism for giving
Whites better conditions than Blacks.

segregation unit a cell for solitary confinement
Am. prison jargon.

select capable of being offered for sale
Shopkeepers' jargon for perishable commodities like tomatoes, which are unsaleable
if rotten. Things so described have rarely
been subjected to any process of selection.
For an estate agent, 'select' also means
better than average – you can reject any
inference that there has been any discrimination in their choice of what they will sell.

selective indiscriminate
Of various military activities, where you wish
to play down the horror. 'Selective

ordnance' is usu. napalm, less widely
destructive than a nuclear blast but hardly
discriminating. A 'selective' strike or
response is one where you don't wipe out all
your enemy. 'Selective facts' are lies.

self-abuse etc. masturbation
Usu. of a solitary male, from the supposition
that it may damage his health or his soul: '. . .
two of them being pretty hopeless cases
through self-abuse' (Richards, 1936). 'Self-
gratification' is rare: 'Nor would loutish self-
gratification quell this imperious, feverish
desire' (Styron, 1976 – the 'desire' was to
copulate). 'Self-indulgence' properly means
giving yourself an undeserved treat: 'Pan-
dora says she is not going to risk being a
single parent . . . . So I will have to fall back
on self-indulgence' (Townsend, 1982).
'Self-pollution' and 'self-pleasuring' are
perhaps ob. 'Self-love' usu. refers only to
female masturbation and does not imply that
she is also narcissistic.

self-catering you buy and prepare your
own meals
Jargon of the tourist industry – you wash up
as well. Often not much of a 'holiday' for the
mother of the family.

self-defence an unannounced military
attack
Specifically the explanation by Iraq for its
September 1980 attack on Iran.

self-deliverance etc. suicide
'Self-deliverance' is the preferred usage of
the supporters of euthanasia but you also find
'self'-execution, immolation or termination.

self publication the circulation of uncen-
sored writings
A translation of the Russian 'samizdat':
'They called it *samizdat*, "self-publishing", a
spoof on the name of the state publishing
house, Godizdat' (Moss, 1985). Uncontrolled printing and duplicating are forbidden in
Communist countries which in some degree
isolates their citizens from truth or independent thought, but severely curtails the
efficient transaction of business.

self-regulation the introduction of that
amount of discipline and openness which
will suffice to ward off statutory control
Used of the City of London's manoeuvres to
stay without the law despite the venality of
traders, bankers etc. Rarely, too, of other
trades.

sell out to betray
But not necessarily for cash: 'You'll sell me

out fast. And you won't have any five thousand dollars' (Chandler, 1958). A 'sell-out' is such a betrayal or, to an extremist, any settlement of a labour dispute.

sell yourself etc. to copulate extra-maritally for payment
Correctly viewed, the transaction is at best one of hire, lease or licence: 'This woman went out on the streets . . . . to keep them both alive . . . . so she sells herself' (Bradbury, 1959). Others may 'sell' their back, body or desires: 'A housewife that, by selling her desires, Buys herself bread and clothes' (Shakespeare, *Othello*). Today too some homosexual use.

send ashore to dismiss from the navy
For misconduct on land or sea.

send down (1) to dismiss from university
The opposite of 'up', in residence. Usu. done because of misconduct or failure to achieve minimal results: 'When I was an undergraduate you got sent down if you were caught riveting a dolly' (Sharpe, 1974).

send down (2) *see* **down the line** (1)

send down the road to dismiss from employment
Usu. at short notice, of one of many employees. Used by employees rather than employers but only heard in BI today among older people.

send home etc. to kill
A Christian might also be 'sent' to heaven, his long account, the skies or other posthumous destinations; an Am. Indian to his happy hunting ground; a Chinese to the happy land: 'The only successful way to get rid of a competitor . . . . is to send him to the happy land of his forefathers by having him "put on the spot"' (Lavine, 1930) or you might 'send him to the land of the lotus blossom' (ibid.). So too for other religions and cultures.

send in your papers as an officer prematurely to retire
From the fig. return to the sovereign of the commission once addressed individually to each Br. officer: '. . . I've put up a fearful black? I'm not sure I shan't have to send in my papers' (P. Scott, 1975).

send over the edge to drive mad
The 'edge of sanity', I suppose, and usu. of a person whose mental balance is already questionable: 'A mental hospital would send him over the edge' (Bradbury, 1959).

send to the showers *see* **take an early bath**

send up to pass a prison sentence upon
An abbr. for 'send up the line' or 'river'. That is where the prisons were and convicts in New York and New Orleans ended up. To 'send up' is also to ridicule and as you may also 'deflate' those whom you 'send up', the etymology is elusive.

senior citizen an old person
In most of Am. over 55 and in Br. a woman over 60 and a man over 65: 'I told them to send half a dozen senior citizens who look a bit sad and just a little threadbare' (L. Thomas, 1979). But do not so describe a High Officer of State, a General or even the geriatric President. Also abbr. to 'seniors': 'Discover Tunisia in the Luxury of our air-conditioned Coach. Seniors a Speciality' (le Carré, 1986 – and suckers too, it would seem, unless I have missed a new meaning of 'discover').

sensible ugly or unfashionable
Of female shoes and clothes, with supposed transference from the wearer: 'Her breasts, neatly harnessed under a dark sweater, did not swing as she walked. She wore the ultimate in "sensible" shoes' (Irvine, 1986).

sensitive payment a bribe
Not the 'sensitive' of police or espionage jargon, meaning secret, but because of its general impropriety and probable illegality in the hands of the recipient. Usu. of excessive 'commissions' etc. paid to Arab or African politicians, princes or other fixers.

sent drunk or under narcotic influence
The subject enjoys another state of consciousness, if not unconscious. Am.

separate to dismiss from employment
Properly, to cause to part, which is I suppose what the employer does. SE too of the voluntary parting of husband and wife during marriage.

separate development the perpetuation of the political and economic supremacy of Whites in S. Africa
The 'apartheid' of the Afrikaans. Despite their economic interdependence Blacks and Whites may not live in the same districts or intermingle. In 19c. Am. the Blacks were 'separate but equal' after the abolition of slavery, which too ensured that they were separate and unequal.

seraglio as brothel
Properly, the palace of the Turkish sultan in

the Golden Horn, of which a part only was the 'harem', or secret spot.

sergeant *see* **top sergeant**

serious credibility gap *see* **credibility gap**

serpent *see* **stung by a serpent**

serum an intoxicant
Properly, the fluid part of the blood after clotting. WWII army usage.

servant a slave
An example of 19c. Am. euphemism which reminds us that these conditions obtained not so very long ago.

serve to copulate with
Properly of male animals but a fruitful ground for innuendo as in the Br. television comedy series set in a store and entitled 'Are you being served?': 'It was a pity there wasn't time and leisure, or I'd have served her as I had once before' (Fraser, 1969, of copulation). Specifically as 'serve your lust': 'I would we had a thousand Roman dames At such a bay; by turn to serve our lust' (Shakespeare, *Titus Andronicus*).

service (1) to copulate with
A rarer form of **serve** (above): 'Aldo had walked in while he was servicing the cigarette girl over his desk' (Collins, 1981). Whence the punning Am. 'service station', a brothel. In SE 'service' is arranged copulation by a male mammal, usu. a stallion or bull.

service (2) a charge additional to the cost of the goods supplied
Levied on you in restaurants etc. regardless of the quality of the attendance. The roadside 'service station' is a misnomer as the motorist is usu. expected to attend to his own needs, except where he finds the apparently tautological announcement 'Attended Service'.

service of military investigation an instrument of repression and torture
Specifically the 1937 Spanish Communist 'Servicio de Investagacion Militar' which provided in its prison cells 'lights to dazzle, noises to deafen, baths to freeze, clubs to beat' (H. Thomas, 1961).

services no longer required dismissal from employment
The blow is supposed to be softened by an inference that the function no longer exists: 'I was given a discharge, ostensibly on the grounds that my services "were no longer

required", this being a curious euphemism' (R. V. Jones, 1978).

set back to have to pay a cost which you cannot easily afford
From the proper meaning, to cause a reverse or relapse: 'Then luncheon, that set me back considerably' (N. Mitford, 1960).

set up (1) to provide living accommodation for a sexual mistress.
From the meaning, to establish or initiate: 'When Christine refused to leave Ward and be set up in a flat, he ceased to meet her' (Green, 1979, of Profumo).

set up (2) to incriminate falsely
As with skittles, for the purpose of knocking them down again: 'They "set up" MacLennan in an attempt to discredit him' (*Private Eye*, July 1980).

set up shop on Goodwin Sands to be shipwrecked off the Kent coast
A low-lying island of some 4,000 acres lying in the English Channel was taken from the Anglo-Saxon Earl Godwin by the Norman conquerors and handed to clerics who neglected the sea walls, a great storm overwhelming it in the year 1100. Since then it has remained a hazard to shipping, emerging above the waves to a varying extent at each low tide. ? ob.

settle to kill
Properly, to reach a conclusion: 'Jack Plenty had settled the Balagnini with a lovely backhand cut' (Fraser, 1977, of a killing).

seven-year-itch a wish for extra-marital sexual variety
Seven years is the classic period of change: 'Time's pace is so hard that it seems the length of seven years' (Shakespeare, *As You Like It*), and *see* **itch**.

sewn up (1) pregnant
Perhaps from the meaning, finally arranged, or from the appearance of a bale packed in sacking. BI.

sewn up (2) drunk
Like a corpse prepared for burial in sacking? Am.

sex (1) copulation
Heterosexually of the male or female: 'I could have asked to wash after sex' (Green, 1979) and also used homosexually.

sex (2) the penis or vagina
From the reproductive functions: 'I rubbed my hot sex against her little button' (Harris, 1925) and: '"Oh, how lovely your sex is!" I

exclaimed . . . . my left hand drew down her head for a long kiss while my middle finger still continued its caress' (ibid.).

sexual act *see* **act (the)** etc.

sexual ambiguity having heterosexual and homosexual tastes
'Ambiguity' in this phrase does not usu. imply doubt or uncertainty – rather it indicates an excess of catholicism: '. . . overstressing his sexual ambiguity, even his deviance with regard to drugs' (Davidson, 1978).

sexual equality the disregard of physical or psychological differences between men and women
The theory is to protect women from exploitation at work; the practice in private employment is to restrict the jobs open to women or in public employment, to put policewomen on riot control duty: '. . . combined classes of bricklayers and nursery nurses so that there was sexual quality' (Sharpe, 1979).

sexual intercourse etc. copulation
Not dealings or conversations between people of either sex but a genteel and journalistic cliché: 'If he gets pinched with a girl in a hotel room, stop sexual intercourse' (Chandler, 1953). 'Sexual commerce' is even more genteel, archaic even, and you don't get paid for your services. 'Sexual knowledge' is legal jargon and does not refer to telling the young about the birds and the bees. 'Sexual relations' may also imply familiarities short of copulation and 'sexual relief' refers to male copulation only, implying that his health might suffer from an excess of celibacy. All these concepts are further explored under **intercourse, commerce, know** and **have** (above).

sexual preference homosexuality
Not of men who prefer blondes or brunettes or of women who fancy moustache-laden kisses: '. . . impossible to ask questions about (as they said on the current affairs programmes) Ron's "sexual preference" ' (Keneally, 1985).

sexual proclivity a sexual preference which is not heterosexual
The phrase could refer to the most traditional of arrangements, but doesn't: 'She discovered her boyfriend's, uh, sexual proclivities' (Sanders, 1986 – he was also homosexual).

sexual variety promiscuity
It does not mean having both male and female forms rather than being hermaphrodite.

shack up to cohabit and copulate extra-maritally
A 'shack' is a roughly built rural residence but the arrangment usu. has a degree of permanence: 'Why not shack up together? . . . . I don't got to drive so far, you got fun' (Bradbury, 1965 – his New York cabbie, in suggesting that they shared a hotel room, misused both the phrase and the verb to get).

shade (1) to reduce in price
Shopkeepers' jargon, making the asking price a 'shade less than it was'. You meet the use in the kind of store where haggling is taboo.

shade (2) a dealer in stolen goods
In Am. underworld speech, he provides some cover for the thief.

shaft to copulate with
Of a male, probably from the insertion of a spindle in a bore: '. . . he was out drinking or shafting someone older and uglier than she was' (Sanders, 1977). A 'shaft' is also a penis or a vagina viewed sexually, the one from the handle of a tool: 'As you thrust your shaft in and out of me, I felt a strange sort of pleasure' (Harris, 1925) and the other from a void in which an object may be inserted or move, such as an elevator shaft.

shag (1) to copulate with
Perhaps from the old meaning to shake or wrestle with – the cormorant is certainly not a renowned sexual performer. Men usu. do the 'shagging': 'Out shagging some quiff' (Sanders, 1982) although they may also be heard to say that a woman 'shags like a rattlesnake' in a cliché which employs daunting imagery. To 'be shagged' of a woman is to be fucked but, of a man, to be weary from any form of toil or exercise.

shag (2) to masturbate
Usu. of boys, again from the shaking. The 19c. Eng. dialect 'shag-boy' was a ghost: 'Fairies and shag-boys! lasses are often skeart at them' (EDD).

shake (1) to rob
By violence or trickery: 'How much you shake him for?' (Chandler, 1953). To 'shake down' is to cheat or rob through deceit, usu. without violence: 'Find out what they're all trying to shake us down for?' (Bradbury, 1976) and a 'shakedown' is a scheme which

defrauds a victim: 'It was a shakedown. For a two-hundred-dollar camera Sony made a hundred and the girl made a hundred' (Theroux, 1973).

shake (2) an arrest
In Am. police jargon, usu. on trivial grounds to show activity or to fill a quota: 'We ain't got no shakes yet today . . . . Maybe we better write a couple of F.I.'s?' (Wambaugh, 1981).

shake hands with the bishop etc. to urinate
Of a male, whose uncircumcised penis may resemble the chessman: 'Help me to the toilet . . . . I have to go and shake the bishop's hand' (Theroux, 1979, quoting Borges). Others may 'shake hands' with their best friend, their wife's best friend or the unemployed.

shake the bushes etc. to watch out for highway police
On Am. CB radio, you entrust this duty to the leading truck in a convoy. Or he may be asked to 'shake' the leaves or trees.

shake the pagoda tree to make a rapid fortune in India
As a foreign colonist and perhaps by dishonest means, punning on the 'pagoda', an Indian gold coin: '. . . won handsome fortunes by "Shaking the Pagoda Tree", by the private trade that then was permitted to John Company's servants' (*Spectator*, 1912, quoted in ODEP – 'John Company' was the East India Company which conquered most of India before handing it over to the Br. crown, demonstrating the truism that the flag follows trade). ob.

shakedown *see* shake

shakes (the) a symptom of a chronic alcoholic
Euphemistic, if at all, in so far as it seeks to minimize the shameful delirium tremens.

shame extra-marital copulation by a woman
What disgraced the female party did not seem to disgrace the male: 'Is't not a kind of incest, to take life From thine own sister's shame?' (Shakespeare, *Measure for Measure*). And 'the shame' was once the devil: 'The shame be on's' (Beattie, 1801).

shanghai to kidnap
Properly, to render senseless and carry on board ship as a crew member from the crime-ridden Chinese city, because some of the crew you arrived with might be absent when you came to sail: 'He'd rue the day he shanghaied me aboard his lousy slave-ship'

(Fraser, 1971) but used of any forceful removal: '. . . shanghai'd might be a more accurate description for all that had happened to her during the last 24 hours' (Price, 1982).

share a bed to copulate
Usu. extra-maritally when it is assumed that such a proximity will always overcome chastity or disinclination: 'I say you share his bed – *puta*' (Deighton, 1981).

share affections knowingly to copulate with someone who is contemporaneously regularly copulating with another
Of either sex: 'The mistress even suggested that his wife should contemporaneously share his affections' (*Daily Telegraph*, 1979).

share favours with to copulate with extra-maritally
In this case the 'sharing' is between the donor and another: 'And who does she pick to share her favours with' (Bogarde, 1981).

share pusher *see* push (4)

sharp and blunt the vagina
Rh. sl. but used only, I think, in the phrase 'a bit of sharp and blunt', a single act of copulation.

sharp with the pen inclinded to overcharge
Of lawyers or retailers who charge 'what the traffic will bear' and, in the latter case, especially when old price tags are changed to reflect inflation.

sharpen your pencil (1) to distort figures in published accounts
This falls short of criminal falsification but involves taking that view on stock valuation, bad debt reserves, etc. which tends towards the desired outcome, showing higher profits or a stronger balance sheet.

sharpen your pencil (2) to alter your stance in bargaining
A commercial usage and injunction to a seller who is asking too much, or a buyer who is offering too little.

sharpen your skates to urinate
One of the improbable excuses for going outside, this time from Am.

sharpener an intoxicant
Usu. whisky and gin, which are supposed to liven you up: 'I managed to escape from Colditz for a sharpener or twain with the Major at the RAC Club' (*Private Eye*, May 1981).

sheath a contraceptive worn by a male
Properly, the covering in which a blade is kept: 'It was typical of Murray to call it a sheath, he thought' (Boyd, 1981 – Murray was a rather pompous Scot).

shed a tear to urinate
Of either sex, I suppose from the bodily secretion of fluid.

sheet a record of criminal convictions
Police jargon, from the paper on which they are written although today we probably are more likely to have a disk: 'A sheet that might inc¹ ⅃e gambling arrests, maybe some boosting' (Sanders, 1973).

sheet in the wind (a) mildly drunk
Even landlubbers know that the 'sheet' is a rope tying a sail to a spar, and not the sail itself. If one or more are loose, the vessel is in some disarray: 'A thought tipsy – a sheet in the wind' (Trollope, 1862). I have never met a drunkard 'two sheets in the wind' although some are 'four' and even more 'three': 'An American lady who was three sheets in the wind said I looked like a movie actor' (Theroux, 1973).

sheets copulation
On the marriage, or any other, bed: 'Happiness to their sheets' (Shakespeare, *Othello*).

shell shock *see* battle fatigue

shellacked very drunk
Properly, covered with shellac, a varnish which is stoved to give a glazed appearance. Mainly Am.

sheltered for those unable to look after themselves
Of accommodation where staff is available to supervise and help geriatrics or invalids who are no longer self-sufficient and whose families cannot or will not help them. In fact, every building is 'sheltered', by its roof and walls.

shelved dismissed from employment
Normally of those asked to retire early through declining powers '. . . so that men who lack drive and imagination can, without undue cruelty, be shelved' (Colville, 1986).

sheriff's hotel a prison
An Am. use now ob. in BI where the post of sheriff is mainly honorific. If you 'danced' at a 'sheriff's ball', you were killed by hanging.

sherpa a senior civil servant
He carries the fig. burden for his Br. political boss.

shield a police badge
And by transference, an Am. policeman or his authority.

shift (1) defecation
From the sense, a movement and usu. as 'do a shift' in male use.

shift (2) to copulate
Again I suppose from the movement involved: 'Let we shift . . . . You give baby me' (Theroux, 1971).

ship to dismiss from employment or to expel from college
Am. commercial imagery, from the dispatch of goods.

ship's lawyer *see* barrack-room lawyer

shirtlifter a bugger
Ignoring the daily occasions on which normal and upright men properly lift their shirts or shirttails: '. . . when you sup with a shirtlifter you should use a very long spoon' (*Private Eye*, January 1987).

(shit is used derogatively of anything which you may disapprove of, and especially of an unwelcome piece of information or poor-grade illicit narcotics: '. . . a junkie with a snootful of shit' (Sanders, 1985).)

shock worker a political prisoner sentenced to forced labour
Communist jargon and an example of what Marx called 'extraeconomic coercion'. A 'shock brigade' is a group of such prisoners.

shoot (1) to kill by a firearm
The word, which may also mean to wound, implies an accurate aim by the person who does the shooting: 'He was condemned to death and shot within two hours' (Goebbels, 1945, in tr.). In BI hunting with a gun is also called 'shooting', 'hunting' being reserved for chasing after foxes on horseback: 'Charles Edouard is shooting, which he calls hunting' (N. Mitford, 1960).

shoot (2) peremptory dismissal from employment
Perhaps a pun on discharge – *see* fire – or from the velocity with which you finally leave your place of work.

shoot (3) diarrhoea in cattle
From its expulsion: 'It piss'd the bed, and shute the bed' (Graham, 1883). ? ob.

shoot (4) to inject an illegal narcotic intravenously
From the direct passage into a vein. To 'shoot gravy' is to inject after mixing the narcotic with your own blood and heating both. A

'shooting gallery' is where you may obtain illegal narcotics.

shoot a lion to urinate
Of a male, usu. out of doors. In Am. you may also say you are going to 'shoot a dog'.

shoot off etc. to ejaculate semen
Usu. prematurely under intense sexual excitement: 'I had to change my underwear when I got back here. That's right. I shot off in my drawers' (Diehl, 1978). The punning 'shoot over the stubble' is to ejaculate in a woman's pubic hair. To 'shoot your roe' refers to any ejaculation. A 'shot' is an ejaculation: 'It's the only one where you get three shots for your money: The shot upstairs (fellatio). The shot downstairs (vaginal copulation), And the shot in the room (whisky)' (Longstreet, 1956, of a brothel). The ob. 'shoot between wind and water' was to infect with venereal disease, puning on the crippling shot to a sailing ship.

shoot the agate to seek out a woman for copulation
From an affected form of strutting used in Black Am. parades which was so named. Am.

shoot the cat to become drunk
Properly, to vomit from any cause. There were many Br. phrases linking cats, vomiting and drunkenness.

shoot the moon *see* **moonlight flit etc.**

shoot with a silver gun to be unable to provide meat by hunting
In season, a Br. gentleman was supposed to be able to keep his family well, and his retainers occasionally, supplied with game birds: 'Shooting with a *silver gun* is a saying among game eaters. That is to say, *purchasing* the game' (Cobbett, 1823). And *see* **catch fish with a silver hook**.

shooting gallery *see* **shoot (4)**

shop (1) to dismiss from employment
The etymology eludes me. Am. ? ob.

shop (2) to give information which leads to arrest
You would think from selling it, but a lot of 'shopping' is done out of malice or self-protection: 'I would have shopped the fellow in an instant . . . . He was most impertinent' (Wilson, 1915). A 'cop shop' is a police station.

shop door is open (the) your trousers are unfastened
An oblique warning to another male, of buttons or zip.

shoplift *see* **lift (1)**

short a spirituous intoxicant
Abbr. for 'short drink', as different from beer: 'A pint of beer, or a glass of "short" (neat gin)' (Mayhew, 1851 – but today 'shorts' are any kind of spirits).

short-arm inspection an examination for venereal disease among men
Punning on the 'small arms inspection' of rifles etc. and the 'short-arm', or penis: 'Periodical medical checks, known as short-arm inspections' (Allen, 1975).

short hairs the pubic hair
Even though they may be more luxuriant than those on the legs etc. The use is almost always in a fig. cliché: 'I think I've got them by the short hairs' (Sharpe, 1974). The 'short and curlies' is specific.

short time etc. a single act of copulation
Prostitutes' jargon for a contract with few preliminaries and no sequel: 'The price for a short time with massage stayed the same' (Theroux, 1973). Less often as a 'short session': 'She's short sessions. Never lets a man stay for more than half an hour' (Archer, 1979). If the hotel clerk asks you whether you need a room for a 'short time' or a 'short-term' occupation etc., he suggests you will use the room for such activity and he will charge you accordingly: 'An overnight stay, sir? Or a short-term residency?' (Keneally, 1985).

shortening the front line (1) retreating under pressure
Soldiers thus excuse a defeat by inferrring that a salient is being voluntarily abandoned.

shortening the front line (2) slimming
Punning on the military euphemism (above) and usu. of fat men.

shorts (the) indigence
Usu. of a temporary nature, short of cash until the next pay day: '. . . if you get the shorts, don't be bashful about asking me for help' (Sanders, 1986). sl.

shot (1) *see* **shoot off etc.**

shot (2) a measure of spirituous intoxicant
I think from the method of discharging, or 'shooting', it into the glass. Frequently in Am., but less so as the years pass, an imprecise measurement depending on your relationship with the barkeep.

shot (3) a narcotic taken illegally
By injection: 'The keepers could sell the

balance . . . . to other prisoners in need of a shot' (Lavine, 1930).

shot (4) drunk
Probably from the sl. meaning, finished or exhausted although the variant 'shot away' suggests derivation from wounding. However drunk, you are unlikely to be ever more than 'half shot': '. . . unlimited wine being dispensed in all the public buildings. The whole population seemed to be half-shot' (Fraser, 1970).

shot in the tail pregnant
A rather tasteless multiple pun.

shot while trying to escape *see* **trying to escape**

shotgun marriage etc. the marriage of a pregnant woman to the baby's father
The man is supposed to come to the altar under duress: 'Princess Caroline of Monaco is finding it impossible to secure an annulment of her 1978 marriage . . . . made even more difficult following a shotgun marriage last December to Italian Stefano Casiraghi' (*Private Eye*, August 1984). Less often as 'shotgun wedding'.

shout (1) (the) peremptory dismissal from employment
Employees still say they have 'had the shout', even if dismissed *sotto voce* or by letter.

shout (2) an obligation to pay for a round of intoxicants
Not euphemistic if you take your turn but perhaps so of someone said 'not to pay his shout' – he cadges from others. To 'shout yourself hoarse' is to be drunk, from having ordered too many drinks.

shove (1) to copulate
Of a male, from the common pushing imagery.

shove (2) (the) peremptory dismissal from employment or courtship
No physical ejection or rejection can be assumed.

shove over to kill
Properly, to overthrow: 'Did you – did anybody – have any idea that she was gonna get shoved over?' (Diehl, 1978). Am.

show (1) to menstruate
Usu. of animals and especially used of mares when breeding is planned. A 'show', menstruation, is a common female usage.

show (2) a battle
Mainly WWI use, minimizing the danger by

reference to a theatrical production: '"I am watching the show over on our right." Some of our new divisions . . . . had advanced through a gap (Richards, 1933).

show your charms as a whore to seek a customer
She may in public reveal more than chaster women but less than the term might suggest, until terms have been agreed: 'A woman was showing a man her private charms, and inviting him to enjoy them' (Masters, 1976).

showers the offer of deviant sexual activities
An Am. code word in the advertisement of prostitutes, from the penchant of some males for sexual antics under jets of water, or, rarely, urine.

shrink *see* **head-shrinker**

shrinkage the amount stolen from retail stores
Properly, a reduction in weight or volume of packed goods due to settlement or dehydration. Retailers' jargon, especially of thefts or embezzlement in supermarkets.

shuffle off this mortal coil to die
The Bard said it first: '. . . left a hundred grand when he shuffled off his mortal coil' (Sanders, 1966). (A distinguished critic has suggested that by being economical with my references, I ask too much of my readers. I prefer to continue to assume that they know what Carlyle threw at his wife, when Churchill adopted the 'Iron Curtain' imagery, and where among his works Shakespeare turned ordinary words into magic.)

sick menstruating
A slightly rarer variant of **ill** (1) (above).

sick leave an additional vacation taken by public servants
Where public employees are entitled to pay for a given number of days in any year when absent due to sickness, the time they spend on recovery and recuperation closely approximates to the days available.

sick out a strike by public service employees
Those prevented by Am. law or contract from going on strike may pretend to be absent due to illness.

side orders sexual practices of unusual or depraved nature
From the dishes served additionally to a main course: 'Alvin C. had been having no

side orders of sex; no arguments either, or drink or drugs' (Davidson, 1978 – although the phrase here could refer to his not copulating outside marriage).

sides pads worn to accentuate a woman's figure
From the days when men seemed to be attracted to wider hips: 'She pulled off a pair of "sides", artificial hips she wore to give herself a good figure' (L. Armstrong, 1954).

sight deprived blind
Perhaps no more than circumlocution despite: 'The blind are now "sight-deprived" as if to refute any suspicion that they got that way voluntarily' (Jennings, 1965).

sigma phi syphilis
Medical jargon from the Greek letters used in shorthand, which also conceals the diagnosis from some of the patients.

sign the pledge to renounce the drinking of intoxicants
Formerly a public renunciation of the 'demon drink' in chapel lore, but now used humorously usu. by those professing remorse after drunkenness. You might also, with less formality, 'take the pledge': 'If they ever start the Little White Ribboners in Russia, all the members will have to be boys, for they'll never get the women to take the pledge' (Fraser, 1973).

silver an unskilled Black worker
ob. Am. local usage in the Panama Canal Zone: 'Race was expressed by the Panama Canal Company not in terms of black and white but by the designations gold and silver. The euphemism was derived from the way workers were paid: the unskilled workers, most of them black, were paid in silver, the skilled workers, nearly all white Americans, were paid in gold' (Theroux, 1979).

simple of small intelligence
Not just lacking knowledge and experience, as in Simple Simon's commercial exchange with the Pieman. 'Simple' is now widely used of idiots considered fit to remain in society.

sin to copulate extra-maritally
Properly, to commit a forbidden act but, since St Paul's obsession with that kind of wrongdoing, now Christian use for any activity which is taboo sexually: 'Most dangerous Is that temptation that doth goad us on To sin in loving virtue' (Shakespeare, *Measure for Measure*). 'Sinful' then means relating to such copulation, as in 'sinful

commerce' and *see* 'live in sin' *under* **live as man and wife** etc.

sing as a criminal to give information to the police
From the imagery of the song-bird in the cage, of your own misdeeds, or of other criminals: '. . . had him under the lights all fuckin' night . . . . and about nine this morning he starts singin' like Frank Sinatra' (Diehl, 1978).

singer a whore
It is a calling to which many prostitutes lay claim, although I am sure that most professional singers lead lives of impeccable and familial virtue. The use comes from the ambience in which they have to work: 'The actress and the singer were considered nothing more than prostitutes with a sideline' (Longstreet, 1956).

singles a chance for people divorced, unmarried or apart from a spouse to meet another person heterosexually
From 'single', unmarried, although women tend on these occasions to hunt in pairs. Thus in Am. you find 'singles' bars, nights and joints where the participants look for anything from a drinking or dancing partner to copulation or marriage: 'Used to be a singles joint but lately it's turned really rough' (Deighton, 1981).

sink a lavatory
Properly, a drain or cesspit: 'Usuph pretended to wander off to the regimental sinks' (Keneally, 1979, writing in 19c. style). ? ob.

sink the soldier to copulate
Of a male, whose 'soldier', an erect penis, is 'standing to attention'.

sip a drink of intoxicant
Properly, anything drunk in small quantities: 'By the time they had had a few sips there was damned little left for us' (Richards, 1933, of a rum ration). The Sc. and N. Eng. 'siper', a drunkard, came from 'sipe', to soak: 'The Hivverby lads at fair drinking are seypers' (Anderson, 1808).

siphon off to steal
Usu. of embezzlement: 'No way he could have spent more than half of what was coming in . . . . The best guess was that Birdsong . . . . was siphoning it off' (Hailey, 1973). Also literally, in the Br. spelling 'syphon', of stealing petrol from motor vehicles.

siphon the python *see* **syphon the python**

sissy a male homosexual
An Am. version of **cissy** (above): 'Little
teeny sissy with gold hair. Looks enough like
a girl to be a queen' (Wambaugh, 1983).

sister a whore
In the Far East pimps claim this kinship: '. . .
pimps accosting you . . . . with promises of
their sister' (Fraser, 1977). The dusky lad
who invites you to copulate with his 'sister,
very white, very clean,' makes three false
assertions. Rarely elsewhere as 'sister of
charity' or 'sister of mercy', both of the same
tendency as **nun** (above).

sit-down job an act of defecation
Usu. of a male, who does not need the western pedestal seat for urination: 'Oh, a sit-
down job, is it?' (Higgins, 1976, of defecation).

sit in a trespass to draw attention to a supposed injustice
Usu. by a body of people, without violence.
A 'sleep-in' continues overnight and during
a 'love-in' the participants while away the
hours in extra-marital copulation.

sit up with a sick friend to spend a night
furtively away from home
A male excuse to cover any taboo act.

sit-upon the buttocks
More common in BI than Am. where 'sit-
upons' in 19c. prudery were trousers, the
equivalent of the Br. 'sit-in-'ems'. Also as
'sit-down-upon', which should be a chair.
An ob. W. Eng. form was a 'sitting': 'She
had a tumour going from her sitting' (EDD
from 1887).

six feet of earth death
The length of a grave rather than its depth:
'Six feet of earth make all men equal'
(Proverb).

six feet underground dead and buried
The regulation coffin depth: 'I'm glad his
father's six feet underground' (G. Greene,
1978).

sixty-nine see **soixante-neuf**

sizzle to be killed by electrocution
One of several Am. culinary images.

skewer to copulate with
Of a male, from the action of transfixing
meat: 'The crooked shadow of Harvey
skewering Hornette' (Theroux, 1978 – they
were copulating during a public performance).

skidmarks the stains of shit in underpants
Mainly Br. boys' use.

skim (1) a bribe or the proceeds of regular
bribery or extortion
The cream taken off the milk: 'A skim of a
hundred and eighty was damned thin for a
bull lieutenant' (Weverka, 1973).

skim (2) illegally to conceal takings
The imagery is the same but the loser is an
employer or the Revenue: 'Skimming is the
term used to describe the removal of gambling revenues before they are counted for
State or Federal taxes' (*Daily Telegraph*, September 1979). To 'skim' may also be to re-
invest such money in a lawful business.

skin a male contraceptive sheath
From its shape and texture. Am.

skin flick a pornographic film
With 'skin' meaning nudity: '. . . bought the
rights on this new Swedish skin-flick'
(Deighton, 1972). A 'skin magazine' contains erotic pictures of naked or partly clad
bodies. A 'skinny-dip' is a bathe in the nude:
'I'm going skinny-dipping . . . . Who's
game?' (Sanders, 1982).

skin off all dead horses to marry your
sexual mistress
A 'dead horse' is something now of small
value but at one time useful. In ob. Ire. use,
to 'work on a dead horse' was to complete a
job for which you had already been paid and
when your task was over you were said to
have 'skinned' it.

skinful an excessive quantity of intoxicants
Usu. of beer, which suggests a distended
human belly or bladder rather than derivation from a wineskin: 'Take it easy, Larry.
You've got a skinful' (Chandler, 1958).

skippy a male homosexual
Taking the female role and using an affected
walk. Am. Black sl.

skirt a woman viewed sexually by a male
The garment is worn only by females –
males call them kilts: 'He's got a nice skirt all
right . . . . I wouldn't say pretty, but a good
figure' (G. Greene, 1932, and not of a transvestite). A 'bit' or 'piece' of 'skirt' is either a
male's partner in copulation or the act itself:
'He enjoyed nothing better in the world than
a nice bit of skirt' (Richards, 1936).

skivvy see **scivvie**

sky piece etc. a wig
Worn by a man. It used to mean a hat. Also
in Am. as a 'sky rug'.

slack to urinate
Of a male. The variant 'slack off' suggests
derivation from loosening or relieving
pressure.

slack fill delivering less than the customer
thinks he has bought
Commercial jargon for the manufacture of
glass etc. containers which look as if they
hold more than they do. Also of not filling
them to full capacity.

slag a sexually promiscuous woman
Often young but not content to form a pair
bond with a single male. Partridge (DSUE)
suggests 'perhaps ex slagger', which was an
ob. term for a bawd but I just wonder,
bearing in mind the social background of
many of those so described, whether it isn't
back sl. for 'gals'. cf. **yob**.

slake your lust to copulate
Of a male, usu. extra-maritally, from 'slake',
to quench or satisfy: '. . . let him slake his
lust on one of his own serf-women' (Fraser,
1973). In ob. Westmorland dialect, a 'sleck-
trough' was a whore – the cooling place into
which a smith plunged his red-hot iron.

slammer a prison
Either from the 'slamming' of the door as
you go in, or the rough treatment you receive
inside: '"You'll turn her into an addict. And
she's – what? Sixteen? Jesus." "She's already
been in the slammer"' (Theroux, 1976).
Rarely abbr. to 'slam': 'Now kin we jist wrap
this up and take me to the slam' (Wambaugh, 1983).

slap and tickle a single act of extra-
marital copulation
Properly no more than heterosexual
courtship.

slash an act of urination
Properly, a splashing or bespattering: 'All I
was doing was quickly relieving myself or, in
plain language having a slash' (Sharpe,
1979). Common use by both sexes.

slate loose (a) idiocy
The imperfect covering of the roof of a
house is transferred to the head. In ob. use a
'slate off' was an idiot: 'He left aw 'at he hed
to his slayatt hoff of a nevvy' (EDD – the
beneficiary was his nephew).

sleep to be dead
When Christians await the resurrection of
the body. Often in compounds according to
the circumstance. Thus to 'sleep in your
leaden hammock' or 'in Davy Jones' locker'
was to have died and been buried at sea:

'Though Drake their famous Captain now
slept in his leaden hammock' (Monsarrat,
1978) and to 'sleep in your shoes' was to be
killed in battle: 'The dreary eighteenth day
of June Made mony a ane sleep in their
shoon; The British blood was split like dew
Upon the field of Waterloo' (Muir, 1816).
By the same token, 'sleep' is death: 'Anyone
who went to sleep in a dug-out where there
was not much air with one of those fires
going . . . . would soon drop into a sleep from
which there would be no awakening'
(Richards, 1933). etc.

sleep around to copulate extra-maritally
and promiscuously
Of either sex, supposedly in various beds:
'. . . sleeping around with a lot of West
Indians. "I never approved of Christine's
lust for black men"' (Green, 1979). In this
and certain following entries, 'sleep' is synonymous with copulation, as though the latter involved something akin to
somnambulation.

sleep over to copulate overnight with an
extra-marital partner at the partner's
residence
Not involving, as you might suppose, the
occupation of bunk beds: 'He wanted her to
sleep over that night' (Sanders, 1982).

sleep together to copulate with
Usu. of extra-marital copulation except in
the negative where it refers to the cessation
of copulation between spouses. Now too of
homosexual activity.

sleep with to copulate with
One of the commonest uses, normally of
extra-marital copulation of either sex. Of a
woman: 'One couldn't accept a fur coat
without sleeping with a man' (G. Greene,
1932) and, of a man: 'East African (European) officers as a whole maintained a very
much stricter code in the matter of sleeping
with African women – sometimes referred to
as "sleeping dictionaries", from their
obvious advantages as language instructors'
(Allen, 1979).

sleeper a spy infiltrating an organization
but staying inactive
Politically usu. of espionage, industrially of
disruption where a union activist is introduced into a company subject in prospect to
fomented unrest. The latter 'sleepers' tend
to wake up as soon as their probationary
period, during which they can be dismissed
without complaint, has been passed: 'Philby,
Burgess and Maclean had little option but to

lie low. As "sleepers" they could secretly console one another' (Boyle, 1979).

sleeping dictionary *see* **sleep with**

sleeping partner someone with whom you regularly copulate extra-maritally
Punning on the partner who takes no active part in the running of a business: '. . . the service of a Somali girl-friend or sleeping partner' (Allen, 1979).

sleepy time girl a whore
Again the 'sleeping' imagery for a wakeful occupation. She may also be a sexual mistress: 'Seems like the bim was one of his sleepy time girls' (Chandler, 1953 – a 'bim' is a female friend).

sleighride the condition of being under narcotic influence
Punning on, and usu. from, 'snow', cocaine.

slewed drunk
Not going straight: 'Mr Hornby was just a bit slewed by the liquor he'd taken' (Russell, c. 1900). Also as 'half-slewed' where, as in other cases, the half equals the whole.

slice to cheat a customer
Retailers' jargon for overcharging or under-delivery, from removing a sliver from cheese etc. which has been weighed for delivery. The ob. 'shave' using the same imagery, was more colourful, especially in the punning phrase to 'shave the gentry.'

slice of the action *see* **action** (1)

slight chill etc. a pretext for not keeping a promised engagement
An indisposition which the draughts of royal palaces seem to induce: '"What shall I tell people? A slight chill?" "That sounds a deal too much like Buckingham Palace. Just say I'm out"' (Ustinov, 1971). Royal personages are also martyrs to 'slight' colds and indispositions.

slip (1) to give premature birth
Usu. of domestic animals: 'Cows slipped their calves, horses fell lame' (Hunt, 1865). Of humans to 'slip a foot' or 'slip a girth' was to give birth to a bastard: 'Slipping a foot, casting a leglin-girth or the like' (W. Scott, 1822). The ob. 'sling', to give premature birth, and its dialect version 'slink', were not used of humans, except as an insult in the sense of an aborted foetus: '. . . the muckle, saft slink o' veal' (Service, 1887 – 'saft' means soft).

slip (2) to die
The concept of gliding easily away: 'The

kid's "slipping". Dying' (Londres, 1928, in tr.). More often in compounds. To 'slip away' is an easy natural death, usu. of old age: 'To "slip awa" within sight of ninety' (Maclaren, 1895). Old people may also 'slip off'. With nautical imagery you may 'slip' your breath, cable, grip or wind: 'He was going to slip his cable with all the good scandal untold' (Fraser, 1971). To 'slip to Nod' is ob.: 'He the bizzy roun' hath trod, An' quietly wants to slip to Nod' (Taylor, 1787 – later in the verse his fate is to 'trudge on Pluto's gloomy shore').

slit the vagina
Properly, a narrow straight incision: 'Her first movement brought her sitting down on the step above me and at once my finger was busy in her slit' (Harris, 1925).

slopped drunk
Spilling over the edge fig., and perhaps also handling your glass maladroitly.

sloppy Joe a policeman
Am. CB sl., perhaps from **slops** (below).

slops the police
Black sl. indicating disrespect: '. . . sent out a girl for the slops' (Sims, 1902).

sloshed drunk
To 'slosh' is to be a glutton but there is also the imagery of an over-full container: '. . . her career of piss artistry, when she could still pretend she got sloshed out of not knowing about alcohol' (Amis, 1986). Often as 'half sloshed' which means no less drunk.

slow stupid
Educational jargon of children and of idiot adults able safely to remain in society.

slowdown a deliberate failure to do work for which you are being paid
The Am. version of the Br. **go slow** (above) as a bargaining tool in a labour dispute, especially when, as for Federal employees, striking may be illegal: '. . . air controllers or postal workers staged "slowdowns"' (*Daily Telegraph*, August 1981 – for the controllers the 'slowdown' shortly became a full stop).

slug (1) a bullet
In the 17c. the gasteropod had much the same shape and colour: '. . . felt that a .38 slug could save wasting a lot of time and the taxpayer's money' (Allbeury, 1975). To 'get a slug' is to be killed or wounded by a bullet but 'slugged' means hit by any agency including a fist or an excess of alcohol.

slug (2) a quantity of spirituous intoxicant
Probably punning on **shot (2)** (above) rather
than from the rare meaning, to swallow.
Usu. in the cliché, a 'slug of whisky'.

slugged drunk
From the hitting, the swallowing or the
measure?

sluggish schizophrenia a pretext under
which sane people are confined and injured
by forced narcotic treatment in a mental
hospital
A Russian Communist excuse for dealing
with sane opponents: '. . . the only uncertainty was whether he would be sent to a
psychiatric institution to be treated for
"sluggish schizophrenia" – a wondrous malady . . . . that had no clinical symptoms – or
consigned to the labour camps' (Moss,
1985).

sluice (1) to copulate with
Properly, to flush: 'She has been sluic'd in's
absence, And his pond fisht by his next
neighbour' (Shakespeare, *Winter's Tale*).
This may well be a spurious entry based on a
single metaphorical use which neither Dr
Johnson nor Sir James Murray recognized
but still more worthy of notice than the Am.
'sluice', to shoot eagles from a helicopter.

sluice (2) a lavatory
From the controlled flow of water: 'He's in
the sluice' (Bradbury, 1959 – he was in a
lavatory and not a mill-stream).

slumber room a morgue
Am. funeral jargon with the commonest
'sleeping' imagery: 'Lavish slumber rooms
where the deceased receives visitors for
some days before the funeral' (J. Mitford,
1980). A 'slumber' cot or box is a coffin and
a 'slumber robe', a shroud.

slush bribery
Properly, 'a soft mixture of grease or oil'
(WNCD). A 'slush fund' is a corporate
bribery budget: 'A non-existent British
Leyland "slush" fund' (*Private Eye*, May
1981).

smack illegal heroin
I suspect it is a corruption of the Yiddish
'schmeck', to sniff rather than derived from
the physical impact or the nickname of the
bandleader James Fletcher Henderson
(1898 – 1952): '"Hey, Johnny, you want
smack?" meaning heroin not punishment'
(Simon, 1979). Mainly Far Eastern use.

small folk etc. the fairies
From their stature in the days when they

were real to countryfolk and, with their
vicious natures, not to be trifled with or
talked about directly. Also as 'small men':
'The small men. I mean the pixies' (Mortimer, 1895) and as 'small people': 'The
small people are believed by some to be the
spirits of the people who inhabited Cornwall
many thousands of years ago' (Hunt, 1865).
Mainly W. Eng.

smallest room the lavatory
Even if, by geometric computation, it isn't:
'The bathroom: restroom. *A facetious
euphemism*' (DAS, in an interesting case of
defining one euphemism by two others).

smashed drunk or under illegal narcotic
influence
Your consciousness, if nothing else, is
destroyed by the substance consumed: 'I was
smashed last night. Some of the guys at this
party were on methedrine with their acid'
(Deighton, 1972). The ob. 'smash the
teapot' was to resume regular drinking of
alcohol after a period of abstinence.

smear (1) to bribe
Properly to spread, whence to spread lar-
gesse: 'A little smearing of the right palm'
(Longstreet, 1956 – he didn't mean to imply
that the left palm wouldn't have served an
equal purpose). The Am. 'schmear' comes
from the German 'schmieren' via Yiddish in
the same sense: 'I got the feeling that a
schmear changed hands somewhere along
the way' (Sanders, 1977).

smear (2) a test for cervical cancer
A vaginal sample is taken for laboratory
analysis. A woman who says 'I've just had my
smear' does not mention the dread and
taboo cancer.

smear (3) to attempt to bring into disrepute
You hope the dirty stain will remain: 'You'll
have to do better than try and smear me'
(Crisp, 1982, of such an attempt).

smear out to kill
A variant of **wipe off** (below): 'The opposition had twice tried to smear me out' (Hall,
1969).

smell the stuff to sniff cocaine as an
addict
Of a general propensity and not a single
experiment. Am.

smile and comb your hair slow down
because of police radar ahead
An Am. CB warning from under another
driver to be on your best party behaviour.

smoke to inhale narcotics illegally
I am assuming that inhaling and expelling
the smoke from tobacco is no longer taboo.
Of narcotics, addicts usu. 'smoke' marijuana: 'A whole lot of girls, real sweet chicks.
And we'll be smoking too' (Bradbury, 1965).
In these circles, 'the smoke' is opium:
'There isn't much record he went for tea-
sticks or the smoke' (Longstreet, 1956). And
prior to the 17c. you 'smoked' only if you
were cremated, burnt to death or went to
hell. The Am. 'smoke', a Black person, was
derogatory and may be ob.: 'Smokes and a
white gal .... Lousy. Crummy' (Chandler,
1939).

smoke it to kill yourself
From putting a handgun in your mouth: 'I
hear some detective from West L.A. smoked
it' (Wambaugh, 1983, of a suicide).

smoke screen a police radar trap for
motorists
An Am. CB warning to approaching drivers
obliquely punning on **smokey** (below).

smokey a policeman
The DAS suggests that it comes from
'Smokey the Bear', the US Forestry Service
symbol, and *see* **bear** (2). In CB sl. there are
many compounds – 'smokey beaver', a
policewoman; 'smokey on four legs', a
policeman on horseback; 'smokey with
camera', police with radar; 'smokey on rubber', police moving in a car; 'smokey with
ears', police with CB radio; etc; and *see*
CBSLD.

smoker the devil
The fire, brimstone, etc. SW Eng. ? ob.

(smooch to engage in prolonged intimate
heterosexual caresses comes from the dialect
'smooch' or 'smoorich', to kiss.)

smooth to distort published accounts
You conceal or try to even out fluctuations
by carrying forward exceptional movements
up or down. This soothes stockholders and
financial commentators.

smother to copulate
Of a male, from his supposed attitude on the
female: 'I've smothered in too many hall
bedrooms' (Chandler, 1939).

snaffle to steal
Properly, to saunter, as many chance thieves
do: 'He cud snaffle the raisins an' currins
away' (Bagnall, 1852).

snake ranch a brothel
From the dangers met in such a place and
punning on Am. sl. 'snake', a penis.

snapper an ampoule of amyl nitrate
The drug is properly used in the treatment
of heart disorders but, as it is popularly supposed in Am. to be an aphrodisiac, it commands a strong illegal market. You use it by
snapping the top off an ampoule, and
sniffing: '... a box of snappers in plain view
on a dresser top' (Sanders, 1977).

snatch (1) a single act of copulation
Usu. extra-maritally. The derivation might
be from any one of several SE meanings of
'snatch' – a snare, an entanglement, a hasty
meal, a sudden jerk – or the sl. **snatch** (2)
(below), a vagina. Shakespeare could have
been using it in either sexual sense: 'It seems
some certain snatch or so Would serve your
turn' (*Titus Andronicus*) but there is no equiv-
ocation in: 'I could not abide marriage, but
as a rambler I took a snatch when I could get
it' (Burton, 1621). The modern use survives
in Am. more than BI.

snatch (2) a vagina
Perhaps from the 'snatch', or portion of hair:
'... if the number of the vaginas .... were
lined up orifice to orifice, there would be a
snatch long enough ...' (Styron, 1976).

snatch(3) to kidnap or steal
From the seizing in either case: 'Snatching
Steven was going to be one big piece of
chocolate cake' (Collins, 1981, of kidnap-
ping). 'The snatch' is the particular execution of the crime.

snatch (4) to arrest a criminal
Either singly, or by taking a ringleader from
a mob. Whence a 'snatch squad' of police,
etc., whose duty it is to make such mob
arrests.

sneak to steal
Properly, to move furtively (whence too the
children's use, to inform against). It was
applied particularly in many phrases to 19c.
robbery from houses: 'He saw Seth
Thimaltwig snake hawf a pahnd o' fresh butter' (Treddlehoyle, 1893). Today we use
only the tautological 'sneak thief'.

sneezer a prison
Possibly a corruption of **freezer** (q.v.) – or
the typist couldn't read Chandler's writing:
'... tossed in the sneezer by some prowl car
boys' (Chandler, 1953).

sniff to inhale narcotics illegally
Uus. cocaine but, among modern children,
glue: '... an increasing number of children
.... have adopted glue-sniffing' (*The Practitioner*, 1977, quoted in Hudson, 1978).

sniff out to kill
Perhaps a corruption of **snuff out** (below) because to 'sniff out' is normally no more than to detect: '. . . before some busybody at the top sniffs out Sniffers' (Manning, 1977 – of killing and not detection but Miss Manning liked to play with words). To 'take a long sniff' – your last deep breath – is more logical: 'Half a dozen horsemen galloped past, firing six-guns into the air. The young cowboy said. "Seems like you might be taking yourself a long deep sniff"' (Deighton, 1972).

snifter a drink of spirituous intoxicants
Properly, a person who sniffs, or who snores. In the 19c. a 'snifter' was a small portion of brandy etc. given to you to let you savour the aroma. The modern use seeks to imply that you do not want more than a small quantity due to your temperate habits.

snip a vasectomy
Medical jargon, punning on the surgical cut and the easy way to earn a fee. 'Snib' and 'snicks' are Eng. dialect words for the castration of lambs and both are likely to come into use of vasectomy.

snort (1) a drink of spirituous intoxicant
Perhaps it makes you exhale noisily: 'There's a pint in the glove compartment. Want a snort?' (Chandler, 1958).

snort (2) to ingest an illegal narcotic
Usu. by sniffing and a 'snort' is a portion: '"I'm not worried about it," she said with a half-smile as she casually spooned two snorts' (Robbins, 1981).

snout a police informer
The nose of the pig: 'I know all about snouts. And I didn't have to pay for this' (James, 1986, of police information).

snow (1) cocaine
In its crystalline or powdered form, from the colour: 'Not all jazz-players smoke marijuana or opium, or sniff snow' (Longstreet, 1956). 'Snowed' is under the influence of illegal narcotics.

snow (2) to present excessive detailed information which makes it hard to grasp the essential factors
Industrial jargon of reports measured in vertical inches, unedited computer print-outs, military six-part specifications, etc. where the recipient is to be induced to reach certain conclusions desired by those who furnish the documentation. A 'snow-job' is

the use of this method of obfuscation. Both come from the blanketing of snow.

snow (3) to confuse or complicate an issue
Usu. to prevent scandal or criminal detection. Unlike **snow** (2) (above) it may imply no more than lies or simple deception: 'Little job? Don't let them snow you, old friend' (Price, 1970). Again the attempt is a 'snow-job': 'A lie, a cover-up, a snow-job was fatal' (Allbeury, 1980).

snowdrop a military policeman
From the white spats worn by Am. WWII police: '". . . we've even put the 787th Military Police Company into the Junior Constitutional Club." . . . . "Your 'snowdrops', you mean"' (Deighton, 1982).

snowing down South the hem of your petticoat is showing
An oblique Am. warning to the wearer. Petticoats were usu. white.

snuff (out) to kill
From extinguishing a candle: 'You mean you make sure he doesn't go off like a mad dog, snuffing people left and right' (Van Lustbaden, 1983). 'Snuff out' is the older version: 'I'd have snuffed out every life in India' (Fraser, 1975). To 'snuff it' is to die: 'An' Ray Tuck's been running Lippy's errands – or was, until Lippy snuffed it' (Price, 1982).

snug drunk
Properly, comfortable. Many Eng. inns have 'snugs', abbr. for 'snug bars' but any pun is, I think, unconscious. Br. estate agents also use 'snug' to gloss over inconveniently restricted space: 'Now he knew "snug" meant tiny' (Theroux, 1974).

so pregnant
From the meaning, in such a situation: 'A euphemism for pregnant . . . . "Mrs Brown is so"' (EDD C. 1900). Less often as 'so-and-so', which may derive from the ob. meaning, in poor health. ? ob.

so-and-so (1) *see* **so**

so-and-so (2) a mild insult
Each 'so' being a substitute for an abusive epithet.

so-so (1) unwell
Properly, mediocre, and usu. how you describe yourself rather than another.

so-so (2) drunk
The common 'unwell' imagery. Of another when he is drunk, or of yourself if suffering from a hangover.

so-so (3)　menstruating
Again, the 'unwell' imagery. DSUE also gives 'so', but I have not heard or read it elsewhere.

soak　a drunkard
In modern use, and 'soaked' is drunk. Formerly, and logically to 'soak' was to drink excessively without showing symptoms of drunkenness: 'A "slug for the drink" is a man who soaks and never succumbs' (Douglas, 1901).

social disease etc.　a venereal disease
Mainly 19c. usage, which you might contract from the 'social evil' prostitution, which, especially in 19c. England, prospered as a result of delayed marriage by men and the fear of repeated pregnancy by women during an era of falling infant mortality: '"He has contracted a social disease, which makes it impossible that he marry." "You mean he's got a dose of clap?"' (Fraser, 1970, writing in 19c. style). A sufferer might also have a 'social infection': '. . . contracting certain indelicate social infections from – hem-hem – female camp-followers' (Fraser, 1975, again in 19c. style).

social evil *see* social disease

social justice　a system which seeks to stop the rich living substantially better than the poor
As political dogma, it sounds well although it means different things to different people, its virtue lying in its imprecision: 'The robbery of the rich is called social justice' (Roberts, 1951). We must always beware any programme which incorporates 'justice' in its title.

social ownership　expropriation
The 1986 Br. socialist version of the economically discredited policy imposed upon the party by its industrial wing, which is the only section of society which thinks it benefits from overmanning and subsidized operation: '. . . the substitution of phrases like "social ownership" for nasty brutal words like "nationalization"' (*Daily Telegraph*, August 1986 – a red rose also replaced the red flag as the party's emblem).

(social science　the study of society and human behaviour has borrowed 'science' from its proper meaning, study of or knowledge about tangible matters capable of precise definition. As FDMT notes: 'Social Studies . . . . frequently fail to exercise scientific stringency.' To observe this is not to denigrate much of the research and teaching done under the misnomer. The status of these studies has sometimes been lowered because of the economy with which courses can be introduced during a time of university expansion, especially when politicians and Principals start playing the 'numbers game'.)

social security　the payment of money by the state to the indigent
The latest and most durable of a line of evasions by which we seek to mask the plight of, and charity to, the poor: 'It was the morning most people went to collect their social security' (L. Thomas, 1979).

social worker　a public employee helping the poor, ineffective, sick or old
Properly, an ant or similarly organized creature. The use does not mean, though it may imply, that work such as manufacturing or compiling a dictionary is anti-social.

socialist　Communist
The use of those who favour autocracy, as in the 'Union of Soviet Socialist Republics'. Like many political labels, 'socialist' means widely different things to different people.

sodomite　a bugger
The Dead Sea city had a reputation for evil: 'She once made a fearful gaffe about Sodomites, mixing them up with Dolomites' (N. Mitford, 1949). 'Sodomy' is buggery: 'It often led to downright sodomy' (Harris, 1925, of masturbation). The abbr. 'sod' is often a mild insult.

soft (1)　imbecile
Abbr. for 'soft in the head': 'She's saft at best, and something lazy' (Burns, 1785).

soft (2)　inflicting less harm than an alternative
The alternative to **hard** (q.v.) in pornography, illegal narcotics, etc. A 'soft' drink is non-alcoholic and will harm your teeth more than your liver. For the soldiers, a 'soft' target is one which is easily attacked. A 'soft option' is a simple solution, with overtones of laziness or cowardice.

soil (1)　extra-marital copulation
Of either sex, from the sullying of reputation: 'Who is as free from touch or soil with her As she from one ungot' (Shakespeare, *Measure for Measure*). ob.

soil (2)　human excrement
From the days of the earth closet or deep-trench latrine, when it had regularly to be removed and, if by night, became **nightsoil** (above). To 'soil' yourself, your pants, etc. is to defecate involuntarily: 'He sometimes soiled his pants here in the park' (McCarthy, 1963).

soixante-neuf simultaneous fellatio and cunnilingus
From the reversible numbers '6' and '9', and the position adopted by the participants. This French form is normal in BI – I speak etymologically – with 'six-à-neuf' being rare: '. . . six-à-neuf meaning a slightly contortive sexual diversion' (Jennings, 1965). The Am. usage, more direct or less Francophone, is 'sixty-nine': '. . . every act from masturbation to "sixty-nine" was indulged in' (ibid.). The participants may also be described as 'sixty-nining'.

solace extra-marital copulation
Supposedly consolement for the absence of a spouse: '". . . seeking that well-known solace." "From two men at the one time?"' (Keneally, 1979). Usu. of women.

soldier (1) *see* sink the soldier

soldier (2) a mobster
At the boss's orders, he threatens, assaults or kills: 'I lend you a couple of soldiers – you frighten the crap outta number one on the list' (Collins, 1981). Am.

solicit to offer sexual services for money
Properly, to request or entreat of anything, like the Br. 'solicitor' who pleads for you in court or the Am. 'solicitor' who is barred from trying to sell you anything in your place of business except between 8.30 and 9.00 a.m. on Monday mornings. Legal jargon of prostitution where the whore does the 'soliciting'. Of homosexuals, it can be either party: 'The defendant was accused of having improperly solicited another man in a public lavatory' (Boyle, 1979, of Burgess). The person who does the asking is a 'solicitor' rather than a 'solicitress' or 'solicitrix', and this leads to much ribald male humour, except among Br. lawyers.

solicitor general the penis
Punning on male promiscuity and the Br. high office of State.

solid waste human excrement
Civil engineering jargon. The term does not include empty tins or potato peelings.

solidarity participation in a strike on behalf of others
In the 19c. it meant, as in modern Poland, the coming together of workers in a single bargaining unit. Now trade union jargon for support given to other unionists engaged in a dispute with a third party.

solitaire suicide
The game that can be played by one person. Am.

solitary sex self-masturbation
Not hermaphroditism. Used of males and females if they indulge in the 'solitary sin'.

something an intoxicant
Usu. in the cliché 'Would you like a little something?' 'Something damp' is more explicit and usu. indicates whisky. 'Something short' is any spirit: 'She pulled out a bottle of gin, asking me if I would have a drop of something short' (Mayhew, 1862). Also as 'something moist': 'I doubt if he were quite as fully sensible of that gentleman's merits under arid conditions, as when something moist was going' (C. Dickens, 1861).

something in the basket pregnant
The 'basket' is the stomach, as in the modern boxing term 'bread basket'. ? ob.

something on you a damaging piece of knowledge about you
Not the clothes you are wearing. In this sense, 'on' means against: 'He's got something on her and she's afraid of him' (Chandler, 1958).

something-something a mild expletive
You invite your auditor to choose his own profanities.

somewhere where he can be looked after off our hands
Used of aged, ill or burdensome dependents, implying that they, not you, will benefit from the care of paid strangers: 'Get him out of here as soon as possible, to somewhere where he can be looked after' (Bradbury, 1959).

son et lumière the clandestine recording of an indiscreet act
Espionage jargon, from the public display which involves lights and music: '. . . a British MP been leaping into bed with a Czech agent, in Prague itself, with full sound and camera coverage, *son et lumière* as the professionals say' (Lyall, 1980).

(son of a bachelor a bastard was probably never used euphemistically. 'Son of a bitch', which also implied bastardy, was a double insult, to the person named and to his mother, and remains so as 'SOB'. Strangely 'son of a gun', which meant the same thing, has lost its insulting connotations.)

song and dance a male homosexual
Rh. sl. for 'nance' and perhaps punning on the supposed tastes of men who dance for a living.

sop a drunkard
Literally, something dipped in liquid or the liquid in which it is dipped. I suspect it is confused with the common **sot** (below).

sore a carcinoma
The symptom, in this case an ulcer, is used for the dread affliction: 'Her own mother had died of a "sore"' (Mann, 1902).

sot a drunkard
Acting like a fool, perhaps. To 'sot' was to become drunk: 'Drover blades, who drink and sot' (Nicholson, 1814).

sought after expensive
Estate agents' puff, when they want to imply a buyer will have plenty of competition. But any property, however humble, is likely to be sought after, at a price, if advertised.

soup illegal explosive materials
Like other criminal speech, its etymoplogy is tenuous but I am drawn to 'jelly', an abbr. of gelignite. The ob. 'souper' was not a safe-blower but an Irish Protestant minister who bribed Roman Catholics for switching allegiance: 'Proselytizers, or soupers, from their offering soup to starving people' (Carleton, 1836). And you too become a 'souper', if you swallowed the bait and the soup: 'I'll turn souper this day for the male' (Barlow, 1892 – 'male' was a meal).

souse a drunkard
The common culinary imagery, this time from soaking in vinegar or the like: 'That much would just get a real souse started' (Chandler, 1953). 'Soused' means drunk: 'I could see that mother was getting soused' (L. Armstrong, 1955).

south (the) the poorer or less indus-trialized countries
From the geographical location of many of them relative to Europe and N. Am. This 1982 version is a happy break from the 'developing' theme but cannot expect much currency in S. Africa or the Antipodes.

South Chelsea Battersea
An example of what happens in most big cities where a fashionable area is bounded by an unfashionable: 'Battersea . . . . South Chelsea, the snobs call it' (Theroux, 1982 – and perhaps, too, the estate agents).

souvenir (1) a bastard
Certainly a lasting memory for the mother: 'I expect in some cases (the troops) had left other souvenirs which would either be a blessing or a curse to the ladies concerned' (Richards, 1933).

souvenir (2) a turd
A reminder of a canine presence: '. . . not many people looking up, preferring instead to study the sidewalks for souvenirs of its vast dog population' (McBain, 1981).

souvenir hunting looting
WWII army usage now used of robbery after a natural disaster or riot, by the thieves.

soviet Russian-controlled
A 'soviet' is a committee and the theory is that committees make the national policy. In the 'Union of Soviet Socialist Republics', one is Russian and the others are conquered or subject states; some of which acquiesce in their condition and some of which might prefer to assert their national identity, as an independent state. So too with nominally independent states under Russian domi-nation, like the 'Czech Soviet Socialist Republic'.

sow your wild oats to behave wildly or irresponsibly
With extravagance or promiscuous seminal distribution like the persistent weed, Avena fatua: 'We all have to sow our wild oats at some time or another' (Sharpe, 1974). SE.

sozzled drunk
Properly, splashed: '"We were all rather sozzled that night." "I wonder if he was drunk when he killed himself"' (Murdoch, 1977). Also as 'half sozzled'.

space a grave
Am. funeral jargon: 'As for other euphemisms . . . . "space" for "grave"' (J. Mitford, 1963) and 'The "space and bronze deal" as it is called by the door-to-door sales specialists' (ibid. – you buy your plot and casket in advance).

spaced under illegal narcotic influence
From the floating sensation, especially after taking a hallucinogen. Am.

Spanish fly a supposed aphrodisiac
No dipterous insect but the cantharis beetle which, by inducing vaginal itch, is said to be an aphrodisiac in women: '. . . they'd put women in a barrel ready mixed with goddam Spanish fly to make 'em saucy' (Keneally, 1979).

Spanish gout syphilis
Br. sailors thought that Spanish girls must have infected them, if not French, Italians or other inferior breeds.

Spanish practices the regular use of dishonest devices by employees fraudulently to reduce hours of attendance and increase pay
The scandal of London's Fleet Street was not so much that the employees customarily and systematically cheated their employers but that the employers tolerated it for so long and the tax authorities turned a blind eye to it: 'A year ago, as well as the overmanning, the exploitative "Spanish practices" and the interrupted production ...' (*The Times*, January 1987). Native-born Englishmen should take no pleasure in observing that it took a part-Iranian, a Czech, a German, an Australian and a Canadian to clean out the stables.

Spanish tummy diarrhoea
The Br. equivalent of the Am. **touristas** (q.v.).

spare tyre obesity at the waistline
Usu. of a male, from the roll of fat overhanging his belt: 'I longed to melt away that spare tyre before it was too late' (Matthew, 1983). In Am. sometimes as 'rubber tire'.

speak to to propose marriage with
This is a rare reminder of the 19c. reticence about marriage: 'When Jamie "spoke to" Janet Carson, who told her people at once, having no opposition to expect ...' (Strain, 1900). The Sc. 'speak for' and 'speak till.' are ob.

speak with forked tongue to deceive
A facility attributed to Whites by Am. Indians, with serpents again getting unfair metaphoric treatment.

speakeasy an establishment selling intoxicants without a licence
Mainly Am. Prohibition use, although noted in 1891 (OED). You had to lower your voice to avoid advertising the transaction.

special (1) ruthless and extra-legal
Usu. in compound phrases concerned with espionage or repression as follow:

  special action the rounding up and murdering of Jews by Nazis, whose phrase it was: '... the incredible *numbers* involved in these Special Actions .... These Jews, they come on and on' (Styron, 1976).

  Special Branch the Br. police etc. concerned with subversion: 'Here you call

your political police the Special Branch, because you English are not so direct in these matters' (Deighton, 1978).

special court a tribunal established by the executive to overrule and supersede an independent judiciary. Thus the Nazi 'Sondergericht' of March 1933 avoided the overt flouting of judgments of established German courts by introducing a tribunal of higher jurisdiction. Today Communists still use such devices.

special detachment an army or police unit used to terrorize dissidents etc. As might be expected, the Nazis perfected the concept by, in Poland, so naming a police force of Jews who worked under control of the SS to harass other Jews: 'Even the Jews of the Special Detachment were reluctant to pick the children up' (Styron, 1976, of Poland in WW II).

special duty an extra-legal or illegal act performed under authority. The phrase is now widely used, and not only by the Communists, but again the concept came from the Nazis whose anti-Jewish street bands were called 'Einsatzgruppen': '"Special duty groups" is a close translation. But the amorphous word "Einsatz" had another shade of meaning ... knightliness' (Keneally, 1982 – the squads were usu. recruited from the Sicherheitsdienst, or SD).

special education a prison regime calculated to kill, cow or indoctrinate dissidents etc. Mainly Communist practice and usage.

special fuzz police concerned with controlling subversion. This is used in BI only of those who come directly in touch with the public: 'A hairy hitchhiking student had only recently complained to him that the special fuzz were becoming hard to pinpoint' (Price, 1971).

special police the police seconded to the control of subversion and civil disorder. The word 'police' seeks to imply a degree of fairness and solicitude for the feelings of the public which seldom characterizes such bodies. A London variant is the 'special patrol group', a riot squad with an occasional penchant for individual weaponry.

special regime a treatment aimed to kill or destroy the health of a prisoner. A 1978 Russian prisoner on 'special regime' would be required to do heavy manual work on 800 calories of food daily, so long as he survived. The other 'regimes' are general (the mildest), intensified and strict.

special squad a unit established by government to murder or harass opponents. A phenomenon of Am. autocracies where the courts have retained some independence of the executive. For the Nazis the 'Sonderkommandos' were used for rounding up and oppressing Jews: '. . . the Sonderkommandos were unleashed to advance with an appropriate sense of racial history and professional detachment into the old Judiac ghettos' (Keneally, 1982, of Poland in WW II).

special treatment the torture and killing of your opponents. This was the treatment accorded by the Nazis to Jews, Gypsies, Slavs and other assorted enemies of the State: '. . . what Sonderbehandlung means, that though it says *Special Treatment*, it means pyramids of cyanosed corpses' (Keneally, 1982). A 1983 British Airways advertisement in Germany was a literal translation of 'You fly frequently. Don't you deserve a little special treatment?'. Many felt the use of 'Sonderbehandlung' was a Freudian slip.

special (2) mentally or physically inferior A 'special' pupil going to a 'special' school may be an idiot or a spastic; 'special' games are for cripples; etc. 'Special' is seldom used in this sense of those of superior attainments, although they may be equally distinctive.

special (3) a part-time policeman Abbr. of the Br. 'special constable' but without political overtones in Eng., Wales or Sc. The N. Ire. 'B Specials' were a para-military force which supported Protestant ascendancy.

special stores nuclear weapons Naval jargon, especially of nuclear depth charges.

specimen a sample of urine Medical jargon and an abbr. of a 'specimen of your urine'. A lot of patients are still confused by it.

speed to take a narcotic illegally Usu. amphetamine despite the fact that a 'speedball' is a mixture of narcotics, and punning on driving a car above a legal limit: 'They were speeding and tripping at the same time' (Deighton, 1972).

spend to ejaculate semen Usu. in copulation: 'Spending his manly marrow in her arms' (Shakespeare, *All's Well*) or, in modern use: 'I could after the first orgasm go on indefinitely without spending again' (Harris, 1925).

spend a penny to urinate Normally of urination by either sex, although only females were required to produce the coin formerly needed to operate the lock of a Br. public lavatory turnstile or cubicle. Rarely of defecation, although in that case men had to 'spend a penny' too.

spend the night with to copulate with extra-maritally Of either sex usu. in a transient relationship: 'She wanted me to go and spend the night with her' (L. Armstrong, 1955). There is also a legal presumption that a male and a female, if not married to each other, cannot spend a night in each other's company without copulating.

sphere of influence a foreign territory which can be controlled politically, militarily and economically without interference from a third party The end product of the colonial cartel, like the 1907 Anglo-Russian Agreement concerning Persia or of the deals done at Yalta: 'In a stroke, we clear the British from India, and extend your majesty's imperial – influence from the North Cape to the isle of Ceylon' (Fraser, 1973, of 19c. Tsarist expansionism).

spike (1) to adulterate an intoxicant Perhaps from 'spiking', or destroying, a gun by driving a metal object through the touchhole or possibly merely from the practice of inserting a hot piece of metal in the glass of fluid. You do it to harm the drinker, or to increase the potency of the intoxicant.

spike (2) to reject for publication Editorial jargon, from the metal spike on which rejects were filed: 'The chances are that no sub-editor is going to spike the story' (Deighton, 1982).

spike (3) a hypodermic needle A specific sharp-pointed piece of metal. Am.

spill (1) to give gratuitous information Normally to the police and an abbr. of 'spill the beans', to pass on damaging information: 'If Hench shot somebody, she would have some idea . . . . She would spill if she had' (Chandler, 1943).

spill (2) to ejaculate semen
In masturbation or copulation: 'Ulf who is
nothing and has no career had spilled himself on their precious sheets' (Seymour,
1980 – they had used the girl's parents' bed).

spill the beans *see* spill (1)

spirits (1) a man's semen
In ob. use, the essence of maleness, whence
the symbol of courage: 'Much use of Venus
doth dim the sight . . . . The cause of
dimness of sight is the expense of spirits'
(Bacon, 1627). The modern **spunk** (below)
has the same duality of meaning.

spirits (2) a spirituous intoxicant
Properly no more than any liquid in the form
of a distillation or essence: 'He gave me a
piece of an honey-comb, and a little bottle of
Spirits' (Bunyan, 1684). Now generically of
whisky, gin, rum, vodka, etc.: '"Spirits don't
seem to agree with you." "They differed
from me sharply this time"' (Amis, 1978).

spit feathers to have a hangover
From the dryness of the mouth. I am sorry
that this useful and graphic phrase seems to
have passed out of use.

splash your boots to urinate
Usu. of a male, but not necessarily out of
doors or even wetting your footwear: 'I was
up splashing my boots' (Theroux, 1971, of
urination).

splice the mainbrace to drink intoxicants
The mainbrace was the rope which held the
mainsail in position and a vessel was in peril
if it broke. In rough weather 'splicing', or
mending by rejoining it, was a hazardous
operation and the seamen deserved a reward
when it was done. For them, it was a double
tot of rum, as it still is to celebrate some
national event in the navy, but for the rest of
us usu. mundane whisky or gin and tonic.

split (1) to inform against
Some children's use, probably from the
sense of dividing: 'It's the meanest thing out
– that splitting on a pal' (Trollope, 1885).

split (2) to copulate
Of the male, with obvious imagery. To 'split
a woman's shape' was to impregnate her.
Whence too 'split-mutton', a penis, and
other vulgarities.

sponge an habitual drunkard
Punning perhaps on the soaking up of intoxicants and his willingness to accept free

refills from others. The Br. 'sponging-
house' was not an inn but a temporary prison
for debtors, where they were relieved, or
'sponged', of cash and valuables before passing into a long-stay debtors' prison.

spoon to caress heterosexually
Perhaps from the phrase 'lie spoons', to
nestle closely with the convex side of one
against the concave side of the other; or from
the old Welsh custom of giving your sweetheart a suitably carved wooden spoon as a
token of your interest. Now rather dated.

sport (the) copulation
Usu. viewed as such by the male: 'He had
some feelings for the sport; he knew the
service' (Shakespeare, *Measure for Measure*
and not of a player of real tennis). In literary
use it becomes the 'amorous sport', 'sport
for Jove', etc. To 'sport' is to copulate: 'Now
let us sport us while we may' (Marvell, c.
1670). In modern use, any 'sporting' copulation is usu. on a commercial basis. Thus a
'sport-trap' is the brothel area of a town:
'Storyville became and stayed the biggest
tourist and sport-trap in the nation'
(Longstreet, 1956 – and it so remained until
1917 when it was shut down to protect Am.
servicemen from temptation and disease). A
'sporting-house' is a brothel: 'She was like a
lot of sporting-house landladies I've known
through life' (L. Armstrong, 1955, of a
bawd). There you might find 'sporting' girls
or women – not hockey-players – who
inhabited the 'sporting section' of the town,
punning on the part of the newspaper given
over to ball games etc. 'You came to the
sporting-section, the cathouses around 22nd
street' (Longstreet, 1956). etc.

sportsman a gambler
The modern equivalent of **gamester**
(above). Usu. of regular or spectacular punters only.

spot (1) a spirituous intoxicant
Suppose an abbr. for a 'spot' of whisky, etc.:
'I think I could do with a spot' (E. Waugh,
1955).

spot (2) to kill
From the entry mark of the bullet, perhaps,
or an abbr. of to **put on the spot** (q.v.):
'That's enough to spot a guy for' (Chandler,
1939).

spot (3) a tubercular infection
Usu. of pulmonary tuberculosis where it is a
hole in the lung but appears as a spot on an
x-ray plate. It is unfortunate that the genetic
ability of N. Europeans to resist and repair a

tubercular infection of the lung by the secretion of repairing fluid now makes them especially prone to emphysema.

sprain your ankle to copulate with a man before marriage
Usu. in the past tense, especially where the woman is pregnant. Br. women also suffered similar inquiries to their knees, elbows and thighs – *see* **break your elbow** etc.

spread for to copulate with
Of a woman, usu. willing, once and extra-maritally. More explicitly to 'spread your legs': 'They must both be paid, cash on the barrel-head, before she would spread her legs' (Monsarrat, 1978) or vulgarly to 'spread your twat': 'Spreading that twat of yours for a cheap, chiseling quack doctor' (Styron, 1976).

spread the greens to hand out tickets for excessive speed
Punning on the colour of the paper used by the Am. police.

spring to secure release from prison before the end of a sentence
Of legal pardon or escape, and rarely of bail before conviction, from the unexpected and positive action of a released coil: 'The proprietor knew how to "spring" them, that is, get them out of jail' (L. Armstrong, 1955).

sprung slightly drunk
Like a ship which leaks but hasn't sunk: 'How's a chap to get sprung, much less drunk' (Westall, 1885). 'Half-sprung' is no less drunk.

spunk a man's semen
Properly, courage and still so used in some innocent circles: '. . . a term Lady Maud found almost as offensive as Colonel Chapman's comment that she was full of spunk' (Sharpe, 1975) but for the less innocent: '. . . right off there, with my fresh spunk in her' (Keneally, 1979). And *see* **spirits** (1). 'Spunk' is rarely used too of the vaginal sexual discharge. The ob. Sc. 'spunkie' was whisky: 'Spunkie ance to make us mellow' (Burns).

spur of the moment passion
unpremeditated extra-marital copulation
Not momentary anger or other forms of suffering: '. . .spur of the moment passion with a married woman' (*Daily Telegraph*, April 1980).

spy in the sky traffic police in a helicopter
Am. CB. sl. punning on orbiting military satellites.

squash to kill
Of humans, treating them as we do insects: '"At best? Two busted kneecaps." "And at worst?" "They'll squash me"' (Sanders, 1980). sl.

squashed drunk
From the way you feel, and not from drinking fruit squash. Am.

squat (1) to defecate
From the posture and perhaps too from the dialect meaning, to squirt: 'The authorities were trying to teach the people not to squat behind their huts' (McCarthy, 1967). Either sex may 'take a squat', which for females may mean urination only.

squat (2) to occupy by trespass
The word in this use originated in Am. but 'squatters' rights' is a concept of the Eng. common law, from the social need in the Middle Ages to see property vacated through plague, etc. brought back into productive use.

squeal as a criminal to give information to the police
There is an implication of duress, with the 'squeal' indicating pain. Of informing on others or confessing your own guilt: '. . . loath to "squeal" or turn him in' (Lavine, 1930).

squeeze to extort from illegally
From the pressure applied: 'The Red Eleven would stick by him and fight anyone who tried to squeeze him' (Theroux, 1973). 'The squeeze' is such extortion but especially the developed and endemic version in the Far East.

squeeze a Malteser to defecate
A 'Malteser' is a small round chocolate.

squib off to murder
Usu. by shooting, from the noise made by a firework: 'The night Joe got squibbed off' (Chandler, 1939).

squiffy intoxicated
Properly uneven or lopsided: '"The man was squiffy," said Aunt Anges. "It was written all over him"' (E. Waugh, 1933).

squirrel tank an institution for the insane
A play on **nut** (q.v.): '. . . the perpetrator went nuts after the accident and is now in the squirrel tank' (Wambaugh, 1975). Am.

squirt to defecate
Normally of diarrhoea, and much used as a mild insult, neither the giver nor the receiver being aware how rude it is: '. . . a very coarse

name, which we can change euphemistically
into – squirts' (Vachell, 1934). Diarrhoea is
also 'skeet', 'squit', 'squitters' or 'skitters':
'"Skitters," I said. "That'll wait for no man.
Run for it. I'll wait." I dashed for the toilet'
(Steinbeck, 1961); and '. . . the senile Labrador that drools and squitters all over the
stairs' (Theroux, 1982).

stab to copulate with
Of a male, using the common imagery of
violence and of pushing: 'He'd stabb'd me in
mine own house . . . . he will foin like any
devil' (Shakespeare, 2 *Henry IV* – 'foin'
means thrust). 'Stabbed with a Bridport dagger' was not copulation with a native of the
Dorset town but death by hanging, Bridport
being famous for rope-making because of a
climate in which flax flourished.

stabilize to conquer
Hitler, and those Communists who have followed his example, have fomented instability
as an excuse for invasion. In other cases
latent instability has been heightened by the
invasion. In either case the aggressor talks of
'stabilizing' the victim.

stable the whores who work for a single
pimp
The common equine imagery.

stag pornographic
From the meaning, male, as in 'stag party':
'But you can get late-night stag movies piped
into our place' (C. Forbes, 1983).

stag month *see* **steg month**

stain to copulate with extra-maritally
Of a male, who pollutes the female morally
rather than seminally: 'Give up your body to
such sweet uncleanness, As she that he hath
stain'd' (Shakespeare, *Measure of Measure*).
ob.

staining minor bleeding
Medical jargon, from the seepage of blood
into bandages.

stake (the) killing by burning
The victim was tied to a pole. The significance of this form of death for heretics was
that nothing remained to reappear and cause
further trouble at the Resurrection.

stake-out a police trap
From the prior exploration of the site of a
suspected future criminal attempt: '. . . he
was running a stake-out . . . . over in the
meat-packing district' (Van Lustbaden,
1983).

stale a whore
Someone already used sexually by others:
'And feeds from home; poor I am but his
stale' (Shakespeare, *Comedy of Errors*). 'Stale'
was also urine, possibly from its common
retention for laundry and other purposes:
'The dung and stale of cattle' (Marshall,
1817). ob.

stall a pickpocket's accomplice
Properly, a decoy bird, whence in Br. use the
person who distracted the victim's attention
while the thief was at work. Thus our modern use, deliberately to postpone, or to lose
airspeed below that necessary for flight.

stand (1) an erect penis
Of obvious derivation: 'When it stands well
with him, it stands well with her' (Shakespeare, *Two Gentlemen of Verona*). The penis
may also be said to 'stand to attention'.

stand (2) to be available for breeding
Of a male quadruped, although 'mount'
might seem more appropriate: '. . . the stallion had stood for three seasons and therefore covered a hundred and twenty mares'
(Francis, 1982). SE.

stand before your Maker etc. to die
It would be presumptuous, I suppose, to sit:
'. . . none should expect Gratitude until it is
his turn to stand before the Father of us all'
(le Carré, 1986).

stand down to be dismissed or prematurely retired from employment
Properly, to end a term of duty or to revert to
a lower state of preparedness after an alert.
The term is used to protect the self-esteem
of a departing employee.

standard small or poor quality
No longer the level of size, quality etc.
against which judgement of other products
can be made. The supermarket 'standard
pack' is small and comparatively expensive; a
'standard' durable product is the one without accessories or elegant styling; etc.

star in the east an undone fly-button
An oblique warning to a male which has not
survived the zip age.

starch an unadulterated illegal narcotic
Presumably from the stiffness and the
colour. Am.

stark naked
'Stark' means quite and this is probably
merely an abbr. of the cliché 'stark naked'.
'Stark as the day they were born' (Buchan,
1898) might be read 'quite as the day etc.'

The ob. meaning, dead, came from a dialect meaning stiff, often in the tautological 'stiff and stark'.

start bleeding to menstruate for the first time
The female concerned will certainly have bled from her nose or a wound on previous occasions: 'Yes, I matured early . . . . I started bleeding at eleven' (Sanders, 1970).

state farm etc. an institution for involuntary detention
Where you keep prisoners, children, geriatrics or lunatics. Also in Am. as 'state' homes, hospitals, (training) schools, etc.

state of heath *see* **condition** (2)

state of nature nudity
The imagery of **nature's garb** (above) but the opposite is not an unnatural state: 'Charles Boon, who scorned pyjamas and was often to be encountered walking about the apartment . . . . in a state of nature' (Lodge, 1975).

state protection the preservation of tyranny
Communist jargon, as the 'Department of State Protection' in Russia which controls political prisons, studies a copy of any original writing, spies on potential dissidents, etc. The Ugandan tyrant Amin used his 'State Research Bureau' for the same purpose.

states' rights the continuation of discrimination against Blacks
Properly, the powers reserved to each individual Am. state as different from federal jurisdiction. The South professed to see federal moves against White supremacy as an attack on the individual rights of each state.

status deprivation being thought badly of
Educational jargon of a child who does badly at school or is objectionable, and therefore not rated highly by teachers or other pupils.

statutory woman *see* **obligatory female**

steady company regular extra-marital copulation
A variant of **keep company with** (above): 'We've been keeping steady company for the past five years now' (McBain, 1981, of a man and his sexual mistress).

steer dishonestly to influence the placing of business
By pretending to give disinterested advice in the selection of an adviser or service when you are receiving a commission or a reciprocal benefit: '. . . bribery of hospital personnel to "steer" cases' (J. Mitford, 1963, describing how funeral firms secured business).

steg month the period around childbirth when a husband might copulate extramaritally with relative impunity
From being a gander in N. Eng. dialect, a 'steg' became an aimless male, wandering about while the goose is hatching the goslings. And *see* **gander-mooner** for a further dissertation and explanation. During this time the unavailable wife was known as a 'steg-widow'. I suspect the 'stag month' and 'stag widow' of other lexicographers, including Partridge, are mistaken corruptions. ob.

step down to be dismissed from employment
Properly, to retire of your own volition: 'Saunders must step down' (*London Standard* headline, January 1987, of a Chairman about to be dismissed).

step off to die
Clearly an abbr. but I'm not sure of what. The ob. Sc. 'step away' also meant to die: 'Garskadden's been wi' his Maker these two hours; I saw him step awa' (Ramsay, 1861).

step on to kill
Again drawn from our habitual treatment of insects: 'Jack and Hyme talk so casually about killing and death. "Should I step on him?" "We should have killed the cocksucker." Like that' (Sanders, 1980). sl.

step out on to copulate with other than your regular sexual partner
Of either sex, perhaps from 'stepping out', courting. Am.

stepney a pimp's favourite whore
The one he treated in other respects as a wife out of a number under his control. A 'stepney' was the fifth wheel carried on the step, or running-board, of a car and only brought into use when one of the other four was out of service. BI ob.

(sterile barren had this meaning before its antiseptic connotations.)

sterilize to destroy
Vietnam jargon for 'purifying' the enemy with bombs: 'We sterilize the area prior to the insertion of the 'R. D. terms' (McCarthy, 1967 – 'R. D.' stood for **rural development** (q.v.)). Of evidence, you 'sterilize' by burning the papers or obliterating the tape.

stern the buttocks
Naval imagery in general use. The punning
'stern-chaser' may have homosexual or heterosexual preferences.

stewed drunk
The common culinary imagery: '... most of
the time in camp .... poor old Abel was
stewed' (Keneally, 1979). And no less drunk
if 'half stewed'.

stews (the) a brothel
Properly, a bath house which often doubled
as a brothel: 'An I could get me but a wife in
the stews' (Shakespeare, 2 *Henry IV*). ob.

stick (1) to kill
Supposedly with a pointed weapon, of cattle
in an abattoir and of wild pigs in hunting. It
used also to mean to wound: 'The black thief
has sticket the woman' (Carrick, 1835).

stick (2) a spirituous liquor added to
another drink
Perhaps you have simply placed, or 'stuck',
one liquid inside another: 'Coffee, if you
like, with a "stick" in it' (Praed, 1890). Still
used in N. Eng. and Australia.

stick (3) to copulate with
Of a male, perhaps from the sl. 'stick', a
penis: 'Said he, with a snicker, As he
watched the guy stick her' (*Playboy's Book of
Limericks*). Also as to 'give stick', punning on
the offering of violence.

stick (4) a marijuana cigarette already rolled
by another
Perhaps an abbr. of 'stick of tea', a thin form
of cigarette. Often in compounds like
'dream-stick' and the punning 'joy-stick'.

stick (5) a handgun
From its shape but **rod (2)** (above) is more
common: 'He hit some East Side apartment
for a bundle. Ice, mostly. Never carried a
stick' (Sanders, 1970, and not of a cripple
sliding into a building). sl.

stick (6) a cluster of bombs dropped from
an aircraft
Perhaps because they fall in a straight line.

stick it into (1) to extort through threats
From fig. wounding with a weapon: 'They
had pictures, who the hell knows what else?
But they stuck it into him' (Diehl, 1978 – the
'pictures' are photographs).

stick it into (2) to copulate with
Of the male and barely euphemistic:
'Brother was sticking it into sister every
night' (Mailer, 1965 – they were committing
incest). The Am. 'stick it on' is rarer: 'Men

liked to think they were sticking it on some
kind of technical virgin' (McBain, 1981).

stick up to rob with a threat of, or with
actual, violence
From the command to 'stick up your hands',
and a 'stick-up' is such a robbery: '"You'll
hold me up, I suppose!" .... "I'm a stick-up
artist now, am I?"' (Chandler, 1939).

sticky a spirituous intoxicant
Usu. a liqueur, from its tacky properties: 'I
spend the next two hours .... with a litre
bottle of some colourless but potent sticky at
my elbow' (*Private Eye*, August 1983).

sticky-fingered thieving
Other people's property adheres to them.
Usu. of embezzlement or chance pilfering.

sticky stranger a clandestine electronic
listening device
Espionage jargon – you have to fix the
apparatus by glue: 'You'll want to look
around for a sticky stranger. If they think
you've got something to hide, they'll plant
another ear' (Francis, 1978 – an 'ear' is also
such a device).

stiff (1) a corpse
From the rigor mortis and an abbr. of the
19c. 'stiff one': 'Would she stick it till she
was a stiff 'un' (Mayhew, 1862) and: 'When
anyone was killed they piled the stiffs outside
the door' (*Scribner's Monthly*, July 1880,
quoted in EDD). The abusive 'stiff', a
moron, may come from this use.

stiff (2) drunk
You often feel and look like a corpse: 'I was
quite stiff by the time we got to the burial
ground' (Styron, 1976 – he was drunk).

stiff (3) having an erection of the penis
Of obvious derivation: '... she approached
me where I lay, stiff as a dagger' (Styron,
1976).

stiff (4) to fail to meet your financial obli-
gations
It is one form of death, I suppose. Also as
the Am. 'stiff out'.

stiffener a spirituous intoxicant
A variant of the common **bracer** (q.v.) and
not because it makes you **stiff (2)** (above).

sting to deprive by trickery
Of robbery, overcharging, cheating or any
other kind of knavery. 'The sting' is the
ultimate coup in an elaborate confidence
trick, as also the title of an Am. novel and
film.

stinking very drunk
Probably not from your 'stinking of drink'
but from the meaning, exceedingly, as in the
cliché 'stinking rich'. At one time corrupted
to 'stinko': 'Are you stinko?' (Chandler,
1953).

stir a prison
Probably from the Romany and not from
what you do to your breakfast **porridge**
(q.v.): 'A friend of mine who's in stir' (Chandler, 1939). To be 'stir-wise' is to be experienced in prison life: 'He's too stir-wise for
me' (ibid. of a convict).

stitched drunk
Mainly military use, using the common
death imagery as a soldier's corpse was sewn
up in canvas before burial. Unhappily not
from the ob. Irish 'stitch in your wig', mild
drunkenness, where to 'stitch' was to rumple
and the imagery is of a wig slightly askew.

stockade a military prison
Properly, a strong fence forming an
enclosure: '. . . you fly or you go to the
stockade' (Deighton, 1982, of Am. WWII
fliers).

stoke Lucifer's fires to be dead
Usu. of one who has led a sinful life for
which he is presumed to be doing penance
into eternity on the end of a shovel: 'There
was a rumour of his death, or he's probably
been stoking Lucifer's fires these thirty
years' (Fraser, 1970, writing in 19c. style).
'Lucifer, for the Christians, was inseparable
from Hell' (*New Larousse Encyclopedia of
Mythology*).

stomach (a) obesity around the waist
Usu. of a male and incorrectly specifying the
internal chamber through which food passes
for digestion. A 'bit of a stomach' also
implies obesity, and not post-surgical deprivation.

stoned drunk or under illegal narcotic
influence
It is hard to see what the discomfort of St
Stephen and others had to do with this common use. Of drunkenness: 'The day Butler's
Military Cross was gazetted they both got
stoned out of their minds' (Price, 1979) and
of narcotics: '. . . happily stoned out of his
mind' (Davidson, 1978).

stones the testicles
Of man and animals: 'A philosopher, with
two stones more than's artificial one'
(Shakespeare, *Timon of Athens*) and an E.
Anglian farmer will say that a castrated

sheep is 'two stone lighter'. The ob. 'stoned-
horse-man' was not a heroin addict but the
groom who took a stallion – 'stony' – around
farms to impregnate mares.

stool pigeon a police informer
Pigeons were tied to stools to lure other
pigeons for capture. To 'stool' is to inform
against: '. . . stooled on a bank job in
Michigan and git me four years' (Chandler,
1939).

stoop your body to pollution to copulate extra-maritally
Of a female, although she is more likely to
have been recumbent: 'Before her sister
should her body stoop To such abhorred
pollution. Then, Isabel, live chaste' (Shakespeare, *Measure for Measure*). ob.

stop one to be killed or wounded
A common WWI use, when snipers still
aimed bullets at individuals: 'We old ones
aren't lucky enough to stop one that way'
(Richards, 1933 – he was referring to a
blighty (above)). To 'stop a slug' is more
specific, except for a keen gardener: 'I wasn't
hired to kill people. Until Frisky stopped
that slug I didn't have no such ideas' (Chandler, 1939). To 'stop the big one' is to be
killed: 'The guy stopped the big one. Cold'
(ibid.).

stoppage (1) an inability to defecate
Medical jargon and also used of nasal and
other bodily malfunctions.

stoppage (2) a strike by employees
Trade union jargon which is still used even
if the factory concerned remains in production.

storage the systematic looting of unoc-
cupied premises
In 1977 the Turks, under some provocation
from Cypriot Greeks, invaded the N. of
Cyprus and plundered those buildings
deserted by fleeing Greeks or foreign
property owners. The Turkish Cypriot
leader, Denktash, asserted that the stolen
items has been taken for 'storage', an
explanation which satisfied the United
Nations officials looking into the matter, but
nobody else.

story a lie
Nursery usage although the punning 'story-
teller' may also be used of an adult. A 'tall
story' implies exaggeration and a 'cock-and-
bull story' is a fabrication.

straddle to copulate with
Of a male, with the common riding imagery:

'I felt a moment's pang at the thought that I'd straddled her for the last time' (Fraser, 1985).

straight not indulging in abnormal behaviour
This is a euphemism of those for whom abnormality is the norm, being used of heterosexuals by homosexuals, of non-addicts by those addicted to illegal narcotics, of honest people by criminals (until they themselves 'go straight'), etc.

straighten to procure for another an illegal narcotic
The person whom you supply cannot act normally, or 'straight', unless under narcotic influence. Am.

straighten out to bribe
You induce another to follow the line which you indicate. The phrase is also used of our forceful, but inevitably unavailing, correction of someone with different opinions from our own.

strangle to cause a horse to run badly in a race
From pulling the bridle surreptitiously: 'Sandie had "strangled" a couple at one stage' (Francis, 1962, of a crooked jockey).

strategic capability the possession of nuclear weapons
The jargon of nuclear armour, it should mean, at most, your ability to work out a plan. From our experience of WW II, anything described as 'strategic' in the way of bombing etc. shows small discrimination between civilian and other targets and a 'strategic nuclear war' delivering 'stragetic warheads' from 'stragetic submarines' is unlikely to prove any different.

strategic withdrawal etc. a retreat under pressure
Any military strategy which involves moving away from the enemy is hardly likely to lead to victory: 'We've admitted a strategic withdrawal . . . . the Jerries are coming hell for leather down the coast road' (Manning, 1965). A 'strategic movement to the rear' seeks to imply, falsely, that some of your side are still in front of you. A 'strategic retreat' is even less of face-saver: 'The Germans announced an Allied retreat. Merely a strategic retreat, said the British News Service' (Manning, 1960).

stray your affection to copulate extramaritally
To 'stray' is to cause to wander: 'Stray'd his

affection in unlawful love' (Shakespeare, *Comedy of Errors*). ob.

streak to run naked in a public place
In this phenomenon of the mid-1970s, the speed was supposed to restrict the visibility. A 'streaker' so behaves.

street (the) prostitution
The place where customers are picked up: '"You're the only person who can save us." "How?" "Why, the street, of course"' (Londres, 1928, in tr., of prostitution). A 'streetwalker', a whore, is dated: 'The modern equivalent of the old-time disorderly house and of the street-walker' (Lavine, 1930). A 'street girl' is also a whore: '. . . her wretched career from housewife to street girl' (Green, 1979 – were both occupations wretched?). The Am. 'street tricking' is finding customers as a whore on the streets: 'This old campaigner we call Mabel the Monster, been street trickin' must be ten years now' (Diehl, 1978). 'On the street(s)' is engaged in prostitution: 'She fell in love with Mary Jack's pimp, who put her on the street' (L. Armstrong, 1955). The ob. Sc./N. Eng. 'Street and Walker's place' meant unemployment, from walking the streets looking for work.

stretch a period of imprisonment
An abbr. of 'stretch of years': 'The bosses always get the longest stretch in the penitentiary' (L. Thomas, 1979).

stretch the hemp etc. to kill by hanging
From the material of the noose: 'Molly Maguire stretching the hemp in the last act' (*Pearson's Magazine*, October 1900, quoted in EDD). Also as 'stretch the neck'. ? ob.

stretch your legs to urinate
Why we say we have intervals in meetings or stops on long journeys: 'Another five or ten minutes, and you'll be able to stretch your legs. And then after that I fancy you'll be able to travel more comfortably' (Price, 1978).

stretcher a lie or exaggeration
From 'stretching' your credulity and the truth: 'Is ole Wheat still telling Gus back there them stretchers regarding his gran' daddy?' (Keneally, 1979). Whence the punning 'stretcher case', an habitual liar and to 'stretch', to lie: 'I ain't about to start stretching at this time of day' (Fraser, 1985 – Flashman isn't often so reticent).

strike out to die
From baseball and therefore confined to Am.

string up to kill by hanging
Usu. in a makeshift manner on the limb of a convenient tree which always seems to be to hand in cowboy films.

stripper a thief
Especially of radios etc. from Am. cars and houses: '. . . our motherfucking car stripper is halfway to Watts' (Wambaugh, 1975). In SE a 'stripper' removes paint or takes off her clothes in public in a manner calculated to entertain male spectators.

stroke off to masturbate
Usu. of the male but used by both sexes.

strong-arm to steal
With the use or threat of force: 'If he had not strong-armed that money out of me I would have given him lots more' (L. Armstrong, 1955 – his own surname originated in the Sc./Eng. borders where for centuries such activity was endemic).

strong waters spirituous intoxicants
Not a fast flowing stream: '. . . it does not one-tenth of the harm that strong waters cause among the poorer classes' (Fraser, 1985, writing in archaic style of opium).

strop your beak to copulate
Of a male, from the movement in sharpening an open razor and the sl. 'beak', a penis. Rarely of masturbation by a male.

structured arranged as a cartel
The concept is of something being put together in an orderly manner but the Am. 'structured competition' covers up illegal agreements on price and other competition.

struggle a political campaign
This was once a fig. usage but riot or violence in public places, especially **demonstrations** (q.v.) or on picket lines, are now commonplace. The Nazi 'struggle' for 'national existence' was not the fight against the Anglo-Americans or the Russians but the extermination of Slavs, Jews and Gypsies: '. . . a struggle for national existence meant racial warfare' (Keneally, 1982).

stubble *see* **take a turn in the stubble** etc.

stuck cheated
Probably an abbr. of 'stuck with a poor bargain': 'I experienced that peculiar inward sinking that accompanies the birth of the conviction that one has been stuck' (Somerville and Ross, 1897, of a horse deal).

stud a male viewed sexually by another
Usu. of a man who is thought to be ready to copulate promiscuously: 'Sex? . . . . No stud in

the world is worth two million dollars' (West, 1979) but also of homosexuals: 'I don't go to no leather joints lookin' for some stud to fistfuck' (M. Thomas, 1980). The derivation is probably from the place where stallions are kept for breeding, their availability, their fee etc. – 'stud farm', 'at stud', 'stud fee' etc. – rather than the imagery of a projecting lug.

student an adult who declines to seek paid employment
The occupation which many agitators profess to follow. As Hudson points out (DDE) the practice of calling all schoolchildren 'students' is 'both flattering and untrue'.

studio a small apartment with no windows at eye level
House agents' jargon, trading on the traditional indirect illumination from a skylight in which some painters choose to work.

stuff (1) any taboo or forbidden substance
Properly, any substance or material. Of semen: 'Put stuff To some she-beggar' (Shakespeare, *Timon of Athens*); of contraband spirits: 'A considerable amount of "stuff" finds its way to the consumers without the formality of the Custom House' (Stoker, 1895); of illegal narcotics: '. . . he smokes too much, and "stuff"' (Bogarde, 1981); etc.

stuff (2) to copulate with
From the physical entry rather than impregnation despite: 'A maid, and stuft! there's goodly catching of cold' (Shakespeare, *Much Ado about Nothing*). Also some use of buggery. Much vulgar fig. use: 'As for the flute, he knew where he could stuff that' (Davidson, 1978).

stung by a serpent made pregnant
Of an unmarried woman, punning on 'serpent', a penis and inferring an unexpected and unwelcome happening. ? ob.

stunt a limited battle
Much more than a trick, but these horrors were played down in WWI: 'If he don't get the Victoria Cross for this stunt I'm a bloody Dutchman' (Richards, 1933).

stunted hare a rabbit
For seamen, the mention of a 'rabbit' is taboo although it is a long time since Br. chandlers substituted salted rabbit meat, which decays quickly, for the conventional salted pork.

stupid drunk
From the drunkard's behaviour rather than the folly of getting like it. Common in Sc. as

'stupid-fou': 'He was na stupid-fou, as was his wont on market days' (Strain, 1900).

(subcompact small was invented by the Am. motor industry to make the ownership of a small car less humiliating.)

subdue to your will to copulate with extra-maritally
Males do it, overcoming female fears or scruples. The woman has to be royal or rich to 'subdue' a man: '. . . the queen has only two uses for foreign men – first to subdue them to her will, if you follow me' (Fraser, 1977).

submit to to copulate with
Of a woman, usu. extra-maritally and with an inference of reluctance: 'They refuse to submit to his pleasure, and will not return him the money' (Mayhew, 1862, of cheating whores).

succubus a whore
Properly, a female demon who copulates with men in their sleep, thus for the fastidious providing an excuse for involuntary seminal ejaculation: '"Yes, thou barbarian," said she, turning to Wagtail, "thou tiger, thou succubus!"' (Smollett, 1748).

succumb (1) to die
Properly, to give way to anything, and usu. of natural death: 'Hibbert . . . . succumbed to a heart attack at his desk' (Candon, 1966).

succumb (2) to copulate extra-maritally
Another form of giving way, by either sex: 'I'm willing to bet you five dollars she doesn't succumb even to the charms of William' (Archer, 1979).

suck daisy-roots to be dead
The common imagery of the churchyard flower seen from below.

suck off to practise fellatio or cunnilingus
Of obvious derivation. Until lately, only spoken but increasingly found in print now that unusual sexual habits have ceased to be matters of literary discretion.

suck the monkey to steal rum
Br. naval use. You inserted a straw in the cask. ob.

suffer the supreme penalty to be killed
Usu. of a convict, flogging, imprisonment and fines being lesser sanctions: 'As for . . . . the murder of her Indian subordinate . . . . eventually one or two men suffered the supreme penalty' (P. Scott, 1973).

suffering cats a mild oath
Partridge said 'Ex caterwauling' (DSUE)

while Wentworth and Flexner said 'A euphem. for "Suffering Christ"' (DAS). They can't both be right.

sugar (1) a bribe
The common imagery of 'sweetening' and a 'sugared' deal is one which involves corruption.

sugar (2) a mild oath
Common genteel usage, for the taboo 'shit'.

sugar (3) an illegal narcotic
In two specific uses, of any white narcotic in crystalline form; and of LSD deposited on a lump of sugar to make it palatable.

sugar daddy a man with a much younger sexual mistress
'Daddy' from his relative age and 'sugar' from the sweet things of life which she may expect from him: 'Kathy's Sugar Daddy Evicted' (*Western Daily Press*, May 1981).

sugar hill a brothel
Presumably from the 'sweet time' given to customers. 'Sugar hill' is also a common name for a brothel area in an Am. Black community, other than Harlem.

sun has been hot today there are signs of drunkenness
Probably from the old Br. habit of putting weak cider or ale in harvest fields. On a hot day a reaper would get progressively more drunk as he slaked his thirst. A drunkard might also be said to 'have the sun in his eyes' or 'have been in the sun': 'We guessed by his rackle as he'd bin i' the sunshine' (Pinnock, 1895 – 'rackle' was riotous conduct).

sun has gone over the yardarm let us drink intoxicants
The sun, in temperate latitudes, sinks in the late afternoon below the 'yardarm', a spar running horizontally from the mast to support a sail: 'Ah well, sun is over the yardarm, so down to work' (*Private Eye*, May 1981, of drinking intoxicants).

Sunday-supplement inaccurate and irresponsible
From the sensation-seeking of some journalists whose scurrilous criticisms and reporting provide continuity for the advertising in colour-printed supplements to Sunday newspapers: 'There were, of course, even then the Sunday-Supplement, New-Yorker Group. Schoolboys in 1939, they now emerged as an elegant shoal of piranhas savaging, on principle, practically anything which was not subtitled' (Bogarde, 1978).

Sunday traveller an illegal drinker of intoxicants at an inn
Only a bona fide traveller could be served with intoxicants on Irish Sundays: '. . . a door consecrated to the unobtrusive visits of so called "Sunday Travellers"' (Somerville and Ross, 1897).

sundowner an intoxicant taken in the evening
Of spirits which in the tropics only an alcoholic would regularly drink during the day because of the effects of additional dehydration. The hard drinking starts at dusk: 'We're all right now, the sun has gone down and we can have a whisky' (Allen, 1979) and 'As he sits there on a hot evening swilling his sundowners' (G. Greene, 1978 – 'there' was in Zaire).

sunset years old age
Trading off the beauty of sunsets rather than the darkness to follow. But still less sickly than the **golden years** (above).

(superior an estate agents' puff has no geographical or other significance. You do not see any 'inferior' properties offered for sale.)

supporters' club the employees of a potential customer improperly favouring a vendor
Punning on an association of sports fans. Commercial use of those who have been influenced by bribes in the form of cash, gifts or lavish entertainment.

sure thing a woman reputed by men to copulate freely and extra-maritally
Probably from the racehorse so described by the tipster, although there are no certainties in either sport: '. . . hardly at all like someone who in her time had been one of the surest things between Bridgend and Carmarthen' (Amis, 1986).

surgical appliance *see* **appliance**

surrender to to copulate with extra-maritally
Of a female with the common imagery of male dominance: 'Girls seemed to prefer the story of her surrendering to Koolman in exchange for a leading role' (Deighton, 1972).

surplus to dismiss from employment
Usu. of a single dismissal with an implication that there was one employee too many. Am.

surveillance spying
Properly, no more than keeping a watch over, as a ward or a prisoner. Now police and espionage jargon for clandestine observation, and 'electronic' or 'technical' surveillance is the use of hidden microphones or other gadgetry of spying.

survivability the extent to which it is thought that a nation can survive a nuclear attack
Military jargon. Mario Pei also gives 'termination capability', the ability to bring to an end a nuclear war, presumably by destroying the other side too.

swallow the bible to perjure yourself
From the taking of an oath in an Am. court: 'They will stick together, stretch conscience and at times "swallow the Bible"' (Lavine, 1930). And *see* also **eat the bible** and **switch the primer.**

swamped drunk
Sunk by too much liquid. In 19c. BI it also meant bankrupted.

sweat it out of to obtain information from by coercion
Am. police jargon and the 'sweat-box' was the room where you did it. The ob. Eng. 'sweat-box' was a cell in any police station.

sweep (1) to kill
Am. Vietnam usage where a 'sweeping' operation was not the cleaning of a barracks and to 'search and sweep' was to go over hostile territory and kill anyone you found there.

sweep (2) to search for clandestine listening devices
Espionage jargon and, like mine-sweeping, barely euphemistic.

sweet momma a man's sexual mistress
Properly, for an Am. Black, any woman of a kindly disposition regardless of age or motherhood. A 'sweet man' is a black woman's extra-marital regular sexual partner.

sweet tooth an addiction to illegal narcotics
An Am. pun on **candy** (above).

sweeten (1) to bribe
The common bribery imagery: 'Now-a-days ane canna' phraise, An' sooth, an' lie, an' sweeten, An' palm, an' sconse' (Lauderdale, 1796 – all the activities were *sui generis* except 'sconce', to trick). A 'sweetener' is such a bribe, often in gift form rather than in cash: 'Giving big commissions, sweeteners, call it bribery if you like' (Lyall, 1980).

sweeten (2) improperly to force up bidding at an auction
Auctioneers' jargon for purporting to accept spurious or non-existent bids.

sweetener *see* **sweeten** (1)

sweetheart an arrangement which improperly benefits two parties at the expense of a third
In various phrases such as the Am. 'sweetheart contract' between an employer and a labour union which benefits the firm and the union officials at the expense of the workers; or a 'sweetheart price' which cheats stockholders: 'And at a real good sweetheart price, too. Less than $6 billion over four years' (M. Thomas, 1980).

swell to be pregnant
Of obvious imagery: 'Unless it swell past hiding, and then it's past watching' (Shakespeare, *Troilus and Cressida*) and in tasteless modern Am. use.

swim for a wizard to test for magical powers of evil
Witchcraft was a fruitful subject of taboo and euphemism, and I include this sample entry to remind us of the social behaviour and beliefs of our recent ancestors: 'So late as 1863, an old man was flung into a mill-stream .... being what is called "swimming for a wizard"' (Harland and Wilkinson, 1867 – presumably, he drowned if he was human and you killed him if he proved himself a wizard by not drowning). Lancs ob.

swing to be killed by hanging
From the rotation of a suspended corpse: 'On high as ever on a tow Swing'd in the widdie' (Anderson, 1826 – 'tow' was hemp, from which hung a noose; and 'in a widdie' was swinging around). Still used fig. of receiving punishment.

swing around the buoy to have an easy job
Br. naval imagery from a ship at anchor, moving with the tides, and the consequent period of relaxation for the crew.

swing both ways to have both homosexual and heterosexual tastes
Probably from 'swing', to be in the fashion as the 'swinging sixties', when open promiscuity and vulgarity were popularised: 'You swing both ways, huh?' (Sanders, 1982 – the male was copulating with a female homosexual).

swing off to die
Not by hanging or even by other violence. The imagery is avian or possibly from jazz music: 'She placed flowers on his grave on the day he swung off' (Longstreet, 1956 – he meant the anniversary).

swing the lamp to boast
Br. naval usage and imagery, probably from the action of a signaller passing a message between ships at night rather than from the moment of a suspended lamp below decks.

swing the lead to pretend unfitness to avoid work or duty
The association with the calling of the leadsman is unclear, unless he is claiming to be grounded while still in clear water: 'The majority were swinging the lead and would do anything to prevent themselves being marked A1' (Richards, 1933).

swing with to copulate with
Not of a trapeze artist. Rarely of a homosexual encounter: 'THOMAS: Did you ever swing with her? CYNTHIA: Twice. No more. THOMAS: Bent – isn't she?' (Sanders, 1970).

swipe to steal
In the original Am. usage, perhaps a corruption of 'sweep' and not from 'swipe', a blow. Usu. of chance pilfering. The ob. Norfolk meaning, to raise lost anchors for an admiralty reward, sounds like a corruption of 'sweep'.

swish to flaunt your homosexuality
Of an Am. male who walks in a manner recognized by fellow homosexuals.

switch-hitter a person with both heterosexual and homosexual tastes
From the Am. ambidexterous baseball player. In ob. Br. use to 'switch' was to copulate, along with to 'swinge' or to 'swive'.

switch on *see* **turn on**

switch the primer to perjure yourself
The Irish 'primer' was a prayer-book and a Roman Catholic would have small regard for the mana of the Protestant bible produced for him to swear upon: 'He switched the primer himself that he was innocent' (Carleton, 1836).

'swounds a mild oath
Punning on 'swound', a fainting fit, and on 'by God's wounds'.

syndicate an association of powerful criminals
Properly, any group of business etc. associates but in this Am. use an abbr. of 'crime syndicate': '"When we talk about the rackets, are we talking about the same guys?"'

"We're talking about the syndicate"'
(Ustinov, 1971).

syphon the python to urinate
Of a male, with the common serpentine
imagery.

syrup a wig
Br. rh. sl. from 'syrup of figs'. Usu. of a male
where the taboo remains strong.

T

tactical done involuntarily under pressure
Properly, relating to the deployment of troops but a 'tactical re-grouping' is a retreat. A 'tactical nuclear weapon' is smaller than a 'strategic', for use primarily against soldiers rather than cities.

tagged (1) hit by a bullet
Properly, labelled and perhaps from the superstition among soldiers that the bullet which hits you 'had your name on it': '"Tagged!" he realized. There was no mistaking it, he had been hit before' (W. Smith, 1979).

tagged (2) detected in the commission of crime
Again I suppose from the identification when you want to remain anonymous: 'Ralph got tagged for stealing stamps' (Steinbeck, 1961). Am.

tail (1) a woman viewed sexually by a male
From 'tail', the buttocks: 'It's tail, Lew. Women' (Bradbury, 1976). More common as a 'bit' or 'piece' of tail: 'She was a piece of Scandinavian tail that he'd picked up ' (Matthew, 1978). Not today usu. of a whore despite Grose's definition 'A prostitute'.

tail (2) to follow surreptitiously
From staying close behind: 'You can do a tail job on him' (Allbeury, 1975 – he was to be so followed).

tail-pulling the publication of a book at the author's expense
Publishers' punning usage, from the meaning teasing, and a synonym of 'vanity' or 'subsidy' publishing.

take (1) to steal
Almost too venerable to be accepted as a euphemism – the OED gives an illustration in this sense from 1200. In modern Am. use, 'the take' is bribery: 'You're on the take from one of the mobs' (Deighton, 1978) and to 'take your end' is to accept a bribe: 'Chicago was a right town then. The fix was in. The dicks took their end without a beef' (Weverka, 1973).

take (2) to copulate with
Usu. of the male: 'To take her in her heart's extremest hate' (Shakespeare, *Richard III*) and in modern use: 'It didn't stop the waves of lust as he took her' (Allbeury, 1976). Rarely, although with rather more logic, the female 'takes' the male: 'Chandra .... had

been the cause of his love affair .... for she had taken him just to forget Chandra' (Masters, 1976).

take (3) to kill
Of animals, by culling or hunting: 'And many of the creatures she allowed to escape. "You take him," she would say' (Mailer, 1965).

take (4) to conceive
Of domestic animals, as of cuttings or grafts: 'Some mares won't "take"' (Francis, 1982, of horse breeding).

take (5) to overcome or master
An omnibus use which describes anything from passing another vehicle on the highway to any kind of villainy: ' He had no doubts he could "take" the apartment at Fontenoy House; he was, after all, one of the best cracksmen in London' (Forsyth, 1984).

take a bath to suffer a heavy financial loss
Your boat is capsized: 'His old man took a bath in real estate about ten years ago, got in the shower, and emptied his brains out with a .45' (Diehl, 1978). In 18c. Eng. to 'go to Bath' meant much the same, so adroit were the frauds and beggars in that spa.

take a bit from to copulate with extramaritally
Usu. of a female on a regular basis: 'Margot Dunlop-Huynegin is taking a little bit now and then from her husband's valet' (Condon, 1966).

take a blinder to die
A 'blinder' here is something unknown, to which you are blind, and not something spectacular, as the sportsman who 'plays a blinder'.

take a break to allow the intrusion of advertisements
Br. television jargon, the advertisements being meant to appear when the continuity of the programme will not be interrupted. This poses a problem for a producer who wants to hold the attention of his audience without unduly contravening the regulations of his licence to transmit.

take a leak *see* leak (1)

take a liberty with *see* take liberties

take a point to listen unsympathetically to a contrary view
A device of politicians who eschew contradicting constituents: 'She received us most cordially and took all the points we

made' (*Daily Telegraph*, February 1980, of Mrs Thatcher).

take a powder to leave without settling your account
From the hasty departure brought on by a laxative and usu. of checking out of a hotel without paying. Some fig. use: '. . . your guys took a powder and the Krauts just came rolling over our support areas' (Deighton, 1981). Am.

take a risk to copulate without contraception
The 'risk' referred to is of conception rather than sexually transmitted disease.

take a turn in the stubble etc. to copulate
The 'stubble' is the female pubic hair as in the punning 'shoot over the stubble', to ejaculate before vaginal entry. According to Grose, a man might take other punning 'turns', in Cupid's Corner, Love Lane, Mount Pleasant and other suggestive locations in and around London; and a woman might 'take a turn on her back' in any part of the kingdom.

take a view to publish a misleading statement
Accountants' jargon and self-justification when they modify published figures by taking a subjective view of reserves, inventory, etc. to please a client.

take a walk to resign from employment
Or less often, to be dismissed: 'I think he should take a walk. Who needs this shit?' (M. Thomas, 1985 – he referred to a troublesome affair and not to the employee). Am.

take a wheel off the cart to bankrupt
Bankers' jargon for demanding repayment of a loan on terms with which the borrower cannot comply. In 1977 a banker who told me he didn't intend to do it, did.

take advantage of to copulate with extramaritally
Of a male, alluding to her weakness and his ungentlemanly conduct: 'My later behaviour in taking advantage of her did no more than damage her self-respect' (Amis, 1978 – but how did he know?). Also in the ob. form to 'take vantage': '"I fear her not, unless she chance to fall" . . . . "God forbid that! for he'll take vantages"' (Shakespeare, 3 *Henry VI*).

take an early bath to be sent off the field for foul play
In BI, too, rarely of being replaced by a substitute after playing badly or being injured. In similar vein, an Am. sportsman may be 'sent to the showers'.

take away no facilities for eating on the premises are provided
Of catering establishments, whence an inference of inferiority as in the fig.: 'We'll be able to advertise Take-Away Degrees' (Sharpe, 1979).

take care to avoid impregnation during copulation
As in **careful** (2) (above): 'I won't hurt you and I'll take care' (Harris, 1925).

take care of (1) to kill
Properly, to look after, whence to account for: 'He might have been afraid you would have him taken care of' (Chandler, 1943).

take care of (2) to bribe
Again from the meaning, to look after: 'Osborne had always known which officials needed to be taken care of' (Archer, 1979).

take for a ride (1) to murder
You bundled your victim into a car and killed him in a secluded place: '. . . takes him for a ride. His death is attributed . . .' (Lavine, 1930). You fared no better if you were 'taken' for an outing or out into the country. Am.

take for a ride (2) to cheat
Damaging, but not terminal.

take home to die of natural causes
The devout, for whom heaven is 'home', are taken there by Jesus. Rarely of an animal: 'If it would please the Lord to take it home' (EDD).

take in your coals to contract venereal disease
Am. male naval usage, punning on the burning sensation and the heat of a coal-fired steamship.

take leave of life to die
Evasive circumlocution as much as euphemism, although it does suggest a voluntary decision where dying is concerned: 'He could eat nothing, not rally his strength; and within ten days he took leave of life' (Monsarrat, 1978).

take liberties to make an unwanted sexual approach to a woman
It covers anything from attempted fondling to copulation: '. . . (the licentious monk) proceeded to take still further liberties' (Lewis, 1795 – the entry of her mother saved the girl from rape). Also as 'take a liberty': 'Nobody

ever tried to take a liberty with her'
(McCarthy, 1963).

take needle to inject a narcotic illegally
Not the action of a sempstress: 'About to
take the needle' (Mailer, 1965, of an addict).

take off to ingest illegal narcotics
From the intended effect. In Am. to be
'taken off' is to be robbed by an addict, of
drugs or the cash to buy them, and a 'take-
off artist' is an addict who thus secures
supplies.

take out (1) to court
The action may also take place in the front
room, if secluded enough.

take out (2) to kill
An abbr. perhaps for 'take out of circulation': 'If a KGB agent named Talaniekov
appeared on the scene he was taken out as
ruthlessly as Schofield' (Ludlum, 1979).
'Take out' is also used of violently over-
powering any opposition: 'Japanese counter-
terrorist people had decided to take out the
headquarters of the fanatical ultra-left Red
Army Faction' (Forsyth, 1984). The ob. Sc.
'take off' also meant to die: 'You were in the
house at the time of his taking off' (Beatty,
1897, of a death).

take precautions *see* precautions

take something to drink an intoxicant or
use a narcotic illegally
In various forms, as the social 'What will you
take?' which offers a choice of intoxicants.
And of narcotics: '"Have you taken anything?" (This meant drugs)' (Murdoch,
1977). 'Drink taken' implies a degree of
drunkenness: 'I had only three bottles o'
porther taken' (Somerville and Ross, 1908).

take steps to initiate proceedings for divorce
Legal jargon, perhaps an abbr. of 'take steps
to end the marriage' – or to secure as much
alimony as you can. Also of other litigation.

take stock of the situation to review the
continuance of a prosecution
Br. legal jargon, using the imagery of
retailing: '(The judge) indicated to prosecuting counsel that it would be a good idea if
he "took stock of the situation" – which
means in judicial language, that he should
throw in the towel' (*Private Eye*, May 1981).

take the air to urinate
From the days when you had to leave the
house: 'Danny rose and said he needed to
take the air, a gentlemanly statement of his
desire to use the outhouse' (Keneally, 1979).

take the can (back) *see* carry the can

take the drop to be killed by hanging
From the scaffold: 'He's as good as taken
the drop already' (G.Greene, 1934). To
'take a drop' is merely to drink intoxicants,
although implying habitual excess, in which
case the victim dies more slowly.

take the gap to emigrate from Rhodesia to
South Africa
Of White inhabitants around 1980 who were
said to be 'gapping': 'The numbers of people
taking the gap (emigrating)' (*Sunday Telegraph*, December 1979). I would like to think
there was a link with the ob. Lancs meaning,
to yield or give in, retreating from the
Northern invaders through the Preston Gap.

take the pledge *see* sign the pledge

take to bed to copulate with
Of either sex and *see* bed (2): 'What does it
matter to me if she lets a man take her to
bed?' (G.Greene, 1932).

take to the cleaners to rob or cheat
The process thoroughly removes all surplus
matter: 'Dantzler's sporting a new Ferrari,
braggin' on the street how he took some
cowboy to the cleaners' (Diehl, 1978).

take to the hills to escape
From captivity, real or fig.: 'I really thought
seriously of taking to the hills with our little
Laura' (B. Forbes, 1983 – a married man
was thinking of leaving his wife for another
woman).

take too much to be drunk
The precise intoxicant is unspecified: 'I very
much fear he has taken too much' (E.
Waugh, 1933 – she thought he was intoxicated). Of a single drinking bout or regular
intemperance.

take under protection as a pimp to control a whore
The jargon of prostitution: 'When a Pole has
chosen a Jewish girl he calls it "taking her
under his protection"' (Londres, 1928, in
tr.).

take up with to cohabit and copulate
extra-maritally with
Properly, no more than to consort with or
support: 'After a quarrel too, a lad goes and
takes up with another young gal' (Mayhew,
1851).

take with you to kill
You would only use the phrase if you
thought you yourself were about to die: '. . . a

few desperate wretches taking as many Sioux with them as they could' (Fraser, 1982).

take your departal *see* **depart this life**

taking your end *see* **take** (1)

take your leave of to die
The final parting: '. . . so absolutely unlike the way Frank would have wished to take his leave of us' (M. Thomas, 1982, of a death).

take your life to kill yourself
As different from 'take your life in your hands', risking it rashly, or just 'taking life as it comes', living life in a casual way: 'Beautiful Young Society Matron Takes Life in Plunge' (Mailer, 1965, of a suicide). To 'take life', to kill, is explicit.

take your name away to copulate with extra-maritally
In such a case, the woman's name is unlikely to be changed by marriage to her partner but her 'good name' or reputation, may be lost: 'The captain of the football team spent a whole year trying to take my dear name away from me' (Mailer, 1965).

take your snake for a gallop to urinate
Of a male,with the common serpentine imagery.

take yourself in hand to masturbate yourself
Punning male usage.'Taken in hand' is of masturbation by another.

taken dead
Not of being killed, as in **take** (3) (above), but from this world to another or as the case may be: 'He was taken with leukaemia' (Ustinov, 1971, giving a cause of death). The dialect 'took' is more emphatic: 'Took he was – in the pride o' his prime' (Ollivant, 1898). A 'taking' or, less often a 'taking hence', is a natural death: 'I was present at her taking, and though I be partial to death-beds . . .' (Zack, 1901) and: 'The early days before the taking hence of her brother John' (Jane, 1897).

taken-away a changeling
The Sc. fairies took your bonny breast-fed child and replaced it by a sad puny creature, weaned on to an inadequate diet, but no corpse was left in the cot for scientific enquiry because 'Whoever lives to see him dee will find in the bed a henweed or a windlestrae, instead o' a Christian corpse' (Galt, 1823 – of a 'ta'en awa'. A 'windlestrae' is a stalk of withered grass). ob.

taken short needing to urinate
Of a male usu. at an inconvenient time or place. I suppose from the days when coaches and trains without corridors used to stop at staging posts or stations, but not between them: 'We used empty bully-beef tins for urinating in. If a man was taken short during the day, he had to use the trench' (Richards, 1933, of WW I).

taking *see* **taken**

talent a woman viewed sexually by a man
Presumably he hopes she has a 'talent for copulation', although he wouldn't put it that way. Also of women so viewed collectively: 'He had no plans to get trapped by just any piece of gash. The talent in the place had to be seen to be believed' (Collins, 1981). The punning 'talent-spotting' is male searching for such females.

talk to the old gentleman *see* **old a' ill thing** etc.

tank a prison cell
From its size and shape. In Am. it is usu. held in reserve for the accommodation of newly arrested prisoners.

tank fight a fraudulent boxing match
One of the fighters 'dives' – collapses voluntarily to the floor – into a fig. water 'tank', whence the pun on the contest between armoured vehicles. Am.

tanked (up) drunk
Am. motoring imagery, which may owe something to the German 'tanken', to fill with fuel: 'He got tanked up one night and stood on his chair and sang' (Theroux, 1973).

tap (1) to drink intoxicants
From piercing a cask with a bung, to draw off liquid: 'I got the square bottle out and tapped it with discretion' (Chandler, 1939). To 'tap the admiral' is reputed to come from the naval habit of sucking liquor furtively through a straw, not excluding rum from the cask in which Admiral Nelson's corpse was being preserved on its return from Trafalgar for a state funeral in London.

tap (2) a clandestine listening device
Espionage jargon for something drawing off sound rather than liquid.

tap (3) to copulate with a virgin
Of a male, the bung going into an unbroken barrel. ? ob.

tap (4) to obtain an advantageous loan or other finance

Again the imagery of the faucet: 'He's invested in movies, I believe, though being a chum I've never tapped him' (C. Forbes, 1983).

tap (5) the constant availability of stock from willing sellers
The inference is that they know more than the prospective buyer. Whence the Stock Exchange saw: 'Where there's a tip, there's a tap'.

tap a kidney to urinate
Of either sex, from the renal function: 'I tapped a kidney in the ladies' room' (Theroux, 1978).

taps (the) death
Am. military use, from the roll of a drum at a funeral.

tapped indigent
Like a cask which has been broached and emptied. Especially of an Am. who has lost a lot of money gambling.

tar opium
From its black, sticky appearance.

tarbrush (the) partial descent from a non-White ancestor
Usu. as a 'touch' or 'lick' of the tarbrush, from the difficulty in eradicating every trace of tar from a brush which you may later wish to use for applying white paint, genes controlling dark pigmentation being equally persistent: 'A little too liberal with the tarbrush perhaps?' (Ustinov, 1971). The use is now thought offensive as implying Black inferiority.

target of opportunity random bombing
The common instruction to WW II bomber crews who might fail to reach the assigned targets bu had to jettison their load to get home and land with safety: 'They bombed "targets of opportunity" .... shutting your eyes, toggling the bombload, gaining height, and getting the hell out' (Deighton, 1982).

tarry-fingered thieving
Sailors in Sc. ports had a reputation for pilfering – the 'tar' came from the tarpaulin he wore: 'To prevent "tarry-fingered" customers, all the hobs were hooked in unison' (Gordon, 1880). ? ob.

tart *see* **jam tart**

taste to copulate with
Of a male, extra-maritally and once only: 'If you can make't apparent That you have tasted her in bed' (Shakespeare, *Cymbeline*). You might also more specifically 'taste her body'. The use survives in the modern Am.

'taste', a single act of extra-marital copulation by a male.

taters the testicles
An abbr. of 'potatoes', and fig. still 'lost' by Eng. Midlanders who act stupidly.

taxi drinker a whore
She introduces herself to potential customers by accepting a drink from them at a bar. Punning perhaps on the 'taxi dancer' whom a solitary male may pay to dance with.

TB *see* **consumption**

tea marijuana
From its likeness when chopped to tea leaves: '. . . marijuana; he called it tea' (Styron, 1976). 'Texas tea' is specific and 'tea sticks' or 'sticks of tea' are marijuana cigarettes: 'There isn't much record he went for tea-sticks or the smoke' (Longstreet, 1956) and: 'Three highballs and three sticks of tea' (Chandler, 1940). Am. 'tea heads' may smoke marijuana illegally at a 'tea party'.

tea leaf a thief
Br. rh. sl.: 'Or go and be a straightforward tea-leaf – thieve, rob' (Kersh, 1936).

tear off a piece of arse etc. to copulate extra-maritally
Of a male, with no actual physical damage to the partner but overtones of haste and a transient relationship. As often with these vulgarisms, for 'piece' read 'bit, and 'ass' for 'arse'.

technical adjustment etc. a sudden fall in stock market prices
It covers anything from an absence of buyers, bad economic news, stock dumping to panic selling. The phrase seeks to imply that jobbers are merely covering their positions by marking prices down without undue selling orders. Beware equally of a 'technical correction' or 'technical reaction'.

technical surveillance *see* **surveillance**

technicolor yawn vomiting due to drunkenness
Of obvious imagery: 'No sooner was Lord Matey allowed back in than he failed to stifle a technicolour yawn and swamped the entire bar' (*Private Eye*, February 1988 – but I don't think the colour film process was ever anglicized as suggested).

temperance *see* **intemperance**

tempered in the forge of labour imprisoned

A Communist phrase, usu. of those shut up for expressing political or nationalistic dissent.

temple (of health) a lavatory
A perhaps ob. genteel usage, based on the medical advantages of regular defecation and the need so to 'worship' daily.

temporary permanent and embarrassing
For the Am. army in Vietnam, a 'temporary' setback, etc.: 'It caused heavy casualities to be announced as light, routs and ambushes to be described as temporary tactical ploys' (Herr, 1977, of the Am. news services). For Harold Macmillan, a 'temporary local difficulty' was a major political crisis. For a firm, a 'temporary liquidity problem' is insolvency: 'Your old man's got a temporary problem of liquidity' (le Carré, 1986). etc.

ten commandments (the) scratches by a woman's fingernails
When she says to a man 'Thou shalt not': 'Could I come near your beauty with my nails, I'd set my ten commandments in your face' (Shakespeare, 2 *Henry VI*). In modern rare use too, of punches by either sex.

ten o' clock girl a whore
After being arrested in London as a prostitute and bailed overnight, she had to attend court at ten o' clock the following morning. ob.

tender a fool to give birth to a bastard
To 'tender' is to attend or wait upon, whence to offer or present. So the punning Polonius: 'Tender yourself more dearly; Or .... you'll tender me a fool' (Shakespeare, *Hamlet*). ob.

tender-loin district the brothel area of San Francisco
Where the choicest **meat** (q.v.) is to be found.

tenure a job for life
University jargon for a teacher confirmed in a post. The security of employment until retirement age is said to be there to encourage fearless thinking (so long as it isn't anti-Black or pro-National Front) but it also protects the idle, the ageing and the incompetent at the expense of students, other teachers and research: 'He set up his tents in various different universities, from all of which he was tactfully evicted. He never achieved "tenure"' (Murdoch, 1983)

terminate (1) to kill
Properly, to end, of anything: 'The people he terminated died for specific reasons' (M.

Thomas, 1980). When killing illegally, the CIA 'terminates with extreme prejudice': 'I'm afraid the project's been terminated. There was prejudice, extreme prejudice' (Lyall, 1980, of such a killing).

terminate (2) to dismiss from employment
Another Am. ending: '... they had been sent home and demoted or else fired – "terminated" was our word' (Theroux, 1982).

terminate (3) to induce an abortion
Yet another ending, usu. of unwanted pregnancies but also where undertaken on medical advice: 'A nice girl from a nice home .... the thought of termination was unthinkable' (Seymour, 1980).

terminological inexactitude a lie
Br. parliamentary usage, to circumvent the convention against calling another member a liar: '... half-lies, or as Erskine May finds more acceptable, terminological inexactitudes' (Howard, 1977).

test the mattress to copulate
Usu. extra-maritally, wtih common imagery: 'I returned unexpectedly .... and found you testing the mattress with our dear old friend Johnny' (Deighton, 1981).

Texas tea *see* tea

thank to bribe
In many places, verbal expressions alone are not enough: '"Have you thanked the captain?" "I always thank everybody," I replied naively' (Simon, 1979, of passing a N. African frontier with a Br. motor cycle). To 'thank' can also be to tip a servant, and a trap for a Br. visitor to Am. I once handed a scantily-clad female in a Philadelphia bar a $5 bill for $1.60 drinks – it must have been long ago – saying in the Eng. fashion 'Thank you'; 'thank yew, sir,' replied the harpie, keeping the change.

that and this urination
Br. rh. sl. for 'piss'.

that time *see* time of the month

that way (1) homosexual
Of either sex: 'I never picked you for a sapphic .... were you always that way?' (McCarthy, 1963). 'Like that' is usu. only of male homosexuals.

that way (2) pregnant
Female use, often of unwanted impregnation.

the worse drunk
An abbr. of 'the worse for drink' etc.: 'She

had never known him the worse for liquor' (Mayhew, 1862).

thick stupid
A synonym for 'dense' and an abbr. of 'thick in the head' but with no imputation of lunacy.

thick of hearing deaf
A W. Eng. variant of the common **hard of hearing** (q.v.): 'Doubtless I may be thick o' hearing' (Quiller-Couch, 1892).

thief the devil
From his evil ways. He is usu. 'old' or 'black', or 'the thief of the world': 'May the thief o' the world turn it all into whishky an' be choked wid it' (Bartram, 1898). Mainly Ire.

thing any taboo object to which you refer allusively
Such as a ghost for which '"Summut" or "Things" is preferred' (*Spectator,* February 1902, quoted in EDD); or a penis or vagina: 'She that's a maid now . . . . shall not be a maid long, unless things be cut shorter' (Shakespeare, *King Lear*) and, in modern use: 'Measured my "thing". It was eleven centimetres' (Townsend, 1982, of a youth); or, for Richard Nixon, an unfortunate series of events, the 'Watergate thing'. In nursery use a 'thingy' or 'thingamajig' is a penis: 'You stand there with your thingamajig in my toothmug' (Sharpe, 1979). etc.

third degree police violence to extract information
Probably from the scale of seriousness of burns, of which 'third-degree' is the worst: 'A veritable catalogue of police third-degree methods is contained in a recent (February 1930) issue of *Harvard Law Review*' (Lavine, 1930). Rarely abbr. to 'third': 'He's giving me a third about a gun' (Chandler, 1934). Etymologists who are also Freemasons may reject the association with **burn** (3) (above) in favour of their own experience at the third stage of their induction into the 'craft', when the ordeal and questioning are reported to be daunting.

third leg a penis
Female rather than male use, and sometimes too as the 'middle leg'.

third world poor and uncivilized
The other two are the Am. and Russian series of alliances: '. . . a wealthy Bostonian, from a family of some distinction, adventuring in Third World philanthropy' (Theroux, 1980). A welcome change from the **developing** (q.v.) routine.

thread (the needle) to copulate
Of a male, with obvious imagery. Perhaps now ob.

three-legged beaver a male homosexual taking the female role
From his penis, and the femininity of **beaver** (q.v.).

three-letter man a male homosexual
Punning, I suppose, on 'four-letter man' (q.v. *under* **four-letter word**): 'The three letters are "f-a-g"' (DAS). In the early days when Latin was more widely acclaimed, and homosexuality less, he was a thief, the letters being 'f-u-r'.

three letters the Russian internal apparatus of repression
A usage in Russia prior to WWII during Stalin's indiscriminate terror: '. . . the Three Letters (a pseudonym used in conversation to avoid mentioning the dreaded GPU)' (Muggeridge, 1972).

three-point play the recruitment of a Black woman
The imagery is from basket-ball. The Am. employer gets a point for taking on another worker, so reducing unemployment; a second point if the worker is female, to show that he is not prejudiced about employing women; and a third point when he contributes to his quota of non-Whites. You get a bonus if the recruit has Red Indian ancestry.

three sheets in the wind *see* **sheet in the wind**

threepennies (the) diarrhoea
Br. rh. sl. for 'threepenny bits', the shits, but now perhaps as rare as the coins themselves.

threesomes a sexual orgy with three participants
Usu. two of one sex, one of the other: 'Young attractive married housewife, AC/DC, like to meet AC/DC people to join well-endowed husband for threesomes and moresomes' (*Daily Telegraph,* May 1980, publishing not an advertisement but an account of a sordid Court case. I seem to recall it was the boastful husband who worded and inserted the entry).

thrill a single act of copulation
Formerly a euphemism for the sexual orgasm (DSUE) but now used in the whore's invitation 'Can I give you a thrill?'.

throne a pedestal lavatory
Some nursery and humorous use, from the shape, elevation and solitary situation.

throw (1) to copulate with
The common violent imagery: 'And better would it fit Achilles much to throw down Hector than Polyxena' (Shakespeare, *Troilus and Cressida*). To-day a male may 'throw a leg over' or 'throw a bop into' his sexual partner.

throw (2) to give premature birth
Usu. of cattle , and still used at least in W. Eng.: 'Sight o' yoes 've a-drow'd their lambs' (EDD – a 'sight o' yoes' is many ewes).

throw (3) to lose deliberately or fraudulently
An abbr. of 'throw away' or of **throw in the towel** (below): 'I heard you were supposed to throw it' (Chandler, 1939, of a boxing match).

throw in the towel to concede defeat
Boxing imagery, where the second does it for his principal. The implication is that a braver person would have held on longer.

throw rocks to commit crimes
From the action of Am. street rioters who may pelt the police etc. with any missiles which come to hand.

throw the book at to charge with every feasible offence
Mainly police jargon, the 'book' being the manual setting out criminal offences: 'You'll just turn to have to throw the book at me . . . . I don't sell out – even to good police officers' (Chandler, 1958).

throw up to vomit
The expulsion may be downwards or only fig.: 'I got so mad I actually threw up. Puked!' (Theroux, 1982).

thud an aircraft crash
Am. Vietnam war, and some later civil, use, from the dull distant noise.

thug a person who does not support Communism
Properly, an Indian robber who strangled his victims having allowed for bodily gases to escape, whence a violent or uncouth person. Now Communist dysphemism for any subject who does not placidly accept the system.

thumb a marijuana cigarette
Because you might suck either for comfort? Am.

thump to copulate with
Of the male, using the common violent imagery: 'Jump her and thump her' (Shakespeare, *Winter's Tale*). And in modern use: 'Well, if I'd had my way, he'd still have been thumping her every night' (Fraser, 1973).

thunder-box a portable pedestal lavatory
The etymology is uncertain – is the 'thunder' the reaction of the chemical dispersant or the noise of defecation? 'When it rained the clients had to row themselves to the thunder-box at the bottom of the yard' (Simon, 1979).

tick a person clandestinely following another
From the parasitic arachnid which sticks to your skin: 'He saw his tick come in through the revolving doors, look around and, spotting Kim, make for the elevator' (Van Lustbaden, 1983).

ticker a heart
But you only speak of it in this way if you have reason to suspect it is likely to cease ticking: '"In any case I have a bad heart." "*My* ticker was none too good," said Mr Flack' (Theroux, 1974 – the conversation was between valetudinarians).

tickle to copulate with
Perhaps from the preliminary caresses, or the association with **tickler** (1) (below): 'When the swollen little girl told her father the name of the man who had been tickling them – and I defy you to find a more revolting terminology' (Condon, 1966 – I fear he might find worse in these pages).

tickle your fancy a male homosexual
Br. rh. sl. for **nancy** (q.v.) and also a pun on the dialect 'tickle your fancy', the viola tricolor, which most of us know better as a pansy.

tickler (1) the clitoris
Perhaps from its significance in sexual arousal: 'I went back to caressing her tickler' (Harris, 1925).

tickler (2) a contraceptive sheath
In Am. only: '. . . a wall-mounted vending machine that dispensed rainbow-coloured French ticklers' (Sanders, 1983).

tiddly slightly drunk
Abbr. of the rh. sl. 'tiddly wink', a drink: 'I poured her wine carefully. "Ma, you'll get tiddly"' (Bogarde, 1983). A 'tiddly wink' or 'kiddlywink' was an unlicensed inn or a pawnshop before it came to mean the game played with counters, no doubt by drinkers.

tie a can on to dismiss from employment
Probably from the attachment of a can to the tail of an unwelcome stray cat, to drive it away, and *see* **can** (2). Am.

tie one on to go on a carouse
The etymology of this Am. phrase is uncertain: 'We could tie one good one on, two days, three days, five empty bottles at the foot of the bed' (Mailer, 1965).

tied up unwilling to see or speak to a caller
If a secretary says her boss is 'tied up', have no fear of bondage or a criminal incursion, nor even that he is moderately overworked – most of the time he just can't be bothered to speak to you. In ob. Eng. use it would have meant that he was constipated: 'I be terrible a-tied up in my inside' (EDD).

tiger sweat an inferior intoxicant
Often bad beer, but with no aspersion cast on 'Tiger' beer from Singapore. Also of spirits: 'King Kong is not a movie, it's cheap alcohol, also known as Tigersweat' (Longstreet, 1956).

tight (1) drunk
The OED suggests a connection with **screwed** (q.v.), but which is a pun on which? 'Well, he got in at last, and he lit a candle then. That took him five minutes. He was pretty tight' (Somerville and Ross, 1897 – to give an example of so common a usage may seem redundant but it allows me to record a more picturesque euphemism in the same story: 'Let it not for one instant be imagined that I had looked upon the wine of the Royal Hotel when it was red').

tight (2) not capable of interception
Am. espionage jargon, the opposite of 'loose', as in 'loose talk': 'And, for the good Lord's sake, use a tight phone' (M. Thomas, 1980).

tightwad a miser
His roll of bills is seldom loosened for the extraction of a banknote: 'Cost him a hundred bucks to cancel which must have killed the old tightwad' (M. Thomas, 1987). 'Tightfisted' is SE of a mean person.

Tijuana bible a pornographic book or picture
Am. visitors to the Mexican border town find erotica openly displayed.

Tijuana taxi a police car
The external lights and signs on some Am. police vehicles call to mind the decoration of Mexican cabs.

time the happening of something subject to a taboo
Of childbirth: 'Elizabeth's full time came that she should be delivered' (St Luke) or, in modern use: 'My wife – she be near her time wi' the eleventh' (M. Francis, 1901); of death: 'Mr Ralph wur to die, his toime had coom' (Antrobus, 1901); and of imprisonment: '"Listen," he said, still softly. "I did my time"' (Chandler, 1939).

time of the month menstruation
Common female usage: 'Could be that time of the day, that time of the month' (Bradbury, 1965).

time sharing a compounded annual rental paid in advance
A number of people are induced to advance capital in respect of the same property, with access limited to each for a stated period in each year. Whence the satirical: 'Don't say two timing, sweetie, think of it as time sharing' (young woman to old man in Smirnoff Vodka cartoon, *Private Eye*, June 1981).

tin handshake a derisory payment on dismissal from employment
A less desirable outcome than the **golden handshake** (above): 'He's sacked, given a tin handshake and left to rot' (Allbeury, 1981).

tincture (1) a partial descent from other than White ancestry
Properly, a pigment, and used of those whose darker skin pigmentation is noticeable: 'She had a tincture herself or she would not have mentioned their race' (Theroux, 1977).

tincture (2) an intoxicant
Properly, in pharmacy, a medical solution in alcohol: 'So while I was shunted off for tinctures with a lot of silly women in leotards' (*Private Eye*, February, 1981).

tinker a gypsy
The trade at which they were once adept, and still used in Ire., as is 'itinerant', for the large and embarrassing numbers who keep their vans and horses on the 'long acre' – the roadside verges – many of whom are not of Romany descent.

tinkle to urinate
Onomatopoeic nursery usage, from the noise of urine against a mild-steel receptacle (a 'tin-pot' would be enormously expensive): 'If you sprinkle when you tinkle Be a sweetie, wipe the seatie' (graffito in lavatory for female use).

tinpot pretentiously assuming the trappings and manner of authority
The etymology comes not from any lack of value in pots made of tin, but from the days when tinkers were wont to pass off inferior articles as such. Now only pejorative and fig. use: '. . . give away every scrap of Empire that remains to any tinpot potentate that asks for it' (*Private Eye*, July 1981).

tint to dye hair
Female and barbers' jargon. It means to colour slightly.

tip (1) to copulate with other than your regular extra-marital partner
An Am. use which I suspect does not come from the dialect 'tip', a corruption of 'tup', and limited to the mating of sheep: 'Tip where you will, you shall lamb with the leave' (Old Proverb).

tip (2) to die
Often in the fuller Eng. expression, to 'tip off', with the common avian imagery: 'They all tipped off an' deed' (Binns, 1889).

tip (3) to drink intoxicants to excess
From the motion of tipping the container: 'You're tipped, darling. You're hurting' (Steinbeck, 1961). To 'tip the bottle' is specific: 'If she "tips the bottle" he knocks her about a little more to teach her to keep sober' (Burmester, 1902). 'Tipped' and 'tipsy' mean drunk: '"Was he tipsy?" "I dare say . . . now you mention it, I think he was"' (E. Waugh, 1933). A 'tiper', 'tipper', or 'tippler' is a drunkard. 'Tip' was ale once sold in Sc. at 2d a pint but 'tipple' is any intoxicant: 'Helpers had brought in the drinks and bits. "Do dig into the tipple," said Serena' (Bradbury, 1976). A 'tippler' used to be an innkeeper, who kept a 'tippling-house': 'No vyattler nor tipler to sell any ale or beer brewed out of town' (Lincoln Corporation Records, 1575).

tip (4) wrongly to warn
An abbr. of 'tip off': '"Who tipped you?" he said, smiling . . . . "If I find him . . . . I'll have his balls"' (Sanders, 1983).

tip off your trolley to go mad
The trolley conveyed the electrical connector of a tram to the overhead supply: 'There are moments when I wonder if I'm tipping off my trolley' (Deighton, 1985).

tip over to rob
From upsetting a stall and stealing some of the goods in the confusion rather than from knocking down your victim. In Am. it applies to any theft and to a sudden police raid.

tire kicking a superficial examination of deep-seated problems
Business jargon, from the inexpert buyer of a used car. Some fig. use: '. . . a simplistic agrarian vision which the war-weary nation had bought without kicking the tires' (M. Thomas, 1980).

tired (1) unwilling to copulate with a regular partner
A female excuse which may or may not have to do with weariness: '. . . a kind of marital signal, looking to her for sexual encouragement, the unspoken suggestion that they would make love, "I'm tired" or "I'm not tired"' (Theroux, 1976).

tired (2) drunk
The symptoms can be the same, and *see* **over-tired** where the sarcasm is stronger.

to the knuckle meanly
All the meat is gone, as with **on your bones** (q.v.): 'It's to the knuckle. It's not MGM or anything. There's no money' (Bogarde, 1983).

toffee ration copulation by the male within marriage
WWII Br. naval usage, in the days when you received a limited but regular supply of sweets.

toilet a lavatory
Properly, a towel, whence washing and the place where the washing was done. And we use 'toilet paper' for wiping rather than washing.

tokenism unfair appointment of a Black
A manifestation of our pigmentation complexes in a predominantly White society: 'There was evidence of "tokenism", employing black staff purely for their colour' (*Daily Telegraph*, June 1984); whence 'token' of an appointment made to placate a pressure group or our social conscience: 'The token black, Dr Clifton R. Wharton, Jr. had gone in 1975' (Lacey, 1986, of the Ford Board of Directors).

Tokyo trots diarrhoea
Not a Japanese race but one of the many alliterative geographical attributions.

tolbooth a prison
Properly, the town hall where tolls were paid. The gaol was often in the same building: 'How many gypsies were sent to the tolbooth?' (W. Scott, 1815).

tom (1) an act of defecation
Br. rh. sl. for 'tom tit' but never used as an
insult. The full expression is also used of
turds: 'All that Tom Tit blown up in the air'
(B. Forbes, 1986 – a sewage works had been
bombed).

tom to act as a whore
I suppose from the sexual reputation of the
cat, although 'queen' might seem the correct
gender.

tomboy a whore
From the feline reputation and perhaps also
a corruption of **tumble** (1) (below): 'A lady
so fair . . . to be partner'd with tomboys'
(Shakespeare, *Othello*). Today it means no
more than a young girl with the athletic and
other tastes of a boy, although some tell us
that boys and girls should not have different
interests.

tomcatting regular extra-marital copulation by a male
Again from the cat's reputation: 'The
tomcatting made history in the form of
songs' (Longstreet, 1956, of New Orleans).

tommy (1) menstruation
Female usage. Except that we choose male
names for taboo objects, the etymology is
unclear.

tommy (2) a penis
Rarer than **dick** (1) (q.v.), commoner than
Harry: 'She . . . . had to use her hand to get
my Tommy in again' (Harris, 1925).

too many sheets in the wind drunk
An uncommon variant of **sheet in the wind**
(q.v.) and its variants in numerical form.

took *see* **taken**

tool a penis
Properly, any instrument whence the punning: '"Draw thy tool" . . . . "My naked
weapon is out"' (Shakespeare, *Romeo and
Juliet*) and in modern use: 'No accountability
could be apportioned anywhere for how his
tool behaved, or failed to behave, while he
slept' (Amis, 1978). For Grose: 'TOOLS.
the private parts of a man'.

tooled up carrying a gun
A 'tool' as a weapon is ob. SE and this use by
modern thieves when about their business
puns on the processes of mass production.

toot a carouse
From the noise: 'Her husband was off on a
toot' (Chandler, 1953). ? ob.

top (1) to copulate with
Either a corruption of the SE 'tup' or from
the position adopted by the male, or from his
supposed dominance: 'Behold her topt?'
(Shakespeare, *Othello*). ob.

top (2) to kill
The imagery is from sylviculture or horticulture: 'Just who did top Ambassador Mobuto?
It came as a great relief to all concerned to
find he had topped himself' (*Private Eye*,
March 1980). To 'top' was much used of
executions and hangings and the ob. 'topping fellow' was a hangman – and a
gruesome pun.

top and bottom *see* **half and half**

top and tail to clean up a baby
Nursery usage with imagery from preparing
gooseberries or root crops, which need
cleaning at either end. The baby is likely to
have vomited as well as defecated.

top-heavy drunk
And unable to stand upright without
swaying: 'We kept on drinking and yarning
until stop-tap. At that time we were getting a
little top heavy' (Richards, 1933).

top sergeant a female homosexual taking
the male role
Am. soldiers in that rank have a reputation
for roughness and toughness. Sometimes
abbr. to 'sergeant'.

top up to conceal inferior goods below
those of higher quality
Usu. of fruit sold by weight where only part
of the purchase is visible: '. . . a few tempting
strawberries being displayed on top of the
pottle. "Topping up," said a fruit dealer'
(Mayhew, 1851).

topless exposing your breasts in public
Beach, bar and entertainment usage: 'As one
of the show-girls who had to strut around
the stage topless' (Green, 1979). Thus a
'topless' bar is not one which is open to the
heavens. However a 'topless' person used to
be, and occasionally still is, bareheaded.

torch of Hymen (the) copulation only
within marriage
Hymen, the god of marriage, was depicted
carrying a torch: 'The torch of Hymen burns
less brightly than of yore' (Mayhew, 1862,
and how undated he remains).

torpedo a hired assassin
As a submarine may fire a single missile
from its hidden place so is he recruited to

undertake a specific murder away from his normal base. Am.

toss (1) an act of copulation
Perhaps alluding to hay – *see* **in the hay** – or from **toss off** (below): 'He had a toss in the hay with his tootsie tonight' (Sanders, 1981). Whence the common vulgarity 'I don't give a toss'.

toss (2) to search another's property
Usu. without consent and looking for illegal narcotics, but also of any incursion: '"How did you find out the apartment had been searched?" .... "She .... knew where everything was kept. She swears the place was tossed"' (Sanders, 1986). The imagery is from throwing things into the air.

toss down to drink an intoxicant
From the movement of the container, but it could be hay off a stack: '"We need to talk," he said, "and toss down a few before you go"' (Shirer, 1984).

toss off to masturbate
Of a male, from the ejaculation: 'I could have another whisky, toss myself off in the loo' (Theroux, 1973).

toss out to feign narcotic withdrawal symptoms
A trick by an addict to induce a doctor to prescribe a fresh supply of narcotics.

tot a drink of intoxicant
Properly, anything small, whence a small drinking vessel or measure, which used to be from quarter to half a pint. Formerly to 'tot' was to drink intoxicants to excess: 'An' th' women folk .... can tot That Dunville's Irish whisky' (Doherty, 1884). 'Totty', a whore, was S. Eng. dialect from the meaning, of evil reputation. This is turn may have punned on a still older meaning, a little bit. I view with some caution Partridge's suggestions in DSUE of derivation from the name Dorothy or from a small girl.

totally dependent an idiot
Am. sociological jargon. It should mean only a young baby or somebody who is paralyzed: 'An idiot, we are informed, is now a "totally dependant"' (Jennings, 1965).

touch (1) to copulate with
Of the male, despite the mutuality: 'You have toucht his queen Forbiddenly' (Shakespeare, *Winter's Tale*) and still heard in Devon: 'I asked her, Did I touch you in the night?' (reported conversation, 1948, after an unplanned pregnancy). For Grose 'To touch up a woman is to have carnal

knowledge of her' but *see* **touch up** (1) (below). To 'touch yourself' is to masturbate, usu. of a female: 'You want to know whether I have touched myself. Sure; all girls have' (Harris, 1925).

touch (2) a theft
Usu. by stealing from a pocket, from the physical contact. Today normally borrowing money which you do not intend to repay: 'A quick ten or twenty dollar *touch*, which of course was never intended to be returned' (Lavine, 1930). The ob. Br. 'touch-crib' was the kind of brothel in which you were liable to be robbed as well.

touch of the tarbrush *see* **tarbrush**

touch signature a fingerprint
Banking jargon when they want positively to identify their customers without accusing them of being crooks: 'The practice is known by the euphemism "touch signature", an approach which one banker described as "part of our back-up security system"' (*Daily Telegraph*, September 1980, of fingerprinting).

touch up (1) digitally to excite the genitals of another
Usu. the male does it to the female, unless they are homosexuals: '. . . it would be ridiculous to keep you from your work just because you touched up some Jewess' (Keneally, 1982). The punning 'touch-hole', a vagina, is ob.

touch up (2) to dye
Barbers' jargon, implying a partial application where in fact the whole is treated.

touched (1) of unsound mind
Abbr. of 'touched in the head', from the supposed effect of the sun or moon on mental stability: '. . . an uncle who had a passion for concrete dwarves .... who his mother said was a bit touched in the head' (Sharpe, 1974).

touched (2) drunk
And usu. only mildly affected by the contact: 'In respect of her liquor-traffic, she was seen "touched" about once a week' (Tweeddale, 1896). ? ob.

tourist inferior
Of hotel accommodation and especially public transport. Airlines use verbal ingenuity in calling the dearer seats for richer holidaymakers something else, like 'club', 'sovereign', 'executive' or 'clipper'.

touristas (the) diarrhoea
Suffered by many an Am. tourist, or 'turista',

whose digestion is unprepared for the diet, climate, cleanliness and excessive alcohol to which it may be subjected on a Mexican vacation.

town house a dwelling built on a small plot
Mainly Br. real estate jargon for a terrace house which may not be located within the urban centre. I don't think there is any implication that the occupant is rich enough to have a country house as well.

town pump a whore
Everyone went there for satisfaction, before domestic supplies were freely available in Am. The rarer 'town bike' was the **ride** (q.v.) available to all.

toy boy a male prostitute
A 1987 in-phrase, which we can only hope proves ephemeral. He is usu. younger than the female retaining his services.

tracks the scars left by repeated illegal narcotic injection
Like Am. railroad lines.

trade (the) prostitution
Prostitutes' jargon everywhere and in Am. the 'trade' is also a whore's customer: 'She doesn't like the trade, she packs it in and goes home' (Diehl, 1978). And *see* **rough trade**. A 'trader' is a whore and 'living by trade' is so working: 'Oh, there's no doubt they live by trading' (EDD, c. 1900).

traffic with yourself to masturbate yourself
Of either sex: 'Having traffic with thyself alone, Though of thyself thy sweet self dost deceive' (Shakespeare, *Sonnets*). ob.

trainable imbecile
Educational and sociological jargon, to distinguish from an idiot who cannot be trained at all. Jennings (1965) also quotes from *Today's Health* 'educable, corresponding to moron'.

tramp a whore
From walking the streets but now in Am. of any promiscuous woman.

translate the truth to lie
A Br. parliamentary evasion to comply with the convention about not calling another member a liar in the House of Commons.

translated drunk
Properly, transferred from one state or place to another, as from life to death or just from one clerical living to another: 'Bless thee, Bottom, thou art translated' (Shakespeare, *Midsummer Night's Dream*). ob.

transported sentenced to exile for a criminal offence
Not merely carried from one place to another. In this use, you went by sea: 'One old offender, who stole the Duke of Beaufort's dog, was transported, not for stealing the dog, but his collar' (Mayhew, 1851 – under Eng. common law dogs were not capable of being stolen). In WW II for Jews 'transported' meant death by the Nazis: '. . . of labour and transport lists, of the lists of living and dead' (Keneally, 1982, of WW II Jewish forced labour in Poland).

travel to cohabit and copulate extra-maritally
Of the homeless poor in 19c. London: 'He could not remember a single instance of his having seen a young Jewess "travelling" with a boy' (Mayhew, 1851). The female 'travelled' with the male.

travel agent a dealer in LSD
Punning on the **trip** (q.v.) on which you might be sent. Am.

traveller an habitual itinerant
Often gypsies although it is a way of life for many Irish families without Romany blood. They are also known generically as the 'travelling people'. In ob. Br. use, to 'travel the road' was to engage in highway robbery.

tread to copulate
Of birds, from their foot movements: 'The cock that treads them will not know' (Shakespeare, *Sonnets*).

treasure the vagina
Viewed sexually by the male, especially when free access is denied to him: 'I fall crazy in love . . . . and she keeps her sweet treasure all locked up' (Styron, 1976).

tree-rat a whore
The small mammal infests the bashas used, among others, by troops in India as billets: 'Any man who availed himself of the "tree rats" or "grass bidis" was properly dealt with' (Allen, 1975).

tree suit a coffin
A modern Am. variant of the ob. 'timber breeches': 'He'll get a good settin'-down some day, afore he gets into his timber breeches' (*Cornhill Magazine*, August 1902, quoted in EDD).

triangular trade (the) trading in slaves
On the first leg, manufactured goods went from England to Africa; on the second leg, slaves went from Africa to America; on the third leg, commodities went from America to

Europe. It was also known as the 'African trade'.

trick a whore's customer
From the limited turn of duty rather than any deception, I suspect: 'Lots of women walking the streets for tricks to take to their "pads"' (L. Armstrong, 1955). To 'call the tricks' was to solicit as a whore: 'They weren't allowed to call the tricks like the girls in Storyville' (ibid.) and to 'trick' was to copulate with the customer: 'And I never tricked him. He never asked for it' (Wambaugh, 1981, of a whore). A 'trick-babe' is a whore but to 'do the trick' is merely to copulate with anyone: 'I dare say would have done the trick if this clown Yei hadn't come' (Fraser, 1985 – Flashman had been alone with a woman). Mainly Am.

trim to copulate with
In modern Am. use of a male, probably from the concept of cutting into shape. To trim your wick is explicit of a male, punning on **wick** (below) and what you used to do to candles: '"You're just getting old. Lucky to be able to –" "Ah, shut up. I got my wick trimmed all right"' (Lyall, 1975). The ob. Br. 'trim the buff' came from 'trim', to beat and 'buff', nudity. 'Trim' is also used of a woman's sexuality, although I have not worked out the etymology – perhaps the imagery is naval.

trip a condition induced by the ingestion of illegal narcotics
Not just those on which you were sent by your **travel agent** (q.v.): 'The kind of thing that hippies switch into when the trips turn sour' (Bradbury, 1975). To 'trip' is to take narcotics illegally: 'They were speeding and tripping at the same time' (Deighton, 1972).

trip up the Rhine copulation
Post-WW II Br. army use, of a single act with a German female.

trolley a single act of copulation
Br. rh. sl. from 'trolley and truck', a fuck.

(trollop a whore or promiscuous woman comes from the Scandinavian 'troll', a witch, and has no non-euphemistic meaning: 'That impudent trollop who is with child by you' (Fielding, 1742).)

trot a whore
The common equine imagery, whence the punning: 'Marry him to . . . . an old trot . . . though she have as many diseases as two and fifty horses' (Shakespeare, *Taming of the Shrew*). The Br. 'trot on your pussy', which

is also ob., meant to copulate of a female and embraced a number of vulgar puns.

trots (the) diarrhoea
The need is too immediate for walking: 'I'd already got the trots. They're supposed to cement you up' (P. Scott, 1975, of pills). A sufferer is said to be 'on the trot'.

trouble any unpleasant or unwanted experience
Euphemistic when the subject is taboo. Of an unwanted pregnancy to a spinster: 'She got into trouble. Through an old white fellow who used to have those coloured girls up to an old ramshackle house of his. I do not have to tell you what he was up to' (L. Armstrong, 1955). Of childbirth: 'When I'm over my trouble I'll come to see you' (M. Francis, 1901). Of menstruation and of any illness of a persistent and unpleasant nature, especially varicose veins and piles. The 'troubles' are fighting or violence in Ire. against the British or between groups whose differences are tribal more than religious: 'The "troubles" – that quaint . . . . word for murder and mayhem' (Theroux, 1983). A 'troubled' child or person , suffers from some mental abnormality, such as urinating in bed. In ob. SW Eng. dialect 'troublesome' was to be haunted: 'Th' old 'ouse up to Park's troublesome 'pon times' (EDD, c. 1900).

truant with your bed to copulate extra-maritally
Not necessarily while you are absent from school without consent: 'Tis double wrong to truant with your bed, And let her read it in thy looks at board' (Shakespeare, *Comedy of Errors*). ob.

truck driver (1) an amphetamine tablet
Punning on the use by Am. truck drivers to keep them awake on long trips.

truck driver (2) a male homosexual taking the male role
From their rough image in Am.

true not copulating with other than your regular sexual partner
The opposite of **false** and **untrue** (q.v.): 'She was true to me all the time we lived together' (L. Armstrong, 1955). The Am. funeral jargon 'true companion crypt', a common grave, suggests posthumous sexual fidelity: 'True Companion Crypt – permits husband and wife to be entombed in a single chamber without any dividing wall to separate them' (J. Mitford, 1963).

trull a whore
Properly, a Scandinavian folk-lore figure:
'Am sure I scared the Dauphin and his trull,
When arm in arm they both came swiftly
running' (Shakespeare, 1 *Henry VI*).

trying to escape in custody
An excuse given for the murder of prisoners:
'Codreanu had not been shot while trying to
escape. He had been assassinated by order
of the king' (Manning, 1962 – the report had
been that he was trying to escape from
custody).

tube buggery
Usu. 'had' or 'laid': '. . . about eight of
them's gonna lay more tube than the
motherfucking Alaska pipeline and your
asshole etc.' (Wambaugh, 1983, of buggery
in prison and the discomfort of an involuntary patient).

tuck away in earth etc. to kill
From the burial but not usu. of natural
death: 'He was going to be quietly tucked
away in earth at the frontier station after
dark' (G. Greene, 1932). To 'tuck under the
daisies' implies burial after natural death,
the daisy being a symbol of the churchyard:
'After me poor old man was tucked under
the daisies' (MacDonagh, 1898).

tumble (1) to copulate with
Of either sex, from the alacrity of the move
into a prone position: 'Quoth she, before you
tumbled me, You promised me to wed'
(Shakespeare, *Hamlet*). Modern use is also
intransitive: 'I'm not a regular girl and you
expect me to tumble' (Weverka, 1973). A
'tumble' is a single act of copulation: 'A
discreet visit in a tri-shaw for a tumble at
Dunroamin' (Theroux, 1973).

tumble (2) an intoxicant
Br. rh. sl. for 'tumble down the sink', a
drink. ? ob.

tumbler a pedestrian who fraudulently
feigns injury
He contrives to fall, to obtain damages
against a motorist: '. . . a crew of repeat
tumblers, of course. The guys with trick
knees and backs who can show the right
X-rays' (Sanders, 1977). Am.

tumescence an erection of the penis
Not just any old swelling. This 19c. word,
unknown to Dr Johnson, is for the pompous
and not generally used in a sexual sense.

tummy ache menstruation
One of the symptoms, but not the most
obvious of them.

tummy bug *see* Tunis stomach

tummy-tuck a cosmetic operation to
reduce frontal flab on the trunk
Not what Billy Bunter sought in the tuck-
shop: 'Felicia Dodat was going to have a
tummy-tuck' (Sanders, 1986).

tumour (a) cancer
Properly, any swelling and for Dryden the
'tender tumour' was an erect penis.

tuned drunk
Electronic imagery, from the heightened
sensitivity perhaps.

Tunis stomach diarrhoea
Contracted by Br. troops in N. Africa in
WW II: 'Everyone got some form of Tunis
stomach' (Bogarde, 1978). We still talk of a
'tummy bug' when we have diarrhoea, and
that is often precisely what is causing the
condition.

turf accountant a person who accepts
bets professionally
The 'turf' is racing and 'accountants' are
supposed to be honest professional men.

Turk a bugger
For Am. use only. In SE he was a fierce
man, who proved more than a match for the
Crusaders, or a ragged boy.

turkey shoot a business deal bringing easy
profits
The bird presents an easy target: '. . . a
chance for a real turkey shoot just turned up'
(M. Thomas, 1982, of a wealthy customer).
But a 'turkey farmer' is a businessman who
fails to make easy money: '. . . at least I'm not
a turkey farmer. My last three films made
money' (B. Forbes, 1983). Am.

Turkish ally an unreliable supporter
From their supposed cowardice and treachery although, etymologically, the Greeks fare
little better: '. . . the rock was a Turkish ally,
ready to change sides if the going got rough'
(Trevanian, 1972).

Turkish medal an inadvertently exposed
trouser flybutton
A warning in the pre-zip days from one male
to another, from the casual way in which
some Turks wear Western-style dress:
'Their flybuttons were undone, and now I
could understand why these buttons were
called "Turkish medals" by British soldiers
in the First World War' (Theroux, 1975).

turn (1) an act of copulation
Male usage, with imagery from the music

hall perhaps and to 'turn up' a woman is to copulate with her extra-maritally.

turn (2) to subvert from allegiance
Espionage etc. jargon: 'The case might be a textbook Soviet attempt to "turn" an American military officer' (*Daily Telegraph*, February 1981). In Am. too to 'turn round' or to 'turn around': '"Why does a feller earning a handsome salary in the American State Department decide to chuck it all in and join a bomb factory?" "I got turned around"' (Theroux, 1976).

turn (3) a sudden illness
Anything from dizziness to a cerebral haemorrhage. This is a 19c. extension of meaning from a word which merits 12 pages in OED.

turn (4) to have predominantly Black residents
Of an Am. neighbourhood formerly occupied only by Whites. In a 'turning' district house prices fall.

turn in to betray to authority
Properly, to hand over to another, as a piece of work to a tutor: '. . . fearing the other might reveal something or even connive to turn in the other' (Sanders, 1980, of criminals). In everyday sl., to 'turn in' means to go to bed; it used also to mean to be killed by hanging.

turn it in to die
Not voluntarily, as might be supposed, of suicides.

turn of life the menopause
An ob. variant of the **change** (1) (above).

turn off (1) to kill
Usu. from hanging and probably with imagery from a lamp rather than from association with the 'turning tree', the gallows on which the corpse rotated: '. . . it gives a man a wonderful appetite for his breakfast to assist at turning off a dozen or more rebels' (Richards, 1936).

turn off (2) not to excite sexually
The opposite of **turn on** (below). In 19c. it meant to dismiss a sexual mistress: 'He can turn a poor gal off, as soon as he tires of her' (Mayhew, 1851).

turn on to excite
Through any taboo or illegal agent, with imagery from a lamp. Of sex: 'He left bruises! I suppose he thought he was – what's the expression – turning me on' (Theroux, 1977). Of illegal narcotics: '"Hey, want to turn on with me? Here, I'll

make you one." He fumbled with his cigarette papers and took out his stash' (Theroux, 1976). And of anything else which grabs you, from whips to carrot juice. To 'switch on' means the same thing.

turn out upon the streets to become a whore
The common **street** (q.v.) imagery: 'Another young girl . . . . advised me to turn out upon the streets' (Mayhew, 1862).

turn the clock back *see* **put the clock back**

turn up (1) *see* **turn** (1)

turn up (2) to give the police information about
From exposing what formerly was hidden but used of an Am. criminal betrayal: 'He would be set free if he "turned up the gang"' (Lavine, 1930).

turn up your little finger etc. to be an habitual drunkard
From a way of holding the glass, although many hold a teacup the same way: 'Ye maun keep unco sober, and no be turnin' up yere wee finger sae aften' (Ballantine, 1869). A Scot might in the same sense 'turn up pinkie': ' So very fond was Tam of "turnin' up his pinkie" that he latterly lost both his credit and his character' (Murdoch, 1895).

turn up your toes etc. to die
Most people are buried on their backs: 'I'll turn merrier toes to th' sky nor thee, lad, when it comes to deeing' (Sutcliffe, 1899). Rarely as 'turn up your heels', implying face-down interment.

turn your bike around to urinate
Of a male out of doors. The imagery of this perhaps ob. phrase is uncertain. Was he going the other way to seek privacy, or is the expression in the **shoot a lion** (q.v.) category?

turn your coat dishonourably to desert a cause
From the days when distinctive clothing facilitated a recognition and indicated allegiance: 'Perhaps wisely they turned coat and told us where he was' (Allen, 1979 – Ali Dinar's spies betrayed him). Some modern fig. use, especially of politicians, and 'turncoat' is SE.

turn your face to the wall to die
Not from the reversal of a picture of a disgraced person but from the privacy sought by the dying: 'Sahib turns his face to the wall

and all is up with him and us' (P. Scott, 1977).

turning tree *see* turn off (1)

tutor a corrupt official in a polling station
He 'instructed' the voter: 'A "tutor" accompanies the voter into the booth to explain the mechanism to him' (Lavine, 1930, of New York City in the days when Tammany Hall had things organized).

twelve annas in the rupee of mixed Indian and White ancestry
Br. Indian derogatory use of those of mixed race, especially if they pretended to be European – there were sixteen annas in the rupee: 'I took the conventional attitude . . . . of making jokes about "blackie-whitie" and "twelve annas in the rupee"' (Allen, 1975). But cf. **not sixteen annas to the rupee**.

twenty-four hour service we have a telephone recording device
A misleading advertisement – annoying when used by a plumber and you have a burst pipe in the early hours.

twilight home an institution for the unwanted old
Not a summerhouse facing the west but from the cliché 'twilight of your life': '. . . arranged for her mother to be packed off to a comfortable and expensive "twilight home"' (Murdoch, 1978). At least it holds out no promise of amelioration, as does the 'Convalescent Home' for the aged in East Haddam, Ct.

twisted drunk or under illegal narcotic influence
A rarer Am. version of **tight** (q.v.). In BI 'twisted' once meant killed by hanging, from the rotation of the corpse on the gallows.

two-backed beast *see* beast with two backs

two-by-four a whore
Br. rh. sl. from the rag used as a pull-through for the .303 army rifle, although we called it a 'four-by-two'.

two-on-one two people sexually using a third
Usu. of two whores with a single male, although it is to be hoped that in practice they take turns: 'If you'd be interested in a two-on-one' (McBain, 1981 – two whores were propositioning a man). Also of male homosexuals: 'Enjoyed more damn two-on-ones with Jimmy up there in Castleviews . . .' (ibid. of convicts).

two stone lighter castrated
Of animals, punning on the **stones** (q.v.) which have been removed and the Br. weight of 14lbs which still mystifies Am. people when those in BI say how heavy they are. I last heard this expression on a Br. farm just after WW II.

two-time to copulate regularly with two people contemporaneously
Properly, in sl. to cheat but cf. **double time**: 'Lonsdale . . . . who is the latest escort of the gracious Princess Margaret, is reputed to be still two-timing with his old flame' (*Private Eye*, December 1981).

Tyburn appertaining to death by hanging
The gallows were located near the modern Marble Arch in London but the district named after the two burns, or streams, has shed its unhappy connotations in the modern St Marylebone. 'Tyburn' was to be found in many phrases. The 'Tyburn' dance, hornpipe or jig was a hanging, of which there were about 2,000 a year at this one location in the 16c., and 12 a year in the 19c. A 'Tyburn tippet' was a noose and the 'Tyburn' tree or triple tree, a gallows, with its 'Tyburn' blossom, a young thief 'who in time will ripen into fruit borne by the deadly never-green' (Grose). The 'King of Tyburn' was the hangman and to 'preach at Tyburn Cross' was to be killed by hanging: 'That souldiers sterne, or prech at Tiborne crosse' (Gascoigne, 1576, quoted in ODEP). A 'Tyburn ticket' was a certificate of exemption from the payment of all taxes in the Parish in which the felony was committed paid to the person who secured a conviction and hanging or, as an alternative, a reward of about £20, which was forty times the minimum value of the stolen property in respect of which a thief could be hanged. A 'Tyburn top' was no more than a wig worn 'in a knowing style' (Grose); etc.

U

Uganda extra-marital copulation
Private Eye use in many forms based on an
alleged incident in which an African
princess, detected in compromising circumstances, explained that she and the man had
been 'discussing Ugandan affairs'. Now also,
in *Private Eye*, of male homosexual activity:
'One second-year student called "Elsie"
offers to discuss Uganda with anyone as an
act of Christian love' (*Private Eye*, May 1981
– he was a candidate for ordination as a
priest). This series of in-jokes has no connection with the seamy sexual reputation of
Whites living in Kenya: 'In Kenya it got to
such a pitch that one used to say, "Are you
married or do you live in Kenya?"' (Allen,
1979, of extra-marital copulation).

ultimate intentions the extermination or
banishment of Jews
A Nazi evasion: 'How did you know this?
About ultimate intentions?' (Keneally, 1982
– the question was asked of a Polish Jew in
WW II). (Without excusing the Nazis, let us
not forget that others were far from innocent
in the matter of persecuting European Jews.
They were proscribed in a pogrom in the
most Catholic city of Limerick in the early
1920s, and few Jews live there to this day. In
1937 the French and Polish governments
direct and the Germans using Pirow, the S.
African Defence Minister, were in serious
negotiation about transporting to and
resettling in Madagascar their indigenous
Jewish populations. It was only after the
onset of WW II that the Nazis abandoned
Madagascar in favour of Zyklon B. For Br.
attitudes to the Jews you have only to study
Franklyn's DRS.)

un-American differing from an accepted
standard
The phrase was introduced in 1844 to
deride the 'Know Nothing' movement and
has been found useful by bigots ever since.
In politics, conservatives find anything other
than conservatism 'un-American': 'It would
be regarded as un-American and therefore
rejected' (Goebbels, 1945, in tr., of
Bolshevism). Anyone who stood up to Senator McCarthy was un-American, along with
numbers who failed to stand up to him. Even
losing your accent by living too long in
Europe puts you at risk: 'They'd be branded
for ever as un-American' (N. Mitford,
1960).

unacceptable damage that degree of
nuclear destruction which involves surrender
Nuclear jargon, assuming that there will be
something left to surrender or, again in the
jargon, that you retain 'survivability'.

unavailable (1) unwilling to accept a caller
Social and business jargon whether the call
is on the telephone or in person. The deceit
implies a willingness to be helpful.

unavailable (2) menstruating
Female usage, especially to a normal sexual
partner.

unavailable (3) evading arrest
Police and underworld jargon: 'Ray Tuck is
"unavailable" at the moment. And we've got
a three-line whip out on him' (Price, 1982).

unbalanced mad
Not just dizziness: 'We have to accept the
position that Ed was unbalanced' (Condon,
1966 – Ed was mentally ill).

uncaring *see* **caring**

uncertain depressed
The jargon of economic projections when
talk of disaster is thought likely to bring it
about: '. . . the economic situation in the UK
remains uncertain' (M. Thomas, 1980).
(And if there were certainty in economic
forecasting, the politicians would soon
restore the state of unpredictability.)

uncle a pawnbroker
Perhaps punning on the Latin 'uncus', the
hook on his scale, and the supposed benevolence of a brother of one of your parents.
In the same sense, although without a classical allusion, the French call a pawnbroker an
aunt and further to confuse things, in ob.
London usage, an 'uncle' was a lavatory.

Uncle Tom a Black who defers unduly to
Whites
From Stowe's *Uncle Tom's Cabin, or, Life
Among the Lowly* of 1851. Some of those who
now use the term derogatively do not know
that the novel was a tract against slavery: '. . .
kissed the right asses, moved on up there.
Fuckin' Uncle Tom shit' (Diehl, 1978).

uncomfortable (1) urgently needing to
urinate
By implication there is no lavatory immediately available.

uncomfortable (2) having an erection of
the penis
A woman's usage of a man whom she does

not know intimately but who wishes so to know her.

under-achiever an idle or stupid child
Properly, a child mentally capable of doing better, especially in examinations, but failing through nervousness or ill-health. This educational jargon seeks to excuse wilfulness under a cloak of misfortune. '. . . "we do have a special course for the Over-active Underachiever," continued the Headmaster' (Sharpe, 1982).

under-arm an armpit
Properly, any of the under part of the arm, a method of lobbing a ball, service at tennis or anything carried in that manner, like the ob. Yorks 'under-arm bairn', a dead child carried by its mother to its grave to save the expense of a coffin. Advertisers especially like to avoid the taboo body-hair and pocket of sweat, or 'under-arm wetness'.

under arrest unmarried and unlikely to marry
Of an Am. female. I have not traced the etymology.

under hatches dead
Br. nautical usage, from the closing of the hold, and of the coffin. The ob. naval 'under sailing orders' meant that you were dying.

under-invoicing a fraudulent device to avoid import duties
Where the importing country imposes high import tariffs and the importer has access to external funds, it is common for the documentation to show a price below that agreed between the parties, the balance of the agreed price being paid by informal transfer and thus not subject to duty. cf. **over-invoicing.**

under the counter illegal
The physical reality with scarce goods in wartime Britian, and for some time thereafter. Now used fig. of criminal transactions involving stolen goods etc.

under the daisies etc. dead
You may also be 'under the sod', 'undersod', 'underground' or 'under the grass' even though you have been cremated: 'If he dhraws thim mountainy men down on me, I may as well go under the sod' (Somerville and Ross, 1908) and: 'Small wonder that th' ghosties stir up an' dahn, time an' time, when them as lig undersod . . .' (Sutcliffe, 1900 – 'lig' means lie) and: 'You can live there when I'm underground, which will be any day now' (Murdoch, 1983).

under the influence drunk
Abbr. of the legal jargon 'under the influence of drink or drugs'. 'Half under' is no less drunk.

under the screw in prison
Punning on the rigours of prison life and the gaoler.

under the table (1) very drunk
You are supposed to end up there after dropping senseless from your chair. Normally today used fig. of someone who is able to consume less intoxicant than his companion: 'I'll drink you under the table, Max. Be warned' (Deighton, 1981).

under the table (2) involving bribery
From the surreptitious passing of the money. Rarely too of any transaction arranged in such a way that tax is avoided.

under the weather (1) drunk
Properly, unwell and therefore also used of someone with a bad hangover.

under the weather (2) menstruating
Again from the meaning, unwell.

underdeveloped poor
One of a series of euphemisms brought into use and then disrepute to avoid offending those whose release from colonialism proved to be merely an interlude between one oppression and the next: 'The use of under-developed is a clue to a state of mind, that of the international do-gooders' (Pei, 1969). Now also of the poorer parts of a city in a rich country: 'All big cities have these little under-developed areas in them' (Theroux, 1982).

underground (1) *see* above ground

underground (2) *see* under the daisies etc.

underground production *see* black economy

underprivileged poor
Properly, lacking honourable distinctions, so that it embraces us all, unless we are royalty, Nobel prize-winners or have been decorated for gallantry: 'One righted the balance by being more than fair to the underprivileged' (Bradbury, 1959).

underweight a young whore
Pimps' jargon, from cattle sent prematurely to market: '. . . women from seventeen to twenty years old. These are *underweight* and must be provided with false papers' (Londres, 1928, in tr.). ? ob.

undiscovered country (the) death
The 'Undiscover'd country, from whose

bourn No traveller returns' (Shakespeare, *Hamlet*) and in modern use: 'I shall have entered the great "Perhaps", as Danton I think called "the undiscovered country"' (Harris, 1925).

undo to copulate with extra-maritally
Of a male, from the loss of reputation rather than the removal of clothing: 'Thou hast undone our mother' (Shakespeare, *Titus Andronicus* – today the children might have said 'thou hast done our mother').

undocumented illegal
Of Hispanic Americans entering the USA illegally, especially when working without a permit.

unfaithful having copulated with other than your regular sexual partner
Of either sex, usu. within marriage: '"She's been unfaithful to me" . . . . "He thinks it's a violation of our marriage because it was someone he didn't like"' (Bradbury, 1965). And of homosexual relationships: '. . . the person he loved was being unfaithful to him in Paris' (N. Mitford, 1949 – the 'person' was male).

unfallen not yet guilty of any sin
The 'falling' is from grace, and not a bicycle. Of either sex, normally, but not necessarily, of sexual adventures: '. . . he felt unfallen and did not yet understand how wickedness began' (Murdoch, 1983).

unfortunate engaged in prostitution
A common 19c. use, especially by women who earned their living in other ways, or not at all: '. . . those unfortunate young women, who . . . . were the juster objects of compassion' (Cleland, 1749, of whores).

unhealthy homosexual
Those who use the phrase do not necessarily regard heterosexual activity as healthy: 'Hattie heard one of the mistresses, talking about her and Pearl, say, "It's an unhealthy relationship"' (Murdoch, 1983).

unhinged mad
The common gate imagery: 'Gordon Masters is quite unhinged – has taken to coming into the Department wearing his old Territorial Army uniform' (Lodge, 1975).

unhorsed knocked out of battle in an armoured vehicle
WW II usage by Br. tank units which were the successors to cavalry regiments but carried on the same traditions, names and jargon: 'He's been unhorsed three times in a fortnight, and the last time he was blown

clean out of his tank by a Tiger' (Price, 1978).

union (1) copulation
Of humans and animals, the making into one: 'The union of your bed' (Shakespeare, *Tempest*). Commonly used too of marriage.

union (2) an institution for the homeless poor
Abbr. of 'union house', set up by a Poor Law Union and still around until after WW II in BI: 'We used to . . . . tramp it from one union to another' (Mayhew, 1862).

union brewed made in a brewery where union membership is compulsory for all employees
You see the statement on Canadian beer cans, etc. but whatever labour unions brew, it is not beer.

Union Jack for the death of
Army usage, from draping the national flag over a soldier's coffin: 'I could see it was the Union Jack for this one, no error. His frame was wasted and yellow' (Fraser, 1972). I have not met an Am. equivalent featuring Old Glory, but I imagine it exists.

unique unusual
Advertising jargon: 'Unique tranquil location adjacent to the Law Courts' (London *Times*, May 1981). Every location is unique nor are there degrees of uniqueness, despite the description of a putting course in Woolacombe, Devon as the 'most unique in Britain'.

united dead
With your 'Maker' etc. or with a spouse who has predeceased you. Monumental usage.

university of Ham the prison in which Louis Napoleon was incarcerated
Prior to the momentous events of 1848, the Prince spent some years as a prisoner in the Castle of Ham. In addition to the concupiscence of which the Governor wrote, he studied deeply and to good effect, being the first ruler to understand the buying power of a modern state and the use to which it could be put in national economic development. Unlike the theorists, he had the chance to put his ideas into effect: 'At the height of his career as Emperor, he was fond of saying . . . . "I took my honours at the University of Ham"' (Corley, 1961).

unknown to men etc. not having copulated
And a man might be 'unknown to women' in

the same sense: 'I am yet unknown to women' (Shakespeare, *Macbeth*).

unlace your sandal to copulate
Of a woman, from the first act of undressing: 'When a *Casita* woman unlaces her sandal from thirty to thirty-five times a day, you can compliment her on being a good worker' (Londres, 1928, in tr.). ? ob.

unlawful extra-marital copulation or bastardy
Our forefathers seemed to be more concerned about the bastardy than the adultery: 'In his unlawful bed, he got This Edward' (Shakespeare, *Richard III*). A bastard was 'unlawful issue': '. . . the unlawful issue that their lust Since then hath made between them' (Shakespeare, *Antony and Cleopatra*), being 'unlawfully born': 'I had rather my brother die by the law than my son should be unlawfully born' (Shakespeare, *Measure for Measure*). But an 'unlawful purpose' covers many vices apart from its criminal connotation, extra-marital copulation being only one: '. . . solicits her In the unlawful purpose (corrupting) the tender honour of a maid' (Shakespeare, *All's Well*).

unlimber your joint *see* joint (2)

unmarried homosexual
Many men choose not to marry without being homosexuals and as usual the euphemism depends on the context: 'Neighbours of unmarried Mr Hamilton contacted police six months ago . . . . a male model and a tenant at Mr Hamilton's house . . . . is acting as Mr Hamilton's agent' (*Sunday Telegraph*, December 1986).

unmentionable disease a venereal disease
Still not spoken of in polite circles: '. . . adding an unmentionable disease to the old lady's dossier of Wilt's faults' (Sharpe, 1979).

ummentionables etc. (1) trousers
19c. prudery which in its extremest form extended to the sexual implications of table legs: 'She had vowed never to change or wash her unmentionables until her husband, Archduke Albert, took the city of Ostend by siege' (Jennings, 1965 – as it held out for three years, she must have kept her vow at the expense of her friends and her marriage). Also as 'unexpressibles', 'unspeakables', 'untalkaboutables', 'unutterables', 'unwhisperables', 'ineffables' and 'inexpressibles': 'They wear all manner of pantaloons and inexpressibles' (James, 1816).

unmentionables (2) haemorrhoids
A female way of talking about piles.

unnatural homosexual
Legal jargon, as in 'unnatural' crime, practice or, rarely, filth: '. . . the severe penalties imposed on unnatural practices in our own country by an Act of 1886 have merely had the effect of advertising them' (Richards, 1936). Also of bestiality and buggery of a female: '. . . trying to sort out which portion of anatomy fitted the next . . . . in what . . . . appeared to be a series of extremely unnatural acts' (Sharpe, 1975).

unregulated free economy the operation of an illegal market
Not the socialist pejorative term for the unregulated supply of goods and services under capitalism which, by succeeding, confounds their dogma but a Zambian euphemism for the **black market** (q.v.).

unscheduled caused by accident or necessity
Airline jargon which seeks to avoid any implication of loss of reliability or safety: 'Engineers have a nice phrase for engine breakdowns. An "unscheduled engine removal"' (Moynahan, 1983).

unsighted blind
Properly, prevented from seeing by an intervening obstruction.

unslated mad
Perhaps ob. N. Eng. imagery from the loss of slates from the roof of a house: 'He's gone clean off his head, unslated' (Brierley, 1886).

unsound not to be trusted
Bureaucratic jargon, of judgement rather than honesty: '". . . Tyler was unsound." "And you can't say worse than that in Whitehall"' (Lyall, 1980). Perhaps from a ship which is not in good condition.

unstanched not having copulated
A 'stanch' is something which stops blood and I think the imagery is from the cessation of menstruation during pregnancy but: 'As leaky as an unstanch'd wench' (Shakespeare, *Tempest*) could as well refer to the absence of a protective towel. ob.

unstoned castrated
Of animals rather than St Stephen. The ob. Eng. dialect 'unpaved' seems to have been quite a good pun, albeit in doubtful taste.

untrimmed not having copulated
The imagery is from a wick rather than from the meaning, to put in order: 'In likeness of a

new untrimmed bride' (Shakespeare, *King John*). ob.

untrue having copulated extra-maritally
The reverse of **true** (q.v.), of either sex:
'The thought that you might have been untrue . . . . would have broken my heart' (Fraser, 1975).

unwaged involuntarily unemployed
It sounds more like a war which didn't take place: 'Claire is trying to get her father to give cheap food to the unwaged' (Townsend, 1982 – he was a greengrocer).

unwell (1) menstruating
From the meaning, ill: '. . . all's well that ends unwell' (Harris, 1925, quoting a woman who had thought she was pregnant).

unwell (2) drunk
Covering up the taboo condition with one of its symptoms: '"Our Mr Fellows" had been "very unwell at the time of the move." "He wasn't unwell," said my sister. "He was drunk"' (Bogarde, 1983).

up (1) to copulate with a woman
Rare, except as 'upped' which is used mainly of rape. The phrase 'up a woman' is explicit: '"When you're up who, Barbara's down on whom?" asks Flora. "Flora, you're coarse," says Howard' (Bradbury, 1975). There are many vulgar puns like 'up her passage', 'up her way' etc.

up (2) under illegal narcotic influence
Especially from amphetamine. Whence 'ups', 'uppers' or 'uppies', such narcotics: 'I knew one 4th Division Lurp who took his pills by the fistful, downs from the left pocket of his tiger suit and ups from the right' (Herr, 1977).

up (2) having forgotten your lines
Am. theatrical sl.

up along old
An Eng. dialect usage which is still heard in the SW. I think the Sc. 'up in life' is ob.: 'Though up in life, I'll get a wife' (Boswell, 1871).

up in arms having an erection of the penis
The common military imagery: 'I'd never have thought to be still up in arms when Susie . . . . was hollering uncle' (Fraser, 1982).

up the creek in severe difficulties
The 'creek' is 'shit creek', or the anus, which, to be 'up', meant that you were a bugger and liable to severe penalties if found out. The abbr. and the full phrases, of which

for most the provenance is fortunately lost, are now only used fig.: '. . . telling them that if they'd followed her this far up shit creek it's long way to walk back' (*Private Eye*, July 1981).

up the loop mad
Army usage with imagery perhaps from railway shunting practice, but perhaps not: 'A lot of us believed he was really up the loop for having played at it so long' (Richards, 1936, of a soldier feigning madness to secure discharge). Whence the more common 'loopy', mad.

up the pole pregnant
Punning on the meaning, in trouble, and on 'pole', the penis: '"We've planned this for a long time." "When you discovered she was up the pole"' (Binchy, 1985 – 'this' was marriage).

up the river in prison
From the location of Sing Sing and other Am. jails relative to their neighbouring cities. And *see* send up.

up the spout pregnant
The imagery is from loading a shell into a rifled barrel from which, the copper band being engaged, it can be extracted from the breech only with danger and difficulty: 'The chorus, four times repeated, was: "She was up the bleeding spout"' (Richards, 1936). Also in ob. usage of bankruptcy.

up the stick pregnant
Perhaps punning on 'stick', a gun barrel and a penis.

uppish drunk
From the sometime feeling of elevation, and perhaps too the cheekiness.

upstairs (1) an allusion to a taboo act or place
'She's gone upstairs' implied that a pregnant woman was about to give birth. Of an invalid 'he's been upstairs two months' indicates the extent of his infirmity. Socially 'would you like to go upstairs?' invites urination. 'Upstairs' too is where the bedrooms are, for copulation: 'Was he going to haul her off upstairs, leaving first-years honours (students) to riot away among the cakes below while he satisfied his passion?' (Bradbury, 1959). For the devout morbid, 'upstairs' is death, where heaven is, and to go 'upstairs out of this world' was to be hanged, punning on the climb up the scaffold.

upstairs (2) in authority.
The senior staff occupy the higher floors:
'And now the pressure put on from upstairs
to put the clamp on the case' (Van Lustbaden, 1983).

urban renewal slum clearance
Not a tidied up business district: 'The abandoned warehouse was in a depressed area
long overdue for urban renewal' (Bagley,
1982).

use (1) to copulate with
Of a male normally outside marriage: 'Be a
whore still: they love thee not that use thee'
(Shakespeare, *Timon of Athens*) and in modern use: 'The fact that her father had used
her killed my liking for Kätchen' (Harris,
1925). There are many explicit phrases like
'use for his vile purposes', 'use to sate his
lusts' and 'use as a woman': 'Do you suppose
that slaver captain has been . . . using her . . .
as a *woman?*' (Fraser, 1971, and not referring
to a mixed tennis partnership).

use (2) to be addicted to illegal narcotics
An abbr. of 'use drugs' etc. and of the jargon
'use some help': '"I think we can use some
help," . . . . he said, passing the vial and the
gold spoon to her' (Robbins, 1981). An Am.
'user' is an addict.

use (3) capable of conception
Of animals usu. as 'in use': '. . . none of the
mares he covered three weeks or more ago
has come back into use' (Francis, 1982).

use of Venus copulation
By a male, Venus being the goddess of love:
'Much use of Venus doth dim the sight'
(Bacon, 1627 – Shakespeare would never
have written that). ob.

use paper to defecate
Hospital jargon, and not of writing a letter
home.

use the facilities etc. to urinate
Of the bathroom or the outhouse: '. . . a
gentlemanly statement of his desire to use the
outhouse' (Keneally, 1979).

use your tin to identify yourself as a policeman
From the Am. badge: 'I'd be in civilian
clothes . . . . Could I use my tin?' (Sanders,
1973, of a policeman).

used second-hand
To relieve the stigma of prior ownership,
especially of cars. But for the Br. 18c. warrior
General Guise 'used up' meant dead or
wounded – he sent for reinforcements after
he had 'used up' his grenadiers in an attack on
Cartagena.

useful fool a dupe of the Communists
Lenin's phrase for the sincere pacifists and
shallow thinkers in the west whom the
Communists manipulate: '. . . the Judas goats
leading what they call "the useful fools" up
the garden path to the knacker's yard – the
brave sons of Ireland in the IRA and the
honest pacifists in CND' (Price, 1982).

utensil a pot for urine
Properly, a container for any use. Now perhaps ob.

V

V-girl a female who might copulate extra-
maritally without payment
To enhance the status of work in WW II Am.
munitions factories, female workers were
called 'Victory Girls'. In the changed
environment and absence from home, many
became sexually promiscuous, as did their
Br. sisters. Abbr. to 'V-girl', servicemen
used the expression of any woman who
'volunteered' to copulate without payment.
Later, when many of the women became
infected with disease, the 'V' came also to
stand for 'venereal'.

vacation a prison sentence
Properly, a holiday which involves any
absence from home: '. . . won a twenty years'
vacation in the Big House' (Lavine, 1930).
Am.

valentine a notice of dismissal from
employment
Punning on the **cards** (q.v.) received by
some on 14 February. It was also used in
Am. of a warning to an employee of conduct
which was unsatisfactory and might lead to
dismissal: 'The captain . . . . may distribute a
few complaints or "valentines" for dereliction of duties' (Lavine, 1930).

vanity publishing *see* **tail pulling**

Vatican roulette the use of the 'safe
period' method of contraception
Punning on the Roman Catholic dogma
against contraception and Russian roulette –
in either case you cannot be quite sure that
there isn't one 'up the spout': 'But it seems
that Vatican Roulette has failed them again
and a fourth little faithful is on the way'
(Penguin blurb for Lodge's *The British
Museum is Falling Down*).

vault (1) to copulate with
Of a male predating the modern **jump** (3)
(above): 'Whiles he is vaulting variable
ramps' (Shakespeare, *Cymbeline*). Whence
the ob. punning 'vaulting-school', a brothel.

vault (2) a cupboard for the storage of a
corpse
Am. funeral jargon. Properly, any structure
with an arched roof which is how some early
tombs were built but: 'That vault we are
describing here is designed as an outer
receptacle to protect the casket and its contents from the elements during their eternal
sojourn in the grave' (J. Mitford, 1963).

vegetarian a whore who will not perform
fellatio
Prostitutes' jargon for one who will not eat
meat (q.v.).

velvet (1) the vagina viewed sexually by a
male
The fabric with a smooth, thick, luxurious
pile: '. . . pitiless calculation of a female with
velvet to sell' (Mailer, 1965).

velvet (2) a payment for which there is no
consideration
Either a bribe: 'Money is deposited in the
"velvet-lined" drawer of my desk . . .'
(Lavine, 1930) or an exceptional profit: '. . .
to get back his original investment in order
to be able to work in "velvet"' (ibid.). Again
from the properties of the cloth.

venereal *see* **Venus**

Venus appertaining to copulation
The Roman goddess of love appears in many
compounds and variations: 'His heart
Inflamed with Venus' (Shakespeare, *Troilus
and Cressida*). 'Venereal', now used only of
sexually-transmitted diseases, once meant
beautiful or lustful and 'venery' once meant
the pursuit of women as well as of deer. The
'venerous act', copulation, is ob.: '. . . it did
afford him some pleasure to see the venerous act performed' (Fowles, 1985, using
archaic language of a voyeur).

verbally deficient illiterate
Not merely having a restricted vocabulary.
Jennings (1965) points out how odd it is that
those who cannot read should need a written
euphemism to conceal their ignorance.

very poorly *see* **poorly** (1)

vibrator *see* **cordless massager**

vicar of Bray a cowardly or opportunistic
trimmer
A cleric held this living in the 16c. during
the reign of four Eng. monarchs, two of
whom were Roman Catholic and three Protestant. (Henry VIII was both.) When the
vicar was accused of being of a changeable
turn he replied: 'No, I am steadfast, however
other folk change I remain Vicar of Bray'
(Alleyn). Elsewhere in the country, livings
were lost and regained with each turn of the
tide, as reference to the names of incum-
bents in many parish churches will illustrate.

victualler the keeper of a brothel
He provides the **meat** (q.v.): '*Falstaff* . . .
suffering flesh to be eaten in thy house con-

trary to the law; for the which I think thou wilt howl. *Hostess* All victuallers do so' (Shakespeare, *2 Henry IV* – note the two sexual puns). Whence the ob. punning 'victualling-house', a brothel.

vigilance informing to the authorities on fellow-citizens
The usage and practice of totalitarian states, to deter or detect any incipient dissident: '... everyone informs right from the nursery .... They call it "vigilance"' (M. C. Smith, 1981, of Russia).

violate to copulate with extra-maritally
The usu. violent imagery and used in this sense since 15c. where a male has used force or blandishments: 'With unchaste purpose, and with oath to violate My lady's honour' (Shakespeare, *Cymbeline*).

viper a person who sells narcotics illegally
Am. dysphemism although we have to point out that the serpent's evil reputation is undeserved: 'Vipers selling a smoke-pot to school kids (Longstreet, 1956). A 'viper' is also an addict to marijuana which is sometimes known as 'viper's weed'.

virtue the property of not having copulated extra-maritally
Properly, conforming with all moral standards, but in this use of women since 16c.: 'Their triumphs over the virtue of girls' (Mayhew, 1851). Whence 'virtuous', not having so copulated: 'Betimes in the morning I will beseech the virtuous Desdemona' (Shakespeare, *Othello*).

visible handicap *see* handicap

visit *see* pay a visit

visiting card urination or defecation in a public place
Of domestic pets: 'He's left his visiting card' (Ross, 1956, of a dog).

visiting fireman a boisterous reveller
Especially if at a distance from his home, from the conduct of Am. males, including firemen, at conventions: '... a visiting fireman in search of a cheap thrill would get mugged and robbed' (McBain, 1981). The phrase is also used of managers sent from a head office to investigate or control an unsuccessful subsidiary.

visitor (a) menstruation
Common female usage, often with punning adjectival adornment. Thus in Am. the 'visitor' may come from 'Redbank'.

vital statistics the measurement of a woman's chest, waist and buttocks
Here, as so often, 'vital' means no more than important, which the information is in the world of entertainment.

vital statistics form a death certificate
Am. funeral jargon which seems singularly inappropriate to death: 'A death certificate would be referred to as a "vital statistics form"' (J. Mitford, 1963).

vitals the testicles
Properly, the parts of the body essential to the continuation of life, whence usu. the organs located in the trunk: '... him so bad with the mumps and all, so that his poor vitals were swelled to pumpkin size' (Graves, 1941).

void water to urinate
An ob. form of **pass water** (q.v.): 'When, at the end, they went too far, she voided her water on the deck' (Monsarrat, 1978, writing in archaic style).

voluntary done under duress or compulsion
As an admission of guilt obtained under duress: '... denied that any coercive measures had been used in obtaining the "voluntary confession"' (Lavine, 1930) or of unpaid work undertaken through compulsion, like chores in the army or the Russian *subbotniki*, extra work which is done on Saturdays.

voluntary patient a person in an institute for the insane
This usage differentiates between those who are confined by legal process and those who are said to be free to leave of their own volition. Provided you are not unconscious at the time, you might be thought to enter a hospital for a physical disorder voluntarily too.

voluntary pregnancy interruption *see* pregnancy interruption

volunteer a person instructed to fight etc. for a third party
Used originally of those who intervened in military formations for the Nazis and Communists during the Spanish Civil War, and now of any organized military interference where you wish to help an ally without declaring war against his enemy: '... intervention on the enemy's side of overwhelming reinforcements of Chinese "volunteers"' (Boyle, 1979, of the Korean War).

voyager a narcotics addict who ingests an hallucinogen
The common Am. travelling imagery.

voyeur a person who enjoys watching the sexual activity of others
Properly, a watcher of anything: 'Hamilton had been an enthusiastic voyeur . . . . In one home, microphones had been installed throughout the bedrooms' (Green, 1979 – an écouteur too, it seems). To 'voyeurize' is so to act: 'That's a hell of a way to get experience . . . . voyeurising ancient broads' (Sharpe, 1977).

Vulcan's badge an indication of cuckoldry
Venus, while married to Vulcan, committed adultery with Mars. Thus, in literary use, to 'wear Vulcan's badge' is to be a cuckold.

vulnerable poor or inadequate
Sociological jargon which forgets that we are all capable of being wounded. On 28 September 1984 the 'Social Services Director' of Dudley, Eng., spoke on BBC Radio 4 of his appointment of a 'Deliberate Self-harm Prevention Officer' to assist those whom he described as 'vulnerable'. Someone was going to keep an eye on attempted suicides.

W

W/WC *see* **water closet**

wad-shifter a person who never drinks intoxicants
A 'wad' is a doughy bun, often taken with 'char', tea. Br. army usage in a society where temperance is taboo: 'If a teetotaller he was known as a "char-wallah", "bun-puncher" or "wad-shifter"' (Richards, 1933).

wages of sin (the) premature death
For devout Christians the posthumous prospects of those said to be so remunerated are poor: 'For the wages of sin is death; but the gift of God is eternal life' (Romans, vi. 23).

wagon *see* **on the wagon**

wake to watch over a corpse
Properly, to keep awake, whence to stay awake by night to ensure that a body is not molested before burial: 'For nobody cared to wake Sir Robert Redgauntlet like another corpse' (W. Scott, 1824). Your vigilance had sometimes to extend after the interment: 'Wauk the kirkyard . . . . to prevent the inroads of resurrection-men' (EDD). Whence our modern 'wake', the feast which may follow a death: '"There's a wake in the family," an euphemistic expression for death' (ibid.).

wake a witch to force a woman to confess to witchcraft
As with **swim for a wizard** (above) this entry is included to illustrate the behaviour of our recent ancestors. Here an iron hoop was placed over the Sc. victim's face, with four prongs in her mouth. Chained to a wall so that she could not lie down, relays of men kept her awake until she admitted she was a witch, after which she might be ducked or burnt to death.

walk (1) to be a whore
Usu. expanded to phrases such as 'walk the streets': 'Women walking the streets for tricks to take to their "pads"' (L. Armstrong, 1955).

walk (2) to be dismissed from employment
This usage wrongly implies a voluntary departure: 'Thing is, I give you maybe three, four years, you'll walk' (Diehl, 1978, of such dismissal). 'Walking papers', notice of dismissal, is also applied to the unilateral ending of an Am. courtship.

walk (3) to be stolen
Of small tools, items of army kit, etc. This ironic usage avoids accusing your mates of theft by attributing the power of locomotion to inanimate objects.

walk (4) to acknowledge dismissal before an umpire's adjudication
Cricket jargon, but euphemistic only in the negative, when 'not to walk' is an imputation of bad sportsmanship by a batsman who knows he has been dismissed but hopes for an umpiring error.

walk (5) to escape deserved punishment
An abbr. of 'walk free' but used only of the guilty': '"Havistock is going to walk, isn't he?" "Sure he is," Al said. "What could we charge him with?"' (Sanders, 1986 – Al was a policeman).

walk out (1) to court
The usage has survived the days when preliminary courtship was a pedestrian affair: 'Caleb was "walkin' a maid out"' (Agnus, 1900). The maid would be said to 'walk out with' or less often to 'walk with' him: 'You'll dance at the hops with me, ride with me, but you won't walk with me' (Cookson, 1967 – a girl was complaining at the limits set by a man to their friendship). Courting couples were said to 'walk with' or 'walk along of' each other.

walk out (2) to go on strike
This does not refer to the departure on foot of workers at the end of a shift and in a 'walk-out', a strike, the majority today leave by car. Usu. of cessation of work at short notice, contrary to agreed conditions of employment and without recourse to negotiating procedures.

walk penniless in Mark Lane *see* **mark**

walk the plank to be murdered by drowning
Favoured by pirates for the disposal of their captives.

wall-eyed drunk
Properly, strabismic, with difficulty in focusing, and drunkenness can cause that too.

wallflower week menstruation
When you stay away from men, or at the least from copulating with them. A 'wallflower' is a woman who has secured no dancing partner, punning on her remaining on a chair around the periphery of a dance-hall and Cheiranthus Cheiri.

wallop the mattress to copulate
To 'wallop' is to beat. Of either party with familiar imagery: 'She'd never have walloped the mattress with me like that if she'd been false' (Fraser, 1975).

wander off to defecate
From the seeking after seclusion and you may say whither you wander: 'The following morning, after we had all wandered off into the appropriate field, and washed at the pump, and breakfasted ...' (Simon, 1979).

wandered slightly mad
From the inability to concentrate: '... sick in mind as in body. He seemed, as my wife's relatives would have said, to be "wandered"' (Fraser, 1969, writing in archaic style). Sc. ? ob.

wank to masturbate yourself
Of a male, from the meaning to beat or thrash, as in the dialect 'wanked', exhausted. A 'wanker' so masturbates: 'Harrison's are a lot of wankers' (Sharpe, 1982, of schoolboys for whom it is a term of abuse as well as self-abuse) and 'wankery' is sexually salacious material for the solitary male: '... locking himself in with a load of new-bought wankery' (Amis, 1978). To 'wank' is rarely to copulate, except in the corruption 'wang' or in 'wang-house', a brothel: 'I had expected the opium parlour to be something like a wang-house filled with sleepy hookers' (Theroux, 1973).

want (1) idiocy
Abbr. for 'want of understanding' etc.: 'I had a want and been daft likewise' (Galt, 1826). Whence the modern 'wanting', imbecile. In Sc. an idiot might 'want some pence in the shilling': '... of rather a wild frantic nature, and seem to want "some pence in the shilling"' (Mactaggart, 1824).

want (2) to wish to copulate with
When you 'want' a man or woman, it is not for social intercourse: 'Yet he wanted my mother, his half-sister, and in trying to get his way with her caused her untold agony of mind' (Cookson, 1969). Specifically you may 'want sex' (which does not mean you are an hermaphrodite) or 'want' relations, intercourse, love, a body, etc.: 'Since she was fifteen, men had wanted her body' (Allbeury, 1976).

want out to wish to kill yourself
Properly, to wish to extract yourself from a deal or arrangement: '"Does the letter signify anything to you?" "Only that he wanted out"' (B. Forbes, 1983, of a suicide note).

war criminal a leader of the enemy
This dysphemism is usu. only applied to the losers, although Goebbels described Churchill and Roosevelt as 'The two war criminals' (1945, in tr.), only to see his companions so arraigned later that year. A 'war crime' is the act of having led a country which has lost a war.

war paint facial cosmetics
Punning jocular female usage, from Redskin adornment before battle: 'Baby was down with a fresh dressing of warpaint' (Sharpe, 1977).

warehouse to hold stocks for a principal seeking to conceal his interest
Stock Exchange jargon for an illegal or clandestine operation, with imagery from holding goods in a store belonging to another: 'It is even suggested that the diminutive legal person could have "warehoused" some of the Howard shares' (*Private Eye*, March 1981).

warm sexually aroused
And sometimes no cooler than **hot** (1) (q.v.): 'The warm effects which she in him finds missing' (Shakespeare, *Venus*). The ob. 'warm one' was a whore whom you might find in a 'warm shop', a brothel. I am sorry that we seem to have lost the descriptive phrase, to 'warm up old porridge', to renew a discontinued sexual relationship, with its gentle reminder that the taste is never quite the same as before.

warning a dismissal from employment
An older form of **notice** (above) but given rather than received: 'If respectable young girls are set picking grass out of your gravel, in place of their proper work, certainly they will give warning' (Somerville and Ross, 1897).

wash (1) urine
As commonly used in the laundry: 'Dochter, here is a bottle o' my father's wash' (Graham, 1883 – it was for medical examination). A 'wash-mug' was a piss-pot. ob.

wash (2) to deal unnecessarily in securities to obtain commission
Br. Stock Exchange jargon, from handling something which remains the same after treatment. The Am. **churning** (above) is more elegant.

wash (3) to bring into open circulation money obtained illegally
A variant of **launder** (above).

wash the baby's head to drink intoxicants in celebration of a birth

There is probably some connection with the rite of Christening: 'To wesh ther heeads e bumper toasts' (Treddlehoyle, 1846). In modern use more as 'wet the baby's head'.

wash your hands to urinate
This is what arriving guests are commonly invited to do, or suggest doing, from the proximity of the lavatory and the hand wash basin. A 'wash and brush up' means much the same thing and 'washroom' is widely used in Am. for lavatory.

wash your hands of to dissociate yourself from anything unpleasant
Like Pilate, who 'took water, and washed his hands before the multitude, saying, I am innocent of the blood of this just person: see ye to it' (Matthew, xxvii 24).

washroom *see* **wash your hands**

waste (1) to kill
From one of the many meanings, to destroy, to use up, to expend needlessly, to spill (as in S. Devon you may 'waste' your milk if you overturn the cup), etc.: 'You wanted a photo of Roger Kope, the cop who got wasted' (Sanders, 1973). Am.

waste (2) to use narcotics illegally
As this is Am. addict sl., probably not from the 'wasting away' of the body of the user.

waste (3) urine or faeces
In Am. particularly of canine excreta, where 'dry waste' is dog shit. And for humans a spacecraft has not a lavatory but a 'waste-management compartment'.

water urine
Used in this sense since 14c. even though the liquid described differs significantly from our concept of the clear and potable compound of hydrogen and oxygen: 'Sirrah, you giant, what says the doctor to my water?' (Shakespeare, 2 *Henry IV*). A male who goes to 'water' his garden, the roses, his nag, etc. will urinate, usu. out of doors. 'Water-shaken' is an ob. term for involuntary urination. 'Waterworks' is a punning reference to the human urinary system, especially when it is not performing properly: '. . . busily at work cauterizing her waterworks' (Sharpe, 1979). etc.

water closet a lavatory with a flush mechanism
Abbr. internationally to 'WC' and rarely in BI to 'W': 'The W is a frequent non-U expression for "lavatory" (W.C. is also non-U)' (Ross, 1956).

water cure a form of torture
A far cry from attending a spa to relieve your rheumatism. The water is applied externally or orally and the torture still persists in modern tyrannies because it is simple, cheap and effective.

water of life whisky
The Sc/Ire. 'usquebaugh' rather than the French *eau de vie*: '"Uisgebeatha?" Murdoch said in Gaelic. "The water of life"' (Higgins, 1976). I suspect in 19c. Sc. it may have been used of any spirituous intoxicant: 'A glass of brandy or usquabae' (W. Scott, 1824).

watering hole a place licensed to sell intoxicants
Punning jocular usage: 'A blinking sign I took to be a watering hole' (Theroux, 1979). He would have been affronted if it offered only water.

waterlogged very drunk
Properly, saturated with water, whence heavy and sluggish, unable to absorb more liquid.

watermelon an indication of pregnancy
The shape of the swelling in Am. phrases 'have a watermelon on the vine' or 'swallow a watermelon seed'.

waterworks *see* **water**

wax to remove unwanted body hair
Female usage and practice: 'Mumsy and I are motoring up to London to have our legs waxed at Fortnums' (*Private Eye*, April, 1981). And *see* **bikini wax**.

way of all flesh (the) death
The biblical: 'I am going the way of all flesh' (Joshua xxiii 4) and made a cliché by Samuel Butler's posthumously (1903) published novel.

way out under illegal narcotic influence
Properly, any wide deviance from a norm, whence too the narcotic elation in which some performers consider they work best.

weakness a tendency towards self-indulgence
Not difficulty in rising from a chair but guilt of one or more of the Seven Deadly Sins and their derivatives. Thus a 'weakness' may be unspecified: '. . . their Mr Fellows *did* have a "weakness"' (Bogarde, 1983 – he was a drunkard) or indicated, as a 'weakness for men' in a woman, profligacy.

weapon an erect penis
Punning on the shape and the use: 'My

naked weapon is out' (Shakespeare, *Romeo and Juliet*) or, less obscurely: '. . . my weapon sheathed itself in her naturally' (Harris, 1925).

wear a bullet to be killed or wounded by shooting
Underworld Am. sl.: '"Who's wearing the bullet?" I asked her' (Chandler, 1958).

wear a smile to be naked
And nothing else. Am. rather than Br. use.

wear away to die a lingering death
Usu. being 'consumed' by pulmonary tuberculosis, the common scourge until WW II, which was also known as 'wearing': 'Sickened, Took the bed, an' wear awa'' (Grant, 1884).

wear Dick's hatband *see* dick (1)

wear down to grow old
Physically accurate and a nice allusion to the burdens of long life: 'I and my Jenny are baith wearin' down' (Rodger, 1838). Sc. ? ob.

wear green garters to remain unmarried after a younger sister's wedding
By Sc. tradition, the unmarried elder sister wore green or yellow garters at the wedding. The taboos which surrounded spinsterhood arose from the plight of women who failed to obtain the support of a husband and were forbidden by convention to support themselves. ob.

wear Hector's coat to be a traitor
The Hector was Hector Armstrong in whose house Thomas Percy, Earl of Northumberland, took refuge after the failure of his rebellion against Queen Elizabeth I in 1569. Armstrong betrayed him for money to the Regent of Scotland, but died in penury.

wear iron knickers not to copulate outside marriage
Women only are fig. so clothed: 'Her Italian father . . . . wanted her to wear iron knickers until she was twenty-one' (Follett, 1979).

wear the breeches etc. to dominate a husband in an unfeminine way
At one time only men wore 'breeches', 'trousers' or the Am. 'pants': 'That you might still have worn the petticoat, And ne'er have stol'n the breech from Lancaster' (Shakespeare, 3 *Henry VI*).

wear your heart upon your sleeve to fail to conceal heterosexual longing
At one time men might advertise their intentions or desires by displaying some keepsake from the woman: 'I will wear my heart upon my sleeve, as one does a lady's favour' (Shakespeare, *Othello*).

wee to urinate
We have a choice of etymology. 'Wee', meaning small, may refer to little jobs (above), or it may be a corruption of the French 'eau'; urine or water (q.v.) are also known as 'wee'. A 'wee-wee' indicates neither greater nor repeated urination: '"Just a minute," said Viola, "I want to wee-wee"' (Bradbury, 1959). Nursery and some genteel use.

wee drop etc. a drink of whisky
Despite the 'wee', the portion is usu. substantial: 'Manis was always fond of the wee dhrap' (Macmanus, 1899). And *see* drop (2). A 'wee half' is less common: '. . . a "wee hauf" held my heart in cheer' (Murdoch, 1873). 'Wee dram' remains common. Mainly Sc./Ire.

wee folk etc. the fairies
The Br. Christmas pantomime tradition makes us forget that especially in Ire. fairies were pretty unpleasant creatures whose malevolence made them the subject of fear and taboo: 'The belief in the "wee folk", or "gentry", is very much more widely spread' (*Cornhill Magazine*, February 1877, quoted in EDD). Also as the 'wee people': '. . . they attribute it to the wee people' (Mason, c. 1815). You had to appease those you feared by speaking kindly of them.

weed (the) marijuana
Formerly tobacco, whence a cigarette, but in this use probably also from the leaf of the pistillate hemp plant: '. . . opened the door and sniffed the weed' (Chandler, 1958 – he could smell cannabis). A 'weedhead' is an habitual smoker of marijuana.

weed killer a chemical defoliant used in warfare
Am. Vietnam jargon for the substance which also destroyed crops, and perhaps the health of those who administered it: '. . . defoliants are referred to as weed-killers' (McCarthy, 1967, of Vietnam).

weekend dishonestly to use a customer's money after the close of business on a Friday
Banking jargon and practice. By delaying putting the credit to a customer's account on a Friday – or even a Thursday – the bank gains for itself interest on the amount until at least the following Monday. All banks do it, but some are more blatant or greedy than others, especially with remittances from abroad and documentary credits. Paying an

inflated charge for telegraphic transfer and advice affords some protection to the customer but I have known a Middle Eastern bank to 'weekend' for upwards of three weeks.

weigh the thumb deliberately to overcharge
From the practice of depressing the scales to give a heavier reading but now used fig. of any overcharging.

weight problem *see* **problem**

weirdie a male homosexual
Also used of anyone whose tastes, dress, politics, etc. differ from our own, as in the dated cliché 'beardies and weirdies'.

welfare state aid to the poor
Properly, prosperity, which is not what it affords its recipients: '. . . his girl friend threatened to call the cops when he took half of her welfare money' (Wambaugh, 1983). The latest (1985) and most persistent of the euphemisms designed to avoid the stigma of giving charity. In a 'welfare state' medical, educational and other services are provided, where available, at a common standard largely paid for by taxation to any who choose to use them. For some the expression has become pejorative because they see the system as perpetuating rather than curing inadequacy and poverty, turning society into a refuge for the idle, and Samuel Smiles, the apostle of self-help, in his grave.

well not menstruating
The opposite of **unwell** (1) (above): '. . . soon after I am well each month' (Harris, 1925).

well away etc. very drunk
You can also be 'well' bottled, in the way, oiled, sprung, corned, etc.: 'I'll nut say drunk, but gay weel cworn'd' (Whitehead, 1896). Some forms are ob.

well built etc. obese
Sometimes of men and women but especially of children because manufacturers know better than to describe somebody's little darling as fat. Formerly as 'well fleshed': 'Well-fleshed men could niver stand up long agen an ale-pot' (Sutcliffe, 1901).

well endowed having large genitalia or mammalia
The person so described may have a tiny dowry, or none at all: '. . . she was probably as pretty, if considerably less well endowed physically' (Price, 1970). 'Amply endowed' has the same meaning but is less common, while 'endowed' on its own is rare.

well hung having large genitallia
Used critically of bulls, stallions and rams but also of men as a variant of **well endowed** (above): 'The blowen was nutts upon the kiddey because he is well-hung' (Grose).

well-informed sources a friend or confidant of the reporter
Properly, an authorised or knowledgeable spokesman. The vague attribution gives weight to a thin or speculative story, or seeks to cover a leak.

wench a whore
Properly, a girl, whence a promiscuous woman: 'Let my lord take wenches by the score' (Blackhall, 1849). To 'wench' is to go whoring of a male, and 'wenching' a tendency in that direction.

West Briton an Anglophile Dubliner
Often Protestant and educated in England, he affects the style, manner and speech of the Br. professional classes and tends to be a successful lawyer or accountant. Some Irish derogatory use, usu. abbr. to 'West Brit'.

wet (1) to urinate
Properly, to damp through any agency but now SE when we 'wet the bed': 'Boys and girls who steal, vandalize, or wet the bed' (Bradbury, 1976). To 'wet yourself' is to urinate in your clothing, perhaps through fear: 'Grooters felt her legs almost doubling underneath her and she wet herself' (Davidson, 1978) as is to 'wet your pants' etc.: 'Merriman thought he was going to wet his pants' (M. Thomas, 1980). The ob. 'wetting' was stale urine used in laundry or cloth manufacture: 'I slat a pot of wettin in his feace' (Wheeler, 1790).

wet (2) a drink of or pertaining to an intoxicant
Rarely on its own: 'Bring me a wet, I'm near parched' (Cookson, 1967). The Br. 'wet canteen' was the one where alcohol was served: 'We spent a very pleasant evening, the First Battalion having a wet canteen, and when we started back we were three sheets in the wind' (Richards, 1933). 'Wet' goods or stuff were intoxicants, especially in Am. Prohibition use: 'The wet goods flowed. You couldn't move all of it' (Longstreet, 1956). A 'wet hand' was a drunkard who might be said to 'wet' his mouth, quill, whistle, etc.: 'Simply must wet m'whistle' (Manning, 1960, who can never be forgiven for Yakimov's untimely death). You 'wet a baby's head' when you celebrate its birth – another rite of Christening – and you 'wet a

bargain' when you drink to steal it: '. . . and be dam we'll wet our bargain' (Somerville and Ross, 1908). A 'wetting' used to be an intoxicating drink: 'The young chaps bring their bottles oot, And ilk ane gets a wettin'' (Lumsden, 1892) but today we talk of a 'wet' or a 'spot of wet'. etc.

wet deck a whore who copulates with one man immediately after another
Nautical usage, from her condition and the sequential action of waves on a ship: 'And who would have the first bout, in any case? I'll not take your wet decks' (Monsarrat, 1978, writing in archaic style of sailors whoring). The ob. 'wet hen' was a whore.

wet dream an involuntary seminal ejaculation while asleep
The experience may be accompanied by an erotic dream: 'Any dreams, wet or non-wet' (Amis, 1978). General and genteel use.

wet for wishing to copulate with
Of a woman, from the vaginal secretion and usu. of extra-marital lust: 'I am rotten-ripe, soft and wet for you' (Harris, 1925).

wet-job a murder
But not necessarily by drowning: 'If anyone fancied the idea of doing a "wet-job" on me then the bomb would go off in hours' (Allbeury, 1983).

wet your dick etc. to copulate
Of a male, usu. extra-maritally: 'And Carlo had tried to wet his wick, because in Oregon that was no big deal, and before the sun was up her father had opened his throat for the ants to have a drink' (Seymour, 1984).

wetness sweat
Genteel female usage.

wetting (1) (2) *see* wet (1) (2)

whack off to masturbate
Of a male – to 'whack' is to pull, among other meanings: 'Zoona – who was eventually thrown out of school for whacking off in full sight of three mothers during parents day' (Collins, 1981).

whacked drunk
Properly, in sl. very tired after being beaten, I think, rather than after sexual activity: '. . . a very wet party. Everyone got whacked out of their skulls' (Sanders, 1982).

what the traffic will bear an excessive but obtainable fee
A principle used by most lawyers etc. when billing corporate, careless or worried clients. The imagery is from transport pricing policy.

what you may call it any taboo object
The lavatory to many females, or the penis or vagina although not necessary in a sexual sense.

whatsit any taboo object
An abbr. of **what you may call it** (above) but usu. of a lavatory only: 'The whatsit is through there if you want it' (B. Forbes, 1983 – a woman was telling a man where the lavatory was). 'Whatzis' is rare: '. . . you'll probably use it to shoot off your whatzis' (Sanders, 1982 – the 'it' was a handgun which might hit the firer's penis).

wheel falsely to inflate the bidding at auction
Probably from the meaning, to keep moving, which the auctioneer does regardless of genuine bids. Whence the cliché, 'wheeling and dealing' as done by 'wheeler-dealers'.

whelp to give birth to a child
A 'whelp' is properly the cub of a bitch, a lioness or a tigress: '. . . she was so close to what she called "whelpin'" that she couldn't be moved' (Keneally, 1979).

whiff to kill
Properly in sl. to hit out at: 'He wasn't alone when you whiffed him' (Chandler, 1939). This Am. usage owes nothing to Carlyle's 'whiff of grapeshot', the firing on the Paris mob by Napoleon through which he established order and his own reputation.

whip to steal
Usu. of small objects, probably from the concept of moving a distant article quickly with the use of a whip.

whip the cat to be drunk
Cats are associated with vomiting, and vomiting with drunkenness.

whistle the penis
Nursery usage, from the shape in a young boy.

whistled drunk
The deviation was probably from the ob. 'whistle-shop', a Br. inn in which you 'wetted your whistle' – *see* wet (2). 'Whistlers' were not drunkards but evil spirits, from the fearful noises they made: '. . . take the calling of a daker hen in the meadow, to be the Whistlers' (Harland and Wilkinson, 1867 – a 'daker' is a corncrake).

whistler a police car
Am. use, from the siren.

whistling poor
Of a narcotics addict unable to buy supplies,

from the wind which whistles through an empty house. Am.

white elephant an unwanted or onerous possession
The King of Siam, also titled the King of the White Elephant, was said to present such a beast to any courtier he wished to ruin. Unable to sell or work the animal, the courtier had to provide for it with no return: 'The £2,000 million white elephant' (*Private Eye*, March 1981, of Concorde).

white eye inferior whisky
Made out of colourless non-potable alcohol and no doubt punning on the rolling of the eyeballs of any so unwise as to drink it. Am.

white feather cowardice
Such a feather in the plumage of a fighting cock was said to indicate poor breeding whence less aggressive behaviour: 'There's a white feather somewhere in the chield's wing, for all he's so big and buirdly' (Hamilton, 1898 – 'buirdly' means fine-looking). In WW I chauvinistic Br. women took the imagery literally, handing out white feathers to young men in mufti, secure too in the knowledge that they were themselves ineligible for service in the trenches.

white-knuckler a small aircraft used on a scheduled service
From the anxious grip of its Am. passengers in poor weather: 'You take a white-knuckler . . . . from Hyannis Airport through sea-fog to Logan' (Theroux, 1978 – Logan is Boston's international airport). Various small carriers enjoy the title of 'White-knuckle line' conferred by their regular passengers.

white lady etc. heroin
Also known as 'white stuff', which can include cocaine and morphine; and as 'white powder': 'He was still getting $100,000 a year . . . . and that bought a goodly amount of the sweet white powder' (M. Thomas, 1982).

white lightning LSD
From its colour and effects.

white man's burden the privileged status of a White in a colonial territory inhabited by Blacks
Kipling invented the phrase but not the concept of the chore of civilizing the natives: '. . . impress the natives with what wonderful things the British were doing for them; the whole idea of the White Man's Burden' (Allen, 1979, of the colonial period). You may recall that in the pictures of intrepid

marches in the interior of Africa by White men, the Black men always seem to be doing the porterage.

white money funds improperly acquired made capable of open spending
The Am. **black money** (above) recycled.

white nigger a poor Southern White
From the days when the Blacks in the South were all poor and poor Whites were also looked down on: 'INGRID: You were poor also . . . *nein*? ANDERSON: Yes. My family was white niggers' (Sanders, 1970). Am. ? ob.

white rabbit-scut cowardice
The 'scut' is the short erect tail, the sign of a fleeing rabbit: 'What, leave Marsh and show the white rabbit-scut to Nicholas Ratcliffe?' (Sutcliffe, 1900).? ob.

white satin gin
The colour and the smoothness: 'White satin, if I must know, was gin' (Mayhew, 1862).

white slave a White whore working outside Europe
Usu. under a pimp's strict control in the Middle East or S. America. Whence 'white slavery': 'White slavery – the seduction and selling, and of course buying, of women for immoral purposes' (Londres, 1928, in tr.) and 'white slaver', the finder or the pimp: 'I'm not a white slaver in case they exist' (James, 1972, of an invitation to a young White woman to go on a journey with a stranger).

white tail a completed but unsold civil aircraft
The manufacturer leaves it in its white undercoat until he can find a buyer who will stipulate the colour scheme. For him, such a stock is a double disaster; the finance charges continue and the existence of unsold aircraft spoils the market.

white wrapper an unmarked police car
It has no advertisement on it. CB sl. Am.

whites the vaginal secretion of a sexually aroused female
Also used of other vaginal secretions due to ill-health, other than bleeding.

whitewash to attempt to hush up an embarrassing or shameful event
Wide political use. 'Whitewash' is made of lime and water, or similar non-permanent materials; quickly and liberally applied to a

surface, it provides temporary cover for the blemishes underneath.

whizz urination
Am. onomatopoeic use: '" I just came down for a whizz." He recoiled at the vulgarity' (Theroux, 1978).

whole can *see* **half a can**

whole hog (the) copulation
Usu. teenage use, after courtship involving exploratory sexual acts: 'She was disappointed. That I didn't go the whole hog' (Amis, 1980). From the meaning, to do something completely which itself has a disputed etymology – either eating all of a roast male pig at a sitting, or drinking all of a hogshead of ale.

wick a penis
Rh. sl. from 'Hampton Wick', a prick, and *see* **Hampton**. This is a unique example of both parts of a rh. sl. phrase being used individually, although 'hampton' and 'wick' are not exact synonyms, 'wick' alone being used fig. as well as literally: 'It gets on my, you know, wick' (Bradbury, 1976).

wide parting (a) baldness
Male humour, used only of speaking about others and unfunny of ourselves.

wide-on (a) female heterosexual lust
I suppose from the inappropriateness of hard-on: 'That's the one thing about lady analyists . . . once in a while they fall in love with a stock, usually because they get a wide-on for the management' (M. Thomas, 1985 – he was speaking fig.). Am.

wife (1) the senior whore of a pimp
Prostitutes' jargon where the pimp has several females in his stable: 'Keep her as your "wife", since she's more use to you than to me, and take me as your sweetheart' (Londres, 1928, in tr.).

wife (2) a male homosexual taking the female role
Homosexual use in a lasting domestic arrangement.

wife (3) a woman who copulates regularly extra-maritally with the same man
Often of a relationship with a male prostitute: 'Several of the other studs had regular customers – their "wives"' (Sanders, 1983).

wife in water colours a sexual mistress
From the impermanent nature of the medium. ? ob.

will a homosexual
Wide Eng. dialect use of either sex, and of a hermaphrodite. Not from the SE 'will', lust but probably an abbr. of 'Will-o'-the-wisp', ignis fatuus, of which the first appearance is deceptive.

will of *see* **have**

willie *see* **willy**

willie-waught a drink of intoxicant
The Sc. 'good willie' means hospitable and 'waught' means to drink deeply: '"And we'll take a right guid willie-waught" was changed to, "We'll give a right guid hearty shake", in deference to temperance principles' (Murray, 1977, writing of Sir James Murray, the creator of the OED and, domestically, the bowdlerizer of Burns).

willing prepared to copulate extra-maritally
Not just any old testatrix, and usu. not of a whore: '. . . there might even be willing mountain women up there to warm his solitude' (Keneally, 1979).

willy a penis
Both nursery and adult use: 'Does your willy rise like a snake out of a basket?' (Theroux, 1978). I can do no better than quote from *Man's Best Friend*: 'There are almost as many names for a man's most intimate possession as there are for man himself. Depending on the self-confidence of the owner, and the degree of esteem that exists between the two parties, these names vary from the optimistic (Big Steve, Oliver Twist) to the pessimistic (General Custer, The Sleeping Beauty); from formality (He Who Must Be Obeyed) to familiarity (Old Faithless); from Tom, Dick and Harry to Jean-Claude, Giorgio and Fritz. The villain of this book is called Willie' (Joliffe and Mayle, 1984).

wilted drunk
The imagery is floral, though from too much liquid rather than too little.

win (1) to steal
Very old general use: 'The cull has won a couple of rum glimsticks' (Grose – a 'glimstick' is a candlestick) but still common in Br. army: 'In the army it is always considered more excusable to "win" or "borrow" things belonging to men of other companies' (Richards, 1936).

win (2) to copulate with
In a bygone age, to 'win' a woman was to do no more than secure her consent to marriage, but the modern use is of extra-marital

sexual conquest: 'I resolved to win her altogether' (Harris, 1925).

win home to die
Christian devout use of the death of others, although the speaker seldom appears anxious to secure a similar victory for himself: 'Thro' a' life's troubles we'll win home at e'en' (Wright, 1897). To 'win your way' is ob.: 'Auld Jamie has giv'en up the ghost And won his way' (Hetrick, 1826).

wind (1) a belch or fart
In genteel use only of belching, about which there are fewer taboos than farting: 'Baked beans, which always give me terrible wind' (Matthew, 1978 – it might apply to either form of expulsion). Whence 'windy', so affected or, of an object, liable to cause such an effect: '... taters .... es windy zorrt o grub' (Agrikler, 1872).

wind (2) summary dismissal from employment
An uncommon Am. variant of **air** (q.v.).

winded incapacitated by a blow to the genitalia
Male sportsmen's jargon. Properly, having received a similarly disabling, but less painful, blow in the stomach which has caused difficulty in breathing.

windfall (1) a bastard
Probably because the 'fruits' arrived on the ground other than by design. ob.

windfall (2) a bribe or other illegal benefit
The fruit which fell to the ground used to be given to whomever wished to pick it up, whence in fig. use anything which you acquired of value without consideration, such as an unexpected legacy or a bribe: 'The cop and those higher up share in the windfall' (Lavine, 1930, of bribery).

window blind a towel worn during menstruation
Punning on the periodical closing of a shop, indicated by the unrolling of a blind to conceal the goods normally on display. BI.

window dressing falsely or fraudulently issuing figures or statements relative to a business
Commercial and banking jargon, using imagery from retail trading. Of attempts to inflate profit, turnover or reserves by improper adjustment, of any suppression or exaggeration designed to enhance the value or prospects of a business and specifically of issuing cheques in your own favour which can only be met from their proceeds: 'The cheques were part of the "window dressing" of the balance sheet at London & County Securities' (*Private Eye*, September 1981).

windy (1) *see* **wind (1)**

windy (2) cowardly
From the WW I use, to get the wind up, to be afraid: '... he may be what the British soldier would call "slightly windy"' (Moss, 1950). In WW I many danger spots in the battle zone were known by the punning 'Windy Corner'.

wing your flight from this world to die
How you made your way to heaven: 'The Bonds of Life being gradually dissolved She winged her Flight from this World in expectation of a better, the 15th January, 1810' (Memorial in Bath Abbey). ob.

winged wounded
Of humans, from the shooting of birds which, if hit in the wing, come to ground alive. WW II and then general use.

winkle a penis
Nursery usage, perhaps from the **willie** (q.v.) in 'Wee Willie Winkle': '... unlikely to hurl himself diagonally across the polished walnut and snatch at his winkle' (Amis, 1978). 'Winkie' is rare: 'Very butch, and he's got a gun trained on your winkie' (B. Forbes, 1986).

wipe off to kill
Of an individual by a natural phenomenon: 'What more useful bird can yer find, as wipes off worms an' grubs' (Patterson, 1895) or through human agency: 'He'll wipe you off' (Chandler, 1939). cf. **wipe out**. The imagery of both is probably from chalk on a blackboard.

wipe out to kill
Usu. of multiple deaths and cf. **wipe off**: 'I worked with three gangs who got wiped out, all except me' (L. Thomas, 1979).

wiped out under the influence of illegal narcotics
Am. addict use.

wire (the) a prison
Especially of a camp for prisoners of war of which the defences often included plain and barbed wire. Thus to be 'behind the wire' is to be in prison.

wired (1) drunk or under narcotic influence
Of the same tendency as **lit** (q.v.) but now usu. of Am. illegal narcotic experience: '"Do you have to go to bed?" he asked. "I'm

wired. I can't sleep"' (Robbins, 1981, of narcotics).

wired (2) subject to clandestine surveillance
This espionage jargon has survived the introduction of devices which are wireless: 'Even the damn cats are wired, no exaggeration' (le Carré, 1980). The device can be carried by the victim or by another knowingly, who may then also be said to be 'wired up': '. . . the defendant remained unaware . . . . that their interrogators were . . . . "wired up"' (*Private Eye*, March 1981). A 'wireman' is an expert in such devices: 'What we need is a first-class wireman. Somebody who can do it right. The apartment. The phone' (Diehl, 1978).

wise man a wizard
And a 'wise woman' was a witch: 'Sure a wise woman came in from Finnaun . . . . and she said it's what ailed him he had the Fallen Palate' (Somerville and Ross, 1908).

with child pregnant
Not just a young woman holding a baby: 'Once he had got a girl with child' (G. Greene, 1932).

with it in your hand always ready for extra-marital copulation
N. Eng. profligate males are said to 'go about' in such a manner. 'It' is the penis.

with Jesus etc. dead
Christian usage in various forms, from the posthumous heavenly gathering of the righteous and others. Other common companions are 'the Lord' and 'your Maker': 'If you make a wrong move, you're with your maker' (Fraser, 1970). A dead fellow-worshipper or clubman may be described as 'with us no more'.

with respect you are wrong
Used in polite discussion and jargon of the Br. legal system where an advocate wants to contradict a judge without prejudicing his chances: 'There is high authority for the view that (with respect) means "You are wrong" . . . . just as "with great respect" means "you are utterly wrong" and "with the utmost respect" equals "send for the men in white coats"' (Mr Justice Staughton quoted in *Daily Telegraph*, February 1987).

withdraw your labour to go on strike
Trade union jargon – it could simply mean to leave one job for idleness, or another. A 'withdrawal of labour' is a strike.

withdrawal to prepared positions a retreat under pressure
One way in which the vanquished seek to mitigate failure. A 'withdrawal in good order' was probably a rout.

without a head unmarried
This ob. Sc. expression refers to the time when an unmarried woman had little security outside her parents' home, poor chances of maintaining herself and almost no protection in law: 'It's no easy thing . . . . for a woman to go through the world without a head' (Miller, 1879). Males who are vexed by the antics of modern feminists should remember that this pendulum once swung the other way.

without baggage to be killed
Of prisoners taken away by Russian Communists for summary execution: 'From time to time someone would depart from the camp "without baggage". Those were sinister words – we all knew what that meant' (Horrocks, 1960, of his 1920 Moscow imprisonment after serving with the White Russian forces). ob.

woman a female viewed by a male for copulation
The man who says 'I feel like a woman tonight' does not postulate an incipient sex-change. Whence 'womanizer', a male profligate.

woman friend a man's sexual mistress
As different from a friend who is a woman, and *see* friend: 'Samoza, his woman friend . . . . and four of his five children' (*Daily Telegraph*, August 1979).

woman in a gilded cage (1) a sexual mistress
Of a female provided with separate accommodation, especially in luxury and the 19c.: 'The companion of a girl's fall might himself be the unconscious utterer of a divine message . . . . the woman . . . . breaking away from her gilded cage' (H. Hunt, c. 1854).

woman in a gilded cage (2) a young woman married to a rich old man
Often coerced into the union by her greedy or ambitious family. Am.

woman named a woman accused by the wife of copulating with her husband during the marriage
Br. legal jargon. In a divorce suit, a male could be joined as a respondent along with the wife by a petitioning husband, and thereby made liable for damages and costs,

but a woman would only be 'named' by the wife, and liable for neither. cf. **co-respondent**.

woman's thing (the) female homosexuality
Not a brassière: 'The virago and her soulmate into, as they would say, the woman's thing' (Theroux, 1978).

woman's things any taboo matter or article exclusive to women
Rarely of menstruation or illness, often of towels worn during menstruation: 'For the curse – you know. Women's things' (W. Smith, 1979, of such towels). Also as 'women's things'.

women a lavatory for exclusive female use
The companion of **men** (above) but no less salubrious than **ladies** (above). Also as 'women's room' etc.

women's disease (the) syphilis
If Br. males could not attribute their misfortune to the French, the Neopolitans or the Spanish, then it had to be the fault of women.

women's liberation aggressive feminism
For most men and many women, a dysphemism. Others believe in and resent male domination and its apparent advantages. Commonly abbr. to 'women's lib': 'Women's lib meant more than burning your bra. It meant total commitment to the programme of women's superiority over men' (Sharpe, 1976). An active proponent of this line is a 'libber': 'She's gone to join some women friends. Libbers, you know' (Murdoch, 1980). Males might feel even less happy about this affront to their manhood if they remembered that the Eng. dialect 'libber' was a castrator of pigs.

women's movement an association of committed feminists
And nothing to do with callisthenics.

women's rights the claim to or enjoyment of economic and social advantages historically exclusive to men
An aspiration of the feminists, who may not necessarily wish to assume the corresponding responsibilities: '. . . extensive literature on Women's Rights and the Feminist movement' (Bradbury, 1976). But before being too dismissive, *see* again **without a head**.

women's room *see* women

women's things *see* woman's things

wooden box etc. a coffin
In ob. forms also as 'wooden' breeches, breeks, coat, overcoat, etc.: 'A pair of wooden breeks Now him doth clede' (Sutherland, 1821). Used too fig. of death: 'The Winston treatment when it finally comes to the wooden box' (*Private Eye*, June 1981 – Churchill had an elaborate State funeral).

wooden hill the staircase
Nursery usage, for children urged to climb it when reluctant to go to bed or, in the double pun, to 'Bedfordshire'.

woodpile a lavatory
From its common location down the Am. yard by the store of logs, which gave women an excuse for going in that direction: 'The average timid woman . . . . I've knowed to take as many as ten trips to the wood-pile before she goes in' (Sale, c. 1930, urging the wisdom of so locating the lavatory).

word from our sponsor a television advertisement
Would that it were only one. Am.

word processing unit a typing pool
Am. bureaucratic jargon from the days before the 'word processor' made the days shorter for copy typists, but the documents longer.

work to copulate
Of females, as in Iago's paradoxical satire: 'You rise to play, and go to bed to work' (Shakespeare, *Othello*). And *see* 'bedwork' *under* **bed** (2).

work brigade a body of Russian prisoners
From the group into which they are organized. The 'shock brigade' undertakes special projects and also consists of convicts.

work of national importance exemption from military service
Br. WW I and II usage which, to the military, suggested that their own activities were of less importance. The timid tended to seek jobs which carried such exemption, while the braver or more robust went to any lengths to escape from a reserved occupation: 'Here they were doing "Work of National Importance" and they were too windy even to join their own town guard' (Richards, 1933 – he spent WW I in the trenches).

work on (1) to extract information from through violence
Properly to persist in treating roughly: '"Shellacking", "messaging", "breaking the

news", "working on the . . .", "giving him the works", . . . express how they compel reluctant prisoners to refresh their memories' (Lavine, 1930, of the NYC police).

work on (2) to copulate with
Of a male, and again from the concept of persistent rough handling rather than from the male posture: 'We could . . . . give you an examination too, and see if you've been working on her tonight' (Mailer, 1965).

work a street to attempt to sell from door to door
Usu. of a dishonest salesman.

work the streets to be a whore
From her public solicitation: 'She worked each side of the street with a skill shared . . . . by the best of streetwalkers' (Mailer, 1965).

work to rule to conduct yourself at work in a manner calculated to obstruct and cause loss
Br. trade union jargon for a device which, if successful, enables the employee to be paid while effectively striking. The employee may purport to be following in all respects a 'Rule Book', which regulates his employment and duties.

work your ticket to contrive an early discharge from contracted service
The Br. 'ticket' was the certificate of honourable discharge. A soldier etc. unwilling to complete the period of his enlistment and unable to buy his release had to use great ingenuity to escape from his commitment with a clean record.

work yourself off to masturbate
Of a male.

workers' control the oppressive rule of an oligarchy
Communist jargon, which tries to perpetuate the fiction that the populace controls the ruling and self-perpetuating oligarchs: 'Within the Leninist model . . . . "Workers' control" here means control of the workers' (*Sunday Telegraph*, August 1980, of Poland).

workhouse an institution for the homeless indigent
The intention was that the unfortunates should work to pay for their keep although the name outlived the concept: 'I was put in the workhouse when I was young . . . . I never knew my father or my mother' (Mayhew, 1862).

working class etc. trade union members
Properly, that section of society occupied in gainful employment or activity. However, when the term is used politically, it infers that those who work are members of trade unions, and that any work of value is done by such people. A modern Br. variant is 'working people', which includes the unemployed: 'I doubt whether working people will be willing to go on making sacrifices of this nature for much longer' (*Daily Telegraph*, January 1977 – the sacrifice was not to be awarded a wage increase unsupported by an increase in productivity and much exceeding the rate of inflation).

working girl a whore
Employed in the **business** (q.v.): '. . . lining up working girls for himself and for clients' (Wambaugh, 1983).

working people *see* working class etc.

workout the use of violence to extract information
Properly, any exercise. Police and Am. underworld jargon: '. . . scream with fear when the "workout" begins' (Lavine, 1930).

workshop a non-industrial activity with political or artistic pretensions
Of threatres and discussion groups where the socialist organizers and participants suffer pangs of guilt because they are not **working people** (q.v.).

World Peace Council an instrument of Russian foreign policy
This represents a fine example of Communist cynicism taking advantage of the **useful fools** (q.v.): 'World Peace Council, see under FRONT ORGANIZATION' (FMDT – which has the same magisterial impact as Fowler's discussing 'same' under 'illiteracies').

worry persistently to attempt to copulate with an unwilling partner
Women use the word of men, of the disturbance rather than their anxiety about the unwanted pregnancy. Properly, to 'worry' was to kill by gripping the throat, of dogs and wild animals, whence by transference mental distress in humans.

worse for wear drunk
Of mild drunkenness: 'Arrived home at four, rather the worse for wear' (Matthews, 1978). And *see* **the worse**.

wrack to copulate with a female virgin
Another form of the more common 'wreck', it means to destroy: 'I fear'd he did but trifle, And meant to wrack thee' (Shakespeare, *Hamlet*). The 'wrack of maidenhead' was the

extra-marital loss of virginity: '. . . the misery is, example, that so terribly shows in the wrack of maidenhead' (Shakespeare, *Titus Andronicus*). ob.

wreak your passion on to copulate with
Of a male, usu. extra-maritally: '. . . over-borne by desire, he had wreak'd his passion on a mere lifeless, spiritless body' (Cleland, 1749). 'Passion', originally the suffering of pain as by Christ, has been used of lust, especially in males, since 16c.

wrecked drunk or under narcotic influence
From the way you feel: 'They were half blitzed, but both Dolly and Dilford were totally wrecked' (Wambaugh, 1983)

wretched calendar (the) I am menstruating
From the female practice of noting the date of the onset. Used especially by apologetic females: 'You must be kind. The wretched calendar' (Fowles, 1977).

wring out your socks to urinate
Br. male usage, perhaps as a facetious explanation of the noise.

wrinklies old people
Used by the young, mindless of 'time's winged chariot': '. . . helping the wrinklies with their heating bills' (*Private Eye*, January 1987). To qualify you do not have to reside in Wrinkle City (Miami).

wrist-job (a) male masturbation
Of the act and, as an insult, of the actor: 'Keen? In my book he's a wrist-job' (C. Forbes, 1983).

write yourself off to be killed in an accident
To 'write off' a vehicle etc. is to remove it from an inventory of serviceable equipment.

written out of the script killed or dismissed from employment
Theatrical usage in a serial play etc.: '. . . he had played a psychiatrist in a soap opera for seven years until he was written out of the script' (Sanders, 1983) whence the fig. use for death: 'One jalopy like that in the flight could get us all written out of the script' (Deighton, 1982, of WW II fliers).

wrong (1) to copulate with extra-maritally
Men 'wrong' women, only marital copulation being 'right': 'Vail your regard Upon a wrong'd, I would fain have said, a maid' (Shakespeare, *Measure for Measure*). To copulate was bad enough, but to impregnate doubly so: 'Ravisht and wrong'd, as Philomena was' (Shakespeare, *Titus Andronicus*).

wrong (2) homosexual
When only heterosexuality was 'right': 'Mildred genuinely suspected something "wrong" with the girl, and "wrong" with Barbie' (P. Scott, 1971). ? ob.

wrong (3) pregnant
N. Eng. dialect, within or outside marriage, but probably of unplanned pregnancies only.

wrong side of the blanket an allusion to bastardy
In addition to the evil of the act, the impregnation supposedly took place on or out of the marital bed, not in it: 'Frank Kennedy, he said, was a gentleman though on the wrong side of the blanket' (W. Scott, 1815).

wrong time of the month the period of menstruation
Female usage, elaborating on **time of the month** (above): 'It's always the wrong time of the month' (Weissman, quoted in Dickson, 1978).

X Y Z

X-ray machine a police traffic radar set
And 'X-raying' is its operation in Am. CB sl.

yard (1) a penis
I hesitate to venture an etymology: '"Loves her by the foot". . . . "He may not by the yard"' (Shakespeare, *Love's Labour's Lost*).

yard (2) to copulate extra-maritally while co-habiting with your spouse
Perhaps you meet the third party just outside your home. Not from the Eng. dialect 'yarding', the first step in courtship in which the parties walked three feet apart, perhaps to be followed by 'aiblen', holding an elbow, and, if your suit prospered, with 'waisting'.

yardbird a prisoner
From the exercise yard in an Am. penitentiary.

year of progress a period of irreversible decline
Look out for this in statements by politicians and company chairmen – it usu. means things have gone badly: 'In the year leading up to the Tet Offensive ("1967 – Year of Progress" was the name of an official year-end report)' (Herr, 1977).

years young old
Journalese for a spry geriatric, described perhaps as '74 years young' to avoid the taboo 'old'. I wonder why it grates so badly.

yellow (1) cowardly
Probably from the paleness of fright, and you find it in many compounds like 'yellow belly', etc. Formerly 'yellow stockings' were a sign of jealousy: 'Remember who commended thy yellow stockings' (Shakespeare, *Twelfth Night*).

yellow (2) a whore of mixed Black and White ancestry
Properly a light-skinned Am. slave, of higher value than a pure-blooded Black and often used as a house servant: 'The yellow girls stood around giggling' (Longstreet, 1956, of New Orleans). Also as 'high-yellow': '. . . end up by being shot in the saloon by a high-yellow girl' (ibid.).

yellow (3) *see* **yellow jacket etc.**

yellow jacket etc. a Nembutal tablet or other illegal narcotic
From the colour, and sometimes abbr. to

'yellow'. Also as 'yellow' angels, bellies, devils, etc. 'Yellow sunshine' is LSD. Am.

Yellowstone Park a concentration of traffic police
A place full of **bears** (2) (q.v.) for an Am. CB user.

yes-girl a female known to copulate promiscuously
Am. male usage, punning on the 'yes-man', or toady. She is not necessarily a whore.

yield to copulate with a man for the first time extra-maritally
From the sense, to submit, with an inference of coercion: 'There is no woeman, Eupheus, but she will yeelde in time' (Lyly, 1579, quoted in ODEP) and: 'I could not get her to yield' (Harris, 1925, in a rare admission of failure). The male may be named: 'My sisterly remorse confutes mine honour, And I did yield to him' (Shakespeare, *Measure for Measure*). The female may also yield to 'desires' or 'solicitation': 'Without much demur I yielded to his desire' (Mayhew, 1862) and: 'The pretty lady's maid will often yield to soft solicitation' (ibid.). Specifically she 'yields' her body, honour or virginity: 'Yielding up thy body to my will' (Shakespeare, *Measure for Measure*) and: 'If I would yield him my virginity' (ibid.). etc.

(**yob** a lout is back-sl. for boy. cf. **slag**.)

you-know-what any taboo subject within the context
Of copulation, as in 'a little of you-know-what'; of a lavatory: '"The you-know-what's in there," she said helpfully. Frensic staggered into the bathroom and shut the door' (Sharpe, 1977); etc.

you know what you can do with that a coarse rebuttal
The reference is to fig. anal insertion: '= stick it. All euphemisms' (DAS). There are a number of similar variants.

young not over 45 years old
Journalistic use for public figures who may have achieved prominence at an earlier age than most of their contemporaries: 'Nick was very young, still in his early thirties' (M. Thomas, 1982). cf. **middle-aged.**

young lady etc. a man's premarital female sexual partner
A genteel usage, implying no more than courtship, as does the more severe 'young woman'. The male partner may be called a 'young man', for which classification youth is less important than for the female.

your nose is bleeding your trouser zip is undone
An oblique Br. warning to another male in mixed company.

youth (guidance) centre an institution for the punishment of young offenders
It could be, as is the Br. 'youth centre', a place where the young can meet socially under mild supervision. For a young Am., attendance may involve involuntary residence under a court order.

yo-yo a male homosexual
Going up and down, it might seem, until he unwinds: 'I just can't see us going across to France with a load of yo-yoes as a crew' (L. Thomas, 1986).

zap to kill violently
Perhaps from Am. strip cartoon language, where it may mean no more than to hit: 'Clever bastards like us, we care about getting zapped' (Seymour, 1984 – but Afghans fighting the Russian invader were braver or more reckless).

zebra a convict
From the striped clothing worn in an Am. jail.

zero a female public display of nakedness
Not directly from nothing but an abbr. of 'zerokini', from 'bikini' punning on 'bi-', or two-piece, via 'monokini', bathing trunks worn without a top by an adult female. Bikini was the atoll in the Marshall Islands used for testing atomic explosions and the use illustrates our slow realization of the long-term effects of nuclear pollution. Such an association with swimwear would be thought in deplorable taste and commercially disastrous, if introduced today.

zoned out drunk or under illegal narcotic influence
The imagery is from defensive play in Am. football and basketball.

zonked drunk
Perhaps from a sl. meaning, hit. Am.

zoo a brothel
Particularly in Am. where the 'animals' on show are of various shades of black and white.

Index

Classification of Entries

Classification under specific headings is necessarily inexact, nor are the lists which follow strictly in alphabetical order. The object is to offer as simple a guide as possible towards any specific area of euphemism. Thus

drop a bundle **drop (4)** *will be found under* drop (4)	
blue **rinse**	rinse
chair-days	chair
state farm	state farm
„ home	state farm

(An entry which incorporates the ditto symbol will be found under the last full entry above it.)
Those entries not easily classified may be discovered under 'General and Miscellaneous'.

Abortion
Age
Auctioneers and Estate Agents
Bankruptcy
Bastardy
Bawds and Pimps
Bi-sexuality
Boasting and Lying
Bribery
Brothels
Charity – Private, National and International
Childbirth
Clothing
Colour and Slavery
Commerce and Industry
Contraception
Copulation
Cosmetics
Courtship and Marriage
Cowardice
Crime other than Stealing
Cuckoldry

Death other than Funerals and Killing
Defecation
Diarrhoea
Dismissal
Drunkenness
Education
Erection and Ejaculation
Espionage
Extortion, Violence and Torture
Farting
Female Genitalia
Funerals
Gambling
General and Miscellaneous
Homosexuality and Sexual Variations
Illness and Injury
Intoxicants
Killing and Suicide
Lavatories
Madness
Male Genitalia

Masturbation
Menstruation
Mistresses and Lovers
Nakedness
Narcotics
Obesity
Parts of the Body other than Genitalia
Police
Politics
Poverty and Stinginess
Pregnancy
Prisons
Religion and Superstitions
Stealing
Sweat
Trade Unions
Unemployment
Urination
Venereal Disease
Vulgarisms and Swearing
Warfare
Whores

Abortion

bring off (2)
criminal operation
D and C
drop a bundle **drop** (4)
illegal operation
misgo **misfortune**
mishap **misfortune**
miss (2)
part with child
     »   Patrick
pick
pregnancy interruption
procedure
sling **slip** (1)
slink **slip** (1
terminate (3)
voluntary pregnancy
   interruption

Age

active
adult (2)
blue hair
blue **rinse**
borrowed time **borrow**
boy
certain age
chair-days
convalescent home
Derby and Joan
distinguished
eventide home
forward at the knees
get along
get on (1)
  » up along
girl (2)
God's waiting room
golden years
home
kid
long in the tooth
make old bones
matron
mature (1)
middle-aged
mutton dressed as lamb
not as young as I was
  » in my first youth
nursing home
of mature years
older woman
resident **residential**
   provision
residential provision
rest home
Roman spring
senior citizen

seniors **senior citizen**
somewhere he can be looked
   after
state farm
  » home
  » hospital
sunset years
twilight home
up along
wear down
Wrinkle City **wrinklies**
wrinklies
years young
young

Auctioneers and Estate Agents

bijou
boost (2)
character
colonial
commodious
convenient
Dutch auction
East Village
eat-in kitchen
estate **agent**
garden city
Georgian
gracious
historic
home
ideal for modernisation
immaculate
in the ring
jolly (2)
knock out
landscaped
marine residence
negotiable
old fashioned
outstanding
part furnished
period (2)
Peter Funk
planned community
planner
planning **planner**
prestigious
realistic
ring (2)
secluded
select
snug
sought after
South Chelsea
superior
time sharing
town house

unique
wheel
zoning **planner**

Bankruptcy

bank
banker **bank**
belly up
bolt the moon
bought and sold
bust (1)
cash flow problem
chapter eleven
close its doors
come to a sticky end (1)
cram down
done for
drown the miller **drown**
   your sorrows
fall at the staves **go** (2)
fall out of bed
flit (1)
fly-by-night (1)
fold
get the shorts
go (2)
  » due north
  » to staves
  » under
  » up Jackson's end
  » up Johnson's end
go for a Burton
go to Bath **take a bath**
haircut
hammer
in Carey Street
lame duck (2)
liquidator **liquidate**
liquidity crisis
moonlight flit
     » flight
     » march
     » touch
     » walk
on the go **go** (2)
on the skids
over-geared
pull the rug
put the skids under
RD
refer to drawer
run (3)
shoot the moon
stiff (4)
     » out
swamped
take a bath
take a wheel off the cart
temporary liquidity problem

uncle
up the spout

Bastardy
basket (1)
bend sinister
born in the vestry
break your elbow
    "   "   leg above
               the knee
by(e)
    " -begot
    " -blow
    " -chap
    " -come
    " -scape
cast a girth
cast a (laggin) girth
chance
    "   -bairn
    "   -begot
    "   -born
    "   -child
    "   -come
chanceling **chance**
child of sin
come in at the window
    " " " back door
    " " " hatch
    " " " side door
    " " " wicket
    " o' will
fly-blow
hop-pole marriage **hop into bed**
illegitimate
indiscretion
left-handed (1)
love child
    " -bairn
    " begotten
    " bird
lover child **love child**
made in the bush **bush** (1)
merry-begot
merry-begotten
midnight baby
misbegot **misfortune**
mishap **misfortune**
misfortune
natural (2)
    " father
nurse-child
one parent family
slip a foot **slip** (1)
slip the girth **slip** (1)
son of a bachelor
    " " bitch
    " " gun

souvenir (1)
tender a fool
unlawful
windfall (1)
wrong side of the blanket

Bawds and Pimps
abbess
bawd
Covent Garden abbess
dab **dabble**
double (2)
handle a woman **handle** (1)
husband (1)
joe
live off **live as man and wife etc.**
live on **live as man and wife etc.**
mackerel
madam
mother
procure
procurer **procure**
procuress **procure**
take under protection
victualler
white slaver **white slave**

Bi-sexuality
AC/DC
all-rounder
ambidexterous
ambivalent
batting and bowling
bisexual
bi **bisexual**
double-gaited
sexual ambiguity
swing both ways
switch-hitter

Boasting and Lying
B S **bull** (2)
blow (3)
blow your own horn
    " your own trumpet
blow smoke
bull (2)
bullshit **bull** (2)
bullshitter **bull** (2)
bunk flying
catch fish with a silver hook
claim
cock-and-bull **story**
creative
credibility gap
draw the long bow
economical with the truth
embroider

evasion
fill in the blank spaces in our history
gild
grandstand **grandstand play**
grandstand play
handle the truth roughly
imaginative journalism
information
inoperative
investigate
investigative journalism **investigate**
martyr to selective amnesia
mis-speak
piggyback
poetic truth
pull the long bow
ride abroad with St George but at home with St Michael
run around the Horn
selective facts
serious credibility gap
shoot with a silver gun
shoot among the doves **draw the long bow**
speak with forked tongue
story
stretch **stretcher**
stretcher
    " case
swing the lamp
tall **story**
terminological inexactitude
translate the truth

Bribery
adjustment (2)
angle with a silver hook
anoint a palm
apple polish
backhander
clean hands
collect
come across (1)
come through
commission
connection
consultant (2)
contract (1)
contribution (2)
cop the drop
cough syrup
cross your palm
cumshaw
cut (4)
distribution

douceur
entertain (3)
entertainment **entertain** (3)
fix (1)
fixer
graft
gratification **gratitude**
gratify
grease (1)
  »   a hand
  »   a palm
  »   a paw
hand-out (2)
hush money
ice (1)
introducer's fee
kickback
lay pipes
look after
lubricate
lunchtime engineering
massage (1)
negotiable
oil
 » the wheels
on the Hill
on the pad
on the side
over-invoicing
palm (1)
  »   -grease
  »   -oil
  »   -soap
palmistry **palm** (1)
pay off (1)
piece off
promotion
questionable
rake-off
schmear
see (2)
sensitive payment
skim (1)
slush
smear (1)
straighten out
sugar (1)
sweeten (1)
sweetener
take (1)
take care of (2)
take your end
thank
under the table (2)
velvet (2)
windfall (2)

Brothels
abode of love

academy
accommodation house
bag shanty **baggage**
bagnio
barrel-house
bat-house **bat** (1)
bawdy-house **bawd**
bed-house **bed** (2)
bird-cage **bird** (1)
bitch
button-hole factory **button** (1)
can (4)
canhouse
casa **case** (1)
case (1)
casito **case** (1)
caso **case** (1)
cat-house **cat** (1)
chamber of commerce
cheap john
chicken ranch **chick**
chippy-joint **chippy** (1)
civil reception
common house
coupling house **couple**
crib
disorderly house
doss-house
escort-agency
fish market **fishmonger's daughter**
fleshpot
fun-house
garden house
gay house **gay** (1)
girlie bar **girl** (1)
 » club **girl** (1)
 » house **girl** (1)
 » parlor **girl** (1)
goat-house
grind-mill
grinding-house **grind**
hook shop **hooker** (2)
hot-house
hot pillow motel
 » sheet
hourly hotel
house (1)
house in the suburbs
house of accommodation
house of assignation
house of civil reception
house of evil repute
house of ill-fame
house of ill-repute
house of pleasure
house of profession
house of resort

house of sale
house of sin
house of tolerance
ill-famed house
immoral house
immoral purposes
improper house
introducing house
  introducer's fee
jag house
joy house **joy** (1)
juke house
kip
knocking shop
  » house
  » joint
ladies' college **lady**
Lahore house
leaping academy **leap**
leaping-house **leap**
loose house **loose** (1)
make-out joint **make** (1)
massage parlour **massage** (3)
meat-house
microwave club
nanny-house
naughty-house
night club
night-house **night club**
nunnery **nun**
panel-house
 » -joint
parlor house
pleasure house
pressure-cooker bar
pushing-school **push** (1)
pushing-shop **push** (1)
queen-house
rag
ramps **ramp**
rap club
red lamp
 » -light
 » lighted number
rib joint
sauna parlor
scalding-house **scald**
seraglio
skivvie-house
snake-ranch
sport-trap
sporting-house **sport**
sporting-section **sport**
stews
sugar hill
tender-loin district
touch-crib **touch** (2)
vaulting-school **vault** (1)

victualling-house **victualler**
wang-house **wank**
warm shop
zoo

Charity – Private, National and International

aid (2)
assistance
benefit
caring
concessional
dole
  » bread
  » money
fly a kite (2)
hand-out (1)
house (3)
  » of industry
income maintenance
live on the high-fly **high** (2)
long-arm **long-arm inspection**
national assistance
negative (income-) tax
on the labour
public assistance
relief (1)
remittance man
sheltered
social security
souper **soup**
tied aid **aid** (2)
uncaring
welfare
workhouse

Childbirth

accouchement
bear (1)
bed (1)
brought to bed
cast
cleanse (2)
come to your time
confined **confinement**
confinement
doorstep
drop (4)
fact(s) of life
fall (3)
  » about
feed
force-put job
free of fumbler's hall **free** (2)
go wrong
gooseberry bush
grass widow

groper **grope**
happy event
hatch
kid
labour (1)
lady in the straw **lady in waiting**
lay in
lie in
lying-in wife **lie in**
nurse
parsley bed
premature
pup
throw (2)
time
trouble
upstairs (1)
whelp

Clothing

Abyssinian medal
appliance
at half mast
athletic supporter
BB **brassière**
bags
body shaper
  » briefer
  » hugger
  » outline
boobytrap **brassière**
box (2)
brassière
built-in emphasis
bust bodice
canteen medal
catch a cold (2)
Charley's dead **Charley**
cheaters
continuations
cup
decent
don't name-'ems
enhanced contouring
falsies
flag of distress **flag is up**
flapper
flying low
foundation garment
gay deceivers **gay** (2)
gazelles are in the garden
indescribables
ineffables **unmentionables** (1)
inexpressibles
jock-strap
Johnnie's out of jail **John Thomas**

medal showing
nappy
one o'clock at the water-works
sensible
shop door is open
sides
sit-in-'ems **sit-upon**
sit-upons **sit-upon**
snowing down South
star in the East
surgical **appliance**
Turkish medal
unexpressibles
  unmentionables (1)
unmentionables (1)
unspeakables
  unmentionables (1)
untalkaboutables
  unmentionables (1)
unutterables
  unmentionables (1)
unwhisperables
  unmentionables (1)
your nose is bleeding

Colour and Slavery

affirmative action
African trade **triangular trade (the)**
apartheid
aryan
black cattle **blackbird**
  » hide **blackbird**
  » pigs **blackbird**
  » sheep **blackbird**
black ivory
blackbird
  » pie
blackbirding **blackbird**
blockbuster
bussing
cattle (1)
Caucasian
chi chi
coloured
community affairs
  » relations
dark (2)
  » gentleman
dark meat (2)
darky **dark** (2)
ethnic
  » minority
fancy
feel a draft
gold
half-baked bread
homelands

honky
immigrant
Jane Crow **Jim Crow**
Jim Crow
Kaffir
itinerant **tinker**
lick of the tarbrush
long acre **tinker**
majority rule
man (3)
middle passage
minorities **minority group**
minority group
minstrel
multi-cultural
native
negress
negro
new commonwealth
non-aryan
non-white
open housing
pigmentation **problem**
poontang
put in the schwartzes to de-
stat
race relations board **racial**
race relations officer **racial**
racial
   » discrimination
racialist **racial**
racist **racial**
salt and pepper (3)
Sam (2)
segregation
separate but equal **separate**
development
separate development
servant
silver
smoke
states' rights
tarbrush
three-point play
tincture (1)
tinker
tokenism
touch of the tarbrush
traveller
triangular trade
turn (4)
twelve annas in the rupee
Uncle Tom
undocumented
white man's burden
yellow (2)

Commerce and Industry

adjust
as planned **planned**
   withdrawal
adjustment (1) (6)
association (2)
bad mouth
best seller
black economy
boiler house
   » room
   » shop
boilerplate
book club
bounce (2) (4)
brand X
brownie points
bucket shop **bucket** (2)
budget
bump (5)
burner
buy jawbone
career interest inventory
carpet (1)
carpet-bagger
chant
chanter **chant**
Chinese copy
Chinese wall
churning
classic
clicker **click**
client
club (2) (3)
colt (2)
come on (2)
commercial gentleman
   commerce
complimentary
concert party
concessional
conference
consumer
controller
convenience (2)
cookie pusher
corner (1)
correction (1)
country
country pay
courtesy
creative
   » accounting
cult
currency adjustment
damp down
dark (1)
demonstrator

direct mail
domestic
downward adjustment
drop the boom
Dutch bargain
Dutch reckoning
easy terms
economic storm
economy
effluent
equity equivalent contingent
   participation
expense account **expenses**
expenses
experienced
expert
   » witness
exterminating engineer
facility (2)
false market
fan club
fast buck
filler
financial products
financial services
flexibility
float paper
fly a kite (1)
for your convenience
free (3)
freeze out
fringe
fringes
front-loading
   » money
greenmailer
grinding employer **grind**
guest artist
hand-tooled
hang a red light on
haute cuisine
health care
hit the silk **bale out** (2)
home equity loan
horse chanter **chant**
hospital job
identification
improvement (1) (2)
improver
in conference
income protection
industrial logic
informal market
inside track
insider
instant best seller
intermission
international best-seller
investment

jawbone
joiner
king-sized
kite
    " -man
knight of the Golden Fleece
lame duck (1)
large (2)
leverage
link prices
low budget
    " cost
    " key
lower the boom on
massage (4)
masterpiece
me-too
medical representative
medium
meeting
member (2)
message
moonlight (3)
motivate
NIH **not invented here**
natural break
near (2)
negative contribution
    " profit contribution
negative growth
negative stock holding
never-never
nominal
non-dairy
non-profit
not invented here
nouvelle cuisine
numerate
operant conditioning
operational difficulties
operator
orderly marketing
    " progress
paper a house
parallel pricing
participate in
patron (2)
pay with the roll of a drum
    pay nature's debt
personal assistant
ping-ponging
plant (2)
poison pill
pop (1)
potboiler
practice development
pre-owned
premium
pressure of work

previously owned
price adjustment
    " revision
price crowding
price **hike**
prime
provision
public relations
pull out of the air
    " " " a hat
punter
qualify accounts
rainmaker
RD
redlining
refer to drawer
regular (2)
restructured
reverse engineering
revision of prices
ring (2)
rodent operator
    exterminating engineer
save
scandal sheet
sculpted
select
self-catering
self-regulation
service (2)
    " station
shade (1)
sharp with the pen
sharpen your pencil (1) (2)
shave (the gentry) **slice**
shoe the colt **colt** (2)
slack fill
slice
smooth
snow (2) (3)
    " -job
spike (2)
standard
steer
structured
    " competition
stuck
subcompact
supporter's club
sweeten (1)
sweetheart
tail-pulling
take a break
take a powder
take a view
take away
tap (4) (5)
technical adjustment
    " correction

    " reaction
tied up
tire kicking
top up
touch signature
tourist
turkey shoot
    " farmer
twenty-four hour service
unavailable (1)
uncertain
under-invoicing
underground production
unregulated free economy
unscheduled
used
vanity publishing
velvet (2)
visiting fireman
warehouse
wash (2)
weekend
weigh the thumb
what the traffic will bear
white knuckler
white tail
window dressing
word from our sponsor
word processing unit
work a street

Contraception

armour
bareback
birth control
bung (2)
cap (1)
cardigan
careful (2)
coil
collapsible container
diaphragm
douche
Dutch cap
F L **French letter**
family planning
fight in armour
French letter
    " renovating pills
    " tickler
froggie
get fitted
intrauterine device
joy bag **joy** (1)
loop (2)
on the loop **loop (2)**
on the pill
pessary

pill (2)
Port Said garters
precautions
preventative
prophylactic
protector (2)
ring (3)
rubber
   » goods
safe
safety
sheath
skin
take a risk
take care
take precautions
tickler (2)
Vatican roulette

Copulation

aboard (2)
abuse a bed **abuse yourself**
accommodate
accommodation house
act
  » of shame
  » of intercourse
  » of love
act like a husband
action (3)
adventure (2)
all the way
amatory rites
amorous favours
     »   sport
     »   tie
amour
antics in bed
any
arse
ashes hauled
ass
astride
athwart your hawse
attend to
attentions
avail yourself of
back
ball
banana
bang
baser needs
basket-making **basket (1)**
be nice to
be with
beast with two backs
beastliness
beat the mattress

bed (2)
  » and breakfast
  » down
  » -hopping
bedwork **bed (2)**
beef
been into
been there
beg a child of
belly to belly
belt
bestride
between the sheets
between the thighs
big prize
bit
blanket drill
block
  » her passage
blow (1)
  » off
  » the groundsels
  » the loose corns
board
board a train **pull a train**
boff (1)
bonk
boom-boom (2)
bounce (1)
break a lance
break your knee **break your elbow**
bring off (1)
buckle to
bull (1)
bullock **bull (1)**
bump (3)
  » bones
bundle
bung up and bilge free
bush patrol **bush (1)**
business
buttock
button-hole **button (1)**
calisthenics in bed
capital act (the)
carnal
    » act
    » knowledge
    » necessities
    » relations
casting couch
catch
cattle (2)
chambering
change your luck
clean up (2)
cleave **chopper (2)**
clicket

climb
  » in with
  » into bed
climb the ladder on your back
cock
  » a leg across
  » a leg athwart
  » a leg over
come
  » about
come across (2)
come off (1)
come on (2)
come over
come to
come together
commerce
completion
compound
compromise (1)
congress
connect (1)
connection
connubial pleasures
conquer a bed
console
consummate
      »   your desires
      »   your relations
contact with
content your desire
continent
conversation
cop a cherry
copulate
corn (2)
corrupt
couple
  » with
cover (1)
crack a Jane
  » a doll
  » a Judy
  » a pitcher
  » a pipkin
crack your whip
cram down
crawl
  » in with
criminal connection
criminal conversation
cross
cut the mustard
  » it
Cythera
dab it up **dabble**
dance the mattress quadrille
    » Haymarket hornpipe

debauch
deed
defile
   "   a bed
defiler **defile**
defloration **deflower**
deflower
dick around **dick** (1)
diddle (2)
dip **Cecil** in the hot grease
dip your wick
dirty deed
disgrace
disport amorously
dissolution (2)
distribute favours
do (1)
   " a perpendicular
   " it
   " what comes naturally
do the trick
dock
double-header
double in stud
droit de seigneur
drop your drawers
   "   "   pants
dry bob
   " run
East-African activities
eat flesh
embrace **embraces**
embraces
employ
enjoy
   "   favours
   "   her person
   "   hospitality of
enter
entertain (2)
exchange flesh
extras
facts (of life)
fall (1)
fate worse than death
favour
favours
feed from home
feed your pussy
filthy
firk
flat on your back
flesh your will
fling
flop
flutter (2)
foin
force your ardour upon
fork

fornicate
foul desire
   "   designs
   "   lusts
   "   way with
frail job **frail** (2)
fraternise
free of your hips
free-lance
free love
friar Tuck
frig
front door
fulfilment
full treatment
fumble
fun
   "   and games
gallant to
gallantry **gallant**
gallop
game (2)
gasp and grunt **grumble**
gentle art (the)
George
get a leg over
   "   "   across
   "   "   dressed
get down to business
get in her pants
get in the **saddle**
get into bed with
get into her bloomers
get it in
get it on
get it up
get laid
get off (2)
get on (2)
get round
get stuffed **stuff** (4)
get there
get through
get up
get your end in
get your greens
get your hook into
get your muttons
get your nuts off
get your rocks off
get your share
get your way with
get your will of
gift of your body
give
give a little
give access to your body
give it to
give out

give stick **stick** (3)
give the time to
give up your treasure
give way
give your all
give your body
give yourself
go all the way
go into
go on
go over the top (1)
go short
go the length
go the whole way
go through
go to bed with
go to it
go with
go wrong
good time
goose (3)
gratification **gratify your passion**
gratify your passion
   "   "   amorous works
   "   "   desires
grease the wheel
  grease (1)
grind
ground rations
grumble
hame
hang it on with **hang a few on**
hanky-panky
haul your ashes
hauled **haul your ashes**
have a man/woman
have a t
have it
   "   away
   "   off
have **pleasure** with
have relations
   "   sexual relations
have sex
have something to do with
have your end off
have your way
   "   filthy way with
have your will of
height of connubial bliss
high jinks
hit (2)
hit the sack with
hochle
hoist your skirt
hop into bed
horizontal (1)

" conquest
" jogging
hot-tailing
hot time
how's your father
human relations
hump
" the mutton
hustle (2)
hymenal sweets
ill-used
illicit
" commerce
" connection
" embraces
" intercourse
impale
impotent
improper suggestion
in (2)
in bed
in circulation
in her **mutton**
in full fling
in the box
in the hay
in the heat **on heat**
in the mood
in the sack
in the saddle
indecency
initiation
" into womanhood
insatiable
intercourse
intimacy
intimate **intimacy**
into the sack
intrigue(s)
invade
it (2)
itch
Jack in the orchard **jack** (1)
jam
jazz
jelly roll
jig **jig-a-jig**
jig-a-jig
jig-jig **jig-a-jig**
jiggle **jig-a-jig**
jiggy-jig **jig-a-jig**
jing-jang **jig-a-jig**
jock
join
jolly (3)
joy (1)
" ride
juggle
juiced up

jump (3)
kind
kiss
knee-trembling **knee-trembler**
knees up
knock **knock off** (2)
knock off (2)
knot
know
know the score
knowledge **know**
lance
last favour
lay
" a leg across
" a leg on
" a leg over
" down
" it
leap
leap on
leave before the gospel
led astray
leg over
leg-sliding
let in
lie together
lie with
" on
lift a leg (1)
light the lamp
limit
line
lose your cherry
" character
" innocence
" snood
" virtue
love
love affair
" -making
lubricate
lumber
make (1)
make arrangements **arrangement**
make it with **make** (1)
make little of
make whoopee **make** (1)
make babies together
make love
make out
make the beast with two backs
make the (bed) springs creak
" " " " squeak
make time with
management privileges

managerial privileges
managerial privileges
massage (3)
mate
mattress
" drill
" extortion
mess (1)
mid-job
mingle bodies
missionary position
misuse
momentary trick
monkey business
mount
national indoor game
natural vigours
naughty
nibble
nice-nice **nice time**
night physic
" baseball
nightwork
no-tell
nocturnal exercise
nookie
oats
oblige
occupy
oestrus
off (2)
offer yourself
" kindness
on the couch
on the job
on the loose
on top of
on your back
one night stand
one nighter **one night stand**
one thing
open-legged
open your legs
outrage
over the broomstick
over the top
park
party (2)
pasture
peel a banana
" fine green banana
penetrate
perform (2)
personal relations
personal services
physic
physical involvement
pile into
plant a man **plant** (1)

play
play around
play games
play hookie
play in the hay
play mothers and fathers
    » mums and dads
play on your back
play the ace against the jack
play the beast with two backs
play the organ
play tricks
play with
please yourself on
pleasure
plough
pluck
    » a rose
plug (2)
plumb
plunge away
pocket the red **pocket pool**
poke (2)
pole **poke (2)**
pom-pom
poontang
pop (1)
possess
pound
    »   the keys
press **attentions**
privy to a bed **bed** (2)
probe
prod
prong
pull (2)
pull a train
pull the trigger
punch
push (1)
pussy
put
    »   a man in your belly
    »   a move on
    »   and take
    »   it about
    »   it in
    »   it up
put out (2)
put to
racy
ram
rattle (1)
ravish
relate
relations
release (3)
relief (3)
relieve of virginity

ride
    »   St George
rifle
rip off a piece of arse
ripple
rivet
rock
rod (1)
rodger **roger** (1)
roger (1)
roll (1)
    »   in the hay
    »   the linen
romp
root **root about**
root about
rootle
rub groins together **groin**
rub the bacon
    »   »   pork
ruin
run out of steam
Russian duck
saddle
score (1)
screw (1)
    »   around
sell yourself
    »   your back
    »   your body
    »   your desires
serve
    »   your lust
service (1)
sex (1)
sexual act
    »   commerce
    »   intercourse
    »   knowledge
    »   relations
    »   relief
shaft
shag (1)
share a bed
share favours with
sharp and blunt
sheets
shift (2)
short time
    »   session
shove (1)
sink the soldier
skewer
slake your lust
slap and tickle
sleep around
sleep over
sleep together
sleep with

sluice (1)
smother
snatch (1)
soil (1)
solace
spend the night with
split (2)
sport
    »   for Jove
sprain your ankle
spread for
spread your twat **spread for**
spur of the moment passion
stab
stain
step out on
stick (3)
stick it into (2)
    »   on
stoop your body to pollution
straddle
stray your affection
strop your beak
stuff (2)
subdue to your will
submit to
succumb (2)
surrender to
swing with
swinge **switch-hitter**
switch **switch-hitter**
take (2)
take a bit from
take a risk
take a turn in the stubble
    »   »   »   »   Cupid's Corner
    »   »   »   »   Love Lane
    »   »   »   »   Mount Pleasant
    »   »   »   on your back
take advantage of
    »   vantage
take **pleasure** with
take to bed
take up with
take your name away
tap (3)
taste
    »   a body
tear off a piece of arse
    »   »   »   »   ass
    »   »   bit of arse
test the mattress
thread (the needle)
thrill
throw (1)
thump
tickle
tip (1)
top (1)

toss (1)
touch (1)
　　" 　up
tread
trim
trim your wick
trip up the Rhine
trolley
trot on your pussy
truant with your bed
tumble (1)
turn (1)
turn up (1)
two-backed beast
two-backed game **beast with
　　two backs**
undo
union (1)
unlace your sandal
up (1)
　" 　her passage
　" 　her way
upstairs (1)
use (1)
　" 　as a woman
　" 　for your vile purposes
use of Venus
vault (1)
venereal
venerous act **Venus**
Venus
violate
virtue
wallop the mattress
wang wank
wank
want (2)
　" 　a body
　" 　intercourse
　" 　love
　" 　relations
　" 　sex
wet your dick
　　" 　wick
whole hog
wide-on
will of
willing
win (2)
work
work on (2)
wrack
wreak your passion on
wrong (1)
yard (2)
yield
　" 　your body
　" 　your honour
　" 　your virginity

ying-yang **jig-a-jig**
you-know-what

Cosmetics

adapt
aesthetic procedure
after shave
beauty care
　　" 　spot
bikini wax
bleach
blue rinse **blue hair**
bring out the highlights
carpet (2)
cleansing lotion
colour-tinted
　　" 　-corrected
cover (2)
dentifrice **dentures**
dentures
enlist the aid of science
ewe mutton
hair stylist
　　" 　sculpture
hairpiece
high forehead (a)
homely
less attractive
mutate
receding
rinse
rug
scalp dolly
sky piece
　" 　rug
syrup
tint
touch up (2)
tummy-tuck
Tyburn top
war paint
wax
wide parting

Courtship and
　　Marriage

air
all right
appetite
apron-string-hold
arousal **arouse**
arouse
asbestos drawers
available **avail yourself of**
axe
baby snatcher
　　" 　farmer
bag (2)
banish your bed

beat the gun
beau
beddable **bed** (2)
bedroom eyes **bed** (2)
bedworthy **bed** (2)
belle mère
betray
bit of **all right**
bit of **arse/ass**
blind **date**
bolt
bolter **bolt**
boondock
bother
bounce (3)
break the pale
broke her elbow at the
　　church **break your elbow**
broomstick match
bundle with
bush marriage **bush** (1)
buttock-mail
by-courting
by-shot
California widow **California
　　blankets**
call down
canned goods
canoe
canoodle **canoe**
carry a torch for
cast sheep's eyes **make
　　sheep's eyes**
catch
chap
chapping **chap**
chase
　　" 　hump
　　" 　skirt
　　" 　tail
cheat
check the seat covers
cherry picker
chuck
clean-living
close the bedroom door
co-respondent
cold (2)
come out
come to a sticky end (1)
come to see
conjugal rights
contingency **incontinent** (1)
cop a **feel**
correspondent
cradle-snatcher
cuckold the parson **cuckoo**
　　(1)
damaged (2)

dance at
dance barefoot
   » in the half-peck
dangerous to women
dark moon
date
dead to priority
   » to honour
   » to social behaviour
dear John
deceive
defend your virtue
degraded
do the right thing
doe
doll (1)
double time
equal pay
exercise your marital rights
experienced
fair sex
faithful
false
fancy
   » seat cover
fast
feather your nest
feel
   » -up
fell design
femme fatale
fidelity
filly
fishing expedition (1)
   » fleet
flapper
flower (1)
follow **follower**
follower
fondle
foxy
frail (2)
frank (1)
free (2)
free a man for duty
free relationship
free samples
freeze **freeze out**
French kissing **enter**
gander-mooner
gash
gate (2)
get off (1)
get off with
give green stockings
good
goose (2)
grass widow
green sickness **green gown**

hand trouble
handle (1)
hang in the bellropes
hang on the bough
hang out the besom
hang out the broomstick
   besom
hang up your hat (1)
   » » » ladle
have a **hard on** for
hawk your meat **hawk your**
   mutton
headache
heavy date
   » necking
   » petting
hen-brass **hen-silver**
honest
honour
hop-pole marriage **hop into**
   bed
horny (2)
hot (1)
hot back
hot for
hot stuff
house-proud
Hyde Park case
improper
in flagrante delicto
in feedom
in name only
inconstancy
incontinent (1)
infidelity
intentions
it (1)
itchy feet **itch**
jail bait
join hands with
jump the besom **jump** (3)
keep your legs crossed
   » » » together
key party
kidnapper
lad
lass
lead apes in hell
leap the broom
leave
leave your pillow unpressed
left-handed alliance **left**
   handed (1)
   » » wife
libber **women's liberation**
liberate (3)
liberation (1)
loose (1)
lose your cherry

   » character
   » innocence
   » reputation
   » snood
mad money
make a **play** for
make sheep's eyes
make up to
marital rights
marriage joys
maul
mouth
neck
nonsense
octopus
old maid
on the make
on the peg
on the shelf
open marriage
out
over-familiar **familiar with**
over-gallant
pass (2)
paw
pet (1)
petting-stone **pet (1)**
pick up
piece (1)
   » of arse
   » of ass
   » of buttered bun
   » of crackling
   » of crumpet
   » of goods
   » of muslin
   » of rump
   » of skirt
pin-up
play gooseberry **gooseberry**
   (1)
play the goat
poppet **popsy**
proposition
pull the pin (1)
pussy-whipped
ram-riding
randy
raunchy
returned empty
right thing
rob the cradle **cradle-**
   snatcher
roundheels
roving eye
ruined in character **ruin**
run away
   » off
saddle-broken

St Colman's girdle has lost
 its virtue
salute upon the lips
San Quentin jail bait
save it
scarlet fever
season
seat cover
seduce
seven year itch
sexual equality
sexual variety
shame
shoot the agate
shove (2)
singles
skirt
smooch
snooded folk **lose your
 cherry**
Spanish fly
speak to
 » for
 » till
spoon
stag month
steg month
 » widow
stud
switch on
tail (1)
take a liberty with
take liberties
take out (1)
take steps
talent
 » -spotting
threesomes
tired (1)
toffee ration
tomcatting
torch of Hymen
true
turn off (2)
turn on
under arrest
unfaithful
unknown to men/women
unlawful
unstanched
untrimmed
untrue
venery **venereal**
walk out (1)
 » along of
 » with
walking-papers **walk** (2)
warm
weakness

wear green garters
wear iron knickers
wear the breeches
 » » pants
 » » trousers
wear your heart upon your
 sleeve
wet for
with it in your hand
without a head
woman
woman in a gilded cage (2)
woman named
women's liberation
 » movement
 » rights
worry
yes girl
young lady
 » man
 » woman

Cowardice
acute environmental reaction
battle fatigue
cold feet
LMF **lack of moral fibre**
lack of moral fibre
shell shock
Turkish ally
vicar of Bray
white feather
white rabbit-scut
windy (2)
work of national importance
yellow (1)
 » belly

Crime other than
 Stealing
above ground
action (1)
ambulance chaser
Arkansas toothpick
assault
assist the police
bend the rules
bent (1)
biographic leverage
bird dog (2)
bite
biter **bite**
black market
black money
 » dollars
 » pounds
blackmail
blow job **blow** (1)
blow the gaff **blow** (5)

blow the whistle **blow** (5)
blue box
boning **bone** (1)
bootleg
bounce (4)
boys (2)
 » upstairs
British justice
bushwack
bust (1)
cannon
care
claim responsibility for
clean
clean up (1)
clock **put the clock back**
cobbler
cocktail (1)
collector **collect**
community alienation
con
 » artist
 » man
cook (2)
cop out
corner (1)
cosa nostra
cough
cover-up **cover story**
diddle (3)
dirt
do (5)
doctor
double-entry
draw the king's picture
eat the bible
fair trader **fair sex**
fall money **fall** (4)
fallaway
family (2)
Federal Hill
feed the meter
finger (1)
 » -man
 » -mob
fix (1)
fleece
form
frame (1)
 » -up
front (2)
fudge (1)
funny money
gaff
gentlemen **gentleman**
goods
gooseberry lay **gooseberry** (2)
grass (1)
green goods

gun (1)
hatchet man
haul in
Havana rider
heat (1)
heavies
help the police (with their enquiries)
Hempshire gentleman **hemp**
highjack
hike
hijack
hook (3)
in the black
in the ring
informal
     "   dealer
irregularity (2)
Jews' **lightning**
kangaroo court
lard
launder
laundry **launder**
lay paper
line your pocket
     "   coat
loaded (2)
low flying
lulu
Lydford law
mark
Michigan roll
mob
mobster **mob**
moonlight (1)
moonraker
muscle
muscleman **muscle**
no show
off the rails
on the chisel
on the square
operator
paperhanging **paper hanger**
penman
piece of the action
pigeon (1)
plant (2)
private enterprise
pull off (2)
put the clock back
put the finger on
questionable
rap
receiver
restorer **restorative art**
rip off
run (1)
runner **run** (1)

salt (1)
score (2)
sell out
set up (2)
shade (2)
shakedown
Shanghai
share pusher
sheet
shop (2)
sing
skim (2)
slice of the action
smear (3)
soldier (2)
soup
spill (1)
spill the beans
split (1)
squeal
sting
stool pigeon
straight
swallow the bible
switch the primer
syndicate
tagged (2)
take (1) (5)
take for a ride (2)
take stock of the situation
throw rocks
throw the book at
tip (4)
     "   off
torpedo
toss (2)
turn in
turn the clock back
turn up (2)
unavailable (3)
under the counter
underground (1)
walk (5)
walk penniless in Mark Lane
wash (3)
white money

Cuckoldry

Actaeon
blow the horn **horn** (2)
forked plague **fork**
freeman of Bucks **freemans**
graft
honour
horn (2)
     "   -maker
knight of Hornsey
member for Horncastle
     member (1)

prey to the bicorn
put horns on
Vulcan's badge
wear a **fork**
wind the horn **horn-maker**

Death other than Funerals and Killing

after life
all up with
alleyed
answer the call (1)
asleep
     "   in Jesus etc.
at rest
     "   peace
at your last **last call**
away (1)
back-gate parole
bath-house
bellyful of lead
better country
     "   world
beyond salvage
big **D**
bite the dust
bonds of life being gradually dissolved
bone (3)
bought it
breathe your last
bring your heart to its final pause
brown (2)
bullet
bump (4)
business
buy it
buy the farm **bought it**
buzzed **buzz on**
call
     "   it a day
call off the bets
call souls
called away **call**
called home **call**
called to higher service **call**
cardiac arrest **cardiac incident**
cash your checks
     "   chips
catch a packet
cement shoes
     "   boots
chair
check out
chips
chop shot **chop** (1)
chuck seven

church triumphant
clink off
close your eyes
clunk
cold (1)
come again
    ” back
come home feet first
come to a sticky end (1)
come to your resting place
    ” ” yourself
concrete shoes
conk (out)
cop a packet **cop** (1)
cop it
cottonwood
count
    ” the daisies
croak
cross the Styx
    ” ” River Jordan
curtains
cut adrift
cut off
cut the painter
    ” adrift
    ” your cable
dance (1)
    ” a twostep in
        another world
    ” at the end of a rope
    ” -hall
    ” off
    ” on air
    ” the Tyburn jig
    ” upon nothing
dancing master **dance** (1)
Davy Jones' locker
dear departed **depart this
  life**
debt of nature
depart this life
departed **depart this life**
departure **depart this life**
die in a horse's nightcap
die in your shoes
die queer
diet of worms
disappear (1)
disinfection
disposal
dissolution (1)
done for
down for good
drop (3)
    ” in your tracks
    ” off the hooks
    ” off the perch
    ” your leaf

drop off
earn the wages of sin
easy way out
electric cure
elimination **eliminate**
end of watch
enter the next world
eternal life
everlasting life
exchange this life for a better
execution **execute**
executive action **execute**
expedient demise
expended
expire
fade away
fall (3)
fall asleep
fall off the hooks
fall out (1)
fallen
feet first
filled full of **lead**
flack out
flit (1)
for the high jump
foul play
gathered to your fathers
get a bullet
get a slug **slug** (1)
get away
    ” it
    ” the call
get the **gas** pipe
get the shaft
give up the ghost
    ” the spoon
go (1)
go away
go aloft
go corbie
go down (1)
go down the nick
go for a Burton
go forth in your cerements
go home
    ” ” feet first
    ” ” in a box
go off (1)
go off the hooks
go on
go out
go over (1)
go right
go round land
go the wrong way
go to a better place
    ” ” glory
    ” ” life eternal

    ” ” rest
go to grass
go to heaven on a string
go to the wall
got to your reward
go to yourself
go up
    ” the chimney
    ” the gate
go upstairs out of this world
  upstairs (1)
go west
God called in the loan **call
  (the)**
gone (1)
goner
gonner **goner**
grave
gravestone gentry **grave**
great certainty
    ” leveller
    ” out
    ” secret
great majority
grim reaper
ground-sweat
grounded for good
had it
hand in your dinner-pail
hang-fair
hang up your hat (2)
    ” ” ” harness
    ” ” ” tackle
hanging judge **hang**
happy release
    ” despatch
    ” hunting grounds
heels foremost
hemp
    ” -string
    ” -strung
hempen fever **hemp**
hempen widow **hemp**
hereafter
high jump
hole in the head **head** (1)
hole in the water **make a
  hole in the water**
hop off
    ” the twig
hot seat
    ” squat
hummingbird
hump it
in Abraham's bosom
in heaven
in the arms of his Maker **in
  heaven**
    ” ” the Lord

in the arms of Jesus
in the cart
jack it (in)
join your dear husband
 » the Great Majority
 » the immortals
 » the many
 » your ancestors
 » your Maker
jump the last hurdle
keel over
keep sheep by moonlight
kick (1)
 » in
 » it
 » off
 » the bucket
 » the wind
 » up
king of **Tyburn**
kingdom-come
kiss the ground
kiss off (2)
kiss St Giles' cup
laid to rest
 » in the lockers
last call
 » bow
 » curtain
 » debt
 » end
 » rattler
 » resting place
 » round up
 » trump
 » voyage
last drop **drop** (3)
last waltz
late (1)
latter end **late** (1)
lay down your life
 »   »   your burden
 »   »   your knife and fork
 »   »   the clay
lead poisoning
leaden fever **lead**
leap in the dark
leave the building
leave the land of the living
 »   » minority
left town **leave the land of**
 the living
lick the dust
life everlasting
little gentleman in black
 velvet
long **count**
long home
 » day

 » journey
 » walk off a short pier
long drop **drop** (3)
Lord has him
lose the vital signs
 » the number of the mess
 » your wind
lost (2)
 » at sea
make the supreme sacrifice
meet with an accident
meet your Maker
 » the Prophet
mole country
napoo
narrow passageway to the
 unknown
next world **better country**
no longer with us
 » more
no right to correspondence
not dead but gone before
 » lost but gone before
not yet returned **NYR**
number is up
NYR
off the voting list
on the end of a shovel
on your shield
on your way out
other side
over Jordan
 » the creek
pack it in
 » up
packet (1)
pass (1)
 » away
 » in your checks
 » on
 » out
 » over
passing
pay nature's (last) debt
 » the extreme penalty
 » the final penalty
 » the supreme penalty
 » your debt to society
peace at last
peg out
planned termination
play your harp
plucked from us
pop off
popping up the daisies
potted (1)
preach at **Tyburn** cross
promoted to Glory
push up the daisies

put away (1)
put in your ticket
put to bed with a shovel
 » to bed with a mattock
 » to bed with a spade
 » under the sod
put to rest
quiet it
quietus
quit
 » cold
reaper
release (2)
released
relocation
remain above ground
removal **remove**
removed **remove**
repose
resign your spirit
rope (1)
routine (nursing) care only
run into a bullet
scragger **scrag**
screwed down
shuffle off this mortal coil
six feet of earth
six feet underground
sizzle
sleep
sleep in your (leaden)
  hammock
 » in your shoes
slip (2)
 » away
 » off
 » to Nod
 » your breath
 » your cable
 » your grip
 » your wind
stand before your Maker etc.
stark
step off
stoke Lucifer's fires
stop one
 » a slug
 » the big one
strike out
suck daisy roots
suffer the supreme penalty
swing
swing off
take a blinder
take a long sniff
  sniff out
take home
take leave of life
take the drop

taken
taking
talk to the old gentleman
taps
time
tip (2)
took
topping fellow **top (2)**
transported
turn in
turn it in
turn up your toes
        » heels
turn your face to the wall
turning tree
twisted
Tyburn
  » dance
  » hornpipe
  » jig
  » ticket
  » tippet
  » tree
  » triple tree
under-arm bairn
under hatches
  » sailing orders
under the daisies
  » the grass
  » sod
underground (2)
undiscovered country
Union Jack for
united
upstairs (1)
wages of sin
way of all flesh
wear a bullet
wear away
westerners **upstairs (1)**
wet-job
win home
  » your way
wing your flight from this
    world
with Jesus
  » the Lord
  » us no more
  » your Maker
without baggage
written out of the script

Defecation

accident (1)
alley apple
ammunition (1)
army form blank
be excused
been

big jobs
bind
bird lime
bodily functions
bodily wastes
body wax **body rub**
bog
Bombay milk-cart
Bombay oyster
boom-boom (1)
bowel movement
bucket (1)
bum fodder **ammunition (1)**
bury a quaker
business
call of nature
cast your pellet
caught short
CC pills
cement
clear out
confined **confinement**
cowpats **horse apples**
crap
crud
defecate
demands of nature
dirty your pants
do a dike **do a bunk**
do a job **do a bunk**
do a rural **do a bunk**
drop the crotte **droppings**
drop the wax **droppings**
droppings
dry waste **waste (3)**
dump (1)
duty
evacuate
evacuation (1)
feel the need
fertilizer
foul
  » yourself
George
go (3)
go about business
go for a walk with a spade
go places
go to ground
go to the bathroom
go upstairs
gold-digger
  » -brick
  » -dust
  » -finder
grunt
honey
  » barge
  » bucket

  » cart
  » dipper
  » wagon
hooky
horse (2)
horse apples
house-trained
incontinent (2)
indiscretions **indiscretion**
irregular
irregularity (1)
job
make a mess
manure
mess (2)
motion (1)
move your bowels
movement (1)
muck **horse apples**
my word
nasty
natural functions
  » purposes
nature's needs
necessities
need
nightsoil
number nine
number two(s)
open your bowels
ordure
pancake **pan**
perform (1)
  » a natural function
pony
poop
pooper-scooper **poop**
post a letter
prairie chips **horse apples**
rear (2)
regular (1)
relieve your bowels **relieve
  yourself**
Richard
road apples
run (4)
sausage
see your aunt **see the
  rosebed etc.**
shift (1)
sit-down job
skidmarks
soil (2)
  » your pants
  » yourself
solid waste
souvenir (2)
squat (1)
squeeze a Malteser

stoppage (1)
take a squat **squat** (1)
tom (1)
top and tail
tied up
use paper
visiting card
wander off
waste (3)

Diarrhoea
Adriatic tummy
Aztec twostep
  ” hop
back-door trot **backdoor-man**
Basra belly
Bechuana tummy
bull-scutter **bull** (2)
Cairo crud
Delhi belly
flying handicap
gastric flu
GI's
gippy tummy
gyppy tummy
Ho Chi-minh
Hong Kong dog
loose (2)
Malta dog
Mexican fox-trot
  Montezuma's revenge
Mexican two-step
  Montezuma's revenge
Mexican toothache
Montezuma's revenge
on the trot (2)
opening medicine
physic
Rangoon runs
runny tummy
runs
scatters
scour
shoot (3)
Spanish tummy
squirt
squit **squirt**
squitters **squirt**
threepennies
Tokyo trots
touristas
trots
tummy bug
Tunis stomach

Dismissal
air
ax(e)

bag (2)
beach
bench
bobtail
boot (1)
bounce (3)
bowler hat
bucket (2)
bullet
bump (1)
bump off
California kiss-off **kiss-off**
  (1)
can (2)
cards
chop (2)
chuck
consultancy
consultant (1)
cop the bullet **cop** (1)
DCM
dispense with assistance
down the road
drop-dead list
early retirement
excess
fire
flush down the drain
for the high jump
  ” it
for the chop **chop** (2)
furlough
gate (2)
general discharge
get on your bike
ghost does not walk
give the air
go (4)
golden bowler
golden handshake
  ” parachute
grand bounce
graze on the common
graze on the plain
grounded
hatchet man
head-count reduction
hike
hoist (3)
hoof
house-cleaning
in the barrel
kick (2)
kiss-off (1)
lay off
leave of absence
let go
let out
New York kiss-off **kiss-off** (1)

notice
off the payroll
order of the boot
  ” ” ” push
out to grass
pink slip
poke (1)
push (2)
put out to grass
railroad
rationalize
reduction in force
  redundant
redundant
release (1)
relieve
  ” of duties
removal **remove**
resign
retrenched
rif
run (5)
running shoes **run** (5)
sack
send ashore
send down the road
separate
services no longer required
shelved
ship
shoot (2)
shop (1)
shout (1)
shove (2)
stand down
step down
surplus
take a walk
terminate (2)
tie a can on
tin handshake
valentine
walk (2)
walking papers **walk** (2)
warning
wind (2)
work your ticket
written out of the script

Drunkenness
aboard (1)
afternoon man
alderman Lushington
arm-bend
bacchanalian
bagged
balmy
bamboozled
bar-fly

barley cap
    " fever
basted
bat (2)
battered
been in the sun **sun has been hot today**
belt (1)
bend
    " the elbow
bender **bend**
bent (2)
binge
blanked
blind
    " -fou
blinder **blind**
blitzed
blown **blow one**
blow your cool etc.
blue (3)
    " -eyed
boiled
bonkers **bonk**
bottled **bottle** (1)
Brahms
breezy
bun on
bun-puncher
bung (1)
Bungay fair **bung** (1)
burn with a low (blue) flame
bust (1)
buzz on
call it eight bells
can on
canned
carry (4)
carry a (heavy) load
catch a fox
celebrate
charwallah
chuck horrors **chucked**
chucked
clobbered
club (3)
cock-eyed
cock the little finger
cocked
cold turkey
cold-water man
comfortable (2)
concerned **concern**
confused
cooked
cop an elephant's
corked
corned
cousin Cis

    " sis
crack a bottle
crock
crocked **crock**
crook the elbow
cupman **in your cups**
cup too many
cure
cut (3)
damaged (1)
deadhead
decks awash
dependency (2)
devotee of Bacchus
dip (2)
    " your beak
    " your bill
discouraged
dissolution (2)
down among the dead men
draw a blank
drink
    " at Freeman's Quay
    " taken
drink(ing) **problem**
drinker **drink**
drop on **drop** (2)
drown your sorrows
    " the miller
drunk
dry (2)
Dutch concert
Dutch courage
Dutch feast
Dutch headache
edged
elbow bender
elephant's
elevate
elevated **elevate**
elevation **elevate**
embalmed
emotional
enjoy a drink
    " a jug
    " a nip
    " the bottle
enjoy a **jar**
fall among thieves
fatigue (2)
feel no pain
fired up **firewater**
five or seven
flash (2)
flawed
floating
fly-by-night (2)
fly one wing low
fogged **foggy**

foggy
forward
fou **full**
four sheets in the wind
foxed
fractured
fragile
frail (1)
fresh
fricasseed
fried
fuddled
full
full of **liquor**
fun-loving
funny (2)
fuzzed
fuzzled **fuzzed**
fuzzy **fuzzed**
gaged **gage** (1)
gas-hound **gassed**
gassed
gay (1)
geared up
geezed up **geezer**
geezer
given to the drink
glass too many
glassy-eyed
glazed
glow on
gone (3)
grape-shot
greased
grog on board
    " -hound
grogged **grog on board**
growler-rushing
half-pint **half a can**
half and half
half canned
    " cooked
    " corned
    " cut
    " foxed
    " gone
    " on
    " screwed
    " shot
    " sprung
    " under
half-seas over
    " sea
hammered
hang a few on
    " one on
hangover
happy
hard drinker

have drink (taken)
hazy
head (3)
headache
heeled (1)
hen-drinking **hen-silver**
high (2)
hit (1)
hit the bottle
  » the hooch
  » it
hoary-eyed
hoist (2)
hold your liquor
hollow legs
honked
horizontal (2)
hot (5)
hung (over) **hangover**
hunt the brass rail
hunt the fox down the red
  lane
illuminated
imbibe
in the Crown Office **in**
  Carey Street
in drink
in liquor
in the down pins **down**
  among the dead men
in the rats
in the sun (shine)
in the tank
in your cups
incapable
indisposed (2)
indulge
intemperance
jag **jag house**
jagged
jet-lag
John Barleycorn
jolly (1)
jugged
juice head **juice** (1)
juiced **juice** (1)
jumbo
keelhauled
kiss the cap
knock it back
knock off (4)
laid out **lay out**
led astray
legless
lift your elbow
  » » arm
  » » little finger
  » » wrist
like a drink

limp
liquored **liquor**
lit
loaded (1)
look upon the wine when it is
  red **tight** (1)
lose your lunch
lubricated
lumpy **lump**
lush
lushed **lush**
lushy **lush**
malt above the meal
malt above the water
malt-sucker
malt-worm
malty **malt**
market **fresh**
merry
migraine
Mozart
muggy
muzzy
nappy
non-drinker **drink**
off the wagon
oil the wig **oiled**
oiled
on (1)
on the bend
on the bottle
on the piss
on the roof
on the **sauce**
on the tiles
on the town (1)
on the wagon
one over the eight
one too many
one wing low
ossified
over-refreshed
  » -excited
  » -indulged
  » -tired
over the bat **bat** (2)
overcome
overdo the Dionysian rites
overindulge **indulge**
package on
paralyzed
paralytic
parboiled
peg
petrified
pickled
pie-eyed
piped
piran

pissed
plastered
polluted
pooped
pot (2)
  » -valour
  » -walloper
potted (2)
powder your hair **powder**
  room
preserved
priest of Bacchus
  bacchanalian
primed
problem drinker
pruned
put away (3)
put it away **put away** (3)
queer (1)
ran-dan **randy**
raunchy
reading Geneva print
ripe
ripped
ripples on **ripe**
rocky (2)
rosy
rush a growler
saturated
Scotch mist
screwed
see a man about a dog
sent
sewn up (2)
shakes
sheet in the wind
shellacked
shoot the cat
shot (4)
shout (2)
  »   yourself hoarse
sign the pledge
skinful
slewed
slopped
sloshed
slugged
smash the teapot **smashed**
smashed
snug
so-so (2)
soak
soaked **soak**
son of Bacchus
  bacchanalian
sop
sot
souse
soused **souse**

sozzled
spit feathers
splice the mainbrace
sponge
sprung
squashed
squiffy
stewed
stiff (2)
stinking
stinko **stinking**
stitch in your wig **stitched**
stitched
stoned
stupid
suck the monkey
sun has been hot today
  » in his eyes
sun has gone over the
  yardarm
Sunday traveller
swamped
take the pledge
take something
take too much
tanked (up)
tap (1)
  » the admiral
technicolor yawn
temperance
the worse
three sheets in the wind
tiddly
tie one on
tight (1)
tip (3)
  » the bottle
tiper **tip** (3)
tipped **tip** (3)
tipper **tip** (3)
tippler **tip** (3)
tipsy **tip** (3)
tired (2)
too many sheets in the wind
toot
top-heavy
toss down
tot
touched (2)
translated
tuned
turn up your little finger
  » » pinkie
twisted
under the influence
under the table (1)
under the weather (1)
unwell (2)
uppish

visiting fireman
wad-shifter
wagon
wall-eyed
wash the baby's head
waterlogged
weakness
well away
  » bottled
  » corned
  » in the way
  » oiled
  » sprung
wet hand **wet** (2)
wet a baby's head **wet** (2)
wet a bargain **wet** (2)
wet your mouth **wet** (2)
wet your quill **wet** (2)
whacked
whip the cat
whistled
wilted
wired (1)
worse for drink
wrecked
zoned out
zonked

Education
academic dismissal
alternative
backward (1)
can (2)
communication
comprehension
comprehensive
concentration problem
custodian
development course
disturbed (1)
dyslexic
exceptional
extended
fair
gate (1)
gifted
graduate
language arts
late developer
less academic
  » able
  » gifted
  » talented
less prepared
limited
maladjusted
mature student **mature** (1)
multiple diplomatosis
no scholar

not a great reader
numeracy
open access
plucked **plucked from us**
precocious
public school
referred
remedial
retarded **retard**
send down (1)
ship
slow
social science
  » scientist
status deprivation
tenure
under-achiever
verbally deficient

Erection and Ejaculation
arousal **arouse**
beat on
blue veiner
bone (2)
bring off (1)
bust your nuts
carnal stump
charge (1)
climax
colleen
come
come aloft
come off (1)
come to a sticky end (2)
completion
cream
Cyprian sceptre
diamond cutter
die
discharge
effusion
erection
essence
expire
finish (2)
fire a shot
  » blanks
  » up
get off
get the upshoot
get your nuts off
go off (2)
go over the top (1)
hard on
have your **banana** peeled
horn (1)
in full fig
Irish toothache

lead in your pencil
loss (2)
machine
man-root
Maria Monk
meat
melt
milk (2)
night loss
nocturnal emission
over the top
piss your tallow **piss pins and needles**
present arms
priapism
pride
  » of the morning
raise a beat
  » a gallop
red-hot poker
release (3)
rise
roe **shoot off**
root (1)
seed
shoot off
  » over the stubble
  » your roe
shot (1)
soldier **sink the soldier**
spend
spill (2)
spirits (1)
spunk
stand (1)
  » to attention
stiff (3)
stuff (1)
tube of meat
tumescence
uncomfortable (2)
up in arms
weapon
wet dream

Espionage
attaché
black operator
blow (5)
bug (1)
  » fix
chauffeur
come across (3)
company (2)
cover story
covert act
deep interrogation
deep sleep
destabilize

disposal facilities
double (2)
drop (5)
ear
electrical surveillance
electronic counter-measures
    » penetration
electronic **surveillance**
executive action **execute**
extreme prejudice
fan club
ferret
firm
fishing expedition (2)
guide
human intelligence
ill (3)
in-depth study
incompatible with status
intelligence
legal resident
letter box
liaison officer
mail cover
military intelligence
    » attaché
mole
negotiation
negotiator **negotiation**
other side (the)
overfly
pavement artist
penetrate
place-man
prejudice **terminate** (1)
safe house
sanitized (2)
secret **agent**
secure house
security risk
security service
sleeper
son et lumière
sticky stranger
surveillance
sweep (2)
tail (2)
tap (2)
technical surveillance
tick
tight (2)
turn (2)
  » around
  » round
wired (2)
wireman **wired** (2)

Extortion, Violence and Torture
appropriate technology
assault
ball money
barker
bell money
benevolence
blackmail
bleed
blood money
bounce (4)
break the news
bunch of fives
burn (3)
cannon
carry (3)
come across (1)
come through
convince
criminal assault
criminally used **criminal assault**
dance (2)
deep **interrogation**
electric methods
enforcer
extreme physical duress
gang-bang
gang-shag **bang** (1)
gang-shay **bang** (1)
handle (2)
heat (2)
heater **heat** (2)
heeled (2)
hen-silver
hook (2)
horse-leech **horse collar**
in protection
indecent assault **indecency**
interfere with
inquisition
interrogation
    » with prejudice
iron (1)
juice (2)
lead
lean on
massage (2)
on the take
pack **heat**
persuade
persuader **persuade**
piece (2)
pitcher
protection
put the arm on
  » black on
  » burn on

       ,,   scissors on
put the bite on
rake-off
razor
refresh your memory
rent
retainer
rod (2)
rodded **rod** (2)
scare
slug (1)
something on you
squeeze
stick (5)
stick it into (1)
sweat it out
third degree
tooled up
voluntary
water cure
work on (1)
workout

Farting
backfire
bad powder
blow (2)
boff (2)
break wind
    ,,   the sound barrier
Bronx cheer
cheeser **cut a cheese**
cut a cheese
    ,,   leg
let off
    ,,   fly
lift a gam **lift a leg** (2)
poop
raspberry (1)
rude noise
wind (1)
windy (1)

Female Genitalia
ace of spades
alcove
amply endowed **well-endowed**
basket (2)
beard (1)
bearded clam **beard** (1)
beaver
    ,,   -shot
bird (3)
bird's nest
box (3)
bubbies **Charlie**
busby
bush (1)

button (1)
cabbage (2)
cat (2)
Charlie
charms
cherry
cleft
cock
cockpit **cock**
cotton
down below
downstairs (2)
endowed
equipment
Eve's custom house
      Adam
fanny
feminine gender
finish off (2)
front door
    ,,   parlour
gap
garden (1)
    ,,   of Eden
gash
gasp and grunt **grumble**
gentleman's pleasure
   garden
   pad (3)
grass (3)
grumble
grummet
hole (2)
    ,,   of contentment
holy of holies (1)
hypogastric cranny **hymenal sweets**
instrument
jugs
keyhole **key**
kitty
knockers
love-juice
Low Countries
lower stomach **lower abdomen**
lungs
meat
monosyllable
mousehole
muff
mutton
naughty bits
nautch girl
nest
nether parts **Netherlands**
nether regions
   Netherlands
Netherlands

nook **nookie**
organ(s)
parts
pen **proud**
pleasure-garden
plumbing (2)
private parts
privates **private parts**
privities **private parts**
privy parts **private parts**
pudendum
puff
purse
pussy
    ,,   -lift
ring (1)
saddle
secret parts
sex (2)
shaft
sharp and blunt
slit
snatch (2)
stubble
thing
tickler (1)
topless
touch-hole **touch up** (1)
treasure
velvet (1)
vital statistics
waterworks
well-endowed
what you may call it
whatsit
whites

Funerals
arrangements conference
   arrangement
at need
black art **black operator**
black job **black operator**
black work **black operator**
blacks **black operator**
body
bone (3)
    ,,   -house
    ,,   -hugging
    ,,   -orchard
    ,,   -yard
box (1)
burial of an ass
case (2)
chapel of ease
    ,,   rest
clay **lay down your life**
cold
    ,,   box

" cart
" cook
" meat
" meat party
" storage
companion spaces
crypt
daisy (1)
dead meat (1)
death benefit
decontaminated
dismal trade
dismal trader **dismal trade**
dismals **dismal trade**
dole meats
double depth
dust
" -bin
dustman **dust**
estate
eternity box **eternal life**
floater (2)
funeral director
garden crypt
garden of remembrance
" honor
grief therapy
" therapist
ground lair **ground sweat**
ground-mail **ground sweat**
hic jacet **hick**
hick
highlandman's burial
home of rest
hygienic treatment
ice box (2)
immediate need
invalid coach
lay out
life insurance
" cover
" office
long home
loss (1)
loved one
lump
marble orchard **marbles**
mausoleum crypt
meat
" wagon
memorial
" association
" counsellor
" home
" park
" society
memorialization **memorial**
narrow bed **narrow**
  passageway to the

unknown
perpetual care fund
personal representatives
pine overcoat
plant (1)
pre-arrangement
" -need
preparation room
professional car
remains
reposing room **repose**
rest room
restorative art
resurrection man
" cove
resurrectionist **resurrection man**
sanitary treatment
slumber room
" box
" cot
" robe
space
" and bronze deal
stiff (1)
" one
tree suit
true companion crypt
vault (2)
vital statistics form
wake
wooden box
" breeches
" breeks
" coat
" overcoat

Gambling
bird dog (1)
bit on
bookmaker
books **book**
broad coves
broad fakers
broad men
broad pitchers
broads **broad**
casino **case** (1)
cleaners
commission agent
creep joint
debt of honour
dissolution (2)
dope
drop anchor
fix (1)
flutter (1)
fruit machine
gamester (2)

gaming **gamester** (2)
handbook
investor
one-armed bandit **fruit-machine**
palm (2)
plant the books
pull (1)
" up
ringer
runner
sportsman
strangle
tank fight
throw (3)
turf accountant

General and Miscellaneous
accident (3)
adverse weather conditions
agent
alternative
anti-
article
B
bags of
baker
bandwagon
barrack-room lawyer
barracks lawyer **barrack-room lawyer**
Bedfordshire
beefcake **beef**
below stairs
below the salt
belt (1)
bench-warmer
Bennett buggy
blow your cool
" cork
" lump
" noggin
" roof
" stack
" top
" wig
blue (2)
born in
brother
bumper **bump** (2)
business
bust (1)
C
cargo
caring
carry the can
case (2)
celebrity

Homosexuality and Sexual Variations

aestheticism **aesthete**
affair
agent
alternative
angel
arse man
aunt (3)
back door
backward (3)
behind
bent (3)
bestiality
bird circuit **bird in the air**
bitch
blow job **blow** (1)
bondage
boondagger **boondock**
Brighton pier
brown (1)
brown-hatter
brownie (1)
Bucklebury **buckle to**
bugger
bull (4)
   » -dyke
bunny (1)
butch
butterfly
camp (1)
   » about
   » it up
capon
chew
chicken
chickenhawk **chicken**
cissy
closet (2)
   » homosexual
   » lez
   » queen
   » queer
come out
   » » of the closet
companion
consenting adults
cookie pusher
cotqueen **queen**
crush
cupcake
curious
daisy (2)
Darby and Joan
Dick's hatband **dick** (1)
dicked **dick** (1)
discipline
dissolution (2)
divergence
do a brown
dominance

down on
drag (1)
dress on the left
drop beads
dyke
écouteur
effeminate
English
   » arts
   » assistance
   » guidance
   » treatment
exhibit yourself
expose yourself
fag
faggot
fairy
   » lady
female (2)
female domination
female oriented
   » identified
femme
finger-artist **finger** (2)
fish (1)
fishwife
fishy
flash (1)
flasher **flash** (1)
flit (2)
fitty **flit** (2)
flower (2)
fluter
frame (2)
freak (1)
   » trick
French (1)
   » kiss
French way
friend
fruit
   » picker
funny (3)
gay (2)
   » liberation front
gear
gender bending
gentleman of the back-door
get it on
ginger
ginger beer
give head
give yourself
go down on
go to bed with
go to Denmark
gobble pork
   » pecker
gobbler **gobble pork**

goose girl **goose** (1)
government inspected meat
Greek way
gross indecency
group sex
half and half
head job
homintern **homo**
homo
hunt
husband (2)
improper
   » suggestion
indecency
indecent exposure
   indecency
indecent offence **indecency**
interfere with
into leather
invert
inverted **invert**
inversion **invert**
iron (2)
Jack of both sides **jack** (1)
Jasper
jocker
jockey **joker**
John (3)
John and Joan **John** (3)
jolly (3)
kife
king Lear
kinky
kiss-off (3)
lavender
   » boys
   » convention
left-handed (2)
les **lesbian**
lesbian
lesbic **lespian**
lez **lesbian**
light (2)
light-footed
like that
Lily
limpwrist
Lizzie
love
lover
make an improper suggestion
   make a suggestion
make the chick scene
male (2)
marge
Mary (1)
Maud
meat
   » -rack

miss Nancy
mother
muff diver
multiple
nameless crime
nance **nancy**
nancy
　　" 　boy
not interested in the opposite
　sex
odd
one of those
one of us
oral sex
other way
pansy
pash **passion**
pass (2)
passion
patient
peculiar
peddle arse
perform (2)
personal relations
petit ami **petite amie**
piccolo player
plate of ham **plater**
play the skin flute
plug (2)
pogey bait **poke (2)**
poke (2)
poof
pooftah **pouff**
poontang
pouff
predilection
proposition
queen
queer (3)
queerdom **queer (3)**
raisin
rap club
ream
relationship
rent
Roman
　　" 　culture
　　" 　way
rough trade
S and M
sad
sapphic
　　" 　attachment
sapphism **sapphic**
Sappho **sapphic**
sergeant
sexual preference
sexual proclivity
shirtlifter

showers
side orders
sissy
six-à-neuf **soixante-neuf**
sixty-nine
skippy
sodomite
sodomy **sodomite**
soixante-neuf
solicit
song and dance
straight
stud
stuff (2)
suck off
swing with
swish
that way (1)
three-legged beaver
three-letter man
tickle your fancy
top sergeant
truck driver (2)
tube
Turk
two-on-one
unhealthy
unmarried
unnatural
　　" 　act
　　" 　crime
　　" 　filth
　　" 　practice
up the creek
vegetarian
voyeur
wear Dick's hatband
weirdie
wife (2)
will
woman's thing
wrong (2)
yo-yo

Illness and Injury
afflicted
alter
amenity
arrange
big C
blighty
bobtail
born in a mill
C
cardiac incident
case (2)
cast for death
catch a packet
challenged

change (3)
claret
　　" 　-jug
clip (2)
comfortable (3)
complications
condition (1)
consumption
cop a packet **cop (1)**
coronary inefficiency
cream crackered
crease
cut (1)
decline
dicky
discomfort
do (2)
　　" 　over
doctor
Down's syndrome
eliminate **manhood**
falling evil
　　" 　sickness
feed the fishes
feminine complaint
fill in **fill full of holes**
fix (2)
funny (1)
gassed **gas**
geed up **G**
get a slug **slug (1)**
go on the box
groper **grope**
growth
gunner's daughter
handicap
handicapped **handicap**
Hansen's disease
hard of hearing
health
hearing-impaired
heart condition
home
Hopkins **hopping-Giles**
hopping-Giles
inconvenienced
Irish hoist
kiss the **gunner's daughter**
kissing disease **French (1)**
knackered
knuckle sandwich
lay a child
lay hands on
lead ballast
lead buttons
left twin
life preserver
lift your hand to
long illness

marry the **gunner's
  daughter**
martyr to
moonlight (2)
motion discomfort
muster your bag
mutt
neoplasm
nick (4)
nip (3)
not very well
 " at all well
 " doing well
old man's friend
old soldier
on the club
 " box
on the panel
one foot in the grave
packet (1)
panel
partially sighted
plug (1)
plumbioscillosis
poorly (1)
prey to
problem
procedure
raspberry (2)
rather poorly
residential provision
restricted growth
ride the wooden horse
sight deprived
smear (2)
snib **snip**
snick **snip**
snip
so-so (1)
sore
spot (3)
staining
stop one
swing the lead
tagged (1)
TB
ten commandments
thick of hearing
throw up
ticker
trouble
tumbler
tumour
turn (3)
uncle Dick **dicky**
unmentionables (2)
unpaved **unstoned**
unsighted
unstoned

upstairs (1)
very poorly
visible handicap
wearing **wear away**
winged

Intoxicants

alcohol
ambrosia
angel foam **angel dust**
anti-freeze
auld kirk
awful experiment
backhander
bar
belt (a)
beverage
 " -host
 " room
blast (3)
blind pig
Bloody Mary
bloody shame
blow one
blue ruin **blue cheer**
blue stone **blue cheer**
booze
bracer
branch water
brother of the bung
brownie (2)
burra peg
bush house **bush** (2)
cactus juice
chaser
chota peg
cocktail (1)
coffin varnish
cooler (2)
cordial (1)
corn (1)
 " -juice
 " -mule
 " -waters
cough medicine
cough syrup
creature
cut (2)
dash (1)
dead soldier
dive (2)
doctor
double (1)
down
dram
drink
drop (2)
 " of blood
dry (1)

Dutch cheer
embalming fluid **embalmed**
eye-opener
fellow commoner
firewater
foot
French article
 " cream
 " elixir
 " lace
Frenchman **French article**
freshen a drink
G
gage (1)
gargle
gas-house **gassed**
gear
geezer
gentleman commoner
giggle water **giggle stick** (1)
glass
 " of something
grape
gravy (1)
groceries sundries
gypsy's warning
hair of the dog
half a can
 " pint
half and half
happy hour
hard
harden a drink **hard**
handware (1)
heel-tap
highball
hooch
hootch **hooch**
hop toad
horn of the ox
hospitality
hush-shop **hush-money**
Irish
jar
jolt
juice (1)
 " joint
libation
Liffey water
lightning
liquid
 " lunch
 " refreshment
 " restaurant
liquor
little something
livener
load (1)
loaded (3)

lotion
lush
　" crib
　" house
　" ken
malt
medicine
mercy
Micky Finn
Moll Thompson's mark
monkey (1)
moonlight (1)
moonshine
mother's ruin
　" milk
mountain dew
mule (1)
nasty (stuff)
neck-oil
needle
Nelson's blood
nightcap
nineteenth
nip (2)
noggin
oil of malt **oiled**
one for the road
package store
panther sweat
parliament
peg
pick-me-up
plasma
poison
Pope's telephone number
prairie oyster (2)
　" dew
prune-juice
public house
public house
purge (1)
quick one
quickie
rag water
red eye
refresher
refreshment
restorative
reviver
river
rosy
saloon
satin
sauce
scour-the-gate
sea food
serum
sharpener
short(s)

shot (2)
sip
slug (2)
snifter
snort (1)
soft (2)
something
　" short
speakeasy
spike (1)
spirits (2)
spot (1)
spunkie **spunk**
stick (2)
sticky
stiffener
strong waters
stuff (1)
sundowner
tiddly wink
tiger sweat
tincture (2)
tip (3)
tipple **tip** (3)
tippling-house **tip** (3)
top and bottom
tot
tumble (2)
Virgin Mary **bloody**
water of life
watering hole
wee drop
　" half
　" hauf
wee **dram**
wet (2)
　" canteen
　" goods
　" stuff
wetting (2)
whistle-shop **whistled**
white eye
white satin
whole can
willie-waught

Killing and Suicide
account for
ace
at a rope's end
auto-de-fé
　" -da-fé
ax(e)
bag (3)
blank (2)
blast (1)
blip off
blot out
blow away

blow your cool etc.
brace
Bridport dagger
brodie
bucket (3)
bump (4)
　" man
bump off
Burke
burn (2)
button (2)
　" man
capital
　" charge
　" crime
　" punishment
carry off
cash in your checks
　" " " chips
catch a packet
chew a gun
chill
chop (1)
chopper (2)
climb the ladder **climb the**
　ladder on your back
clip (2)
　" the wick
compromise (2)
contract (2)
cook (1)
cool (1)
cow
crease
croak
cull
cut (6)
cut down on
deep six
deliberate self-harm
　vulnerable
demote maximally
deprive **deprived**
despatch **dispatch**
destroy
diddle (3)
dispatch
do (2)
" for
" in
" yourself in
do the **Dutch**
draw a bead on
drill
drop (1)
　" down the chute
dump (2)
dust (2)
Dutch act

Lavatories

boys (1)

  " room

bucket (1)

bum fodder **ammunition** (1)

buoys

can (1)

chamber

  " -pot

chamber of commerce

chapel of ease

chic sale

cloakroom

close stool

closet (1)

coffee shop **coffee grinder**

comfort station

commode

common house

convenience (1)

corner (2)

cousin John

crapping case **crap**

crapping-castle **crap**

crapping ken **crap**

dolls

duck

EC

earth closet

Eve

facility (1)

female (1)

fountain palace

fourth

gang **go** (3)

gentlemen

gentlemen's convenience

gents **gentlemen**

geography

gulls

guys

head(s) (2)

holy of holies (2)

hopper

house (2)

  " of commons

  " of ease

  " of lords

  " of office

jakes

jane (2)

Jericho **jerry**

jerry

jockum **jock**

joe

john (1)

Jordan

ladies

  " convenience

  " room

  " toilet

lads

lassies

latrine

lavabo

lavatory

little boys' room

little girls' room

little house

loo

looking glass

male (1)

men

men's room

modern conveniences

Mrs Chant

Mrs Jones **aunt** (2)

nappy

necessary

  " house

  " woman

night bucket

night stool

no-man's-land

outdoor plumbing **outhouse**

outhouse

pan

parliament

personal hygiene station

petty house

pig

place

plumbing (1)

pot (3)

potty **pot** (3)

powder room

private office

privy

  " stool

public convenience

quaker's burial ground

rears **rear** (2)

rest room

retiring room

retreat

sanctum sanctorum

sanitary man

sanitized (1)

sink

sluice (2)

smallest room

temple (of health)

throne

thunder-box

toilet

uncle

upstairs (1)

utensil

W

WC

wash-mug **wash** (1)

washroom

waste-management

  compartment **waste** (3)

water closet

what you may call it

whatsit

whatzis **whatsit**

women

women's room

woodpile

you-know-what

Madness

acorn academy

adjustment (3)

ape

asylum

backward (1)

balance of mind disturbed

barmy **balmy**

bananas

barred window boys

bats (in the belfry)

batty **bats in the belfry**

bin

blue-devil factory **blue**

 cheer

bonkers **bonk**

booby

  " -hutch

both oars in the water

brick short of a load

bug-house

by yourself

camisole

certifiable **certified**

certified

change (2)

changeling **change** (2)

commit

content

control unit

counsellor

crack-brained **cracked**

cracked

crackers **cracked**

cuckoo (2)

dateless **date**

Deolalic tap **do-lally-tap**

devil's mark

distressed

disturbed (2)

do-lally-tap

dope

dotty

dummy

eccentric

educable **trainable**
educationally sub-normal
fatigue (1)
fifty cards in the pack
flake
fruitcake
funny (4)
  » farm
  » house
  » place
gears have slipped
God's child
half deck
Harpic
head-case
headshrinker
hospital (1)
ill-adjusted
in left field
institutionalize
laughing academy
light in the head
limited
loco
loopy **up the loop**
loose in the attic
  » » » head
lose your **marbles**
maladjustment
  (**maladjusted**)
meathead
mental
mentally handicapped
  mental
mentally retarded **mental**
natural (1)
nervous breakdown
not all there
not sixteen annas to the
  rupee
nut
 » box
 » college
 » farm
 » house
 » hutch
nutter **nut**
nuts **nut**
nutty **nut**
off his **nut**
off at the side
 » the wall
 » your chump
 » » gourd
 » » head
 » » trolley
 » » turnip
out of your mind
 » » » head

» » » senses
» » » skull
out to lunch
potty
psycho
put away (2)
queer (2)
residential provision
retard
right **Charlie**
rocky (1)
round the bend
screw loose
  » factory
screwy **screw loose**
seclusion
section eight
send over the edge
shrink
simple
slate loose
  » off
slow
soft (1)
special (2)
squirrel tank
state farm
  » home
  » hospital
  » (training) school
thick
  » in the head
tip off your trolley
totally dependent
touched (1)
trainable
troubled **trouble**
unbalanced
unhinged
unslated
up the loop
voluntary patient
wandered
want (1)
want some pence in the
  shilling **want** (1)
wanting **want** (1)

Male Genitalia

Aaron's rod
abdomen
abdominal protector
  abdomen
acorns
Adam's arsenal
affair
amply endowed
appendage
balls

basket (2)
batter **belt**
beak **strop your beak**
beef
berries **berry**
Big Steve **willy**
Cecil
Charlie
chopper (2)
cluster
cobblers
cobs **cobblers**
cock
corner (3)
crown jewels
dick (1)
ding **ding-a-ling**
ding-a-ling
ding-dong **ding-a-ling**
dong **ding-a-ling**
down below
downstairs (2)
endowed
engine
equipment
essentials
exhibit yourself
expose yourself
exposure **expose yourself**
family jewels
finish off (2)
foreskin
Fritz **willy**
fun **stick**
gear
General Custer **willy**
giggle stick (1)
Giorgio **willy**
goolies
groin
gun (3)
Harry **willy**
hampton
he who must be obeyed **willy**
head (4)
honk
hung like
implement
indecent exposure
  indecency
instrument
jack (1)
Jean-Claude **willy**
jewels
jock
John Thomas
  » Willie
joint (2)
joy stick **joy** (1)

key
knackers
knocker
little finger
load (2)
loins
long-arm inspection
Low Countries
lower abdomen
     " stomach
man-root
manhood
marbles
meat
     " and two veg.
member (1)
membrum virile **member (1)**
middle leg
most precious part
natural parts **natural**
    functions
naturals **natural functions**
naughty bits
nether parts **Netherlands**
nether regions **Netherlands**
Netherlands
Nimrod
nuts
Old Faithless **willy**
old man (2)
Oliver Twist **willy**
orchestras
organ(s)
parts
pecker
peculiar members
pencil
Percy
person
personal parts
peter
pickle **pump your pickle**
pill (1)
pills
pin
pistol
pole **up the pole**
pork (2)
prairie oyster (1)
prick
private parts
privates
privities **private parts**
privy parts **private parts**
process
purse
rocks
rod (3)
roger (2)

sausage
secret parts
serpent
sex (2)
shaft
short-arm inspection
short hairs
    " and curlies
Sleeping Beauty **willy**
snake ranch
soldier (1)
solicitor general
split-mutton **split (2)**
stick **up the stick**
stones
taters
tender **tumour**
thing
thingy **thing**
thingamajig **thing**
third leg
Tom **willy**
tommy (2)
tool(s)
two stone lighter
vitals
well endowed
well hung
what you may call it
whatsit
whatzis **whatsit**
whip **crack your whip**
whistle
wick
willie
willy
winded
winkie **winkle**
winkle
yard (1)

Masturbation
abuse yourself
auto-erotic habits
bash the bishop
beastliness
beat your meat
    " off
    " your dummy
belt your batter **belt (1)**
blanket drill
body rub
boff (1)
box the Jesuit and get
    cockroaches **box (1)**
bring off (1)
caress yourself
chicken choker **choke your**
    chicken

choke your chicken
come to a sticky end (2)
come your mutton
cordless massager
corporal and four
diddle (2)
do it (with) yourself **do (1)**
duff
extras
filthy
finger (2)
finish yourself **finish (2)**
five-fingered widow
flog off
    " the bishop
    " your beef
    " your donkey
    " your dummy
    " your mutton
fluff your duff
fondle
fool (about) with yourself
frig
fudge (2)
gallop your maggot
genital sensate focussing
grind
hand job
J Arthur
jack off
jazz yourself
jerk off (1)
    " your maggot
    " your turkey
jiggle
levy
make **love** to yourself
manual exercise
marital aid
milk (2)
mother five fingers
mount a corporal and four
mutual abuse
mutual pleasuring
onanism
personalized message
    personal relations
play
play at hot cockles
play the organ
play with
pocket pool
    " job
pork puller **pork (2)**
pull off (1)
    " the pudding
    " the wire
    " yourself
pump your pickle

     „   shaft
rub off
   „   up
   „   yourself
secret vice
   „   indulgence
   „   sin
self-abuse
   „   -gratification
   „   -indulgence
   „   -love
   „   -pleasuring
   „   -pollution
shag (2)
solitary sex
   „   sin
stroke off
strop your beak
take yourself in hand
toss off
touch yourself **touch** (1)
traffic with yourself
vibrator
wank
wanker **wank**
wankery **wank**
whack off
work yourself off
wrist job

Menstruation

ammunition (2)
Aunt Flo **aunt** (2)
bad news
bad week
baker flying
bends (the)
bloody
   „   flag is up
bunny (2)
caller
captain is at home
cardinal is at home
change (1)
Charlie
clout
come around
come on (1)
country cousins **relations**
   have come
courses
cramps
curse
   „   of Eve
danger signal is up
fact(s) of life
fall off the roof
female physiology
flag is up

   „   of defiance
flowers
flux
fly the red flag
friend has come
   „   to stay
grandmother to stay
have the painters in
holy week
hygiene
ill (1)
in heat
in use **use** (3)
indisposed (1)
irregular
irregularity (1)
Kit has come
late (2)
leaky
little **friend**
little visitor
manhole cover
mense(s)
miss (2)
monthlies
monthly **flowers**
monthly period
   „   courses
number one London
off duty
off games
old faithful
out of circulation
over your time
pad (3)
padlock **pad** (3)
painters are in
pause (1)
period (1)
personal hygiene
pleasure-garden padlock
poorly (2)
problem days
rag(s) on
red flag is up **red rag**
red rag (is up)
Red Sea is in
redhaired visitor
reds
regular (1)
relations have come
ride the red horse
road is up for repairs
roses
run on
sanitary napkin
   „   towel
show (1)
sick

so **so-so** (3)
so-so (3)
start bleeding
that time
time of the month
tommy (1)
tummy ache
turn of life
unavailable (2)
under the weather (2)
unstanched
unwell (1)
use (3)
visitor
   „   from Redbank
wallflower week
well
window blind
woman's **problem**
woman's things
women's things
wretched calendar
wrong time of the month

Mistresses and Lovers

à trois
admirer
adventuress
affair
affaire **affair**
affinity
amateur
amour
arse man
assignation
association (1)
athlete
back-door man
beard (2)
bedfellow **bed** (1)
bit on the side
boy friend
brother starling
camp down with
canary
carry on with
chère amie
close friend
cocksman **cock**
cohabit
company (1)
consort with
constant companion
cookie
cracked in the ring
crackling
cruise (1)
crumpet
crush

cuckoo (1)
daddy
dalliance **dally**
dally
dear friend
dirty old man
dirty weekend
dish
don Juan
enjoyed **enjoy**
errant
escort
extra-curricular activity
    ,,   ,,   sex
extra-marital excursion
fair lady **fair sex**
fallen woman
familiar with
fancy man
fancy woman
friend
fun-loving
gallant
garconnière
gentleman friend
girl friend **boy friend**
girler **girl** (1)
goat
gold-digger
good friends
good natured
grass widow
green gown
grope(r)
hand-fast
heavy date
    ,,   involvement
homework (1)
honey man
horn of fidelity **horn** (1)
hot stuff
housekeeper
hussy
john (2)
Judy
just good friends
keep
keep company with
keep **old boots**
keeper **keep**
kept mistress **keep**
kept wench **keep**
kept woman **keep**
lady friend
lady of intrigue
lay
learn on the pillow
leave shoes under a strange
    bed

liaison
liberal
light (1)
light-footed
light-heeled **light-fingered**
live as man and wife
    ,,   in sin
    ,,   tally
    ,,   together
    ,,   with
live in
live off
loose (1)
    ,,   fish
    ,,   in the hilts
lothario
love nest
lover
make a suggestion
    ,,   an improper
         suggestion
make yourself available to
man (1)
    ,,   -friend
ménage à trois
miss (1)
mistress
molest
more than a good friend
mouse **mousehole**
muslin
mutton
    ,,   -monger
native comfort
new cookie
no better than she ought to
         be
,, ,, ,, ,, should be
nose open
not inconsolable
old Adam
old boots
old man (3)
on the side
other woman
parallel parking
paramour
patron (1)
pay for your dinner
peculiar
pet (2)
petite amie
piece of **arse**
    ,,   ass
piece on a fork **piece** (1)
pillow partner
play-fellow
playmate **play**
protector (1)

relationship
rich friend
ride in **old boots**
riding master **ride**
romance
rough trade
run around with
secretary
see (1)
set up (1)
shack up
share affections
share **embraces**
sin
sinful **sin**
skin off all dead horses
slag
sleeping dictionary
sleeping partner
sleepy time girl
steady company
sugar daddy
sure thing
sweet momma
    ,,   man
take up with
travel
turn off (2)
two-time
Uganda
warm up old porridge
wife (3)
wife in water-colours
woman friend
woman in a gilded cage (1)

Nakedness
as Allah made him
,, God made him
au naturel
birthday suit
    ,,   attire
    ,,   finery
    ,,   gear
bottomless **bottom**
buff
in the altogether
in the raw
in the skin
    ,, ,, buff
in your naturals **natural**
    functions
nature's **garb**
naturist **nature's garb**
raw
skin flick
    ,,   magazine
skinny-dip **skin flick**
stark

state of nature
streak(er)
wear a smile
zero

Narcotics

A
A bomb
Acapulco gold
acid
    " fascism
African black
angel dust
arctic explorer
artillery
B-bomb A
B-pill
baby
bag (4)
baling
balloon room
bang (2)
beat the gong
    " pad
bee
belt (1)
benny
black beauty
black stuff
    " pills
    " smoke
blast (3)
    " party
blocked
bloke
blow (6)
    " Charlie
    " horse
    " snow
    " stick
blow your cool etc.
blue cheer
    " devil
    " flags
    " heaven
    " jay
    " velvet
bomb (2)
bombed out **bomber**
bomber
bombita **bomber**
boot (2)
brick
brownie (3)
burn (3)
burn out
bush (2)
business
bust (1)

    " a cap
buzz on
C
California sunshine
    California blankets
can on
candy
    " man
canned **can on**
cap (2)
carry (2)
cement
channel
charge (2)
charged up **charged** (2)
chef
China-white **Chinese tobacco**
Chinese tobacco
chippy (2)
chuck horrors **chucked**
clean
clear up
co-pilot
coast
cocktail (2)
coke
    " -hound
coked **coke**
cold turkey
Columbian gold
come down
come off (2)
connect (2)
connection
controlled substance
cook (3)
cookie pusher
cool (2)
cop (3)
crash
cruise (2)
cube
    " head
    " juice
cure
cut (2)
dabble
deal
deck
    " up
dependency (2)
dirty
dissolution (2)
doctor
doll (2)
dope
dope-**fiend**
downs

drag (2)
dream dust
    " stick
drop acid
dust
dynamite
Eastern substances
eat
equipment
eye-opener
feed your nose
fiend
fix (3)
flight
floating
fly (2)
flying **fly** (2)
foil
forwards **forward**
freak (2)
    " out
French blue
fruit salad
gage (2)
gay (1)
gear
geezed up **geezer**
get off (3)
get on (3)
giggle stick (2)
girl (3)
go up
God's (own) medicine
gold dust **golden triangle**
golden trianagle
gom **God's (own) medicine**
gone (3)
goof
goofball **goof**
goofed **goof**
gow
grass (2)
    " -weed
green grass
Guatemala
gun (2)
H
" and C
habit
happenings
happy dust
hard
hash
    " -head
hay
head (5)
    " -kit
headache-wine
heaven dust

» and hell
heavenly blue **heaven dust**
hemp
herb
high (2)
hit (4)
hold
hook (4)
hooked
hop
» -head
» -joint
hopped (up) **hop**
horner
horse (4)
horsed **horse** (4)
hot shot
hustle(r) (1)
ice cream
» » habit
» » man
icecreamer **ice cream**
Indian hay
Indian hemp
J
» smoke
» stick
jab a vein
» off
jerk off (2)
joint (1)
jolt
joy (2)
» flakes
» popper
» powder
» rider
» smoke
» stick
juju
junk
junked up **junk**
junker **junk**
junkie **junk**
junkman **junk**
kick stick
» party
» the gong around
kick the habit
kilo connection
lamp habit
leaf
lid
life
lift (2)
lit
loaded (1)
low
Lucy in the sky with

diamonds
M
M J **Mary** (2)
mainline
Mary (2)
» Anne
» Jane
merchandise
Mexican brown
» green
» mushroom
» red
mezz
molecular roulette
monkey (2)
Morocco
mother's blessing
mud
mule (2)
needle park
O
on (3)
on a cloud
on the needle
operator
ounce man
pharmaceuticals
pharmacy
piece (3)
pill (3)
pillhead **pill** (3)
pop (1)
popper **pop** (1)
pot (4)
purple heart
push (4)
pusher **push** (4)
re-entry
red devil
» cross
» dirt
reefer
roach
root (2)
rope (2)
salt (2)
salt and pepper (1)
sent
shoot (4)
» gravy
shooting gallery
shot (3)
sleighride
smack
smashed
smell the stuff
smoke
snapper
sniff

snort (2)
snow (1)
snowed **snow** (1)
soft (2)
spaced
speed
spike (3)
starch
stick (4)
» of tea
stoned
straight
straighten
stuff (1)
sugar (3)
sweet tooth
switch on
take needle
take off
take something
tar
tea
» head
» party
Texas tea
thumb
toss (2)
toss out
tracks
travel agent
trip
truck driver (1)
turn on
twisted
up (2)
uppers **up** (2)
uppies **up** (2)
ups **up** (2)
use (2)
user **use** (2)
viper
» 's weed
voyager
waste (2)
way out
weed
weedhead **weed**
white lady
» powder
» stuff
white lightning
wiped out
wired (1)
wrecked
yellow (3)
yellow jacket
» angel
» belly
» devil

    „   sunshine

Obesity

ample
battle of the bulge
bay window
big-boned
big girl
bit of a **stomach**
brewer's goitre
buxom
calorie counter
chubby
classic proportions
contour
cure
full -figured
    „ -bodied
larger woman **older woman**
mature (2)
middle-age spread **middle aged**
reduce your **contour**
rubber tire
shortening the front line (2)
spare tyre
stomach
weight problem
well-built
    „ fleshed

Parts of the Body other than Genitalia

after part
back passage
    „ garden
    „ way
backseat **backside**
backside
basement
behind
benders **bend**
bottom
bronze eye **second eye**
can **canhouse**
cheeks
    „   near cunnyborough
cleavage
cow brute
dark meat (1)
derrière
double **jug**
drumstick
elephant and castle
end
fanny
fleshy part of the thigh
game chicken
he-biddy

    „ cow
Johnny Bum **arse**
Khyber
latter end
    „ part
limb (1)
little Mary
lower limb **dark meat** (1)
posterior(s)
rear (1)
    „ end
ring (1)
rooster
seat
second eye
sit-down-upon **sit-upon**
sit-upon
sitting **sit-upon**
stern
tassel **pencil**
trotter **dark meat** (1)
under-arm

Police

accommodation collar **collar** (2)
arm
B specials **special** (3)
badge bandit
bear (2)
    „ bait
    „ bite
    „ food
    „ in the air
    „ trap
bearded buddy **bear** (2)
bears are crawling **bear** (2)
bent copper **bend the rules**
big brother
bill
bird in the air
black and whites
blow the whistle
blue (1)
    „ and white
    „ -belly
    „ jeans
    „ lamp
    „ police
bluebird **blue** (1)
bluebottle **blue** (1)
blucoat **blue** (1)
bobby
bogy
boned **bone** (1)
boy scouts
bracelets **brace**
brown paper bag
bull (3)

bust (1)
busy
button (3)
camera
canary
Charlie
chirp
clown
co-operator (2)
collar (2)
cop (2)
    „ house
    „ shop
copper
country Joe
decoy
dick (2)
dickless tracy **dick** (2)
do your paperwork
drop the hook on
eye in the sky
feed the bears
fireman
flash tin **flash** (1)
flat **flatfoot**
flatfoot
floater (1)
fly (1)
    „ ball
    „ bob
    „ bull
    „ cop
    „ dick
folding camera
frog
front office
fuzz
G-man
Gestapo
grasshopper
green stamp collector
gum-shoe
harness bull
hawk
head-hunter (2)
horny (1)
house man
internal affairs
jack (2)
    „ rabbit
jacket
john (4)
    „ Law
KGB
Kojak
lady bear
lift (3)
limb (2)
    „ of the law

little bears
local bear
  » boy
  » yokel
lower the boom on
man (2)
men in blue
morals squad **moral**
mug-shot
night crawlers
nightingale
old Bill
open season
paddy wagon
paper hanger
peel **peeler**
peeler
penny
piece of paper
pig
pigeon (2)
pinch (2)
pink panther
plain brown wrapper
polar bear
preventative man
pull in
question
radical squad
red squad
rubber heel
runner
running bear
salt and pepper (2)
Sam (1)
secret (state) police
shake (2)
shake the bushes
  » » leaves
  » » trees
shield
sloppy Joe
slops
smile and comb your hair
smoke screen
smokey
  » beaver
  » on four legs
  » on rubber
  » with camera
  » with ears
snatch (4)
  » squad
snout
snowdrop
special (3)
special branch
special fuzz
special police

  » patrol group
spread the greens
spy in the sky
stake-out
state-bear **bear** (2)
stool-pigeon
Tijuana taxi
use your tin
whistler
white wrapper
X-ray machine
Yellowstone Park

Politics (C or N indicate Communist or Nazi)

action (2) N
activist
adviser
alternative
anarchistic groups C
anti-fascist C
anti-socialist elements C
aryan N
bag job **bag** (1)
bandit C
bath-house N
bederipe **droit de seigneur**
benevolence
big brother
black order N
blackshirt N
blue police **blue** (1) N
boat people C
boonwork **droit de seigneur**
boys in the backroom **boys** (2)
boys uptown **boys** (2)
business-like and friendly
camp (2) C N
campaign
carry a card C
certain regarder
charter of labour N
cheap money
chisel
civil rights
class warfare C
  » conflict C
  » education C
  » law C
  » literature C
co-ordination N
colony
come into the public domain
Comecon C
committed
Committee of State
  Security C

Committee for the protection
  of the revolution C
common ground
comrade C
concentration camp N
concern
confederation
controlled economy C
controversial
cordial (2)
correct C N
correctional labour camp
  corrective training C
correctional labour colony
  corrective training C
corrective training C
counter-revolution C
cross the floor
cultural revolution
cut (5)
decadent C N
decontaminate
  decontaminated
democracy
democratic
demonstration
departmental view
dependency (1)
deselect
developing
development area **developing**
deviation C
dictatorship of the proletariat
  C
direct action
disinfection N
disinvestment
dollar shop C
draw too much water
East Asia All-one-Culture
encirclement C N
Endlösung N
era of pacification **pacify**
evacuation (2) N
exchange of views
executive measure N
fair-haired boy
fair rent
fat cat
fellow traveller C
fifth column N
final solution N
fireman N
flexibility
flexible **flexibility**
for the good of the cause C
forced labour C N
Fortress America
  » Europe N

frank (2)
free trade
  » enterprise
  » -for-all
free world
freeze
friendly C
front (1) C
full and frank
full employment
German N
  » chemistry N
  » mathematics N
German Democratic
  Republic C
Germanization **German** N
Gestapo N
go native
go over (2)
  » » the wall
great and the good (the)
great leap forward C
guerrillas
guide C
guidelines
harmful elements C
hawk
hegemony C
hinterland
Holy Alliance
Holy Roman Empire
holy wars
hooligan C
hostile class elements C
house trained
human rights
in place of strife
information
initiative
inner city
internal affairs C
internal security
involved
involvement **involved**
Iron Curtain
jolly (1)
KGB C
king over the water
lame duck (1)
leak (2)
leakage **leak** (2)
leaky **leak** (2)
lease-lend
Lebensborn **living space** N
Lebensraum N
left
left-wing
liberal
living space N

log-roller
love boonwork **droit de**
  seigneur
love-in **sit-in**
low profile
Malayan People's Anti-
  Japanese Army C
masses C
masters
National Front N
national security guard
National Socialist N
nationalize
new economic zones C
New Order N
  » Society
news management
no comment
non-aligned
non-person C
on the road to reform C
over-civilized N
OVRA N
party member C
pause (2)
Pax Britannica
peace C N
  » council C
  » campaign C
  » initiative C
  » offensive
  » women
people's
people's army
people's car N
people's court C N
people's democracy C
people's justice C N
people's militia C
people's republic C
People's War C
place of safety N
plumber
policy of realism **Realpolitik**
political and social order
political education C
  » re-education C
popular front C
population transfer C N
pork (1)
  » barrel
  » chopper
post-war credit **benevolence**
Potomac fever
Pravda C
preliterate
prime the pump
procedure N
progressive C

proletarian C
  » democracy C
  » internationalism
    C
propaganda
protect **protectorate**
protective custody N
provocation C N
public feeling
public sector borrowing
  requirement
public tranquillity
purification of the race N
put the file in order
racial purity N
racial science N
radical N
re-educate C
re-introduced to society C
Realpolitik
redistribution of wealth
regularize (1)
rehabilitate C
relevance
relocation N
resettlement N
restraint
revisionist C
revolutionary organs of
  power C
right-wing
salami tactics C
samizdat C
self publication C
service of military
  investigation C
sherpa
shock worker C
  » brigade C
sick leave
sit in
sleep-in **sit-in**
sluggish schizophrenia C
so-called Austrian **problem** N
social justice
social ownership
socialist
soviet C
special (1)
special action N
special branch
special court N
special detachment N
special duty C N
special education C
special fuzz
special squad N
special treatment N
sphere of influence

squat (2)
state protection C
  » Research Bureau
struggle
  » for national
       existence N
student
take a point
temporary local difficulty
three letters C
thug C
transported N
troubles **trouble**
tutor
ultimate intentions N
un-American
uncaring
unsound
useful fool C
vigilance C
war criminal
  » crime
welfare state
whitewash
workers' control C
workshop
World Peace Council C

Poverty and Stinginess
backward (2)
basket case
big house
bolt the moon
boracic
California blankets
careful (1)
carry the banner
  » » balloon
casual
church house
claimant
  » 's union
close
culturally deprived **cultural**
demographic strain
deprivation **deprived**
deprived
developing
disadvantaged
emergent
emerging **emergent**
financial assistance
finangler
fledgling nation
flit (1)
fly-by-night (1)
fumble
gentleman at large
hard up

hearts
law and order
less developed
lesser developed **less
   developed**
low income
moonlight flit
  » flight
  » march
  » touch
  » walk
moth in your wallet (a)
near (1)
negatively privileged
nickel and dime
on **assistance**
on the board **on the club**
on the box **on the club**
on the parish
  » parochial
on the ribs
on the town (2)
on your bones
other side of the tracks
privileged
raise the wind
relative deprivation
remittance man
seen better days
set back
shoot the moon
shorts (the)
social worker
south
tapped
third world
tied aid **aid** (2)
tightwad
to the knuckle
uncle
underdeveloped
underprivileged
union (2)
urban renewal
vulnerable
walk penniless in Mark Lane
whistling
white nigger
workhouse

Pregnancy
accident (2)
afterthought
anticipating
away the trip **away** (2)
awkward
bear (1)
beat the gun
belly plea

big
  » belly
bump (2)
bun in the oven
carry (1)
carrying
caught (1)
certain condition
cheat the starter
club (1)
colt (1)
come to a sticky end (1)
condition (2)
costume wedding
delicate condition
do the right thing
do your duty by
eat for two
enceinte
expectant
expecting **expectant**
fact(s) of life
fall (2)
  » for a child
  » in the family way
  » wrong to
family way
fill a pannier **fill full of holes**
force-put job
full in the belly
get with child
gone (2)
grass widow
great
have a **watermelon** on the
  vine
heavy date
high in the belly
how's your father
in a certain condition
in calf
in for it
in foal
in heat
in kindle
in oestrus
in pig
in pod
in pup
in season
in the club
  » (plum(p)) pudding club
in the family way
in trouble
interesting condition
Irish toothache
join the club
jolly (1)
kid

knock up
labour (1)
lady in waiting
large (1)
lined **line**
little stranger
lumpy **lump**
make a child **make babies together**
make an honest woman of
mistake
off-white wedding
on (2)
on heat
on the nest
on the way
overdue (1)
plum(p) pudding club
proud
　" 　in the pen
pudding club
pup
quick
rank
riding time **ride**
right thing
ring the bell
rush job
sewn up (1)
shot in the tail
shotgun marriage
　" 　wedding
so
so-and-so (1)
something in the basket
split a woman's shape **split** (2)
stand (2)
state of health
sterile
stoned-horse-man **stones**
stung by a serpent
swallow a **watermelon** seed
swell
take (4)
that way (2)
trouble
up the pole
up the spout
up the stick
watermelon
wear the belly high **belly plea**
with child
wrong (3)

Prisons

adjustment (3)
approved school

around the horn
assembly centre
attendance centre
away (2)
back-gate parole
bag (5)
bear cage **bear** (2)
behind the **wire**
big house
　" 　pasture
　" 　school
bird (2)
birdcage **bird** (2)
black hole
board school **residential provision**
boat **boat people**
book
boom-passenger **boom-boom** (2)
both hands
brig
bucket (2)
bullpen **bull** (3)
buried
cage
camp (2)
can (3)
canary
　" 　-bird
chokey
chuck horrors
clink
cock-chafer
come to a sticky end (1)
community treatment **community alienation**
cooler (1)
coop
cop (2)
correction (2)
correctional
　" 　facility
　" 　officer
corrective training
cross bar hotel
custody suite
deep freeze
detainee
detention **detainee**
down the line (1)
enjoy Her Majesty's hospitality
entertain (1)
fall (4)
Fanny Hill
fistful
five fingers
flowery

fly a kite (3)
forced labour
freezer
G
glass house
go down (2)
　" 　up the river
go over the hill **go over** (2)
go over the side **go over** (2)
go over the wall **go over** (2)
grind the wind
guest
　" 　of Her Majesty
　" 　of Uncle Sam
gulag
handful
hit the hump **hit the bricks**
hole (3)
holiday
home
hoosegow
horse (3)
hospital (2)
house of correction
　" 　detention
hulk(s)
ice box (1)
　" 　house
ill (3)
in (1)
in care
in need of supervision
in the bag
indoctrination camp
inside
jolt
jug
kiss the counter
kiss the clink
kitty
labour education
landing officer
last shame **last favour**
length
limbo **limb**
little school
man (2)
municipal farm
nab the stoup
Newgate
nick (3)
on ice **ice box** (1)
on the rockpile
on the trot (1)
out of town
periodic rest
place of safety
　" 　" 　correction
poke (3)

political education
porridge
Potsdam
preventive detention
protective custody
put away (2)
quod
railroad
residential provision
resisting arrest
rock crusher
room and board with Uncle
   Sam
school
screw (2)
seclusion
segregation unit
send down (2)
send up
sheriff's hotel
shock brigade **work brigade**
shot while trying to escape
slam **slammer**
slammer
sneezer
special education
special regime
sponging-house **sponge**
spring
state farm
   "   home
   "   (training) school
stir
   " -wise
stockade
stretch
sweat-box **sweat it out of**
take to the hills
tank
tempered in the forge of
   labour
time
tolbooth
transported
trying to escape
unauthorised departure
   depart this life
under the screw
University of Ham
up the river
vacation
wire
work brigade
yardbird
youth (guidance) centre
zebra

Religion and
Superstition

auld
auto-de-fé
   " -da-fé
bad lad
   " man
Beelzebub **Lord of the flies**
black gentleman
   "   lad
   "   man
   "   prince
   "   Sam
   "   spy
black **thief**
blazes
butch
cargo cult
charm
charmer **charm**
child of God
cloot
clootie **cloot**
clootie's croft **cloot**
cock
creative conflict
cunning man
dark man
David Jones **Davy Jones'**
   locker
devil's books **book**
dickens
dipper **dip** (1)
Eumenides
Euxine **Eumenides**
father of lies
fetch
fiend
flowery language
fly-by-night (1)
forspeak
forspoken **forspeak**
foul ane
   " thief
furry thing
game-fee **game** (2)
gentle people
   "   thorns
gentry
given rig
glamour
   "   gift
go again
go over (2)
good folk
   "   neighbours
   "   people
good man
goodman's craft **good man**

goodman's field **good man**
goodman's rig **good man**
goodman's taft **good man**
gooseberry (1)
grunter
guidance towards change
Harry
horny (1)
hot place **hot seat**
ill **ill-man**
ill man
   " bit
   " place
irregular situation
lift the books **lift** (1)
little folk
   "   people
look in a cup
lord Harry
Lord of the flies
mark
nick (1)
nicker **nick** (1)
nickie **nick** (1)
night man **night job**
night rider **night job**
night whistler **night job**
old a' ill thing
   " bendy
   " blazes
   " bog(e)y
   " boots
   " boy
   " chap
   " child
   " cloutie
   " dad
   " davy
   " driver
   " gentleman
   " gooseberry
   " Harry
   " hornie
   " lad
   " mahoon
   " Nick
   " one
   " poger
   " poker
   " Roger
   " ruffin
   " Sandy
   " scratch
   " serpent
   " smoker
   " sooty
   " thief
   " toast
old man (1)

old man's fold **old a' ill
   thing**
overlook **oversee**
oversee
overshadow **oversee**
playboy **play**
plotcock **plot**
scratch (1)
shag-boy **shag** (2)
shame
small folk
   » men
   » people
smoker
souper **soup**
stunted hare
swim for a wizard
taken-away
thief
wake a witch
wee folk
   » people
whistlers **whistled**
wise man
   » woman

Stealing
acquire
adjustment (5)
alienate
all-night man **all-nighter**
appropriate
badger game
bag (1)
bag job
black George **black
   gentleman**
blackfisher **black
   gentleman**
bleed the monkey
bone (1)
borrow
brethren of the coast
brotherhood of the coast
   **brethren of the
   coast**
browse
cabbage (1)
cadge(r)
canary
cannon
carpet-bagger
carry the can
   » » » back
chisel
claim
cleaners
click
clicker **click**

clickem fair **click**
clickem inn **click**
clip (1)
   » -artist
   » -joint
clout
collar (1)
convey
conveyance **convey**
conveyancing **convey**
conveyer **convey**
cop (1)
crack
cracksman **crack**
crib man
cut out
Davy Jones' natural children
   Davy Jones' locker
dip (1)
dipper **dip** (1)
dive (1)
diver **dive** (1)
do (3)
   » over
   » the dirty
drop (5)
earn
fair trader **fair sex**
fall off the back of a lorry etc.
fence
fetch
fiddle
fillet
find
finder **find**
finger-blight
fish hook
five-fingered discount
flash panney **flash** (1)
fly the blue pigeon
footpad
forage
free (1)
free load
free trade
freemans
freeze on to
G
gain
gap-maker
gentleman of the road
gentleman of fortune
gentleman's master
glean
glue
go on the account **account
   for**
gooseberry (2)
grab

graze
half inch
haul
heist
help yourself
high law **highwayman**
high lawyer **highwayman**
high pad **highwayman**
highgrade(r)
highwayman
hit (3)
hoist (1)
hoister **hoist** (1)
hold-up
hook (1)
hooker (1)
hot (2)
hot wire
hustle (1)
hustler **hustle** (1)
inventory leakage
it's a big firm
job
joy ride
jump (1) (2)
knight of the road
knock off (3)
liberate (2)
life
lift (1)
lifter **lift** (1)
light-fingered
made at one heat
make (2)
make away with (2)
make off with
merchandise
milk (1)
Monday man
mooch
move
mudlark **mud-kicker**
mug
mugger **mug**
mush
nab
   » the snow
neighbourhood connection
Newgate bird
nick (2)
nicks **nick** (2)
nip (1)
nipper **nip** (1)
obtain
on the **chisel**
on the hoist
on the hook **hooker** (1)
pad (2)
phantom

pickle **pick**
pick
pigeon **fly the blue pigeon**
pike **pick**
pinch (1)
plot
pocket
porch climber
ramp
redistribution of property
rent
ride out **ride up Holborn
  Hill**
roll (2)
rumble
running rumbler **rumble**
salvage
scrump
seepage
shake (1)
shoplift
shrinkage
siphon off
snaffle
snatch (3)
sneak
souvenir hunting
stall
stick up
sticky-fingered
storage
stripper
strong-arm
swipe
syphon **siphon off**
tarry-fingered
tea leaf
three-letter man
tip over
touch (2)
travel the road **traveller**
Tyburn blossom
walk (3)
whip
win(1)

Sweat
BO **body odour**
bedewed
body odour
glow
under-arm wetness
wetness

Trade Unions
brother
bug (2)
bump (1)
comparable

custom and practice
day of protest
  " action
dispute
feather-bed
flying picket
furry tail **furry thing**
go slow
hit the bricks
industrial action
  " relations
job action
kangaroo court
  " club
lock out
movement (2)
organize
parity
productivity deal
provocative **provocation**
ratten
sell out
sick out
slowdown
solidarity
Spanish practices
stoppage (2)
sweetheart
union brewed
walk out (2)
withdraw your labour
work to rule
working class
working people

Unemployment
at liberty
between shows
employment
furlough
gentleman
Irish promotion
Irish(man's) rise
job turning
jump ship
labour (2)
Mexican raise
  " promotion
on the beach
on the labour
pull the pin (2)
resting
send in your papers
Street and Walker's place
unwaged

Urination
accident (1)
accommodate yourself

adjourn
answer the call (2)
back teeth afloat
bale out (1)
be excused
beat a **retreat**
bedwetting
been
benny
bodily functions
bodily wastes
bottle (2)
break your neck
burst
business
bust (2)
call of nature
cash a check **cash in your
  checks**
caught short
chamber-lye
cock the leg
comfortable (1)
comfy **comfortable** (1)
commit a nuisance
consulting Mrs Jones
continent
contribution (1)
cover your feet **cover** (1)
demands of nature
Dicky Diddle **diddle** (1)
diddle (1)
dirty your pants
disappear (2)
do a bunk
  " dike
  " shift
drain off
ease springs
  " your bladder
  " yourself
empty your bladder
feed a dog
  " a goldfish
  " a horse
  " a parrot
feel the need
forget yourself
freshen up
gather a daisy **pick a daisy**
gather a pea **pick a daisy**
gather a rose **pick a daisy**
go (3)
  " on the coal
  " over the heap
  " round the corner
  " to Cannes
  " to the bathroom
  " upstairs

grow your greens
house-trained
incontinent (2)
indiscretions **indiscretion**
Jerry riddle **Jimmy**
Jimmy
 » Riddle
leak (1)
leaky
leave the class
 »   room
lift a leg (2)
little jobs
littles **big jobs**
look at the garden
 » » compost heap
 » » crops
 » » flowers
 » » lawn
 » » roses
 » » vegetable garden
mail a letter
make a call
make a mess
make room for tea etc.
make water
mess (2)
Micky
Mike Bliss
minor function
natural functions
 » purposes
nature's needs
necessities
need
night water **nightsoil**
nuisance
number one
on the coal
P
pass water
pay a visit
 » » to the old soldiers'
  home
pee
perform (1) (a natural
 function)
pick a daisy
 » a pea
 » a rose
pluck a daisy
point Percy at the porcelain
powder your nose
powder your puff **powder
 room**
puddle
pull a daisy etc. **pick a daisy
 etc.**
pump ship

 » bilges
rattle (2)
relief (2)
relieve yourself
run (4)
run-off **run off the
 bathwater**
run off the bathwater
sample
scatter **scatters**
see a man about a dog
see the rosebed etc.
 » your aunt
shake hands with the bishop
 » » » the
     unem-
     ployed
 » » » your best
     friend
 » » » your wife's
     best
     friend
sharpen your skates
shed a tear
shoot a lion
 » a dog
siphon the python
slack
 » off
slash
specimen
spend a penny
splash your boots
stale
stretch your legs
syphon the python
take a leak
take the air
take your snake for a gallop
taken short
that and this
tinkle
turn your bike around
uncomfortable (1)
unlimber your joint
use the facilities etc.
visit
visiting card
void water
wash (1)
wash your hands
 » and brush up
waste (3)
water
 » shaken
 » your garden
 » your nag
 » your roses
wee

 » -wee
wet (1)
 » the bed
 » your pants
 » yourself
wetting (1)
whizz
wring out your socks

Venereal Disease

bang and biff **bang** (1)
bareback rider
black pox
blood disease
 » -poison
blue balls
bone ache **bone** (2)
break your shins against
 Covent Garden rails
burn (1)
 » your poker
burner **burn** (1)
catch a cold (1)
catch a packet
catch the boat up
caught (2)
clap
clean
come home by Clapham
communicable disease
contagious and disgraceful
 disease
cop a packet **cop** (1)
Covent Garden ague
crabs
disease of love
docked smack smooth **dock**
dose
Drury Lane ague
dry pox **dry bob**
FFI **free from infection**
free from infection
French ache
 » disease
 » fever
 » gout
 » measles
 » pox
garden gout
general paralysis of the
 insane **incurable bone-
 ache**
get a marked tray
gone after the girls **gone** (2)
hat and cap
hazard of the town
high (1)
horse (1)
hot (3)

ill (2)
incurable bone-ache
jack in the box **jack** (1)
ladies' fever **lady**
malady of France
Neapolitan bone-ache
　　　" 　　favour
old Joe
packet (2)
pick up a nail
piled with French velvet
piss pins and needles
poison the blood of the
　　nation
pox
pro-pack
rail
Rangoon itch
rusty rifle
scald
secret disease **blood disease**
shoot between wind and
　　water **shoot off**
short-arm inspection
sigma phi
social disease
　　" 　infection
Spanish gout
specific blood poison **blood**
　　disease
take in your coals
unmentionable disease
Winchester goose **goose** (1)
women's disease

Vulgarisms and Swearing

Anglo-Saxon
B
B fool
B off
basket (1)
beggar
berk **Burke**
berry
bespattered
bestiality
Billingsgate
blank (1)
blanking **blank** (1)
blast (2)
blasted **blast** (2)
bleating **blast** (2)
bleeding
blooming
blow (4)
Burke
Charlie
chicken choker **choke your**

chicken
cram it **cram down**
D
dad
darn
dash (2)
effing
F
Fanny Adams
feather plucker
flowery language
forget yourself
foul-fa **foul ane**
foul may care **foul ane**
foul skelp ye **foul ane**
four-letter word
　　" 　man
French (2)
friar Tuck
frigging **frig**
gee **G**
golly
gum **golly**
Gordon Bennet(t)
H
hail Columbia
horse collar
jerk **jerk off**
Joe
language
mercy
Mrs Duckett
muck
P off
pheasant plucker
pissed off
P.O.'d **pissed**
potty mouth **pot** (3)
pound salt
　　" 　sand
poxy **pox**
prick
rabbit **rat**
rat
rose-coloured **roses**
round objects
ruddy
sanguinary
silly **B**
so-and-so (2)
sod **sodomite**
something-something
stiff (1)
suffering cats
sugar (2)
'swounds
tinpot
toss (1)
wanker **wank**

you know what you can do
　　with that

Warfare

active (air) defence
aid (1)
air support
alternative
America first
Anschluss
anti-personnel
appeasement
bale out (2)
bomb (1)
border incident
boys in the bush **boys** (2)
brew
brushfire war
bug out
cease-fire
Charlie
chemical warfare **agent**
chopper (1)
clean
cleanse (1)
co-belligerent
co-operate (1)
collaborator
collaborationist **collaborator**
come up with the rations
conflict
confrontation
conventional
counter-force capability
　　" 　-force weapon
　　" 　-value capability
counter insurgency
counterattack
cross the road
cruise (3)
D notice **defence**
de-rehabilitation
　　rehabilitate
defence
　　" 　　budget
　　" 　　debate
　　" 　　procurement
　　" 　　strategy
　　" 　　votes
defensive victory
deliver
delivery vehicle
device
ditch
do (4)
done for
dove
draw the enemy into a trap
drop your flag **drop your**

drawers
egg
emergency
enhanced radiation weapon
escalate
expendable **expended**
fire has gone out
first strike
     „   capability
fizzer
flap
frag
free a man for duty
freedom fighters
French leave
friendly fire
gapping
garden (2)
General Winter
go over the side **go over** (2)
go over the top (1)
Greater East-Asia Co-
   prosperity Sphere
groceries
hardware (2)
hawk
hot (4)
incident
incursion
Indian National Army
intervention
late disturbances
  „ unpleasantness
liberate (1)
limejuice
limited action
lot
militia
milk run
Ministry of Defence
Molotov cocktail
mop up
national service
nerve agent
Nuremberg trials
obstacle detachments
occupied
pacification **pacify**
pacify
party (1)
patriotic front
peace-keeping action
peace-keeping force
pioneer
planned withdrawal
police action
political change
pre-dawn vertical insertion
pre-emptive strike

preparedness
preventive war
protectorate
purge (2)
push (3)
quarantine
ranch hands
rectification of frontiers
regularize (2)
relocation camp
resistance
resources control
returned to unit
reverse
run (2)
rural construction
    „ development
scratch (2)
second front
second strike
    „   „   capability
selective
self-defence
shortening of the front line (1)
show (2)
soft (2)
special stores
stabilize
sterile
strategic capability
    „   nuclear war
    „   submarine
    „   warhead
strategic withdrawal
    „   movement to the
          rear
    „   retreat
stunt
survivability
search and sweep **sweep** (1)
tactical
    „ nuclear weapon
take a powder
take the gap
target of opportunity
temporary setback
temporary tactical ploy
termination capability
    survivability
thud
turn your coat
unacceptable damage
unhorsed
used up
volunteer
wear Hector's coat
weed killer
withdrawal to prepared
          positions

    „   in good order

Whores
abandoned
academician **academy**
actress
all-nighter
alley cat
ammunition wife
  ammunition (2)
arse-peddlar
article
aunt (1)
B girl **bar**
bachelor's wife
bad
badger
bag (6)
baggage
bang-tail **bang** (1)
banger **bang** (1)
bar girl
bash
bat (1)
bed-faggot **bed** (2)
beef
belly-piece **belly to belly**
belter **belt** (1)
besom
besomer **besom**
bibi
bidi **bibi**
biddy
bint
bird (1)
bit
bitch
black-eyed Susan
black velvet
blow (1)
blowen **blow** (1)
board lodger
bobtail
bona-roba
bottle (3)
bottom woman
brass
break luck **break a lance**
broad
brother of the gusset
bum
bun
business
    „   woman
buttered bun
buttock
    „   and file
    „   and twang
buy love

call-button girl
call girl
   „ boy
call the tricks
camp follower
can (4)
cannibal
case vrow **case** (1)
cat (1)
cattle (2)
cavalry
champagne trick
charity girl
   „   dame
Charlie
chick
chickie **chick**
child of Venus
chippy (1)
cockatrice **cocktail** (1)
cocktail (1)
coffee grinder
common customer **common**
   house
common jack **common**
   house
common maid **common**
   house
common sewer **common**
   house
common tart **common**
   house
commoner o' th' camp
   common house
convenient
country club girls
courtesan
Covent Garden
   „   „   goddess
   „   „   nun
creamer **cream**
creature of sale
Cressida
cross girl
cruiser **cruise** (1)
Cyprian
dance-hall hostess
dance a Haymarket hornpipe
   dance the mattress
   quadrille
dasher **dash** (2)
daughter of the game
dead meat (2)
demi-mondaine
   „ -rep
doe
dolly
   „   -common
   „   -mop

doxy
dress for sale
   „ -lodger
Drury Lane vestal **Drury**
   Lane ague
Dutch widow
easy woman
edie
escort
ewe mutton
faggot
fallen woman
feather-bed soldier
filth **filthy**
fish (1) (2)
fishmonger's daughter
fix up
flapper
flash girl **flash** (1)
flash tail **flash** (1)
flash woman **flash** (1)
flat-backer **flat on your**
   back
flutter a skirt **flutter** (2)
forty-four
frail sister **frail** (2)
free ride
fresh and sweet **dead meat**
   (2)
fresh meat
fruit fly
game (2)
   „ pullet
gamester (1)
gay girl **gay** (1)
gay it **gay** (1)
gay ladies **gay** (1)
gay life **gay** (1)
girl (1)
   „ of the streets
girlie **girl** (1)
go case
go into the streets
go to Paul's for a wife
goat-milker
good-time girl
goose (1)
grande horizontale
grass bibi
grass bidi
guinea-hen
gull
harlot
hawk your mutton
   „   pearly
head chick **head job**
hetaerism
high yellow girl
hobby-horse

hold-door trade
hooker (2)
horizontal life **horizontal** (1)
hostess
husband (1)
hustle (2)
hustler **hustle** (2)
immoral
   „ girls
   „ earnings
Immorality Act **immoral**
in circulation
in the business
in the game **game** (2)
in the trade
infantry **cavalry**
jam tart
jane (1)
jerker **jerk off** (1)
Jezebel
john (5)
joy girl **joy** (1)
joy sister **joy** (1)
Judy
kerb crawling
kife
knee-trembler
lady
lady boarder
lady of a certain description
lady of easy virtue
lady of no virtue
lady of pleasure
lady of the night
ladybird
liberated **liberate** (2)
lie backwards and let out
   your front rooms **lie with**
life
life of infamy
   „ shame
light skirts **light-fingered**
little bit
living by **trade**
lost (1)
low girls **low budget**
Magdalene
masseuse
messer **mess** (1)
mixer
mob
model
moll
moose
mud-kicker
Murphy
mutton
nanny
nautch-girl

nice time
night club hostess
night job
nightingale
nocturne
nun
nymph
oldest profession
on the bash
on the gad **oestrus**
on the game
on the grind
on the loose
on the road to Buenos Ayres
on the street(s)
on the stroll
on the town (1)
pad (1)
pagan
painted woman
panel **panel-house**
Paphian
park woman
party girl **party** (2)
pavement princess
peddle arse
piece of trade **piece** (1)
pin-money
plater
popsy
presenter **present arms**
prima donna **princess**
princess
privateer
pro
profession
professional (woman)

profession
quail
queen
quick time
quickie
receiver-general
remount
renter **rent**
sand rat
scarlet woman
scivvie
scrubber
scupper
sea gull
show your charms
singer
sister
   "   of charity
   "   of mercy
skivvy
sleck-trough **slake your lust**
sleepy time girl
social evil
solicit
solicitor **solicit**
sporting girls **sport**
sporting women **sport**
stable
stale
stale **meat**
stepney
street
   "   girl
   "   tricking
   "   walker
succubus

tail (1)
tart
taxi drinker
ten o'clock girl
tom (2)
tomboy
totty **tot**
town pump
   "   bike
toy boy
trade
trader **trade**
tramp
tree rat
trick
   " -babe
trollop
trot
trull
turn out upon the streets
two-by-four
underweight
unfortunate
V-girl
vegetarian
walk (1) (the streets)
warm one
wench
wet deck
   "   hen
white slave
   "   slavery
wife (1)
work the streets
working girl
yellow (2)